Critical Essays on

HERMAN MELVILLE'S
MOBY-DICK

CRITICAL ESSAYS
ON
AMERICAN LITERATURE

James Nagel, General Editor
University of Georgia, Athens

Critical Essays on

HERMAN MELVILLE'S
MOBY-DICK

edited by

BRIAN HIGGINS

and

HERSHEL PARKER

G. K. Hall & Co. / *New York*
Maxwell Macmillan Canada / *Toronto*
Maxwell Macmillan International / *New York   Oxford   Singapore   Sydney*

G. K. Hall & Co.
Macmillan Publishing Company
866 Third Avenue
New York, New York 10022

Maxwell Macmillan Canada, Inc.
1200 Eglinton Avenue East
Suite 200
Don Mills, Ontario M3C 3N1

Macmillan Publishing Company is part of the Maxwell Communication Group of Companies.

Library of Congress Cataloging-in-Publication Data

Critical essays on Herman Melville's Moby Dick / edited by Brian
    Higgins and Hershel Parker.
        p.   cm. — (Critical essays on American literature)
    Includes bibliographical references and index.
    ISBN 0-8161-7318-4:
    1. Melville, Herman, 1819-1891. Moby Dick. 2. Whaling in
literature.   I. Higgins, Brian, 1943-   II. Parker, Hershel.
III. Series.
PS2384.M62C75   1992
813'.3—dc20   92-16874
                                                                    CIP

The paper used in this publication meets the minimum requirements of American National Standard for Information Sciences—Permanence of Paper for Printed Library Materials. ANSI Z3948-1984. ∞ ™

10   9   8   7   6   5   4   3   2   1

Printed in the United States of America

Contents

♦

LITERARY INFLUENCES AND AFFINITIES

x ◆ CONTENTS

THE WHALE, AHAB, AND ISHMAEL

Moby-Dick   395
  LEWIS MUMFORD

In Nomine Diaboli   408
  HENRY A. MURRAY

Moby-Dick: Work of Art   421
  WALTER E. BEZANSON

Ahab's Greatness: Prometheus as Narcissus   440
  THOMAS WOODSON

"Loomings": Yarns and Figures in the Fabric   456
  HARRISON HAYFORD

The Meaning of the Whale   470
  EDWARD F. EDINGER

GENESIS

Unnecessary Duplicates: A Key to the Writing of Moby-Dick   479
  HARRISON HAYFORD

NEW ESSAYS

Moby-Dick and the Impress of Melville's Learning   507
  JOHN WENKE

"Its wood could only be American!":
Moby-Dick and Antebellum Popular Culture   523
  DAVID S. REYNOLDS

Moby-Dick and Domesticity   545
  HERSHEL PARKER

x ◆ CONTENTS

THE WHALE, AHAB, AND ISHMAEL

GENESIS

NEW ESSAYS

General Editor's Note

◆

This series anthologizes the most important criticism on a wide variety of topics and writers in American literature. Our readers will find in various volumes not only a generous selection of reprinted articles and reviews but original essays, bibliographies, manuscript sections, and other materials brought to public attention for the first time. This volume, *Critical Essays on Moby-Dick*, is the most comprehensive collection of essays ever published on one of the most important novels in English. It contains both a sizable gathering of early reviews and a broad selection of more modern scholarship as well. Among the authors of reprinted articles are Virginia Woolf, Carl Van Doren, Van Wyck Brooks, D. H. Lawrence, Nathalia Wright, Merton M. Sealts, Jr., Leon Howard, and Harrison Hayford. In addition to a substantial introduction by Brian Higgins and Hershel Parker that provides an overview of the history of scholarship on the novel, there are also three original essays commissioned specifically for publication in this volume, new studies by John Wenke on Melville's reading and education, David S. Reynolds on the novel and popular culture, and Hershel Parker on *Moby-Dick* and Melville's domesticity. We are confident that this book will make a permanent and significant contribution to the study of American literature.

JAMES NAGEL
University of Georgia, Athens

Publisher's Note

◆

Producing a volume that contains both newly commissioned and reprinted material presents the publisher with the challenge of balancing the desire to achieve stylistic consistency with the need to preserve the integrity of works first published elsewhere. In the Critical Essays series, essays commissioned especially for a particular volume are edited to be consistent with G. K. Hall's house style; reprinted essays appear in the style in which they were first published, with only typographical errors corrected. Consequently, shifts in style from one essay to another are the result of our efforts to be faithful to each text as it was originally published.

Introduction

◆

BRIAN HIGGINS AND HERSHEL PARKER

Moby-Dick, the greatest American adventure story, is a book filled with Herman Melville's exuberant bookishness, a remarkably "literary" work capable of captivating, and even transforming audiences from widely divergent classes: the book has been prized by highly educated, sophisticated literary men and women, but it has also been treasured by readers with little formal education.[1] In the 1870s a dainty little Englishwoman carried the three volumes of *The Whale* (as the first English edition was titled) aboard a trading schooner in the Samoas and gave them to the grizzled Scottish captain with the recommendation that they contained the saddest, strangest story she had ever read. The captain, the one well-educated man on the ship, read the volumes aloud to the crew during that voyage. Louis Becke, one of the crew, recalled the experience a quarter century or so later, after he had become a popular novelist:

> The mate and myself were not always in perfect accord with him [the captain], and often bitter words had passed between us; but "Moby Dick" brought us happily together again. For "the old man" had a deep, resonant voice, and he read the story to us from beginning to end. And although he would stop now and again, and enter into metaphysical matters, we forgave him, for we knew that he too, like us, was fascinated with mad Captain Ahab and brave mate Starbuck and the rest of the ill-fated crew of the "Pequod."

Critical Essays on Herman Melville's Moby-Dick contains this account and several other stories of intense first encounters with the book, readings that often converted innocent readers or listeners into lifelong enthusiasts for Melville. To adapt Thoreau's words in *Walden* (chapter 3, "Reading"), many a reader has dated a new era in his or her life from the first acquaintance with *The Whale* or *Moby-Dick*.

This extraordinary book, so thickly allusive to other books, was the work of a largely self-educated young man. Born in 1819 into a patrician

family, his father the son of a hero of the Boston Tea Party and his mother
the daughter of the hero of Fort Stanwix, Melville for ten years was reared in
luxury in New York City, with long vacations among pampering relatives in
upstate Albany and Boston, as well as other parts of New England, including
an estate on Narragansett Bay.[2] Between the ages of ten and twelve he
suffered first the profound disruption of a removal to Albany under the cloud
of his father's failure in business, then the catastrophe of his sudden death,
after which he was taken out of school and put to work as a clerk in a bank.
Thereafter Melville's formal education was spotty, though in the way of the
time he was thought, at eighteen, qualified to teach in a rural school in the
Berkshires. In 1838 his mother, unable to afford Albany prices, moved her
family to Lansingburgh, across the Hudson and a dozen miles north, and in
the fall Melville took a course in surveying and engineering at the local
academy. At nineteen he went to sea, on a summer's voyage to Liverpool, and
on his return taught at a school just east of Albany (Leyda, 42). At
twenty-one, after a vain attempt to find employment in Galena, Illinois,
where his uncle Thomas was living, he signed on a whaler bound for the
Pacific, where he deserted ship in the Marquesas Islands and spent three
weeks with one of the tribes there. After two subsequent brief voyages on
whaling ships and short stays in Tahiti and Hawaii, Melville enlisted in the
navy, returning to Boston aboard the frigate *United States* in October 1844
(Leyda, 102). Reunited with his family (two brothers now lawyers in New
York City and the rest of the family still in Lansingburgh), he soon turned
to the composition of his first book, *Typee*, which purported to be the
unvarnished truth about his stay among the natives in the Marquesas; the
composition was facilitated by the fact that in "many a night-watch at sea"
he had already tried out many of the episodes (including no doubt the more
sexually titillating ones) on his shipmates.[3]

During Melville's youth his brother Gansevoort, four years older (just
turned sixteen when their father died, but having finished more years of
schooling than Herman ever received), had carried on with some ostentation
a campaign of continuing self-education. For at least four years, probably
beginning in 1837, he made careful notes on his wide reading, in 1839
devouring Irving's *The Sketch-Book* and in 1840 reading widely in the novels
of Sir Walter Scott (Leyda, 60–62).[4] During these years Herman Melville
was probably already an equally voracious reader, although the evidence is as
spotty as his education was. His first known pieces of writing, "Fragments
from a Writing Desk" (published in a local newspaper in May 1839), contain
allusions to many writers—Robert Burton (*The Anatomy of Melancholy*), Lord
Chesterfield, Thomas Campbell ("The Pleasures of Hope"), Lord Byron
(*Childe Harold*), Swift (*Gulliver's Travels*), Milton ("L'Allegro"), Coleridge
("Genevieve"), Shakespeare (*Hamlet* and *Romeo and Juliet*), Edmund Burke
(*Reflections on the Revolution in France*), Richard Sheridan (*The Rivals*), and *The
Arabian Nights*.[5] At sea Melville made do with what he found in whaleships

or in the *United States*, the man-of-war he returned home aboard. He later described some of the books written by "choice old authors" that his character "White Jacket" found aboard the *Neversink*—not the books in the ship's official library but those in "various parts of the ship, among the inferior officers," books such as Morgan's *History of Algiers*, Knox's *Captivity in Ceylon*, Walpole's *Letters*,

> and some odd volumes of plays, each of which was a precious casket of jewels of good things, shaming the trash nowadays passed off for dramas, containing "The Jew of Malta," "Old Fortunatas," "The City Madam," "Volpone," "The Alchymist," and other glorious old dramas of the age of Marlow and Jonson, and that literary Damon and Pythias, the magnificent, mellow old Beaumont and Fletcher, who have sent the long shadow of their reputation, side by side with Shakspeare's, far down the endless vale of posterity.[6]

In this account in *White-Jacket* Melville emphasized the pleasures of random reading and the joys of books come upon by chance: as "every book-lover must have experienced before me," he wrote, "the books that prove most agreeable, grateful, and companionable, are those we pick up by chance here and there; those which seem put into our hands by Providence; those which pretend to little, but abound in much."[7] For *Typee* and his second book, *Omoo* (the partly autobiographical account of his experiences and observations in Tahiti and a neighboring island), Melville's reading was a purposeful plundering of books on the South Seas for information to ballast the narrative of his own experiences. At the same time he probably continued his more random reading of choice old authors: in *Omoo* Long Ghost's familiarity with Virgil, Hobbes, and Butler may reflect Melville's own current reading, but long-familiar biblical echoes and cadences resound throughout the prose of this work.[8]

    Early in 1847, engaged to Elizabeth Shaw, the daughter of a friend of his father's family, Lemuel Shaw, Chief Justice of Massachusetts, Melville went to Washington, hoping to gain a political appointment, but failed. By spring he had begun writing his third book, *Mardi*.[9] After his marriage that August (now a professional writer, almost by default), he and Elizabeth took up residence in New York City with his younger brother Allan, also recently married, and with his mother and four unmarried sisters. In January 1848 he bought a membership in the New York Library Society, and around the same time he began to borrow volumes from the large private library of Evert Duyckinck, a new friend, who had been editor of Wiley and Putnam's Library of American Books when *Typee* appeared there. In these first months of 1848, while still at work on *Mardi*, Melville borrowed Esais Tegnér's *Frithiof's Saga* and volumes by Rabelais and Sir Thomas Browne from Duyckinck (Leyda, 255–73). "Melville reads old Books," Duyckinck wrote in March 1848 to his brother George, then in Europe: "He has borrowed Sir Thomas Browne of me and says finely of the speculations of the *Religio Medici* that Browne is a kind of 'crack'd Archangel'" (Leyda, 273). Melville's love of old books, and of the "cracked archangel" in particular, was soon apparent in *Mardi*, where he fused colloquial nautical raciness with Elizabethan vocabulary and sentence structure. Accompanying Melville on this literary voyage was a crew of great men he had met in books and become intimate with—"my gentlemanly friend Stanhope," "my old uncle Johnson," "my Right Reverend friend, Bishop Berkeley," "my fine frank friend, poor Mark [Antony]," "my glorious old gossiping ancestor, Froissart," "my late eloquent and prophetic friend and correspondent, Edmund Burke," "my Peloponnesian friend Thucydides."[10] This sense of being an equal of worthy literary and historical figures from the past and his ambitious ranging among ideas in *Mardi* marked Melville's new concept of himself, not as whaler, deserter, and beachcomber (his roles in *Typee* and *Omoo*) but as earnest truth-seeker and as (he was prematurely daring to hope) one of the great writers of the world.

In early 1849 Melville took his wife to Boston so that their first child could be born at her family home. Before that trip he had known many works by two older American writers, Washington Irving and James Fenimore Cooper, but he did not know all the rising American authors. He had "only glanced" at one of Ralph Waldo Emerson's books in Putnam's store in New York.[11] At the beginning of February, he heard Emerson lecture in Boston and, despite reservations, thought him "a great man" (*Letters*, 77). Later that month, just after the birth of his son, Melville discovered—momentously for *Moby-Dick*—a set of Shakespeare in print large enough for him to read comfortably. He wrote to Duyckinck:

> Dolt & ass that I am I have lived more than 29 years, & until a few days ago, never made close acquaintance with the divine William. . . . I am mad to think how minute a cause has prevented me hitherto from reading Shakspeare. But until now, every copy that was come-atable to me, happened to be in a vile small print unendurable to my eyes which are tender as young sparrows. But chancing to fall in with this glorious edition, I now exult over it, page after page.
>
> (*Letters*, 77)

This "glorious" Shakespeare was most likely the seven-volume edition (now at Harvard) that he heavily marked and annotated. He soon acquired two other works that he drew on extensively in *Moby-Dick*: in Boston he bought "a set of Bayle's dictionary" and either there or afterwards in New York he acquired Milton's *Poetical Works* in the same format as his Shakespeare. The intention he announced to Duyckinck, "to lay the great old [Bayle] folios side by side & go to sleep on them thro' the summer, with the Phaedon in one hand & Tom Brown in the other," was thwarted by the critical and commercial failure of *Mardi* (*Letters*, 83–84).[12] The summer of 1849 was swallowed up by his rapid composition of *Redburn* and *White-Jacket*, "two *jobs*," as he later described these books to his father-in-law, "which I have done for money—being forced to it, as other men are to sawing wood" (*Letters*, 91).

On his voyage to England that October (carrying the proof sheets of *White-Jacket* to secure in person the best terms for the book's English publication). Melville had leisure for more congenial activities. One of his fellow voyagers, George Adler, a friend of Duyckinck's, was a scholar of German philosophy and literature—and "author of a formidable lexicon, (German & English)," as Melville recorded in his journal.[13] With Adler, who was "full of the German metaphysics, & discourses of Kant, Swedenborg &c," Melville had long conversations about "Fixed Fate, Free-will, fore-knowledge absolute"—that is, the topics debated by Milton's fallen angels and later reflected in the preoccupations of Ishmael and Ahab (*Journals*, 4). During the voyage, as Melville later wrote R. H. Dana, Jr., he "found a copy of Lamb in the ship's library—& not having previously read him much . . . dived into him, & was delighted." In London he used Dana's letter of introduction to Lamb's publisher, Edward Moxon, who regaled him with stories of that "rare humorist & excellent hearted man" and later sent him his collected works (*Letters*, 108).

For Melville, London was a bookman's paradise. Wandering through bookstalls and bookstores, he kept an eye out for De Quincey's *Confessions of an English Opium Eater*, and when he "at last got hold of" it he began it at once, calling it "A wonderful thing, that book." The next day he finished it and wrote in his journal, "A most wondrous book," and the day after that he mentioned again that "marvelous book" (*Journals*, 46–47). Melville searched for books, read them avidly, treasured the reading experience, and cherished the long-lingering aftereffects. He had come to love, too, not only choice old authors, but also fine old copies, elegantly bound, on good paper, with quaintly printed and curiously worded title pages redolent of the past, to which he felt linked by both the words of the author and the physical book that had outlived its original owner. At "Stribbs's in the Strand" he bought for Duyckinck "a fine old spicy duodecimo mouthful in the shape of 'Hudibras,'" which led him to reflect: "Are they not delicious, & full flavored with suggestiveness, these old fashioned London imprints?" (*Letters*, 102–103). Behind the frequent references to old volumes and the cataloging of whales according to their folio, quarto, and duodecimo sizes in *Moby-Dick* lies this intense relish for the physical characteristics, as well as the contents, of old books. In London and on his short side-trip to the Continent, Melville acquired many other books, a number of which he used in *Moby-Dick* besides De Quincey's *Confessions*—among them Thomas Hope's *Anastasius*, Mary Shelley's *Frankenstein*, and Laurence Sterne's *Tristram Shandy*.[14]

Back in New York in early February 1850, Melville began the book that became *Moby-Dick*, continuing to take time for reading—often reading he wanted to plunder for his whaling book. But his reading about whaling had begun years before. Even before he went to sea on a merchant ship he may have read J. N. Reynolds's "Mocha Dick: or the White Whale of the Pacific," which was first published in the *Knickerbocker Magazine* in May 1839. His first whaling ship, the *Acushnet*, gammed in the Pacific with a ship aboard which he met a young son of Owen Chase, who loaned him a copy of his father's *Narrative of the Essex*, famous for being sunk by a sperm whale in the Pacific, near the latitude and longitude where Melville met young Chase.[15] In New York he already had on hand J. Ross Browne's *Etchings of a Whaling Cruise*, which he had reviewed for the *Literary World* (6 March 1847), Frederick Debell Bennett's *Narrative of a Whaling Voyage round the Globe*, which he had drawn on in *Mardi*, and the *Penny Cyclopaedia of the Society for the Diffusion of Useful Knowledge*, which contained an article on "Whales" that paraphrased passages from Thomas Beale's standard work, *The Natural History of the Sperm Whale*. To these works he added others, including the Rev. Henry T. Cheever's *The Whale and His Captors* (published while he was abroad) and Beale's book (both major sources for *Moby-Dick*), and later his father-in-law, Judge Shaw, acquired for him a copy of Chase's *Narrative*.[16] From Duyckinck in June or July 1850 he borrowed Thoreau's *A Week on the Concord and Merrimack Rivers*, possibly in preparation for his trip to Pittsfield in July, since he had probably heard that the book contained a section on Mount Greylock. He also borrowed Carlyle's *Sartor Resartus*, *On Heroes, Hero-Worship, and the Heroic in History*, and later that summer *German Romance*, (Leyda, 376–77).[17]

Melville's deepest literary engagement at this time was with Shakespeare, and in all likelihood a problem tormenting him at the time he broke off for a vacation in the Berkshires was how an American writer could hope to rival Shakespeare without slavishly imitating him and the other great Elizabethan dramatists. On 5 August, Melville met Nathaniel Hawthorne for the first time, on a now-famous excursion to Monument Mountain that also included Oliver Wendell Holmes, Evert Duyckinck and his friend Cornelius Mathews, and Hawthorne's publisher, James T. Fields. The meeting stirred Melville to write an essay on Hawthorne's *Mosses from an Old Manse*, in which he ranked Hawthorne close to Shakespeare in the process of articulating his broodings about how an American writer could achieve literary greatness.[18] In the same essay he placed Emerson after Hawthorne in a list of American writers, and one morning the following month during a visit to the Hawthornes' cottage at Lenox, Melville read (as Mrs. Hawthorne recorded) "Mr Emerson's Essays."[19] In October Melville moved with his wife, infant son, mother, and three of his sisters to a farm near Pittsfield that he named Arrowhead, and after several weeks he resumed work on his whaling book. The family continued its practice of reading aloud at night, and that winter Melville probably heard in this way Schiller's *The Ghost Seer* and Dickens's *David Copperfield*.[20]

In July 1851, after further interruptions in the composition of the book (incompletely chronicled in his occasional letters to Hawthorne), Melville finished his masterpiece, the culmination of his reading and assimilation of great literature as well as of his own creative genius. Among its literary forebears, besides Shakespeare, were the Bible, Rabelais, Burton, Sir Thomas Browne, Milton, Byron, De Quincey, and Carlyle ("Historical Note," 646–47). In London Melville's English publisher, Richard Bentley, brought out *The Whale* in three volumes on 18 October 1851; in New York Harper & Brothers published *Moby-Dick* (the last-minute change of title) in a single volume on 14 November. The two editions differed in other respects: for some reason in *The Whale* the "Extracts" appeared at the end of the work (not at the beginning as in *Moby-Dick*), and the "Epilogue" was not included. Bentley or one of his readers had also excised or modified most passages that might be considered blasphemous or otherwise irreverent or sexually suggestive, so that *The Whale* was a tamer and safer book than the one the Harpers published in New York ("Historical Note," 659–89). British reviewers consequently had little to say about what American reviewers referred to as Melville's "sneers at revealed religion" or his "irreverence or profane jesting," frequent causes of offence among American reviewers. Some objected, however, to Melville's violation of the literary conventions (a three-volume novel published by Bentley was expected to be a love story), and because of the truncated narrative (without the "Epilogue" Melville's narrator seemed to perish at the end) several reviewers complained of the book's violation of the commonsensical rule that first-person narrators should survive the events they depict.[21]

The majority of American reviews were perfunctory; the reviewers— usually less professional, less well-educated, and less sophisticated in literary taste than their British counterparts—were simply not up to the challenges posed by the book.[22] Many London reviewers of *The Whale*, however, and a few American reviewers of *Moby-Dick* responded with gusto akin to Melville's own, praising his remarkable achievement and often celebrating affinities between his work and those of writers he cherished. The reviewer in the London *Morning Advertiser* (24 October 1851) declared that the "whalers' hostelrie" at New Bedford and its inmates were "pencilled with the mastery and minuteness of Washington Irving" and (hearing an echo of Charles Lamb) quoted a passage from "Breakfast" on the value of affording others a laugh at one's own expense. This reviewer also recognized now "a Carlylism of phrase, then a quaintness reminding us of Sir Thomas Brown, and anon a heap of curious out-of-the-way learning after the fashion of the Burton who 'anatomised' melancholy." Even the *Athenaeum* (25 October), which was contemptuous of *The Whale* as "an ill-compounded mixture of romance and matter-of-fact," saw "a wild humorous poetry in some of his [Melville's] terrors which distinguishes him from the vulgar herd of fustian-weavers" and cited "his interchapter on 'The Whiteness of the Whale'" as being "full of ghostly suggestions for which a Maturin or a Monk Lewis would have been thankful." The *Leader* on 8 November quoted "a splendid passage from our greatest prose writer," De Quincey, as "a fit prelude to the thrilling pages of Melville's *Whale*." The New York *Commercial Advertiser* (28 November) called *Moby-Dick* "a salmagundi of fact, fiction and philosophy, composed in a style which combines the peculiarities of Carlyle, Marryatt and Lamb." On 6 December the great New York sporting magazine, *The Spirit of the Times*, contrasted Melville with the novelists and romanticists who "stick to the same overdone incidents, careless of the memories of defunct Scotts and Radcliffs":

> it is only now and then when genius, by some lucky chance of youth, ploughs deeper into the soil of humanity and nature, that fresher experiences—perhaps at the cost of much individual pain and sorrow—are obtained; and the results are books, such as those of Herman Melville and Charles Dickens. Books which are living pictures, at once of the practical truth, and the ideal amendment: books which mark epochs in literature and art.

Despite reservations on the score of taste and morals, William A. Butler (an acquaintance of Melville's) in the Washington *National Intelligencer* (16 December) declared that Melville's descriptive powers were unrivaled and that language in his hands became "like a magician's wand." Melville displayed "a strange power to reach the sinuosities of a thought," his "delineation of character" was "actually Shakespearean," and his humor was "of that subdued yet unquenchable nature which spreads such a charm over the pages of Sterne." Butler also saw traces in the book "of that 'wild imagining' which throws such a weird-like charm about the Ancient Mariner of Coleridge."

Such acknowledgment of Melville's literary affinities by reviewers of *The Whale* and *Moby-Dick* went for little or nothing toward the establishment of a lasting reputation. His next book, *Pierre* (1852), was not published in England, for Melville refused his English publisher's terms—that the book be published at half profits, without an advance, and that Melville let the publisher "make or have made by a judicious literary friend" such alterations as were "absolutely necessary" if the book were to be "properly appreciated" there (*Letters*, 151, n.5). The consequence was that the great British reviewers did not have a chance to make up their minds about *Pierre* or to reconsider *The Whale* in the light of the new book. Subsequently none of the few known London reviews of Melville's next books, *Israel Potter* (1855) and *The Piazza Tales* (1856), mentioned any of his earlier works by name; known London reviews of *The Confidence-Man* (1857) contain only one reference to *The Whale* and *Pierre* ("Historical Note," 698–700,710). American reviewers, in the summer and fall of 1852, took *Pierre* as an offense against public morals and aesthetic standards, and scorned it more nearly unanimously and more viciously than any significant American novel of the century.[23] Thereafter Melville's reputation never recovered during his lifetime. Despite a few surveys of his career in important periodicals in the mid-1850s, Melville's general reputation faded rapidly after 1852, and during the next decades *Moby-Dick* and *The Whale* were seldom mentioned in American and English literary periodicals. In England, however, *The Whale* (and *Moby-Dick*, as a few copies were imported) found a very slowly widening circle of admirers, most often associated with an overlapping set of groups, the Pre-Raphaelite Brotherhood, the workingmen's movement, Fabian Socialists, and writers about the sea and remote lands. A hallmark of such admirers was interest in Walt Whitman or Henry David Thoreau (or both), two other American writers then not often considered by Americans to be among the country's great writers ("Historical Note," 732–49).

Among the earliest published tributes in England to the all but forgotten Melville was one by the poet James ("B.V.") Thomson in an article on Whitman in the radical magazine *National Reformer* in 1874. Melville in Thomson's eyes was the "one other living American writer" who approached Whitman "in his sympathy with all ordinary life and vulgar occupations, in his feeling of brotherhood for all rough workers, and at the same time in his sense of beauty and grandeur, and his power of thought." The English sea-novelist W. Clark Russell in 1884 singled out "The Forecastle" (chapter 40 of *Moby-Dick*) for special praise: what Melville made to pass among sailors, and the sayings he put into their mouths, "might truly be thought to have come down to us from some giant mind of the Shakespearean era." *Moby-Dick* was like a drawing by William Blake or "better yet" it was "of the 'Ancient Mariner' pattern, madly fantastic in places, full of extraordinary thoughts, yet gloriously coherent." The poet-dramatist Robert Buchanan in 1885 published a poem ("Socrates in Camden") celebrating Whitman but also glancing at Melville's *Typee* and what he called *The White Whale*. He felt called upon to identify Melville in a footnote, where he declared him to be "the one great imaginative writer fit to stand shoulder to shoulder with Whitman" on the North American continent. Henry S. Salt, the biographer of Thomson and Thoreau, published articles on Melville in 1889 and 1892, lauding *Moby-Dick* in the second as "the supreme product of a master mind." No one, Salt declared, should "presume to pass judgment on American literature unless he has read, and re-read" it. In 1893 the London branch of Putnam's published *Moby-Dick* and three others of Melville's early books imported from the United States in the editions prepared by Arthur Stedman in consultation with Melville's widow. Reviewing the books in the *Spectator*, J. St. Loe Strachey acknowledged Melville as a great artist, despite his tendency to let the last great master of style he had been reading run away with him. A few years later, at the turn of the century, a reviewer of a series of sea novels described *Moby-Dick* in the London weekly magazine *Literature* as "a most astounding epic," in which Ahab "hunts the whale that dismembered him through the seas of the earth as the Opium Eater was hunted through the forests of Asia." *Moby-Dick* was the only book in the series that was "supremely great and undoubtedly a work of genius."

From the years around Melville's death in 1891 until the centenary of his birth, 1919, such tributes slowly accumulated in England and began to appear from year to year in the United States, without, however, bringing Melville into the canon of American literature as it was being taught in high schools or "academies" (and a few colleges) in the United States, where the greatest American writers of the nineteenth century were Cooper, Irving, Emerson, Hawthorne, Longfellow, and a few others, never including Melville. In the United States between 1851 and 1919 the most enthusiastic praise of *Moby-Dick* came in 1893 in a New York *Critic* review of the new edition prepared by Authur Stedman:

> In this story Melville is as fantastically poetical as Coleridge in the "Ancient Mariner," and yet, while we swim spellbound over the golden rhythms of Coleridge feeling at every stroke their beautiful improbability, everything in "Moby Dick" might have happened. . . . The author's extraordinary vocabulary, its wonderful coinages and vivid turnings and twistings of worn-out words, are comparable only to Chapman's translations of Homer. The language fairly shrieks under the intensity of his treatment, and the reader is under an excitement which is hardly controllable. The only wonder is that Melville is so little known and so poorly appreciated.

At the end of the century and in the early 1900s, William Livingston Alden, the London correspondent for the *New York Times*, wrote about Melville in several of his columns; in 1899 he called for the founding of a Melville society, devoted to securing Melville the reputation he deserved—as "far and away the most original genius that America has produced." It was "a National reproach," Alden declared, that Melville "should be so completely neglected."[24] The same year a young Canadian professor, Archibald Mac-Mechan, who had written Melville an admiring letter in 1889, published the first article ever devoted to *Moby-Dick* (aside from the reviews). In "The Best Sea Story Ever Written" MacMechan emphasized the "distinctly American" quality of *Moby-Dick* in subject and in style: it was "large in idea, expansive," with "an Elizabethan force and freshness and swing" and, "above all, a free-flowing humour, which is the distinct *cachet* of American literature." The chief charm of its style—perhaps "more rich in figures than any style but Emerson's"—was "its freedom from all scholastic rules and conventions." Melville was "a Walt Whitman of prose." MacMechan was an academic, but he was also a literary discoverer out to elevate a neglected book to its rightful literary ranking. With *Moby-Dick*, he concluded, Melville "takes rank with Borrow, and Jefferies, and Thoreau, and Sir Richard Burton; and his place in this brotherhood of notables is not the lowest." MacMechan's article (which was published in a Canadian magazine, then reprinted in a minor London journal in 1901 and in a collection of MacMechan's essays in 1914) probably had little influence in the United States (no one who wrote on Melville in his centennial year, 1919, referred to it). Despite Alden's proselytizing (and a small flurry of correspondence about Melville in the *New York Times Saturday Review of Books* in 1905) Houghton Mifflin in 1906 refused a young American admirer, Frank Jewett Mather, an advance for a biography, on the grounds that Melville "was a hopelessly bad risk, and one that no prudent publisher could undertake even to the extent of a few hundred dollars." [25] Most academics who commented on Melville in these decades between his death and the centenary of his birth showed no such knowledge of *Moby-Dick* as MacMechan's and were usually content to categorize Melville among minor writers—as a rival of William Gilmore Simms, for instance, surpassed like Simms by Cooper.

From the 1880s through the early 1920s *The Whale* or *Moby-Dick* and other works by Melville were often passed by hand from one Melville lover to another, especially in England. In August 1884 James Billson, a young Oxford graduate who practiced law in Leicester, wrote to Melville that his books were "in great request" but hard to come by: "as soon as one is discovered (for that is what it really is with us) it is eagerly read & passed round a rapidly increasing knot of 'Melville readers'" (*Letters*, 275, n. 1). (Billson had by this time read *Moby-Dick* and the rest of Melville's books, with the exception of *White-Jacket*, *Battle-Pieces*, and *Clarel*.) Testimonies to other such sharing accumulated at the centennial and for several years afterward. In 1922 Henry S. Salt looked back to the beginnings of his own interest in Melville in the 1880s, when he had written the first of his two articles on Melville and exchanged letters with him on (among other matters) their mutual interest in the poetry of Thomson:

> It was from that widely-read student of good books, Bertram Dobell, that I first heard of Melville's works; and so grateful was I for the information that I sedulously passed it on to others. I remember, in particular, bringing *The Whale* to the notice of William Morris, and how a week or two afterwards I heard him quoting it with huge gusto and delight.

In the 1890s W. H. Hudson, who wrote about *Moby-Dick* in *Idle Days in Patagonia* (1893), introduced the book to Morley Roberts. Later Roberts recalled how they had wondered "how it was that the Americans still looked forward to some great American book when all they had to do was to cast their eyes backward and find it." Roberts added that "Hudson knew it [*Moby-Dick*] and learnt from it and spread its name." [26] Augustine Birrell in "The Great White Whale: A Rhapsody" (1921) credited his own introduction to Melville to "that exquisite judge of a good book, Sir Alfred Lyall," at whose instigation he had bought *Typee, Omoo,* and *The Whale,* though he had let the three volumes of the latter remain unread for a decade. After taking them down one "happy day" and reading them, Birrell wrote, "I have discovered that all this time I had intimate friends, and even relatives, not much addicted to holding their peace, who knew all about Ahab and Bildad and Peleg and Moby Dick, and yet never gave me a hint of their existence."

In September 1922 the strange subterranean reputation *The Whale* or *Moby-Dick* had sustained until the last two or three years was summed up by a writer in the London *Nation and Athenaeum* (H. M. Tomlinson, who retold the story the following month in the *Christian Science Monitor*):

> That book . . . appears to have been a wonder treasured as a sort of secret for years by some select readers who had chanced upon it. They said little about it. We gather that they had been in the habit of hinting the book to friends they could trust, so that "Moby Dick" became a sort of cunning test by which the genuineness of another man's response to literature could be proved. If he was not startled by "Moby Dick," then his opinion on literature was of little account.

Such a phenomenon could have taken place only with a neglected work by a neglected writer—nothing by Byron or Scott or Tennyson or Dickens, for instance, could have achieved such cult status.

A spate of articles at the centenary of Melville's birth and the publication the following year (1920) of a new inexpensive edition of *Moby-Dick* (in the Oxford "World's Classics" series) helped bring about the "Melville Revival" of the 1920s, when extensive publicity in newspapers, magazines, and books put Melville's name before a mass audience and transformed his masterpiece from cult status to public property. His name and the American title of his masterpiece, at least, would henceforth be famous. In January 1921 in the *Nation* John Middleton Murry testified to the contagion of the fever of the revival. H. M. Tomlinson (not named in the article) had read *Moby-Dick* and written an ecstatic article on it; while Murry was struggling with it, "wondering what the deuce it could mean," he received a letter about *Moby-Dick* from Augustine Birrell (identified only as "a famous literary man") "marked on the outside 'Urgent,' and on the inner scroll of the MS. itself 'A Rhapsody.'" Upon observing yet another article on *Moby-Dick* (perhaps that of E. L. Grant Watson, who the previous month had called the book the "history of a soul's adventure"), Murry began to read it for himself and declared his surrender: "I hereby declare, being of sane intellect, that since letters began there never was such a book, and that the mind of man is not constructed so as to produce such another."

A remarkable part of the new publicity was the ranking of *Moby-Dick* with other masterpieces of world literature. Murry himself made a pugnacious ranking of Melville (on the basis of *Moby-Dick*) "with Rabelais, Swift,

Shakespeare, and other minor and disputable worthies." Tomlinson in June 1921 placed it "amongst the world's great works of art," then a few months later was more specific:

> I have no doubt "Moby Dick" goes into that small company of big, extravagant, generative books which have made other writers fertile in all ages—I mean the books we cannot classify, but which must be read by every man who writes—"Gargantua and Pantagruel," "Don Quixote," "Gulliver's Travels," "Tristram Shandy," and the "Pickwick Papers." That is where "Moby Dick" is, and it is therefore as important a creative effort as America has made in her history.

In the following year T. E. Lawrence referred in his correspondence to his "shelf of 'Titanic' books (those distinguished by greatness of spirit, 'sublimity' as Longinus would call it)"—*The Brothers Karamazov*, *Thus Spake Zarathustra*, and *Moby-Dick*. Tomlinson was prophetic in seeing *Moby-Dick* as a book that would make other writers fertile: Lawrence was inspired by *Moby-Dick* and the other two works "to make an English fourth." (Over the next several years he re-inventoried the books on the shelf, always listing *Moby-Dick* but at times citing other companions to it, *Leaves of Grass*, *War and Peace*, Rabelais, and *Don Quixote*.)[27] Other writers who read Melville during the revival were not inspired to write their own equivalent of *Moby-Dick* but responded profoundly: D. H. Lawrence (who first read *The Whale* in 1916 and subsequently published his fervid essay on *Moby-Dick* in his *Studies in Classic American Literature*, 1923); the poet John Freeman (who in 1926 published the first book in England on Melville); E. M. Forster (who discussed both *Moby-Dick* and the newly published *Billy Budd* in his influential 1927 study, *Aspects of the Novel*); and Virginia Woolf (who published a centennial article on Melville in the *Times Literary Supplement*, at which time she apparently did not know *Moby-Dick*, and then compared *Moby-Dick* and *Wuthering Heights* at some length in her 1929 essay "Phases of Fiction").[28]

As early as 1923 J. W. M. Sullivan tried to account for this strange phenomenon of the Melville revival: "The recent emergence of a large public for Melville's work," he wrote, "is one of the most interesting indications of the change which is taking place in the general mind." Melville's "complete lack of popularity in his own time was due to the great dissimilarity between his personal vision and the general *Weltanschauung*" of the Victorians: their "material world was a perfectly clear-cut and comprehensible affair, and everything that was not material was merely moral. . . . They were islanders who lived unconscious of the sea." Sullivan went on to try to define the new post–World War Zeitgeist:

> It is characteristic of our time that there is a sense of unprecedented possibilities; the firm lines of our accustomed world are growing indistinct. In

science and philosophy, chiefly, we feel that the soul of man has started on new adventures. We get glimpses of greater and perhaps more lonely seas than man has ever adventured on before. . . . We are aware of possibilities; man is once more a mystery to us, and a greater mystery than ever before. We feel that Melville's oceans and leviathans are credible symbols. That man hunts through a great deep who looks into himself.

Three years later in his *Gifts of Fortune*, H. M. Tomlinson told a story of the new fame of *Moby-Dick*:

On a winter's night, only a year or two ago, I was intrigued into a drawing-room in a London suburb to hear a group of neighbours, who were men of commerce, discuss this book of Melville's. They did so with animation and the symptoms of wonder. It could not have happened before the war. Was some unseen door now open? Were we in communication with influences that had been unknown to us?

In "Two Americans and a Whale" (also 1926) Tomlinson answered his question of why Melville spoke to the postwar generation, seeing his new popularity as a symptom of the changes in public consciousness. Unlike Sullivan, he did not try to define the change in the spirit of the times, but he felt that things "in which once only odd men and women delighted" had acquired a significance for the general populace: "Where it was all dark, now most people may see something. Melville, in his own day, was addressing an intelligence which was hardly awake. To-day it is apprehensive" (that is, alert, comprehending).

Appropriately enough, in this article Tomlinson, a Londoner, was responding to the wonderment of two Americans concerning the new popularity of *Moby-Dick*. The Melville revival was primarily a London-based phenomenon built upon scattered but long-sustained English interest in Melville. Some of the journalists who had written about Melville around the time of his death were still active at the time of the centennial and the revival. Henry S. Salt and J. St. Loe Strachey were two such men who bridged the decades, and many others were alive in the 1920s who had loved some of Melville's books for decades. Furthermore, London literary society was, on the whole, much more sophisticated than that in the United States—where there were few literary journalists and fiction writers as talented and highly educated as those in England.

In the United States the revival of Melville was promoted most by Carl Van Doren, who had begun reading Melville in 1914 in order to write about him in the *Cambridge History of American Literature* (1917). His three and a half pages on Melville in a section on "Contemporaries of Cooper" was the most comprehensive and sympathetic treatment that had yet appeared in any literary history or textbook. Too busy to write a full biography of Melville, he set Raymond M. Weaver to the task. Weaver's *Herman Melville: Mariner and Mystic* (1921) was in almost every respect a poor book—inadequately researched, disproportionate (heavily weighted to the earlier years, bulked out with information about whaling, meager on the last four decades of Melville's life), derivative in critical judgments, packed with unassimilated documents (often badly transcribed), and awkwardly written in a bombastic style. Nonetheless, in the eyes of publishers in the 1920s Weaver had first claim on Melville, and he provided introductions for the Boni edition of several of Melville's books, including *Moby-Dick* (1924–1925), for the Modern Library edition (1926), and for the Liveright edition of the *Shorter Novels* (1928). He also transcribed *Billy Budd* for the English Constable Edition (1924, its first publication), revising his transcription for *The Shorter Novels*. The only American rival to Weaver as a propagandist for Melville in the 1920s was Van Wyck Brooks, who wrote a series of articles in the New York *Freeman*, revising upward his judgment of Melville's craftsmanship in *Moby-Dick* with his rereadings of the book, coming to defend the cetological matter as ballast that an epic must carry.

For his 1929 biography Lewis Mumford did almost no new research of his own and like Weaver assumed that *Redburn*, *Typee*, *Omoo*, and *White-Jacket* (in that order) could safely be taken as autobiography. In his chapter on *Moby-Dick*, however, Mumford offered the most sustained analysis yet made of the character of Ahab and of the role of the white whale. As a selection of the Literary Guild, Mumford's biography reached into many thousands of American homes, so that during the 1930s and beyond it was available to anyone who wanted to know something about Melville, as Weaver's less well-distributed book was not. In the years before Mumford's book appeared, another American, Henry A. Murray, had become fascinated with *Moby-Dick* and had begun a study of Melville that lasted through the next six and a half decades of his life, during which he became an eminent psychologist. In his introduction to *Endeavors in Psychology: Selections from the Personology of Henry A. Murray* (1981), the thanatologist Edwin S. Shneidman tells the remarkable story of the beginning of the influence of *Moby-Dick* on Murray's life and work. Early in the 1920s, Murray, "then a young doctor, was on his annual trip to England and the Continent on one of the Cunard liners when, three days out to sea, the captain of the ship developed acute appendicitis, necessitating an emergency-at-sea operation."

The ship's surgeon invited Murray, inasmuch as he was also a physician, to assist him by administering the chloroform and, in their conversation, mentioned his admiration of Herman Melville. Indeed, on this trip to the States the surgeon had taken special pains to go to New Bedford to see the Whalemen's Chapel. By pleasant coincidence, Murray had had a copy of *Moby-Dick* "forced upon" him by a friend and had begun to read it on that voyage. Thus, during the decade of the Melville Revival, an Englishman and a Boston Brahmin, almost literally over their captain's anesthetized body, discussed America's masterpiece. Appropriately, while at sea, Murray finished this great oceanic book.

The effect of Murray's first reading of *Moby-Dick* was magical. In one elevating and insightful experience, Melville's book revealed to Henry Murray the vast mysterious world of the unconscious—a topic that had previously never occupied his mind and subsequently never left it.

Thus began Murray's central lifelong interest—soon thereafter made alive by his contact with Freud and his intense relationship with Jung—in the workings and wonders of the unconscious elements of the human mind.[29]

In the second half of the 1920s, aside from Mumford's feint at research, Murray was alone in doing basic biographical research on Melville. He made contact with Julian Hawthorne, who remembered Melville from his child-hood and from a visit he had paid Melville in the 1880s; he became acquainted with Melville's granddaughter Eleanor Melville Metcalf and with Melville's surviving grandnieces and grandnephews, the Morewood grand-children of Melville's brother Allan. Murray began accumulating books Melville had owned and various family documents, and continued to do so for many years.[30] He wrote many sections of a biography of Melville but did not publish it; indeed he seldom published anything on Melville, but his introduction to the Hendricks House *Pierre* (1949) and his essay on *Moby-Dick*, "In Nomine Diaboli" (1951), brought a clinically based profes-sionalism to the psychological interpretation of Melville and his works, rather than the amateur psychologizing that had prevailed since the 1920s.

In the 1920s enthusiasts for *The Whale* or *Moby-Dick*, mainly non-academics, often literary journalists, made the work famous—so famous that two movies, *The Sea Beast* (1926) and *Moby Dick* (1930), both starring John Barrymore as Ahab, were loosely based upon it.[31] During this decade the book was widely accessible in both Great Britain and the United States in the Everyman and World's Classics editions and several other inexpensive editions and was also available in two volumes of the Constable limited edition of Melville's writings (London, 1922–1924), as well as in the Modern Library edition in the United States. In the 1930s, over a few baffled protests that the re-estimate of Melville had "overshot the mark" (as Ludwig Lewisohn complained),[32] Melville entered the canon of American literature, a decade or so after that literature began to be taught in American colleges with some regularity. Even through the 1930s only a few professors devoted much class time to *Moby-Dick* (the only work of Melville's then likely to be taught). By the late 1930s, the professional study of *Moby-Dick* had begun, soon largely replacing the enthusiastic essays which had established its reputation. By the late 1940s courses in American literature of the nineteenth century regularly included *Moby-Dick*.

After the decade of the Melville Revival (counting from the centennial of Melville's birth in 1919 until the publication of Mumford's critical biography in 1929), criticism on *Moby-Dick* was transformed. By 1930 or so, it became hard for a new reader of the book to get his or her rapturous response to it into print: by then a belated enthusiast was as boring as a writer today who discovers the marvels of word processing and raves about those marvels to friends who have already written articles and even books on computers. In England, the main scene of the Melville Revival, there virtually ceased to be any important writing about Melville for several decades, although novelists such as Angus Wilson absorbed Melville and alluded to him in their works. About the only way to get an article on the book into print as late as the 1940s was to write an introduction to a new edition, as Montgomery Belgion did.[33] There were few academic outlets in England, where American literature was rarely taught in colleges and universities and where fewer journals were established to publish academic criticism on British literature, let alone American. In 1951 Ronald Mason, a civil servant, published *The Spirit Above the Dust*, the first book on Melville by an English critic since John Freeman's (1926). Few books—and few significant articles—by English critics have followed. Even as late as the 1970s and 1980s when university courses in American literature had become more common, the new writing on *Moby-Dick* in England tended to be derivative, repeating (often in more elegant style than American academic writing) some of the commonplaces of American criticism. This was a curious eventuality in a nation where previous generations had kept Melville's fame alive and at last had exalted his reputation internationally. English critics discovered *Moby-Dick* in the 1920s and after 1930 pretty much left it for Americans to write about.

As *Moby-Dick* gradually began to be taught in more colleges in the United States during the 1930s (usually by young instructors who had never studied the book in their own college days and now [as Robert Spiller recalled to Hershel Parker] had to wait years before their senior colleagues would give them an opportunity to teach it), academics began publishing scholarly studies of the book. In 1932 William S. Ament first drew attention to the fact that the English edition had been expurgated, thereby initiating textual study of *Moby-Dick*.[34] Constance Rourke in *American Humor* (1931) discussed the book's folklore elements, and articles began to appear identifying whaling books that Melville seemed to have drawn on.[35] In the first of these Leon Howard (1934) revealed Melville's possible indebtedness in plot to Joseph C. Hart's anonymously published novel *Miriam Coffin, or The Whale Fisherman*, and Frederick B. Adams, Jr. (1936) demonstrated that Melville had used and humorously satirized William Scoresby's *An Account of the Arctic Regions*.[36] In 1939 Charles R. Anderson devoted part of his *Melville in the South Seas* to a more extensive study of Melville's whaling sources. During this decade, with the help of Melville's granddaughter Eleanor Melville Metcalf and other family members, Charles Olson began locating books that survived from Melville's library.

In the academic study of *Moby-Dick* in the 1930s, new lines of interpretation and analysis proliferated. George C. Homans (1932) developed a line of interpretation begun by Carl Van Vechten in the early 1920s: *Mardi*, *Moby-Dick*, and *Pierre* were a trilogy, a tragedy in three acts, each of them dramatizing Melville's pursuit of the Ultimate or search for the secret of the universe, and his failure to find it.[37] In the introduction to his anthology *Herman Melville: Representative Selections* (1938), which became for the next two decades the indispensable companion to Melville studies, Willard Thorp also saw the three books as a trilogy dramatizing Melville's quest for the Ultimate, and attempted to read *Moby-Dick* as an "allegory of Melville's spiritual state in 1851."[38] In *Maule's Curse* (1938) Yvor Winters gave a detailed exposition of what he took to be the symbolism of *Moby-Dick*, central to which was the antithesis between the land (representing the known and mastered in human experience) and the sea (representing "the half-known, the obscure region of instinct, uncritical feeling, danger, and terror").[39] Like Van Wyck Brooks and Lewis Mumford, Winters argued that the book is less a novel than an epic poem, but a tragic rather than a traditionally heroic epic. In contrast to Winters, who celebrated *Moby-Dick* as "one of the most carefully and successfully constructed of all major works of literature,"[40] R. P. Blackmur (1938) used *Moby-Dick*, along with *Pierre*, to support his claim that Melville never attained mastery of the formal devices of fiction.[41] At the end of the decade, Stanley Geist in his Harvard honors thesis, revised as *Herman Melville: The Tragic Vision* (1939), explored what he considered to be a dominant theme in *Moby-Dick* and *Pierre*: the importance and greatness of the tragic vision, the vision essential, in Melville's view, to true heroism.[42]

By the end of the 1930s *Moby-Dick* (along with a few other items in the Melville canon) was clearly established as attractive territory for academic explorations. Thereafter, the volume of commentary on *Moby-Dick* expanded rapidly. As Brian Higgins notes in the introduction to the second volume of his Melville bibliography, "Commentary on Melville accumulated steadily during the 1930s and the first half of the 1940s, then proliferated so rapidly in the years following World War II that by 1950 Robert Spiller claimed that Melville was 'the most thoroughly studied of all American authors.'"[43] In the following decades scores of books, several hundred dissertations, and several thousand articles, chapters, and notes on Melville have been published, as well as numerous introductions to new editions and reprints of his works. Though very few critics would now endorse the recurrent assertion of the Revival that Melville was a "one-book author," *Moby-Dick* has continued to receive far more attention than any of his other works. Thus, any account of commentary on the book since the 1930s, however ordered, is apt to seem a foredoomed attempt to classify what Melville in chapter 32 of *Moby-Dick* calls "the constituents of a chaos."

A number of major trends and developments can be identified, nevertheless. Knowledge has accumulated, albeit unsteadily, on a range of mainly factual topics, such as the composition and textual history of *Moby-Dick*, its place in Melville's literary career, its initial reception, its literary influences and affinities, and its place in the contexts of nineteenth-century politics, philosophy, and religion.

By the late 1930s and early 1940s scholars dissatisfied with Weaver's and Mumford's accounts began to make their way to Mrs. Metcalf in order to see Melville's surviving papers and also to the manuscript archives in the New York Public Library and other libraries in search of biographical evidence, including the date and circumstances of the composition of *Moby-Dick*. Luther S. Mansfield's dissertation, "Herman Melville: Author and New Yorker, 1844–1851" (Chicago, 1938), was a notable achievement here. In the 1940s academic study of Melville's life burgeoned, with *Moby-Dick* the central document to be understood. Several lines of biographical investigation converged. Leon Howard pursued his researches in a notable 1940 article ("Melville's Struggle with the Angel"), and through a chance meeting he encouraged the free-lance researches of Jay Leyda, who in the late 1940s gathered the documents which he published as *The Melville Log* in 1951, the same year in which Howard's biography, based on it, appeared.[44] Meanwhile, at Yale, Stanley T. Williams directed a series of dissertations on Melville's life and works, including Harrison Hayford's study of Melville and Hawthorne, a central section of which dealt with the meeting of the two authors in early August 1850 and the composition of "Hawthorne and His *Mosses*."[45] Howard's and Leyda's 1951 books were followed in 1952 by the lavishly annotated Hendricks House edition of *Moby-Dick*, edited by Luther S. Mansfield and Howard P. Vincent.[46] In 1948 Mrs. Metcalf had published an edition of the journal Melville kept during his trip to London and the Continent just before he began *Moby-Dick*, and in 1953 she published *Herman Melville: Cycle and Epicycle*, which drew on documents not already printed, on family stories, and on her own memories of Melville.[47] Newton Arvin pronounced that Metcalf's book was the last documentary work needed on Melville;[48] this was premature, but in fact few new documents relating to *Moby-Dick* were published in the next four decades. Complete texts of all of Melville's known letters that bear on the composition of *Moby-Dick* (previously extracted in *The Melville Log*) were first published together in *The Letters of Herman Melville* (1960), edited by Merrell R. Davis and William H. Gilman (two of Stanley T. Williams's students).[49] New evidence concerning the composition of *Moby-Dick* surfaced when Harrison Hayford and Hershel Parker, collating the English and American editions for the Norton Critical Edition (1967), established that some of the English readings were in fact Melville's revisions.[50] Their work went into the Northwestern-Newberry edition (1988), which they coedited with G. Thomas Tanselle.[51]

Since the 1920s *Moby-Dick* has frequently (if somewhat casually) been discussed in relation to Melville's other books; critics have less often attempted to place it in Melville's literary career through documentary evidence. An important exception, William Charvat (1968), drew on Melville's letters to his publishers and reviews of his books, focusing specifically on Melville's developing relationship with his audience as it affected the way that he wrote.[52] Charvat concluded that *Moby-Dick* "has never been properly understood as the work of a writer who was in a state of creative tension with a reading public whose limitations he had at last defined. Many of its devices, and to some extent its form and its greatness, can be explained in terms of that tension."[53] Another study, G. Thomas Tanselle's "The Sales of Melville's Books" (1969), put in accessible form much information previously unknown or incomplete that allowed readers to gauge the extent to which Melville had succeeded in making his masterpiece "saleable" in comparison with his other works;[54] and in "Contract: *Moby-Dick*, by Herman Melville" (1971), Harrison Hayford studied the contract for *Moby-Dick* in relation to Melville's other contracts with the Harpers.[55] In *Melville's Reviewers* (1961) Hugh W. Hetherington discussed the known reviews of *Moby-Dick*, including some that he and others had found since the publication of *The Melville Log*.[56]

A number of Melville's sources in *Moby-Dick* have been explored in considerable detail. The fullest published treatment of Melville's whaling sources is Howard P. Vincent's *The Trying-Out of MOBY-DICK* (1949).[57] All students of Melville's sources have acknowledged the importance of the King James Bible, the use of which is most elaborately documented in Nathalia Wright's *Melville's Use of the Bible* (1949). Shakespeare's major influence on *Moby-Dick* has become an acknowledged commonplace of Melville criticism in the last five decades, yet the treatments by Olson (1938), Howard (1940), and F. O. Matthiessen (1941) remain the most provocative and enlightening.[58] Olson was the first to discover and analyze Melville's annotations and markings in his set of Shakespeare and his jottings on the last fly-leaf of the last volume, and to relate them to aspects of *Moby-Dick*. Olson saw *King Lear* as central to Melville's relation to Shakespeare and directly behind the creation of *Moby-Dick*. In particular, Olson noted the correspondence between Ahab's relationship with Pip and Lear's with the Fool and Edgar. Howard argued that the influence of Shakespeare on Melville during the composition of *Moby-Dick* filtered through the medium of Coleridge's lecture on *Hamlet*, enabling him to create for the first time a lifelike tragic hero, instead of fictitious "humor" characters. Matthiessen, emphasizing the dramatic elements in *Moby-Dick*, drew attention to Shakespeare's influence on the composition of particular scenes.

More than three decades before Melville's annotated set of Milton's poetry surfaced in 1984, Henry F. Pommer (1950) through internal evidence accurately identified Miltonic language throughout Melville's works and explored the "poetic" and "epic" influences of *Paradise Lost* on *Moby-Dick*.

Other scholars have argued for the lesser, but contributory, influence of Homer, Dante, Rabelais, Cervantes, Burton, Sterne, and Goethe, as well as Luiz de Camoëns and Pierre Bayle.[59] Thomas Carlyle's influence appears now to have been even more extensive than alert contemporary reviewers thought it to be. Leon Howard (1951) thought that of all the novels Melville read during the gestation of *Moby-Dick* Carlyle's *Sartor Resartus* seemed to have made the greatest impression on him and became the one most frequently reflected in his writing. Howard and James Barbour (1976) have explored the influence of that book on the conclusion of *Moby-Dick*;[60] and Jonathan Arac (1979) has argued that the characterization of Ahab as manager and manipulator of his crew owes something to the section on Cromwell in Carlyle's "The Hero as King."[61] Howard further explores the influence of *Sartor Resartus* and speculates on the influence of *Heroes and Hero Worship* in the posthumous pamphlet *The Unfolding of MOBY-DICK* (1987).

Of American influences on *Moby-Dick* critics point first to that of Nathaniel Hawthorne, who was Melville's friend and neighbor during the last half or more of the time he was working on the book. There is no clear consensus on how much was specifically literary influence on the book and how much was personal influence on Melville's moods and ambitions. Lincoln Colcord (1922) felt that the last two-thirds of *Moby-Dick* were damaged by Hawthorne's impact on Melville; others have generally viewed the older man's influence in a more positive light, paying tribute to both Hawthorne and the "blackness" of his works as shaping forces in the *Moby-Dick* Melville ultimately conceived and completed. Richard H. Brodhead's chapter on *Moby-Dick* (1976) is a detailed attempt to demonstrate that Melville was putting into practice what he had recently learned from Hawthorne.[62]

Little has been done to place *Moby-Dick* in relation to contemporary American fiction writers other than Hawthorne. A number of critics, however, following Constance Rourke, have stressed the book's roots in American folk humor. Richard Chase (1949), in particular, emphasized this element, finding folk humor in Ishmael and Ahab, as well as in lesser characters and in the legends and tall tales the book employs. In *Melville's Humor: A Critical Study* (1981), Jane Mushabac disputed a number of Chase's broader claims. Acknowledging that Chase had made "important suggestions" in attempting to define the American element in Melville's humor, Mushabac held that American folklore is only one part of what Melville was absorbing and building upon in *Moby-Dick*, namely "the whole tradition of prose humorists who, from the Renaissance on, played with the excitement of the opening of the frontier, of land and knowledge, of the new man of infinite potentials." Perry Miller in 1953 tentatively explored the relations of Melville's writings, including *Moby-Dick*, to popular "romance" in both contemporary American and English fiction.[63] Since then the most wide-ranging argument for the relation of contemporary American popular literature to *Moby-Dick* has been David S. Reynolds's treatment in *Beneath the American Renaissance* (1988).[64] A study such as Reynolds's points up the absence of a comprehensive examination of the influence on *Moby-Dick* of British and European literature from the mid-eighteenth to the mid-nineteenth century—from Smollett to Scott to De Quincey to Dickens.

A few critics have tried to place *Moby-Dick* within nineteenth-century literary movements or political, philosophical, or religious contexts. John Stafford (1952) argued that Melville's literary chauvinism during the composition of *Moby-Dick* was a result of his association with a small New York group who were calling for—and trying to call forth—a great national literature.[65] Perry Miller's *The Raven and the Whale* (1956) and other studies of American literary nationalism have carried forward the research Stafford pioneered.[66] At the end of the 1950s and the start of the 1960s different critics argued that *Moby-Dick* is a political allegory which cannot be understood without keys to contemporary political events and personalities; they came to mutually contradictory identifications on the basis of similar arguments: Ahab is William Lloyd Garrison, Ahab is Daniel Webster, Ahab is John C. Calhoun.[67] A recent variation on these essays, Michael Paul Rogin's *Subversive Genealogy* (1983), sees these earlier interpretations as wrongly politicizing *Moby-Dick* "at the expense both of Melville's political imagination and of his actual subject," but nevertheless takes the book as a political allegory which remains "above politics."[68] Rogin's reading belongs to the Marxist-derived New Historicism:

> The sea devours and dissolves the object world; commodities provide humans with their sense of power over nature. Instead of being consumed, humans consume commodities. The white whale reverses that process. It drives Ahab back to the original human helplessness against which commodity creation defended. When Moby Dick shears off Ahab's leg, it reopens the wounds of nature's antagonism. Ahab is, his wound forces him to see, vulnerable to nature's power. Capitalist appropriation has failed him (as it failed [Melville's father] Allan Melvill), returning him to the devouring danger of mother nature.[69]

Both Rogin and James Duban (1983) find oblique commentary in *Moby-Dick* on the abuses of Manifest Destiny and the related issue of whether to extend slavery into the territory acquired as a result of the Mexican War.[70] Another recent New Historicist reading, Donald Pease's discussion of "the scene of cultural persuasion" (1986), links Ahab's rhetoric to the rhetoric of orators and politicians in the early 1850s and its supposed effect on listeners.[71]

Serious study of Melville's interest in philosophy was pioneered by Merton M. Sealts, Jr., in his 1942 Yale dissertation (under Stanley T. Williams) and later studies. In "Melville and the Platonic Tradition" (1982) Sealts examines Ishmael and Ahab as Platonists and explores "the implications of Platonic thought for the book as a whole."[72] John Wenke (1986) examines Melville's use of various philosophers and schools of thought in *Moby-Dick* (and Melville's other works) and supplements Sealts's treatment of Platonic elements in the book.[73] Transcendentalism, a movement influenced by Platonism and encompassing the issue of literary nationalism as well as issues in politics, religion, and philosophy, has been frequently discussed in relation to *Moby-Dick*, as critics have attempted to demonstrate Melville's Transcendentalist or anti-Transcendentalist sympathies. Like many later critics, Matthiessen (1941) argued that in *Moby-Dick* Melville shared "key positions" with the Transcendentalists, though Ahab represents in part Melville's reaction against the destructiveness of Emerson's "self-enclosed individualism."[74] Nina Baym (1979) has made the largest claims for Emerson's impact on *Moby-Dick,* arguing that Melville's contact with Emerson's thought was the single most significant influence on the shape of the book, that it reflects an Emersonian view of fiction and reading, and that Emerson's concepts of truth and the divine authorship of nature and language, expressed in the "Language" section of *Nature*, are wrought into its texture and form.[75] In his meticulous evaluation of Melville's knowledge of Emerson (1980, 1982), however, Sealts was unconvinced by Baym's claims but found parallels between passages in *Moby-Dick* and passages in "Intellect," "The Transcendentalist," and *Representative Men*.[76]

Melville's religious dilemmas as evidenced by *Moby-Dick* were first discussed at length in William Braswell's *Melville's Religious Thought* (1943).[77] Since then the fullest attempt to relate the book to Melville's religious training in childhood and to contemporary religious controversies has been T. Walter Herbert, Jr.'s *MOBY-DICK and Calvinism: A World Dismantled* (1977). Herbert argues that Melville's "religious perplexities were shaped by the fact that he absorbed in childhood the opposing theories of Unitarianism and the most conservative orthodoxy"; he assembles evidence that Melville's "spiritual exploration in *Moby-Dick* employs specific themes and motifs of Calvinist and liberal theology, and of the controversy between them."[78] Rowland Sherrill's "Melville and Religion" (1986) discusses the issues involved in Melville's "religious life"and surveys other treatments of his religious thought.[79]

Studies like these that relate *Moby-Dick* to movements or ideas current in Melville's time have been less common than studies that focus on the words of the book (in whatever text that is being used) without recourse to evidence about Melville's life, his reading, or his times. Among the topics frequently argued from internal evidence are the problem of who the hero is and the related issues of the consistency of the narration and the roles of Ishmael and Ahab.

When the question of identifying the hero of *Moby-Dick* has arisen, the whale himself has had a few advocates (most notably Mumford), but until the 1950s Ahab was regularly regarded as the hero. Most critics of the 1920s took that for granted: in Henry A. Murray's interpretation (formed contemporaneously with Mumford's though published much later) the name Ishmael does not even occur. According to Murray, the "tragic hero" of the book is "Ahab-Lucifer." There is no aesthetic distance between author and satanic hero: "Ahab-Melville's aggression was directed against the object that once harmed Eros with apparent malice and was still thwarting it with presentiments of further retaliations." Despite his specialized interpretation, Murray represented the dominant tendency of the 1920s to identify Ahab in various ways with Melville. In contrast, Mumford (while barely mentioning Ishmael) distinguished clearly between Ahab and Melville: Ahab fights evil and "therein lies his heroism and virtue: but he fights it with its own weapons and therein lies his madness"; Melville, through writing *Moby-Dick*, "conquered the white whale in his own consciousness." Art, "in the broad sense of all humanizing effort," Mumford argued, is man's answer to the "inscrutable, unfathomable, malicious" universe. Thorp (1938), in different terms, also distinguished between author and character (Melville "hurled, not himself, but Ahab, his creature, at the injurious gods").[80] William Ellery Sedgwick (1944), the first critic to devote sustained attention to Ishmael since Evert Duyckinck reviewed *Moby-Dick* in the *Literary World*, held that Ishmael's story "turns on his mortal need to maintain himself against the strong drag he feels towards Ahab," and later critics who have discussed Melville's relation to Ahab have tended to sound variations on Thorp's notion that Melville's sympathy for Ahab stopped short of total identification and Sedgwick's suggestion that Ahab and Ishmael represent "opposite pulls" of Melville's temperament.[81]

Critics in the 1940s were inclined, like Matthiessen and Sedgwick, to treat Ahab as both hero and villain, paying tribute to various aspects of his greatness, yet far more alive than most earlier critics to his tragic flaws—most notably his excessive, anti-social individualism. At the end of the decade, Richard Chase cited Ahab as an example of the false hero or false Prometheus (whom he took to be a recurrent figure in Melville's works), one who "betrays his humanity through some monstrous pride, some titanic quest for moral purity, some obsessed abdication from the natural ambiguities of life in quest of the absolute and the inviolable, or some moral treachery which involves his companions as well as himself in a final catastrophe." Newton Arvin (1950) also stressed Ahab's rejection of the common ties of humanity. The alternative to Ahab's "raging egoism" (which is akin to the hubris of Greek tragedy and the Christian sin of pride but is "neither quite the one nor quite the other"), Arvin argued, is "a strong intuition of human solidarity as a priceless good." This "affirmation" was Melville's version of Hawthorne's "magnetic chain of humanity" and Whitman's "manly attachment," an essentially humanistic and secular rather than Christian principle.[82] Similarly, Henry Nash Smith (1953) decided that Ahab was "an exemplification of any of a number of wrong and dangerous attitudes"; Ishmael was the hero of *Moby-Dick* because he embodied Meville's "affirmations" of brotherhood or community.[83]

In the face of such emphasis on Ahab's moral shortcomings, Lawrance Thompson's iconoclastic, pun-mongering interpretation of Melville's "quarrel with God" (1952) attempted to re-establish Melville's identification with un-Christian Ahab.[84] Braswell had concluded that *Moby-Dick* "contains evidence apart from what Ahab says that Melville thought of God as not wholly benevolent."[85] Thompson went much further: *Moby-Dick* is Melville's "personal declaration of independence not only from the tyranny of Christian dogma but also from the sovereign tyranny of God Almighty." Melville "ultimately chooses to justify himself by glorifying Ahab's declaration of independence from man and God; to justify himself by representing Ahab as a supremely tragic hero who rises to his highest grandeur . . . even in the face of that ultimate and inevitable God-bullying indignity, death." Thompson argued that there is in fact a close identity of viewpoints between Ishmael and Ahab, that Melville only *pretends* a contrast between their viewpoints.[86] Despite Thompson's efforts, critics have continued to dwell upon Ahab's failings in brotherhood and love.

Mumford's example shows that even the most elaborate analysis of *Moby-Dick* could be written in the 1920s with no more than a passing mention of Ishmael. Critics of the 1930s tended to mention him in accounting for a narration that seemed to shift back and forth from Melville's own voice to that of his narrator. The hyphenated term "Ishmael-Melville" (or "Melville-Ishmael") began to be used, sometimes as a formula for identifying the narrator of passages Ishmael could not literally have witnessed or heard about at secondhand; often as a way of implying a community of attitude between Melville and his narrator. Reacting to such casual identification of narrator and author, Charles Olson (1938) protested that Ishmael had been "confused with" Melville too long; Ishmael, he insisted, "is fictive, imagined, as are Ahab, Pip and Bulkington."[87] Walter E. Bezanson, in his highly regarded "*Moby-Dick*: Work of Art" (delivered as a lecture in 1951 and first printed in 1953), argued cogently against "any one-to-one equation of Melville and Ishmael" or use of the phrase "Melville-Ishmael," unless it were defined to mean either Melville or Ishmael, not both. "For in the process of composition," Bezanson cautioned, "even when the artist knowingly begins with his own experience, there are crucial interventions between the act that was experience and the re-enactment that is art—instruments of time, of intention, and especially of form, to name only a few."

Without specifically designating Ishmael as the hero, Bezanson argued that *Moby-Dick* "is not so much about Ahab or the White Whale as it is about Ishmael" and proposed that "it is he who is the real center of meaning and the defining force of the novel." Bezanson was the first critic to distinguish clearly between "forecastle Ishmael," or the younger Ishmael of "some years ago," and "narrator Ishmael," who is "merely young Ishmael grown older," and whose voice recounts the adventures of young Ishmael "as a story already fully experienced" but "not fully understood." Bezanson was also the first critic to offer an elaborate analysis of the qualities of Ishmael's mind—qualities that uniquely fit him for the telling of *Moby-Dick*. Paul Brodtkorb in *Ishmael's White World* (1965) attempted an even more rigorous demonstration that "in a major sense" Ishmael "*is* the book," that his "overt character and history are consistent with his emotions, which in turn constitute his universe of space, time, body, and others," and that "that universe is totally coherent, even if it occasionally seems not to be."[88] The crucial difference between these two influential analyses is that Bezanson finally stressed the sense of "wonder" in Ishmael while Brodtkorb stressed a kind of "boredom, dread, and pervasive despair" as the "unity" of Ishmael's consciousness and of his book (Brodtkorb, 112). Other critics have followed Brodtkorb in arguing that the "prime experience" for the reader of *Moby-Dick* is "the narrator's unfolding sensibility," but few have assented entirely to Brodtkorb's characterization of that sensibility. In one subsequent treatment of Ishmael, Warwick Wadlington (1975) occupies middle ground between Bezanson and Brodtkorb, finding Ishmael's "central and saving mood" to be a "ludic combination of his psychic extremes—on the one hand the black despair of alienation and on the other a genial expansive delight in fellowship with humankind and with the All."[89]

The most sophisticated analysts of the narration of *Moby-Dick* have attempted to explain apparent narrative discontinuities through their definition of Ishmael's role. Thus, Glauco Cambon (1961), confronting those passages where Ishmael tells things he could not have witnessed, argued that Ishmael "is a conjurer endeavoring to evoke, to make present, his improbable hero." In this perspective, the asides and soliloquies of Ahab, Starbuck, and others "are the conjuring narrator's imaginative reconstruction of the characters he knew, the *As If* of imagination becoming a presentational *Here*." Cambon saw Ishmael as "the artist in the act of telling us, and struggling to understand, his crucial experience": his "vanishing from the stage after a certain point does not constitute a breach of poetical continuity, but a dialectical movement that reproduces and expands the repeated transition from narrative to drama, from memory to visionary actuality, from conjuring subjectivity to conjured objectivity."[90] Brodtkorb developed the most complexly ratiocinative justification for regarding Ishmael as narrator throughout, to the point of saying that "formally" Ishmael, not Melville, "is the one who is inconsistent when he does not accurately remember something he has written, and later writes something at odds with it." It should not be surprising, Brodtkorb held, "that curiously Ishmaelean traits and attitudes appear in other characters":

At such times, Ishmael imagines another character to be like himself if only because at all times he *is* whatever character he reports, even when he reports what logically he could not know; for he is the writer, entering into the souls of others by virtue of his—somewhat imperfect, to be sure—Keatsean negative capability. And, similarly, when he disappears from the action, he quite simply *is* the action; why should he not be? Why should he remain a separate observer for the dubious sake of low-mimetic unity when the existential fact he is formally demonstrating is that he was *not* separate: that he also had given himself up "to the abandonment of the time and the place."

(Brodtkorb, 7–8)

Problems remain, not entirely solved—for instance, by Brodtkorb's ascribing to Ishmael rather than Melville an uncle in Dorchester, Massachusetts, named John D'Wolf; but unquestionably Cambon and Brodtkorb influenced the way in which the narration has been discussed. Few later critics casually assert that Ishmael "disappears" somewhere in the middle of the book. The implications of Harrison Hayford's account (1978) of the genesis of *Moby-Dick* (and of related "Discussions of Adopted Readings" in the Northwestern-Newberry edition [1988]) have yet to be explored in a thorough analysis of the narration.

The attention devoted to Ishmael in the 1950s eventually provoked protests from such critics as Merlin Bowen (1960), who (while acknowledging Ishmael's importance) insisted that "the book lives in our memories, and surely this was the author's intention, as Ahab's story, not as Ishmael's."[91] Thomas Woodson (1966) agreed that in "the popular mind *Moby-Dick* has always been Ahab's book," even though literary critics, "more concerned with the intellectual issues raised by Melville's art than with the adventurous plot, have turned their attention from Ahab to Ishmael, the author's narrator and spokesman." Noting that Ishmael "insists that Ahab is a great man, a tragic hero," Woodson reexamined Ahab's character, "with sympathy towards this judgment, leaving the ethical atmosphere in the background, and concentrating on what actually is said about him in Ishmael's narrative and in his own words." The most strenuously argued advocacy of Ahab's greatness, however, came from Brodtkorb, who, despite his rigorous commitment to the centrality of Ishmael in *Moby-Dick*, was part of the reaction against recent estimates of Ahab. Brodtkorb claimed that the tendency to condemn him "often involves a prior reduction of the sort of stature granted Ahab by Ishmael's presentation of him" (Brodtkorb, 158, n.16). On the question of Ahab's "final moral status," Brodtkorb argued, Ishmael is as "self-divided" as Ahab is, but he presents him as a kind of religious hero: "the behavior in relation to God that Mapple advocates is . . . seen to be Ahab's behavior; and it is the behavior of a saint" (Brodtkorb, 78,73). In their defense of "Ahab's greatness," both Brodtkorb and Woodson proceed through discussion of Ishmael in a way critics never did before the 1950s, and no corrective scholarship seems likely to relegate Ishmael again to a minor position in *Moby-Dick*, however long his lay aboard the *Pequod*. Robert Zoellner's book-length study, *The Salt-Sea Mastadon* (1973), which distinguishes between "the Ahabian and the Ishmaelian epistemologies," is typical of the continuing tendency among critics in the 1970s and 1980s to see both Ishmael and Ahab as central to whatever meaning they find in the book.[92]

Among the other characters aboard the *Pequod*, the mates, the harpooneers (especially Queequeg), Bulkington, Father Mapple, and Pip have all received voluminous commentary. Bulkington and Father Mapple's sermon have both often been regarded as central to interpretation of the book. In 1938 Yvor Winters claimed that Melville praised Bulkington and condemned Ahab because Bulkington lives "by perception trained in principle, in abstraction, to the point where it is able to find its way amid the chaos of the specific," while Ahab rejects "living by judgment" (as when he destroys his quadrant),[93] and since then critics have argued over whether Bulkington is a similar or antithetical character to Ahab. Notably, in Harrison Hayford's hypothetical account of the composition of *Moby-Dick* (1978) Bulkington plays a central role. Critics have also played numerous variations on Howard P. Vincent's argument (1949) that "Ahab no less than Father Mapple is in search of an Absolute" but unlike Mapple "acknowledges no law but his own; his search will be carried on in self-assertion, not in self-submission."[94]

Several of the fuller critical examinations have dealt with the structure of the book. Olson and Matthiessen helped popularize a comparison to a five-act play or a symphony with five movements. Arvin, who thought the book was an epic, not a tragedy, said it moved in four "waves": first, the chapters up to the sailing; then a "second unmistakable wave" that "comes to its crest in the scene on the quarter-deck"; then the central portion of the book; and a fourth beginning with "The Symphony." Bezanson distinguished two chapter forms besides the usual novelistic chapters devoted to "the movement of narrative or to character analysis": the dramatic chapters (such as "Midnight, Forecastle," "The Quarter-Deck," and "The Candles") and the sermonic-essayistic chapters (such as Father Mapples's sermon and Fleece's sermon in "Stubb's Supper," and chapters like "The Line," "The Blanket," and "The Funeral"). Bezanson also identified various kinds of mutual relations of chapters such as "chapter sequences" (whether of narrative or theme), "chapter clusters," and "balancing chapters," relating the structure of the book, like everything else, to "the organic mind-world of Ishmael whose sensibility rhythmically agitates the flux of experience." Leo Marx (1964) pointed out another sort of patterning: "The try-works episode stands in the same relation to 'A Squeeze of the Hand' as the quarter-deck scene to the masthead revery: it is an evocation of explosive power following a pastoral interlude."[95] More recently Wadlington argued that one "of the basic structural and rhetorical patternings" of *Moby-Dick* is the repetition of "enchantmentlike captivations or commitments and the subsequent releases from them, a cycle that establishes Ishmael's self-being as both character and narrative consciousness."[96]

In the last four decades *Moby-Dick* has been subjected to every fashionable academic approach, Freudian, Jungian, Marxist, neo-Christian, existential, New Critical, mythic, structuralist, post-structuralist, reader-response, deconstructionist, New Historicist, in addition to a multitude of thematic studies. In this introduction we have been able to offer merely the draft of a systematization of Melville criticism, to point only to some of its main tendencies and to suggest something of its extreme diversity.[97] The predominant characteristic of writing on *Moby-Dick* in the last forty years is clear enough: whatever approaches writers used, those approaches were almost always derived from critical theories rather than from documentary evidence—and were in that sense critical rather than scholarly. In these years Melville enthusiasts made few exciting documentary discoveries relating to *Moby-Dick*, not because everything had been found but because the academic climate did not encourage professors to hunt for new documents or to tease more precise meaning out of the documents already known. Few academics tried to build on the biographical work of the late 1930s and 1940s. Since the early 1950s only a few old-fashioned source studies of *Moby-Dick* have appeared (though a hundred and sixty sources have been cited by writers on Melville beginning with the first reviewers of *The Whale*). Only half a dozen scholars have attempted to understand the stages of the book's composition on the basis of external evidence and its internal anomalies.[98]

We seem to have witnessed recently, however, the beginning of a new era in Melville scholarship. In 1983 the New York Public Library acquired the greatest previously unknown cache of Melville documents, the surviving portion of the papers of Melville's sister Augusta, which included many family letters from the period of *Moby-Dick* and her record of correspondence for the entire time Melville was working on his masterpiece. In the second half of the 1980s, several substantial studies were published close together. G. Thomas Tanselle in *A Companion to Melville Studies* (1986) surveyed "Melville and the World of Books" in an essay that ranged "from Melville's own reading and book-buying to the collecting of and commentary on the books he wrote, including the efforts to establish reliable texts of his works for future readers."[99] While Tanselle dealt with all of Melville's writings, he necessarily devoted most attention to *Moby-Dick*. No other American writer has evoked such a detailed and learned biographical, bibliographical, and historical exposition as this essay by Tanselle. In 1987 Mary K. Bercaw published *Melville's Sources*, a study that lists the books which allusions in Melville's own writings show that he must or may have read, although no one has been able to link particular copies to him in many instances. Bercaw defined her study so as to include what was excluded from Merton M. Sealts, Jr.'s *Melville's Reading*, which appeared in a revised edition in 1988. Together

Sealts and Bercaw have provided an astonishingly comprehensive (although necessarily incomplete) record of the reading that went into the creation of *Moby-Dick* and Melville's other works. In 1988 the long-planned Northwestern-Newberry edition of *Moby-Dick* was published. There, in addition to a critical text, the editors (Hayford, Parker, and Tanselle) included detailed information about bibliographical and textual matters, elaborate discussion notes on editorial decisions, as well as a monograph-length "Historical Note" on the composition, publication, reception, and later critical history of the book. In this edition the "Augusta Papers" were used to help retell the history of the composition, as were documents in Parker's forthcoming study of the effect on *Moby-Dick* of the English forger Thomas Powell (who may have helped to precipitate Melville's break with the older generation of American writers and to direct his thinking about the relationship between originality and greatness, in Shakespeare and in his whaling book). Rather than closing off research, the "Historical Note" pointed up just how much new research still needs to be done, particularly on the history of the British reputation of first *The Whale* and then *Moby-Dick*. Kevin J. Hayes and Hershel Parker's revision of the 1975 *Checklist of Melville Reviews* by Steven Mailloux and Parker was published in 1991 by Northwestern University Press. The results of other recent research are forthcoming. The Northwestern-Newberry volume of Melville's *Correspondence*, completely re-edited and annotated by Lynn Horth (and supplemented by additional letters and by surviving letters to Melville) is set for publication in 1992. As this G. K. Hall volume goes to press, Hershel Parker is finishing a draft of the first full-scale biography (one to run two or three times the length of Weaver's or Howard's), to be published by W. W. Norton in 1994. About the same time Parker expects to publish his expansion of Jay Leyda's 1951 two-volume *The Melville Log* into the three-volume *The New Melville Log* (Gordian Press). Thus for the first time since around 1950, the early 1990s mark a new stage in scholarship on *Moby-Dick*. Factual information is once again, for the most part, consolidated (or about to be consolidated) in a few books rather than being scattered through scholarly articles and notes.

The essays in this collection bear witness to the vital part that Melville's reading and assimilation of both old and newer authors played in the creation of his masterpiece. We reprint here several significant reviews from 1851; extracts from articles that surveyed Melville's career in the mid-1850s; commentary from 1874 to 1919, the centenary of Melville's birth; and several of the most rhapsodic pieces of the Melville Revival. In subsequent sections we include early and more recent studies of the literary influences on *Moby-Dick* and of its literary affinities; some of the best commentary on Ahab, Ishmael, and the Whale; and Harrison Hayford's work on the genesis of *Moby-Dick*, the most sustained analysis of its internal anomalies in the context of the phases of Melville's work on the book. The final section of new essays includes John Wenke's study of Melville's use of Mary Shelley's *Frankenstein* and De Quincey's *Confessions of an English Opium Eater* (which draws on Hayford's essay); David S. Reynolds's essay on the affinities between *Moby-Dick* and popular literature of the 1840s and 1850s (which extends his work on *Moby-Dick* in his recent study *Beneath the American Renaissance*); and Hershel Parker's study of the influence of Melville's domestic circumstances on the composition of *Moby-Dick*. While the essays in this collection testify to the magnitude of Melville's achievement in *Moby-Dick* and to the enduring fascination the book has always evoked (and often sustained for decades) in its warmest admirers, they are also chosen to celebrate a special kind of literary intertextuality, where the book-loving author shares his immense, extravagant, and exuberant range of literature with a book-loving reader who responds to *Moby-Dick* from the strength of his or her own range of literary enthusiasms.

Notes

1. In this introduction mentions of books and articles on *Moby-Dick* are footnoted only when the passages referred to are not reprinted in this collection.

2. See the chronology in Jay Leyda, *The Melville Log* (1951; rpt., with supplement, New York: Gordian Press, 1969), 2; hereafter cited in the text as Leyda.

3. Herman Melville, *Typee: A Peep at Polynesian Life*, ed. Harrison Hayford, Hershel Parker, and G. Thomas Tanselle (Evanston and Chicago: Northwestern University Press and The Newberry Library, 1968), xiii.

4. See the forthcoming study by Hershel Parker and Kevin J. Hayes of Gansevoort Melville's record of his reading in two surviving volumes of John Todd's *Index Rerum*, preserved in the Berkshire Athenaeum.

5. Herman Melville, *The Piazza Tales and Other Prose Pieces, 1839–1860*, ed. Harrison Hayford, Alma A. MacDougall, G. Thomas Tanselle, and others (Evanston and Chicago: Northwestern University Press and The Newberry Library, 1987), 191–204 and 622–624.

6. Herman Melville, *White-Jacket*, ed. Harrison Hayford, Hershel Parker, G. Thomas Tanselle (Evanston and Chicago: Northwestern University Press and The Newberry Library, 1970), 168.

7. *White-Jacket*, 169.

8. For Long Ghost's reading, see Herman Melville, *Omoo*, ed. Harrison Hayford, Hershel Parker, and G. Thomas Tanselle (Evanston and Chicago: Northwestern University Press and The Newberry Library, 1968), 12; for evidence of Melville's own "learning," see Harrison Hayford and Walter Blair, eds., *Omoo* (New York: Hendricks House, 1969) , xxxix, 350-51.

9. For new evidence on the date Melville began *Mardi*, see Herman Melville, *Moby-Dick*, ed. Harrison Hayford, Hershel Parker, and G. Thomas Tanselle (Evanston and Chicago: Northwestern University Press and The Newberry Library, 1988), 618.

10. Herman Melville, *Mardi*, ed. Harrison Hayford, Hershel Parker, and G. Thomas Tanselle (Evanston and Chicago: Northwestern University Press and The Newberry Library, 1970), 41, 63, 69, 78, 79, 104.

11. *The Letters of Herman Melville*, ed. Merrill R. Davis and William H. Gilman (New Haven: Yale University Press, 1960), 79; hereafter cited in the text as *Letters*.

12. For further discussion of Melville's editions of Shakespeare and Milton, see the Northwestern-Newberry edition of *Moby-Dick*, 956–57; for the comparative failure of *Mardi*, see *Letters*, 85–89, and Leyda, 298–311.

13. Herman Melville, *Journals*, ed. Howard C. Horsford with Lynn Horth (Evanston and Chicago: Northwestern University Press and The Newberry Library, 1989), 4; hereafter cited in the text as *Journals*.

14. See the facsimile of Melville's list of "Books obtained in London," *Journals*, 145.

15. See "Melville's Memoranda in Chase's *Narrative of the Essex*" in *Moby-Dick*, 971-95.

16. For Melville's whaling sources for *Moby-Dick* and the dates he acquired them, see *Moby-Dick*, 635–47, 971–77.

17. For *Sartor Resartus* and *On Heroes*, see Merton M. Sealts, Jr., *Melville's Reading* (Columbia: University of South Carolina Press, 1988), 163.

18. For the composition of Melville's essay on Hawthorne, see the "Historical Note" in *Moby-Dick*, 611–15, and the documentation in *The New Melville Log*, ed. Jay Leyda and Hershel Parker, forthcoming.

19. "Supplement" to *The Melville Log* (1969 edition), 925.

20. *Moby-Dick*, "Historical Note," 626; hereafter cited in the text.

21. For British reviews of *The Whale*, see section 7 of the "Historical Note" in *Moby-Dick*, 700–710. All the then known reviews of *Moby-Dick* and *The Whale* are reprinted in Hershel Parker and Harrison Hayford, *MOBY-DICK as Doubloon* (New York: W. W. Norton, 1970). All reviews yet discovered are listed (not reprinted) in Kevin J. Hayes and Hershel Parker's *Checklist of Melville Reviews* (Evanston: Northwestern University Press, 1991), a revision and expansion of the 1975 *Checklist* compiled by Steven Mailloux and Hershel Parker.

22. For American reviews, see section 7 of the "Historical Note" in *Moby-Dick*, 712–28, and the works cited in the previous footnote.

23. All the reviews of *Pierre* known in 1983 are reprinted in Brian Higgins and Hershel Parker, eds., *Critical Essays on Herman Melville's PIERRE; OR, THE AMBIGUITIES* (Boston: G. K. Hall, 1983).

24. George Monteiro, "'Far and Away the Most Original Genius that America has Produced': Notations in the New York *Times* and Melville's Literary Reputation at the Turn of the Century," *Resources for American Literary Study* 5 (1975): 69–80.

25. George Monteiro, "Mather's Melville Book," *Studies in Bibliography* 25 (1972): 226–27.

26. Morley Roberts, *W. H. Hudson: A Portrait* (New York: E. P. Dutton, 1924), 131.

27. See *MOBY-DICK as Doubloon*, 149, 173.

28. See "Herman Melville," *Times Literary Supplement* 916 (7 August 1919), 423, unsigned but identified as Woolf's in B. J. Kirkpatrick, *A Bibliography of Virginia Woolf*, rev. ed. (London: Rupert Hart-Davis, 1967), 110 (C 161). See Brian Higgins's summary in "A Centennial Essay by Virginia Woolf," *Melville Society Extracts* 45 (February 1981): 10–12. See also Virginia Woolf, "Phases of Fiction," [New York] *Bookman* 69 (June 1929): 408–10.

29. Shneidman's introduction to the section on "Personology" in *Endeavors in Psychology: Selections from the Personology of Henry A. Murray* (New York: Harper & Row, 1981), 5.

30. Murray's Melville collection, including his copies of twentieth-century studies of Melville, are now in the Melville Room, which he founded at the Berkshire Athenaeum in Pittsfield, Massachusetts. For details of the unpublished biography of Melville, see Forrest Robinson's biography of Murray, forthcoming from Harvard University Press.

31. See M. Thomas Inge, "Melville in Popular Culture," in *A Companion to Melville Studies*, ed. John Bryant (Westport, Conn.:Greenwood Press, 1986), 695–739, especially 696–701.

32. Ludwig Lewisohn, *Expression in America* (New York: Harper, 1932), 186–93; excerpted in the Norton Critical Edition of *Moby-Dick*, ed. Harrison Hayford and Hershel Parker (New York: W. W. Norton, 1967), 634.

33. Montgomery Belgion, "Introduction," in Herman Melville, *Moby Dick* (London: The Cresset Press, 1946), vii–xxvii.

34. William S. Ament, "Bowdler and the Whale: Some Notes on the first English and American Editions of *Moby-Dick*," *American Literature* 4 (March 1932): 39–46.

35. Constance Rourke, *American Humor: A Study of the National Character* (New York: Harcourt, Brace, 1931). Critics of the Revival did not usually interest themselves in Melville's whaling sources, though Carl Van Doren (1923) pointed as a possible source to J. N. Reynolds's "Mocha Dick," *Knickerbocker Magazine* 13 (May 1839): 377–92 (reprinted in the Norton Critical Edition of *Moby-Dick*, 571–90).

36. Leon Howard, "A Predecessor of *Moby-Dick*," *Modern Language Quarterly* 49 (May 1934): 310–11; and Frederick B. Adams, Jr., "The Crow's Nest," *Colophon* n.s. 2 (Autumn 1936): 148–54.

37. George C. Homans, "The Dark Angel: The Tragedy of Herman Melville," *New England Quarterly* 5 (October 1932): 699–730; and Carl Van Vechten, "A Belated Biography," *Literary Review* 2 (31 December 1921): 316.

38. Willard Thorp, *Herman Melville: Representative Selections* (New York: American Book Co., 1938), lxxiv.

39. Yvor Winters, "Herman Melville and the Problems of Moral Navigation," in *Maule's Curse: Seven Studies in the History of American Obscurantism* (Norfolk, Conn.: New Directions, 1938), 53.

40. Winters, 73.

41. R. P. Blackmur, "The Craft of Herman Melville," *Virginia Quarterly Review* 14 (Spring 1938): 266–82.

42. Stanley Geist, *Herman Melville: The Tragic Vision and the Heroic Ideal* (Cambridge: Harvard University Press, 1939).

43. Brian Higgins, *Herman Melville: A Reference Guide, 1931–1960* (Boston: G. K. Hall, 1987), xi; the reference in the quotation from Higgins is to Robert E. Spiller, "Melville: Our First Tragic Poet," *Saturday Review of Literature* 33 (25 November 1950): 24–25.

44. Leon Howard, "Melville's Struggle with the Angel," *Modern Language Quarterly* 1 (June 1940): 195–206; Howard, *Herman Melville: A Biography* (Berkeley: University of California Press, 1951); and Jay Leyda, *The Melville Log: A Documentary Life of Herman Melville, 1819–1891*, 2 vols. (New York: Harcourt, Brace, 1951).

45. Harrison Hayford, "Melville and Hawthorne: A Biographical and Critical Study," unpublished dissertation, Yale University, 1945.

46. Herman Melville, *Moby-Dick*, ed. Luther S. Mansfield and Howard P. Vincent (New York: Hendricks House, 1952).

47. Herman Melville, *Journal of a Visit to London and the Continent*, ed. Eleanor Melville Metcalf (Cambridge: Harvard University Press, 1948); and Eleanor Melville Metcalf, *Herman Melville: Cycle and Epicycle* (Cambridge: Harvard University Press, 1953).

48. Newton Arvin, "Those Close to Melville," *New York Times Book Review* (8 November 1953), 6.

49. *The Letters of Herman Melville* (New Haven: Yale University Press, 1960).

50. Herman Melville, *Moby-Dick*, ed. Harrison Hayford and Hershel Parker (New York: W. W. Norton, 1967), 471–98.

51. Herman Melville, *Moby-Dick*, ed. Harrison Hayford, Hershel Parker, and G. Thomas Tanselle (Evanston and Chicago: Northwestern University Press and The Newberry Library, 1988).

52. William Charvat, *The Profession of Authorship in America, 1800–1870*, ed. Matthew J. Bruccoli (Columbus: Ohio State University Press, 1968), 204–61.

53. Charvat, 240–41.

54. G. Thomas Tanselle, "The Sales of Melville's Books," *Harvard Library Bulletin* 17 (April 1969): 195–215

55. Harrison Hayford, "Contract: *Moby-Dick*, by Herman Melville," *Proof*, vol. 1, 1–7.

56. *Melville's Reviewers: British and American, 1846–1891* (Chapel Hill: University of North Carolina Press, 1961), 189–226. Because of the unreliability of this book, students should go to the reviews published in *MOBY-DICK as Doubloon*, ed. Hershel Parker and Harrison Hayford (New York: W. W. Norton, 1970); reviews discovered after 1970 are listed in Kevin J. Hayes and Hershel Parker, *Checklist of Melville Reviews* (Evanston: Northwestern University Press, 1991). See n. 21.

57. The fullest treatment of Melville's whaling sources is Sumner W. D. Scott's unpublished dissertation, "The Whale in *Moby Dick*" (Chicago, 1950). For further discussion of the whaling sources and attempts by scholars to date the composition of parts of the book on the basis of Melville's use of them, see section 4 of the "Historical Note" in the Northwestern-Newberry edition of *Moby-Dick*, reprinted below.

58. Extracts from the works cited in the preceding sentences of this paragraph are included in this G. K. Hall volume except for Howard's "Melville's Struggle with the Angel," already cited in n. 44.

59. Mary K. Bercaw, *Melville's Sources* (Evanston: Northwestern University Press, 1987).

60. James Barbour and Leon Howard, "Carlyle and the Conclusion of *Moby-Dick*," *New England Quarterly* 49 (June 1976): 214-24.

61. Jonathan Arac, *Commissioned Spirits: The Shaping of Social Motion in Dickens, Carlyle, Melville, and Hawthorne* (New Brunswick: Rutgers University Press, 1979), 139–63.

62. Richard H. Brodhead, *Hawthorne, Melville, and the Novel* (Chicago: University of Chicago Press, 1976), 134–62. See also the chapter on "Hawthorne, Melville, and the Fiction of Prophecy" in Brodhead's *The School of Hawthorne* (New York: Oxford University Press, 1986), 17–47.

63. Perry Miller, "Melville and Transcendentalism," *Virginia Quarterly Review* 29 (Autumn 1953): 556–75.

64. David S. Reynolds, *Beneath the American Renaissance: The Subversive Imagination in the Age of Emerson and Melville* (New York: Alfred A. Knopf, 1988).

65. John Stafford, *The Literary Criticism of "Young America": A Study in the Relationship of Politics and Literature, 1837–1850* (Berkeley: University of California Press, 1952).

66. Perry Miller, *The Raven and the Whale: The War of Words and Wits in the Era of Poe and Melville* (New York: Harcourt, Brace, 1956).

67. See Willie T. Weathers, "*Moby-Dick* and the Nineteenth-Century Scene," *University of Texas Studies in Literature and Language* 1 (Winter 1960): 477–501; Charles H. Foster, "Something in Emblems: A Reinterpretation of *Moby-Dick*," *New England Quarterly* 34 (March 1961): 3–35; and Alan Heimert, "*Moby-Dick* and American Political Symbolism," *American Quarterly* 15 (Winter 1963): 498–534. These articles are excerpted in *MOBY-DICK as Doubloon*, 272–84, 306–18.

68. Michael Paul Rogin, *Subversive Genealogy: The Politics and Art of Herman Melville* (New York: Alfred A. Knopf, 1983), 108.

69. Rogin, 115.

70. James Duban, *Melville's Major Fiction: Politics, Theology, and Imagination* (DeKalb: Northern Illinois University Press, 1983).

71. Donald Pease, "Melville and Cultural Persuasion," in *Ideology and Classic American Literature*, ed. Sacvan Bercovitch and Myra Jehlen (Cambridge: Harvard University Press, 1986), 384–417.

72. Merton M. Sealts, Jr., "Herman Melville's Reading in Ancient Philosophy,"

unpublished dissertation, Yale University, 1942; see a section revised from the dissertation, "Melville and the Platonic Tradition," in Sealts, *Pursuing Melville, 1940–1980: Chapters and Essays* (Madison: University of Wisconsin Press, 1982), 300–19.

73. John Wenke, "'Ontological Heroics': Melville's Philosophical Art," in *A Companion to Melville Studies*, ed. John Bryant (Westport: Greenwood Press, 1986), 567–601.

74. For further commentary on *Moby-Dick* and Transcendentalism, see Brian Higgins, "Herman Melville," in *The Transcendentalists: A Review of Research and Criticism*, ed. Joel Myerson (New York: Modern Language Association of America, 1984), 348–61.

75. Nina Baym, "Melville's Quarrel with Fiction," *PMLA* 94 (October 1979): 909–23.

76. Sealts, *Pursuing Melville*, 263–70, 317–19.

77. William Braswell, *Melville's Religious Thought: An Essay in Interpretation* (Durham: Duke University Press, 1943).

78. T. Walter Herbert, Jr., *MOBY-DICK and Calvinism: A World Dismantled* (New Brunswick: Rutgers University Press, 1977), 5–6, 10.

79. Rowland A. Sherrill, "Melville and Religion," in *A Companion to Melville Studies*, ed. John Bryant (Westport: Greenwood Press, 1986), 481–513.

80. Willard Thorp, *Herman Melville: Representative Selections*, lxxv.

81. William Ellery Sedgwick, *Herman Melville: The Tragedy of Mind* (Cambridge: Harvard University Press, 1944), 120, 125.

82. Newton Arvin, *Herman Melville* (New York: William Sloane, 1950), 179, 181.

83. Henry Nash Smith, "The Image of Society in *Moby-Dick*," in *MOBY-DICK Centennial Essays*, ed. Tyrus Hillway and Luther S. Mansfield (Dallas: Southern Methodist University Press, 1953), 75, 74.

84. Lawrance Thompson, *Melville's Quarrel with God* (Princeton: Princeton University Press, 1952), 147–243.

85. Braswell, 69.

86. Thompson, 147, 153, 151.

87. See also Olson, *Call Me Ishmael* (New York: Reynel and Hitchcock, 1947), 57.

88. Paul Brodtkorb, *Ishmael's White World* (New Haven: Yale University Press, 1965), 4, 102; hereafter cited in the text.

89. Warwick Wadlington, *The Confidence Game in American Literature* (Princeton: Princeton University Press, 1975), 74.

90. Glauco Cambon, "Ishmael and the Problem of Formal Discontinuities in *Moby Dick*," *Modern Language Notes* 76 (June 1961): 522, 522–23, 523.

91. Merlin Bowen, *The Long Encounter: Self and Experience in the Writings of Herman Melville* (Chicago: University of Chicago Press, 1960), 252.

92. Robert Zoellner, *The Salt-Sea Mastadon* (Berkeley: University of California Press, 1973), 11.

93. Winters, 57.

94. Vincent, 75.

95. Leo Marx, *The Machine in the Garden: Technology and the Pastoral Ideal in America* (New York: Oxford University Press, 1964), 305–6.

96. Wadlington, 78. *Moby-Dick* has been so minutely explicated that almost every chapter has been the center of controversial exegeses. For recent discussions of individual chapters, see Rodolphe Gasché's deconstructionist reading of chapter 32, "Cetology" ("The Scene of Writing: A Deferred Outset," *Glyph* 1 [1977]: 150–71); Carolyn Porter's Bakhtinian reading of chapter 24, "The Advocate," and chapter 45, "The Affidavit" ("Melville's Realism," *New Orleans Review* 12 [1985]: 5–14); and P. Adams Sitney's reading of chapter 132, "The Symphony" ("Ahab's Name: A Reading of 'The Symphony,'" in *Herman Melville*, ed. Harold Bloom [New York: Chelsea House, 1986], 223–37), which Bloom describes (x) as "radically advanced."

97. Useful guides to this long-since overwhelming mass of commentary include the bibliography of *Moby-Dick* studies in *MOBY-DICK as Doubloon*, ed. Hershel Parker and Harrison Hayford (New York: W. W. Norton, 1970); Nathalia Wright's chapter on Melville in *Eight American Authors*, ed. James Woodress (New York: W. W. Norton, 1971); Brian Higgins's *Herman Melville: An Annotated Bibliography, 1846–1930* and *Herman Melville: A Reference Guide, 1931–1960* (Boston: G. K. Hall, 1979, 1987); the annual chapters on Melville in *American Literary Scholarship* (Durham: Duke University Press, 1963 to the present; and "Sources" of the "Historical Note" in the Northwestern-Newberry edition of *Moby-Dick* (1988), 756–62.

98. See the "Historical Note" (648–59) and "Sources" (758–59) in the Northwestern-Newberry edition of *Moby-Dick* (1988). A convenient recapitulation of discussion on the composition of *Moby-Dick* is in James Barbour, "'All My Books are Botches': Melville's Struggle with *The Whale*," in *Writing the American Classics*, ed. James Barbour and Tom Quirk (Chapel Hill: University of North Carolina Press, 1990), 25–52, especially 49 n.2.

99. *A Companion to Melville Studies*, 781–835; the quotation is from 783.

REVIEWS
◆

Morning Advertiser (London)

To convey an adequate idea of a book of such various merits as that which the author of "Typee" and "Omoo" has here placed before the reading public, is impossible in the scope of a review. High philosophy, liberal feeling, abstruse metaphysics popularly phrased, soaring speculation, a style as many-coloured as the theme, yet always good, and often admirable; fertile fancy, ingenious construction, playful learning, and an unusual power of enchaining the interest, and rising to the verge of the sublime, without overpassing that narrow boundary which plunges the ambitious penman into the ridiculous: all these are possessed by Herman Melville, and exemplified in these volumes.

In the first chapter, bearing the title of "Loomings," we are introduced to the author, who on its threshold desires us to call him Ishmael. The very name being significant of a propensity to wander, we are prepared for an adventurer's acquaintance.

We have said that the writer is philosophically playful, and we will back his opening chapter, descriptive of New York, with its disquisitions on men's motives, the sea, nay water in the abstract as well as the concrete, against the same amount of prose in any book of fiction for the last dozen years, with a couple of exceptions, which we shall keep to ourselves. He tells us that a ship, when "the soul's November" comes up on him, is what a charged pistol is to a hypochondriac; and thence he plunges into a dissertation on the sea, its uses, glories, and beauties, enough to tempt a hydrophobic patient to a voyage, or at least a cold bath. He resolves to go a whaling voyage. Ishmael sets forth from "Old Manhatto" for New Bedford, and puts up at the "Spouter Inn." This whalers' hostelrie and its inmates are pencilled with the mastery and minuteness of Washington Irving. The strange bedfellow of Ishmael, Queequeg, a South Sea cannibal, who deals in embalmed men's heads, goes to bed with his tomahawk, pipe, and razor-like harpoon, and is a skilful "harpooneer," figures prominently in the after portion of the story. The cannibal turns out to be a good, a generous, and a feeling fellow, and Ishmael consoles himself with the reflection "that it is better to sleep with a sober cannibal than a drunken Christian." And the oddly-assorted couple become sworn friends.

"In New Bedford, fathers give whales for dowers to their daughters, and portion off their nieces with a few porpoises a-piece. You must go to New

Reprinted from the London *Morning Advertiser* (24 October 1851).

Bedford to see a brilliant wedding, for, they say, they have reservoirs of oil in every house, and every night recklessly burn their lengths in spermaceti candles." After a sketch of this queer whaling town, "where they tell us the young girls breathe such musk, their sailor sweethearts smell them miles off shore, as though they were drawing near the odorous Moluccas instead of these Puritanic sands," he exhibits his faculty of passing

"From gay to grave, from lively to severe,"

by taking us into the whaler's chapel.

Then describing the "silent islands of men and women, who sat steadfastly eyeing certain small marble tablets set on the walls," to the memory of whalemen lost in the far-off seas, he proceeds:—"Here were assembled the victims of unceasing grief; here you might mark those, in whose unhealing hearts the sight of those bleak tablets sympathetically caused the old wounds to bleed afresh."

"Oh, ye, whose dead lie buried beneath the green grass

*   *   *

stave my soul—who can do this" [ch. 7, paras. 4–7, condensed].

Many a bold fellow may have thought thus before our author, but which of them could thus analyze his thoughts, or thus express the ideas which in ordinary men refuse to shape themselves in words?

We remember reading in the life of Whitefield, a story of his power over the passions of uncultivated hearers. The anecdote runs that he was preaching to a congregation of seamen on the perils of sin and of the judgment-day, when he so worked upon them by his vivid description of the perils of a storm, that, maddened with the reality of the sinking ship thus word-painted before them, the entire auditory jumped up, and in reply to his question:—"Oh my brethren, what will you do then?" shouted out, "Take to the long-boat!" The unsophisticated reply was well used by the preacher. Let those who would read such a sermon as that which we have lost of Whitefield's, turn to the 9th chapter of this book, and he may realise the idea by a perusal of the discourse of Father Mapple.

The odd pair, our hero and Queequeg, reach Nantucket in due time, when we get the biography of Queequeg. He is the son of a savage king, and, impelled by curiosity, has shipped himself on board a whaler. His skill as a "harpooneer" has made him valuable, and the roving life of a whaleman at present suits him.

There is a kernel of philosophy in the quiet little anecdote of Queequeg, who, unaware of the application of a wheelbarrow, to the great derision of the Sag Harbour people, fixes his luggage thereon, and placing it on his back, carries the whole load by means of the handles; and "didn't the people laugh?" Queequeg retorts by telling a story of "a grand sea captain," who visited Kokovoko, his native isle. He was invited to a grand ceremonial, where a bowl, according to the country's custom, was introduced, into which the High Priest dips his finger as an act of consecration, ere any partake thereof. The sea captain, taking the holy cup for a sort of large finger-glass, followed the example by washing his hands in the beverage. "Now," said Queequeg, "what you tink now? did *our* people laugh?" The savages were the best-mannered here. What follows reminds us of Charles Lamb.

"A good laugh is a mighty good thing

*   *   *

there is more in that man than you perhaps think for" [ch.5, para. 2].

Our hero and his companion enter on board a whaler, "The Pequod," whose owners, Captains Bildad and Peleg, are such samples of Nantucketers, as must interest every student of the social varieties of man. Quakers by descent, Nantucket having been originally settled by that sect, they retain many of the peculiarities of the Friends, modified most anomalously by things and pursuits altogether incongruous —some of these Quakers being the most sanguinary and resolute of whale-hunters. In truth, fighting Quakers, swearing Quakers, and drinking Quakers, are no rarity in Nantucket.

The portraits of these men, which you can see must have been taken from the life, and that they are the types of a class, are exquisitely finished. The signing ship's articles, by our hero and Queequeg, with the latter's fast, or ramadan, and the reasoning thereon, to which that ceremony gives rise, will well repay perusal. Captain Ahab, who is the hero of the whaling voyage, the commander of the Pequod, and thereafter the soul of the romance, is now introduced.

We will not weaken the effect which must be produced upon every one fortunate enough to obtain this work, by such brief extracts as we could here give: suffice it to say, that the fierce monomaniac, Ahab, has long pursued in the vast southern ocean a white whale, of unparalleled ferocity, size, and cunning. Not only has this monster of the deep baffled him, but in his last voyage has added to the destruction of his boats and stores a fearful mutilation; no less than the tearing off with its fearful jaws of the old whaler-captain's leg. The deficient limb is characteristically supplied by a supplemental piece of fish ivory, whereon the fierce old whale-hunter supports himself, steadied, when on deck, by a couple of socket-holes made in the ship's floor on each side of the vessel, at convenient holding-distance from the shrouds of the mizenmast. As a sample of Herman Melville's learning, we may refer to the chapter headed "Cetology," in the second volume; and that we have not overrated his dramatic ability for producing a prose poem, read the chapter on the "whiteness of the whale," and the scene where Ahab nails the doubloon to the mast, as an earnest of the reward he will give to the seamen, who just "sights" "Moby Dick," the white whale, the object of his burning and unappeasable revenge. Then come whale adventures wild as dreams, and powerful in their cumulated horrors. Now we have a Carlylism of phrase, then a quaintness reminding us of Sir Thomas Brown, and anon a heap of curious out-of-the-way learning after the fashion of the Burton who "anatomised" "melancholy." Mingled with all this are bustle, adventure, battle and the breeze. In brief the interest never palls, although we are free to confess that in the latter scenes of Ahab's fierce madness we were fain to exclaim, "Somewhat too much of this!" Finally, we have a series of fierce combats with "the white whale," ending, on the third day's chase, with the death of Ahab, and a mysterious Parsee "harpooneer," in the boats. Thereafter the white whale, "Moby Dick," attacks the fated ship, staves her, the catastrophe is complete, and thus sinks the Pequod into the wild waste of waters. "Now small fowls fly screaming over the yet yawning gulf, a sullen white surf beat against its steep sides, then all collapsed, and the great shroud of the sea rolled on as it rolled five thousand years ago."

As a sample of pleasantry, take the author's view of his task:—

"By good right the whale should only be treated of in imperial folio. Fain are we to stagger to this emprise under the weightiest words of the dictionary. And here be it said, that whenever it has been convenient to consult one in the course of these dissertations, we have invariably used a huge quarto of Johnson, purchased for this especial purpose; because that famous lexicographer's uncommon personal bulk more fitted him to compile a lexicon to be used by a whale author."

In another place this is a small part of his defence of the pursuit of leviathan:—

"But though the world scouts at us whalehunters

*   *   *

But this is not the half: look again" [ch. 24, paras. 4–7, condensed].

Did space permit us we might be tempted to the injustice of giving more of the defence; as it is, we can only again refer the reader to the volumes, than which three more honourable to American literature, albeit issued in London, have not yet reflected credit on the country of Washington Irving, Fenimore Cooper, Dana, Sigourney, Bryant, Longfellow, and Prescott.

Atlas (London)

In all Mr. Melville's previous works, full of original genius as they are, there was to be found lurking a certain besetting sin of extravagance. Sometimes we saw merely the tendency—at others, we traced a startling development of the tendency unchecked. We might get over a volume smoothly enough, delighted with the fancy, profoundly impressed with the descriptive powers, not a little pleased with a quaint and original vein of philosophy of the author, when suddenly the sluice would be lifted, the torrent would burst forth, and for a score of chapters, perhaps for the remainder of the book, we would wade wearily through a waste of satirical or quasi-philosophical rhapsody, vainly longing and vainly looking for an island of firm treadable common sense, on which to clamber out of the slough, it might be of clever, but after all, of vain and unprofitable words. The book before us offers no exception to the general rule which more or less applies to all Mr. Melville's fictions. In some respects we hold it to be his greatest effort. In none of his previous works are finer or more highly soaring imaginative powers put forth. In none of them are so many profound, and fertile, and thoroughly original veins of philosophic speculation, or rather perhaps philosophic fancy, struck. In none of them, too, is there a greater affluence of curious, quaint, and out of the way learning brought to bear upon the subject in hand. In none of them are the descriptions of seafaring and whaling matters so wonderfully graphic, and in none of them is there to be found a more thorough command over the strength and the beauties of our language. Extravagance is the bane of the book, and the stumbling block of the author. He allows his fancy not only to run riot, but absolutely to run amuck, in which poor defenceless Common Sense is hustled and belaboured in a manner melancholy to contemplate. Mr. Melville is endowed with a fatal facility for the writing of rhapsodies. Once embarked on a flourishing topic, he knows not when or how to stop. He flies over the pages as Mynheer Von Clam flew over Holland on his steam leg, perfectly powerless to control the impulse which has run away with him, and leaving the dismayed and confounded reader panting far behind. We open one of the volumes at random, and we find the mate of a whale ship soliloquising over a Spanish doubloon as follows:

Reprinted from the London *Atlas* (1 November 1851), 697–98.

THE DOUBLOON

"There now's the old Mogul

*　　　*　　　*

So, so; he's beginning."

(ch.99, para. 9)

And this unbridled extravagance in writing, this listless and profitless dreaming, and maundering with the pen in the hand, is as it were supported and backed by the wildness of conception and semi-supernatural tone of the whole story. The author tells it *in propria persona*. He is a fore-mast man on board a South Sea whaler, the Old Peequod, of New Bedford. Ere he embarks, he seems to have left this mortal world, and lived in wild limbo of signs and portents. First he falls in with a strange, wild, savage harpooneer, a tatooed cannibal from a South Sea island, called Queequeg between whom and Melville a strange and mystic sympathy springs up. In Queequeg he recognises the sublimity of the animal man, and the grandeur of the savage hero. The scenes in which the harpooneer and Melville pay adoration to Yojo, the god of the former, a deformed little graven image, and those in which Queequeg keeps his Ramadan, sitting fasting for six and thirty hours, with his wooden god upon his head, are strange specimens of powerfully imaginative writing. So again is the interview between Melville and the two retired whaling captains, the owners of the Peequod, one of them a generous old sailor, the other a griping old screw; but both pervaded with a certain species of quaint mystery, breaking out in strange hints and prophecies and allusions to the captain who is to sail the ship,—Captain Ahab, a morbidly strange conception of character, on which the notion of the book chiefly turns. Melville and the savage harpooneer do not embark without multitudinous warnings as to the "grand ungodly godlike man, Captain Ahab." A strange beggarly-looking personage, who calls himself Elijah, and utters whole sybilline leaves, full of mysterious hints about the terrible captain, haunts the newly-engaged sailors, appears suddenly to them round corners, whispers ghostly words in their ears, mopes and momes, and says "morning to ye, morning," when they would question him, and flits away, and is seen no more. Melville, however, screws up his courage, pronounces this gentleman a humbug, and they sail.

Once afloat, we soon find out what Captain Ahab is. In the first place, "he looked like a man cut away from the stake when the fire has overruningly wasted all the limbs without consuming them, or taking away one particle from their compacted, aged robustness." Furthermore, Ahab is one-legged, his missing limb being supplied by a leg fashioned from the bone of the jaw of the sperm whale, and a strange livid scar, said to run from his forehead all down his body, marks him like Cain. This personage is a sort of unearthly monomaniac. For years and years he has been chacing one particular whale—a white, albino whale, a huge livid unnatural monster, awful in his cunning, his strength, and his ferocity. This whale is called Moby Dick. All the South Sea whale-men know him. He has smashed boats by dozens, drowned men by scores. His name is a word of fear upon the ocean. He swims round and round the world stuck full of harpoons, and minds them no more than pins. He is, in fact, the very Old Bogey of Cetology, and he is the particular Old Bogey of Captain Ahab. Among all the whalers, Ahab has devoted himself to the destruction of Moby Dick. A dozen of times has he given him battle; as often has Moby Dick been the conqueror, and in the last struggle, in a gale off Cape Horn, the whale has smashed his assailant's leg into a jelly. This injury results in delirium, which drives Ahab fairly out of his senses. Thenceforth, to slay Moby Dick is his mission in the world. All his being, all his energies, all his soul, are, as it were, melted and fused into one undying mass of intensest hate for Moby Dick. To kill Moby Dick and then die is all he wants—vengeance, vengeance on Moby Dick, is burning the very life out of him; give him that vengeance, and even, as some spirit whose task is accomplished vanishes from the night, so Captain Ahab will become void and silent, and be heard of no more.

It will be acknowledged that there are fine poetic elements in this conception. Wild and extravagant as it is, Captain Ahab would strongly move us, were it not that the intensity of the conception is continually impaired by the constant rigmarole rhapsodies placed in the monomaniac's mouth. A little of this sort of thing would be well in character, and might be made very effective; but pages and chapters of it become simply tedious. A model speech of Captain Ahab's, however, the reader shall have. He has nailed a golden doubloon to the mast, to be the property of the man who first descries the white whale, and then calls on all the crew to swear a solemn oath that they will never desert him in the hunt:

THE BAPTISM OF THE HARPOONS.
"Drink and Pass!"

*   *   *

and Ahab retired within his cabin.

(ch. 36, paras. 44–50)

And so the Peequod turns her bows to that part of the Indian Ocean where the ancient Captain, well versed in the mysterious peregrinations of whales—knowing the ocean currents with which they float—and the season when and the place where their food principally abounds—expects to find Moby Dick. Melville's sketches of his shipmates are amongst the poorest things he has done. We recognise no flesh and blood aboard the Peequod. The sailors might have voyaged with the "Ancient Mariner," or have been borne on the hooks of the "Flying Dutchman." The three mates are mere phantoms—stupid, characterless phantoms, too. The black cook is a caricature. Pip, the negro boy, is a clumsy monstrosity. Queequeg and his fellow-harpooneers, both savages, one of them a Red Indian from the lakes, the other a coal-black man from Africa, are the happiest, because the most fanciful of the minor sketches. Nor is the forecastle more happily painted. Most of the conversation allotted to the seamen is in the wild, rhapsodic vein to which we have alluded—destitute either of sense, appropriateness, or character, and, as a specimen of which, we would refer to the nightwatch colloquy in Chapter 39 of Vol. I [ch. 40 in first American edition].

Meantime, while the Peequod is cruising hither and thither in pursuit of sperm whales in general and the white whale in particular, Herman Melville also cruises backwards and forwards in all manner of philosophic, philologic, physiologic, zoologic, and metaphysic reveries as regards whales and whaling. Over all these the sin of rhapsody more or less extends; but, granting this fault, the portion of the book in question is full of strange and novel beauties. Herman Melville plunges, as it were, among the whales as if he loved them, and accounted them the grandest and most glorious of the creatures of the globe. Upon the whale, its mysteries, and its terrors, he dwells as if the subject had enchantment for him. If Captain Ahab was bewitched by Moby Dick, Mr. Melville is not the less spell-bound by Leviathan in general. He pours into multitudinous chapters a mass of knowledge touching the whale—its habits and its history—its haunts in the sea, and its peregrinations from ocean to ocean—the minutest details of its feeding, or sporting, or swimming, strangely mixed with ingenious and daring speculation on the more mysterious habits and peculiarities of the great brute—the whole written in a tone of exaltation and poetic sentiment which has a strange effect upon the reader's mind in refining and elevating the subject of discourse, and at last making him look upon the whale as a sort of awful and unsoluble mystery—the most strange and the most terrible of the wonders of the great deep. That Herman Melville knows more about whales than any man from Jonah downwards, we do really believe. He has studied their written history like a bookworm, and he must have passed years and years in hunting them, always closely observing their habits, always fixing on them an eye which, if we be not mistaken, nothing could escape—an eye which would see strange things where less favoured organs found but barrenness, and always, too, as may be well believed, picking up and profiting by the practical experience of older, if not wiser, mariners. The sum, then, of Mr. Melville's experience induces him to reject as a bit of finical refining, the common dictum that a whale is not a fish. Animals, he says, which live in the sea, not being amphibious, are fish, and it is mere scientific cant to prate about warm blood and the characteristics of the mammalia. A whale, says Mr. Melville, is "a spouting fish with a horizontal tail," and as even humble porpoises spout in a small way, and carry horizontal tails, Mr. Melville does not scruple to say that they are little whales. All creatures of the species he divides into three families, classing them ingeniously enough by the technical terms applied to the size and shape of books. Thus we have the *folio* whale, comprising all the big fellows, such as the Greenland whale, the sperm, the fin-back, the hump-backed, the razor-back, and the sulphur bottom whales. Next we have the *octavo* whale, typified by the grampus, the narwhal, and such middling-sized monsters. And, thirdly, we come to the *duodecimo* whale, of which, as we have said, the porpoise tribe is the most common representative. The whale which people in general know most of, and that which they generally refer to when they use the word—the Greenland whale—Mr. Melville treats with summary contempt as an interloper and an impostor, in so far as he wears the crown of the kingdom of the whales. The sperm whale, the oil of which is infinitely more valuable, and which is generally larger, swifter, more ferocious, and more cunning, he considers to be the true monarch of the ocean. The descriptions of this creature are wonderfully minute. Inside and outside Mr. Melville surveys him inch by inch, leaving not a muscle of his flesh or a barnacle on his sides unvisited—these minute details being constantly enlivened and elevated by the peculiarly exalted and enthusiastic tone of the writer, by the strong flash of what we cannot but call a certain poetic light, even although it play upon oil-casks and blubber, with which he constantly invests even the meanest subject which he takes in hand. We have already referred to the curious hints given of the peregrinations of the whales, and of the skill with which an old hunter will follow the fish from bank to bank and zone to zone of the Indian Ocean and the Southern Sea. In connexion with this part of the subject Mr. Melville gives a number of curious details and speculations, coming to the conclusion that could the sperm whale be well watched and closely observed all over the world, his movements would be found to be as regular and guided by as unswerving a law as those of the herring or the swallow. While on this subject, we may add that the identification within a very short period, by two ships, of a whale—first, in the North Atlantic, and afterwards in the North Pacific Ocean—seems to prove to Mr. Melville's mind that the secret of the north-west passage, so long a problem to man, has never been a problem to the whale. Of the individual whales noted, and which have received names from mariners, Mr. Melville mentions several, and thus apostrophises four of the most famous:

But not only did each of these famous whales

＊   ＊   ＊

or Sylla to the classic scholar.

(ch. 45, para. 5)

Atlas (London)

We must now hasten after the Peequod, only pausing for a moment to note that in this encyclopædia of information, rhapsody, and speculation about the whale, Mr. Melville carefully examines all great pictures and representations of whaling, unmercifully cuts up Cuvier, and, more or less, all the scientific naturalists, who, he declares, know nothing about the matter; pronounces the plates of whales in most natural history books to be unutterable humbugs; dives deep into the theologic and mythologic history of the whale; and is especially great upon Jonah, continually alternating with the strangest coolness from the grandest to the smallest themes, leaping from the world before the flood, with its megatheria and mastadons, to a discussion upon the merits, in a culinary point of view of whales' steaks, and oscillating from rhapsodically expressed tirades upon the doctrine of metempsychosis to a closely argued demonstration that the skin of a whale is its blubber. Meantime the Peequod is rapidly filling her empty barrels with sperm oil; while, to the unspeakable wonder of the crew, the first time that the look-out man from the hull of the main-royal mast sings out, "There she blows," a tawny Indian boat's crew—"tiger-yellow" Manilla men—who had never before been heard of in the ship, suddenly spring, no one knows from where, like theatrical demons, up trap-doors, and leap into Ahab's boat. This mystic crew seem the coadjutors of Captain Ahab in his crusade against Moby Dick, and the steersman is a semi-supernatural sage, who ultimately, when the excitement is properly wound up, in mysterious and doubtful terms, prophecies his own fate and that of his master. The ordinary whaling adventures, before Mr. Moby Dick is descried, are told with rare and impassioned power. The "first lowering," *i.e.* of the boats in pursuit, is thwarted by the sudden outburst of a southern squall. The scene is magnificently told. The four boats are in pursuit of a shoal or "school" of whales:

AFTER THE WHALE.

Meanwhile, all the boats

*　　　*　　　*

merely grazed by the iron, escaped.

(ch. 43, paras. 37–45)

Now and then whalers are met with, and the crews "gam," that is, go and visit each other and give mutual dinners. On these occasions wild

Reprinted from the London *Atlas* (8 November 1851), 714–15.

whaling legends are told; one of them being to the effect that the white whale, or Moby Dick, is no less a personage than the incarnation of the God of the Shakers! Strange details are also given of "brit" and "squid," the food of the Greenland and sperm whale. The former is a yellow slimy weed, covering the sea to the horizon, so that the ship seemed to be sailing through boundless fields of ripe and golden wheat. In this ocean pasture is descried a shoal of whales, and painted, as it were, with one dash of the brush, in this magnificently picturesque sentence:

> As morning mowers, who side by side slowly and seethingly advance their scythes through the long wet grass of marshy meads, even so these monsters swam, making a strange, grassy, cutting sound; and leaving behind them endless swaths of blue upon the yellow sea.

The "squid" is a species of polypus animal, which, when it rises from the depths of the sea, is said to forebode death to the man who sees it. "A vast pulpy mass, furlongs in length and breadth, of a glancing cream-colour, it lay floating in the water, innumerable long arms radiating from its centre, and curling and twisting like a nest of anacondas. . . . No perceptible face or front did it have—no conceivable token of either sensation or instinct; but undulated there on the billows—an unearthly, formless, chance-like apparition of life."

At length another shoal of sperm whales is discovered, and thus is the capture of the first described:

THE DEATH OF THE WHALE.
"Start her, start her, my men!

*   *   *

His heart had burst!

(ch. 61, paras. 11–20)

After the death of this the first whale, copious and interesting details are given of the equipments of the whale boats; of the gear used, in all its minutiæ, and of the entire processes gone through in attaching the dead monster to the ship, in cutting off his blubber and hoisting it into the hold, in bucketting up the true sperm from the cavity in his head, and in "trying out" or expressing the other oil from the masses of fishy lard piled in the blubber-room. We heartily wish that we had room for copious extracts of these details, but we must refer the reader to the book itself, where he will find a picture of life on board a South-Sea whaleman, with the *rationale* of all the operations in relation to the prey, living and dead, painted in colours which will not soon be forgotten. We, however, must hurry past. As Captain Ahab nears the seas wherein he expects to find Moby Dick, his monomania rises into frenzy. A number of beautifully told episodes are introduced, apropos of the different whalers of many nations, whom he hails for news of his huge enemy. One has seen him and allowed him to pass undisturbed. One has fairly fled from him. The captain of another, the Samuel Enderby, of London, holds up his whalebone arm. He has been maimed by the monster. A third ship exhibits her stoven boats, smashed by a blow of his flukes. A fourth has maimed corpses lying on the gratings by the gangway, ready for burial, the victims of the same all-potent conqueror. Ahab becomes furious in his mania, and not being able to ascend the shrouds, has himself hoisted to the heel of the royal mast, where he clings from dawn to dark, gazing after Moby Dick. At length the white whale is espied, and by the captain himself, and away go the four boats in hot and eager chase. For an account of the long struggle which ensues we must refer to the book. For three days is it kept up, boat after boat falling victims to the crush of Moby Dick's jaws, or the blow of his tail—Captain Ahab uselessly planting harpoon after harpoon in the blubber of the monster, which seems immortal and invincible. On the second day, while pulling hard in the wake of the whale, the "tiger-yellow" Indian, the steersman of the captain's boat, is suddenly seized with the spirit of prophecy, and predicts that Ahab will die but one day after himself; that he will die by hemp, and that before he dies he will see two hearses—one of them made of American wood. This strange jumble of prediction soothes Ahab, who does not deem the apparition of hearses in the middle of the Pacific Ocean a very likely one. It is hardly made, however, when a new "iron" is fixed in the white whale, and Fedallah is carried overboard, entangled in the line, which is speedily exhausted by the deep sounding of the monster, and obliged to be cut. With difficulty regaining the ship, Ahab passes the night in delirious raving. The next morning he is after Moby Dick again; and as the whale rises, rushing from a thousand-fathom dive, he sees borne upon his back, entangled in the twisted line, the stark-staring corpse of Fedallah. "Aha!" says Ahab—a light breaking in upon him—"the First Hearse." The second is soon provided. Leaving the boat, the vast whale rushes headlong at the ship. A yell of unutterable despair bursts from Ahab. He feels in his soul that Moby Dick, predestined to conquer, is about to fulfil his destiny. But Herman Melville must speak for himself:

THE TRIUMPH OF MOBY DICK.

From the ship's bows

*   *   *

as it rolled five thousand years ago.

(ch. 135, paras. 55–62)

The last word quoted is the last in the book, and as we close it we feel as if waking from what was partly a gorgeous vision, partly a night-mare dream, but both vision and dream intense, over-mastering in their power, the spell of magician who works wildly, recklessly, but with a skill and a potency which few, we should think, will be disposed either to deny or resist.

Leader (London)

Want of originality has long been the just and standing reproach to American literature; the best of its writers were but second-hand Englishmen. Of late some have given evidence of originality; not *absolute* originality, but such genuine outcoming of the American intellect as can be safely called national. Edgar Poe, Nathaniel Hawthorne, Herman Melville are assuredly no British offshoots; nor is Emerson— the *German* American that he is! The observer of this commencement of an American literature, properly so called, will notice as significant that these writers have a wild and mystic love of the supersensual, peculiarly their own. To move a horror skilfully, with something of the earnest faith in the Unseen, and with weird imagery to shape these Phantasms so vividly that the most incredulous mind is hushed, absorbed—to do this no European pen has apparently any longer the power—to do this American literature is without a rival. What *romance* writer can be named with Hawthorne? Who knows the terrors of the seas like Herman Melville?

The Whale—Melville's last book—is a strange, wild, weird book, full of poetry and full of interest. To use a hackneyed phrase, it is indeed "refreshing" to quit the old, wornout pathways of romance, and feel the sea breezes playing through our hair, the salt spray dashing on our brows, as we do here. One tires terribly of ballrooms, dinners, and the incidents of town life! One never tires of Nature. And there is Nature here, though the daring imagery often grows riotously extravagant.

Then the ghostly terrors which Herman Melville so skilfully evokes, have a strange fascination. In vain Reason rebels. Imagination is absolute. Ordinary superstitions related by vulgar pens have lost their power over all but the credulous; but Imagination has a credulity of its own respondent to power. So it is with Melville's superstitions: we believe in them imaginatively. And here we will take the occasion to introduce the reader to a splendid passage from our greatest prose writer, descriptive of the superstitious nature of sailors—(you divine that we are to quote from De Quincey). He says they are all superstitious. "Partly, I suppose, from *looking out so much upon the wilderness of waves empty of human life*; for mighty solitudes are generally fear-haunted and fear-peopled; such, for instance, as the solitudes of forests where, in the absence of human forms and ordinary human sounds, are discerned forms more dusky and vague not referred by the eye to any

Reprinted from the London *Leader* 2 (8 November 1851), 1067–69.

known type, and sounds imperfectly intelligible. Now, the sea is often peopled amidst its ravings with what seem innumerable human voices, 'ancestral voices prophesying war'; often times laughter mixes from a distance (seeming to come also from distant times as well as distant places) with the uproar of waters; and, doubtless, shapes of fear or shapes of beauty not less awful are at times seen upon the waves by the diseased eye of the sailor. Finally, the interruption habitually of all ordinary avenues to information about the fate of their dearest relatives; the consequent agitation which must often possess those who are reëntering upon home waters; and the sudden burst, upon stepping ashore, of *heart-shaking news in long-accumulated arrears*—these are circumstances which dispose the mind to look out *for relief towards signs and omens as one way of breaking the shock by dim anticipations.*"

This passage is a fit prelude to the thrilling pages of Melville's *Whale.* The book is not a romance, nor a treatise on Cetology. It is something of both: a strange, wild work with the tangled overgrowth and luxuriant vegetation of American forests, not the trim orderliness of an English park. Criticism may pick many holes in this work; but no criticism will thwart its fascination. As we mean you to read it and relish it, we shall give no hint of the story: an extract or so by way of whet to the appetite is all you must expect.

Here is a picture of

AHAB WITH THE IVORY LEG.
"So powerfully did the whole grim aspect

       *   *   *

flowered out in a smile."

(ch. 28, paras. 4–7)

There is a chapter on the "Whiteness of the Whale" which should be read at midnight, alone, with nothing heard but the sounds of the wind moaning without, and the embers falling into the grate within. From it we quote this on—

THE ALBATROSS A BIRD OF TERROR.
"I remember the first albatross

       *   *   *

as when I beheld the Antarctic fowl.

(ch. 42, footnote to para. 5)

Here you have a glimpse into—

THE MERCILESS SEA

"But, though to landsmen in general

*   *   *

thou canst never return!"

(ch. 58, paras. 6–11)

Let us first tell you that the sharks are in fierce shoals tearing away at the flesh of a dead whale fastened to the ship, and you will then listen with pleasure to—

THE NIGGER'S SERMON TO SHARKS

" 'Fellow-critters: I'se ordered here to say

*   *   *

till dey bust—and den die."

(ch. 64, paras. 14–28)

Although this is not a set treatise of Whales, it contains a large amount of information on the subject, and the materials for a treatise evidently were collected. We have no room for a tithe of the curious things he tells us; but we must give a passage from his chapter on the "Monstrous Pictures of Whales." He expresses the most emphatic disapprobation of almost all the portraits that have been published of his favourite fish. Nay, even these given by such eminent naturalists as Lacépède and F. Cuvier, are pronounced monstrous absurdities. He adds, however:

"But these manifold mistakes

*   *   *

touching this Leviathan."

(ch. 55, paras. 12–14)

Post (Boston)

We have read nearly one half of this book, and are satisfied that the London Athenæum is right in calling it "an ill-compounded mixture of romance and matter-of-fact." It is a crazy sort of affair, stuffed with conceits and oddities of all kinds, put in artificially, deliberately and affectedly, by the side of strong, terse and brilliant passages of incident and description. The Athenæum's notice throughout seems to us a fair one, and we copy the greater portion for the sake of economy and good taste. . . .

The production under notice is now issued by the Harpers in a handsome bound volume for *one dollar and fifty cents*—no mean sum, in these days. It seems to us that our publishers have gone from one extreme to the other, and that instead of publishing good books in too cheap a form, they are issuing poor books, in far too costly apparel. "The Whale" is not worth the money asked for it, either as a literary work or as a mass of printed paper. Few people would read it more than once, and yet it is issued at the usual cost of a standard volume. Published at *twenty five cents*, it might do to buy, but at any higher price, we think it a poor speculation.

Excerpted and reprinted from the Boston *Post* (20 November 1851).

Independent (New York)

(The following communication is from the pen of one whose familiarity with the scenes described in the volume, renders his judgment particularly valuable. This alone leads us to admit a book-notice not strictly editorial.)

MOLY-DICK, or THE WHALE. By Herman Melville, author of Typee, Omoo, etc., pp. 635. Harper & Brothers.

The name given to this burly volume reminds us of an observation of Burton in his Anatomy of Melancholy, where he says that it is a kind of policy in these days to prefix a fantastical title to a book which is to be sold, because as larks come down to a day-net, many readers will tarry and stand gazing like silly passengers at an antic picture in a painter's shop, that will not look at a judicious piece. There are harlequin writers at this day as ready as in Burton's time to make themselves Merry-andrews and Zanies, in order to raise the wind of curiosity about their literary wares.

In the volume before us there are some of the queerest specimens of ground and lofty tumblings in the literary line, to which the world has been lately treated. Up to the middle of the book the writer is half the time on his head, and the other half dancing a pirouette on one toe. By the time these *outré* gayeties are a little spent, the reader gets an inkling that Moly-Dick is a very famous and most deadly Monster, a Sperm Whale of an uncommon magnitude and malignity, having as many lives as a cat, and all of them immortal. After this the realities and the fabrications of whaling life are dashed into with a bold hand; and mixed with a great deal of myth and mystery, there are exciting descriptions, curious information, and strange adventures, which would have not a shade of probability, were not truth in whaling life often stranger than fiction.

The writer evinces the possession of powers that make us ashamed of him that he does not write something better and freer from blemishes. And yet we doubt if he could, for there is a primitive formation of profanity and indecency that is ever and anon shooting up through all the strata of his writings; and it is this which makes it impossible for a religious journal heartily to commend any of the works of this author which we have ever perused. Let his mind only turn on the poles of truth, and be fixed with the desire to do good rather than to tickle and amuse by the exposure of his

Reprinted from the New York *Independent* (20 November 1851).

foolish vagaries, and few could do more than the author of Moly-Dick to furnish instructive literary aliment for the Sons of the Sea.

The Judgment day will hold him liable for not turning his talents to better account, when, too, both authors and publishers of injurious books will be conjointly answerable for the influence of those books upon the wide circle of immortal minds on which they have written their mark. The book-maker and the book-publisher had better do their work with a view to the trial it must undergo at the bar of God.

Literary World (New York)

A difficulty in the estimate of this, in common with one or two other of Mr. Melville's books, occurs from the double character under which they present themselves. In one light they are romantic fictions, in another statements of absolute fact. When to this is added that the romance is made a vehicle of opinion and satire through a more or less opaque allegorical veil, as particularly in the latter half of Mardi, and to some extent in this present volume, the critical difficulty is considerably thickened. It becomes quite impossible to submit such books to a distinct classification as fact, fiction, or essay. Something of a parallel may be found in Jean Paul's German tales, with an admixture of Southey's Doctor. Under these combined influences of personal observation, actual fidelity to local truthfulness in description, a taste for reading and sentiment, a fondness for fanciful analogies, near and remote, a rash daring in speculation, reckless at times of taste and propriety, again refined and eloquent, this volume of Moby Dick may be pronounced a most remarkable sea-dish—an intellectual chowder of romance, philosophy, natural history, fine writing, good feeling, bad sayings—but over which, in spite of all uncertainties, and in spite of the author himself, predominates his keen perceptive faculties, exhibited in vivid narration.

There are evidently two if not three books in Moby Dick rolled into one. Book No. I., we could describe as a thorough exhaustive account admirably given of the great Sperm Whale. The information is minute, brilliantly illustrated, as it should be—the whale himself so generously illuminating the midnight page on which his memoirs are written—has its level passages, its humorous touches, its quaint suggestion, its incident usually picturesque and occasionably sublime. All this is given in the most delightful manner in "The Whale." Book No. 2 is the romance of Captain Ahab, Queequeg, Tashtego, Pip & Co., who are more or less spiritual personages talking and acting differently from the general business run of the conversation on the decks of whalers. They are for the most part very serious people, and seem to be concerned a great deal about the problem of the universe. They are striking characters withal, of the romantic spiritual cast of the German drama; realities of some kinds at bottom, but veiled in all

Reprinted from the New York Literary World, No. 251 (22 November 1851), 403–4.

sorts of poetical incidents and expressions. As a bit of German melodrama, with Captain Ahab for the Faust of the quarter-deck, and Queequeg with the crew, for Walpurgis night revellers in the forecastle, it has its strong points, though here the limits as to space and treatment of the stage would improve it. Moby Dick in this view becomes a sort of fishy moralist, a leviathan metaphysician, a folio Ductor Dubitantium, in fact, in the fresh water illustration of Mrs. Malaprop, "an allegory on the banks of the Nile." After pursuing him in this melancholic company over a few hundred squares of latitude and longitude, we begin to have some faint idea of the association of whaling and lamentation,and why blubber is popularly synonymous with tears.

The intense Captain Ahab is too long drawn out; something more of *him* might, we think, be left to the reader's imagination. The value of this kind of writing can only be through the personal consciousness of the reader, what he brings to the book; and all this is sufficiently evoked by a dramatic trait or suggestion. If we had as much of Hamlet or Macbeth as Mr. Melville gives us of Ahab, we should be tired even of their sublime company. Yet Captain Ahab is a striking conception, firmly planted on the wild deck of the Pequod—a dark disturbed soul arraying itself with every ingenuity of material resources for a conflict at once natural and supernatural in his eye, with the most dangerous extant physical monster of the earth, embodying, in strongly drawn lines of mental association, the vaster moral evil of the world. The pursuit of the White Whale thus interweaves with the literal perils of the fishery—a problem of fate and destiny—to the tragic solution of which Ahab hurries on, amidst the wild stage scenery of the ocean. To this end the motley crew, the air, the sky, the sea, its inhabitants are idealized throughout. It is a noble and praiseworthy conception; and though our sympathies may not always accord with the train of thought, we would caution the reader against a light or hasty condemnation of this part of the work.

Book III., appropriating perhaps a fourth of the volume, is a vein of moralizing, half essay, half rhapsody, in which much refinement and subtlety, and no little poetical feeling, are mingled with quaint conceit and extravagant daring speculation. This is to be taken as in some sense dramatic; the narrator throughout among the personages of the Pequod being one Ishmael, whose wit may be allowed to be against everything on land, as his hand is against everything at sea. This piratical running down of creeds and opinions, the conceited indifferentism of Emerson, or the run-a-muck style of Carlyle is, we will not say dangerous in such cases, for there are various forces at work to meet more powerful onslaught, but it is out of place and uncomfortable. We do not like to see what, under any view, must be to the world the most sacred associations of life violated and defaced.

We call for fair play in this matter. Here is Ishmael, telling the story of this volume, going down on his knees with a cannibal to a piece of wood, in the second story fire-place of a New-Bedford tavern, in the spirit of amiable and transcendent charity, which may be all very well in its way; but why dislodge from heaven, with contumely, "long-pampered Gabriel, Michael and Raphael." Surely Ishmael, who is a scholar, might have spoken respectfully of the Archangel Gabriel, out of consideration, if not for the Bible (which might be asking too much of the school), at least for one John Milton, who wrote Paradise Lost.

Nor is it fair to inveigh against the terrors of priestcraft, which, skilful though it may be in making up its woes, at least seeks to provide a remedy for the evils of the world, and attribute the existence of conscience to "hereditary dyspepsias, nurtured by Ramadans"—and at the same time go about petrifying us with imaginary horrors, and all sorts of gloomy suggestions, all the world through. It is a curious fact that there are no more bilious people in the world, more completely filled with megrims and head shakings, than some of these very people who are constantly inveighing against the religious melancholy of priestcraft.

So much for the consistency of Ishmael—who, if it is the author's object to exhibit the painful contradictions of this self–dependent, self-torturing agency of a mind driven hither and thither as a flame in a whirlwind, is, in a degree, a successful embodiment of opinions, without securing from us, however, much admiration for the result.

With this we make an end of what we have been reluctantly compelled to object to this volume. With far greater pleasure, we acknowledge the acuteness of observation, the freshness of perception, with which the author brings home to us from the deep, "things unattempted yet in prose or rhyme," the weird influences of his ocean scenes, the salient imagination which connects them with the past and distant, the world of books and the life of experience—certain prevalent traits of manly sentiment. These are strong powers with which Mr. Melville wrestles in this book. It would be a great glory to subdue them to the highest uses of fiction. It is still a great honor, among the crowd of successful mediocrities which throng our publishers' counters, and know nothing of divine impulses, to be in the company of these nobler spirits on any terms.

Weekly News and Chronicle (London)

This is a wild, weird book, full of strange power and irresistible fascination for those who love to read of the wonders of the deep. The poetry of the great South Seas, the rude lawless adventure of the rough mariners who for years of continuous voyaging peril themselves on its waters, the excitement and the danger of the fishery for the sperm whale, the fiercest and hugest monster "of all who swim the ocean stream," combine to make these pages attractive and interesting to many different classes of readers. Artists and sportsmen, the lovers of scenery, and the lovers of excitement, will alike find in them ample material of gratification. The blemish of the book is its occasional extravagance and exaggeration—faults which mar the effect they were intended to heighten, and here and there, as in the character of Captain Ahab, make a melodramatic caricature of what, with a little more simplicity, might have been a striking and original picture.

The story of the book is brief; the supposed voyager having been long desirous of seeing somewhat of the whale fishery, takes ship at Nantucket, United States, on board the "Pequod" of that port, commanded by Captain Ahab—a veteran whaler, who, having lost a leg on his last voyage, in an encounter with a vast sperm whale—the terror of the Pacific—called by the sailors "Moby Dick,"—sails on his present cruise with the fixed intention of never returning till he shall have slaked his vengeance in the blood of his monstrous enemy. The whole narrative consists of the search through the vast Pacific, for this fierce and formidable antagonist, of his final discovery, of the life-and-death contest which ensues between the enraged Leviathan and the fated crew of the "Pequod." The catastrophe with which the book terminates, viz., the sinking of the ship in mid ocean from the effects of a direct charge by "Moby Dick" on her quarters, is not to be set down amongst the extravagancies of Herman Melville. It is on credible record, that in the year 1820 precisely such a casualty befel the ship "Essex;" and, even as we write, our eye rests on an extract from the *New Bedford Mercury*, given in the *Times* of Friday, the 21st ult., containing a circumstantial account of the destruction by a sperm whale of the ship "Ann Alexander," Captain J. Deblois, of New Bedford, United States. In this case the whale had previously destroyed the boats, and the chase was being continued in the ship, against which the monster rushed at the rate of about fifteen knots an hour, and, striking her about two feet from the keel, abreast the foremast,

Reprinted from the London *Weekly News and Chronicle* (29 November 1851).

knocked a great hole entirely through her bottom, from the effects of which she foundered in less than ten minutes.

This may serve to show that the peril of the sperm whale fishery is by no means imaginary: in these volumes the excitement felt about the mysterious monster "Moby Dick"—the great White Whale—the terror of all whalers—is singularly increased by every kind of dramatic artifice. Every one of the crew on board the "Pequod" has some tale about him—every solitary whale-ship which the "Pequod" encounters in her long years of wandering over the great world of waters, has some tidings to give of the destructive prowess of the monster; so that, to all who can enter into the spirit of the book, the eagerness of expectation becomes at last most pleasurably painful. Another point which shows the power of the writer, is the utter "whalish-ness" (we must coin the word) of everything that meets you in his volumes, from the first page to the last. You feel yourself at once in a new and strange element. The snugly-curtained room and the cheery fire-side are forgotten as you read: the hand of a master carries you far away into wild scenes and the companionship of wilder men, you are sailing under the moonshine over the broad Pacific, watching from the mast head if haply you may discern some stray whale-spout jetting up amid the interminable waste of waters, or it may be the great White Whale himself, gliding phantom like through the solitudes of the midnight ocean.

But it is time to let Ishmael, the whaler, speak for himself. This is his description of the "Spouter Inn," at New Bedford, where he put up before sailing on his four years' cruise:

"Entering that gable-ended Spouter-Inn

> *　　　*　　　*

dearly sells the sailors deliriums and death."

(ch. 3, paras. 1–5)

Once abroad upon the great Pacific, Ishmael, like the rest of the crew, has to take his turn at the mast-head, which he thus moralises:—

"The three masts are kept manned!

> *　　　*　　　*

a convenient closet of your watch-coat."

(ch. 35, paras. 5–6)

Our readers doubtless would like to learn something of the great White Whale himself. Here are some dim intimations of him:

"I, Ishmael, was one

               *   *   *

to encounter the perils of his jaw."

(ch. 41, paras. 1–5)

Here we must pause. The extracts we have given will serve to show the quality of this book—which is, to our minds, by far the most powerful and original contribution that Herman Melville has yet made to the Romance of Travel. And be it remembered that, though abounding in the wild and imaginative, the book is, by no means, deficient in accurate information. The chapter on Cetology contains an admirable analysis of the different varieties of the whale tribe, while the various processes of capturing the fish and extracting the oil are described with the minute and graphic vividness which no mere literary ability could have accomplished, and which evidently betoken the close observation of an attentive and gifted eyewitness. To the artist, the naturalist and the general reader these volumes may be confidently recommended as among the freshest and most vigorous that the present publishing season has produced.

Churchman (New York)

Moby Dick, or *the Whale*, by Herman Melville, (Harpers,) pp. 467, is a strange compound of rare ability, stirring adventures, brilliant descriptions, and apparently an accurate knowledge of the nature, form, and habits of this monster of the deep, with much wild rhapsody and bad philosophy, many violations of good taste and delicacy, and we are sorry to add, frequent displays of irreligion and profanity. Had these latter features been excluded, the book would have been diminished one third in bulk, and infinitely more readable. The character of the monomaniac Captain Ahab is a novelty, and powerfully drawn, and the final catastrophe is most horrible: but it is pitiable to see so much talent perverted to sneers at revealed religion and the burlesquing of sacred passages of Holy Writ.

Reprinted from the New York *Churchman* (6 December 1851).

Spirit of the Times (New York)

Our friend Melville's books begin to accumulate. His literary family increases rapidly. He had already a happy and smiling progeny around him, but lo! at the appointed time another child of his brain, with the accustomed signs of the family, claims our attention and regard. We bid the book a hearty welcome. We assure the "happy father" that his "labors of love" are no "love's labor lost."

We confess an admiration for Mr. Melville's books, which, perhaps, spoils us for mere criticism. There are few writers, living or dead, who describe the sea and its adjuncts with such true art, such graphic power, and with such powerfully resulting interest. "Typee," "Omoo," "Redburn," "Mardi," and "White Jacket," are equal to anything in the language. They are things of their own. They are results of the youthful experience on the ocean of a man who is at once philosopher, painter, and poet. This is not, perhaps, a very unusual mental combination, but it is not usual to find such a combination "before the mast." So far Mr. Melville's early experiences, though perhaps none of the pleasantest to himself, are infinitely valuable to the world. We say *valuable* with a full knowledge of the terms used; and, not to enter into details, which will be fresh in the memory of most of Mr. Melville's readers, it is sufficient to say that the humanities of the world have been quickened by his works. Who can forget the missionary *expose*—the practical good sense which pleads for "Poor Jack," or the unsparing but just severity of his delineations of naval abuses, and that crowning disgrace to our navy—flogging? Taken as matters of art these books are amongst the largest and the freshest contributions of original thought and observation which have been presented in many years. Take the majority of modern writers, and it will be admitted that however much they may elaborate and rearrange the stock of ideas pre-existant, there is little added to the "common fund." Philosophers bark at each other—poets sing stereotyped phrases—John Miltons re-appear in innumerable "Pollock's Courses of Time"—novelists and romances stick to the same overdone incidents, careless of the memories of defunct Scotts and Radcliffs, and it is only now and then when genius, by some lucky chance of youth, ploughs deeper into the soil of humanity and nature, that fresher experiences—perhaps at the cost of much individual pain and sorrow—are obtained; and the results are books, such as those of Herman Melville and Charles Dickens. Books which are living pictures, at once of the

Reprinted from the New York *Spirit of the Times* 21 (6 December 1851), 494.

practical truth, and the ideal amendment: books which mark epochs in literature and art.

It is, however, not with Mr. Melville generally as a writer that we have now to deal, but with "Moby Dick, or the Whale," in particular; and at first let us not forget to say that in "taking titles" no man is more felicitous than our author. Sufficiently dreamy to excite one's curiosity, sufficiently explicit to indicate some main and peculiar feature. "Moby Dick" is perhaps a creation of the brain—"The Whale" a result of experience; and the whole title a fine polished result of both. A title may be a truth or a lie. It may be clap-trap, or true art. A bad book may have a good title, but you will seldom find a good book with an inappropriate name.

"Moby Dick, or the Whale," is all whale. Leviathan is here in full amplitude. Not one of your museum affairs, but the real, living whale, a bona-fide, warm-blooded creature, ransacking the waters from pole to pole. His enormous bulk, his terribly destructive energies, his habits, his food, are all before us. Nay, even his lighter moods are exhibited. We are permitted to see the whale as a lover, a husband, and the head of a family. So to speak, we are made guests at his fire-side; we set our mental legs beneath his mahogany, and become members of his interesting social circle. No book in the world brings together so much whale. We have his history, natural and social, living and dead. But Leviathan's natural history, though undoubtedly valuable to science, is but a part of the book. It is in the personal adventures of his captors, their toils, and, alas! not unfrequently their wounds and martyrdom, that our highest interest is excited. This mingling of human adventure with new, startling, and striking objects and pursuits, constitute one of the chief charms of Mr. Melville's books. His present work is a drama of intense interest. A whale, "Moby Dick"—a dim, gigantic, unconquerable, but terribly destructive being, is one of the persons of the drama. We admit a disposition to be critical on this character. We had doubts as to his admissibility as an actor into dramatic action, and so it would seem had our author, but his chapter, "The Affidavit," disarms us; all improbability or incongruity disappears, and "Moby Dick" becomes a living fact, simply doubtful at first, because he was so new an idea, one of those beings whose whole life, like the Palladius or the Sea-serpent, is a romance, and whose memoirs unvarnished are of themselves a fortune to the first analist or his publisher.

"Moby Dick, or the Whale," is a "many-sided" book. Mingled with much curious information respecting whales and whaling there is a fine vein of sermonizing, a good deal of keen satire, much humor, and that too of the finest order, and a story of peculiar interest. As a romance its characters are so new and unusual that we doubt not it will excite the ire of critics. It is not tame enough to pass this ordeal safely. Think of a monomaniac whaling captain, who, mutilated on a former voyage by a particular whale, well known for its peculiar bulk, shape, and color—seeks, at the risk of his life and the lives of his crew, to capture and slay this terror of the seas! It is on this idea that the romance hinges. The usual staple of novelists is entirely wanting. We have neither flinty-hearted fathers, designing villains, dark caverns, men in armor, nor anxious lovers. There is not in the book any individual, who, at a certain hour, *"might have been seen"* ascending hills or descending valleys, as is usual. The thing is entirely new, fresh, often startling, and highly dramatic, and with those even, who, oblivious of other fine matters, scattered with profusest hand, read for the sake of the story, must be exceedingly successful.

Our space will not permit us at present to justify our opinions by long quotations; but, at the risk of doing Mr. Melville injustice by curtailment, let us turn to the chapter headed "The Pequod meets the Rose Bud," pp. 447, in which a whaling scene is described with infinite humor. The "Pequod"—our author's ship—was sailing slowly "over a sleepy, vapory, mid-day sea," when "the many noses on her deck proved more vigilant discoverers than the three pair of eyes aloft."

"Presently the vapors in advance

*　　　*　　　*

blasted whales in general."

(ch. 91, paras. 3–4)

[Summary, with extract from ch. 91,
"and this was the romantic name

*　　　*　　　*

'Yes,' rejoined a Guernsey man from the bulwarks".

(paras. 7–12).

*　　　*　　　*

"He now perceived that

*　　　*　　　*

get out of this dirty scrape."

(ch. 91, paras. 19–25)]

Stubb now sounds the Guernsey man, and finds he has no suspicion of the ambergris, and that the Captain has not the slightest knowledge of English. Stubb thereupon plots with the mate of the Rose Bud to compel the Captain to cast off from the blasted whale. The Guernsey man is to act as interpreter, and being quite willing to see his Captain satirized, the following dialogue—which is a fine comedy in itself—ensues.

"By this time their destined victim

*　　　*　　　*

would bid them good bye."

(ch. 91, paras. 29–49)

Did our limits permit we would gladly extract the fine little episode, contained in the chapter called "The Castaway," as a favorable specimen of Mr. Melville's graphic powers of description. But we must conclude by strongly recommending "Moby Dick, or the Whale," to all who can appreciate a work of exceeding power, beauty, and genius.

Morning Chronicle (London)

When the author of "Omoo" and "Typee" appeared, we were happy to hail a new and bright star in the firmament of letters. There was vast promise in these finely imagined fictions. Sea stories had been gradually waning in attraction. A vast number of respectable sailors, who never ought to have had their hands blacked in any fluid save tar, were discolouring them in ink. Cooper was not much imitated, but Marryat had a shoal of clumsy followers, who believed that the public liked to read of the most ordinary naval manœuvers told in technical language, and who imagined and let loose upon the world a swarm of *soi-disant* naval characters, who were either weak and conventional, or wildly extravagant and clumsily caricatured. Herman Melville was a man of different mettle: originality—thorough originality—was stamped upon every line he wrote. There never was a fresher author. He took up a new subject, and treated it in a new fashion. Round his readers he flung a new atmosphere, and round his fictions a new light. Herman Melville, in fact, gave the world a new sensation: springing triumphantly away from the old scenes of naval romances, abjuring the West Indies, and the English Channel, and the North Sea; recognising as classic ground neither the Common Hard nor Portsmouth Point—treating us to no exciting frigate battles—absolutely repudiating all notion of daring cuttings out of French luggers moored under batteries of tremendous power—never chasing slavers, and never being chased by pirates—inventing no mysterious corsairs, and launching no renowned privateers, Herman Melville flung himself entirely into a new naval hemisphere. The Pacific, with its eternally sunny skies and tranquil seas—the great ocean of the world—with its mysterious inhabitants—its whales, to which the whales of Greenland are babies, and its ships—worn, battered, warped, and faded ships, cruising for months and months, and years and years in that great illimitable flood—its glorious isles, too—ocean Edens—the very gardens of the south, coral girt and palm crowned, set in sparkling surf, smiled over by everlasting summer skies, and fanned by never-dying summer breezes—the birth-place of a happy, mirthful, Epicurean race, living in the balmy air and the tepid seas—pure and beautiful in their wildness, loving and kind, simple and truthful—such was the semi-fairy world into the gorgeous midst of which Herman Melville, like a potent and beneficent magician, hurled his readers. The power and the skill of the new literary enchanter were at once admitted. With a bursting

Reprinted from the London *Morning Chronicle* (20 December 1851), 2–3.

imagination, and an intellect working with muscles which seemed not likely soon to tire, Herman Melville bid high for a high place among the spirits of the age. There never was an author more instinct with the flush of power and the pride of mental wealth. He dashed at his pages and overflowed them with the rushing fulness of his mind. A perception of the picturesque and of the beautiful—equally powerful and equally intense—an imagination of singular force, and capable of calling up the wildest, most vivid, and most gorgeous conceptions, and a genuine, hearty, warm, and genial earnestness—in all he imagined, and in all he wrote—marked Herman Melville, not for a man of talent and a clever writer, but for a genius. And his style was just as thoroughly characteristic. Its strength, its living energy, its abounding vitality, were all his own. He seemed to write like a giant refreshed. He bounded on and on, as if irresistibly impelled by the blast of his own inspiration, and the general happiness of phrase, and the occasional flash of thought rendered in the most deliciously perfect words, were subsidiary proofs of the genuineness of the new powers which addressed the world.

But still, even in the best parts of the best books of the American sailor, there lurked an ominous presence which we hoped would disappear, but which, as we feared, has increased and multiplied. We could not shut our eyes to the fact that constantly before us we saw, like a plague spot, the tendency to rhapsody—the constant leaning towards wild and aimless extravagance, which has since, in so melancholy a degree, overflown, and, so to speak, drowned the human interest—the very possibility of human interest—in so great a portion of Herman Melville's works. First, indeed, there was but a little cloud the size of a man's hand. Unhappily it has overspread the horizon, and the reader stumbles and wanders disconsolately in its gloom. It was in "Mardi" that the storm of extravagance burst fairly forth. The first volume was charming. What could be more poetic, yet life-like, than the picture of the sea-worn whaler, with her crew yearning again for a sight of a clod of dry green land—what finer than the canoe voyage—what more strangely thrilling, yet truth-like, than the falling in with the island schooner, with her grass ropes and cotton sails, drifting with two savages along the sea? So far Melville had held his fine imagination in curb. It had worked legitimately, and worked right well. It had proceeded by the eternal rules of art and the unchanging principles of the truthful and the symmetrical. But with the second volume the curb of judgment is removed. Common sense, which Herman Melville can depose or keep enthroned at will, was driven out by one *coup d'état*, and the two last volumes are melancholy rhodomontade—half raving, half babble—animated only by the outlines of a dull cold allegory, which flits before the reader like a phantom with a veiled face, and a form which is but the foldings of vapour wreaths. You yearn for the world again—for sea and sky and timber—for human flesh, white or brown—for the solid wood of the ship and the coarse canvass of the sail—as did the whaler's crew for land and grass. What are these impalpable shadows to you? What care you for these misty phantoms of an indefinite cloud land? You want reality—you want truth—you want *vraisemblance*. Close the book—there are none in the last two volumes of "Mardi."

Next, if we remember rightly, came a three-volume series of sketches called "White Jacket." They depicted life on board an American frigate in the Pacific—the severe, and in many points brutal, discipline of a Transatlantic ship of war, elaborated with such daguerreotype exactitude and finish, so swarming with the finest and minutest details, and so studded with little points never to be imagined, that you are irresistibly impelled to the conclusion that, from the first word to the last, every syllable is literal, downright truth. Here Herman Melville rushes into the other extreme from "Mardi." In one he painted visions, in the other he engraves still life. The first is all broad, vague dashes—the second all carefully finished lines. You look at one book, as it were, through a hazy telescope with many coloured glasses—at the other, through a carefully cleaned microscope, which shows you every infinitesimal blister of the tar in the ship's seams—every fibre in a topsail haulyard, and every hair in a topman's whisker. And yet, every now and then, even in the midst of all this Dutch painting, comes a dash at the old fashion of raving. Every now and then a startling chapter lugs you from the forecastle, or the cock-pit, or the cable-tiers, or the very run, up into the highest, bluest Empyrean—you are snatched up from bilge-water to the nectar of the Gods—you are hurried from the consideration of maggots in biscuits, to that of the world beyond the stars or the world before the flood: in one chapter there is a horrifying account of the amputation of a man's leg—in the next you are told how the great mountain peaks of the Andes raised all their organ notes to peal forth hallelujahs on the morning when the world was born.

One other work by Herman Melville divides his wildly extravagant "Mardi" from the little less extravagant fiction before us. It is called, if we remember right, "My First Voyage," and is the literally and strongly told experiences of a sailor boy on his first trip from New York to Liverpool. The work smacks strongly of reality, but it is written in a lower, less buoyant, and less confident key than the earlier fictions. It seemed to us, also, as we read it, that some, at all events, of the virtue of the author had departed, and that he knew it. He walked feebly and groped. The inward sunshine was wanting, and the strong throb of the vigorous brain was neither so full nor so steady as before.

Here, however—in "The Whale"—comes Herman Melville, in all his pristine powers—in all his abounding vigour—in the full swing of his mental energy, with his imagination invoking as strange and wild and original themes as ever, with his fancy arraying them in the old bright and vivid hues, with that store of quaint and out-of-the-way information—we would rather call it reading than learning—which he ever and anon scatters around, in, frequently, unreasonable profusion, with the old mingled opulence and happiness of phrase, and alas! too, with the old extravagance, running a perfect muck throughout the three volumes, raving and rhapsodising in chapter after chapter—unchecked, as it would appear, by the very slightest remembrance of judgment or common sense, and occasionally soaring into such absolute clouds of phantasmal unreason, that we seriously and sorrowfully ask ourselves whether this can be anything other than sheer moonstruck lunacy.

Let us put it to our readers, for example, what they think of the following as the speech of a whaling captain to his crew:—

CAPTAIN AHAB.

" 'Drink and pass!'

*   *   *

hunt Moby Dick to his death!' "

(ch. 36, paras. 44–50)

But it may be replied that Captain Ahab is represented as being a monomaniac. So be it: but the crew are not, and what is to be thought of such a conversation as the following amongst the hands of a whaler:—

FORECASTLE TALK.
MATE'S VOICE FROM THE QUARTER-DECK.

"Eight bells there forward

*   *   *

showest thy black brow, Seeva!"

(ch. 40, paras. 3–23)

And so on indefinitely.

But it is high time to inform our readers what they may expect to find in "The Whale." The author tells the story, as usual *in propria persona*. He determines to sail from the harbour of New Bedford on board a whaler, for a four years' cruise in the Pacific. In a sailors' tavern, roughly and powerfully drawn, he is put to sleep with a South Sea Island harpooner, a tatooed cannibal, and a Pagan who worships a wretched little black graven image called Gogo, and in whom Herman recognises a noble and heroic soul— insomuch, indeed, that with certain philosophic mental reservations—he does not scruple to go on his knees to Gogo, set upright in the empty grate as a shrine, and join the orisons of his South Sea acquaintance. As soon as this personage appears, the story assumes that nightmare unreality, and becomes overshadowed by that uncertain looming of imaginative recklessness, which is only here and there dispersed by the intensely-written whaling adventures, and the minute truth of the descriptions not only of the whales themselves, but of the utensils used for capturing them, and the process of cutting up the monsters and extracting the oil. Queequeg, the harpooneer, and Herman Melville embark on board the Pequod, an ancient whaler—a sort of mystic prophet of evil—a strange sepulchral voiced phantom-like man having several times warned them against the voyage in vain. All this, and in fact the entire book, except the portions we have mentioned, reads like a ghost story done with rare imaginative power and noble might of expression. The captain of the Pequod—Captain Ahab—is a mystery of mysteries. He looms out of a halo of terrors—scents prophecies, omens, and auguries. He is an ancient mariner—an ancient whaler—and there seems on him a doom and a curse. His destiny is linked to the destiny of a certain whale—a strange horrible whale—perfectly white—an albino whale, a monster famous since the South Sea fisheries began for his ferocity, his cunning, and his strength. This white whale's name is "Moby Dick." He is held to be hundreds, if not thousands, of years old. He has ploughed the oceans before a sail was set above them. He may have been, for all Captain Ahab knows, the very whale who swallowed Jonah. Well, this whale has Captain Ahab pursued voyage after voyage. This whale he has chased, we know not how many times round the earth; to kill this whale he has devoted all his means, all his energies, all his thoughts in this world, and, so far as we can make out, is supposed to have bartered all his prospects in the next. Often has he encountered it, but Moby Dick bears a charmed life. There are scores and scores of rusted harpoons wedged deeply in his blubber. He trails miles of line behind him, until the hemp rots off and sinks in the brine. He has smashed boats by scores—drowned men by dozens. Every South Sea man knows the "white whale," and, taught by dread experience, gives him a wide berth. The sailors tell dreadful tales of him in the sleepy mid-watch. He is, in fact, a sort of ocean fiend—a tremendous *bogey* of the sea—an apparition which no one seeks but Captain Ahab, whose destiny is bound up in the doomed pursuit. So, then, the Pequod turns her battered bows to the Indian Ocean, and Captain Ahab commences his final hunt of Moby Dick.

The personages introduced as the author's shipmates are even more phantom-like, un-human, and vaguely uninteresting than the Captain. There are three mates—Starbuck, Stubb, and Flash—mere talking shadows—and rare rhapsodies of nonsense they sometimes talk. Queequeg, the Pagan harpooner, is the only flesh and blood like portraiture, and he is little save an animal. A cook and a carpenter, and a half-witted negro called Pip, are absolutely shadows. The voyage out to the whaling grounds is told with all those extraordinary plunges into all manner of historical, allegorical, and metaphysical disquisitions and rhapsodies which distinguish the author; but, mixed up with these, there are very many chapters devoted to the natural history of the whale, containing, in our view, some of the most delightful pages in the book. Herman Melville, we believe, knows more about whales than any man alive, or who ever lived. He seems to have read every page upon the subject of cetology ever written. Theoretic naturalists and practical harpooneers, he has them all at his finger ends, publishing, indeed, as if to show his lore, in an Appendix an extraordinary collection of sentences touching whales, from texts in Genesis down to songs sung by Nantucket harpooneers. Mr. Melville treats our old friend the Greenland, or, as he calls it, the "right whale," with considerable contempt. He is neither fierce nor cunning, and his oil is coarse and of little value. The Sperm whale of the South Sea is declared to be the rightful monarch of the ocean, and the only creature worthy of the deadly iron flung by the brawny arm of a true Nantucketer. The whole tribe of whales, Herman Melville divides into three classes; taking his illustrative titles from the technical language of the book trade, and dividing the blubbery monsters of the deep into folio whales, of which the sperm whale is a type; octavo whales, typified by the grampus and the norwhal; and duodecimo whales, typified by the propoise. Flinging overboard—not, however, by any means after stating satisfactory reasons why—the commonly received hypothesis that a whale is not a fish, as a mere empty and useless mystification—Melville defines a whale to be "any spouting fish with a perpendicular tail," and under that definition he ranges numerous tribes of animals, such as the porpoise, which are not above four feet long. So much for the scientific divisions of whales. Their appearance, their habits, their manner of swimming, diving, breathing, spouting, and so forth, are described in wonderful detail, and with a vivid picturesqueness and freshness of language which brings the mighty animals at once before us. Let anybody who wants to understand the full difference between drawing at once from nature and merely copying from books, contrast one of Herman Melville's descriptions with a page from, say, Goldsmith's "Animated Nature," or any book of the same class. How utterly uneffective and unsatisfactory the cold prosy general truths about the animal described, compared with the bright variety of confident detail into which Melville enters, familiar as he seems with every motion, gesture, and peculiarity of Leviathan, as we are with the dogs and cats of our own fire-side.

Arrived first in the Indian Ocean, the whale hunt begins. We have already quoted the scene in which Captain Ahab makes the crew decide to follow Moby Dick to the death; but the captain is not quite mad enough not to "lower" in pursuit of the other whales which chance to come first in the way. Only the first time the boats are in the water after the cheering cry of "there she spouts," Captain Ahab's boat appears manned by a crew of "Zigo Yellow" and turbanned Manilla men, or Chinese, who then, for the first time, make their appearance, leaping up at the summons from some unknown recess of the ship in which they had hitherto been buried. The steersman of this strange company is a semi-supernatural personage, who prophesies in a mystic way his own death, and then Captain Ahab's, in the last encounter with Moby Dick, and the whole band are looked upon by the whalers as something half demoniac. Turning, however, from the jumble of mysticism and rhapsody with which all that appertains to Captain Ahab is enveloped, we prefer setting before our readers a few extracts from certainly the most vivid accounts of whaling ever written. A magnificent sperm whale is descried, and the boat starts furiously in chace:—

THE KILLING OF THE WHALE.

"'Start her, start her, my men.

*   *   *

His heart had burst!"

(ch. 61, paras. 11–22)

Wandering here and there, up and down through the trackless wastes of the southern seas, the Pequod pursues her trade of sperm-whale killing; Captain Ahab of course keeping a bright look-out for Moby Dick. Mingling with rhapsodic outbursts about all imaginable subjects, we have masses of vivid detail about whale fishing; dissertations of remarkable interest, on the ocean wanderings of the great leviathans, dependent upon the set of the currents and the drift of their food—"brit," a slimy, yellow, vegetable substance, through which the ship sails for leagues, as through meadows of golden grain, and "squid," a white pulpy mass seemingly of the polypus order—"furlongs and furlongs in length, of a glancing cream colour— innumerable long arms radiating from its surface, and curling and twisting like a nest of anacondas, as if blindly to clutch at any object within reach. No perceptible face or front did it have—no conceivable token of either sensation or instinct, but undulated there on the billows, an unearthly, formless, chancelike apparition of life." This substance, or animal, is imagined by whalemen to be the largest living thing in the ocean, and to furnish its sole food to the sperm whale; and Herman Melville hazards the conjecture that "squid" is no more or less than the kraken of good old Bishop Pontoppidan. The substance is so seldom seen on the surface, that its appearance is reckoned ominous. "The great live squid," says one of the mates, "which few whale ships ever beheld and returned to their ports to tell of it." Then we have pleasant details of "gamming," that is of the visits paid by one whale crew to another on the ocean, wild legends told by dark mid-watches of battles with whales, and desperate mutinies thousands of miles from land. Then the author will suddenly start into a consideration of the "honour and glory of whale fishing"—next, perhaps, into a wild and whirling rhapsody on the origin of whales—on the huge monsters of the sea contemporary with the mastodons and the megatheria of the pre-adamite world—anon he will discourse greatly and learnedly upon the anatomy of the whale—next, perhaps, he will take to discussing all known pictures of the whale, or to smashing all theories of stay-at-home cetologists. After a chapter on the excellence of whale steaks, and the perfect possibility of enjoying a blubber supper, we may look out for one chapter of critical inquiry into the history of Jonah, followed, perhaps, by a sort of prose pœan upon the delights of squeezing half congealed sperm oil with the bare hands. To form anything like an idea of this strange conglomeration of fine description, reckless fancy, rhapsodic mistiness, and minute and careful Dutch painting, the book itself must be referred to. We can only give a faint and outlined idea of its strange contents. After passing through the Straits of Sunda, an immense herd or school of whales is descried. The boat in which Herman Melville pulls an oar is forced by the frantic motions of the bewildered creatures into the centre of the squadron—the grand armada the author calls it—in which are swimming the females and young ones of the herd. The following is a magnificent piece of painting:—

THE BABY WHALE.
"Now, inclusive of the occasional wide intervals

*   *   *

in eternal mildness of joy."

(ch. 87, paras. 21–70)

We could fill a whole page with extracts, but we forbear. We have already given one of the harpooning scenes, and we will add to it a very minute and curious account of the management of the whale line, showing how it so often sweeps an unwary or an unlucky man overboard:—

THE WHALE LINE.
"The whale line is only two-thirds

*   *   *

could never pierce you out."

(ch. 60, paras. 4–9)

At length, deep in the third volume, Moby Dick is descried. Ship after ship had been met with, and battered boats, and maimed and drowned men have told of her conflicts with the fearful whale. Captain Ahab's delirium waxes to its full fury. The enemy of his life, and the destroyer of his reason, Moby Dick, is before him. For three days he chases the fated whale. Twice is his boat smashed, and he himself rescued by a miracle. His crew would fain flee from the monster; but it is not to be. Captain Ahab fascinates them. They all obey him, as enchanted men a charm. His Manilla men pull him like fiends, and work his will as imps obey a conjuror. On the second day, Fedallah prophesies that Captain Ahab will be killed by hemp, after he has seen two hearses—one of them made of American wood. This extraordinary prediction is thus fulfilled—Fedallah, carried over by a hitch of the line, is lost. The next day his body is seen borne by Moby Dick upon his back, enveloped in twisted whale lines. This is hearse the first. Then comes the last attack. Moby Dick, wounded by the harpoon of Captain Ahab, suddenly rushes, not at the boat, but at the ship, and smiting it with his vast forehead, crushes in its bows. The sinking Pequod is hearse the second, and, of course, made of American wood. As Ahab sees his foundering ship, and knows that the white whale has conquered, he bursts out into one of his delirious rhapsodies, and with this, and the magnificent piece of writing describing the disappearance of the whale-ship, we close our notice of this strange and unaccountable book:—

THE LAST OF AHAB.

"'I turn my body from the sun.

*   *   *

as it rolled five thousand years ago."

(ch. 135, paras. 58–62)

Southern Quarterly Review (Charleston)

In all those portions of this volume which relate directly to the whale, his appearance in the oceans which he inhabits; his habits, powers and peculiarities; his pursuit and capture: the interest of the reader will be kept alive, and his attention fully rewarded. We should judge, from what is before us, that Mr. Melville has as much personal knowledge of the whale as any man living, and is better able, than any man living, to display this knowledge in print. In all the scenes where the whale is the performer or the sufferer, the delineation and action are highly vivid and exciting. In all other respects, the book is sad stuff, dull and dreary, or ridiculous. Mr. Melville's Quakers are the wretchedest dolts and drivellers, and his Mad Captain, who pursues his personal revenges against the fish who has taken off his leg, at the expense of ship, crew and owners, is a monstrous bore, whom Mr. Melville has no way helped, by enveloping him in a sort of mystery. His ravings, and the ravings of some of the tributary characters, and the ravings of Mr. Melville himself, meant for eloquent declamation, are such as would justify a writ *de lunatico* against all the parties.

Reprinted from the Charleston, S.C., *Southern Quarterly Review* 5 (January 1852), 262.

Democratic Review (New York)

Mr. Melville is evidently trying to ascertain how far the public will consent to be imposed upon. He is gauging, at once, our gullibility and our patience. Having written one or two passable extravagancies, he has considered himself privileged to produce as many more as he pleases, increasingly exaggerated and increasingly dull. The field from which his first crops of literature were produced, has become greatly impoverished, and no amount of forcing seems likely to restore it to its pristine vigor. In bombast, in caricature, in rhetorical artifice—generally as clumsy as it is ineffectual—and in low attempts at humor, each one of his volumes has been an advance upon its predecessors, while, in all those qualities which make books readable, it has shown a decided retrogression from former efforts. Mr. Melville never writes naturally. His sentiment is forced, his wit is forced, and his enthusiasm is forced. And in his attempts to display to the utmost extent his powers of "fine writing," he has succeeded, we think, beyond his most sanguine expectations.

The truth is, Mr. Melville has survived his reputation. If he had been contented with writing one or two books, he might have been famous, but his vanity has destroyed all his chances of immortality, or even of a good name with his own generation. For, in sober truth, Mr. Melville's vanity is immeasurable. He will either be first among the book-making tribe, or he will be nowhere. He will centre all attention upon himself, or he will abandon the field of literature at once. From this morbid self-esteem, coupled with a most unbounded love of notoriety, spring all Mr. Melville's efforts, all his rhetorical contortions, all his declamatory abuse of society, all his inflated sentiment, and all his insinuating licentiousness.

"Typee" was undoubtedly a very proper book for the parlor, and we have seen it in company with "Omoo," lying upon tables from which Byron was strictly prohibited, although we were unable to fathom those niceties of logic by which one was patronized, and the other proscribed. But these were Mr. Melville's triumphs. "Redburn" was a stupid failure, "Mardi" was hopelessly dull, "White Jacket" was worse than either; and, in fact, it was such a very bad book, that, until the appearance of "Moby Dick," we had set it down as the very ultimatum of weakness to which its author could attain. It seems, however, that we were mistaken.

We have no intention of quoting any passages just now from "Moby Dick." The London journals, we understand, "have bestowed upon the work

Reprinted from the New York *Democratic Review* 30 (January 1852), 93.

many flattering notices," and we should be loth to combat such high authority. But if there are any of our readers who wish to find examples of bad rhetoric, involved syntax, stilted sentiment and incoherent English, we will take the liberty of recommending to them this precious volume of Mr. Melville's.

ARTICLES AND ESSAYS

◆

[A Literary Doppelganger]

"Sir Nathaniel" [Francis Jacox]

For so successful a trader in "marine stores" as Mr. Melville, "The Whale" seemed a speculation every way big with promise. From such a master of his harpoon might have been expected a prodigious hit. There was about blubber and spermaceti something unctuously suggestive, with him for whaleman. And his three volumes entitled "The Whale" undoubtedly contain much vigorous description, much wild power, many striking details. But the effect is distressingly marred throughout by an extravagant treatment of the subject. The style is maniacal—mad as a March hare—mowing, gibbering, screaming, like an incurable Bedlamite, reckless of keeper or strait-waistcoat. Now it vaults on stilts, and performs *Bombastes Furioso* with contortions of figure, and straining strides, and swashbuckler fustian, far beyond *Pistol* in that Ancient's happiest mood. Now it is seized with spasms, acute and convulsive enough to excite bewilderment in all beholders. When he pleases, Mr. Melville can be so lucid, straightforward, hearty, and unaffected, and displays so unmistakable a shrewdness, and satirical sense of the ridiculous, that it is hard to suppose that *he* can have indited the rhodomontade to which we allude. Surely the man is a Doppelganger—a dual number incarnate (singular though he be, in and out of all conscience):—surely he is two single gentlemen rolled into one, but retaining their respective idiosyncrasies—the one sensible, sagacious, obser-vant, graphic, and producing admirable matter—the other maundering, drivelling, subject to paroxysms, cramps, and total collapse, and penning exceeding many pages of unaccountable "bosh." So that in tackling every new chapter, one is disposed to question it beforehand, "Under which king, Bezonian?"—the sane or the insane; the constitutional and legitimate, or the absolute and usurping? Writing of Leviathan, he exclaims, "Unconsciously my chirography expands into placard capitals. Give me a condor's quill! Give me Vesuvius' crater for an inkstand! Friends, hold my arms!" Oh that his friends had obeyed that summons! They might have saved society from a huge dose of hyperbolical slang, maudlin sentimentalism, and tragi-comic bubble and squeak.

His Yankeeisms are plentiful as blackberries. "I am tormented," quoth

Excerpted and reprinted from "American Authorship. No. IV—Herman Melville," *New Monthly Magazine* [London] 98 (July 1853), 307–8.

he, "with an everlasting itch for things remote." Remote, too frequently, from good taste, good manners, and good sense. We need not pause at such expressions as "looking a sort of diabolically funny;"—"beefsteaks done rare;"—"a speechlessly quick chaotic bundling of a man into eternity;"—"bidding adieu to circumspect life, to exist only in a delirious throb." But why wax fast and furious in a thousand such paragraphs as these:—"In landlessness alone resides the highest truth, indefinite as the Almighty. . . . Take heart, take heart, O Bulkington! Bear thee grimly, demi-god! Up from the spray of thy ocean-perishing—straight up, leaps thy apotheosis!"—"Thou [scil. Spirit of Equality] great God! who didst not refuse to the swart convict, Bunyan, the pale, poetic pearl; Thou who didst clothe with doubly hammered leaves of finest gold the stumped and paupered arm of old Cervantes; Thou who didst pick up Andrew Jackson from the pebbles; who didst hurl him upon a war-horse; who didst thunder him higher than a throne!"—"If such a furious trope may stand, his [Capt. Ahab's] special lunacy stormed his general sanity, and carried it, and turned all its concentrated cannon upon its own mad mark. . . . then it was, that his torn body and gashed soul bled into one another; and so interfusing made him mad."—"And the miser-merman, Wisdom, revealed [to a diving negro] his hoarded heaps; and among the joyous, heartless, ever-juvenile eternities, Pip saw the multitudinous, God-omnipresent, coral insects, that out of the firmament of waters heaved the colossal orbs. He saw God's foot upon the treadle of the loom, and spoke it; and therefore his shipmates called him mad."

The story itself is a strange, wild, furibund thing—about Captain Ahab's vow of revenge against one Moby Dick. And who is Moby Dick? A fellow of a whale, who has made free with the captain's leg; so that the captain now stumps on ivory, and goes circumnavigating the globe in quest of the old offender, and raves by the hour in a lingo borrowed from Rabelais, Carlyle, Emerson, newspapers transcendental and transatlantic, and the magnificent proems of our Christmas pantomimes. Captain Ahab is introduced with prodigious efforts at preparation; and there is really no lack of rude power and character about his presentment—spoiled, however, by the Cambyses' vein in which he dissipates his vigour. His portrait is striking—looking "like a man cut away from the stake, when the fire has overrunningly wasted all the limbs without consuming them, or taking away one particle from their compacted aged robustness"—a man with a brow gaunt and ribbed, like the black sand beach after some stormy tide has been gnawing it, without being able to drag the firm thing from its place. Ever since his fell encounter with Moby Dick, this impassioned veteran has cherished a wild vindictiveness against the whale, frantically identifying with him not only all his bodily woes, but all his feelings of exasperation—so that the White Whale swims before him "as the monomaniac incarnation of all those malicious agencies which some deep men feel eating in them, till they are left living on with half a heart and half a lung." The amiable cannibal Queequeg occasions some stirring and some humorous scenes, and is probably the most reasonable and cultivated creature of the ship's company. Starbuck and Stubb are both tiresome, in different ways. The book is rich with facts connected with the natural history of the whale, and the whole art and process of whaling; and with spirited descriptions of that process, which betray an intense straining at effect. The climax of the three days' chase after Moby Dick is highly wrought and sternly exciting—but the catastrophe, in its whirl of waters and fancies, resembles one of Turner's later nebulous transgressions in gamboge.

[A Book "Composed in an Opium Dream"]

[William Hurton]

The last work we have to notice is a large one, entitled "The Whale," and it is quite as eccentric and monstrously extravagant in many of its incidents as even "Mardi;" but it is, nevertheless, a very valuable book, on account of the unparalleled mass of information it contains on the subject of the history and capture of the great and terrible cachalot, or sperm-whale. Melville describes himself as having made more than one cruise in a South-sea-whaler; and supposing this to have been the fact, he must nevertheless have laboriously consulted all the books treating in the remotest degree on the habits, natural history, and mode of capturing this animal, which he could obtain, for such an amazing mass of accurate and curious information on the subject of the sperm-whale as is comprised in his three volumes could be found in no other single work—or perhaps in no half-dozen works—in existence. We say this with the greater confidence, because we have written on the sperm-whale ourselves, and have consequently had occasion to consult the best works in which it is described. Yet the great and undeniable merits of Melville's book are obscured and almost neutralised by the astounding quantity of wild, mad passages and entire chapters with which it is interlarded. Those who have not read the work cannot have any conception of the reckless, inconceivable extravagancies to which we allude. Nevertheless, the work is throughout splendidly written, in a literary sense; and some of the early chapters contain what we know to be most truthful and superlatively-excellent sketches of out-of-the-way life and characters in connexion with the American whaling trade.

*   *   *

Perhaps we have so far indicated our opinion of the merits and demerits of Herman Melville in the course of the foregoing remarks, that it is hardly necessary to state it in a more general way. Yet, in conclusion, we may sum up our estimate of this singular author in a few short sentences. He is a man of genius—and we intend this word to be understood in its fullest literal sense—one of rare qualifications too; and we do not think there is any living author who rivals him in his peculiar powers of describing scenes at sea and

Excerpted and reprinted from "A Trio of American Sailor-Authors," *Dublin University Magazine* 47 (January 1856), 53–54.

sea-life in a manner at once poetical, forcible, accurate, and, above all, original. But it is his *style* that is original rather than his *matter*. He has read prodigiously on all nautical subjects—naval history, narratives of voyages and shipwrecks, fictions, &c.—and he never scruples to deftly avail himself of these stores of information. He undoubtedly is an original thinker, and boldly and unreservedly expresses his opinions, often in a way that irresistibly startles and enchains the interest of the reader. He possesses amazing powers of expression—he can be terse, copious, eloquent, brilliant, imaginative, poetical, satirical, pathetic, at will. He is never stupid, never dull; but, alas! he is often mystical and unintelligible—*not* from any inability to express himself, for his writing is pure, manly English, and a child can always understand what he *says*, but the ablest critic cannot always tell what he really *means;* for he at times seems to construct beautiful and melodious sentences only to conceal his thoughts, and irritates his warmest admirers by his provoking, deliberate, wilful indulgence in wild and half-insane conceits and rhapsodies. These observations apply mainly to his latter works, "Mardi" and "The Whale," both of which he seems to have composed in an opium dream; for in no other manner can we understand how they could have been written.

Such is Herman Melville! a man of whom America has reason to be proud, with all his faults; and if he does not eventually rank as one of her greatest giants in literature, it will be owing not to any lack of innate genius, but solely to his own incorrigible perversion of his rare and lofty gifts.

[Whitman and Melville:
The Earliest Comparison?]

B. V. [James Thomson]

. . . [Whitman] sings, in the great section termed *Calamus*, as it has
scarcely been sung before, the perfect love of comrades, the superb friendship
of man and man, deep as life, stronger than death. His genius expatiating
over all his vast country, he sings it, north and south, east and west; revelling
in long enumerations (often each item a distinct and glowing picture) of its
lands, its rivers, its cities, its various occupations, which pass as in
many-coloured processions that will never end, till the mind is bewildered
with beholding them. In the words of Mr. Conway: "He notes everything,
forgets nothing. His brain is indeed a kind of American formation, in which
all things print themselves like fern in coal." I know but one other living
American writer who approaches him in his sympathy with all ordinary life
and vulgar occupations, in his feeling of brotherhood for all rough workers,
and at the same time in his sense of beauty and grandeur, and his power of
thought; I mean Herman Melville, the author of "Typee," "Omoo," "Mardi,"
"The Whale," etc.; but Melville is sometimes strangely unequal to his better
self, and has lavished much strength in desultory doings; while Whitman has
concentrated himself from the beginning on one great strenuous endeavor,
with energies reinforced and multiplied by the zeal and enthusiasm of the
consciousness of a mission. Above all the rest, if preference there be, his heart
leaps with exultation at the vision of the great West, and his voice never
swells more proudly than when singing the ever-advancing armies of the men
of the West; the earth-subduers, deploying by scores, by hundreds, by
thousands, from the rising to the setting sun, from the Alleghanies to the
Rocky Mountains, and over these to the Pacific; large-natured with daring
and endurance, strong and haughty, wild and generous; the "resistless,
restless race" of his *Pioneers! O Pioneers!*

Excerpted and reprinted from "Walt Whitman," *National Reformer* [London], new ser. 24 (30 August
1874), 135.

[A Medley of Noble Impassioned Thoughts]

W. Clark Russell

Cooper pleases and has pleased, and is to this day read and admired by thousands; but speaking from a sailor's point of view, I really have no words to express the delight with which I quit his novels for the narratives of his countrymen, Dana and Herman Melville.

Whoever has read the writings of Melville must I think feel disposed to consider "Moby Dick" as his finest work. It is indeed all about the sea, whilst "Typee" and "Omoo," are chiefly famous for their lovely descriptions of the South Sea Islands, and of the wild and curious inhabitants of those coral strands; but though the action of the story is altogether on shipboard, the narrative is not in the least degree nautical in the sense that Cooper's and Marryat's novels are. The thread that strings a wonderful set of fancies and incidents together, is that of a whaler, whose master, Captain Ahab, having lost his leg by the teeth of a monstrous white whale, to which the name of Moby Dick has been given, vows to sail in pursuit of his enemy. The narrator embarks in the ship that is called the *Pequod*, which he describes as having an "old-fashioned, claw-footed look about her."

> "She was apparelled like any barbaric Ethiopic Emperor, his neck heavy with pendants of polished ivory. She was a thing of trophies. A cannibal of a craft, tricking herself forth in the chased bones of her enemies. All round her unpanelled, open bulwarks were garnished like one continuous jaw, with the long sharp teeth of the sperm-whale, inserted there for pins to fasten her old hempen thews and tendons to. Those thews ran not through base blocks of land wood, but deftly travelled over sheaves of ivory. Scorning a turnstile wheel, at her reverend helm she sported there a tiller; and that tiller was in one mass, curiously carved from the long narrow jaw of her hereditary foe. The helmsman, who steered by that tiller in a tempest, felt like the Tartar when he holds back his fiery steed by clutching its jaw. A noble craft, but somehow a most melancholy! All noble things are touched with that."

Melville takes this vessel, fills her full of strange men, and starts her on her insane quest, that he may have the ocean under and around him to muse upon, as though he were in a spacious burial-ground, with the alternations

Excerpted and reprinted from "Sea Stories," *Contemporary Review* [London] 46 (September 1884), 356–57.

of sunlight and moonlight and deep starless darkness to set his thoughts to. "Moby Dick" is not a sea-story—one could not read it as such—it is a medley of noble impassioned thoughts born of the deep, pervaded by a grotesque human interest, owing to the contrast it suggests between the rough realities of the cabin and the forecastle; and the phantasms of men conversing in rich poetry, and strangely moving and acting in that dim weather-worn Nantucket whaler. There is a chapter where the sailors are represented as gathered together on the forecastle; and what is made to pass among them, and the sayings which are put into their mouths, might truly be thought to have come down to us from some giant mind of the Shakespearean era. As we read, we do not not need to be told that seamen don't talk as those men do; probabilities are not thought of in this story. It is like a drawing by William Blake, if you please; or, better yet, it is of the "Ancient Mariner" pattern, madly fantastic in places, full of extraordinary thoughts, yet gloriously coherent—the work of a hand which, if the desire for such a thing had ever been, would have given a sailor's distinctness to the portrait of the solemn and strange Miltonic fancy of a ship built in the eclipse and rigged with curses dark. In "Typee," and "Omoo," and "Redburn," he takes other ground, and writes—always with the finest fancy—in a straight-headed way.

[Melville, Sea-Compelling Man]

[ROBERT BUCHANAN]

Meantime my sun-like music-maker,
   Shines solitary and apart;
Meantime the brave sword-carrying Quaker
   Broods in the peace of his great heart,—
While Melville,† sea-compelling man,
Before whose wand Leviathan
Rose hoary white upon the Deep,
With awful sounds that stirred its sleep,
Melville, whose magic drew Typee,
Radiant as Venus, from the sea,
Sits all forgotten or ignored,
While haberdashers are adored!
He, ignorant of the drapers' trade,
   Indifferent to the art of dress,
Pictured the glorious South-sea maid
   Almost in mother nakedness—
Without a hat, or boot, or stocking,
A want of dress to most so shocking,
With just one chemisette to dress her
She *lives*—and still shall live, God bless her!
Long as the sea rolls deep and blue,
   While heaven repeats the thunder of it,
Long as the White Whale ploughs it through,
The shape my sea-magician drew
   Shall still endure, or I'm no prophet!

Excerpted and reprinted from "Socrates in Camden, With a Look Round," *Academy* [London] 28 (15 August 1885), 102–3.
†Hermann Melville, author of *Typee, The White Whale,* &c. I sought everywhere for this Triton, who is still living somewhere in New York. No one seemed to know anything of the one great imaginative writer fit to stand shoulder to shoulder with Whitman on that continent.

[Dramatic Vigour and a Sort of Epic Grandeur]

H. S. SALT

Moby Dick; or, The White Whale (1851) is perhaps more successful as a whole than *Mardi*, since its very extravagances, great as they are, work in more harmoniously with the outline of the plot. Ishmael, the narrator, having embarked on board a whaling-vessel with a savage harpooner named Queequeg, whose character is admirably drawn, gradually discovers that they are committed to an extraordinary voyage of vengeance. It seems that, in a former expedition, Captain Ahab, their commander, a mysterious personage, who 'looked like a man cut away from the stake when the fire has overrunningly wasted all the limbs without consuming them,' had lost one of his legs, which had been 'reaped away' by Moby Dick, a famous white sperm-whale of unequalled strength and malignity. Frenzied by his loss, he was now devoting the rest of his life to the single object of destroying Moby Dick, who 'swam before him as the monomaniac incarnation of all those malicious agencies which some deep men feel eating in them.' The book is a curious compound of real information about whales in general and fantastic references to this sperm-whale in particular, that 'portentous and mysterious monster,' which is studied (as the bird is studied by Michelet) in a metaphysical and ideal aspect—'a mass of tremendous life, all obedient to one volition, as the smallest insect.' Wild as the story is, there is a certain dramatic vigour in the 'quenchless feud' between Ahab and Moby Dick which at once arrests the reader's attention, and this interest is well maintained to the close, the final hunting-scene being a perfect nightmare of protracted sensational description.

*   *   *

His literary power, as evidenced in *Typee* and his other early volumes, is also unmistakable, his descriptions being at one time rapid, concentrated, and vigorous, according to the nature of his subject, at another time dreamy, suggestive, and picturesque. The fall from the mast-head in *White Jacket* is a swift and subtle piece of writing of which George Meredith might be proud; the death of the white whale in *Moby Dick* rises to a sort of epic grandeur and intensity.

Excerpted and reprinted from "Herman Melville," *Scottish Art Review* [London] 2 (November 1889), 188–89.

[A Queer Yarn]

Anonymous

I see that he [Melville] is dead after a life of mingled storm and almost sluggish calm. Do boys between the ages of 10 and 70 read his books now? I fear not, for some of them are out of print; and yet I was mightily pleased at finding the copy of "Moby Dick"—and what a queer yarn it is—thumbed beyond repair, and with broken back, the testimony of the appreciation of frequenters of the Public Library. What a grand fellow that harpoon man was—I have forgotten his name—who, when he was in the New Bedford inn, began dressing by putting on his stove-pipe hat.

*　　*　　*

To me Herman, the spinner of yarns, was more real than Herman the quiet man who found a post in the New York Custom House. His stories were not ruined by allusions to science; his sailors were either naturally simple or crazed by strange sights at sea; they were not akin to the creations of the ingenious Verne, and the books in which they figured taught no useful lesson for the benefit of the priggish boys. I wish there were more stories like them. And I wish Melville had explained before his death the reasons of the fierce and long-established hatred between the White Whale and Captain Ahab.

Excerpted and reprinted from "Here in Boston," Boston *Post*, 2 October 1891.

The Literary Wayside

Herman Melville, one of the most original and virile of American literary men, died at his home on Twenty-sixth street, New York, a few days ago, at the age of 72. He had long been forgotten, and was no doubt unknown to the most of those who are reading the magazine literature and the novels of the day. Nevertheless, it is probable that no work of imagination more powerful and often poetic has been written by an American than Melville's romance of "Moby Dick; or the Whale," published just 40 years ago; and it was Melville who was the first of all writers to describe with imaginative grace based upon personal knowledge, those attractive, gentle, cruel and war-like peoples, the inhabitants of the South Sea islands.

*   *   *

Although as aforesaid Melville's early novels are not now read, they are as well worth reading as the more sensuous stories of Pierre Loti, or the vivacious ventures of Robert Louis Stevenson, whose scenes are laid in the same region of "lotus eating," to describe in a fit phrase the common life of the Pacific Islands. "Typee," particularly, would be found to retain its charm for even the sophisticated readers of to-day. But the crown of Melville's sea experience was the marvelous romance of "Moby Dick," the White whale, whose mysterious and magical existence is still a superstition of whalers,—at least such whalers as have not lost touch with the old days of Nantucket and New Bedford glory and grief. This book was dedicated to Nathaniel Hawthorne, and Hawthorne must have enjoyed it, and have regarded himself as honored in the inscription. This story is unique; and in the divisions late critics have made of novels, as it is not a love-story (the only love being that of the serious mate Starbuck for his wife in Nantucket, whom he will never see again), it is the other thing, a hate-story. And nothing stranger was ever motive for a tale than Capt Ahab's insane passion for revenge on the mysterious and invincible White whale Moby Dick, who robbed him of a leg, and to a perpetual and fatal chase of him the captain binds his crew. The scene of this vow is marvelously done, and so are many other scenes, some of them truthful depictions of whaling as Melville knew it; some of the wildest

Excerpted and reprinted from the *Springfield Republican*, 4 October 1891.

fabrications of imagination. An immense amount of knowledge of the whale is given in this amazing book, which swells, too, with a humor often as grotesque as Jean Paul's, but not so genial as it is sardonic. Character is drawn with great power too, from Queequeg the ex-cannibal, and Tashtego the Gay Header, to the crazy and awful Ahab, the grave Yankee Starbuck, and the terrible White whale, with his charmed life, that one feels can never end. Certainly it is hard to find a more wonderful book than this Moby Dick, and it ought to be read by this generation, amid whose feeble mental food, furnished by the small realists and fantasts of the day, it would appear as Hercules among the pygmies, or as Moby Dick himself among a school of minnows.

[The Crown and Glory of the Later Phase]

HENRY S. SALT

As "Typee" is the best production of the earlier and simpler phase of Melville's authorship, so undoubtedly is "The Whale" (or "Moby Dick," as it is sometimes styled) the crown and glory of the later phase; less shapely and artistic than "Typee," it far surpasses it in immensity of scope and triumphant energy of execution.[1] It is in "The Whale" that we see Melville casting to the winds all conventional restrictions, and rioting in the prodigality of his imaginative vigour. It is in "The Whale" that we find the fullest recognition of that magical influence of the sea—the "image of the ungraspable phantom of life"—which from first to last was the most vital inspiration of his restless and indomitable genius. ("The ocean," he finely wrote in a later volume, "brims with natural griefs and tragedies; and into that watery immensity of terror man's private grief is lost like a drop.") Ostensibly nothing more than a wild story of a strange voyage of vengeance, a "quenchless feud" between a fierce old sea-captain and a particular white sperm-whale of renowned strength and audacity, the book, which abounds with real facts concerning the details of the whale-fishery, has a mystic esoteric significance which lifts it into a wholly different category. In the character of Captain Ahab, who "looked like a man cut away from the stake when the fire has overrunningly wasted all the limbs without consuming them," we see a lurid personification of the self-destructive spirit of Hatred and Revenge, while Moby Dick, the white whale, "swam before him as the monomaniac incarnation of all those malicious agencies which some deep men feel eating in them." To quote detached passages from a work of such ambitious conception and colossal proportions would be worse than useless; I must therefore content myself with saying that "The Whale," faulty as it is in many respects, owing to the turgid mannerisms of Melville's transcendental mood, is nevertheless the supreme production of a master mind—let no one presume to pass judgment on American literature unless he has read, and re-read, and wonderingly pondered, the three mighty volumes of "The Whale."

The increasing transcendentalism of Melville's later thought was accompanied and reflected by a corresponding complexity of language, the

Excerpted and reprinted from "Marquesan Melville," *Gentleman's Magazine* [London] 272 (March 1892), 252–54, 256–57.

limpid simplicity so remarkable in "Typee," and "Omoo," and "White Jacket" being now succeeded by a habit of gorgeous and fantastic word-painting, which, though brilliantly effective at its best, degenerated, at its worst, into mere bombast and rhetoric, a process which had already been discernible in the concluding portions of "Mardi," while in "Pierre" (or "The Ambiguities," as it was appropriately designated) it reached the fatal climax of its development.

*　　*　　*

His love of literature was fully sustained to the end. I have before me a most interesting batch of letters, dated between 1884 and 1888, addressed by him to Mr. James Billson, of Leicester, and mostly dealing with the poems of James Thomson ("B.V."), of which he was a great admirer. Some of these comments and appreciations are in Melville's best style. " 'Sunday up the River,' " he writes, "contrasting with the 'City of Dreadful Night,' is like a Cuban humming-bird, beautiful in faery tints, flying against the tropic thundercloud. Your friend was a sterling poet, if ever one sang. As to pessimism, although neither pessimist nor optimist myself, nevertheless I relish it in the verse, if for nothing else than as a counterpoise to the exorbitant hopefulness, juvenile and shallow, that makes such a muster in these days—at least in some quarters."

"Exorbitant hopefulness" could indeed have been hardly otherwise than distasteful to one who, like his own "John Marr" (a retired sailor whose fate it was to live on a "frontier-prairie," among an unresponsive inland people who cared nothing for the sea), had so long experienced the solitude of disappointed genius. But it is impossible to believe that this undeserved neglect can be permanent. The opinion of those competent judges who are students of Melville's works is so clear and emphatic in his favour,[2] that it is not too much to say that to read his books is generally to appreciate them; nor is it only those who have what is called an "educated taste" who are thus impressed, for I have been told of instances in which English working-men became his hearty admirers. It is satisfactory to know that a new edition of his best books is forthcoming, both in America and England, and that the public will thus have an opportunity, I will not say of repairing a wrong done to a distinguished writer, for, as I have already shown, the decay of his fame was partly due to circumstances of his own making, but at least of rehabilitating and confirming its earlier and truer judgment. Herman Melville will then resume his honorable place in American literature (for, to end as I began, I hold that the existence of an American literature is a fact and not a supposition), as the prose-poet of the Pacific—

the sea-compelling man,
Before whose wand Leviathan
Rose hoary-white upon the deep,

With awful sounds that stirred its sleep;
Melville, whose magic drew Typee,
Radiant as Venus, from the sea.[3]

Notes

1. *The Whale* was dedicated to Hawthorne, and is referred to in his "Wonder-Book." "On the hither side of Pittsfield sits Herman Melville, shaping out the gigantic conception of his 'White Whale,' while the gigantic shadow of Greylock looms upon him from his study window."

2. I may instance Mr. William Morris, Mr. Theodore Watts, Mr. R. L. Stevenson, Mr. Robert Buchanan, and Mr. W. Clark Russell.

3. Robert Buchanan's *Socrates in Camden*.

[A Marvellous Odyssey]

Anonymous

It was not until this remarkable romance came out, over forty years ago, that Herman Melville, that strange compound of Dutch, English and Huguenot blood, merited the name of the American prose Victor Hugo. In fact it was after the publication of "Moby-Dick" that Hugo's really great romances of the sea and land came out; so that one might truthfully turn the tables and almost say that Victor Hugo was the French Melville. So striking, so suspicious is the resemblance between "Moby-Dick" and "Les Travailleurs de la Mer," that one is sorely tempted to the enticing accusation of a certain sort of plagiarism on the part of the Sage of Guernsey, of that general and diffusive kind which critics love to point out between Swift and Lucian, Goethe and Marlowe, Faust and Manfred, and Coleridge and Mme. de Staël. A gigantic devil-fish is one of the *dramatis personæ* of "Moby-Dick" as it is of "The Toilers of the Sea," and the fantastic learning, the episodic style, the wonderful picturings of the sea in all its beauty and terror, and the peculiar manipulation of imaginative effects in both books, emphasize the fact of their essential kinship. Hugo was familiar enough with English literature to command it completely, and it is far from incredible that he knew the works of Melville. Hawthorne paid the warmest tribute to Melville's surpassing imagination, and to him "Moby-Dick" was very appropriately dedicated.

Indeed there is no romance of Hawthorne's that surpasses this whaling-story in witching power, in grasp on the pulse, in almost supernatural strength of description, and in ability to quicken the blood. The undreamt poesy lying in the lives of Nantucket whalers in the fifties has for once received epical treatment, and the result is a marvellous Odyssey of adventure in warm seas and in icy, in halcyon and in purgatorial latitudes, over such a range of sunlit or storm-smitten billows as could occur only in actual experience before the mast in search of real whales on the real deep. Hugo never travelled; and therefore his lovely poems of the sea or his "Hans d'Islande" are conceived from the shore—powerful but shadowy idealizations of things he had never really seen. His empty shells Melville fills full of the living breath, the roar, the music, the vibration of the living sea, Whitmanesque in its intensity and realism, the memories of one who had

Excerpted and reprinted from the *Critic* [New York], new ser. 19 (15 April 1893), 232.

lived years in the troughs or on the mountain-crests of Homeric waves, and who therefore in his work simply transcribed ineffaceable impressions. Mohammedanism has been described as mere "paint"; even so Hugo's seas are painted seas as compared with the streaming or starlit or surging oceans of this real mariner. To depict the guillotining of Louis XVI. it is not necessary indeed to feel the actual flash of the axe itself across one's arteries, but a certain amount of actual knowledge is always welcome if not indispensable in depicting the mighty phenomena of great voyages, great emotions or great deeds. This Hugo did not possess, and his phantom romances are mere husks, mere *larvæ* or *simulacra*, illumined by an unnatural interior light, like a jack o'lantern, as compared with the healthy, wholesome, rude but terrible realities of such books as "Moby-Dick."

In this story Melville is as fantastically poetical as Coleridge in the "Ancient Mariner," and yet, while we swim spellbound over the golden rhythms of Coleridge feeling at every stroke their beautiful improbability, everything in "Moby-Dick" might have happened. The woe-struck captain, his eerie monomania, the half-devils of the crew, the relentless pursuit of the ever-elusive vindictive white whale, the storms and calms that succeed each other like the ups and downs of a mighty hexameter, all the weird scenery of the pursuit in moonlight and in daylight, all are so wonderfully fresh in their treatment that they supersede all doubt and impress one as absolutely true to the life. Even the recondite information about whales and sea-fisheries sprinkled plentifully over the pages does not interfere seriously with the intended effect; they are the paraphernalia of the journey. The author's extraordinary vocabulary, its wonderful coinages and vivid turnings and twistings of worn-out words, are comparable only to Chapman's translations of Homer. The language fairly shrieks under the intensity of his treatment, and the reader is under an excitement which is hardly controllable. The only wonder is that Melville is so little known and so poorly appreciated.

[This Epic of Whaling]

[J. St. Loe Strachey]

Mr. Stevenson would have deserved well of the republic of letters if he had done nothing but bring the South Seas into fashion again. Our fathers and grandfathers revelled in the stories of that wonderful region "to the su'thard of the line," where, as De Quincey's sailor-brother declared, the best arguments against ghosts and the voices and strange shapes that haunt the vast solitudes of the sea are of no avail; and where, as a later poet has told us,—

> "The blindest bluffs hold good, dear lass,
> And the wildest tales are true."

For some thirty years, however, a strange veil of dullness fell upon the face of the Pacific Ocean; and if we heard at all of its islands and its surf-drenched reefs, it was in the prosaic narratives of Lady Brassey and other such long-distance tourists. A fortunate accident, however, took Mr. Stevenson to the South Seas, and at the magic of his voice the calm of commonplace has disappeared, and once more our fancy can possess that region of high romance.

With this renaissance of the South Seas, it was inevitable that there should come a demand for the republication of *Typee* and *Omoo*—those wonderful "real romances" in which the inspired usher, who passed his time between keeping school at Green Bush, N.Y., and sailing among the islands, told the world how he had lived under the shadow of the bread-fruit trees, a life which, as far as sensuous delight and physical beauty were concerned, could only be compared to that of ancient Hellas. There, in vales lovelier than Tempe, and by waters brighter than those of the Ægean, he had seen the flower-crowned and flower-girdled Mænads weave the meshes of their rhythmic dance; had sat at feasts with youths whose forms might have inspired Lysippus and Praxiteles; had watched in amazement and delight the torches gleaming through the palm-groves, while the votaries of mysteries, like those of Demeter or Dionysus, performed their solemn rites and meet oblations; and yet, in spite of all, had yearned with a passionate yearning for

Reprinted from "Herman Melville," *Spectator* [London] 70 (24 June 1893), 858–59. Occasioned by the publication of *Typee, Omoo, White-Jacket*, and *Moby-Dick* by G. P. Putnam's Sons.

the pleasant fields of New England and the wholesome prose of modern life—the incomparable charities of hearth and home.

Though Melville has not the literary power of Mr. Stevenson, the description in *Typee* of the life he led among a cannibal tribe in the Marquesas islands has a charm beyond the charm of *The Wrecker*, the *Island Nights*, or those studies of the Marquesas which Mr. Stevenson contributed to the earlier numbers of *Black and White*. *Typee* is the "document" *par excellence* of savage life, and a document written by one who knew how to write as well as to look. We have said that Mr. Melville does not write as well as Mr. Stevenson, but this does not mean that he is not a literary artist. Mr. Melville is no mean master of prose, and had his judgment been equal to his feeling for form, he might have ranked high in English literature on the ground of style alone. Unfortunately, he was apt to let the last great master of style he had been reading run away with him. For example, in *Moby Dick*—one of the best and most thrilling sea-stories ever written—Mr. Melville has "hitched to his car" the fantastic Pegasus of Sir Thomas Browne. With every circumstance of subject favourable, it would be madness to imitate the author of *Urne Burial*. When his style is made the vehicle for describing the hunting of sperm-whales in the Pacific, the result cannot but be disastrous. Yet so great an artist is Mr. Melville and so strong are the fascinations of his story, that we defy any reader of sense to close this epic of whaling without the exclamation,—"With all its faults I would not have it other than it is." Discovering a right line in obliquity and by an act of supreme genius forcing his steed to run a pace for which he was not bred, Mr. Melville contrives, in spite of Sir Thomas Browne, to write a book which is not only enchanting as a romance, but a genuine piece of literature. No one who has read the chapter on "Nantucket" and its seafarers, and has learned how at nightfall the Nantucketer, like "the landless gull that at sunset folds her wings and is rocked to sleep between billows," "furls his sails and lays him to his rest, while under his very pillow rush herds of walruses and whales," will have the heart to cavil at Melville's style. In *White Jacket*—a marvellous description of life on a man-of-war—we see yet another deflection given to Mr. Melville's style, and with still worse results. He had apparently been reading Carlyle before he wrote it; and Carlylisms, mixed with the dregs of the *Religio Medici*, every now and then crop up to annoy the reader. In spite, however, of this heavy burden, *White Jacket* is excellent reading, and full of the glory of the sea and the spirit of the Viking. And here we may mention a very pleasant thing about Mr. Melville's books. They show throughout a strong feeling of brotherhood w :h the English. The sea has made him feel the oneness of the English kin, and he speaks of Nelson and the old Admirals like a lover or a child. Though Mr. Melville wrote at a time when English insolence and pig-headedness, and Yankee bumptiousness, made a good deal of ill-blood between the two peoples, he at heart feels that, on the sea at least, it is the English kin against the world.

We have left ourselves no time to quote, as we desired to do, either the enchanting description of how Mr. Melville, while a prisoner in the "island valley" of Typee, came upon the image of the dead chief seated in his canoe with his sails set, like a Viking for Valhalla; or the exquisite picture of the forest glade, in which stood the great monoliths, placed there, like our own Druid stones, by some forgotten and perished people. Nor can we give his picture of Fayaway, the beautiful genius of the vale. Typee and the South Seas our readers must explore for themselves. Instead, we will quote the account of the Quaker whalers who sail out of the Island of Nantucket, though some of the syntax is quite indefensible:—

"Now, Bildad, like Peleg, and indeed many other Nantucketers, was a Quaker

*　　　*　　　*

it only results again from another phase of the Quaker, modified by individual circumstances."

(ch. 16)

Nantucket itself must also claim notice. Here is the description of the islanders, and what they have done:—

"And thus have these naked Nantucketers

*　　　*　　　*

while under his very pillow rush herds of walruses and whales."

(ch. 14)

If there is not high imagination and true literature in this, we know not where to find it.

The Best Sea Story Ever Written

Archibald MacMechan

Anyone who undertakes to reverse some judgment in history or criticism, or to set the public right regarding some neglected man or work, becomes at once an object of suspicion. Nine times out of ten he is called a literary snob for his pains, or a prig who presumes to teach his betters, or a "phrase-monger," or a "young Osric," or something equally soul-subduing. Besides, the burden of proof lies heavy upon him. He preaches to a sleeping congregation. The good public has returned its verdict upon the case, and is slow to review the evidence in favour of the accused, or, having done so, to confess itself in the wrong. Still, difficult as the work of rehabilitation always is, there are cheering instances of its complete success; notably, the rescue of the Elizabethan dramatists by Lamb and Hazlitt and Leigh Hunt. Nor in such a matter is the will always free. As Heine says, ideas take possession of us and force us into the arena, there to fight for them. There is also the possibility of triumph to steel the raw recruit against all dangers. Though the world at large may not care, the judicious few may be glad of new light, and may feel satisfaction in seeing even tardy justice meted out to real merit. In my poor opinion much less than justice has been done to an American writer, whose achievement is so considerable that it is hard to account for the neglect into which he has fallen.

This writer is Herman Melville, who died in New York in the autumn of 1891, aged eighty-three [72]. That his death excited little attention is in consonance with the popular apathy towards him and his work. The civil war marks a dividing line in his literary production as well as in his life. His best work belongs to the *ante-bellum* days, and is cut off in taste and sympathy from the distinctive literary fashions of the present time. To find how complete neglect is, one has only to put question to the most cultivated and patriotic Americans north or south, east or west, even professed specialists in the nativist literature, and it will be long before the Melville enthusiast meets either sympathy or understanding. The present writer made his first acquaintance with *Moby Dick* in the dim, dusty Mechanics' Institute Library (opened once a week by the old doctor) of an obscure Canadian village, nearly twenty years ago; and since that time he has seen only one copy of the book

Reprinted from *Queen's Quarterly* (Kingston, Ont.) 7 (October 1899), 120–30.

exposed for sale, and met only one person (and that not an American) who had read it. Though Kingsley has a good word for Melville, the only place where real appreciation of him is to be found of recent years is in one of Mr. Clark Russell's dedications. There occurs the phrase which gives this paper its title. Whoever takes the trouble to read this unique and original book will concede that Mr. Russell knows whereof he affirms.

Melville is a man of one book, and this fact accounts possibly for much of his unpopularity. The marked inferiority of his work after the war, as well as changes in literary fashion, would drag the rest down with it. Nor are his earliest works, embodying personal experience like *Redburn* and *White Jacket*, quite worthy of the pen which wrote *Moby Dick*. *Omoo* and *Typee* are little more than sketches, legitimately idealized, of his own adventures in the Marquesas. They are notable works in that they are the first to reveal to civilized people the charm of life in the islands of the Pacific, the charm which is so potent in *Vailima Letters* and *The Beach of Falesà*. Again, the boundless archipelagos of Oceanica furnish the scenes of *Mardi*, his curious political satire. This contains a prophecy of the war, and a fine example of obsolete oratory in the speech of the great chief Alanno from Hio-Hio. The prologue in a whale-ship and the voyage in an open boat are, perhaps, the most interesting parts. None of his books are without distinct and peculiar excellences, but nearly all have some fatal fault. Melville's seems a case of arrested literary development. The power and promise of power in his best work are almost unbounded; but he either did not care to follow them up or he had worked out all his rifts of ore. The last years of his life he spent as a recluse.

His life fitted him to write his one book. The representative of a good old Scottish name, his portrait shows distinctively Scottish traits. The head is the sort that goes naturally with a tall, powerful figure. The forehead is broad and square; the hair is abundant; the full beard masks the mouth and chin; the general aspect is of great but disciplined strength. The eyes are level and determined; they have speculation in them. Nor does his work belie his blood. It shows the natural bent of the Scot towards metaphysics; and this thoughtfulness is one pervading quality of Melville's books. In the second place, his family had been so long established in the country (his grandfather was a member of the "Boston tea-party") that he secured the benefits of education and inherited culture: and this enlightenment was indispensable in enabling him to perceive the literary "values" of the strange men, strange scenes and strange events amongst which he was thrown. And then, he had the love of adventure which drove him forth to gather his material at the ends of the earth. He made two voyages; first as a green hand of eighteen in one of the old clipper packets to Liverpool and back; and next, as a young man of twenty-three, in a whaler. The latter was sufficiently adventurous. Wearying of sea-life, he deserted on one of the Marquesas Islands, and came near being killed and eaten by cannibal natives who kept him prisoner for four months. At last he escaped, and worked his way home on a U.S. man-o'-war. This adventure lasted four years and he went no more to sea.

After his marriage, he lived at Pittsfield for thirteen years, in close intimacy with Hawthorne, to whom he dedicated his chief work. My copy shows that it was written as early as 1851, but the title page is dated exactly twenty years later. It shows as its three chief elements this Scottish thoughtfulness, the love of literature and the love of adventure.

When Mr. Clark Russell singles out *Moby Dick* for such high praise as he bestows upon it, we think at once of other sea-stories,—his own, Marryat's, Smollett's perhaps, and such books as Dana's *Two Years before the Mast*. But the last is a plain record of fact; in Smollett's tales, sea-life is only part of one great round of adventure; in Mr. Russell's mercantile marine, there is generally the romantic interest of the way of a man with a maid; and in Marryat's the rise of a naval officer through various ranks plus a love-story or plenty of fun, fighting and prize-money. From all these advantages Melville not only cuts himself off, but seems to heap all sorts of obstacles in his self appointed path. Great are the prejudices to be overcome; but he triumphs over all. Whalers are commonly regarded as a sort of sea-scavengers. He convinces you that their business is poetic; and that they are finest fellows afloat. He dispenses with a love-story altogether; there is hardly a flutter of a petticoat from chapter first to last. The book is not a record of fact; but of fact idealized, which supplies the frame for a terrible duel to the death between a mad whaling-captain and a miraculous white sperm whale. It is not a love-story but a story of undying hate.

In no other tale is one so completely detached from the land, even from the very suggestion of land. Though Nantucket and New Bedford must be mentioned, only their nautical aspects are touched on; they are but the steps of the saddle-block from which the mariner vaults upon the back of his sea-horse. The strange ship "Pequod" is the theatre of all the strange adventures. For ever off soundings, she shows but as a central speck in a wide circle of blue or stormy sea; and yet a speck crammed full of human passions, the world itself in little. Comparison brings out only more strongly the unique character of the book. Whaling is the most peculiar business done by man upon the deep waters. A war-ship is but a mobile fort or battery; a merchantman is but a floating shop or warehouse: fishing is devoid of any but the ordinary perils of navigation; but sperm-whaling, according to Melville, is the most exciting and dangerous kind of big game hunting. One part of the author's triumph consists in having made the complicated operations of this strange pursuit perfectly familiar to the reader; and that not in any dull, pedantic fashion, but touched with the imagination, the humor, the fancy, the reflection of a poet. His intimate knowledge of his subject and his intense interest in it make the whaler's life in all its details not only comprehensible but fascinating.

A bare outline of the story, though it cannot suggest its peculiar charm, may arouse a desire to know more about it. The book takes its name from a monstrous, invincible, sperm whale of diabolical strength and malice. In an encounter with this leviathan, Ahab, the captain of a Nantucket whaler, has had his leg torn off. The long illness which ensues drives him mad; and his one thought upon recovery is vengeance upon the creature that has mutilated him. He gets command of the "Pequod," concealing his purpose with the cunning of insanity until the fitting moment comes: then he swears the whole crew into his fatal vendetta. From this point on, the mad captain bears down all opposition, imposes his own iron will upon the ship's company, and affects them with like heat, until they are as one keen weapon fitted to his hand and to his purpose. In spite of all difficulties, in spite of all signs and portents and warnings, human and divine, he drives on to certain destruction. Everything conduces to one end, a three day's battle with the monster, which staves and sinks the ship, like the ill-fated "Essex."

For a tale of such length, *Moby Dick* is undoubtedly well constructed. Possibly the "Town-Ho's Story," interesting as it is, somewhat checks the progress of the plot; but by the time the reader reaches this point, he is infected with the leisurely, trade-wind, whaling atmosphere, and has no desire to proceed faster than at the "Pequod's" own cruising rate. Possibly the book might be shortened by excision, but when one looks over the chapters it is hard to decide which to sacrifice. The interest begins with the quaint words of the opening sentence: "Call me Ishmael"; and never slackens for at least a hundred pages. Ishmael's reasons for going to sea, his sudden friendship with Queequeg, the Fijian harpooneer, Father Mapple's sermon on Jonah, in the seamen's bethel, Queequeg's rescue of the country bumpkin on the way to Nantucket, Queequeg's Ramadan, the description of the ship "Pequod" and her two owners, Elijah's warning, getting under way and dropping the pilot, make up an introduction of great variety and picturesqueness. The second part deals with all the particulars of the various operations in whaling from manning the mast-heads and lowering the boats to trying out the blubber and cleaning up the ship, when all the oil is barrelled. In this part Ahab, who has been invisible in the retirement of his cabin, comes on deck and in various scenes different sides of his vehement, iron-willed, yet pathetic nature, are made intelligible. Here also is much learning to be found, and here, if anywhere, the story dawdles. The last part deals with the fatal three days' chase, the death of Ahab, and the escape of the White Whale.

One striking peculiarity of the book is its Americanism—a word which needs definition. The theme and style are peculiar to this country. Nowhere but in America could such a theme have been treated in such a style. Whaling is peculiarly an American industry; and of all whale-men, the Nantucketers were the keenest, the most daring, and the most successful. Now, though there are still whalers to be found in the New Bedford slips, and interesting as it is to clamber about them and hear the unconscious confirmation of all Melville's details from the lips of some old harpooneer or boat-header, the industry is almost extinct. The discovery of petroleum did for it. Perhaps Melville went to sea for no other purpose than to construct the monument of whaling in this unique book. Not in his subject alone, but in his style is Melville distinctly American. It is large in idea, expansive; it has an Elizabethan force and freshness and swing, and is, perhaps, more rich in figures than any style but Emerson's. It has the picturesqueness of the new world, and, above all, a free-flowing humour, which is the distinct *cachet* of American literature. No one would contend that it is a perfect style; some mannerisms become tedious, like the constant moral turn, and the curiously coined adverbs placed before the verb. Occasionally there is more than a hint of bombast, as indeed might be expected; but, upon the whole, it is an extraordinary style, rich, clear, vivid, original. It shows reading and is full of thought and allusion; but its chief charm is its freedom from all scholastic rules and conventions. Melville is a Walt Whitman of prose.

Like Browning he has a dialect of his own. The poet of *The Ring and the Book* translates the different emotions and thoughts and possible words of pope, jurist, murderer, victim, into one level uniform Browningese; reduces them to a common denominator, in a way of speaking, and Melville gives us not the actual words of American whalemen, but what they would say under the imagined conditions, translated into one consistent, though various Melvillesque manner of speech. The life he deals with belongs already to the legendary past, and he has us completely at his mercy. He is completely successful in creating his "atmosphere." Granted the conditions, the men and their words, emotions and actions, are all consistent. One powerful scene takes place on the quarter-deck of the "Pequod" one evening, when, all hands mustered aft, the Captain Ahab tells of the White Whale, and offers a doubloon to the first man who "raises" him:

> "'Captain Ahab,' said Tashtego, 'that White Whale must be the same that some call Moby Dick.'
>
> *　　　*　　　*
>
> If man will strike, strike through the mask!'"

(ch. 36)

Then follows the wild ceremony of drinking round the capstan-head from the harpoon-sockets to confirm Ahab's curse. "Death to Moby Dick. God hunt us all, if we do not hunt Moby Dick to the death!" The intermezzo of the various sailors on the forecastle which follows until the squall strikes the ship is one of the most suggestive passages in all the literature of the sea.

Under the influence of Ahab's can, the men are dancing on the forecastle. The old Manx sailor says:

"I wonder whether those jolly lads bethink them of what they are dancing over. I'll dance over your grave, I will—that's the bitterest threat of your night-women, that beat head-winds round corners. O, Christ! to think of the green navies and the green-skulled crews."

Where every page, almost every paragraph, has its quaint or telling phrase, or thought, or suggested picture, it is hard to make a selection; and even the choicest morsels give you no idea of the richness of the feast. Melville's humour has been mentioned; it is a constant quality. Perhaps the statement of his determination after the adventure of the first lowering is as good an example as any:

"Here, then, from three impartial witnesses, I had a deliberate statement of the case.

*   *   *

'Queequeg,' said I, 'come along and you shall be my lawyer, executor and legatee.'"

(ch. 49)

The humour has the usual tinge of Northern melancholy, and sometimes a touch of Rabelais. The exhortations of Stubb to his boat's crew, on different occasions, or such chapters as "Queen Mab," "The Cassock," "Leg and Arm," "Stubb's Supper," are good examples of his peculiar style.

But, after all, his chief excellence is bringing to the landsman the very salt of the sea breeze, while to one who has long known the ocean, he is as one praising to the lover the chiefest beauties of the Beloved. The magic of the ship and the mystery of the sea are put into words that form pictures for the dullest eyes. The chapter, "The Spirit Spout," contains these two aquarelles of the moonlit sea and the speeding ship side by side:

"It was while gliding through these latter waters that one serene and moonlight night, when all the waves rolled by like scrolls of silver; and by their soft, suffusing seethings all things made what seemed a silvery silence, not a solitude; on such a silent night a silvery jet was seen far in advance of the white bubbles at the bow. Lit up by the moon it looked celestial; seemed some plumed and glittering god uprising from the sea.

*   *   *

Walking the deck, with quick, side-lunging strides, Ahab commanded the t'gallant sails and royals to be set, and every stunsail spread. The best man in the ship must take the helm. Then, with every mast-head manned, the piled-up craft rolled down before the wind. The strange, upheaving, lifting tendency of the taffrail breeze filling the hollows of so many sails made the buoyant, hovering deck to feel like air beneath the feet."

In the chapter called "The Needle," ship and sea and sky are blended in one unforgettable whole:

"Next morning the not-yet-subsided sea rolled in long, slow billows of mighty bulk, and striving in the "Pequod's" gurgling track, pushed her on like giants' palms outspread. The strong, unstaggering breeze abounded so, that sky and air seemed vast outbellying sails; the whole world boomed before the wind. Muffled in the full morning light, the invisible sun was only known by the spread intensity of his place; where his bayonet rays moved on in stacks. Emblazonings, as of crowned Babylonian kings and queens, reigned over everything. The sea was a crucible of molten gold, that bubblingly leaps with light and heat."

It would be hard to find five consecutive sentences anywhere containing such pictures and such vivid, pregnant, bold imagery: but this book is made up of such things.

The hero of the book is, after all, not Captain Ahab, but his triumphant antagonist, the mystic white monster of the sea, and it is only fitting that he should come for a moment at least into the saga. A complete scientific memoir of the Sperm Whale as known to man might be quarried from this book, for Melville has described the creature from his birth to his death, and even burial in the oil casks and the ocean. He has described him living, dead and anatomized. At least one such description is in place here. The appearance of the whale on the second day of the fatal chase is by "breaching," and nothing can be clearer than Melville's account of it:

"The triumphant halloo of thirty buckskin lungs was heard

*   *   *

to the dim mistiness of an advancing shower in a vale."

(ch. 134)

This book is at once the epic and the encyclopaedia of whaling. It is a monument to the honour of an extinct race of daring seamen; but it is a monument overgrown with the lichen of neglect. Those who will care to scrape away the moss may be few, but they will have their reward. To the class of gentleman-adventurer, to those who love both books and free life under the wide and open sky, it must always appeal. Melville takes rank with Borrow, and Jefferies, and Thoreau, and Sir Richard Burton; and his place in this brotherhood of notables is not the lowest. Those who feel the salt in their blood that draws them time and again out of the city to the wharves and the ships, almost without their knowledge or their will; those who feel the irresistible lure of the spring, away from the cramped and noisy town, up the long road to the peaceful companionship of the awaking earth and the untainted sky; all those—and they are many—will find in Melville's great book an ever fresh and constant charm.

[A Most Astounding Epic]

Anonymous

Considering to what an extent the sea must necessarily influence the literature of a maritime race, it is, perhaps, not so easy as it might seem on the first glance to pick the six best sea novels or stories written by Englishmen and Americans. The selection made in FAMOUS NOVELS OF THE SEA (Sampson Low, 21s. net) contains among the six only one by a living writer. It would, we think, have been better to confine the series altogether to writers who are dead than to include Mr. Clark Russell. For though the "Wreck of the Grosvenor" is his best book, he cannot stand in the same rank with Michael Scott, Herman Melville, George Cupples, and Captain Marryat, who, with Fenimore Cooper, make up the authors of this series. Nor, indeed—though for other reasons—has Fenimore Cooper the least right to be in the same bookshelf with his four great companions. What Fenimore Cooper knew of the sea by actual experience was extremely little, and it only needs to open any one of his sea stories to perceive his ignorance. His claims to the title of the "American Scott" are only justified by the steady tiresomeness which characterizes him and the least interesting stories of the Wizard of the North.

But as regards the four books remaining of the six nothing can be said against their right to speak on behalf of the sea and on behalf of sailormen of all sorts and conditions. "Midshipman Easy" has been made a classic by the united boyhood of England, and has sent more boys to sea than anything else except the very smell of tar and salt water. It is truly the model for an adventure book, and has neither a dull moment nor a dull sentence in it. Marryat, who was naturally soaked in salt water, showed his knowledge by what he left out. The chief fault of amateur sea-writers, and there are many of them, is the desire to show that they know their subject. The results are too often laborious failures which excite the sombre derision of the seaman. Marryat knew what to omit, and his power of humour and character-sketching has given the world a series of portraits which must live so long as the sea excites the imagination of the English race.

But strong and humorous as was Marryat, it is doubtful whether his greatest admirers would claim genius for him. For genius implies something

Excerpted and reprinted from *Literature* [London] 7 (17 November 1900), 386–87.

that gives a book permanent value, not only for its subject, but as literature pure and simple. In Michael Scott's "Tom Cringle's Log" there are undoubtedly flashes of real genius. The book is astoundingly fluent, absolutely natural, and contains passages of descriptions which are true, unforced, and brilliant. Indeed, Michael Scott was one of the few writers who can use "description" properly as a background, and not as padding. And Scott knew not only the naval man but the English and American merchant seaman. There is no air of his having learnt anything. The narrative flows like a river, and has, like a tropical mountain stream, a thousand glimpses of the unexpected. His humour at times partakes of the pantomime, but even so it is unforced and boyish. And when he touches the tragic string his feeling is utterly sincere. Even his greatest villain is not without touches of real humanity. Few who have read the book once but will be ready to read it again.

The signs of real knowledge at first hand, not gathered from books nor noted by a passenger on the "fo'c'sle head," are visible in George Cupples' "Green Hand." Perhaps he invented the trick, now done to death, of the passenger who is also a seaman and plays the *deus ex machina* when the inevitable and necessary disaster at last occurs. The trick in the "Green Hand" is, at any rate, well done, and any man who reads the book through and understands it must have a competent knowledge of seamanship, even if he acquires an unjustifiable contempt for the seamanlike qualities of the merchant service.

But of all these six books the one, the only one, which is supremely great and undoubtedly a work of genius is Herman Meville's "Moby Dick." And it just as surely has no claim to be in the collection at all. It is not a novel. It is hardly a story. It is an epic, and a most astounding epic too. The human hero is nothing to the great white whale which dominates the intense and imaginative narrative. For this book is the first and, properly speaking, the last book ever written upon the greatest big game hunting of the world. The cachalot, singly and collectively, in the huge personality of Moby Dick, is the theme. And the book is an encyclopædia. Its knowledge is deep, inclusive and conclusive. No man after reading it can hope to exceed or to equal or even to comment upon it. It has peculiar qualities; the peculiar qualities of Melville. In one place he names the world as one might name an inn. He calls it "At the Sign of the Thunder Cloud." The book is half a nightmare; it is like a thunder-storm in the brewing; there are spaces of clear sky, and great blurs of gloom in it. It is natural history raised to the highest power of tragedy. It is monstrous, inchoate, suggestive, and full of speculation and astonishment. Ahab Peleg, the demoniac Captain, hunts the whale that dismembered him through the seas of the earth as the Opium Eater was hunted through the forests of Asia. But the drugged one here is the hunter, and the cold, acute, and horrible intellect of the epic whale dominates the play upon the mighty stage of the wandering sea. The book is full of pictures. They are pictures of imagination, fervid and deep. The characters are types, human but superhuman. The humour is tragic humour; the talk of the players is astounding. The scheme of the book is no scheme, but it grows Æschylean and concludes inevitably upon an inexorable vortex. Only those who have not read the book may conclude that this is the language of indiscriminate eulogy. A reprint of it upon this side of the Atlantic has so long been desired by the few who knew its value that the series will be welcome if only for the work of perhaps the greatest natural genius produced upon American soil.

[The Power and Fascination of Melville]

Louis Becke

Many years ago, when the present writer was supercargo of a small trading schooner, sailing from the beautiful port of Apia, in the Samoan group—those lovely clustering gems of the blue Pacific, whose names are now familiar and endeared to all English-speaking people through the memory of the man who rests on the verdured slopes of Vailima Mountain,—there came on board our ship, one day, a sweet, dainty little English lady, whom we rough wandering island traders loved, and feared as well; for with all the gentleness that filled her woman's heart, she could, as we knew at times by our burning cheeks of shame, be very, but justly, bitter to us when we had done those things which we ought not to have done. And in Samoa, in those days, men did those things which they ought not to have done very frequently.

"I have brought you some books," she said to our grizzled old captain; "and among them are three volumes by an American writer—Herman Melville. It is called 'The Whale,' and it is the strangest, wildest, and saddest story I have ever read."

.   .   .   .

Strange, wild, and sad indeed is this tale of "Moby Dick," or, as it was first known, "The Whale." Some there are who profess to see in the tale, story, narrative, phantasy—call it what you will—nothing but the "mad rhetoric and bombast, the fantastic and unintelligible creation of a mind losing, or that had lost, its balance."

To such critics, who write from a high and unbending standpoint of the ethics of literary style, plan, and plot, I would say that their criticism is based upon the unstable foundation of absolute ignorance of the strange conditions and environment of the whaleman's life, as so truly portrayed by Herman Melville; the one man who knew his subject and knew how to write about it, though much of his brilliancy of description is too often marred and obscured by a headlong and purposeless dash away from his main theme into the vague realms of weird and fantastic metaphysical imagination.

Reprinted from "Introduction," in *Moby Dick* (London: G. P. Putnam's Sons, 1901), pp ix–xii.

115

But to me, and, I doubt not, to all sailormen who have read any single one of Melville's books,—whether "Typee," Omoo," "White Jacket," "Mardi," or this present work,—his writings possess that power and fascination that no other sea-writer, excepting Marryat, can exercise. He was of the sea; he loved it. Its hardships, its miseries, its starvation, its brutalities, and the grossness and wickedness that everywhere surrounded him in his wanderings through the two Pacifics, held but little place in the mind of a man who, ragged and unkempt as was too often his condition, had a soul as deep and wide and pure as the ocean itself, a soul that for ever lifted him up above all mean and squalid things. How I wish I could say I have met the man! How I should have loved to grasp his hand, if only for the sake of the words he once wrote—

"Oh, give me again the rover's life, the thrill, the joy, the whirl! Let me feel them again: old sea! Let me leap into thy saddle once more! I am sick of these 'Terra Firma' toils and cares, sick of the dust and reek of towns! Let me sniff thee up, sea-breeze, and whinney in thy spray!"

Those three volumes of "Moby Dick" (published by Bentley, in London, in 1851) were the first of Melville's books I ever read; and I and my old comrades shall always cherish the memory of the dainty little lady who brought them to us. For she too, like Melville, has gone beyond, and gone as he, I think, would have liked to go himself—the deep Pacific, which *he* loved so well, is *her* last resting-place.

The captain of our little schooner was the one well-educated man of our ship's company—a man with a very heavy hand and a very kindly Scotsman's heart. The mate and myself were not always in perfect accord with him, and often bitter words had passed between us; but "Moby Dick" brought us happily together again. For "the old man" had a deep, resonant voice, and he read the story to us from beginning to end. And although he would stop now and again, and enter into metaphysical matters, we forgave him, for we knew that he too, like us, was fascinated with mad Captain Ahab and brave mate Starbuck and the rest of the ill-fated crew of the "Pequod."

I am no critic of literary "style," and only attempt thus poorly to express my opinion—that of a scantily educated seaman—of what I regard as one of the best "sea-books" ever written. For to Melville truly, like the ancient helmsman of Longfellow's "Secret of the Sea," was given some of the meanings of the great deep; and all mariners—those who love the sea and those who hate it—and all who have not read "Moby Dick" will, when they do read it, say from their hearts, "Here is a man indeed who has braved the dangers of the sea and seeks to teach some of its mystery!"

And from my own hard-won knowledge, I think that a whaleman does know and comprehend more of the mysteries and dangers and wonders of the ocean than any other sea-going man. The author of "Moby Dick" was, like many of his gallant New England countrymen, who, more than a hundred years ago, carried their nation's proud flag throughout the South and North Pacific in pursuit of leviathan, and helped to civilise (*and not to brutalise*, as so often has been written) the natives of the Pacific Islands,—a born whaleman, a sailor, and a "perfect gentleman."

[Almost the Greatest Sea Story in Literature]

WILLIAM P. TRENT

Fortune, which seemed not long since to have deserted HERMAN MELVILLE (1819–91) as completely as Simms, has at last smiled again upon the former since a generation fond of narratives full of not too improbable adventure and of tropical glow has accepted, with at least fair complacency, the republication of books that won the warm commendation of Robert Louis Stevenson. The author of *Typee* was born in New York, and ultimately died there, after a long period of seclusion. He had no special incentive save his own love of adventure to desert farming at an early age and go to sea as a cabin-boy. He then tried teaching, but shipped again in 1841, this time on a whaler bound for the South Seas. The cruelty of his captain caused him—with a companion, the Toby of *Typee*—to desert the ship as she lay in a harbour in the Marquesas. Then followed the adventures so interestingly told in *Typee*, which was published in 1846, soon after Melville's return to civilization. His book was very successful in both England and America, although some persons refused to give credence to it or to *Oomoo,* which immediately followed it. Marriage and literary success then transformed the adventurer into a fairly prolific man of letters. But as early as 1848 the quasi-speculative, chaotic romance entitled *Mardi* gave premonition of aberration and of the eventual frustration of a promising career. Melville's greatest achievement still awaited him, however, for after two other fair books of adventure he published, in 1851, his masterpiece, *Moby Dick, or the White Whale.* If it were not for its inordinate length, its frequently inartistic heaping up of details, and its obvious imitation of Carlylean tricks of style and construction, this narrative of tremendous power and wide knowledge might be perhaps pronounced the greatest sea story in literature. The breath of the sea is in it and much of the passion and charm of the most venturous of all the venturous callings plied upon the deep. It is a cool reader that does not become almost as eager as the terrible Captain Ahab in his demoniacal pursuit of Moby Dick, the invincible whale, a creation of the imagination not unworthy of a great poet. In this uneven, but on the whole genuine, work of genius, Melville probably overtasked himself. He published several other books while, like his friend Hawthorne, attending to his duties in the

Excerpted and reprinted from *A History of American Literature, 1607–1865* (New York: D. Appleton, 1903), 389–91.

custom-house, but nothing comparable to his earlier works. One, *Israel Potter*, deserved Hawthorne's praise because of its spirited portraits of Franklin and Paul Jones, but no revival of their author's fame will justify the republication of these productions of his decline.

[Melville's Finest Performance]

W. Clark Russell

"Moby Dick; or, The Whale," is generally and with justice regarded as Melville's finest performance. It is, indeed, taken on the whole, a very noble piece. Some of the conversations among the sailors remind one for their strength, sweetness and courage of such passages in Dekker, Webster, Massinger, Fletcher, and other old dramatists as Charles Lamb loved to select. The opening chapters of this book are extraordinarily impressive. He gives us a picture of New Bedford by night. His sketch of the Spouter Inn, its hoarse, salt landlord, its delicious clam chowder, the frightful Mowrèe harpooner whose bed the hero has to share, enchant the imagination and chisel the memory with the delights and impressions produced by a masterpiece in Dutch painting.

Yet it is easy to understand why "Moby Dick" should never reach the popularity of "Typee" or "Omoo." In parts it is too obscure. The reader, moreover, is harassed by the frequent interpolation of a transcendental mysticism which often ill-fits the mouths of the rough tarpaulins who are made to deliver their minds of the sublimated fancies which appear to oppress them even more than the brine-hardened food they consume.

Excerpted and reprinted from "Editor's Preface," *Typee* (London: John Lane, 1904), vii–viii.

The Letters Column of the New York Times Saturday Review of Books in 1905: A Forum for Discoverers of Moby-Dick

◆

[A Recommendation to Kipling and Bullen: Read *Moby-Dick*]

ANONYMOUS

Mr. Sidney Low, in The London Standard, has been taking to task both Rudyard Kipling and Frank Bullen for seeming to know nothing whatever of Herman Melville and "Moby Dick," which Mr. Low justly calls "the splendid prose epic of the South Sea fishery." A new edition of Mr. Bullen's admirable "Cruise of the Cachalot" has appeared in London, and simultaneously a letter to Mr. Bullen from Mr. Kipling, full of compliments to the book, has been printed. Mr. Bullen is of the opinion that his book contains the first account of a cruise of a South Sea whaler from the seaman's point of view. And Mr. Kipling infers that no other book "has so completely covered the whole business of whale fishing, and at the same time given such real and new pictures." Mr. Low urges both these gentlemen to make the acquaintance of Melville and his "Moby Dick" without delay. Melville's book, by the way, is out of print in England, though it still may be obtained here. We trust that Mr. Low's sensible remarks may soon lead to the early publication of a new English edition.

Reprinted from the *New York Times Saturday Review of Books* (20 May 1905), 321.

[That Good Old Story *Moby-Dick*]

C[harles] F[rancis] A[dams]

I was interested in an editorial comment on that good old story "Moby Dick" a few weeks ago. There is some character drawing in that book which is unequaled, and as for the whale fishing information Mr. Bullen is "not in it." The opening chapters about the cannibal harpooner is great. But what I wished to say was that the query you made had been already answered in your "Readers' Column" by Peter Toft about five years ago in a very entertaining letter, in which he describes calling Mr. Bullen's attention to "Moby Dick" and the author's remark that he "did not think much of the melodramatic features of the book."

It was, however, totally unknown to Mr. Bullen at the time he wrote "The Cruise of the Cachalot," and evidently equally so to Kipling, in spite of his universal knowledge.

Reprinted from the *New York Times Saturday Review of Books* (15 July 1905), 470.

[*Moby-Dick* as Tone Poem]

"Cosmopolitan"

I thought I had laid down my pen for good. Mr. Hall's last letter contained nothing which had not before been discussed in these columns. I have also been "zu sehr viel anderswo engagiert." But meanwhile I have found time to read Herman Melville's books, and wish to thank The New York Times Book Review for introducing us to that author in an April number. It gives a jaded reader fresh courage to find that an author worth while existed a half-century since and undiscovered until now. There may be others!

"Melodramatic," says Mr. Bullen. To be sure; there is enough in his books for selection and rejection by varied moods and tastes. But throughout he is a man. That is to say, a God-fearing man.

For my part, I find in "Moby Dick" even more than the "grand prose epic" of Mr. Sidney Low. It is one of those rare books which suggest tone poems. Having no musical education, I still seem to hear through it operatic strains far more grand than Wagner's "Flying Dutchman." I mean, of course, always without any trickery of language.

Excerpted and reprinted from the *New York Times Saturday Review of Books* (22 July 1905), 486.

Melville and Bullen

George Stephen

I read with interest a letter which, under the initials of C. F. A., appeared in your "From Readers" page July 15, on the subject of Herman Melville's "Moby Dick," and Mr. Frank Bullen's quoted remark therein, that "he did not think much of the melodramatic features of the book."

Let any American whaleman take side by side Melville's "The Whale; or, Moby Dick," (as his book was first entitled,) and Mr. Bullen's "Cruise of the Cachalot," and compare the two works, and then judge if Mr. Bullen has any right to speak of Melville as being melodramatic. The major part of Bullen's book is true, but he has spoiled the effect of his tale by narrating in detail two "incidents" that never occurred.

Excerpted and reprinted from the *New York Times Saturday Review of Books* (26 August 1905), 562.

Mr. Bullen and Melville

Frank T. Bullen

Although as a rule I take no part in newspaper controversies, I feel that I ought once more to make clear that I did not, for many reasons, ever say anything derogatory of Herman Melville's wonderful work.

What I did say to Mr. Peter Toft was, "Had I read 'Moby Dick' first, I should never have dared to write 'The Cruise of the Cachalot.'" Mr. Toft thereupon asked me if I could account for the general neglect of Melville's masterpiece. I answered that perhaps it was partly on account of its length and partly because of the wonderfully transcendental and melodramatic story woven in with his splendid narrative of facts. And for this I am accused of depreciating the work of a man whose shoelatchets (in a literary sense) I have never felt worthy to unloose, and since I have known his work I have always said so.

The plain fact is that until long after I wrote the "Cachalot" I had never read any book dealing with the South Seas or sperm whaling except Bennett's voyage round the world, and from that I borrowed nothing because I needed nothing. As for Mariner's "Tonga," I did not even know that there was such a book until last year, when I read the "Diversions of a Prime Minister." The only aid I had in writing the "Cachalot" was my own memory of events happening to me personally.

Reprinted from the *New York Times Saturday Review of Books* (30 September 1905), 642.

Bullen and Melville

M. U. O.

I am very glad that Mr. Frank Bullen made an exception to his rule, by writing the letter in the last number of THE NEW YORK TIMES BOOK REVIEW. Glad also that he did not read "Moby Dick" before he wrote "The Cruise of the Cachalot." The world would have been the loser indeed if the latter book had not been written. Melville's book simply carried me away. "The Cruise of the Cachalot" I had read several times before I read "Moby Dick," and am ready to read it as many times again, after having read the older book. I think in these days everybody prefers a well-written narrative of facts to a poem as a steady diet. Although Mr. Bullen has no reason to be as modest as he expresses himself, it is pleasant to know that he was misrepresented in the quotations, one of which I used at second or third hand.

Reprinted from the *New York Times Saturday Review of Books* (7 October 1905), 658.

[The Deterioration of Melville's Style]

William B. Cairns

Moby Dick, or the White Whale, is a story of a crazed sea captain who pursued around the world the invincible white whale that had maimed him for life. Many incidents are told with a detail that suggests that they were actual experiences of the author's own whaling voyage. The conception of the story is a powerful one, but it is not adequately sustained. By this time (1850) the author had become deeply interested in abstruse philosophy, and especially, it is said, in Sir Thomas Browne. As a result his style suffered a complete and disastrous change from the directness of *Typee* and *Omoo.* The beginnings of this change are seen in *Moby Dick;* and it is more marked in the author's later prose works, which are hardly readable. *Battle Pieces and Aspects of the War* is a collection of poems, mostly crude and formless, but written with much enthusiasm. Melville's early work is so good as to cause serious regret at the deterioration of his style.

Excerpted and reprinted from *A History of American Literature* (New York: Oxford University Press, 1912), 369–70.

[Simms versus Melville]

W. P. Trent and John Erskine

It was in the fertility and excitement of his plots that Simms excelled Cooper, and in this phase of the development of the American novel he in turn is rivalled by the friend of Hawthorne, Herman Melville.

*   *   *

The work of Simms, for its extent and its contemporary importance, is far more worthy of attention than all of Melville's writing, with the one exception of *Moby Dick;* and the character of Simms was most engaging. But the Southerner's novels are now hardly known by name, whereas the praise of Stevenson and some other craftsmen near at hand has given Melville's best work a new lease of life. Yet above them both Cooper still keeps his secure place, not much injured by unsympathetic modern criticism, nor even by some condescending praise.

Excerpted and reprinted from *Great Writers of America* (London: Williams & Norgate, 1912), 55–57.

[A Strange Mixture]

John Calvin Metcalf

But the great work of Melville is *Moby Dick* (1851), the story of the chase of the great white whale by Captain Ahab and his crew in revenge for the loss of one of the Captain's legs in the monster's mouth. Known among sailors as Mocha Dick, this legendary white whale was pursued by the old sea captain with implacable hatred. "All the subtle demonisms of life and thought," says Melville; "all evil, to crazy Ahab, were visibly personified, and made practically assailable in Moby Dick." The terrible white whale becomes a symbol of nature against which man is in the end helpless, for ship and crew are defeated in the struggle. *Moby Dick* is a strange mixture of adventure and philosophy, of realism and fantasy, invested with the poetic coloring of romance. It is one of the greatest books of its kind in literature and links the name of its author with other masters of the sea story from Defoe to Joseph Conrad. Melville was the first American writer to put the old whaling vessels picturesquely into literature and to reveal the mysterious fascination of those exotic Pacific islands which have of late furnished the background for many romances. Because of the tributes of certain well-known English writers and several American scholars, and of an increasing interest in South Sea explorations, Melville, long neglected, is again widely read at home and abroad.

Excerpted and reprinted from *American Literature* (Richmond: Johnson, 1914), 390–91.

[A German View]

LEON KELLNER

MELVILLE.—This group of writers [the Transcendentalists] had a most original compeer in Herman Melville, the author—almost unknown in Germany—of the sea tale "Typee" (a journey to the Marquesas Islands), 1846; "Omoo" (descriptions of the South Sea), 1847; "Mardi," 1848; "White Jacket, or the World in a Man-of-War," 1850; "The White Whale, or Moby Dick," 1851, etc.

These tales are characterized by a realism which anticipates the Zolas and Goncourts, but surpasses them in verity, inasmuch as every particular was seen and experienced. In "Moby Dick," his most widely read work, the writer narrates in the first person how a certain Ishmael enlists on a whaler as a common sailor, and gives all his experiences until the foundering of the vessel. That Ishmael was Melville himself. What Kipling admired so greatly in Frank T. Bullen's "Cruise of the Cachalot" was accomplished by the American nearly fifty years earlier, and that with a considerable measure of wordly wise humor. Unfortunately, Melville fell at an early day under the influence of Carlyle and the spiritualists; that proved very detrimental to his delineation, and particularly to his style. He represents his hero, Captain Ahab, a whaler, as a mysterious fire-eating figure of colossal proportions who outdoes himself in high-sounding phrases and indulges in a quantity of exclamatory words. And at the same time, behind palpable events of the most commonplace sort, the cosmic soul of things is constantly sought.

Excerpted and reprinted from *American Literature,* trans., Julia Franklin (Garden City: Doubleday, Page, 1915), 116–17.

[The Immense Originality of *Moby-Dick*]

Carl Van Doren

In *Mardi* for the first time appear those qualities which made a French critic call Melville "un Rabelais américain," his welter of language, his fantastic laughter, his tumultuous philosophies. He had turned, contemporaries said, from the plain though witty style of his first works to the gorgeous manner of Sir Thomas Browne; he had been infected, say later critics, with Carlylese. Whatever the process, he had surely shifted his interest from the actual to the abstruse and symbolical, and he never recovered from the dive into metaphysics which proved fatal to him as a novelist. It was, however, while on this perilous border that he produced the best of his, and one of the best of American, romances; it is the peculiar mingling of speculation and experience which lends *Moby Dick* (1851) its special power.

The time was propitious for such a book. The golden age of the whalers was drawing to a close, though no decline had yet set in, and the native imagination had been stirred by tales of deeds done on remote oceans by the most heroic Yankees of the age in the arduous calling in which New England, and especially the hard little island of Nantucket, led and taught the world. A small literature of whaling had grown up, chiefly the records of actual voyages or novels like those of Cooper in which whaling was an incident of the nautical life. But the whalers still lacked any such romantic record as the frontier had. Melville brought to the task a sound knowledge of actual whaling, much curious learning in the literature of the subject, and, above all, an imagination which worked with great power upon the facts of his own experience. Moby Dick, the strange, fierce white whale that Captain Ahab pursues with such relentless fury, was already a legend among the whalers, who knew him as "Mocha Dick."[1] It remained for Melville to lend some kind of poetic or moral significance to a struggle ordinarily conducted for no cause but profit. As he handles the story, Ahab, who has lost a leg in the jaws of the whale, is driven by a wild desire for revenge which has maddened him and which makes him identify Moby Dick with the very spirit of evil and hatred. Ahab, not Melville, is to blame if the story seems an allegory, which Melville plainly declared it was not; but it contains, nevertheless, the semblance of a conflict between the ancient and

Excerpted and reprinted from "Contemporaries of Cooper," *The Cambridge History of American Literature*, ed. W. P. Trent et al., vol. 1 (New York: G. P. Putnam's Sons, 1917), 322–23.

scatheless forces of nature and the ineluctable enmity of man. This is the
theme, but description can hardly report the extraordinary mixture in *Moby
Dick* of vivid adventure, minute detail, cloudy symbolism, thrilling pictures
of the sea in every mood, sly mirth and cosmic ironies, real and incredible
characters, wit, speculation, humour, colour. The style is mannered but
often felicitous; though the book is long, the end, after every faculty of
suspense has been aroused, is swift and final. Too irregular, too bizarre,
perhaps, ever to win the widest suffrage, the immense originality of *Moby
Dick* must warrant the claim of its admirers that it belongs with the greatest
sea romances in the whole literature of the world.

Note

1. See Reynolds, J. N., *Mocha Dick, Knickerbocker Magazine,* May, 1839.

[Inexhaustible Literary Energy]

PERCY H. BOYNTON

Like most other great narrative literature, it [*Moby Dick*] offers an appeal for youthful readers in the external story alone. This concerns Captain Ahab, who had lost a leg in an encounter with the terror of the South Seas, Moby Dick, the great white whale; and tells of his consuming hatred for the monster, and of his voyage after revenge, which ends with his death in conflict with the foe. Two thirds of the chapters might be culled to present this relentless sequence in the form of a so-called boys' book. Yet even so presented the story would contain more than meets the eye. However great it is as a straight whaling adventure—and there is nothing equal in literature—in a secondary sense it is just as great a story of life which happens to be told in terms of whales and whalers. This is the story of Eve and of Prometheus, the perennial struggle of man for spiritual freedom in the midst of an externally physical world—his attempt to make a conquest of circumstances. "All visible objects, man," says Captain Ahab, "are but as pasteboard masks. But in each event—in the living act, the undoubted deed—there some unknown but still reasoning thing puts forth its features from behind the unreasoning mask. If man will strike, strike through the mask! How can the prisoner reach outside, except he thrust through the wall?" The tale is not an allegory, but it is so innately true that it has all the revealing significance of allegory to him who can perceive it.

As a piece of writing "Moby Dick" serves as a reminder that the greatest stories in literature are never the most neatly constructed. The plot of this one has before it an inevitable ending; one is drawn toward it as down a high-walled stream to the edge of a cataract. Yet all the way along it is told with the utmost leisureliness. While there is no escape, there is no haste. With an inexhaustible literary energy, and an abounding flow of varying emotion, Melville combines thrilling episodes, minute discussions of whaling lore, visionary symbolism, ironic allusion and sustained satire, vivid characterization, and picturesque beauty. The present "Melville revival" can be accounted for partly by the present-day vogue of South Sea literature and partly by the post-war temper of skepticism, but more because in Melville has been rediscovered one of the immensely energetic and original personalities of the last hundred years.

Excerpted and reprinted from *A History of American Literature* (Boston: Ginn and Company, 1919), 307–8.

[A Book Like the Eternal Sea]

HOLBROOK JACKSON

He who provides us with the means of departing to the ends of the earth without the trouble of leaving our armchair deserves well of time, and it is unlikely, so long as human interest in adventure in strange places survives, that the principal works of Herman Melville will be forgotten. Over seventy years have passed since he gave to the world those entrancing distillations of adventurous experience known as 'Typee' and 'Omoo,' and although imitators have arisen, sometimes possessing greater artistry in fiction, these books more than survive the devastating struggle for existence to which all written records are subjected.

*　　　*　　　*

Herman Melville was only secondarily creative; his imagination needed the stimulus of experience. Left to invent he moidered into metaphysics and lost himself and his readers in the labyrinthine ways of the darkling woods of thought—where no birds sing! So long as he was content to play the part of the retired seaman spinning the thread of experience and weaving it into the stuff of fiction he was sure of a hearing, though he could never hope to achieve the imaginative heights of the untravelled Englishman who invented Robinson Crusoe. It must be noted, however, to the credit of his inventiveness that his seafaring years were almost as few as James Boswell's period of direct association with Dr. Johnson.

*　　　*　　　*

Herman Melville had more energy than art and more thought than imagination. A less laborious mind would have given to the world more compact narratives, and a keener sense of the artistry of a story would have impelled him to weed his garden of adventure of those reflective deviations which cumber it, and annoy all but the most devoted of readers. The vice of intellectual enlargement of his theme grew. He never learned how to eliminate what Walter Pater called the otiose. He could not resist the temptation to philosophize, and at times he varied his discursiveness by becoming deliberately informative. Curiously enough those latter deviations

Excerpted and reprinted from "Herman Melville (1819–1891), " *Anglo-French Review* [London] 2 (August 1919), 59–64.

from the true path of narrative fiction are often of extraordinary interest. Particularly is this so in 'Moby Dick,' which is at once a story of the perils of the deep and a technical and historical account of whaling. The chapter entitled 'Cetology' is itself a scholarly treatise on the whale, revealing evidence of painstaking research and the rare gift of attractive elucidation of a little-known subject. Readers of 'Omoo' will, of course, recall the excellent chapter on 'The Cocoa Palm' in that book; and there are similar dissertations in all of the three masterpieces I have named which, although, superfluous from the point of view of artistry, are not lacking in charm or value. It was only when his innate love of deviation became a dominating habit, when, as in his later books, the tail wagged the dog, that this 'transcendentalist in oilskin,' as one writer has it, becomes unreadable.

That, however, rarely if ever occurs in his best works.

*   *   *

Melville places you under no illusions as to the desirability of the life barbaric. He consorted with savages, happily kindly savages, by accident, and although he greatly admired their free yet orderly lives, in a climate which left man little work to do, he had no particular desire to become decivilized. His stay in the Valley of Typee was in the nature of exile and he took the first opportunity to get among his own kind. To his credit also it should be said that he never, in after life, sentimentalized over the joys of barbarism. He spun his yarn and left it at that. At the same time it is impossible to read 'Typee' and 'Omoo' without the conviction that Herman Melville felt whilst writing those books the sort of joy certain people feel in visualising some realm of bliss, some islands of the blest. Just as those 'sea-shouldering whales' in 'Moby Dick' symbolise for him the mighty forces of Nature with which men eternally wage war, so in the earlier narratives the happy riot of untrammelled folk among the cocoa palms and bread-fruit trees of the Pacific archipelagoes symbolize for him a triumph over the tribulations and complexities which beset civilized races.

The temptation to dwell upon the fascinating records of barbaric life which Herman Melville has given the world and with which his name is most definitely linked, is inevitable. But he was equally successful in recording and depicting the rougher and more adventurous incidents in seafaring life. The sea has inspired many masterpieces of literature, particularly in the language of our sea-girt islands, but there are few of them greater than Melville's 'Moby Dick.' This crowded narrative, with its riches of observation, its store of knowledge, its thrills and hairbreadth escapes, its massive and rolling wildness, is like the eternal sea itself. 'Moby Dick' tastes and smells of the sea and its very formlessness makes it more real. It is a rolling panorama of seascapes humanised by ships. In one sense it shows a bigger man than the Melville who wrote 'Typee' and 'Omoo' and wields a pen of greater strength. Perhaps time will be avenged of the charm which has given greater prominence to the island narratives, by prolonging the life of Herman Melville's epic of the sea beyond that of his other works.

[Melville and Borrow]

F. C. OWLETT

Coming at last to treat of "Moby Dick," one feels the utter futility of any attempt to convey a just idea of that marvellous tale. "In that wild, beautiful romance"—the words are Mr. Masefield's—"Herman Melville seems to have spoken the very secret of the sea, and to have drawn into his tale all the magic, all the sadness, all the wild joy of many waters. It stands quite alone; quite unlike any other book known to me. It strikes a note which no other sea writer has ever struck." Here is a book about which Criticism is wonderfully agreed. Whatever the faults of it, there is only one opinion—as far as I have been able to discover there has never been more than one opinion touching its greatness. Writing people who have read it and have written around it—however diverse the judgments they may have pronounced on other books, and whatever the critical doctrines they may severally swear to—unite in acclaiming "Moby Dick" as the finest sea book ever written in English. That a finer will ever be written is simply not to be conceived. The crown of this king of the sea writers is secure as Shakespeare's own.

*　　　*　　　*

Mr. Shorter and others have styled Melville the American Borrow. To a certain extent the implied comparison is just. Both were vagabonds, in the sense of Alexander Smith's delightful essay of that title; both knew how to turn their vagabondisings to good account in the weaving their experiences into fascinating narrative; both had the poetic vision; both had humour.

Melville, however, was much more of the idealist than Borrow, who at bottom was a realist. Melville's idealism frequently became transcendentalism. In transcendental mood he conceived and fashioned "Moby Dick." It is the finest sea story in the world. In transcendental mood he wrote "Mardi," "Pierre," and other books equally unreadable. The robuster humour of Borrow saved him from perpetrating a "Pierre"; his greater matter-of-factness prevented his ever giving to the world a "Moby Dick."

Melville's humour is of a subtler and more intimate quality than

Excerpted and reprinted from "Herman Melville (1819–1891): A Centenary Tribute," *Bookman* [London] 56 (August 1919), 164–67.

137

Lavengro's. It permeates his work—is, indeed, the vital essence of it—charging it through and through, and playing on it from without as it were, lambent always save in those great moments when it breaks and surges in riot. His style is spontaneous, buoyant, rich—with the richness of seventeenth century prose (Mr. Strachey has pointed out the literary kinship of Melville with Sir Thomas Browne). His best descriptive passages reach the highest level of impassioned prose, and even in those books where he falls farthest from literary grace, he never loses his sense of the force and the colour of words. It may even be contended that the badness of his worst work is due to an overdevelopment of this same sense, which, in its relation to our author's other excellent qualities, exhibited at times the dangerous tendencies of an Aaron's rod. Let it be conceded that Borrow on occasion achieves greater effects, in spite of—shall we say because of?—his terser statement of fact, and the simplicity and angularity that are the marks of his style. The throes of composition were very real with Borrow; his books were produced only after sore travail. He (who never confessed anything) might have confessed with Milton that he wrote prose as it were with his left hand (which is not to say that the Lavengro ever wrote, or was capable of writing, poetry).

Both Melville and Borrow were men of dauntless spirit. When, however, one reads of how Melville's apprehension of a flogging came nigh causing him to hurl his captain overboard, one hardly dares to speculate—not on what Borrow in a like situation would have done, so much, as at what moment precisely he would have done it—an important consideration under all the circumstances. In other days, and under other conditions, Borrow would have been a Drake. The singeing of a papistical potentate's beard would have been an operation after his own heart. His defiant humour would have anticipated Van Tromp's broom. Melville was a more tractable being. His father belonged to an old Scottish family, his mother to the Dutch family of Gansevoort. Such blood-mingling affords as sufficient a warranty for coolness and discretion as for intrepidity.

Of the two men, Borrow was the more thoroughgoing rebel. Each was capable of great overthrowings, but Melville had what Borrow lacked—the imagination that constructs. It is significant that Borrow never created a character. If his characters live (and who shall deny that they live?) it is in spite of him, and because they are not the creatures of his imagination. He had met them one and all—had dwelt with them, fought with them, conjugated Armenian verbs with them, drunk ale with them. His supreme moments were his aggressive moments, and they, unlike Campbell's hours of bliss, were neither few nor far between. Melville has his iconoclastic passages—and very effective they are—but if we would match the "Appendix" to the "Romany Rye," we must go back to such masters of vituperative prose as Milton and Swift. Finally, if the investing the commonplace with the indefinable spirit of Old Romance be held to be an achievement greater than the intensifying a fascination already exerted by circumstances of distance and unsatisfying rumour, then there can be only one Borrow. In which view, be it clearly understood, there is nothing at all derogatory to the genius of the American romancer.

Melville and Our Sea Literature

The romancer born a century ago alludes in the early pages of "Moby Dick" to the unconquerable love Americans then had for the sea. "Circumambulate the city on a dreamy Sabbath afternoon," from Corlear's Hook to Coenties Slip, and what do you see? "Posted like sentinels all round the town, stand thousands upon thousands of mortal men fixed in ocean reveries. Some leaning against the spiles; some seated upon the pier heads; some looking over the bulwarks of ships from China; some high aloft in the rigging"—all landsmen, magnetically attracted. When Melville took to the ocean in his twenties because his merchant father left him penniless, seafaring was a lure for great numbers of young Americans. Our mariners, when Melville was born, were enjoying the still fresh laurels of their exploits against Britain. Our whalers were scouring every sea as he grew up; as he reached manhood our merchant marine reached its greatest strength. Yankee exploits on the ocean have not been neglected by prose writers. Dana's classic and Cooper's sea novels were damp from the press when Melville became author; he had not left off when Nordhoff and Wise, to mention lesser figures, began. But he stands foremost.

Melville's strange literary career—his sun rising so early and brilliantly and disappearing midway under such a heavy cloud of mental aberration—was marked by three great exploits. He was the first who ever burst into the South Seas with a romancer's pen in hand, and he seized his opportunity. Stevenson himself, coming half a century later and praising "Omoo" and "Typee" in Melville's last days, has not displaced him. Our literature of the whaler is scanty, but it includes one book of undying interest, "Moby Dick." Finally, the life of the American sailor on the frigate, noblest of war vessels, has never been pictured so well as in "White Jacket"; Marryat himself, with all his superiority at an imaginative yarn, cannot teach us so much. Some part in the obscuring of Melville's genius may have been played by the simple exhaustion of his materials of experience, for he was not a man to repeat himself; it is regrettable that he did not explore other seas, or become better acquainted with the merchant marine, to which he did nothing like justice in "Redburn." He was twenty-one when he embarked for the Pacific sperm

Reprinted from the *New York Evening Post*, 2 August 1919.

fishery; an eighteen months' cruise, desertion in the Marquesas, imprisonment by a savage tribe, escape, mutiny on a ship in the Society Islands, and return home from Honolulu on the frigate United States, made him twenty-five when he reached Boston in 1844.

The South Sea tales present the most manifold appeal to the reader—an appeal historical, geographical, human, and romantic. The loveliness of the scenery is yet there, but the enchanting life of the untouched natives in the Marquesas has given way to the still picturesque but very different existence familiar through travellers and Joseph Conrad. The Typees have gone forever, and with them the valley scenes nearest to Eden in all literature, the morning bath, the meal of *poee-poee,* bananas, breadfruit, and cocoanut milk, the daily employment of making war-gear, canoes, and mats, the boating, the evening dances, the total innocence, with light skirmishing against another tribe to avert *ennui.* Two-thirds of the story would be a beautiful idyll were we not always conscious that the keen Yankee observer is noting everything barbaric as well as picturesque—the Feast of Calabashes, the idol in his bamboo temple, the canoe and effigy serving as monument to a dead chieftain, the beautiful maiden eating raw fish. In "Omoo" is described in detail the ruinous process of Christianization as it appeared when the Society Islanders began passing under the simultaneous sway of religion and vice. The documented narrative makes doubly bright the existence of the good-humored. Kory-Kory and pretty Fayaway in their jungle fastness, but the Tahitians are far from unattractive. In this book are episodes more unforgettable than any in the equable "Typee"—the wretched life of the sailors on their rotten Sydney bark, their amusing but effective rebellion, the friction between Protestant Anglo-Saxons and Catholic French, and the adventures of the wandering narrator, culminating in his inglorious exit from Queen Pomaree's "palace."

But is is undoubtedly in "Moby Dick" that Melville has engaged the warmest affections of his readers. It has a stormy impetuosity which makes its atmosphere unique; regarded from a critical angle, its story seems a wild farrago, an application of Eugéne Sue plot-making and Carlylean style to the tale of a New England sea captain. But its rare merits greatly outweigh its defects. Chief among them is the unrivalled account it gives of the natural history of leviathans, the business of catching them, cutting them up, and salvaging their veritable lakes of oil—a marvel of lucidity and interest, achieved through not only perfect command of the subject, but an enlivening play of fancy and illustration. What dulness might not another writer have given the description of a sperm whale's reservoir?

> The upper part of the head, known as the case, may be regarded as the great Heidelburgh tun of the sperm whale. And as that famous great tierce is mystically carved in front, so the whale's vast plaited forehead forms innumerable strange devices for the emblematical adornment of his wondrous

tun. Moreover, as that of Heidelburgh was always replenished with the most excellent of the wines of the Rhenish valleys, so the tun of the whale contains the most precious of all his oily vintages; namely, the highly prized spermaceti, in its absolutely pure, limpid, and odoriferous state. Nor is this precious substance found unalloyed in any other part of the creature. Though in life it remains perfectly fluid, yet upon exposure to the air after death it soon begins to concrete, sending forth beautiful crystalline shoots, as when the first thin delicate ice is just forming in water.

Of only less merit is the depiction of the typical New England whaling crew, or rather crews. The glimpse we have of the New England background in the visit to New Bedford, where men give whales for dowries to their daughters, and a few porpoises to nieces, and where grizzled sea dogs who attack leviathans undauntedly face tavern strangers bashfully, is inimitable. Capt. Peleg and Capt. Bildad afford close views of these worthies. Withal, for the story itself much may be said. The determination of the half-demented Capt. Ahab to take the whale which had cost him his leg; his resolution to keep on after each fresh disappointment; the final desperate chase, and its terrible culmination when the white whale rams his ship and sinks it, fulfilling a prophecy Ahab had often heard—no boy, no matter how grown-up, ever tired of this. By way of compensation to oldsters, the book is full of that philosophy which makes Melville unique among sea writers.

[Again, a Great Opium Dream]

Raymond M. Weaver

Born in hell-fire, and baptized in an unspeakable name, "Moby-Dick, or the Whale" (1851), reads like a great opium dream. The organizing theme of the book is the hunting of Moby-Dick, the abhorred white whale, by the monomaniac Captain Ahab. To Ahab, this ancient and vindictive monster is the incarnation of all the vast moral evil of the world; he piles on the whale's white hump the sum of all the rage and hate of mankind from the days of Eden down. There are in "Moby-Dick" long digressions, natural, historical, and philosophical on the person, habits, manners, and ideas of whales; there are long dialogues and soliloquies, such as were never spoken by mortal man in his waking senses, conversations that for sweetness, strength, and courage remind one of passages from Dekker, Webster, Massinger, Fletcher, and the other old dramatists loved by Charles Lamb; perhaps a fifth of the book is made up of Melville's independent moralizings, half essay, half rhapsody; withal, the book contains some of the most finished comedy in the language. If one logically analyzes "Moby-Dick," he will be disgusted, just as Dr. Johnson, who had no analysis but the logical, was disgusted with "Lycidas." And so with Melville's novel. If one will forget logic and common sense, and "abandon himself"—as Dr. Johnson would contemptuously have said—to this work of Melville's, he will acknowledge the presence of an amazing masterpiece. But neither "Lycidas" nor "Moby-Dick" should be read by philistines or pragmatists.

Excerpted and reprinted from "The Centennial of Herman Melville," *Nation* [New York] 109 (2 August 1919), 146.

[Loving Melville: Like Eating Hasheesh]

Frank Jewett Mather, Jr.

My introduction to Herman Melville is due to Edwin Lucas White, the author of "El Supremo" and of much verse equally notable, if too little known. Amid the rigors of philology, to which we were then both bound, we kept certain private delectations of a literary sort. One afternoon he took me to his study and instead of the expected sonorous passage from Victor Hugo's "Légende des Siècles" he read me the following words out of a stout, shabby, cloth-bound book named "Moby Dick, or The Whale":

> To a landsman, no whale, nor any sign of a herring, would have been visible at that moment; nothing but a troubled bit of greenish white water, and thin scattered puffs of vapor hovering over it, and suffusingly blowing off to leeward, like the confused scud from white rolling billows. The air around suddenly tingled and vibrated, as it were, like the air over intensely heated plates of iron. Beneath this atmospheric waving and curling, and partially beneath a thin layer of water also, the whales were swimming.

(Then began the chase)

> It was a sight full of wonder and awe! The vast swells of the omnipotent sea; the surging, hollow roar they made, as they rolled along the eight gunwales, like gigantic bowls in a boundless bowling green; the brief suspended agony of the boat, as it would tip for an instant on the knife-like edge of the sharper waves that almost seemed threatening to cut it in two; the sudden profound dip into the watery glens and hollows; the keen spurrings and goadings to gain the top of the opposite hill; the headlong, sled-like slide down its other side—all these, with the cries of the headsmen and harpooners, and the shuddering gasps of the oarsman, with the wondrous sight of the ivory Pequod bearing down upon her boats with outstretched sails, like a wild hen after her screaming brood—all this was thrilling. Not the raw recruit marching from the bosom of his wife into the fever heat of his first battle; not the dead man's ghost encountering the first unknown phantom in the other world—neither of these can feel stranger and stronger emotions than that man does, who for the first time finds himself pulling into the charmed, churned circle of the hunted sperm whale.

Excerpted and reprinted from "Herman Melville," *Review* [New York] 1 (9 August 1919), 276–78; (16 August 1919), 298–301.

The tang of this was unforgettable. That reading made a Melvilleite out of me. I bought everything Melville published—it took me ten years to do it, and my collection was only completed with the two privately printed pamphlets of poems, through the gracious gift of Melville's daughter. I read my collection up and down with increasing delight. Gradually I learned that to love Melville was to join a very small circle. It was like eating hasheesh. Robert Louis Stevenson and Charles Warren Stoddard had given him brave praise. John La Farge told me of meeting in the South Seas two American beachcombers lured towards the Marquesas by the spell of "Typee." La Farge made the charming drawing of Fayaway standing in the bow of a canoe and serving as mast and sail. It was for the ill-fated reprint of "Typee" and "Omoo" edited by the late Arthur Stedman, and I saw another charming Fayaway in clay in the studio of the sculptress, Miss Elizabeth Cornwall. I owe to my enthusiasm for Melville acquaintance with extraordinary persons on both sides the seas; for no ordinary person loves Melville. So on the centenary of his birth it is a double debt of gratitude which I repay most inadequately in giving some account of one of the greatest and most strangely neglected of American writers.

*   *   *

Melville, in prose, for he was also no mean poet, had three styles, like an old master. The swift lucidity, picturesqueness, and sympathy of "Typee" and "Omoo" have alone captured posterity. Melville lives by his *juvenalia*. "Redburn" and "White Jacket" are straightforward manly narratives, less colorful than their predecessors. They have not stood the competition with Dana's quite similar "Two Years Before the Mast." They are not quite as solid as that classic, but their chief fault was merely in being later. Then Melville developed a reflective, mystical, and very personal style, probably influenced by Carlyle, which the public has from the first eschewed. It asserts itself first in the strange allegory, "Mardi, and a Voyage Thither," 1849, it pervaded "Pierre, or the Ambiguities," 1852, and other later books. "Moby Dick" shows an extraordinary blend of the first and the last style—the pictorial and the orphic; is Melville's most characteristic and, I think, his greatest book. Still, for the average reader Melville is merely the author of "Typee" and "Omoo."

*   *   *

Melville was one of the earliest literary travelers to see in barbarians anything but queer folk. He intuitively understood them, caught their point of view, respected and often admired it. Thus "Typee" in a peculiar sense is written from the inside. The ready tolerance that Melville had learned in the forecastle had not blunted the gentleman in him, but had prepared him to be the ideal spectator of a beautiful life that has forever passed. As having distinctly saved a vanishing charm for posterity, "Typee" is perhaps Melville's most important book.

*   *   *

In one sense "Typee," the adventure and the book, made Melville. At twenty-seven, from being an oddity of the forecastle, he jumped into fame. From "Typee" and his antecedent experience at sea came the subject of every book of his that has lived. In another sense "Typee" undid Melville. Its success barred other roads. Surviving himself by nearly forty years, Melville tried restlessly in one direction and another to work out a sort of philosophic romance in which he relatively failed. The sojourn under King Mehevi's palm trees had made a skeptic of Melville, yet a skeptic with philosophical yearnings and profoundly religious intuitions. It had destroyed also all political and social theories and gone far to efface conventional maxims of morality.

These may seem only long words for the forecastle mood, which "bolts down all events, all creeds, and beliefs, and persuasions, all hard things visible and invisible; as an ostrich of potent digestion gobbles down bullets and gunflints." It is a mood, however, endurable only for one who thinks little, and Melville thought tremendously. To doubt everything, yet to retain certain saving intuitions became his avowed programme. This work of critical destruction and reintegration was that of Melville's times—the Victorian mood. But few of Melville's contemporaries had gone so far in disillusion, few had razed prejudice so thoroughly, few had lived so much. What might have been a triumphant process of reconstruction—for Melville had the intelligence and apparently the force—lapsed through invalidism and misfortune into occasional strenuous gropings not without their nobility and pathos. Herman Melville was gradually eaten up by his desire to understand the eternal mysteries, and his activities were not of a sort to clarify his quest. His fate superficially was that of the Ohio honey hunter, described in "Moby Dick," who "seeking honey in the crotch of a hollow tree, found such exceeding store of it, that leaning too far over, it sucked him in, so that he died embalmed. How many think ye, have likewise fallen into Plato's honey head, and sweetly perished there?"

The human interest of Melville's later and forgotten work is so great that I can not follow my predecessors and betters in criticism who have agreed to ignore it as unreadable. We may best approach Herman Melville's cavernous phase from the vantage point of the great transitional romance "Moby Dick."

II

In 1849, about two years before "Moby Dick," appeared that strangest of allegories, "Mardi, and a Voyage Thither." The two works are companion pieces: "Mardi" is a survey of the universe in the guise of an imaginary voyage of discovery, "Moby Dick" is a real voyage skilfully used to illustrate the cosmos; "Mardi" is a celestial adventure, "Moby Dick" an infernal. "Mardi" is highly general—the quest of a mysterious damsel, Zillah, a sort of Beatrice, a type of divine wisdom; "Moby Dick" is specific, the insanely vengeful pursuit of the dreaded white whale. The people of "Mardi" are all abstractions, those of "Moby Dick" among the most vivid known to fiction. "Mardi" was far the most ambitious effort of Melville's, and it failed. Personally I like to read in it; for its idealism tinged with a sane Rabelaisianism, for its wit and rare pictorial quality, for the strange songs of Yoomy, which, undetachable, are both quaintly effective in their context, and often foreshadow oddly our modern free verse. It is often plethoric and overwritten, it drops out of the Polynesian form in which it is conceived, and becomes too overt preaching and satire. It justifies the Bacchic philosopher Babbalanja's aphorism—"Genius is full of trash"; but it is also full of wisdom and fine thinking. It represents an intellectual effort that would supply a small library, and I suppose it is fated to remain unread. Perhaps its trouble is its inconclusiveness. Again Babbalanja is enlightening:

> Ah! my lord, think not that in aught I've said this night, I would assert any wisdom of my own. I but fight against the armed and crested lies of Mardi, that like a host, assail me. I am stuck full of darts; but tearing them from out of me, gasping, I discharge them whence they came.

The very seriousness of "Mardi" tells against it. One feels something, a breaking heart under the literary horseplay. Thus it can not hold its own either with such neatly fashioned ideal republics as Edward Bellamy's "Looking Backward," nor with the Horatian elegance of Samuel Butler's "Erewhon," nor of course with the grim impassivity of "Gulliver's Travels." The occasional delver in "Mardi," however, will pluck out of it all sorts of surprises from foreshadowings of the superman to an anticipation of Samuel Butler's vitalism.

"Moby Dick" has the tremendous advantage of its concreteness. Captain Ahab's mad quest of the white whale imposes itself as real, and progressively enlists and appalls the imagination. Out of the mere stray episodes and minor characters of "Moby Dick" a literary reputation might be made. The retired Nantucket captains, Bildad and Peleg, might have stepped out of Smollett. Father Mapple's sermon on the Book of Jonah is in itself a masterpiece, and I know few sea tales which can hold their own with the blood feud of Mate Radney and sailor Steelkilt. The style still has the freshness and delicate power of "Typee," but is subtler. Take the very modern quality of a passage which a Loti might envy:

It was while gliding through these latter waters that one serene and moonlight night, when all the waves rolled by like scrolls of silver; and by their soft, suffusing seethings, made what seemed a silvery silence, not a solitude; on such a silent night a silvery jet was seen far in advance of the white bubbles at the bow. Lit up by the moon, it looked celestial; seemed some plumed and glittering god uprising from the sea.

There is also a harsher note befitting the theme. The tang of it is in the passage with which this essay opened. The tragic and almost incredible motive of the quest of the demon whale gains credibility from the solid basis of fact, as mad captain Ahab himself is based, so to speak, on his ivory leg. The insane adventure itself grows real through the actuality of its participants: Was there ever such a trio as the savage harpooners? Their very names, Feddallah, Tashetego, Queequeg, are a guarantee of good faith. A reader instinctively hurrahs at the deeds of such mates as Starbuck and Stubbs while with them he cowers under the fateful eye of Captain Ahab. Throughout the book are shudders, sympathies, and laughs.

But "Moby Dick" is more than what it undisputedly is, the greatest whaling novel. It is an extraordinary work in morals and general comment. In the discursive tradition of Fielding and the anatomist of melancholy, Melville finds a suggestion or a symbol in each event and fearlessly pursues the line of association. As he and Queequeg plait a mat on the same warp, the differing woofs and resulting surfaces become a symbol for man's free will asserting itself against the background of fate. Such reflections are in a grave, slow-moving style in which Burton has counted for much and Carlyle for something. It is the interplay of fact and application that makes the unique character of the book. As for the Christian fathers the visible world was merely a similitude or foreshadowing of the eternal world, so for Melville the voyage of the Pequod betokens our moral life in the largest sense. An example may best show the qualities and defects of the method. "Ishmael" (Herman Melville) is at the wheel at night gazing at the witches' kitchen of "trying out" the blubber. The glare sends him into a momentary doze and a strange thing happens:

> Starting from a brief standing sleep, I was horribly conscious of something fatally wrong. The jaw-bone tiller smote my side, which leaned against it; in my ears was the low hum of sails just beginning to shake in the wind.

> *   *   *

> Look not too long in the face of the fire, O man! Never dream with thy hand on the tiller! Turn not thy back to the compass; accept the first hint of the hitching tiller, believe not the artificial fire when its redness makes all things look ghastly. Tomorrow, in the natural sun, the skies will be bright; those who glared like devils in the forking flames will show in far other, at

least gentler relief; the glorious, golden, glad sun, the only true lamp—all others but liars.

Upon the reader's slant towards this sort of parable will very much depend his estimate of "Moby Dick." Are we dealing with trimmings or essentials?—that is the critical question. Cut out the preachments, and you will have a great novel, some readers say. Yes, but not a great Melville novel. The preachments are of the essence. The effect of the book rests on the blend of fact, fancy, and profound reflection, upon a brilliant intermingling of sheer artistry and moralizing at large. It is Kipling before the letter crossed with Sir Thomas Browne, it comprises all the powers and tastes of Herman Melville, is his greatest and most necessary work. So while no one is obliged to like "Moby Dick"—there are those who would hold against Dante his moralizing and against Rabelais his broad humor—let such as do love this rich and towering fabrique adore it whole-heartedly—from stem to stern, athwart ships and from maintruck to keelson.

In a sense "Moby Dick" exhausted Melville's vein. At thirty-two he had put into a single volume all that he had been in action, all that he was to be in thought. The rest is aftermath. . . .

[A Much-Ignored Book]

Viola Meynell

Within limits most people could say what special form of writing they prefer. Even the most just literary judgment may be subject to preferences for one kind of greatness over another kind. If the great book which is the subject of this article has in some way just missed people's preferences, that and nothing else may account for the neglect of it. It is possible that many of those even who are alert for treasure have an unconscious preference for finding it elsewhere than in a story about a whale-hunt. This much-ignored book is *Moby Dick*, written in 1851 by Herman Melville, and it is the story of the hunting of whales in general and of a white whale in particular.

Though it tells with scientific accuracy of every part of the whale and every detail of its capture, it is a work of wonderful and wild imagination. His whale is real, like Blake's tiger, but in thinking of it he occasionally loses hold of reality as we know it—as Blake's imagination also flies loose from his sinewy tiger to infinity. Herman Melville has that rarest quality, rare even in genius, of wildness, imagination escaping out of bounds. But the whale is the cause—this natural object, and its order, and the truth that we know of it, and its laws, are the occasion of his wildness. There may be people who do not love such an occasion for imagination. There are all those, one must always remember, who like to find imagination, for instance, in fairies, fantasies, trees with living limbs, imps, gnomes, etc. If they can enter by that easy open door, how should they expect that a whale, its measurements, its blubber, its oil, its lashless eyes, its riddled brow, and harpoons and ropes and buckets are the way to imagination? Preferences will range people into two groups in this regard. One group requires that imagination shall begin in facts, and in its wildest flights shall still owe an acknowledgment to fact, and requires, too, to believe that Truth is at the other unseen end of that imagining. The other group distrusts reality or the natural object even for a start, and would not wait to measure a whale, but hastens after a fairy whom fancy can make as large or as small as it likes. Or, since terms of fact, such as colour, must be used in description, then mere profusion is supposed to lend fancy. The fairy's robe may be of many colours, there is no reason why one should be excluded. Is that profusion imagination?—or will imagination

Excerpted and reprinted from "Herman Melville," *Dublin Review* 166 (January–March 1920), 96–97.

not rather spring from some great restriction, such as the whiteness of this whale—whiteness "which strikes more of panic to the soul than that redness which affrights in blood?" Fairies have no starting-place in valuable reality, and, what is worse, no ultimate reality to arrive at. Fairies begin and end in themselves. The very freedom allowed to fancy in that world of fairy (or faerie as believers like it written) is somehow fatal to its interest; it has the deadly freedom of being utterly outside truth.

But it is of facts and figures that the imagination in *Moby Dick* is made.

"Moby Dick"

E. L. Grant Watson

An imaginative writer can never be more pertinent nor convincing than when writing his autobiography. If he will but tell the story of himself, it is the best he can give. We well know the charm of the simple narration of events, events which find their significance in their simplicity (as in the works of Jefferies or Hudson), lightening with a mild lucidness the occasions of everyday life. This is the imagination of nature in a tranquil mood, and the beauty that is there revealed is of a harmony between man's spirit and the spirit of all that is unknowable. But there are degrees of intensity for the creative passion, and there are those who beat with fierce hands upon the walls of the unknowable. There are men touched so deeply by the vivid consciousness of living that they need to create beyond-worlds for their imagination, wherein, by means of symbols, they indicate the history of their perceptions. Shakespeare created his enchanted island, peopling it with men and spirits, each but a part and symbol of his own experience. Ibsen, in his last play, *When We Dead Awaken*, has told in direct and simple speech the story of his soul. He tells of his failure as a great artist, his bitter repentance, and his resurrection. In this play the chief actors are but symbols, and the world in which they move is no "real" world. It is an imaginary creation of the artist; the air breathed is so thinly diffused that each word and idea uttered takes a mystical significance, so that we draw back appalled at the abysses over which human actions are suspended.

Melville also has his story to tell, and he also has his transcendental values; but his story is not told so simply as is Ibsen's. In *Moby Dick or the White Whale*, which is Melville's greatest and best-known work, there is a richness of material that might well puzzle the casual reader. He plunges, in the first pages, into schoolboy adventures with cannibal chiefs, to be followed quickly by rhetoric, by sermons, the magic of embarkation, the magic of voyages, of the sea and of ships. There is natural history, text-books on cetology, wayside philosophisings, realistic descriptions of whale hunts, pictures of the sea and of the sea's dread and beauty such as no other man has penned, and, winding through the whole, giving cohesion and intensity, is the story of the author's own fiercely vivid life-consciousness, which, like the

Reprinted from "Moby Dick," *London Mercury* 3 (December 1920), 180–86.

vindictive *Pequod*, journeys upon the most adventurous of all quests, drawn always onward by the beauty and terror of that symbol of madness, the white whale. This inner history is well hidden amongst high adventures. The lives of real men whom Melville has known and loved enfold it. It is tossed with the *Pequod* round all the seas of the ocean, yet once fairly sighted, the story of the soul's daring and of the soul's dread is never lost, but holds the reader in a grip of awful anticipation, till at the end he is left aghast at the courage of one who dares with unflinching perception follow into the heart of its uttermost ocean that quality which, in our cowardice, we call madness.

The separate elements of personality, their divisions and their affinities are well known to Melville; he analyses with a marvellous lucidness the stages of his own peculiar mentality. The *Pequod*, with her monomaniac captain and all her crew, is representative of his own genius, and in this particular sense that each character is deliberately symbolic of a complete and separate element. Yet all are equally involved in the case, their fates are not to be separated. The interplay and struggle between them are but portrayals of the vehement impulsion and repercussion of a richly-endowed spirit that draws inevitably, and yet of its own volition, towards the limit of human sanity. Moby Dick is the symbol of the nameless thing that they pursue; he is the sensuous symbol of nature's beauty and terror:

> A gentle joyousness, a mighty mildness of repose in swiftness invested the white whale. . . . No wonder there had been some among the hunters who, namelessly transported and allured by all this serenity, had ventured to assail it; but had fatally found that quietude but the vesture of tornadoes. Yet calm, enticing calm, oh, whale! thou glidest on, to all who for the first time eye thee, no matter how many in that same way thou may'st have bejuggled and destroyed before. And thus through the serene tranquillities of the tropical sea, among waves whose hand-clappings were suspended by exceeding rapture, Moby Dick moved on, still withholding from sight the full terrors of his submerged trunk, entirely hiding the wretched hideousness of his jaw.

In this story the white whale is the symbol or mask of that outer mystery, which, like a magnet, for ever attracts, and in the end overwhelms the imagination. Ahab, the monomaniac captain of the *Pequod*, that godlike, godless old man, is its counterpart. He is the incarnation of the active and courageous madness that lies brooding and fierce, ever ready to spring to command, within the man of genius. He is the atheistical captain of the tormented soul.

On his last voyage Ahab had encountered Moby Dick; he had had one of his legs bitten off at the hip. He had been pulled on board unconscious, and had lain for weeks raging with fever. In a straight-jacket he had swung to the rocking of the gales; but later he had seemed to recover and "bore that firm, collected front, and issued his calm orders once again." Melville describes the metamorphosis of his malady:

Human madness is ofttimes a cunning and most feline thing. When you think it is fled, it may but become transfigured into still subtler form. Ahab's full lunacy subsided not, but deepeningly contracted.. . . . But as in his narrow-flowing monomania not one jot of Ahab's broad madness had been left behind, so in that broad madness not one jot of his great natural intellect perished. That before living agent now became the living instrument. If such a furious trope may stand, this special lunacy stormed his general sanity, and carried it, and turned all its concentrated cannon upon its own mad mark; so that far from having lost strength, Ahab to that one end did now possess a thousand-fold more potency than he had sanely brought to bear upon any one reasonable object.

In his heart Ahab has a glimpse of his power: "All my means are sane, my motive and object mad." To the outward world he appears to be recovered. A new leg has been made for him by the ship's carpenter of the bone of a whale's jaw. He is much changed by his suffering and mutilation, but apparently sane, though he had grown morose and fierce. On this account the owners of the *Pequod* think him the better fitted to be the captain of a Nantucket whaler. They have no suspicion of his madness, and only when the ship is far out to sea does he make his appearance. He then calls all hands upon the quarter-deck and tells them that they are upon no ordinary cruise, but that his chief purpose is to hunt and kill Moby Dick, that "great gliding demon of the seas of life." By his magnetic enthusiasm he carries with him all but Starbuck, the chief mate. Starbuck, the brave, the chivalrous, the humane honest man, the symbol of unaided virtue and right-mindedness, tragically destined to be overborne by madness, he alone protests. He calls it blasphemy to pursue a dumb brute with such vindictive rage. Ahab takes him aside, concentrating all his imaginative *puissance* against Starbuck's outraged amazement.

All visible objects, man, are but pasteboard masks. But in each event, in the living act, the undoubted deed, there, some unknown but still reasoning thing puts forth the mouldings of its features from behind the unreasoning mask. If man will strike, strike through the mask. How can the prisoner reach outside except by thrusting through the wall? To me the white whale is that wall, shoved near to me. Sometimes I think there's naught beyond. But 'tis enough. He tasks me; he heaps me; I see in him outrageous strength, with an incurable malice sinewing it. That inscrutable thing is chiefly what I hate; and to be the white whale agent or to be the white whale principal I will wreck that hate upon him. . . .

Thus Ahab! In his madness he carries the crew with him. Stubb, the second mate, the laughing philosopher, merely laughs and bends to his will. The others are as if intoxicated by Ahab's passion, and so for the time Starbuck is silenced; but never is he vanquished; the struggle between sanity and madness continues to the end. A wild oath is forced upon the crew: "Death to Moby Dick! God hunt us all if we do not hunt Moby Dick to his death." In this first contest Ahab is wholly victorious. Later in his cabin he sits gazing out over the sea:

> What I've willed I've dared, and what I've willed I'll do. They think me mad. . . . Starbuck does; but I am demoniac, I am madness maddened! The wild madness that's only sane to comprehend itself! . . . Swerve me? The path to my fixed purpose is laid on iron rails, whereon my soul is grooved to run. Over unsounded gorges, through the rifled hearts of mountains, under torrents' beds, unerringly I rush. Naught's an obstacle, naught's an angle to the iron way!

Starbuck, leaning against the mast, also soliloquises.

> My soul is more than matched; she's overmanned; and by a madman. Insufferable sting, that sanity should ground arms on such a field. But he drilled deep down and blasted all my reason out of me. I think I see his impious end; but feel that I must help him to it. Will I, Nill I, the ineffable thing has tied me to him; tows me like a cable I have no knife to cut. Horrible old man! Who's over him? he cries; aye, he would be a democrat to all above; look how he lords it over all below! I plainly see my miserable office, to obey rebelling, and worse yet to hate with touch of pity! For in his eyes I read some lurid woe would shrivel me up, had I it.

So much for their first glimpse of their divergence. As the story continues they become bound by an indissoluble love; Starbuck perceives more clearly that "lurid woe," and his pity makes mild and tender his opposition. But as yet he knows little of Ahab's foresight and cunning; for when whales are first sighted, up out of the hold come five tiger-yellow Manilla men and their leader, the white-turbaned Fedallah. These men Ahab has smuggled on board as an extra boat's crew, so that he in person, contrary to general custom, may be enabled to follow in the hunt.

The first sight of Fedallah inspires the crew with a feeling of awe and fear. He takes his stand on the prow of Ahab's boat. One tooth evilly protrudes from his steel-like lips. A rumpled Chinese jacket of black cotton funereally invested him; but strangely crowning this ebonness was a glistening, white plaited turban, the living hair braided and coiled round and round upon his head. As the voyage continues, the superstitious sailors regard him as an evil spirit. He represents the fatal inspiration of Ahab's madness. There is a compact between the two. They are bound by invisible bonds, and it is Fedallah who strengthens Ahab with prophecies of his invulnerability, prophecies which encompass their mutual doom, and which yet seem to guard against disaster. Fedallah is but a symbol, a ghostly shadow, a spirit of madness, he and Ahab are as shadow and substance; but he is metallic like moonshine or a reflection; he has no human quality.

> At times, for longest hours, without a single hail, they stood far parted in the starlight; Ahab in his scuttle, the Parsee by the mainmast; but still fixedly gazing upon one another; as if in the Parsee Ahab saw his overthrown shadow, in Ahab, the Parsee his abandoned substance. And yet somehow did Ahab, in his proper self, as daily, hourly, and every instant, commandingly revealed to his subordinates, Ahab seemed an independent lord; the Parsee but his slave. Still again both seemed yoked together, and an unseen tyrant driving them; the lean shade siding the solid rib. For be this Parsee what he may, all rib and keel was solid Ahab.

Yet on the one occasion, when softened by Starbuck's entreaty to about helm and abandon the chase, Ahab relents for a moment from his iron purpose. Fedallah is near him, his eyes *reflected* in the calm water gazing up as an evil and scarce earthly reminder of that purpose.

As the voyage continues and other whales are encountered and killed, Ahab's hatred against Moby Dick waxes fiercer. As the *Pequod* nears that part of the Pacific which is the white whale's most accustomed haunt, adverse gales would blow her westward. A hurricane strips the ship of her canvas, but Ahab is nothing daunted. He now discards all outward semblance of sanity; he destroys his sextant, and steering without compass or log, holds his course in the teeth of adverse winds towards the sunrise. Auguries and warnings are not lacking; all, save Ahab, believe that they are doomed, but have not the power to break the iron of his will. Upon Starbuck the ordeal falls most heavily. He feels that he alone might be able to save the ship, but how control the uncontrollable? Have Ahab overpowered and bound? The thought of Ahab in bonds sears his imagination. The fury of those howls would madden the whole ship's company. He thinks of killing Ahab, takes down a musket and, invoking God's aid, levels it; but it is not within Starbuck's compass to kill his captain. However good his cause, he cannot do it.

Ship after ship passes the *Pequod;* they are homeward bound. Some are well laden with oil and full of merriment, others carry awful tidings of the white whale, of his terrible power and malignant strength. Each and all of these ships, whether stricken or successful, offer a marked contrast to the *Pequod*. Whatever fortune has befallen them, they at least are sane. The *Pequod* alone fights her way eastward against contrary winds towards that amazing calm, that entrancing mildness in which she is to encounter Moby Dick.

Each story that the passing captains tell adds fuel to Ahab's madness. He inspires his crew with his spirit, making his cause their own. They no longer appear as men, but as instruments of his will. The elements of personality are now flowing together; the increasing power of madness is too strong to allow them to remain separate.

Ahab has nailed a golden doubloon to the mainmast, a reward to the man who first sights Moby Dick. This coin possesses a significant and mystical quality. Each man in turn is attracted to stand musing before it, and read therein the secrets of his life. Ahab stands before it regarding the three Andes' summits engraved thereon, upon one a flame; a tower on another; on the third a crowing cock.

> There's something ever egotistical in mountain tops and towers, and all other grand and lofty things; look here, three peaks as proud as Lucifer. The firm tower, that is Ahab; the volcano, that is Ahab; the courageous, the undaunted, and the victorious fowl, that, too, is Ahab; all are Ahab; and this round globe is but the image of the rounder globe, which, like a magician's glass, to each and every man in turn but mirrors back his own mysterious self. Great pains, small gains, for those who ask the world to solve them; it cannot solve itself. . . . From storm to storm, so be it, then. Born in throes, 'tis fit that man should live in pains and die in pangs! So be it then! Here's stout stuff to work on. So be it then.

Starbuck follows him, and reads in the coin an interpretation of his own ordeal.

> A dark valley between three mighty, heaven-abiding peaks, that almost seems the Trinity, in some faint, earthly symbol. So in this vale of death God girds us round; and over all our gloom, the sun of righteousness still shines a beacon and a hope. If we bend down our eyes, the dark vale shows her mouldy soul; but if we lift them, the bright sun meets our glance half way to cheer. Yet, oh, the great sun is no fixture; and if, at midnight, we would fain snatch some sweet solace from him, we gaze for him in vain! This coin speaks wisely, mildly, truly, but still sadly to me. I'll quit it, lest Truth shake me falsely.

In this scene and throughout the story, Ahab and Starbuck present the chief elements of the drama; but there are others symbolised no less completely. There is Stubb, the second mate, whose philosophy is founded on a broad basis of good-humoured carelessness, who laughs at the most terrible auguries, and is undaunted not only by all the terrors of the sea, but by the subtler fears of introspection. There is Flask, the third mate, the cockney mediocrity, with "courage as fierce as fire and as mechanical," who will stoop to wanton cruelty, and will joke at the piteous terror and dumb agony of the dying whale. Yet these, and all the crew, like Starbuck, though in personality less separate and conscious than he, are drawn on by Ahab to their inevitable doom. Pip, the ship's boy, the little curly-headed negro, who went to sea by mistake, and who, terrified by the strange fierceness of life, became more and more of a coward, until frightened beyond all endurance, he lost his wits; he also is bound to furious Ahab by invisible ties of affinity. His gentle idiocy is the counterpart of the old man's fierceness, and Ahab, as his madness waxes, reads in Pip's strangely illuminated utterances oracular sayings. He takes the boy to live with him in his cabin. The two antithetical poles of human perception, the one intensified by fear, the other by courage: the one gentle and wayward, the other fierce and concentrated, live side by side, while a strange love enfolds them. On deck Fedallah watches like the hungry embodiment of a madman's purpose. For the most part he is silent, but when he speaks it is only to whisper intimations and prophecies of the end. He is feared and hated by the crew, who, in so far as they are separate from Ahab, remain sane, and whose only madness is that they are bound by his iron purpose.

At last Moby Dick is sighted. Ahab himself is the first to descry the white hump, for, like that dark impulse that overpowers the lemmings and compels them to cast themselves into a destroying sea, so has Ahab's insanity responded to the more transcendental, more far-reaching potency of Moby Dick. The white whale is the magnet that has drawn the *Pequod* round all the seas of the world. He embodies the stark forces of Nature; he is the symbol of imaginative life, of life which surpasses itself and continues beyond into realms where few men dare follow; and his strange whiteness is both the sign and veil of his mystery.

To this quality of whiteness Melville devotes a long chapter. It has for him an *unearthly* significance, combining the grandeur of snow-capped mountains, the treachery of rock-broken waters and the dread of phantoms. The absence of all colour which is the concrete of all colours leads beyond the bounds of personality and reason. He struggles to explain this mystical, well-nigh ineffable quality. "But," he cries, "how can I hope to explain myself here? And yet in some dim random way explain myself I must, else all these chapters might be naught." And explain himself he does, in so far that as we read we feel that it is the whiteness of Moby Dick that bestows upon him so surpassing a beauty, so malevolent a cunning. The white whale's whiteness is the whiteness of insanity; "the concrete of all colours, yet the absence of all colour." Only Godlike, godless Ahab would have courage to pursue and meet in deadly strife so terrible a monster. Ahab's is the history of a man who sees the world as the creation of a suffering and malignant Deity, a Deity whose highest thought is inferior to his own high courage. This demon who is his god and his apotheosis he will meet with contempt, exultation, and the rapture of conflict.

In the last chapters this passionate meeting is described. Three days of chase and conflict lead to the inevitable end; but never is Ahab's courage broken. Though boats are smashed beneath him, though the prophecies of Fedallah are one by one fulfilled with such contrary cunning as only a malign fate could contrive, though sharks nibble at the oars, and though his bone leg is severed a second time he follows with unquenchable fury. He is the needle drawn by the magnet. His madness is of such quality that the white whale and all that is there symbolised needs *must* render its consummation or its extinction.

Melville finishes his book upon a note of such seeming extravagance that to any but a symbolical interpretation it would appear bombastic. If, however, the undercurrents of his thought are perceived, the concluding incidents are of the inevitable structure of the tragedy. And this use of symbols does not only concern the main characters, but can be traced into the smallest details.

As a writer upon the sea, Melville's power of description is unsurpassed. It would be easy to multiply the quotation of passages of nobility and beauty. Again and again the reader pauses in a kind of spell-bound intoxication before the grandeur of his vision. Where, indeed, could be found an equal to his description of the sea the morning after the storm? And yet this extreme richness of the work tends towards its misinterpretation. That its high quality as a piece of psychological synthesis has been so much neglected is due to this very richness of material. A casual reader might often skip the more transcendental passages, and classify it as a mere book of adventure. It is indeed a book of adventure, but upon the highest plane of spiritual daring. A profound wisdom is here joined with a suffering and a courage which gropes beyond the limits of sanity. "There is a wisdom that is woe, and there is a woe that is madness." Both the wisdom and the woe are here mingled in this history of a soul's adventure.

[A Deposition From a New Reader]

"A Wayfarer" [John Middleton Murry]

It is clear that the wind of the spirit, when it once begins to blow through the English literary mind, possesses a surprising power of penetration. A few weeks ago it was pleased to aim a simultaneous blast in the direction of a book known to some generations of men as "Moby Dick." A member of the staff of THE NATION was thereupon moved in the ancient Hebrew fashion to buy and to read it. He then expressed himself on the subject, incoherently indeed, but with signs of emotion as intense and as pleasingly uncouth as Man Friday betrayed at the sight of his long-lost father. While struggling with his article, and wondering what the deuce it could mean, I received a letter from a famous literary man, marked on the outside "Urgent," and on the inner scroll of the MS. itself "A Rhapsody." It was about "Moby Dick." Having observed a third article on the same subject, of an equally febrile kind, I began to read "Moby Dick" myself. Having done so I hereby declare, being of sane intellect, that since letters began there never was such a book, and that the mind of man is not constructed so as to produce such another; that I put its author with Rabelais, Swift, Shakespeare, and other minor and disputable worthies; and that I advise any adventurer of the soul to go at once into the morose and prolonged retreat necessary for its deglutition. And having said this, I decline to say another word on the subject now and for evermore.

Reprinted from the *Nation* [London] 28 (22 January 1921), 572.

The Great White Whale: A Rhapsody

Augustine Birrell

The Whale; or, Moby Dick. By Herman Melville. 3 vols. (Richard Bentley, 1851.)

Moby Dick; or, The Whale. By Herman Melville. With an Introduction by Viola Meynell. "The World's Classics." (Oxford University Press. 2s. 6d. net.)

> Where the sea beasts ranged all round
> Feed in the ooze of their pasture ground,
> Where the sea-snakes coil and twine,
> Dry their mail and bask in the brine;
> Where Great Whales come sailing by,
> Sail and sail with unshut eye
> Round the world for ever and aye.
> —Matthew Arnold

And amongst these great whales, first, foremost and immortal, is Moby Dick, the Great White Whale.

It is seventy years, just the measure of my own lifetime, since the white head and hump of Moby Dick suddenly loomed out of the blue water not very far to leeward. "There she blows, there she blows, a hump like a snow-hill. It is Moby Dick."

Earlier in the same year "The Whale" had been published in New York, and at once, as indeed might have been expected, aroused the enthusiasm of Nathaniel Hawthorne, but, though "Moby Dick" has been reprinted in England three or four times since 1851, none of these reprints has attracted sufficient attention.

Books have their fates no less than their authors, and it must not for one moment be supposed that this masterpiece of eloquence, character and adventure, despite a small circulation, hard to explain even in the year of "Uncle Tom's Cabin," fell flat. It did nothing of the kind, for from the very first it numbered good intellects among the "grown ups," and excited the same enchanted admiration among a limited number of fortunate children as then did and do now the books of that kindred spirit, though of the Earth and not the Sea, George Borrow.

Reprinted from the *Athenæum* [London], no. 4735 (28 January 1921), 99–100.

Among those lucky youngsters, the godchildren of Apollo, were included some subsequently celebrated writers who, having been allowed to feed their infant genius on the quintessential oils and the delectable blubber of this incomparable Beast, have risen into fame and attained a circulation quite beyond the dreams of the New Yorker who, born in 1819, of (so Miss Meynell tells us) mixed Dutch and English stock, went to sea as a cabin-boy on a vessel trading to Liverpool, and wrote "Moby Dick" in his thirty-second year. The sea remained Melville's element through a life which ended in 1891. The ocean he loved best was the Pacific, which "rolls the midmost waters of the world."

But though there is no need to commiserate Herman Melville on his limited "sales," it was none the less a hideous deprivation to a man of my age never to have encountered in the days of his youth, amid his various book-adventures, the Great White Whale, the ship "Pequod," the mono-maniacal and crippled Captain Ahab for ever pursuing Moby Dick round the world, the tattooed lovable cannibal Queequeq with his pocket idol, the mysterious stranger Fedallah, the unaccountable Elijah, Starbuck, Stubbs and Flask, and the rest of the crew of the doomed whaler.

How this came about I cannot guess, for the house was otherwise well-stored with masterpieces, but so it was; nor was it until I was some years older than Melville when he wrote "Moby Dick" that I first heard his name. I owned my introduction to "Omoo," "Typee" and "The Whale" to that exquisite judge of a good book, Sir Alfred Lyall, who was shocked at my ignorance, and most emphatically urged me to read "Omoo" and "Typee"; but, as ill luck would have it, he did not specially dwell upon "The Whale." To hear was, in those days, to obey, and a second-hand bookseller almost at once supplied me with these three books. Even then I was not out of the Wood of Ignorance, for though I was greatly taken with "Omoo" and "Typee" I was not so bewitched by them as to begin at once upon the three volumes of "The Whale"—which I allowed to remain for a whole decade unread. One happy day I took them down, and then and then only did Moby Dick swim into my ken. Oh, woeful waste! Is there, I wonder (looking all round me), another such book lying neglected in this very room? And yet now, when full of my wrongs, I have discovered that all this time I had intimate friends, and even relatives, not much addicted to holding their peace, who knew all about Ahab and Bildad and Peleg and Moby Dick, and yet never gave me a hint of their existence. What on earth were they talking about all these years! I cannot remember. Now that "Moby Dick" is in the "World's Classics," and can be had for half-a-crown of all booksellers, the excuses of Ignorance or Concealment can no longer be urged on anyone's behalf in the High Court of Taste.

The two striking features of this book, after allowing for the fact that it is a work of genius and therefore *sui generis*, are, as it appears to me, its most amazing eloquence, and its mingling of an ever-present romanticism of style with an almost savage reality of narrative.

Eloquence is no common quality in English books, for to be really eloquent in cold print requires great courage, almost impudence, mixed with an extreme sensitiveness of nature; and sensitive men are apt to be timid with their pens and to hesitate long before beginning a sentence with the particle O! "I think it may be observed," says Dr. Johnson, in his "Life of Pope," "that the particle O at the beginning of a sentence always offends." Like most of the sayings that issued from the Johnsonian Mint, this dread *dictum* has a ring of truth about it, but it will not bear close examination. In the June number of the *Gentleman's Magazine* for 1787 a learned critic, signing himself J. A., had no difficulty in supplying the cultivated readers of that admirable periodical with a number of famous passages both of prose and poetry, culled from Hebrew, Latin and English authors of the greatest celebrity, all beginning with this bold particle. (See Walker's "Selection from the *Gentleman's Magazine*," vol. ii. p. 341.)

I own to thinking but little of any author, be he poet or proseman, who dares not occasionally run the risk (and it is a risk) of beginning a sentence with an O! George Borrow never hesitated, and though Herman Melville is not so prodigal, he provides his readers with some splendid examples of this audacity; nor can I think that any reader of "The Whale" will deny the claim of its author to be one of the most eloquent of our English writers. To give curtailed examples, torn from the context of a book, the absorbing interest of which is all hung upon one peg—the pursuit of Moby Dick by the monomaniacal captain whose leg had been devoured by the sea-monster—would be a blunder, so I pass on to the second feature.

That most distinguished writer known to us all as R[obert] L[ouis] S[tevenson], who, in his bundle of good humours, had one especially delightful shaft which he often employed to make fun of himself, invented a new word whereby to describe his method of "dressing up" a romance. He called it *tushery*. Now there is no "tushery" in "The Whale." It is romantic from end to end, and eloquent throughout, but it is also grim and real. As an acute feminine critic once said to me about Melville's style in "The Whale," "it bruises you all over." You not only share the feelings, but all the hardships of the crew of the "Pequod," and your bones ache accordingly.

To give quotations, as I have already said, would be ridiculous, but to those who fight shy of a book they know nothing about, "The Town-Ho's story" (as told at the Golden Inn, Lima), or the chapter entitled "The Whiteness of the Whale," may safely be recommended to timid beginners.

It will be curious to observe whether a generation of readers brought up on another kind of fare will repair the injustice done by their grandparents in 1851.

Here and there a page or even a chapter of "The Whale" may be skipped with comparative impunity, but nobody but a sea-gudgeon can ever be sent to sleep between its pages. "And whereas all the other things, whether beast or vessel, that enter into the dreadful gulf of the whale's mouth, are immediately lost and swallowed up, the sea-gudgeon retires into it in great security *and there sleeps*" (Montaigne in his "Apology for Raimond de Sebonne").

> We're not as "gudgeons" are;
> Smith, take a fresh cigar!
> Jones, the tobacco-jar!
>   Here's to thee, "Melville"!

The King of Them All [The Melville Revival in England and the United States]

CHRISTOPHER MORLEY AND H. M. TOMLINSON

One we have mentioned several times before, who knows what he is talking about, writes to us from London. We hope he won't mind our quoting a portion of his letter, which was not intended for print:

> I've been reading again a writer I've never heard an American mention. Not once. I cannot recall that I've ever seen him referred to in a book on American letters. (You'll be surprised, perhaps alarmed, to hear that Concord, Mass., is a place of such august memories to me that perhaps it is best I should never visit it.) But this writer—an American all right—puts it across *all* the sea writers I know. For that sort of work your side of the water not only holds the belt, but is going to keep the championship. The title *cannot* be contested. You have held the championship since 1851. Conrad, Masefield, Marryat— not on your life! They're not in it. I regret to have to say it, but there it is. This very sea book (which I have not named to you) was, in my presence this week, admitted by Arnold Bennett, Augustine Birrell, Massingham, John Middleton Murry, and Swinnerton, to be the—well, to be IT. There ain't nothing like it. There never will be again. What book is that? My stars, I'd belt some of you Americans over your really tremendous classic when you bring forward the English sea writers.
>
> The way America has taken to Conrad, considers Masefield a classic, and has even bought up an edition of *Old Junk*, and another of *The Sea and the Jungle*, makes writers on this side very grateful. But MOBY DICK . . . ah, the secret is out! That's the Immense book of the sea.
>
> H. M. Tomlinson

But it does seem a little odd to us that Mr. Tomlinson has never seen *Moby Dick* mentioned in American journalism. Melville, like Dana, has so long been accepted as a classic over here that he is more or less taken as a matter of course (as a matter of college course too often, we fear) and too little mentioned. Yet we have never seen a year go by without a little Melville racket cropping up somewhere. In 1919, the year of his centennial, there was a big Melville hullabaloo over here. *Moby Dick* has lately been reissued in

Reprinted from Christopher Morley's "Bowling Green" column in the *New York Evening Post* (5 February 1921).

England (by the Oxford University Press, in its admirable *World's Classic* [sic] series) which has brought it to the eye of English reviewers. (It went into the blessed company of *Everyman's Library* in 1907.) We must confess, for our own part, that we never read it until 1919, when the Melville centennial came along. But all that Mr. Tomlinson says is true. No man of sense needs to read sixty pages of *Moby Dick* to know it is one of the world's great books. Its fertile mysticism, its extraordinary humor and melancholy ("All noble things are touched with that"), betray an author "with a globular brain and a ponderous heart."

The only reason we can give for Mr. Tomlinson's not having seen Melville praised in American print—and we would like to give it as politely and deferentially as possible—is, quite simply, that, like most English journalists, he probably does not read the American prints nearly as thoroughly as we do the British. Now, let us be honest. When we get back to the office we will send him an accurate list of the British journals which are subscribed to by the *Evening Post*. Will he, in turn, tell us how many American papers and magazines are taken in the office (his own) of the London *Nation?* We have always been amazed at the complete agnosticism of many British editors as to what is going on over here in a literary way. The favorite preoccupation of most intelligent American editors is more mutualism among the English-speaking peoples. In reply to which we are greeted by that recent novennial quaintness from Mr. Punch. Mr. Tomlinson, for whom we have such affectionate regard, will not misunderstand our gentle plea. We speak for the good of the house.

[Not Everybody's Book]

Frank Swinnerton

Another great discovery of the London critics is Herman Melville, of whose works there is to be a collected edition. Years ago I read "Typee", "Omoo", and "Moby Dick", and then came to the conclusion that the later books of Melville were unreadable. "Omoo" and "Typee" have long been popular works. "Moby Dick" has for some time been included in the excellent "Everyman's Library". But only lately have the quidnuncs discovered the latter book, of which a new edition has just appeared in "The World's Classics" with an introduction by Viola Meynell. This edition has called forth just such another chorus of praise from the critics as has the Keats centenary. "Moby Dick" has been formally "found" and placed as one of the masterpieces of all time. It can never again be wholly forgotten; but I wonder how long it will be before it is half forgotten. Not long, I fear. For one thing, it is not everybody's book. It is too fervid, as the author's later works are superabundantly too fervid. It is magnificent, full of color, a glorious example of what can be done with words urged to their task by a willing spirit. I do not question the virtue of Melville. But I find it hard to believe that his recent discoverers have done more than scratch the soil above the treasure of "Moby Dick"; and when once another old book has been rediscovered their enthusiasm will flow easily into the new channels with hardly a trace of memory to savor the fresh allegiance. Let us hope I am wrong. I have noticed, however, other discoveries and their precarious hold upon the attention of booklovers. The complete edition will doubtless do much to establish Melville as a permanent figure. Will not somebody discover the best of Marryat's work? It would be a kindly task, and one most grateful to those who are forever losing patience with what is current and representative of our own time. The time is with us, and it is easier to retrieve a classic than to make a new one, particularly if the author be alive.

Excerpted and reprinted from "The Londoner," *Bookman* [New York] 53 (May 1921), 239.

[Melville's Insecure Artistic Control]

Van Wyck Brooks

For some time now vague rumours have been going about of the presence of a great lost author in the cloudy depths—or the beclouded shallows, if you will—of our American literary history. The name of Herman Melville, an obscure clerk in the New York custom-house, dead these thirty years, the centenary of whose birth passed, two summers ago, unnoticed, is to-day in every one's mouth. Melville is emerging, portentous as his own White Whale: next month is to witness the publication of the first book that has been written about his life. "Though I wrote the Gospels in this century," he himself remarked to his friend Hawthorne, "I should die in the gutter." Melville did not die; for forty years after his great work was done he lived, unseen, forgotten, in the city where he was born. He did not even die in the historical manuals: the rising generation was assured, on the contrary, that his talent was quite as great as that of a dozen seventh-rate poets and romancers who had been his contemporaries. That his talent was a sovereign talent, or had at least its sovereign moments (let us insist only on the moments), his fellow-countrymen had not observed: it was only in England that he had been justly appreciated. For how many years I do not know, but certainly for many, it has been a common experience for American travellers in England to be asked why it is that no one has written a biography of Herman Melville. Well, it was only a question of time: sooner or later the darkness that surrounds this extraordinary man was certain to yield before our indefatigable national appetite for investigation and research. Next year Melville will have been forgotten again. The "hatred of literature," as Flaubert called it, which prevents our literary authorities from recognizing a genius prevents them also from retaining the memory of one. But for the next six months there is to be a Melville boom. Ishmael is to emerge at last: he is to have his little hour. And there will be a few hundred or a few dozen readers, moreover, who, discovering him for the first time in this limelight, will seize upon his gift as a permanent possession.

A complete edition of Melville's works is said to be in preparation, to follow the appearance of Professor Weaver's biography. The publishers of "Everyman's Library," meanwhile, have just issued reprints of their editions

Reprinted from "A Reviewer's Notebook," *Freeman* [New York] 4 (26 October 1921), 166–67.

of "Omoo," "Typee" and "Moby Dick." The first two of these books have already had their hour of late, thanks to the vogue of the South Seas. It is in "Moby Dick," however, that Melville rises to his real height and reveals himself not as a chronicler but as a creator. All these books were written before he was thirty-two. Thereafter the transcendental mystic got the best of the "man of this world": in "Moby Dick" itself there are strange lapses into the inexpressible that show us how insecure the artistic element was in its control over the various parts of Melville's mind. Melville seems to have been constitutionally unable to keep his eye on his subject, he was devoid of the sentiment of form: an artist of miraculous power in the minting of a phrase, a paragraph, a sudden, sharp, momentary episode, he wanders, when it comes to a large composition, like a garrulous old man who can not recall, at the conclusion of a discourse, the idea with which he began. This weakness was the ultimate undoing of him as a writer. It is sufficiently pronounced in his one masterpiece.

To those, indeed, for whom literature is a question of the theme, of the intention, no book could be more exasperating than "Moby Dick." The great characters, that of the narrator, that of the cannibal Queequeg, vanish in the midst of it as if one had not been led to suppose that they, with Captain Ahab, were the chief strands in the rope of the tale. Captain Ahab himself, who emerges at the end so superbly, disappears for hundreds of pages in the middle. The author forgets his story, he loses himself in the details of cetology, he tells us about ambergris and about the erroneous and the "less erroneous" pictures of whales by Hogarth, by Guido, by Dürer; he has a chapter on the tails of whales, another on the spouting of whales, another on "Jonah Historically Regarded"; he speculates, he mythologizes, he indulges, like some incorrigible old Burton, every quaint conceit, every whim of the bookworm in the dressing-gown. Does one regret it? I am speaking of the opportunity he appears to miss by such a procedure. If Coleridge had permitted the ancient mariner to tell his story in his own language, we should have no doubt a thousand pages of entrancing talk. Something was gained, however, by Coleridge's taking the words out of his mariner's mouth and shaping them with the last severity. Melville has an ancient mariner, too, that strange Elijah who plucks Ishmael's sleeve on the wharf at Nantucket and warns him against putting to sea in the "Pequod." What a place "Moby Dick" would have had among the great stories of the world if its author, having seized upon that thread, had held it firmly in his hand and followed it, with a single eye!

If Melville had been capable of this, moreover, he might have given us many another great book. As well ask a George Borrow to write like a Prosper Mérimée! Melville is an American Borrow, a Borrow of the sea: to say that is to surrender all one's regrets and simply yield to the delight of the anomalous. "He lived in the world," our author says of Captain Ahab, "as the last of the grizzly bears lived in settled Missouri." Melville was himself a sort of unique anachronism. One can easily discern here and there in his writings the traces of his age. There is the touch of mystical democratism which he shares with Whitman; there is the occasional note of "Sartor Resartus" in his ecstatic soliloquizings. For the style, for the method of "Moby Dick," one has to go back, on the other hand, to the seventeenth century. "Out of the trunk the branches grow; out of them the twigs. So, in productive subjects, grow the chapters." True enough, if the subject happens to be the Anatomy of Melancholy or the Religio Medici. When Melville begins to discuss the theme of standing mastheads do not expect him to stop until he has told you that the earliest successful standers-of-mastheads were the Egyptians, inasmuch as the great stone mast of the builders of Babel went down with the first gale, that Simeon Stylites was dauntless in this pursuit and that something is to be claimed even for Napoleon, who has held his place for some years on the top of a column; do not, when the chapter happens to be concerned with the "honour and glory of whaling," look for the last word till our author has explained how Perseus was the first whaleman and how Hercules and St. George have the right to be enrolled in this guild, not to mention Jonah and Vishnu. If Melville's learned loquacity takes one back three hundred years, so does his use of language. He can carry an apostrophe to the length of a page, and his words have the strong natural flavour of Shakespeare's prose, or of Southdown mutton. No seasoning there! It would be difficult to find in any other American book pages to compare with his in this power of retaining the primitive juices of the English tongue. And I am not speaking of the temperament of the man, which is that of an Elizabethan voyager, "boldly dipping," to quote a phrase of his own, "into the Potluck of both worlds."

To return, however, to "Moby Dick." If Melville constantly loses the thread of his tale, he more than makes up for this by the intensity with which he returns to it. He has a ravenous eye, he clings to the visible fact as a pouncing hawk clings to its prey. What has ever been more fiercely seen than such episodes, for example, as that of the great squid, or Captain Ahab's watch, or the appalling chase of the White Whale? Melville somewhere expresses the fear that his book will be taken for a "hideous and intolerable allegory." An allegory it is, and he is in general at no pains to conceal the fact: this white-headed whale with his wrinkled brow, his crooked jaw and his high, snowy hump, personifies, our author frankly tells us, "the heartless voids and immensities of the universe," and again "all that most maddens and torments, all that stirs up the lees of things, all truth with malice in it, all that cracks the sinews and cakes the brain, all the subtle demonisms of life and thought." He is fate, this Moby Dick, and the terrible old Captain Ahab is the tragic will of man which defies it and tracks it down, only to be overwhelmed and to perish by it. But no allegory could less confuse the reader's imagination, seized as it can not fail to be by the personal tragedy of the terrible old man himself, a truly Shakespearean figure. I have spoken of the opportunity which Melville appears to miss by wandering from his main theme. The marvel of the book is that he leaves one, after all, so much at the mercy of the single impression he has done his best to destroy.

An American Borrow, a Borrow of the sea: let us return to this. Let us remark in conclusion, however, that Melville was indeed the "word-master" that Borrow professed to be and was not. Who excels him in the gift of the phrase? Recall, for example, how Queequeg darts from the side of the ship "with a long living arc of a leap." In the ability to flash a sudden picture upon the retina? Who can forget that moment in the "'Town-Ho's' Story" when the White Whale emerges from the sea and the dogged crew eye askance "the appalling beauty of the vast milky mass, that lit up by a horizontal spangling sun, shifted and glistened like a living opal in the blue morning sea"? Who can forget the last appearance of the whale, emerging on the third day of the chase to give battle to the doomed "Pequod" and all its men?

> Suddenly the waters around then slowly swelled in broad circles; then quickly upheaved, as if sideways sliding from a submerged berg of ice, swiftly rising to the surface. A long rumbling sound was heard, a subterranean hum; and then all held their breaths, as, bedraggled with trailing ropes, and harpoons, and lances, a vast form shot lengthwise, but obliquely, from the sea. Shrouded in a thin drooping veil of mist, it hovered for a moment in the rainbowed air; and then fell swamping back into the deep. Crushed thirty feet upwards, the waters flashed for an instant like heaps of fountains, then brokenly sank in a shower of flakes, leaving the circling surface creamed like new milk around the marble trunk of the whale.

To these blinding moments some will prefer such scenes as the old black cook's sermon to the sharks or Queequeg the cannibal's prostration before his idol in the chamber of the New Bedford inn. But Melville is himself, like the White Whale, emerging again. He does not need to be pointed out.

A Clue to "Moby Dick"

H. M. Tomlinson

Many years ago I was discussing the literature of the sea with a Fleet Street colleague, a clever and well-read man against whose volatile enthusiasms experience had taught me to guard myself well. He began to talk of "Moby Dick." Talk! He soon became incoherent. He swept aside all other books of the sea with a free, contemptuous gesture. There was only one book of the sea, and there never would be another worth mentioning. I fear that a native caution has shut me from many good things in life, so I smiled at my friend; yet, in the way of a cautious man, I smiled at him with sound reason. I had not read the White Whale; I had only heard rumors of it. But I knew "Typee" and "Omoo," and I knew my colleague even better. I may point out that a brief experience on the Somme battlefield unbalanced his mind, and he died insane. Now "Typee" and its mate are brisk and attractive narratives of travel and adventure, exuberantly descriptive, lively with their honey-colored girls and palm groves, jolly with the talk of seamen in fo'castles of ships sailing waters few of us know, though we all wish we did, and full of the observation of an original mind in a tropic world that is no more. But they are not great literature. I knew perfectly well that the author of "Typee" was not the man to rise to that stellar altitude which moved my colleague to rapture and wonder. That was not Melville's plane, and having read the American writer's first two books, I thought a busy man, amid a wilderness of unread works, need not bother himself about this White Whale, for hardly a doubt it was just a whale.

I was wrong. My friend who was unbalanced by the war was right. I do not know whether Americans are aware of the position of their Melville as a writer, but I find it difficult to write of his great book within measure, for I have no doubt "Moby Dick" goes into that small company of big, extravagant, generative books which have made other writers fertile in all ages—I mean the books we cannot classify, but which must be read by every man who writes—"Gargantua and Pantagruel," "Don Quixote," "Gulliver's Travels," "Tristram Shandy," and the "Pickwick Papers." That is where "Moby Dick" is, and it is therefore as important a creative effort as America has made in her history. I will sing "The Star-Spangled Banner," if that is the

Reprinted from the *Literary Review* [New York] 2 (5 November 1921), 141–42.

right hymn, with fervor and the deepest sense of debt and gratitude, at any patriotic thanksgiving service for "Moby Dick." I would assist any future body of Pilgrim Fathers to any place on earth if on their venture depended the vitality of the seed of such a book as that. The inchoate jungle of human society flowers, and in a sense is justified, in its great books, carrying in them in microcosm its fortunate future, or, if there is no future for it in the future, then its sad but heroic story.

Melville's extraordinary yarn about the White Whale came my way only recently. I had always recognized that it was a book I ought to look at, and when by chance a new edition coincided with some leisure I began to experiment upon it. I must confess that my mind to-day is not what it was in 1914. It is, as a polite alienist might say, possessed. I think all day of but one thing, and at night I dream about it. The Somme did not make me insane like my colleague, but I am not in the least surprised by his fate. I set out, with small hope, with Ahab after Moby Dick. I was at once caught in an awful adventure in which men, ships, seas, harpoons, and Leviathan are but dread symbols, and in a sense I have never returned from that trip. I became missing as soon as the Pequod was out of sight of Nantucket. While the book was unfinished there was no home, there were no duties, and time and space were figments. It was an immense experience.

I have been trying to puzzle it out. In the search for a clue to the mystery of "Moby Dick" I have been reading Melville's "White Jacket," "Redburn," "The Confidence Man," "Piazza Tales," "Pierre," "Battle Pieces," and "Mardi." But they give me no clue to the White Whale. The secret is not there, and I doubt whether it can be found in any book of Melville's that I have not read. "Moby Dick" is still elusive as a dream, shadowy but vast, an inimical but compelling portent; it is as though after reading it we felt sure that Fate had interrupted our trivialities with a veritable half-word; we have the feeling that we were just not quick enough to catch an answer to all our secret questioning, questioning to which we had never expected any answer, for we had supposed there was Nothing to answer us. We have to discover how it came about that the breezy writer of a pedestrian book called "White Jacket," a yarn not free even from facetiousness—not a deadly sin, but the mark of a mediocre mind—came to write a masterpiece. Not a small masterpiece either, but a work great in length, various in matter, though borne on a simple plan; as full of digressions as a tropical wild is astonishing with the easy abundance of life at its source; sustained throughout its mass by the original force of its inspiration; taken to the stars and kept there, as great tragedy should be; and, when we look back at it, we see it dark with foredoom, remotely lighted by faint but unfailing points of hope. The forlorn region of its drama, where nothing moves but the winds, the seas, and a little company of lost and insignificant souls, seems to us charged with the memory of the high but lost endeavors of all humanity, and witnessing then with indifference the effort of yet another handful of indomitable men, set to an achievement against the winds of chance and implacable destiny itself, but given to the fate which waits below the horizon for us all.

How did the author of "Typee" find it in him to write that masterpiece? If "Moby Dick" were Melville's only work the question would not arise. That would be his mark. But he has made his mark elsewhere, in many volumes, and so we may judge his qualities. His other books are sometimes admirable, more often curious, as of the imitative efforts of an able but erratic man trying to go beyond his powers—an important point—and frequently dull or stilted or even incoherent. But for one thing, that it was the author of "Moby Dick" who wrote them, they would be lost with the Victorian things—now dead and forgotten—amid which they first appeared; except, of course, "Typee" and Omoo," which are delightful records that have been indorsed by good judges like R. L. Stevenson, who once declared it was these books which sent him to the South Seas. In none of them, however, do I see much to indicate the possibility of the mysterious whale, nor to explain in what profound sea that creature had birth. I wish it were possible. For if we could discover what happened to Melville of "White Jacket" when he began upon Ahab and his voyage we might go far towards learning what are the qualities of mind and character, and in what lucky circumstances they must coincide, which produce great literature. For Melville clearly transcended his powers in "Moby Dick." A whimsical character, with an occasional erratic fancy and diverting liveliness, suddenly magnified into the high dignity and dominion and the measureless fertility of a master mind! How did it happen? Melville is an enigma whose secret concerns the very springs of genius.

For, naturally, he always had it in him. We want to know what gave full liberty to his powers. What was it that removed his inhibitions? We hear that Melville became "unbalanced"; but it can be easily understood that the man whose mind imagined the scenes in the "Try Pots" Inn of Nantucket would be thought mad by those who are never moved except by common sense; for the commonest sense, as Thoreau once pointed out, is that of men asleep, which they express by snoring, and most of us would be thought at least a little queer by our friends if we went any distance beyond that safe and verifiable noise in everybody's language.

Some English friends of mine are inclusive Melville enthusiasts, and this light way of dismissing his many books, with the enthusiastic exception of "Moby Dick," may be serious for me. James Billson, to whom I am indebted for nearly a full reading of Melville, has a complete collection of his publications and reveres him. It should be explained that even the British Museum is without copies of some of Melville's books. I remember that when about a year ago I hailed "Moby Dick" without any careful modulation of praise, some critics, who, it appeared had known him for years, but had said nothing about it, asked in noticeable scorn: "What about 'Mardi'"? They included in their test of my right to speak the "Piazza Tales" and other books whose names confused my ignorance. But now I ask: Well, what about them? I have now read them, and I declare that they only deepen the mystery of "Moby Dick." If all we knew of Shakespeare was some stuff like, say, the "Euphues," with one exception, and "Macbeth" that exception, I think Shakespeare would be an even more engaging enigma than he is. I confess that Melville's other books have a fascination for me. I envy Mr. Billson his complete set of first editions. Yet I think the principal value of these volumes is documentary; though that is a value indeed when the evidence concerns a man like Melville. We cannot be grateful enough to those who shrewdly discerned so many years ago the importance of their contemporary and treasured all of him they could discover.

What is the literary value of Melville's other books? The "Confidence Man" is almost unreadable. "Pierre" must be tackled in the way of a problem. One's sole pleasure in reading them is that one is looking for a clue to Ahab and the carpenter, Queequeg, and Father Mapple's sermon. Now, in all these other books there is no evidence that Melville was really a confident writer. He had the high spirits which go with full vitality and an enjoyment of life's good things; but he knew the cheat in appearances, and his recurrent intellectual melancholy would enter and wag solemnly at his fun, which then was embarrassed into elephantine jocosity. He had studied the many philosophies to the extent of treating them all with veiled contempt, as a vanity. When reading him on the South Seas you will come on a passage that is startling because the book has suddenly begun to speak with the entirely different voice of another personality. "Heavens," you exclaim, "there's Sir Thomas Browne!" Melville, is it clear, had read extensively and acutely. He was a lover of rare ideas in fine prose. He had peeped into every corner of the library; he had travelled widely, and his mind was alive with vivid recollections of strange men, foreign scenes, and queer events. His memory seems to have been highly charged and not under control; his admiration for the achievements of other artists was so warm, and his own ability so great, that his mimicry was unconscious. I should say he was a modest man, impatient with himself, condemning his own qualities in unnecessary comparisons, and allowing his want of confidence in himself to deflect his aims. It looks as though when writing he was haunted by gaunt admonitions, irresponsible imps, and seductive follies, whose importunities kept his purpose distracted. He did not burn one clear, steady light, but experimented with a large variety of illuminations, and even with fireworks. One, therefore, sees his object but fitfully, and then fantastically distorted.

Yet there is never a doubt that he was an original, and, more than that, a wise and tolerant man. His "Battle Pieces," poems of the Civil War, are startling in their appeal to us to-day. This generation, too, can respond to that language. His prose supplement to those poems, an address to the heated and distracted people he found around him after the war, might have been written last week. It is meant for us, too. I wish I could persuade any American who feels he has a title to a bitter grudge against the British or the

Germans to read that lofty and persuasive appeal. It leaves no doubt about the spaciousness and benignity of Melville's nature. Yet, when considering him as a writer, look at this of his from "Pierre":

> Pierre was the only son of an affluent and haughty widow; a lady who externally furnished a singular example of the preservative and beautifying influences of unfluctuating rank, health, and wealth when joined to a fine mind of medium culture, uncankered by any inconsolable grief, and never worn by sordid cares.

That sort of thing requires a considerable resolution to persevere with it for some time. "Redburn" and "White Jacket" are both plain narratives of voyages—one of a merchant ship, the other of a warship. They are, to me, enjoyable books because of Melville's extreme particularity in his descriptions of the ships and sea life in an era the very memory of which is fading. They cannot be compared with Dana's book, but they are invaluable records.

Now, "Mardi" is entirely different. It opens handsomely on a whaler in the Pacific, and the innocent reader moves through the opening chapters with hope brightly rising. He regards the bulk of the book and sees it is great; but its bulk, under such a promise, is a chief merit. Suddenly, without warning, with all his awakened and lively interest bright in his eyes, the unlucky reader is dropped out of the certainty of the veritable Pacific, its calms and storms, its sharks and monsters, and the wonders of its days and nights seen from an open boat, into the vacuity of a sham dream world of ladies who are not what they seem (one is named Yillah!), philosophical savages, and nebulous islands of both the blest and the damned. And that transformation scene Melville, with most of the book before him, tries to maintain as a fascinating illusion when he has never succeeded in making it more than a disappointment in the first place. He becomes—indeed, having taken the plunge, he has no choice—hortatory, shrilly ecstatic, and expansively rhetorical. But the task is beyond him. The magic does not come. We see no more than a faery land where the wonders are of limelight and the stage carpenter, and the ethereal ladies cannot disguise their green-room aids, and where the wires along which move the visiting sprites are occasionally visible.

It is in "Piazza Tales," I think, that we come nearest to the Melville of "Moby Dick." One strange yarn in that collection, "Benito Cereno," though it holds well enough, yet still leaves a reader aware that his critical faculties are unsubdued, for they tell him that here is first rate material which has been crudely handled. The authentic Melville, with all the many voices stilled in his mind and speaking for himself, is manifest, however, in the "Encantadas," an account of the Gallipagos Islands. That is the real thing. I can quote only part of his description of the tortoises of those stark and forsaken tropic rocks, but in its total effect it is rather like a nightmare.

As I lay in my hammock that night, overhead I heard the slow, wearing draggings of the three ponderous strangers along the encumbered deck. Their stupidity or their resolution was so great that they never went aside for any impediment. One ceased his movements altogether just before the mid-watch. At sunrise I found him butted like a battering ram against the immovable foot of the foremast, and still striving, tooth and nail, to force the impossible passage. That these tortoises are the victims of a penal, or malignant, or perhaps a downright diabolical enchanter, seems in nothing more likely than in that strange infatuation of hopeless toil which so often possesses them. I have known them in their journeyings ram themselves heroically against rocks, and long abide there, nudging, wriggling, wedging, in order to displace them, and so hold on their inflexible path. Their crowning curse is their drudging impulse to straightforwardness in a belittered world.

Of that passage there can be no doubt. It is confident, firm, direct, simple, and nervous English; it is excellent prose. But it is more than that. It has in it the signs of what can never be taught or learned. It is the writing of a master who possibly is unaware of what it is he does, who is himself perhaps blind and deaf to the starglints and echoes from the deeps in the measure of his own words.

We come to "Moby Dick." When one enters that book one is instantly aware of an overshadowing presence. From the opening there is no doubt about it. Nor is it now a fitful presence. It meets us at that entrance which is quite rightly entitled "Loomings." We go at once into a world where all is familiar—streets, ships, men, sea, and sky—but where all has been enchanted. Another spirit is there, creative, dominant, which knows us, but is itself unknown. What has happened it is impossible to say. We hear Melville's voice. It is easily recognizable. His words are familiar and the rhythm of their ordering. But they are somehow changed. They have been transmuted. They shine with an unearthly light. Their music can be even terrifying, like nameless sounds heard at night in the wilderness.

These, of course, are generalities. But who has resolved poetry into its elements? We know it only from the thrill it gives, neither of joy nor of fear, but something of each, when we encounter it. "Moby Dick" is a supreme test. If it captures you, then you are unafraid of great art. You may dwell in safety with fiends or angels and rest poised with a quiet mind between the stars and the bottomless pit.

[The Crown of
Melville's Artistic Achievement]

J. C. SQUIRE

The reputation of Herman Melville has had curious vicissitudes. Seventy years ago, for a brief period, he was widely known on both sides of the Atlantic. After "Moby Dick" he lapsed into a semi-obscurity which lasted for the remaining forty years of his life. New editions of his principal works came out at rare intervals; now and again some writer peculiarly interested in the sea—Stevenson, Clark Russell, and, later, Mr. Masefield—celebrated his genius; periodic attempts were made by critics who had come across him to induce a wide public to read him. But his death in 1891 was almost unnoticed, and for nearly thirty years after that he continued to be what he had been—to the few a great classic, to the many barely a name. And when I say the many I mean not the greater many, but the many who are in the habit of reading good books. Some strange inhibition seems to have operated. You could tell an intelligent man about Melville; he might remark that somebody else had told him about Melville; and he would then go away and leave Melville unread. Possibly Melville's titles—"Typee," "Omoo," "Moby Dick"—may have had something to do with it. At any rate, there it was. In 1919 Melville's centenary was celebrated; that is to say, it occurred. The last two years have seen articles, and good articles, about him in most of the leading critical journals; the Oxford Press has reissued "Moby Dick" precisely as the author wrote it; and now an American enthusiast, with the help of family papers, has compiled a biography [Raymond M. Weaver, *Herman Melville: Mariner and Mystic*, 1921]. Can we hope that these latest attempts to incorporate Melville in the list of authors with whom every reading person must have some familiarity will be more successful? Possibly what seems like a curse may still be in operation; but here at least is one more effort.

*   *   *

By the time he was forty he had written all the most important of his books. For the rest of his life he was externally a customs officer, of whom the world

Excerpted and reprinted from *Books Reviewed* (New York: George H. Doran, (1922), 214–22.

became increasingly oblivious, and his inner life was that of an imaginative philosopher, whose writings were scattered with obscure splendours and speculations of terrifying sombreness. A few people knew him as a bronzed and bearded recluse who had had a rather disreputably violent past and now read Kant and Plato. They might think what they chose. He felt himself to be growing perpetually, but he ceased to be very much interested in what others thought of him. "I have come to regard this matter of fame as the most transparent of all vanities. I read Solomon more and more, and every time see deeper and deeper and unspeakable meanings in him."

What could be more pessimistic, more disillusioned? It certainly would be impossible to describe Melville as anything but a pessimist. He habitually faced the harshest facts in the universe; they hurt him, and he had no explanation for them. Looking for an image of his attitude when in contemplation one thinks inevitably of the gentle and meditative mate Starbuck, looking over the side of the "Pequod" as she floats over the silken sunlit Pacific, and thinking of the world of horror under that lovely surface, the perpetual massacre, the vile writhing shapes, the ruthless rows of teeth. The whole book—and "Moby Dick" is quintessential Melville as well as the crown of his artistic achievement—has been resolved into an allegory of despair. The mad captain, Ahab, sleeplessly chasing the great White Whale, who had mutilated him, is that innermost ego to the nature and insistence of which Melville so often recurs. The mates, quiet Starbuck, and jovial Stubb, and commonplace Flask, are the recurrent moods with which he must keep company. The chase is the chase of life, the thing hunted an invulnerable brutality and an inevitable defeat. Again and again the theme is directly and openly returned to; the eternal problem of evil is posed in all its manifestations; sentences and pages are written which momentarily open black abysses of despair or present to the mind with irresistible force pictures of nightmare horror. No writer could more powerfully convey such pictures to the imagination; none has exceeded Melville in the gift of using a single word or phrase which stabs the heart and leaves it throbbing with dread. Whenever Moby Dick is seen he seems "the gliding great demon of the seas of life." Ahab, momentarily softening to the poor black boy, Pip, speaks to him of "omniscient gods oblivious of suffering man; and man, though idiotic, and knowing not what he does, yet full of the sweet things of love and gratitude." Consider, says the author, the eternal wars of the sea:

> Consider all this; and then turn to this green, gentle, and most docile earth; consider them both, the sea and the land; and do you not find a strange analogy to something in yourself? For as this appalling ocean surrounds the verdant land, so in the soul of man there lies one insular Tahiti, full of peace

and joy, but encompassed by all the horrors of the half-known life. God keep thee! Push not off from that isle, thou canst never return.

Melville himself pushed off; at least in the sense that he became lost in speculation. Perhaps it was inevitable, as Miss Meynell suggests in her excellent little introduction to the new edition ["The World's Classics," Oxford University Press, 1920], that this should happen to the author of "Moby Dick." There are depths so great that if the diver reaches them he sinks to return no more. But in "Moby Dick" itself, the struggles of the intellect with the enigma are not yet out of the control of the artist; moreover, one is liable to give a false impression in saying that the book is pessimistic. It has nothing in common with the grey miseries of the enfeebled. Its darkest passages are passionate in the writing and produce an exhilaration in the reader; both the glory as well as the awfulness of life are celebrated at white heat; and the moods of the book are as varied as the "Pequod's" crew. The jovial Stubb and the matter-of-fact Flask get their turns with Starbuck and the captain. Every variety of marine experience, all the beauty and terror of the South Seas, a world of human character and lively external incident, are here. At one moment we are watching a bloody fight on deck, at another listening to a story in a café at Lima, at another boiling down whale-blubber in the fire-lit night; there are enough battles and storms and encounters to make a dozen books for boys. Not only does one feel that there was a Conrad and a Stevenson in Melville, but frequently one is forcibly reminded, in chapters at a time, of Dickens and Defoe. How could a book open more briskly and humorously and excitingly? In what novel can one find a record of fact so elaborate, a collection of odd learning so amusing and peculiar, as in that large section of the book which describes the whole history, structure, and fate of the whale, and epitomises the manners and customs of whalers?

Melville's laugh is as loud as his brooding is deep, and no recorder of the surface of life ever had a keener eye for every kind of detail or a more retentive memory. And the whole wealth of his passion and knowledge, humour and suffering is poured out in language which is at its best unsurpassed, and in a curious mixed form—plain narrative is broken up by essays, treatises, dramatic dialogues—which superbly justifies itself.

He lapsed sometimes into excesses of rhetoric; his love for Sir Thomas Browne sometimes betrayed him; but he equalled Browne's sentences and De Quincey's apostrophes when he was thinking of neither, and none of his numerous South Sea successors has approached him in the power of natural description. "I will add," he says, when discussing ropes, "that Manilla is much more handsome and becoming to the boat than Hemp. Hemp is a dusky, dark fellow, a sort of Indian; but Manilla is a golden-haired Circassian to behold." "For," he says in parentheses, "there is an æsthetics in all things." That there was to him, that he was a born poet, is evident everywhere—except sometimes in his poetry. Imagery pours out of him, and everything he mentions is touched with light. I should like to reprint the whole marvellous chapter on "The Whiteness of the Whale."

*   *   *

There have been more profuse great writers than Melville, and, as some may think, wiser men; but I do not believe that there exists a greater work of prose fiction in English than "Moby Dick."

Revival of "Moby Dick"

FAIRFAX LEE

Is the *Evening Post* not entitled to very much of the credit—for such I think it—of bringing about the revival of interest in Herman Melville and his books, the best of which, of course, is "Moby Dick"? I think so. I read "Moby Dick"—a first edition—when I was a lad, and that in the cabin of the old and now forgotten Horner Jubilee, running out of Baltimore to 'Frisco. I was an apprentice. Every sailor lad read it then and I venture to say that this book sent to sea many and many an American sea captain and a good many still sailing under the American ensign. In those days "Moby Dick" was read as a part of the curriculum of every marine school and training ship in this country, and by hearsay I know that every apprentice aboard British ships was compelled or expected to read it.

I left the sea thirty-two years ago. In that interval I cannot recall hearing the book spoken of by a landsman but once, and this man was a graduate of the old schoolship St. Mary's. Seamen have spoken to me of it, but none of the younger ones had until within the last two years. Nowadays—Glory be!—lots of them are speaking of it, and reading it, too.

About a year and a half ago I saw "Moby Dick" mentioned in print for the first time in more than a quarter of a century. It was in the *Evening Post*, in "The Bowling Green." Mr. Morley wrote quite a little piece about it—made it the chef d'œuvre of his literary menu for that day. It made me run around in circles for a few minutes and then I sailed east to Manhattan, bought three copies and sent 'em around to friends to be passed around. One of them is on the way home from Port Adelaide in an American freighter. The last I heard it had passed through fifty-two sets of hands and, though very much autographed and weak in the back, it was going strong.

Now, Mr. Morley, broached the subject quite a year before the recent book about Melville was announced. It was scarcely a month before some publisher announced a new edition of "Moby Dick" because of an increased demand for it. I first thought to write Mr. Morley personally, but I've read in the "Green" about what he does with his mail and to his clients, so I feel safer with you.

Reprinted from the *New York Evening Post*, 9 February 1922.

[Well-known Admirers of Melville]

Henry S. Salt

As a good many Rationalists probably know, James Thomson was a great admirer of Melville, and Melville in his turn highly valued "B. V.'s" poems, especially *The City of Dreadful Night*. In a letter which I received from him in 1890, he wrote: "B. V. interests me much. *The City of Dreadful Night* is the modern book of *Job*, under an original form, duskily looming with the same aboriginal verities." Other remarks of Melville's are quoted in my *Life of James Thomson*. It was from that widely-read student of good books, Bertram Dobell, that I first heard of Melville's works; and so grateful was I for the information that I sedulously passed it on to others. I remember, in particular, bringing *The Whale* to the notice of William Morris, and how a week or two afterwards I heard him quoting it with huge gusto and delight. Among other well-known men who realized Melville's genius have been Robert Buchanan, R. L. Stevenson, Edward Carpenter, Clark Russell, and John Masefield. Stevenson is said to have considered Melville's books about the South Seas to be the best ever written on the subject.

Excerpted and reprinted from "Herman Melville," *Literary Guide* [London], new ser. 311 (May 1922), 70.

[The Spell of Balzac]

J. St. Loe Strachey

Anything about Herman Melville and his books is sure to be interesting. But, though this is true, I cannot say that Mr. Weaver's *Herman Melville: Mariner and Mystic* is a great book, or even a satisfactory book. It might so easily be much better and tell us so much more than it does. The chief point of interest is Mr. Weaver's account of Melville's neglected and unrevived novels. Everyone who knows anything about literature knows *Typee, Omoo, White Jacket,* and *Moby-Dick,* but the other books are for the most part unknown to the world. Yet it is obvious from the quotations that they are full of strange and good things.

*　　　*　　　*

Whenever in a passage we get Melville's words, they are full, not only of animation, but of distinction. How excellent is the phrase "spontaneously an atheist"! So, too, are Jackson's last words, "Haul out to windward!" as he broke a blood vessel and died in a torrent of his own blood. It is always said that Melville based his style upon Sir Thomas Browne and Carlyle, which superficially and perhaps consciously he did; but I am strongly inclined to think that there was another influence at work which has not been noticed. I believe him to have come very strongly under the spell of Balzac. Whether Melville actually studied the *Comédie Humaine* I do not know, and it does not really matter, for the influence which I mean is not so much a verbal as a spiritual influence. It is shown, not so much in the phrases as in the structure of the novels. There were, no doubt, plenty of translations of Balzac to be found in America during Melville's youth and even middle life.

*　　　*　　　*

I do not mean that Melville, though a great man of letters in many ways, had anything like the universal touch, the full scope of genius that belonged to Balzac. Yet Melville undoubtedly felt, as did the author of *The Human Comedy,* that he was seated in the gallery of a great theatre and seeing men and women "play their fantastic tricks before High Heaven," or perhaps one should say before the Lords of Hell.

Excerpted and reprinted from "Herman Melville: Mariner and Mystic," *Spectator* [London] 128 (6 May 1922), 559–60.

Before I leave the subject of Melville I should like to point out that the latest biographer of the great American does not seem to realize how strong the feeling about Melville has always been in England. I well remember some thirty years ago writing a review in the *Spectator* on a new edition of Melville's works which had just appeared. A reference thereto shows that a Melville boom was then proceeding. But this is not all. I remember that when my article appeared a lady of letters who could remember the 'fifties remarked to me that she was glad to see people were reading Melville again, and added: "I can't tell you how enthusiastic we all were, young and old, at the end of the 'forties and beginning of the 'fifties, over *Typee, Omoo,* and *Moby-Dick.* There was quite a furore over Melville in those days. All the young people worshipped him."

As a further proof of that, I have just been turning over a reprint of *The Whale,* issued as a three-volume novel by Bentley in 1851. It is interesting, though rather sad, to note that in this seventy-year-old book the paper is for the most part spotless, firm, and crisp, and the print exquisitely clear. It is to be feared that our post-War, and even many of our pre-War novels will not be anything like as legible at the beginning of the twenty-first century.

Melville, I venture to say, will never be forgotten either here or in America. So long as the English language survives—and who dare prophesy its extinction?—so long will people read and wonder at the eccentric mariner, who described a whale-hunt in the terms of Urn Burial. He was an uncanny throw-forward, and did not in his day quite fit into either the life or the literature of his age. If he were living and writing now, he would be one of the world's greatest-sellers and would thoroughly deserve his success.

Notes on "Moby Dick"

LINCOLN COLCORD

I

Fresh from a second reading of Melville's "Moby Dick," I am surprised by the heterodoxy of certain strong impressions. It is a book which leads to violent convictions. I first read it as a boy, on shipboard, somewhere about the world; I was enthralled by the story, but beyond a keen sensation of pleasure I retained no definite recollection of it. Thus, upon a second reading, the book had for me all the delight of a new discovery. Again I was enthralled, this time by more than the story; by all the infernal power and movement of the piece, by that intangible quality which, through suggestion and stimulation, gives off the very essence of genius. I do not mean atmosphere— Conrad creates atmosphere—but something above atmosphere, the aura of sublime and tragic greatness; not light but illumination, the glance of a brooding and unappeasable god.

The art of "Moby Dick" as a masterpiece of fiction lies in the element of purposeful suspense which flows through the tale from beginning to end in a constantly swelling current; and in the accumulating grandeur and terror evoked by the whale-*motif*. This achievement which, like every such feat of genius, defies either description or criticism, is what makes the book superlatively great. Melville performs the most difficult task of literary creation—that of encompassing and fixing the vague form of a tremendous visionary conception.

The high-water mark of inspiration in the book is reached in the dramatic dialogue between Ahab and the carpenter over the making of the wooden leg. This scene is preceded by the finest piece of descriptive characterization in the volume, written in Melville's own style (not aped after Sir Thomas Browne): the sketch of the old ship-carpenter. Starting abruptly from the heights of this description, the dialogue soars straight to the realm of pure literary art. It is the equal of Shakespeare's best dialogue. One longs to hear it given by a couple of capable actors: the scene, the confusion of the "Pequod's" deck by night on the whaling-grounds; the lurid flame of the smithy in the background, in the foreground the old bewhiskered carpenter

Reprinted from "Notes on 'Moby Dick,'" *Freeman* [New York] 5 (23 August 1922), 559–62; (30 August 1922), 585–87.

planing away at Ahab's ivory leg; before the footlights an audience familiar with the book, or, lacking this, any intelligent audience, the want of special knowledge being supplied by a plain prologue. The scene exactly as it stands is magnificently dramatic.

This, however, is a burst of inspiration. The ablest piece of sustained writing in "Moby Dick" unquestionably is the extraordinary chapter on "The Whiteness of the Whale." Here we have a *tour de force* without excuse in the narrative, a mere joyous rush of exhilaration and power, a throwing out of the arms with a laugh and a flash of the eye. "The Whiteness of the Whale," I said to myself, as I came to this chapter; "what the devil have we now?" I feared that Melville would exceed his licence, that he might be going to strain the case a little. For it seemed an inconsequential heading for a chapter; and when I ran over the leaves, noting how long the effort was, my heart misgave me. But before a page is finished, the reader catches the idea and perceives the masterliness of the attack. Throughout the chapter, as one watches the author play with his theme, letting it rise and fall naturally (nothing is ever still that comes from Melville's hand—even his calms shimmer and shake with an intensity of heat); as one follows this magically dexterous exercise, all of which, apart from its intrinsic beauty, contributes in some ineffable manner to the charm and mystery of the tale; one is aware of the thrill which comes but seldom in a lifetime of reading.

As a piece of sheer writing, this chapter on the whiteness of the whale is a remarkable achievement. Its creator could do anything with words. I wonder that it has not been more commonly utilized in the higher teaching of English; I know of no effort in the language which affords a better study of what can be accomplished by the magic of literary power.

II

"Moby Dick" stands as one of the great nautical books of the world's literature. What I have to say of it on this score, therefore, may to Melville's public, which is almost exclusively a shore-public, appear to be malicious heresy. But I am concerned only with establishing what seems to me an interesting verity; I want to find the real Melville, because he is so well worth finding; I would not be engaged in criticism had I not first become engaged in love and admiration.

I am surprised, when all is said and done, to find how little of real nautical substance there is in "Moby Dick." It would not be overstating the case to say that the book lacks the final touch of nautical verisimilitude. In criticizing the book from this viewpoint, one must, of course, make due allowance for the refining and rarifying influence of the imaginative pitch to which the whole work is cast; an influence which naturally tends to destroy a share of nautical realism, as, indeed, it tends to destroy all realism. Yet, when this allowance is made, there remains in "Moby Dick" a certain void, difficult of estimate or description, where the shadows, at least, of nautical reality should stand.

This void, of course, appears only to the sailor who reads the book; no one else would notice it. It is not that the book lacks the framework of nautical reality; it would be idle for me to attempt to deny what plainly exists. "Moby Dick," indeed, is in the generic sense of the term a nautical piece; it is a tale of ships, sailing, and the sea. We have a view of the "Pequod," of certain seafaring scenes and operations; we have a picture of the business of whaling, the handling of boats, the cutting in of the great fish alongside the ship, the final labours on deck and in the hold; we have a general background of nautical affairs, so that the scenes inevitably stand out against a tracery of sails, clouds, horizon and sea; and all this is correctly written, from the nautical standpoint, save in a few insignificant particulars. Melville's treatment of the whaling-industry, in fact, is classic. No one else has done such work, and no one ever will do it again; it alone serves to rescue from oblivion one of the most extraordinary episodes of human enterprise.

But this fidelity to the business of whaling is not precisely what I mean by nautical verisimilitude. How, then, shall I define the lack of this verisimilitude which I find in "Moby Dick"? Shall I put it that there is not quite enough of sure detail, in any instance where a nautical scene or evolution is described, to convince the sailor-reader that the man who wrote the words understood with full instinctive knowledge what he was writing about? A sailor, a seaman in the real sense of the word, would involuntarily have followed so closely the scene or evolution in hand, that he could not have fallen short of the final touch of realism; he would himself have been a part of the picture, he would quite unconsciously have written from that point of view, and the added colour and particularity, in the case of "Moby Dick," far from detracting from the strength and purpose of the work, would on the contrary have considerably augmented them.

Melville, quite unconsciously, did not write the book that way. To his eye, indeed, it plainly was not so much a nautical work as it was a study in the boundless realm of human psychology. Yet, having taken the sea for his background, he could not have failed, had he been a sailor, to fill the void I mention. From this one gets a measure of Melville's spiritual relation to seafaring.

Most mysteries submit to a simple explanation; they are no mysteries at all. In the present case, a closer view of seafaring alone is needed. All Melville's seafaring experience lay before the mast. He gives no indication that he was in the least degree interested in this experience as a romantic profession; he speaks of obeying orders, admitting that those who commanded his activities on the sea had a right to require him to do anything under the sun; but I have never seen a passage in which he celebrated the task of learning to be a good seaman—except as a piece of extraneous description—or one showing the slightest interest in the sea professionally. He was decidedly not looking towards the quarter-deck. When afloat, he seems simply to have been mooning around the vessel, indulging his fancy to the full, chiefly observing human nature; realistically intent on the ship's company, but merely romanticizing over the ship herself; in short, not making any advance towards becoming himself a sailor, towards the acquisition of those instinctive reactions which make man and ship dual parts of the same entity.

I would not be thought so absurd as to blame Melville for not becoming a true sailor; I am merely trying to run the fact to earth. He was divinely inefficient as a seaman; he never learned the lore of a ship, beyond attaining the necessary familiarity with her external parts, with the execution of simple commands, and with the broader features of her control and operation. His nautical psychology was that of the forecastle, the psychology of obeying orders. For months on end, at sea, he felt no curiosity to know where the ship was or whither she was going; he never understood exactly why she was made to perform certain evolutions; he helped to execute the order, and watched the result with a mild and romantic perplexity. The psychology of the quarter-deck, the psychology of handling a vessel, was foreign to him.

This is why his nautical atmosphere is made up of relatively unimportant details and insignificant evolutions, such as a green man before the mast would have compassed; while infinitely more important details and more significant evolutions, and the grasp of the whole ship as a reality, all of which would have been in the direct line of the narrative, and would only have intensified the effect he was striving to produce, were passed over in silence because they were beyond his ken. He might have made the ship, as well as the whale, contribute to the mysterious grandeur of the book's main theme; in no single instance does he attempt to do so. The "Pequod," to all intents and purposes, is a toy ship; when, indeed, she is not a ship nautically fictitious, a land-lubber's ship, a ship doing the impossible.

If Captain Ahab says "Brace the yards!" once, he says it a hundred times; whereas there are dozens of commands that he might have shouted with stronger effect, both realistic and literary; whereas, furthermore, the order to "brace the yards" means nothing in particular, without a qualifying direction, and never would be given in this incomplete form on a ship's deck. This is a minor instance; but the sum of these nautical ineptitudes throughout the book is fairly staggering.

To cite a major instance, the account of the typhoon off the coast of Japan is a sad failure; it might have been written by one of your Parisian arm-chair romanticists, with a knowledge of the sea derived from a bathing-beach experience. The ship is an imaginary piece of mechanism; no coherent sense of the storm itself is created; no realization of the behaviour of a vessel in a typhoon runs behind the pen. Ahab's battered quadrant, thrown to the deck and trampled on the day before, is allowed to come through the storm reposing as it fell, so that his eye may be caught by it there when the weather has cleared. In fact, both as a piece of writing and as an essential of the tale, the scene wholly fails to justify itself. It serves no apparent purpose; it seems to have been lugged in by the ears.

How a man with an experience of some years on the sea, a man who could write the superlative chapter on the whiteness of the whale, should fail so completely to present an adequate or even an understanding picture of a ship beset by a heavy circular storm—here is a mystery not so easy of solution. It would seem to be plainly evident that Melville had never passed through a typhoon, and never, probably, had been on the Japan whaling-grounds. But he must have seen plenty of storms at sea. With all his passionate descriptive power, however, he is strangely handicapped when he comes to imagine a scene beyond the range of his experience; his literary equipment did not readily lend itself to the translation of an imaginative picture in terms of reality.

Certainly Melville had in his blood none of the "feeling of the sea," that subtle reaction which is the secret animating spring of the real sailor. Romantic appreciation he had, and imaginative sentiment; but these must never be confounded with seamanship. Yet, in defence of his nautical laxity in the latter half of "Moby Dick," it should be recognized that, by the time he had reached these chapters, he must have been exhausted with the intensity of the emotional effort; and that, after juggling with forms for two-thirds of the volume, he had now definitely forsaken all attempts at realism. Ahab alone would have worn out an ordinary man in short order.

III

I do not remember having seen in print a discussion of the extraordinary technical development of "Moby Dick." In terms of the craft of writing, the book is a surpassing feat of legerdemain. Briefly, "Moby Dick" is the only piece of fiction I know of, which at one and the same time is written in the first and the third persons. It opens straightforwardly as first-person narration. "Call me Ishmael"—"I thought I would sail about a little"—"I stuffed a shirt or two into my carpet bag, tucked it under my arm, and started for Cape Horn and the Pacific." So it runs, throughout the opening scenes in New Bedford and Nantucket; the characters are real persons, seen through Ishmael's eyes; they speak real speech; the scenes are delineated with subjective realism. Melville is telling a story. His (or Ishmael's) meeting with Queequeg, and their first night together in the big feather bed at the Spouter Inn, are intensely human and alive. Even Bildad and Peleg are creations of realism. The first note of fancifulness is introduced with the Ancient Mariner who accosts Ishmael and Queequeg on the pier in Nantucket. The book, however, still holds to the technical channel of first person narration; and it is through Ishmael's eyes that one sees the "Pequod" sail from Nantucket.

Then, without warning, the narrative in Chapter twenty-nine jumps from the first to the third person; begins to relate conversations which could not possibly have been overheard by Ishmael and to describe scenes which his eye could not possibly have seen; follows Ahab into his cabin and Starbuck into the recesses of his mind, and launches boldly on that sea of mystical soliloquy and fanciful unreality across which it sweeps for the remainder of the tale. As it progresses, Ishmael sinks farther and farther from sight, and the all-seeing eye of the third person comes more and more into play.

Yet, even at this stage, the technical form of first-person narration is not entirely abandoned; is kept along, as it were, like an attenuated wraith. As the "Pequod" sights ship after ship, the narrative momentarily reappears, only to be discarded once more at the first opportunity; so that, of the main body of the book, it may truly be said that it is written in both the first and the third persons. For instance, chapter ninety-one, "The 'Pequod' Meets the 'Rosebud'": "It was a week or two after the last whaling-scene recounted, and when we [not they] were slowly sailing over a sleepy, vapoury, midday sea. . . ." This is a recurrence to first person narration in the midst of pages of third-person soliloquy. But turning to Chapter CXXVIII, "The 'Pequod' Meets the 'Rachel'": "Next day, a large ship, the 'Rachel,' was descried, bearing directly down upon the 'Pequod,' all her spars thickly clustering with men"—this might be either first or third person; the context shows it to be the latter. Ishmael has been definitely forsaken, and hereafter remains in abeyance until the end of the book; when, suddenly, he re-emerges in the epilogue.

The quarrel between the persons, however, does not by any means comprise the whole technical irregularity of "Moby Dick." There is the introduction of the form of dramatic dialogue; an innovation singularly successful, and remarkably in keeping both with the mood of the moment when it is introduced and with the general tone of mystical formlessness pervading the whole work. There is the adroit suspending of the narrative by those absorbing chapters of plain exposition, descriptive of whales and whaling; the gradual revealing of the secrets of the whale, while the final nameless secret is withheld, while fancy and terror feed and grow on suspense. There is the totally ideal development of the characterization, as Ahab and Starbuck and Stubbs and all the rest indulge themselves in the most high-flown and recondite reflections and soliloquies. Finally, there is the bizarre method of chaptering—each chapter a little sketch, each incident having its own chapter; some of the chapters only half a page in length, others a page or two; a hundred and thirty-five chapters in all, together with forewords on etymology and extracts, and an epilogue. In short "Moby Dick" as a technical exercise is utterly fantastic and original. Melville has departed from every known form of composition; or rather, he has jumbled many forms into a new relation, choosing among them as fancy dictated.

It is safe to say that no literary craftsman of the present day would so much as dream of attempting the experiment which "Moby Dick" discloses on its technical side. Such an attempt would be answered by both critics and public with the ostracism which modern Western culture reserves for irregularity. Here we have a striking commentary on the rigidity of our present literary technique; a technique which rules style and matter, and dominates the literary field, as never before. We speak of ourselves as individualists, freely developing new forms; we like to regard the period of 1840 as a time of stilted and circumscribed literary expression. Yet the truth of the matter seems to be quite otherwise. We are slaves to the success of a literary convention, while the writers of 1840 were relatively free. I am not aware that "Moby Dick" was received at the time of its publication with any degree of surprise at its technical form, whatever surprise or opposition may have been called forth by its content. Neither am I aware that Melville himself felt that he was doing an extraordinary thing in adopting a unique but natural technical form for the expression of an original creative effort. His letters to Hawthorne during the composition of "Moby Dick" betray no self-consciousness on this score. In fact, he seems to have retained a perfectly free relation with his technical medium.

IV

The exhaustion in the latter part of "Moby Dick," of which I have already spoken, seems to me to become startlingly apparent at the crisis of the book, which is reached in the last chapter. Cavilous as the criticism may sound from the viewpoint of a broader appreciation, I sincerely feel that Melville failed to reap in his crisis all that he had sown throughout the body of the tale. The chase of the white whale is splendid; in the daily fight between Ahab and this sinister embodiment of evil Melville is at his best, everything goes magnificently up to the very last; but the final attack of Moby Dick on the ship, and the sinking of the "Pequod" with all her company, are inadequate to the point of anticlimax.

There should have been a more generous descriptive effort at this pass; Melville could picture a scene superbly, and he should have spared no pains to do it here. He seems instead to have adopted an affectation of simplicity. He will rest on his oars now, let the momentum of the book carry it forward, allow the various lines of suspense and horror to culminate of their own accord; in fine, he will sketch the winding up of the piece, leaving the actual descriptive effort to the reader's imagination.

But in this he made a critical error; while it is a fine thing to utilize the reader's imagination, it is disastrous to tax it too far. The last pages of "Moby

Dick" do not give us the ending for which we have been prepared; which, with the keenest anticipation, we have been awaiting. Having created such intense suspense, Melville was under the imperative obligation to provide for its satisfaction a flash of equally intense realism. The imagination, having too readily devoured the feast that he has set forth, and finding its hunger only increased thereby, is suddenly let down and disappointed. In this unhappy, defrauded state, it fastens upon the first thing at hand, which is the catastrophe itself; recognizing at once the fantastic nature of that complete oblivion which so causelessly descends on the "Pequod" and her company. For, as a matter of sober fact, a ship of her size would not, in sinking, have drawn down into her vortex an agile cat, much less a crew of whalers, used to being pitched out of boats in the open sea, and surrounded with quantities of dunnage for them to ride when the decks had gone from under.

Turning to the last chapter of "Moby Dick," one may note that it contains but a brief paragraph describing the whale's frantic attack on the vessel. No horror is created, no suspense, no feverish excitement. It is another of art's vanished opportunities. There should have been a close-packed page or two of tumultuous visualization; then, with the gigantic whale dashing head-on toward the devoted "Pequod," a pause in the narrative, to let suspense rankle, while a few paragraphs were occupied with a dissertation on the sinking of vessels—not the sinking of vessels by whales, which matter has already been examined, but the sinking of vessels; about how difficult, how unusual, it would be for a ship to carry her whole company beneath the waves; about Starbuck's knowledge of this fact; about their frantic preparations for escape—then, loosing every ounce of reserve literary power, a description of the crash, the catastrophe, the peculiar and malignant combination of circumstances, easily to be imagined, which, in spite of common experience, did actually destroy this whole ship's company. The whale should have dashed among the debris and floating men, after the ship had gone down, to complete the work of destruction. The scene should have been cast in the form of first-person narration, and Ishmael should have been near enough to see it all. (He was adrift, it will be remembered, and did not go down with the vessel; but the return to the first person is reserved for the epilogue, while the crisis of the story is told in an especially vague form of the third person.) We should have been given a final view of the white whale, triumphantly leaving the scene and resuming the interrupted course of his destiny. In short, there are dozens of strokes of realism neglected in this chapter which plainly demand to be driven home.

Melville chose to end the book on a note of transcendentalism; he himself does not seem to have visualized the scene at all. The influence of Hawthorne, one suspects, was largely responsible for this grave error. Hawthorne was living just over the hill in the Berkshires that summer. The intense and lonely Melville had fallen under his fascination; he thought that he had at last found a friend. He was captivated, also, by that vague imaginative method of thought and style out of which Hawthorne wove his tales; and, quite naturally, his own work reflected this influence. For Melville was that man of genius known as the passionate hunter; he was the taster of all sensations, the searcher of all experience, the sampler of every form and style. And, as so often happens with such people, it was his tragic fate never entirely to find himself. The secret quarry of life constantly eluded him.

The influence of Hawthorne is painfully evident throughout the last two-thirds of "Moby Dick"; painfully evident, because it is so incongruous with Melville's natural manner which is that of narrative realism; he must be there in person—he makes the scene alive with amazing vitality where he stands. In the same sense, his natural power of characterization is in the descriptive or analytical field; I am not aware that he has ever put into the mouth of a single character a realistic speech. Wherever, in "Moby Dick," he gets his best effects, he gets them through the exercise of his natural manner. Certain scenes stand out vividly. Certain pages of analytical characterization are instinct with truth and greatness. The natural impulse keeps bursting through. But the bulk of the characterization is cast in a method artificial to him; he constantly tries to raise the pitch of the tale, to inflate the value of the words. Too much of the descriptive matter likewise is forced through unnatural channels, losing the air of mastery in its adaptation to the less vigorous form of the third person.

Thus the book, in its composition, represents a struggle between realism and mysticism, between a natural and an artificial manner. It begins naturally, it ends artificially. This in a measure explains the strange confusion of the technique, the extravagant use of the two separate persons. Only the most extraordinary creative power could have struck art and achievement from such an alien blend.

What, then, of the allegory?—for we are told that "Moby Dick" is a masterpiece of this form of composition. I must confess that I did not follow the allegory closely, and did not find that it was forced on my attention; and now that I look back on the book, I fail exactly to see wherein it lies. What, for instance, does Ahab represent, and what the white whale? I am not certain that Melville meant the story to be an allegory. In fact, does he not somewhere fiercely disclaim the imputation? But it is the fate of all work done in the manner of transcendentalism to land sooner or later in the rarified atmosphere of allegory, whether it means anything or not, whether or not the allegory seems to point anywhere in particular. Transcendentalism is the stuff of allegory. Melville hated allegory, and would have hated transcendental-ism, had he not just then happened to come under the influence of a transcendentalist. This put him in a bad fix, and made him, whether he willed it or not, write a book which looked like allegory. Do we need a better explanation of his turning so fiercely against the imputation?

Not because of its allegorical significance, and not, indeed, because of its mysticism, considered as a thing apart, does this book of the chase of the white whale live among the immortal works of literature; but rather because of its irrepressible triumph of realism over mysticism, because of the inspired and gripping story that builds itself up out of a passionate flow of words. For my part, I like Ahab as Ahab, not as a symbol of something or other; and Ahab lives as Ahab, marvellously enough, in spite of the wild unreality of his constant meditations and ebullitions. Yes, and because of it; the overshadowing demoniac terror of the story lends reality to unreality, charm and substance to mystical formlessness. This is the mark of genius in the creator. Yet even genius may carry things too far; Ahab manages to live as Ahab, but Starbuck—well, Starbuck struts and swells a little, betrayed by an overdose of transcendentalism.

V

If I have seemed to wish that "Moby Dick" had been written in the form of unalloyed narrative realism, that Melville had left off altogether his dalliance with transcendentalism, I would correct the impression now. As a piece of pure realism, the book obviously would not have been the inspired achievement that it is in its present form. The creative struggle that Melville was undergoing at the time of its composition was the intensifying medium through which the work rose to superlative heights. The chapters flow easily, as though he did not realize their duality of form and temper, but felt them to be parts of a unified, continuous product; but the grievous battle taking place within him caused him to produce what actually are gigantic fragments, struck from mountains of fire and anguish, which slowly and ponderously arrange themselves into the delineation of a majestic idea.

"Moby Dick" is not the allegory of Ahab's struggle with destiny; it is rather the story of Melville's struggle with art and life. Without this struggle, there would have been no agonizing greatness; only another "Typee," a splendid tale, a perfect example of literary realism. But, given the struggle, there had to be from page to page this singular conflict in style and form and matter, the confused, reflected gleams of a hidden conflagration; so that to wish the conflict away would be to wish away the book's divinity.

The Vogue of Herman Melville

[H. M. TOMLINSON]

Typee; Omoo. The Prose Works of Herman Melville. Standard Edition in
Twelve Vols. (Constable. 10 guineas the Set.)

Three years ago perhaps six literary critics in a national congress of their kind
might have been able to name the author of "Piazza Tales," "Mardi," and
"The Confidence Man," though that is doubtful; it is fairly certain, however,
that not more than two of the six could have said that they had read those
books. This reviewer, so long ago, would have had to admit his ignorance to
be complete. Even the British Museum, at that time, did not possess a copy
of "Piazza Tales," and no doubt even a good second-hand bookseller would
have let a copy of it go for a shilling or two. We heard last week that £30
was being asked in London for a first edition of it; not an unreasonable price
either, for, though incorrectly described as the only example of its kind in the
country, we know of the existence of but two other copies.

The demand here and in America for the very rare first editions of
Melville's books—the fire many years ago at Harpers of New York destroyed
a large stock of his early editions—arises from a simple cause. A recent cheap
edition of "Moby Dick" has resulted in a common confession that the book
is a masterpiece, and in a general curiosity about its author. That book,
indeed, appears to have been a wonder treasured as a sort of secret for years
by some select readers who had chanced upon it. They said little about it.
We gather that they had been in the habit of hinting the book to friends they
could trust, so that "Moby Dick" became a sort of cunning test by which the
genuineness of another man's response to literature could be proved. If he was
not startled by "Moby Dick," then his opinion on literature was of little
account. It should be observed, however, that the victim was never told this,
because this test was made by those who seemed scared by the intensity of
their own feelings aroused by the strange, subliminal potency of the monster
called the White Whale. And they observed, too, that "Moby Dick" was not
a book whose merits, so remarkable to them, had been noted by the
authorized surveyors of literature. They were confident in their opinion, but
they were in the position of the amateur astronomer who feels sure that, with
a home-made telescope, he has discovered a star of the first magnitude, yet

Reprinted from the *Nation and Athenæum* [London] 31 (30 September 1922), 857–58.

hardly cares to announce it because Greenwich is strangely silent about this obvious celestial wonder.

To-day, Herman Melville is admitted to be one of the best things America has done. So whole-hearted, indeed, has been the admiration of English critics for "Moby Dick" that the more intellectual of the American critics have, quite naturally, retorted that the White Whale is not such a fine whale after all. It might have been bigger, or different. It is not the kind of whale to which a modern American man of letters would have given birth. Which, we will admit, is probable; yet, nevertheless, the significance of "Moby Dick" is so portentous that a deep curiosity concerning its author and his other works is natural. Owing to Messrs. Constable's enterprise, Melville's other books, which not only were out of print but were almost forgotten, will now be accessible—at least, to those with the requisite guineas for a praiseworthy investment.

To those who know only "Omoo" and "Typee"—the initial volumes of this standard edition—and "Moby Dick," Melville's other books may prove not only puzzling, but disappointing. Some of his novels and narratives are but pedestrian, others are flamboyant and wild, and there are others so congested and tough that it is only the drive of one's desire to find a clue to the mind of so extraordinary a man which gets one through them. An interest which will carry a reader through even an attractive writer's worst work is rare. Darwin, too, was an extraordinary man, but a reading of the "Origin of Species" does not awaken a passion to learn all that is to be known about him. Nor is the desire to read all that Melville wrote merely a hopeful expectation of finding another book like "Moby Dick." One knows at once, or ought to know, that that book is unique.

What makes it so remarkable a book is not easy to define. It is certain, however, that its writer was as different from the majority of his species as a man is from a sheep. Melville gives hints, in his masterpiece, that his mind at times moved to a plane where he saw things in a way we will call phantasmal, because our intelligence cannot do it. What he knew cannot be related to anything we know, and some of us, therefore, are likely to explain it as a vagary of dementia. But that will not do. The exquisite poise, so perilously maintained throughout "Moby Dick," mocks us out of that explanation. There are moments in great music when the listener can believe he has heard echoes out of deeps he cannot know. There are such thrills in great poetry, as those hints and warnings which transcend the drama of "Macbeth." It is this fearful apprehension, the suspicion that there was a sound from beyond our horizon, which moves us at times in reading "Moby Dick." An ardent curiosity concerning all that its author has written is, therefore, natural.

Herman Melville's "Moby Dick"

D. H. Lawrence

Moby Dick, or the White Whale.

A hunt. The last great hunt.

For what?

For Moby Dick, the huge white sperm whale: who is old, hoary, monstrous, and swims alone; who is unspeakably terrible in his wrath, having so often been attacked; and snow-white.

Of course he is a symbol.

Of what?

I doubt if even Melville knew exactly. That's the best of it.

He is warm-blooded, he is lovable. He is lonely Leviathan, not a Hobbes sort. Or is he?

But he is warm-blooded, and lovable. The South Sea Islanders, and Polynesians, and Malays, who worship shark, or crocodile, or weave endless frigate-bird distortions, why did they never worship the whale? So big!

Because the whale is not wicked. He doesn't bite. And their gods had to bite.

He's not a dragon. He is Leviathan. He never coils like the Chinese dragon of the sun. He's not a serpent of the waters. He is warmblooded, a mammal. And hunted, hunted down.

It is a great book.

At first you are put off by the style. It reads like journalism. It seems spurious. You feel Melville is trying to put something over you. It won't do.

And Melville really is a bit sententious: aware of himself, self-conscious, putting something over even himself. But then it's not easy to get into the swing of a piece of deep mysticism when you just set out with a story.

Nobody can be more clownish, more clumsy and sententiously in bad taste, than Herman Melville, even in a great book like *Moby Dick*. He preaches and holds forth because he's not sure of himself. And he holds forth, often, so amateurishly.

The artist was so *much* greater than the man. The man is rather a tiresome New Englander of the ethical mystical-transcendentalist sort:

Reprinted from *Studies in Classic American Literature* (New York: Thomas Seltzer, 1923), 214–40.

Emerson, Longfellow, Hawthorne, etc. So unrelieved, the solemn ass even in humour. So hopelessly *au grand serieux,* you feel like saying: Good God, what does it matter? If life is a tragedy, or a farce, or a disaster, or anything else, what do I care! Let life be what it likes. Give me a drink, that's what I want just now.

For my part, life is so many things I don't care what it is. It's not my affair to sum it up. Just now it's a cup of tea. This morning it was wormwood and gall. Hand me the sugar.

One wearies of the *grand serieux.* There's something false about it. And that's Melville. Oh, dear, when the solemn ass brays! brays! brays!

But he was a deep, great artist, even if he was rather a sententious man. He was a real American in that he always felt his audience in front of him. But when he ceases to be American, when he forgets all audience, and gives us his sheer apprehension of the world, then he is wonderful, his book commands a stillness in the soul, an awe.

In his "human" self, Melville is almost dead. That is, he hardly reacts to human contacts any more: or only ideally: or just for a moment. His human-emotional self is almost played out. He is abstract, self-analytical and abstracted. And he is more spell-bound by the strange slidings and collidings of Matter than by the things men do. In this he is like Dana. It is the material elements he really has to do with. His drama is with them. He was a futurist long before futurism found paint. The sheer naked slidings of the elements. And the human soul experiencing it all. So often, it is almost over the border: psychiatry. Almost spurious. Yet so great.

It is the same old thing as in all Americans. They keep their old-fashioned ideal frock-coat on, and an old-fashioned silk hat, while they do the most impossible things. There you are: you see Melville hugged in bed by a huge tattooed South Sea Islander, and solemnly offering burnt offering to this savage's little idol, and his ideal frock-coat just hides his shirt-tails and prevents us from seeing his bare posterior as he salaams, while his ethical silk hat sits correctly over his brow the while. That is so typically American: doing the most impossible things without taking off their spiritual get-up. Their ideals are like armour which has rusted in, and will never more come off. And meanwhile in Melville his bodily knowledge moves naked, a living quick among the stark elements. For with sheer physical, vibrational sensitiveness, like a marvellous wireless-station, he registers the effects of the outer world. And he records also, almost beyond pain or pleasure, the extreme transitions of the isolated, far-driven soul, the soul which is now alone, without any real human contact.

The first days in New Bedford introduce the only human being who really enters into the book, namely, Ishmael, the "I" of the book. And then the moment's hearts-brother, Queequeg, the tattooed, powerful South Sea harpooner, whom Melville loves as Dana loves "Hope." The advent of Ishmael's bedmate is amusing and unforgettable. But later the two swear "marriage," in the language of the savages. For Queequeg has opened again the flood-gates of love and human connection in Ishmael.

"As I sat there in that now lonely room, the fire burning low, in that mild stage when, after its first intensity has warmed the air, it then only glows to be looked at; the evening shades and phantoms gathering round the casements, and peering in upon us silent, solitary twain: I began to be sensible of strange feelings. I felt a melting in me. No more my splintered hand and maddened heart was turned against the wolfish world. This soothing savage had redeemed it. There he sat, his very indifference speaking a nature in which there lurked no civilized hypocrisies and bland deceits. Wild he was; a very sight of sights to see; yet I began to feel myself mysteriously drawn towards him."—So they smoke together, and are clasped in each other's arms. The friendship is finally sealed when Ishmael offers sacrifice to Queequeg's little idol, Gogo.

"I was a good Christian, born and bred in the bosom of the infallible Presbyterian Church. How then could I unite with the idolater in worshipping his piece of wood? But what is worship?—to do the will of God—*that* is worship. And what is the will of God?—to do to my fellowman what I would have my fellowman do to me—*that* is the will of God."—Which sounds like Benjamin Franklin, and is hopelessly bad theology. But it is real American logic. "Now Queequeg is my fellowman. And what do I wish that this Queequeg would do to me. Why, unite with me in my particular Presbyterian form of worship. Consequently, I must unite with him; ergo, I must turn idolater. So I kindled the shavings; helped prop up the innocent little idol; offered him burnt biscuit with Queequeg; salaamed before him twice or thrice; kissed his nose; and that done, we undressed and went to bed, at peace with our own consciences and all the world. But we did not go to sleep without some little chat. How it is I know not; but there is no place like bed for confidential disclosures between friends. Man and wife, they say, open the very bottom of their souls to each other; and some old couples often lie and chat over old times till nearly morning. Thus, then, lay I and Queequeg—a cozy, loving pair—"

You would think this relation with Queequeg meant something to Ishmael. But no. Queequeg is forgotten like yesterday's newspaper. Human things are only momentary excitements or amusements to the American Ishmael. Ishmael, the hunted. But much more, Ishmael the hunter. What's a Queequeg? What's a wife? The white whale must be hunted down. Queequeg must be just "KNOWN," then dropped into oblivion.

And what in the name of fortune is the white whale?

Elsewhere Ishmael says he loved Queequeg's eyes: "large, deep eyes, fiery black and bold." No doubt, like Poe, he wanted to get the "clue" to them. That was all.

The two men go over from New Bedford to Nantucket, and there sign on to the Quaker whaling ship, the *Pequod*. It is all strangely fantastic, phantasmagoric. The voyage of the soul. Yet curiously a real whaling voyage, too. We pass on into the midst of the sea with this strange ship and its incredible crew. The Argonauts were mild lambs in comparison. And Ulysses went *defeating* the Circes and overcoming the wicked hussies of the isles. But the *Pequod's* crew is a collection of maniacs fanatically hunting down a lonely, harmless white whale.

As a soul history, it makes one angry. As a sea yarn, it is marvellous: there is always something a bit over the mark, in sea yarns. Should be. Then again the masking up of actual seaman's experience with sonorous mysticism sometimes gets on one's nerves. And again, as a revelation of destiny the book is too deep even for sorrow. Profound beyond feeling.

You are some time before you are allowed to see the captain, Ahab: the mysterious Quaker. Oh, it is a God-fearing Quaker ship.

Ahab, the captain. The captain of the soul.

> "I am the master of my fate.
> I am the captain of my soul!"

Ahab!

"Oh, captain, my captain, our fearful trip is done."

The gaunt Ahab, Quaker, mysterious person, only shows himself after some days at sea. There's a secret about him? What?

Oh, he's a portentous person. He stumps about on an ivory stump, made from sea-ivory. Moby Dick, the great white whale, tore off Ahab's leg at the knee, when Ahab was attacking him.

Quite right, too. Should have torn off both his legs, and a bit more besides.

But Ahab doesn't think so. Ahab is now a monomaniac. Moby Dick is his monomania. Moby Dick must DIE, or Ahab can't live any longer. Ahab is atheist by this.

All right.

This *Pequod,* ship of the American soul, has three mates.

1. Starbuck: Quaker, Nantucketer, a good responsible man of reason, forethought, intrepidity, what is called a dependable man. At the bottom, *afraid.*

2. Stubb: "Fearless as fire, and as mechanical." Insists on being reckless and jolly on every occasion. Must be afraid too, really.

3. Flask: Stubborn, obstinate, without imagination. To him "the wondrous whale was but a species of magnified mouse, or water-rat—"

There you have them: a maniac captain and his three mates, three splendid seamen, admirable whalemen, first class men at their job.

America!

It is rather like Mr. Wilson and his admirable, "efficient" crew, at the

Peace Conference. Except that none of the Pequodders took their wives along.

A maniac captain of the soul, and three eminently practical mates. America!

Then such a crew. Renegades, castaways, cannibals: Ishmael, Quakers. America!

Three giant harpooners, to spear the great white whale.

1. Queequeg, the South Sea Islander, all tattooed, big and powerful.

2. Tashtego, the Red Indian of the sea-coast, where the Indian meets the sea.

3. Daggoo, the huge black negro.

There you have them, three savage races, under the American flag, the maniac captain, with their great keen harpoons, ready to spear the *White* whale.

And only after many days at sea does Ahab's own boat-crew appear on deck. Strange, silent, secret, black-garbed Malays, fire-worshipping Parsees. These are to man Ahab's boat, when it leaps in pursuit of that whale.

What do you think of the ship *Pequod,* the ship of the soul of an American?

Many races, many peoples, many nations, under the Stars and Stripes. Beaten with many stripes.

Seeing stars sometimes.

And in a mad ship, under a mad captain, in a mad, fanatic's hunt.

For what?

For Moby Dick, the great white whale.

But splendidly handled. Three splendid mates. The whole thing practical, eminently practical in its working. American industry!

And all this practicality in the service of a mad, mad chase.

Melville manages to keep it a real whaling ship, on a real cruise, in spite of all fantastics. A wonderful, wonderful voyage. And a beauty that is so surpassing only because of the author's awful flounderings in mystical waters. He wanted to get metaphysically deep. And he got deeper than metaphysics. It is a surpassingly beautiful book. With an awful meaning. And bad jolts.

It is interesting to compare Melville with Dana, about the albatross. Melville a bit sententious.—"I remember the first albatross I ever saw. It was during a prolonged gale in waters hard upon the Antarctic seas. From my forenoon watch below I ascended to the over-crowded deck, and there, lashed upon the main hatches, I saw a regal feathered thing of unspotted whiteness, and with a hooked Roman bill sublime. At intervals it arched forth its vast, archangel wings.—Wondrous throbbings and flutterings shook it. Though bodily unharmed, it uttered cries, as some King's ghost in supernatural distress. Through its inexpressible strange eyes methought I peeped to secrets not below the heavens—the white thing was so white, its wings so wide, and in those for ever exiled waters, I had lost the miserable warping memories of traditions and of towns.—I assert then, that in the wondrous bodily whiteness of the bird chiefly lurks the secret of the spell—"

Melville's albatross is a prisoner, caught by a bait on a hook.

Well, I have seen an albatross, too: following us in waters hard upon the Antarctic, too, south of Australia. And in the Southern winter. And the ship, a P. and O. boat, nearly empty. And the lascar crew shivering.

The bird with its long, long wings following, then leaving us. No one knows till they have tried, how lost, how lonely those Southern waters are. And glimpses of the Australian coast.

It makes one feel that our day is only a day. That in the dark of the night ahead other days stir fecund, when we have lapsed from existence.

Who knows how utterly we shall lapse.

But Melville keeps up his disquisition about "whiteness." The great abstract fascinated him. The abstract where we end, and cease to be. White or black. Our white, abstract end!

Then again it is lovely to be at sea on the *Pequod,* with never a grain of earth to us.

"It was a cloudy, sultry afternoon; the seamen were lazily lounging about the decks, or vacantly gazing over into the lead-coloured waters. Queequeg and I were mildly employed weaving what is called a sword-mat, for an additional lashing to our boat. So still and subdued and yet somehow preluding was all the scene, and such an incantation of reverie lurked in the air that each silent sailor seemed reselved into his own invisible self.—"

In the midst of this preluding silence came the first cry: "There she blows! there! there! there! She blows!"—And then comes the first chase, a marvellous piece of true sea-writing, the sea, and sheer sea-beings on the chase, sea-creatures chased. There is scarcely a taint of earth,—pure sea-motion.

"'Give way men,' whispered Starbuck, drawing still further aft the sheet of his sail; 'there is time to kill fish yet before the squall comes. There's white water again!—Close to!—Spring!' Soon after, two cries in quick succession on each side of us denoted that the other boats had got fast; but hardly were they overheard, when with a lightning-like hurtling whisper Starbuck said: 'Stand up!' and Queequeg, harpoon in hand, sprang to his feet.—Though not one of the oarsmen was then facing the life and death peril so close to them ahead, yet their eyes on the intense countenance of the mate in the stern of the boat, they knew that the imminent instant had come; they heard, too, an enormous wallowing sound, as of fifty elephants stirring in their litter. Meanwhile the boat was still booming through the mist, the waves curbing and hissing around us like the erected crests of enraged serpents.

"'That's his hump. *There! There,* give it to him!' whispered Starbuck.—A short rushing sound leapt out of the boat; it was the darted iron of Queequeg. Then all in one welded motion came a push from astern,

while forward the boat seemed striking on a ledge; the sail collapsed and
exploded; a gush of scalding vapour shot up near by; something rolled and
tumbled like an earthquake beneath us. The whole crew were half-suffocated
as they were tossed helter-skelter into the white curling cream of the squall.
Squall, whale, and harpoon had all blended together; and the whale, merely
grazed by the iron, escaped—"

Melville is a master of violent, chaotic physical motion, he can keep up
a whole wild chase without a flaw. He is as perfect at creating stillness. The
ship is cruising on the Carrol Ground, south of St. Helena.—"It was while
gliding through these latter waters that one serene and moonlight night,
when all the waves rolled by like scrolls of silver; and by their soft, suffusing
seethings, made what seemed a silvery silence, not a solitude; on such a silent
night a silvery jet was seen far in advance of the white bubbles at the bow—"

Then there is the description of Brit. "Steering northeastward from the
Crozello we fell in with vast meadows of brit, the minute, yellow substance
upon which the right whale largely feeds. For leagues and leagues it
undulated round us, so that we seemed to be sailing through boundless fields
of ripe and golden wheat. On the second day, numbers of right whales were
seen, secure from the attack of a sperm whaler like the *Pequod*. With open
jaws they sluggishly swam through the brit, which, adhering to the fringed
fibres of that wondrous Venetian blind in their mouths, was in that manner
separated from the water that escaped at the lip. As moving mowers who,
side by side, slowly and seethingly advance their scythes through the long
wet grass of the marshy meads; even so these monsters swam, making a
strange, grassy, cutting sound; and leaving behind them endless swaths of
blue on the yellow sea. But it was only the sound they made as they parted
the brit which at all reminded one of mowers. Seen from the mast-heads,
especially when they paused and were stationary for a while, their vast black
forms looked more like masses of rock than anything else—"

This beautiful passage brings us to the appariation of the squid.

"Slowly wading through the meadows of brit, the *Pequod* still held her
way northeastward towards the island of Java; a gentle air impelling her keel,
so that in the surrounding serenity her three tall, tapering masts mildly
waved to that languid breeze, as three mild palms on a plain. And still, at
wide intervals, in the silvery night, that lonely, alluring jet would be seen.

"But one transparent-blue morning, when a stillness almost preternatural spread over the sea, however unattended with any stagnant calm; when
the long burnished sunglade on the waters seemed a golden finger laid across
them, enjoining secrecy; when all the slippered waves whispered together as
they softly ran on; in this profound hush of the visible sphere a strange
spectre was seen by Daggoo from the mainmast head.

"In the distance, a great white mass lazily rose, and rising higher and
higher, and disentangling itself from the azure, at last gleamed before our
prow like a snow-slide, new slid from the hills. Thus glistening for a

moment, as slowly it subsided, and sank. Then once more arose, and silently gleamed. It seemed not a whale; and yet, is this Moby Dick? thought Daggoo—"

The boats were lowered and pulled to the scene.

"In the same spot where it sank, once more it slowly rose. Almost forgetting for the moment all thoughts of Moby Dick, we now gazed at the most wondrous phenomenon which the secret seas have hitherto revealed to mankind. A vast pulpy mass, furlongs in length and breadth, of a glancing cream-colour, lay floating on the water, innumerable long arms radiating from its centre, and curling and twisting like a nest of anacondas, as if blindly to clutch at any hapless object within reach. No perceptible face or front did it have; no conceivable token of either sensation or instinct; but undulated there on the billows, an unearthly, formless, chance-like apparition of life. And with a low sucking it slowly disappeared again."

The following chapters, with their account of whale-hunts, the killing, the stripping, the cutting up, are magnificent records of actual happening. Then comes the queer tale of the meeting of the *Jereboam,* a whaler met at sea, all of whose men were under the domination of a religious maniac, one of the ship's hands. There are detailed descriptions of the actual taking of the sperm oil from a whale's head. Dilating on the smallness of the brain of a sperm whale, Melville significantly remarks—"for I believe that much of a man's character will be found betokened in his backbone. I would rather feel your spine than your skull, whoever you are—" And of the whale, he adds:

"For, viewed in this light, the wonderful comparative smallness of his brain proper is more than compensated by the wonderful comparative magnitude of his spinal cord."

In among the rush of terrible, awful hunts come touches of pure beauty.

"As the three boats lay there on that gently rolling sea, gazing down into its eternal blue noon; and as not a single groan or cry of any sort, nay not so much as a ripple or a thought, came up from its depths; what landsman would have thought that beneath all that silence and placidity the utmost monster of the seas was writhing and wrenching in agony!"

Perhaps the most stupendous chapter is the one called *The Grand Armada,* at the beginning of Volume III. The *Pequod* was drawing through the Sunda Straits towards Java when she came upon a vast host of sperm whales. "Broad on both bows, at a distance of two or three miles, and forming a great semi-circle embracing one-half of the level horizon, a continuous chain of whale-jets were up-playing and sparkling in the noonday air." Chasing this great herd, past the Straits of Sunda, themselves chased by Javan pirates, the whalers race on. Then the boats are lowered. At last that curious state of inert irresolution came over the whales, when they were, as the seamen say, gallied. Instead of forging ahead in huge martial array they swam violently hither and thither, a surging sea of whales, no longer moving on. Starbuck's boat, made fast to a whale, is towed in amongst this howling

Leviathan chaos. In mad career it cockles through the boiling surge of monsters, till it is brought into a clear lagoon in the very centre of the vast, mad, terrified herd. There a sleek, pure calm reigns. There the females swam in peace, and the young whales came snuffing tamely at the boat, like dogs. And there the astonished seamen watched the love-making of these amazing monsters, mammals, now in rut far down in the sea.—"But far beneath this wondrous world upon the surface, another and still stranger world met our eyes, as we gazed over the side. For, suspended in these watery vaults, floated the forms of the nursing mothers of the whales, and those that by their enormous girth seemed shortly to become mothers. The lake, as I have hinted, was to a considerable depth exceedingly transparent; and as human infants while sucking will calmly and fixedly gaze away from the breast, as if leading two different lives at a time; and while yet drawing moral nourishment, be still spiritually feasting upon some unearthly reminiscence, even so did the young of these whales seem looking up towards us, but not at us, as if we were but a bit of gulf-weed in their newborn sight. Floating on their sides, the mothers also seemed quietly eyeing us.—Some of the subtlest secrets of the seas seemed divulged to us in this enchanted pond. We saw young Leviathan amours in the deep. And thus, though surrounded by circle upon circle of consternation and affrights, did these inscrutable creatures at the centre freely and fearlessly indulge in all peaceful concernments; yea, serenely revelled in dalliance and delight—"

There is something really overwhelming in these whale-hunts, almost superhuman or inhuman, bigger than life, more terrific than human activity. The same with the chapter on ambergris: it is so curious, so real, yet so unearthly. And again in the chapter called *The Cassock*—surely the oldest [oddest?] piece of phallicism in all the world's literature.

After this comes the amazing account of the Try-works, when the ship is turned into the sooty, oily factory in mid-ocean, and the oil is extracted from the blubber. In the night of the red furnace burning on deck, at sea, Melville has his startling experience of reversion. He is at the helm, but has turned to watch the fire: when suddenly he feels the ship rushing backward from him, in mystic reversion.—"Uppermost was the impression, that whatever swift, rushing thing I stood on was not so much bound to any haven ahead, as rushing from all havens astern. A stark, bewildered feeling, as of death, came over me. Convulsively my hands grasped the tiller, but with the crazy conceit that the tiller was, somehow, in some enchanted way, inverted. My God! What is the matter with me, I thought!"

This dream-experience is a real soul-experience. He ends with an injunction to all men, not to gaze on the red fire when its redness makes all things look ghastly. It seems to him that his gazing on fire has evoked this horror of reversion, undoing.

Perhaps it had. He was water-born.

After some unhealthy work on the ship, Queequeg caught a fever and was like to die.—"How he wasted and wasted in those few, long-lingering days, till there seemed but little left of him but his frame and tattooing. But as all else in him thinned, and his cheek-bones grew sharper, his eyes, nevertheless, seemed growing fuller and fuller; they took on a strangeness of lustre; and mildly but deeply looked out at you there from his sickness, a wondrous testimony to that immortal health in him which could not die, or be weakened. And like circles on the water, which, as they grow fainter, expand; so his eyes seemed rounding and rounding, like the circles of Eternity. An awe that cannot be named would steal over you as you sat by the side of this waning savage—"

But Queequeg did not die—and the *Pequod* emerges from the Eastern Straits, into the full Pacific. "To my meditative Magian rover, this serene Pacific once beheld, must ever after be the sea of his adoption. It rolls the utmost waters of the world—"

In this Pacific the fights go on.—"It was far down the afternoon; and when all the spearings of the crimson fight were done; and floating in the lovely sunset sea and sky, sun and whale both died stilly together; then such a sweetness and such a plaintiveness, such inwreathing orisons curled up in that rosy air, that it almost seemed as if far over from the deep green convent valleys of the Manila isles, the Spanish land-breeze had gone to sea, freighted with these vesper hymns.—Soothed again, but only soothed to deeper gloom, Ahab, who has steered off from the whale, sat intently watching his final wanings from the now tranquil boat. For that strange spectacle, observable in all sperm whales dying—the turning of the head sunwards, and so expiring—that strange spectacle, beheld of such a placid evening, somehow to Ahab conveyed wondrousness unknown before. 'He turns and turns him to it; how slowly, but how steadfastly, his home-rendering and invoking brow, with his last dying motions. He too worships fire; . . .'"

So Ahab soliloquizes: and so the warm-blooded whale turns for the last time to the sun, which begot him in the waters.

But as we see in the next chapter, it is the Thunder-fire which Ahab really worships: that living sundering fire of which he bears the brand, from head to foot.—It is storm, the electric storm of the *Pequod,* when the corposants burn in high, tapering flames of supernatural pallor upon the masthead, and when the compass is reversed. After this all is fatality. Life itself seems mystically reversed. In these hunters of Moby Dick there is nothing but madness and possession. The captain, Ahab, moves hand in hand with the poor imbecile negro boy, Pip, who has been so cruelly demented, left swimming alone in the vast sea. It is the imbecile child of the sun hand in hand with the northern monomaniac, captain and master.

The voyage surges on. They meet one ship, then another. It is all ordinary day-routine, and yet all is a tension of pure madness and horror, the approaching horror of the last fight. "Hither and thither, on high, glided the snow-white wings of small unspecked birds; these were the gentle thoughts of the feminine air; but to and fro in the deeps, far down in the bottomless blue, rushed mighty leviathans, sword-fish and sharks; and these were the strong, troubled, murderous thinkings of the masculine sea—" On this day Ahab confesses his weariness, the weariness of his burden. "But do I look very old, so very, very old, Starbuck? I feel deadly faint, and bowed, and humped, as though I were Adam staggering beneath the piled centuries since Paradise—" It is the Gethsemane of Ahab, before the last fight: the Gethsemane of the human soul seeking the last self-conquest, the last attainment of extended consciousness—infinite consciousness.

At last they sight the whale. Ahab sees him from his hoisted perch at the masthead.—"From this height the whale was now seen some mile or so ahead, at every roll of the sea revealing his high, sparkling hump, and regularly jetting his silent spout into the air."

The boats are lowered, to draw near the white whale. "At length the breathless hunter came so nigh his seemingly unsuspectful prey that his entire dazzling hump was distinctly visible, sliding along the sea as if an isolated thing, and continually set in a revolving ring of finest, fleecy, greenish foam. He saw the vast involved wrinkles of the slightly projecting head, beyond. Before it, far out on the soft, Turkish rugged waters, went the glistening white shadow from his broad, milky forehead, a musical rippling playfully accompanying the shade; and behind, the blue waters interchangeably flowed over the moving valley of his steady wake; and on either side bright bubbles arose and danced by his side. But these were broken again by the light toes of hundreds of gay fowl softly feathering the sea, alternate with their fitful flight; and like to some flagstaff rising from the pointed hull of an argosy, the tall but shattered pole of a recent lance projected from the white whale's back, and at intervals one of the clouds of soft-toed fowls hovering, and to and fro shimmering like a canopy over the fish, silently perched and rocked on this pole, the long tail-feathers streaming like pennons.

"A gentle joyousness—a mighty mildness of repose in swiftness, invested the gliding whale—"

The fight with the whale is too wonderful, and too awful, to be quoted apart from the book. It lasted three days. The fearful sight, on the third day, of the torn body of the Parsee harpooner, lost on the previous day, now seen lashed on to the flanks of the white whale by the tangle of harpoon lines, has a mystic dream-horror. The awful and infuriated whale turns upon the ship, symbol of this civilized world of ours. He smites her with a fearful shock. And a few minutes later, from the last of the fighting whale boats comes the cry: " 'The ship! Great God, where is the ship?'—Soon they, through the dim, bewildering mediums, saw her sidelong fading phantom, as in the gaseous Fata Morgana; only the uppermost masts out of the water; while fixed by infatuation, or fidelity, or fate, to their once lofty perches, the pagan harpooners still maintained their sinking lookouts on the sea. And now concentric circles seized the lone boat itself, and all its crew, and each floating oar, and every lance-pole, and spinning, animate and inanimate, all round and round in one vortex, carried the smallest chip of the *Pequod* out of sight—"

The bird of heaven, the eagle, St. John's bird, the Red Indian bird, the American, goes down with the ship, nailed by Tastego's hammer, the hammer of the American Indian. The eagle of the spirit. Sunk!

"Now small fowls flew screaming over the yet yawning gulf; a sullen white surf beat against its steep sides; then all collapsed; and then the great shroud of the sea rolled on as it rolled five thousand years ago."

So ends one of the strangest and most wonderful books in the world, closing up its mystery and its tortured symbolism. It is an epic of the sea such as no man has equalled; and it is a book of exoteric symbolism of profound significance, and of considerable tiresomeness.

But it is a great book, a very great book, the greatest book of the sea ever written. It moves awe in the soul.

The terrible fatality.

Fatality.

Doom.

Doom! Doom! Doom! Something seems to whisper it in the very dark trees of America. Doom!

Doom of what?

Doom of our white day. We are doomed, doomed. And the doom is in America. The doom of our white day.

Ah, well, if my day is doomed, and I am doomed with my day, it is something greater than I which dooms me, so I accept my doom as a sign of the greatness which is more than I am.

Melville knew. He knew his race was doomed. His white soul, doomed. His great white epoch, doomed. Himself, doomed. The idealist, doomed. The spirit, doomed.

The reversion. "Not so much bound to any haven ahead, as rushing from all havens astern."

That great horror of ours! It is our civilization rushing from all havens astern.

The last ghastly hunt. The White Whale.

What then is Moby Dick?—He is the deepest blood-being of the white race. He is our deepest blood-nature.

And he is hunted, hunted, hunted by the maniacal fanaticism of our white mental consciousness. We want to hunt him down. To subject him to our will. And in this maniacal conscious hunt of ourselves we get dark races and pale to help us, red, yellow, and black, east and west, Quaker and fire-worshipper, we get them all to help us in this ghastly maniacal hunt which is our doom and our suicide.

The last phallic being of the white man. Hunted into the death of upper consciousness and the ideal will. Our blood-self subjected to our will. Our blood-consciousness sapped by a parasitic mental or ideal consciousness.

Hot-blooded sea-born Moby Dick. Hunted by monomaniacs of the idea.

Oh God, oh God, what next, when the *Pequod* has sunk?

She sank in the war, and we are all flotsam.

Now what next?

Who knows? *Quien sabe? Quien sabe, señor?*

Neither Spanish nor Saxon America has any answer.

The *Pequod* went down. And the *Pequod* was the ship of the white American soul. She sank, taking with her negro and Indian and Polynesian, Asiatic and Quaker and good, businesslike Yankees and Ishmael: she sank all the lot of them.

Boom! as Vachel Lindsay would say.

To use the words of Jesus, IT IS FINISHED.

Consummatum est!

But *Moby Dick* was first published in 1851. If the Great White Whale sank the ship of the Great White Soul in 1851, what's been happening ever since?

Post mortem effects, presumably.

Because, in the first centuries, Jesus was Cetus, the Whale. And the Christians were the little fishes. Jesus, the Redeemer, was Cetus, Leviathan. And all the Christians all his little fishes.

[A Third Look at Melville]

Van Wyck Brooks

So much has been written lately about "Moby-Dick" that I hesitate to bring the subject up again; but the beautifully clear and spacious pages of the new collected edition of Melville to which I referred last week have beguiled me into reading the book a third time, and I am wondering if all its felicities have dawned even yet on people's minds. It seems to me now less chaotic, better shaped, than it seemed at first: nothing has surprised me more than to discover how conscious Melville was of what he was doing. I had taken too seriously the statement with which he opens Chapter 82: "There are some enterprises in which a careful disorderliness is the true method"—or rather, I had not placed enough weight on this word "careful." It seemed to me intolerable that he had not removed the chapters on whales in general, on whaling, whales' heads, pitchpoling, ambergris, the try-works, etc., and published them separately: they were glorious, but I could not believe that they had been deliberately introduced to retard the action. It struck me that the action should have been retarded as it were within the story. I do not feel this now. The book is an epic, and an epic requires ballast. Think of the catalogue of ships in Homer, the mass of purely historical information in the "Æneid," the long descriptions in "Paradise Lost": how immensely these elements add to the density and the volume of the total impression, and how they serve to throw into relief the gestures and activities of the characters! This freight of inanimate or partially inanimate material gives "Moby-Dick" its bottom, its body, in the vintner's phrase; and I am convinced that Melville knew exactly what he was about.

It is only when we have grasped the nature of the book that we begin to perceive how cunning is its craftsmanship throughout. Of the larger lines I shall speak presently; but glance for a moment at the single episode of Father Mapple's sermon in the Whaleman's Chapel. Why is it that, once read, this episode seems to have built itself permanently into the tissues of our imagination? It is because of the skill with which Melville has excluded from our minds every irrelevant detail. He wishes, first, to establish the nautical character of the preacher, so he has him stoop down, after he has climbed into the pulpit, and drag up the ladder step by step, till the whole

Reprinted from "A Reviewer's Notebook," *Freeman* [New York] 7 (16 May 1923), 238–39.

is deposited within. This may have been taken from reality, for Father Mapple is known to have been drawn from Father Taylor, Emerson's friend, the apostle to the sailors in Boston. But Melville's skill here consists in not remarking that Father Mapple might have been boarding a ship: the image already conveys this connotation—Melville uses it to heighten our sense of the preacher's momentary "withdrawal from all outward worldly ties and connexions." This nautical character, moreover, is preserved by every detail of the sketch. When Father Mapple kneels and prays, his prayer is so deeply devout that he seems to be "kneeling and praying at the bottom of the sea." When he rises, he begins to speak "in prolonged solemn tones, like the continual tolling of a bell in a ship that is foundering at sea in a fog." This impression, once established, is maintained by the imagery of the sermon; but, to pass to another point, why do we remember the sermon so vividly? Partly because of the storm that is beating outside the chapel. We are never allowed to forget this storm. It shrieks and drives about us as we enter the chapel, it pelts the door from without, it howls between the hymn and the sermon, it appears to "add new power to the preacher, who, when describing Jonah's sea-storm, seemed tossed by a storm himself." The effect of all this is to redouble the solemn intimacy of the scene. The chapel is cut off from the world like the cabin of a ship; our minds are focused with an almost painful intensity upon the visible and audible facts that immediately surround us.

I have dwelt on this episode because it shows with what deliberate art Melville has ensnared his readers. To turn now to the work as a whole: how carefully, with what prevision, he has built up the general scheme: the pitch of the book, the "mystery" of the White Whale, the character of Captain Ahab. First of all, the pitch: with what a mighty rhythm the "Pequod" starts on its voyage:

> Ship and boat diverged; the cold, damp night breeze blew between; a screaming gull flew overhead; the two hulls wildly rolled; we gave three heavy-hearted cheers, and blindly plunged like fate into the lone Atlantic.

There we have the note of the saga; and this is consistently sustained by a dozen different means. Take the portraits of the three mates, Starbuck, Stubb and Flask, "momentous men" all; and the three fantastic harpooneers, the cannibal Queequeg, Tashtego, the Gay Head Indian, and Daggoo, the gigantic Negro. By a process of simplification that heightens their effect without removing it from reality, Melville invests these characters with a semblance as of Homer's minor heroes:

> Daggoo retained all his barbaric virtues, and erect as a giraffe, moved about the decks in all the pomp of six feet five in his socks. There was a corporeal

humility in looking up at him; and a white man standing before him seemed a white flag come to beg truce of a fortress.

[Tashtego.] To look at the tawny brawn of his lithe snaky limbs, you would almost have credited the superstitions of some of the earlier Puritans, and half believed this wild Indian to be a son of the Prince of the Powers of the Air.

This method of characterization, indeed, prevails throughout the book. Take the captain of the "Jeroboam," for instance:

A long-skirted, cabalistically cut coat of a faded walnut tinge enveloped him; the overlapping sleeves of which were rolled up on his wrists. A deep, settled, fanatic delirium was in his eyes.

We are living from beginning to end in a world by one degree larger than life. The constant mythological allusions, the sweep of the style, the bold splendour of the similes support this impression, till at last the battles with the whales begin and we feel beneath the book the very pulse of the ocean itself. "Give me a condor's wing!" Melville exclaims in the excitement of his inspiration. "Give me Vesuvius's crater for an inkstand!" And then he adds, proudly conscious of his achievement: "Such, and so magnifying, is the virtue of a large and liberal theme! We expand to its bulk. To produce a mighty book, you must choose a mighty theme."

No less extraordinary is the development of the legend of "Moby-Dick," of the sense of impending fatality. Towards the end it may be thought that Melville strains a point or two in order to produce this latter effect. I am thinking especially of the chapter in which the sea-hawk darts away with Ahab's hat; but the chapters on the "candles" and the needle are open to the same objection. There is an electrical storm and the corposants appear on the yardarms; and soon afterwards it is found that the compasses have been turned. All these phenomena are natural, but they are certainly exceptional; and, occurring so close together, they seem to me to overshoot their mark, which is, of course, to inform the reader that the calamitous whale is approaching. Machinery of this kind is much more in place in works like "The Ancient Mariner" that frankly embody supernatural elements. But consider, at the outset of the book, the apparition of Elijah. Consider that astonishing chapter on the whiteness of the whale. Consider the reports of Moby-Dick that come to us, one after another, from the sailors, from wandering sea-captains encountered during the voyage, from the mad Gabriel of the "Jeroboam," from the captain of the "Samuel Enderby" whose arm the monster has torn away as he tore away Ahab's leg. The fabulous whale torments our imagination till we, like Gabriel, think of him as "no less a being than the Shaker God incarnated"; and all this, be it noted, without a word of direct description on Melville's part. Until he reveals himself just before the chase, we see Moby-Dick solely through the consequences of his actions and the eyes of superstitious men.

I should like to linger over another aspect of the fabulous element of the book—fabulous but entirely consonant with reality. I mean the theme of the "five dusky phantoms" who appear midway in the story, suddenly surrounding Ahab and as if "fresh formed out of air." We get our first hint of their existence in the dark words of Elijah, when Ishmael and Queequeg encounter him near the wharf in the grey dawn:

> But he stole up to us again, and suddenly clapping his hand on my shoulder, said, 'Did ye see anything looking like men going toward that ship a while ago?'
>
> Struck by this plain matter-of-fact question, I answered, saying, 'Yes, I thought I did see four or five men; but it was too dim to be sure.'
>
> 'Very dim, very dim,' said Elijah. 'Morning to ye.'
>
> Once more we quitted him; but once more he came softly after us; and touching my shoulder again, said, 'See if you can find 'em now, will ye?'
>
> 'Find who?'
>
> 'Morning to ye! Morning to ye!' he rejoined, again moving off.

Later, on the voyage, Stubb remarks that Captain Ahab is always disappearing at night: "Who's made appointments with him in the hold? Ain't that queer, now?" These vaguely defined Orientals are satisfactorily accounted for as the story moves on; but they remain dim, and their presence and their dimness and the pale, opalescent light that emanates from them spread I can hardly say what magic through the book. It is to be observed, moreover, that all this fantasy in "Moby-Dick" has behind it everywhere a substantial fabric of fact: that is why we never feel that we are reading a romantic novel, why, even at the most extravagant moments, we accept every detail as veracious. There were actually to be seen, in the Nantucket of the 'forties, such figures as Queequeg and Fedallah, just as there were old "fighting Quakers, Quakers with a vengeance," lords of whales like Bildad and Peleg, with their "thousand bold dashes of character, not unworthy a Scandinavian sea-king, or a poetical pagan Roman." We can trace the whole story, trunk, branches and twigs, back to the scene out of which it springs, and which we feel between the lines, just as we can trace the Arabian genie back to Aladdin's lamp; and this, by enabling us to compare the fact with the treatment, inevitably and immensely heightens the effect of the latter.

Of Captain Ahab I should never stop talking if I once began. But here again, to recur to the aspect of the book upon which I have been dwelling, how admirable is Melville's power of construction. "Ahab's soul's a centipede that moves upon a hundred legs." So he himself asseverates, in the midst of the chase; and this character of a "mighty pageant creature, formed for noble tragedies" is developed and sustained with uncanny adroitness. First we are presented with the other captains who give us the scale of the Nantucket whale-masters in general. Then we see him through a cloud of strange rumors, and not till the ship is well at sea does he appear at all. Suddenly he emerges; he stands on the quarter deck, and Melville describes him minutely in a magnificent passage. Then he vanishes again, to remain omnipresent but only intermittently visible, the soul, the brain, the will of the ship, and in the end the embodiment of a bedevilled humanity. We are never permitted to become familiar with him: he is never mentioned, he never appears, indeed, save to the accompaniment of some superb phrase, some new majestic image. He is a "grand, ungodly, godlike man," a "good man—not a pious good man, like Bildad, but a swearing good man"; he is a "khan of the plank, a king of the sea, and a great lord of leviathans"; he "lives in the world as the last of the grizzly bears lived in settled Missouri." It can fairly be said that by the time the chase begins, Ahab is as mighty and terrible a figure in our minds as Moby-Dick himself. The two fabulous characters have grown, by similar means, side by side.

Much more might be said of the form of the book—of the shredded Shakespearean drama, for example, the scraps and fragments of which, among other diverse elements, have been pressed into the moving mass of the narrative. But I can not attempt to develop these points. "The great task of an artist," said Taine, "is to find subjects which suit his talent." Melville had this good fortune once and once only; but his masterpiece is worth more than libraries of lesser books. "Moby-Dick" is our sole American epic, no less an epic for being written in prose; and has it been observed that it revives in a sense the theme of the most ancient epic of the English-speaking peoples? Grendel in "Beowulf" might almost be described as the prototype of the White Whale. Was not Grendel also the symbol of "all that most maddens and torments, all that stirs up the lees of things, all truth with malice in it, all that cracks the sinews and cakes the brain, all the subtle demonisms of life and thought, all evil—visibly personified"?

[Melville's Lonely Journey]

[J. W. N. Sullivan]

Herman Melville is one of those writers who make it clear beyond all controversy that much of the apparatus of literary criticism which has been elaborated up to our time is fit only to deal with unessentials. In the greatest work of Herman Melville we are in the presence of a kind of literature where the "scientific" analysis of Taine would be solemn buffoonery, and where the delicate sensibility of Pater would be irrelevant. The principles for the formation of a proper literary taste, the principles so carefully expounded in old lectures on rhetoric, with their subdivisions of "character-drawing," "description," "style," and so on, tell us, when applied to Melville, nothing of the slightest consequence. "Who touches this book," said Whitman of his own, "touches a man." It is to that kind of literature that Melville's best work belongs. We are not in the presence of what is usually called a work of art, something that can be separated off from its author in the same way, although not to the same degree, as a scientific theory can be separated off from its originator. "Moby Dick" is not, as it has been so often called, the greatest of sea stories; it is not a vast, elaborate account of the hunting of a mighty and mysterious whale. It is an account of the mighty, mysterious, and troubled soul of Herman Melville.

It is possible that "Moby Dick" is a great work of art. Those wonderful descriptions of New Bedford, the Spouter Inn, Father Mapple's sermon, fair and foul weather at sea, the technique of whale-hunting, probably satisfy all the canons. And possibly there are some to whom Ahab, Starbuck and the rest of them are credible and satisfying sea heroes. But as the great whale grows more imminent even the most resolutely realistic reader must have strange qualms. Is this a ship, are these men, and is the great whale really a whale? Can anything which happens on a real sea evoke this dark, profound passion; make natural the terrible tension of this hardly controlled prose; justify these sudden soundings to depths of which we were unconscious? We realize that the great ocean itself and the leviathans that inhabit it are scarcely big enough to shadow forth the real deeps and the real monsters with which Melville is concerned. And the story, which perhaps seemed so clear, becomes a veil. Melville, we realize, is dealing with things that even great

Reprinted from "Herman Melville," London *Times Literary Supplement*, no. 1123 (26 July 1923), 493–94. Occasioned by publication of the Constable and Cape editions of Melville.

writers rarely touch; he is trying to say things which are not fully to be said. But it is only in so far as we have understood the inexpressible that we have read Melville.

There has been, we must suppose, a growth of consciousness in man. The journey from the sub-microscopic organism or the amœba, or whatever began it all, has been a very long one. And who can say what kinds of awareness, what other sorts of consciousness, were not implicit in those beginnings? Who can say what price we have paid for being what we are? Many men must be suspicious at times that these clear, adequate minds of ours extend very little beyond their usefulness, that they are, essentially, reasonably successful devices of accommodation. A premium has been put upon a part of us; a certain kind of environment has made incessant demands upon us. But we have grown to this, and it may be that we shall grow beyond it. It is unreasonable to suppose that the whole of us is exhausted by what we have now to be. And it seems, now and then, that a man appears in whom our fast-slumbering faculties have been stirred to a little life. He has a little escaped from the bond of circumstance; he can see, very dimly, shapes lurking in our featureless blackness. He sees our world differently; the happenings of life are differently pregnant for him. If he be a writer, this vision will give a curious quality to his writing: he will be trying to say something language was not invented to say, and it will only be in so far as our world affords symbols for what he has to say that he will be able to communicate with us. Even so, he may wait a long time for an audience.

The recent emergence of a large public for Melville's work, as testified by these collected editions, is one of the most interesting indications of the change which is taking place in the general mind. Melville's complete lack of popularity in his own time was due to the great dissimilarity between his personal vision and the general *Weltanschauung*. The world of the Victorians was hardly a mysterious world. Their material world was a perfectly clear-cut and comprehensible affair, and everything that was not material was merely moral. Every aspect of their world, as it seems to us now, was most strangely finite and most strangely clear; their most comprehensive schemes left out so much. Perhaps it was only in that age that the biological theory of evolution could have been welcomed as a world philosophy; when it was objected to, it was objected to as "degrading." Important people felt their dignity to be outraged, but the entire irrelevance of the theory to the central mystery of man himself seems hardly to have been remarked either by the antagonists or the supporters of the theory. The severer science of that time, splendid as it was, was equally naïve. "Matter," it was accepted everywhere, was the sort of stuff that made up the stone Dr. Johnson kicked—and obviously there was no mystery about that. To the kind of awareness possessed by Herman Melville it must have seemed that his contemporaries understood hardly anything. Even to us there is often something invisibly superficial about their outlook. They were islanders who lived unconscious of the sea. No murmur from far-off regions could reach their ears. The rumblings of "Moby Dick" were quite inaudible to them, and even that most mystical of composers, Beethoven himself, became somebody remarkable for the elevation of his style and the nobility of his sentiments. This is not to say that there were no exceptions. But to the general consciousness of that age Melville probably had less to say than he would have had in almost any other age, and certainly much less than he has to say to us. And it may be mentioned, incidentally, that the complete lack of comprehension he encountered was hardly a good thing for Melville. A kind of recklessness in fantasy, the growing lack of a sense of proportion, observable in Melville's later work, sprang, we think, from the complete lack of public understanding of his essential purpose. He became more and more content to make less and less effort to communicate to others the profundities of his inner life. It is not without significance that whereas "Moby Dick" is dedicated to Nathaniel Hawthorne, "Pierre" is dedicated to no human being, but to Greylock, the mountain near which Melville lived. And it is in "Pierre" that Melville shows a more bitter scorn for his contemporaries than it is good for a man, so little shallow, to have.

> So beforehand he felt the unrevealable sting of receiving either plaudits or censures, equally unsought for, and equally loathed ere given. So beforehand he felt the pyramidical scorn of the genuine loftiness for the whole infinite company of infinitesimal critics. His was the scorn which thinks it not worth the while to be scornful. Those he most scorned never knew it.

But worse things come of this lonely and implacable voyaging than loss of contact with one's fellows. As Melville says later, "But man does not give himself up thus, a doorless and shutterless house for the four loosened winds of heaven to howl through, without still additional dilapidations."

As we say, we think there has been a change in the general mind. It would seem that there is a *Zeitgeist* swaying peoples as a whole; it seems that man's consciousness develops, or at least acquires a new direction. Things which were dark become clear; there is a perpetual shifting up and down of great ones on their thrones; the region of the possible becomes enlarged, and more and more adventurous spirits are driven to peep over the edge of the world. In our own time we think that science has been the chief agent in liberating men from the clear but too finite world of the Victorians. There is a great difference between the random collocations of atoms which were supposed to produce us and the modern universe whose matter, space, and time, it appears, are largely creations of our own. Such ideas do not nestle isolated in the mind. They subtly modify the whole of a man's outlook; they make a sensitive surface where there was nothing but a blind integument; they create dim centres of vision for what was before total darkness. It is characteristic of our time that there is a sense of unprecedented possibilities;

the firm lines of our accustomed world are growing indistinct. In science and philosophy, chiefly, we feel that the soul of man has started on new adventures. We get glimpses of greater and perhaps more lonely seas than man has ever adventured on before. And although the general consciousness may have no more than the dimmest apprehension of what is being attempted, it is aware that something is afoot. It stirs, a little blindly, but not much more blindly than the most far-sighted man amongst us. These troubled waters may presage some great tidal movement, but no man can yet say what the direction will be. And we are now sufficiently tremulous, sufficiently sensitive, for that strange class of writers to which Melville belongs to be, not perhaps intelligible, but certainly not meaningless. We are aware of possibilities; man is once more a mystery to us, and a greater mystery than ever before. We feel that Melville's oceans and leviathans are credible symbols. That man hunts through a great deep who looks into himself.

It is in "Moby Dick" that Melville first became unintelligible to his age and valuable for ours. In his earlier writings the Melville who revealed himself in "Moby Dick" seems to be almost wholly absent. This cannot have been more than very slightly due to circumspection, to the reluctance of a young author to attempt a theme beyond his powers; we must suppose that a rapid, almost sudden, change occurred in Melville shortly before he undertook "Moby Dick." There is a letter to Hawthorne which bears out this surmise. We cannot, of course, know in any intimate way what happened, but such sudden liberations of a man's powers are by no means unprecedented. Thus Einstein has testified to the extraordinarily sudden release of his energies—"like a storm breaking loose"—which occurred in the year he composed his first paper on relativity. Until "Moby Dick" is reached, Melville is not, truth to tell, a very interesting writer. His South Sea stories and accounts of voyages have often extraordinary felicities of expression, but, unless we embark on a minute detective hunt, there is little of great interest in the mind revealed to us. As being what they profess to be, these earlier stories doubtless have merits, but they are not very pertinent to the real problem presented by Melville. Perhaps a partial exception should be made in the case of one of the worst constructed and most inchoate books that can ever have been written—"Mardi." In this extraordinary work the fantastic reflections, the laboured and wearisome satires, the clumsy humour, and the curiously naïve and extreme romanticism are the incoherent and, as it were, scattered manifestations of a mind which is merely flying loose. Perhaps no one could have said that there was real promise in "Mardi," and yet perhaps most people could find promise in it after knowing what Melville went on to do. It is interesting as showing how great was Melville's need of discipline. For him to gain true austerity and depth it was necessary for him to confine himself, as it were, within the limits of an iron scheme, to think out a coherent group of symbols within which he could give some sort of definite body and shape to his perceptions. This is magnificently realized in "Moby Dick," whose mechanism is by far the most comprehensive and flexible that Melville ever invented. In "Pierre" he may be concerned with something even profounder, but the mechanism is comparatively puerile. Even in "Moby Dick" Melville has his resting places. There are whole chapters where the hunt is abandoned, and Melville will discourse on species of whales or on methods of extracting spermaceti with a practical and sometimes incongruous realism. Melville was never fully in control of his own vision; he was always more dominated than dominating.

At the time of writing "Moby Dick" the problem that was always to haunt Melville was, as it were, fairly straightforward. The great white whale may be said to symbolize what some old theologians have called the evil principle of the universe. It is something which can be ignored; men need not encounter it. But there is an experience which comes to some men, and which Melville more than once likened to setting out alone on an uncharted sea, when this principle of evil, this sinister underside of things, becomes their dominating problem. One is irresistibly reminded of Dostoevsky's Polar expeditions, and his broodings over the problem of whether all things are lawful. To Melville the matter is, in a way, more simple. He does not doubt, at the time of writing "Moby Dick," the existence of the white whale; there is evil and there is good. It is clear to Melville that the spirit of man is at enmity with the whale. The horror of the thing to Melville is that he sees the whale will be victorious. Opposed to the whale is the giant heroism and resolution of Ahab, but in the person of Ahab Melville introduces another aspect of the general problem. Ahab is at the very pinnacle of human self-assertion against the vast and mystically apprehended forces which are at enmity with all human ideals. He is one of the few who have the courage and the insight necessary to be a champion of mankind. He is one whose unshakable strength of purpose fits him to be a hunter of the whale. It is a lonely, sad eminence, and it has its own danger. It brings with it a terrible pride. Again and again Melville stresses this Lucifer-like pride until we realize, in some subtle way, that it is Ahab's pride, as much as the awful power of the whale, which foredooms him to destruction. It would seem that Melville is here describing something which is profoundly true. Dostoevsky's hero, Stavrogin, who is also one of those who assert the human will against whatever else there may be, is also like Lucifer in his pride, and his pride contributes to his final destruction. So that the old religious warning against the danger of taking glory to oneself may contain a profound human experience. Melville's problem becomes less clear-cut in "Pierre," but already in "Moby Dick" there are foreshadowings of Melville's later perception of the confusing beauty of evil—a beauty which can lead one to doubt whether there is any real distinction between evil and good, and which led Melville to give "Pierre" the second title, "The Ambiguities." Melville's description of the whale, just before the final battle is joined, hints at this perplexing fascination:

> A gentle joyousness—a mighty mildness of repose in swiftness—invested the gliding whale. Not the white bull Jupiter swimming away with ravished Europa clinging to his graceful horns; his lovely, leering eyes sideways intent upon the maid; with smooth bewitching fleetness, rippling straight for the nuptial bower in Crete; not Jove, not that great majesty Supreme! did surpass the glorified White Whale as he so divinely swam. On each soft side— coincident with the parted swell, that but once leaving him, then flowed so wide away—on each bright side, the whale shed off enticings.

But although in "Moby Dick" the real voyage is a spiritual voyage, it is apparent that Melville is still interested in the objective world. To regard "Moby Dick" merely as a sea story is to misunderstand it, but it is true that it is incidentally incomparably the finest sea story in the language. Melville has a passion for the actual sea; the impulse that sent him voyaging as a young man has not yet completely ebbed. The infinite vagaries of the sea, every stick and board in a ship, are still dear to the still youthful Melville, the born sea-rover. No one else can communicate so overwhelming an impression of the boundlessness and profundity of the sea; no one else has floated so gently and tenderly in its azure calms. And this may explain his strange lingerings over what seems unessential to his main purpose. He catalogues with infinite zest all the species of whale. Every operation of a whale ship, from the fierce technique of the actual hunt to the messy labour of storing the blubber, is described by a loving hand. Almost reluctantly, it seems at times, he brings his stormy Ahab on the deck. But he had to obey his demon. There was that in him which looked into greater deeps than those of the ocean, and which knew vaster monsters than the whale. By the time Melville came to write "Pierre" he seems wholly concerned with the inner life. The disparity between the symbolism of this story and the meaning that Melville forces his symbols to carry is so great as to be occasionally ludicrous and even repulsive. An ardent young man who wishes to spare his father's name the stigma of having had an illegitimate daughter; the extravagant device, therefore, of pretending to marry his unacknowledged sister, rejecting the girl he had promised to marry and breaking his mother's heart—none of this produces the slightest illusion of reality. The book has been dismissed as unintelligible, as the work of a man too abnormal to be called sane. But it is sane enough. It is profound. But Melville, either perfunctorily or through that curious lack of a sense of proportion which he exhibits in all his writings, has tried to embody his thoughts in a vehicle which cannot contain them. Isabel, the unacknowledged sister, is Melville's last and subtlest presentment of the white whale. But Isabel, beautiful and mysterious, is as attractive as any angel of light. And perhaps the deepest point at which Melville had arrived is his conviction that it was the very nobility of Pierre, his faultless and unswerving grasp of the good, which led him to abandon Lucy and marry Isabel. Isabel is no siren; if she be the principle of evil, then evil is not to be distinguished from good. Is there good and evil? Melville seems to ask. Are we aware of anything but ambiguities? Isabel herself, so far as any human insight can pierce, is wholly good. In cleaving to her Pierre unfalteringly obeyed the god within him. And his end is the hopeless, pointless, irremediable destruction of himself and those he loves. The world is a lie, through and through a lie, is Melville's final conclusion. In this world it is hopeless to distinguish good from evil, or even to know whether there is any distinction. There is nothing but ambiguities. There is despair in this book and much bitter wisdom. Melville's lonely journey has taken him into a deeper and deeper night. There is no room here for heroic purpose or unyielding pride. For there is no foe, except in the sense that the whole context of things is at enmity with the soul of man, poisoning his virtue and giving heavenly radiance to his vice, entangling him in ambiguities, leaving him with nothing indubitable, no loyalties and no aspirations. It is a comfortless last word, but we must take Melville as we find him. He is one of the men who have adventured far; perhaps one has to go farther yet to find light. We are convinced that Melville's knowledge was no empty fantasy. He has a high place amongst those who adventure even if we believe, as we prefer to believe, that there are others who have adventured farther and passed through Melville's night.

[Melville's Magnificent Achievement]

Morley Roberts

In another place, when noting some of Hudson's favourite haunts, "some woods of Westermain" or an ancient city, I shall have to speak of his powers of historic vision which were allied to this mystic animism, and therefore shall not dilate upon it here. But I cannot leave this favourite book of mine without noting that it was to Hudson that I owed my first knowledge of Herman Melville and his magnificent achievement, *Moby Dick*. Often Hudson and I wondered how it was that the Americans still looked forward to some great American book when all they had to do was to cast their eyes backward and find it. Some day they will turn upon their path and see that in the cloud and mist which covered their passage they have missed one of their two great monuments of literature. It is obvious, of course, that *Moby Dick* is not flawless. There are pages of it in that fatal style which is not prose and yet has not the majesty of poetry, but when we contemplate it as a whole it has a strange unequalled power, an insight into character hardly to be surpassed by its grasp of great natural phenomena, and with all its terror there is also laughter. It is said to be a book of the whale. It is also a book of the ship and of the sea and of man, and Hudson knew it and learnt from it and spread its name.

Excerpted and reprinted from *W. H. Hudson: A Portrait* (New York: E.P. Dutton, 1924), 131.

[The Strength and Sadness of *Moby-Dick*]

JOHN FREEMAN

Moby-Dick is a novel, if it can be termed a novel, to consider in isolation. It is lifted above the rest of Melville's work as nobly as the flying sails above the sea.

Melville's characteristics faults, his digressions and his delays, are found in *Moby-Dick*, and are hardly less frequent than in most of his books; but they have little power to retard the reader. Even when he suspends the action, in order to discourse upon the technicalities of whaling, the suspension is not fatal; and though the symbolism is prominent, and readers are impatient of symbolism, it is not capable of marring the drama of Ahab and Moby-Dick, but rather heightens it. Subject and mood are perfectly matched, and since that "matching" is essential to drama, and the form needed here was not verse (as with *Pierre*) but supple, variable prose, he attained a simple and final felicity in the writing of *Moby-Dick*.

The subject calls out something new in him, a humour which most of his writing lacks and forbids. It is a rather sly, inconstant quality, but it is discovered as soon as the young whaler visits the inn frequented by whaling crews, and finds himself sharing a bed with the apparitional Queequeg, a tattooed savage, once a prince among cannibals, now an emblazoned harpooner with bald purplish skull. More conspicuous is it in the chapter toward the close of the story, when the "Pequod" hails the "Samuel Enderby", and the grimness of Ahab and his wild crew is dreadfully sharpened by contrast with the extravagant good spirits of the stranger. The height of Melville's great argument—which is Ahab's madness in challeng-ing the world for pride—is measured by the simple jolly humour of the English ship, a humour that the author might have borrowed from Marryat if he needed it. But it is not a humorous book, though there is this unfamiliar bright seam in the darkness of the mine. The story that Melville is possessed with is that of the whaler "Pequod", sailing on its last great voyage one Christmas Day under mad, morose Ahab, with Ishmael the chronicler on board, and a crew vividly presented one after another, Starbuck, Stubb and Flask, the harpooners, the sinister Parsee Fedallah and the inspired idiot Pip. They all alike speak with tongues that were never

Excerpted and reprinted from *Herman Melville* (London and New York: Macmillan, 1926), 114–29.

224

native to mortal men; every man's lips are at times prophetic, full of dark wisdom and pregnant philosophy; and all alike are subdued to their captain's imperious will. In an earlier voyage he had lost a limb in chasing the monstrous, almost mythical White Whale, Moby-Dick; and now, though his pretext is whale-hunting for profit, his real purpose is to destroy his enemy—Ahab and the whale, the prototypes of an eternal bloody strife between opposites. If you ask for a definition of these opposites, the answer is not very easy; they are, in one view, spirit against flesh, eternity against time; in another view, pride against pride, madness against madness, unreason against unreason. Indeed, the opposition is not an essential one, as Melville presents it; rather than a clashing of opposites there is a contest of rivals. One matches the other, man and whale are alike vindictive and remorseless; the same nature, the same necessity, urges both; the conflict has been set from the foundation of the world. Ever since the first fatal encounter, when he had lost his leg, "Ahab had cherished a wild vindictiveness against the whale, all the more fell for that in his frantic morbidness he at last came to identify with him, not only all his bodily woes, but all his intellectual and spiritual exasperations. The White Whale swam before him as the monomaniac incarnation of all those malicious agencies which some deep men feel eating in them, till they are left living on with half a heart and half a lung. That intangible malignity which has been from the beginning . . . all the subtle demonisms of life and thought"—it is this and these that haunt Ahab's heart as they haunt Melville; in the author they are subdued to a metaphysical view or half-view of the world, but in his Ahab they are freed and enlarged into domination.

> Of man's first disobedience and the fruit
> Of that forbidden tree whose mortal taste
> Brought death into the world and all our woe
> With loss of Eden—

this is Melville's theme as it was Milton's, but the name of the great enemy is not Lucifer, but Leviathan. The never-to-be-ended combat typified by Milton's Lucifer and Archangels is typified as boldly by Melville's Moby-Dick and Captain Ahab. Vindicating his pride against almightiness, Lucifer is overthrown but unsubdued; but vindicating his perverted spirit against a malignity not less perverse, Ahab is slain by the White Whale. The conflict is told in terms of whaling, and told with circumstance and detail that might obscure the greatness of the issue but for the intensity of passion and the exaltation of Ahab's hate: never is the spiritual encounter forgotten in the material. It is a parable of an eternal strife. You may read it as a mere narrative of wonders, you may read it as an allegory of the ancient war between spirit and sense, or between the simple lust of domination and the more primitive lust of strength and freedom; or as Mr. D. H. Lawrence has seen it, you may read it as a parable of another conflict, in which Moby-Dick is "the deepest blood-being of the white race; he is our deepest blood-nature. And he is hunted, hunted, hunted by the maniacal fanaticism of our white mental consciousness. . . . Hot-blooded sea-born Moby-Dick, Hunted by monomaniacs of the idea".

Into this many-rooted, many-branched conflict Melville has poured himself prodigally, spending his genius, his spirit, his strength upon the pursuit of the great theme. There is no question now of reserve and suppression; he has forgotten himself, he has identified himself with Ahab and the crew and the whale; his personality is submerged in the strife which he animates and informs with light. His own loneliness and loftiness of spirit, his communings, griefs and consolations—almost all that is expressed in his other books is here unexpressed but more subtly present. By an unlaboured, instinctive infusion he has passed into his creation, and is to be found there, not in words so much as in spirit. Imagination not simply as a faculty of picture and metaphormaking, but as a strong shaping spirit—it is this that he uses, obedient as a horse to his hand, and swift as a horse to bear him to his desire. Extravagancies might well be pardoned in speaking of *Moby-Dick*, but they are not necessary, for there is no other book with which to compare it. A sea narrative such as Dana's is lacking in the primary power of Melville's, for it is a story of externals only, nor can one say more for such an excellent invention as Mr. Kipling's *Captains Courageous*; and it is, nevertheless, only with what are conveniently called sea-stories that *Moby-Dick* can be compared, since the sea is no mere background, but is numbered among the *dramatis personae*. What, however, removes Melville's work from comparison is his particular kind of imagination, or the particular direction of his imagination. It is active not simply in the material, but also in the spiritual sphere; it is a spiritual and moral imagination of visible and invisible worlds. "Oh, what quenchless feud is this, that Time hath with the sons of men!" cried Melville, in *Pierre*; and whatever form it takes, under whatever figure it may be expressed, the feud is quenchless, and the sons of men are partners in it. The common feud between man and man, the rarer feud between man and men, the subtler feud between man and woman, Melville ignores these—most of all this last humorous and tragic feud, so often and so briefly reconciled—and so ignoring them, passes on to the deeper, universal feud of man with fate and infinity. Ahab against the White Whale, like against like, man against himself, infinite against infinite: under this aspect the conflict is heroic and desolate. The warmth of strife dies into the coldness of resistance, and stars mock the end.

Subordinate to this unique purpose there are a thousand strange and wonderful things floating in the sea of *Moby-Dick*. Never to be forgotten is the sermon preached by Father Mapple in the whaleman's conventicle. Preaching to whalemen and their black-liveried relicts, he preached such a sermon as Donne might have delivered to a people over whom the wrath of

God hung hawk-like visible. Sombre in dehortation, noble in its familiar wave-like rhythm, it has something peculiarly Melvillian in its doctrine. "Woe to him who seeks to please rather than to appal! Woe to him whose good name is more to him than goodness! Woe to him who, in this world, courts not dishonour! Woe to him who would not be true, even though to be false were salvation. . . . Eternal delight and deliciousness will be his, who coming to lay him down, can say with his final breath—O Father!— chiefly known to me by Thy rod—mortal or immortal, here I die. I have striven to be Thine, more than to be this world's, or mine own. Yet this is nothing; I leave eternity to Thee; for what is man that he should live out the lifetime of his God?" Never to be forgotten, again, are certain digressive chapters, such as that concerning the whiteness of the whale, where a single magnificent paragraph, buoyant and shining with a light like that of Shelley's *Prometheus Unbound*, becomes a prose hymn to whiteness, ending with fear and terror:—"and though among the holy pomps of the Romish faith, white is specially employed in the celebration of the Passion of our Lord; though in the Vision of St. John, white robes are given to the redeemed, and the four-and-twenty elders stand clothed in white before the great white throne, and the Holy One that sitteth there white like wool; yet for all these accumulated associations, with whatever is sweet, and honourable, and sublime, there yet lurks an elusive something in the innermost idea of this hue, which strikes more of panic to the soul than that redness which affrights in blood." True these digressions delay the progress of the story, and another episode is brought suddenly into the narrative, like a small craft swinging across the course of a great ship; but as nevertheless the crisis is slowly approached, digressions become less frequent, and nothing dulls the impact of that crisis upon the reader's sense and intelligence, nor obscures the metaphysical purpose. Indeed, there is something like design, the skill of a deliberate and consummate artist, in the effect produced by the recurring asides, the incidental excitements, the grave meditations, with which the latter half of *Moby-Dick* is diversified. Hamlet-like soliloquies, a Shakespearean idiot who breathes wisdom in his pleading fidelity, passages of the intensest dramatic value turning upon ordinary matters and vivifying the theme with continually fresh energy, these are not only singularly powerful in themselves; they are also powerful in their contributory effect. [1]

And of these scenes nothing is more wonderful and more overwhelming in its revelation of the native forces of the sea than the chapter "The Grand Armada"—a living Armada of whales herding in the Straits of Malacca and Sunda. Amid that strange, incredible multitude the "Pequod" was embayed at once, hunter and hunted; great regiments and infant nurseries, whales in friendly, fearless companies—"Like household dogs they came snuffling round us, right up to our gunwales.

*   *   *

The delicate side-fins, and the palms of his flukes, still freshly retained the plaited crumpled appearance of a baby's ears newly arrived from foreign parts." He is describing in this and succeeding pages the "subtlest secrets of the seas . . . surrounded by circle upon circle of consternations and affrights".

Scarcely more wonderful, but more terrible and overpowering to the imagination that mounts with Melville's as the last scenes are unmasked, is the final narrative of the three-days' chase of the White Whale. Thrice the whale is attacked by Ahab's insane vindictiveness; the boats are smashed, Ahab killed, and then the "Pequod", herself done to death by Leviathan, fades into the sea.

"Diving beneath the settling ship, the whale ran quivering along its keel

                *   *   *

then all collapsed, and the great shroud of the sea rolled on as it rolled five thousand years ago." [ch. 135]

Not the least attractive feature of this prodigious invention is the voluble and vivid detail in which the history and craft of whaling are set forth; for, as I have suggested, Melville's distinction lies partly in the fact that he inhabits contemporaneously two worlds. A recent book on whaling by Mr. Charles Boardman Hawes traces the development of the perilous trade, and bears constant witness, both direct and indirect, to the truth and comprehensiveness of Melville's accounts in *Moby-Dick*; page after page being cited to show what he can show better than any one else. Perhaps the most valuable instance is Mr. Hawes's account of the deliberate attack upon and sinking of a whaler by an infuriated whale, on 20th August 1851, only a few weeks before the publication of *Moby-Dick*; the intelligent deliberation of the whale that sank the "Ann Alexander", and the manœuvres of ship and whale, precisely remind a reader of the prolonged and cunning conflict that ended in the loss of the "Pequod".

But now the whaling industry is almost dead, the harpoons that Queequeg and Tashtego flung from the boats of the "Pequod" were ousted by a harpoon gun of 1864, that exploded within the helpless creature a phial of sulphuric acid; and few are the ships needed now. Mr. Hawes says that a short time ago he went to New Bedford to see the fitting-out of the "Wanderer", last of the big whalers, and lost in August 1924; "when first she slid down the ways she joined some of the very ships that lay in port when hesitating Ishmael of *Moby-Dick* first passed 'The Crossed Harpoons' and 'The Swordfish Inn'". The literality thus supported gives an additional value and fascination to Melville's narrative, for these minutiae of whaling practice do not merely make a background for the emotional synthesis, but also supply the interest which the young have always found in the story of the great White Whale.

Real strength, says Melville, never impairs beauty or harmony, but often bestows it; in everything imposingly beautiful, strength has much to do with that magic. It is *strength* that survives as the dominant impression of *Moby-Dick*, if you ask what personal characteristic is chief. Strength first, but sadness next. The man that has more of joy than sorrow in him, he declares, cannot be true. The Man of Sorrows was the truest of all men, the truest of all books is Solomon's, and Ecclesiastes the fine-hammered steel of woe. Against this conviction no one need inveigh; it is Melville's conviction, and it shapes the character and destiny of his mad and tragical Captain Ahab. Sadness is at the heart of the fated hunter, and in the secret mood of the mates and crew of his ship—the sadness that comes from thinking, not from mere indulged melancholy. The disease of thought has sailed with the "Pequod", creeping through the crew, making them bold and desperate, but never glad, and loosening, you might think, the very rivets of the ship until the mere spout of Moby-Dick had power to dismember and destroy it. The disease of thought had assailed Melville himself, the energy of imagination rose to resist it, and out of that prolonged, incensed struggle *Moby-Dick* was born.

The intangible malignity which has been from the beginning— Melville's phrase cannot but recall the work of a writer whom perhaps he never read, William Blake, the greatest of English mystics. But if Melville had never read Blake when he wrote *Moby-Dick* he had been gifted with somewhat of the same power of intuition and the same confidence in his intuition. He too has been called a mystic, and for once it may be admitted that the term is not improperly used. His whole apprehension of the world is mystical. He does not, like Blake, ignore the world, and never declares, as Blake did, that natural objects weaken, deaden and obliterate imagination in him. Nature means to Melville what it meant to another than Blake, to Wordsworth, whose apprehension of the unapparent was born of a steady gazing at the apparent. Susceptible as he was in an intense degree to the beauty and energy of natural phenomena, as *Moby-Dick* abundantly shows, that beauty and energy became as the screen through which he could endure to gaze at the Burning Bush. As was said a moment since, his Ahab is a Miltonic figure; but when we turn to Blake we can speak more precisely. In Blake's doctrine a central point is found in his assertion of a divine unity—even identity, God being seen as the original of Good and Evil alike, and Good and Evil two aspects of the one Power. Energy is Eternal Delight, is Blake's cry, and that is the avowed reverse of other gnomic perceptions, such as "Energy, called Evil, is alone from the Body; and Reason, called Good, is alone from the Soul". Obscure because of contradictions as so much of Blake needs must seem, his unmistakable brightness in essentials sheds a strong light on Melville's attitude, especially in his imagination of Captain Ahab. Ahab's cardinal sin is that of selfhood and single vision. He too might have mourned, in Blake's words:

> I will go down to self-annihilation and eternal death
> Lest the Last Judgement come and find me unannihilate,
> And I be seized and given into the hands of my own Selfhood.

It is the burning concentration upon his own injury by the White Whale, his proud vindictive passion, that draws Ahab down to self-annihilation. The Energy that is eternal delight became in him evil, but delight and evil are both from God.

This conviction, implicit in Ahab's story, is but a part of the grand idea which *Moby-Dick* presents half in light and half in cloud, in the long slow course of the narrative. Immanent and immutable, the divinity of the unseen is opposed to the unstable apparitional visible world; the unseen haunts Ahab and his officers and the crew of the fated "Pequod", and all alike, in that years-long isolation, are exposed to visitations of the invisible. Hence even the "unreasoning" carpenter, who perhaps had not a soul, had a subtle something within that kept him endlessly soliloquizing; Starbuck ponders an unfathomable loveliness in all that his eye beholds, and cries, "Let faith oust fact; let fancy oust memory; I look deep down and do believe"; while Stubb, still irrepressible, leaps fishlike "in that same golden light", the beauty and truth of which is derived from its hidden fountain in the unapparent. How can this one small heart beat, breathes Ahab, imploring the darkness, and this one small brain think thoughts, unless God does that beating, does that thinking, does that living, and not I? For God is in all and beneath all and over all the thoughts and deeds of the "Pequod", and slowly Ahab and his men have come to apprehend this wonderful, affrighting truth, taught by danger, solitude and silence during the long discipline of the voyage. Ahab is wiser in his madness than ever in his saneness, but his wisdom is defeated by his pride. He has seen God, but only as Lucifer might, from a deep inner hell. And his crew, too, have seen God (as masked by clouds), though with spirits not inflamed by the demonism that possessed their unhappy misleader.

If the doors of perception were cleansed, said Blake, everything would appear to man as it is—Infinite. To Ahab, with his exasperated perception, everything was infinite; and it seems that when Melville was looking back at his own whaling experiences, and seeing them through the eyes of his gigantically imagined Ahab, he saw everything as infinite. Nothing existed temporally or for itself, but all timelessly and in relation to an immanent Infinite. This "cleansed" perception was rare, but it endured during all the excitement of his writing of *Moby-Dick*. The matter of his speculations and his general proneness to metaphysics may have come as the result of his reading, though it was no philosopher, but a poet—Dante himself—who "opened to his shuddering eyes the infinite cliffs and gulfs of human mystery and misery", if his remark concerning Pierre Glendinning may be transferred to his own story. But his spiritual perception was not learned, it was native.

There is no evidence of any knowledge on his part of Blake's wild and exalted doctrines; few in England and probably none in America knew more than the name of Blake in 1851. But it has been commonly remarked that the great mystics are essentially at one in their vision, and it is because Melville depended not upon "the Daughters of Memory", but upon "the Daughters of Inspiration", that he saw what others saw, and uttered in the great imagination of *Moby-Dick* the apprehension which others have uttered in verse, prayer and picture.

Imagination, as Blake declares, is eternity, and it was in eternity that Melville's spirit moved when he wrote his greatest book.

When *Moby-Dick* was published in 1851 it was received with a little respect and a great deal of derision. In England the *Examiner* lamented the author's carelessness and wilfulness, and found nothing since Tom Thumb to compare with the last tragedy of Ahab and the Whale. There was so much more about whales than any human interest that the critic could but deplore the fact that a writer of such imagination and mastery of language should have committed himself to such an extravaganza. The *Athenæum*, hostile and voluble, would not even concede a point of style, but denounced Melville's mad rather than bad English, the *dénouement* of the story, the frenzy of invention, the rant and the ravings. Unlike Mr. Hawes, the *Athenæum* would not allow any value even as history to this unfortunate masterpiece. "Mr. Melville has to thank himself only if his horrors and his heroics are flung aside by the general reader, as so much trash belonging to the worst school of Bedlam literature, since he seems not so much unable to learn as disdainful of learning the craft of an artist." The craft of criticism, as I am here reminded, is not less difficult, and reproaches may be spared. But that Melville himself was discouraged is clear, and except in two shorter stories he never resumed the free powers of imagination that dictated *Moby-Dick*.

Note

1. "People have criticized *Moby-Dick* because it is formless and full of irrelevancies; but the truth is that the irrelevancies are an essential part of its form, and had Melville attempted to reduce the bounds of his universe to the scene required for a slick story of the sea, that universe would not have been the multitudinous and terrible thing he sought to create." *Aesthetics, a Dialogue.* By Lewis Mumford. (Privately printed at the Troutbeck Press, New York, 1925.)

Two Americans and a Whale

H. M. TOMLINSON

My two friends from New York looked out to the Thames from an upper window of the Savoy Hotel. I know that scene well. When I used to glance up from printer's proofs in an Adelphi office that same picture of the Thames, for six years, was the warning of something more lasting to any man inclined to attach undue importance to affairs that were temporal. The two Americans were evidently impressed. It was an autumn afternoon. The golden dusk over London conjured its buildings into the unsubstantial palaces of a city no man has ever reached, though we all seek it. That city lay beyond the foliage of the Embankment, and perhaps beyond Time itself; Cleopatra's monolith, in the near foreground, was the prominent black interrogation mark of our own wonder and surprise. The Thames itself was a gulf of light. The bridges which spanned it appeared to be at an immense height above the earth, as though they crossed from one cloud to another.

Naturally, I said nothing. I had nothing to say. If there was anything to be said, perhaps the Americans knew it. Besides, I felt that vision of London was theirs as much as mine. It was English, like Shakespeare's poetry; but oddly enough whatever is transcendently national belongs to the world. We may keep our parliamentary institutions, our coal mines, and cotton factories, and our rates of exchange, but the best that we have and do becomes the property of whoever can understand it. How can Americans claim their Revolution as their own? Its impulse at once entered into the body of English political thought and regenerated it. If you read the story of the Reform Bills in English history you will find it working there, and even then must remember that the impulse did not cease. Such impulses never do. Who could name the day when it became certain that there would be a Labor Government at Westminster?

*   *   *

The three of us began to discuss English and American writers. We were painfully polite to one another. We made free concession of our pawns, as it were, as though we did not wish to win the game. My friends submitted, and I freely confessed, the vitality and significance of the literary

Excerpted and reprinted from "Two Americans and a Whale: Some Fruits of a London Luncheon," *Harpers Magazine* [New York] 152 (April 1926), 618-21.

impulses in contemporary America. No doubt about that vitality. But they regretted that America could not match the old country yet with any star of the first magnitude—no Shelley, no "Ode to the Nightingale," no "Christabel," no *Pickwick Papers*; nothing of that size.

Heavens, I said to myself, what do these men want! What would they call a big star? My mind fumbled backwards to the 'fifties when, within a few years of one another, there appeared in the United States *Leaves of Grass, Walden,* and *Moby Dick*. Enough to satisfy any quiet community for a century! I glanced at my friends, thought I could see how it was, and therefore made bread pills, silently and respectfully. Evidently I was faced at this luncheon with a very fine exhibit of transatlantic modesty. They did not want me to feel sorry because England had nothing to show of quite the stamp of those three works. I was forced at last to congratulate my friends on their noble sacrifice of an impregnable position. No doubt could remain any longer of the friendship of the two Anglo-Saxon peoples. "If an Englishman," I assured them, "had told the story of the White Whale we should not pretend that we thought it of no more than the usual significance, not for all the Americans in America. And we could not have grown *Leaves of Grass* at all. Victorian England was simply incapable of it."

*   *   *

As for *Moby Dick*—but that is different. Even the young men who, half a century ago, looked upon *Leaves of Grass* as a happy release from the repellent materialism of their age and from the bondage of learning's formalities, saw Melville's masterpiece without understanding. How could they tell that it was one of the most important things that had happened in America since the Revolution? I do not find it easy to speak in moderation of that book. One might, as a reader, point out that it contains one of the best sermons ever written, that it reports a church service which is unique in English literature, that its pictures of ships and the sea make the best in other books look no more than happy and lucky photographs, that there are no such good stories of taverns and wayward men as Melville gives us outside books of the size of *Pickwick* and *Don Quixote*; that in its opening chapter it gets off the earth we know, so that when we are reading it for the first time we suspect that its author, though he begins in a glorious madness, yet must at once become sane and shrewd again, and hesitant, like the rest of us.

Yet no, Melville leaves the earth in the first chapter, the earth we know and accept, and maintains himself thereafter among the stars. If America had produced in its short life as a separate nation nothing but *Moby Dick*, that would be enough to justify her revolution and separation. We may say it is the greatest book of the sea in English literature; which, I suppose, means that it is the best in all literature. But that, we must remember, is because it is more than a book of the sea. The whale which was hunted by Captain Ahab and the men of Nantucket was a more wonderful quarry than all the oceans of this world could hold. That mythical whale left this earth and, a gigantic but elusive shadow, it led those men up among the very stars. The good ship *Pequod* navigated the constellations in pursuit of it and hurled spears, so to speak, at the Great Bear. Something like a long voyage! It is a book to put with the world's greatest. There are places in it which are like the soliloquies of Macbeth; and you know it is possible to argue that "Macbeth" is the best thing the English have done. I read only recently an American criticism of *Moby Dick* in which the courageous young man pointed out that Melville missed some opportunities for fine writing in the final chapters of his work. Melville could, for instance, have described the feelings of the sailors and the look of the whale as the final calamity swiftly approached. Ah! And if to some of us had come the chance of writing the "Moonlight Sonata," how different it would have been! And if only I myself could have daubed some red slabs across the sunset which my American friends witnessed from the Savoy Hotel one day, how much more remarkable London would have appeared to them!

"Why is it, then," asked one of the Americans, "that *Moby Dick* is only now being noticed? That book was forgotten till recently. Do you tell me a book as good as you say could have been overlooked without sufficient cause?"

Now that question is addressed to a mystery of the human mind. There has been such a change, in ten years, in the public consciousness that things in which once only odd men and women delighted have acquired a significance for the general. Where it was all dark, now most people may see something. Melville, in his own day, was addressing an intelligence which was hardly awake. To-day it is apprehensive.

[A Trilogy and a Crescendo]

Anonymous

This latest addition to the "English Men of Letters" series [John Freeman's *Herman Melville*] seeks to fulfil a crying need, being the first English book on perhaps the most astonishing literary figure of the last century. Professor Raymond Weaver led the way in America with his "Herman Melville, Mariner and Mystic"; and certainly Melville was a spiritual mariner, his sharp, peering eye ever on the human compass. The facts of the life are yet sparse, and several "tease the sense with unconfirmed significance," to quote from "Clarel," the interminable strange poem published toward the end of Melville's days. In "Pierre" he wrote that not to know gloom and grief is not to know anything an heroic man should learn: an aphorism that comes pat to the mind reflecting on Melville, who, as a thinker, is even more heroic than his valiant Ahab; and, like Paracelsus, at once longs to trample on and to save mankind. In his maturity he produced two great prose tragedies, "Moby Dick" and "Pierre," and a short one, "Bartleby" in the "Piazza Tales," works without parallel; and if Hawthorne spoke truth, there was a deep, dark tragedy in Melville's own life, for he could neither believe nor accept unbelief. He too strove angrily with God for a blessing and probed far into the mystery of iniquity.

August 1, 1919, was the hundredth anniversary of his birth, and from that hour, in the incalculable giddy dance of public favour and criticism, his renaissance as an author began: he literally arose from the dead to enchant and to puzzle the world. A thick harvest of reviews and articles followed promptly, the many rhetorical, a few hysterical, concerned in the main with "Moby Dick"; in fact, Melville was paraded and trumpeted as a one-book man, an author of romantic sea tales, who damned himself finally and drowned his genius in a metaphysical vat. The standard English edition of his works revealed another Melville, notably in "Mardi," "Pierre" and "Bartleby." His greatness, standing foursquare for inspection, appeared vast and obscure enough to promote a new literature; his life-work offered a labyrinth for anyone with sufficient temerity and patience to blaze paths here and there. One path only has been cleared and can be taken with a relative ease; and though Mr. Freeman, in his short study, glances to right and left, makes tentative steps, loiters with his eye on this and that sombre, entangled

Excerpted and reprinted from "Herman Melville," London *Times Literary Supplement*, no. 1268 (20 May 1926), 337.

byway, he is content generally to follow rather than boldly to lead, though he amplifies and extends the analysis of "Moby Dick," making skilful use of Blake's Good and Evil doctrines to help him by analogy in his exposition of that mighty human synthesis. Melville, however, reaching as he did to the opaque core of life, demands a critic as doughty and indomitable as his own Ahab; for he fascinates and imperils like the White Whale.

*　　　*　　　*

. . . Mr. Freeman ascribes Melville's so-called pessimism to a reaction of mind against the task of incessant composition: surely a trivial notion to account for an inborn and developed habit of mind, a predisposition of temperament, diffused throughout Melville's big works and affining him spiritually to Dante, Shakespeare, Ecclesiastes, Schopenhauer, Hartmann and the like masters of a profound and unflinching philosophy of life.

*　　　*　　　*

Mr. Freeman examines the works in detail, doing his duty as critic and expositor faithfully and well, until he comes to "Mardi"; and here, and specifically in "Pierre," either because his peculiar prejudice is too stubborn, or because his critical equipment is too narrow, he is less successful; and unquestionably his difficulties were great. He fails to see a trilogy and a crescendo in "Mardi," "Moby Dick" and "Pierre," and is therefore hampered at the outset; nor does a fear of or a distaste for metaphysics separate him from many of his fellows. He sees allegory in "Mardi," but will not allow its place in "Moby Dick" or in "Pierre," though he stresses the symbolism of the White Whale; and he has a plaguey suspicion that there may be something of the kind in the tragic story of young Glendinning.

*　　　*　　　*

Other readers may see in "Mardi" a prefatory review of human experience and endeavour and collapse, a survey of all philosophies and creeds and myths, at times reminding one of Flaubert's "Saint Antony"; in "Moby Dick" yet another search for the Absolute, limited by mundane law and leading to disaster; in "Pierre" a cosmic drama worked out in vividly human symbols involving enemy-impulses and the primordial urge of the whole universe.

When Herman Melville Was "Mr. Omoo"

JULIAN HAWTHORNE

My own apology for considering this work [John Freeman's *Herman Melville*] (aside from the courteous invitation from the Editor of THE INTERNATIONAL BOOK REVIEW), is that I knew Melville in the flesh. This, of course, is a distinction which few living persons share with me; he was in his thirty-second year and I in my sixth when our acquaintance was formed. And my last sight of him was in 1883, when he was sixty-four: he died in 1891, aged seventy-two. Our friendship lasted, then, for two and forty years, and would seem to imply that I ought to have known him well. On the other hand, long stretches of years passed during which we were removed from sight and sound of each other; and perhaps the period of my child-acquaintance with him might hardly be thought to count.

That last, however, is open to question. I have discovered, in looking back over my life, that the impressions of my childhood were very keen and particular; it is memories more recent that fade.

I can see plainly the man in the shaggy coat and bushy dark beard, ploughing his way through the snow, from Pittsfield, six miles away, to the door of our little red cottage on the brow of the hill overlooking frozen Lenox Bowl, and Monument Mountain beyond. He is companioned by a black Newfoundland dog, shaggy like himself, good natured and simple. Between our front door and the road intervenes a small yard, with a dark fir tree on either side of the path—(on a bough of one of which we had found that morning a little frozen bird that had missed its way in the southward flight of its kindred). Out steps my father, tall, dark-haired, heavy browed, with smiling blue eyes, to welcome the wayfarer's arrival; and my mother behind him, on the threshold, small, kind, gentle, incarnation of spontaneous goodness and joyful hospitality, with the eyes of an artist and a wise, tranquil brain. Soon my sister Una and I are fraternizing with the warm wet dog, on whose amiable back "Mr. Omoo," as we call him, sets us astride: the baby, Rose, is in her cradle within. We show our guest the grave of the dead bird, beneath the snow, dug in the frozen soil, from which we hope it will arise transfigured in the spring. Now we troop inside and fill the little sitting-room. We sit expectant, for we know that presently will begin the

Excerpted and reprinted from *Literary Digest International Book Review* [New York]4 (August 1926), 561–64.

tales, more affecting than those of Queen Scheherezade, of wild adventures in tropic seas and forests: of graceful brown girls and tattooed men, of strange festivals, banquets, combats, amid the hot scents, white sea-beaches and thundering reefs of the remote equator. There are dangers and doubts beneath the torrid sunshine and mysterious shadows; the tall palms sibilate overhead, there is peril in the dense thickets, as we glance aside at moments from the rhythmic dances and chantings, timed to the pulsations of our hearts, and drink the sweet, exciting liquor from the bowls that pass from hand to hand. Is that a serpent or a savage stirring stealthily in yonder obscurity? But lithe and lovely Fayaway rises and takes us by the hand, and we follow her to the inland pool, plunging into its coolness in her sparkling wake. The beauty of life banishes its misgivings.

Later, the bearded improvisatore with the strange, introspective eyes, withdraws with his tall host into the miniature chamber, in which were written "The House of Seven Gables" and the Wonder-Book tales, there to discourse, perhaps, of life and death, the destiny of the soul, the problems of the Infinite, and the peerings of German metaphysics. Hawthorne, the musing man of near fifty, has long since passed beyond the lure of these speculations; he speaks at need, only, at intervals and briefly, but with aim and depth; his guest pours forth his thoughts in a mingled torrent, with the eagerness of one seldom finding an adequate listener, questioning, surmising, rejecting, finding no secure footing between heaven and earth, wandering in a mirage which promises and deceives. Does not that grave figure opposite hold a secret in his keeping, which he will not disclose, which would correct fallacies and solve ambiguities?—or is he only a spectator of life, finding as much and as little mystery in the growing grass as in the riddle of the Sphinx?—saying, "These things are given, not to be explained, but to form and temper the receiver." And in the evening the restless pilgrim ploughs back to Pittsfield through the snow, with his faithful dog and his haunting problems, and falls to work once more upon his "gigantic conception of the White Whale."

The fascination of Mystery begins with the savage, and still besets the ultra-civilized man of science, and like the butterfly which the boy thought he has caught under his hat, it flutters unscathed away. The Ancients figured it as Proteus, of countless forms, but in essence unattainable: reason labors vainly on its trail forever; only unreasoning faith can overtake it, for faith is of its own brotherhood and quality, and is the Mystery of mysteries. But it is futile to preach such doctrine; unless it be born in the inmost deeps of the nature, it is alien and incomprehensible. No hand can be stretched to save the drowning man, who is already drowned.

One may guess that the situation between Hawthorne and his younger and impatient friend was somewhat like this; and some adumbration of it may be surmised in the tragic pursuit of Ahab after the Whale, and in Taji's of Yillah, in "Mardi," which seem to indicate that Melville had caught a fragmentary glimpse of his goal, but could not grasp it. The posture of his mind was amiss; repose and acquiescence were impossible to him; he must whirl with the planet, instead of abiding its turning. This lack of mental control was partly due to lack of early education and training; his physical adventures preceded his explorations in the realm of thought. But, more than that, the explanation of his failure lies in the insecurity of his mental structure itself.

Little is known of Melville's conditions in boyhood, but an uneasy mind rather than a genuine impulse to adventure was the cause of his leaving home, and once afloat he accomplished nothing, and after his return did nothing but write of what he had experienced. In spite of the excellence of the descriptive ability which he thus discovered in himself, at times rising to genius, he could not see that his proper function was description of things seen and known; he wanted to probe and solve the moral universe. For this, he was equipped neither by nature nor education, and he drifted upon the rocks. The catastrophe inflamed his malady, and brought it from latent to positive disease. His case was plainly pathological; he had already begun to succumb to it in the latter chapters of "Moby Dick," and in "Pierre" it became rampant. The ruin was accompanied by fitful blazings-up of passion and even of insight, which produce a powerful and even splendid impression, tho never an agreeable one; insanity must always be a painful spectacle, tho the normally hidden faculties may be at moments brilliantly in evidence, like explosions of gunpowder in a sinking hull. They achieve a sensation in the beholder, but it leads to nothing. It was otherwise with a mind such as Goethe's, which can pass untroubled through the visions of the Second Part of Faust: the fruits of his journey are a better understanding of human limitations and possibilities. Imagination holds its wholesome integrity, and knows its course.

*　　　*　　　*

Melville's own era appraised him justly enough. As long as he did good and sane work, he was widely read and extolled; when he fell to metaphysical rubbish, his audience turned to more agreeable books. Why should we be asked to share his crazy resentment at what was inevitable? I return to my appreciation of Mr. Freeman's conscientiousness, method and diligence; but discerning literary criticism does not weave ropes out of sand. Melville, in his young manhood, was a likable, even lovable man, and richly endowed as a writer: it was his infirmity, not his fault, that beguiled him into mistaking the true nature and limitations of his gifts.

[Prophetic Song in *Moby-Dick*]

E. M. Forster

Moby Dick is an easy book, as long as we read it as a yarn or an account of whaling interspersed with snatches of poetry. But as soon as we catch the song in it, it grows difficult and immensely important. Narrowed and hardened into words the spiritual theme of *Moby Dick* is as follows: a battle against evil conducted too long or in the wrong way. The White Whale is evil, and Captain Ahab is warped by constant pursuit until his knight-errantry turns into revenge. These are words—a symbol for the book if we want one—but they do not carry us much further than the acceptance of the book as a yarn—perhaps they carry us backwards, for they may mislead us into harmonizing the incidents, and so losing their roughness and richness. The idea of a contest we may retain: all action is a battle, the only happiness is peace. But contest between what? We get false if we say that it is between good and evil or between two unreconciled evils. The essential in *Moby Dick*, its prophetic song, flows athwart the action and the surface morality like an undercurrent. It lies outside words. Even at the end, when the ship has gone down with the bird of heaven pinned to its mast, and the empty coffin, bouncing up from the vortex, has carried Ishmael back to the world—even then we cannot catch the words of the song. There has been stress, with intervals: but no explicable solution, certainly no reaching back into universal pity and love; no "Gentlemen, I've had a good dream."

The extraordinary nature of the book appears in two of its early incidents—the sermon about Jonah and the friendship with Queequeg.

The sermon has nothing to do with Christianity. It asks for endurance or loyalty without hope of reward. The preacher, "kneeling in the pulpit's bows, folded his large brown hands across his chest, uplifted his closed eyes, and offered a prayer so deeply devout that he seemed kneeling and praying at the bottom of the sea." Then he works up and up and concludes on a note of joy that is far more terrifying than a menace.

> Delight is to him whose strong arms yet support him when the ship of this base treacherous world has gone down beneath him. Delight is to him who gives no quarter in the truth, and kills, burns and destroys all sin though he pluck it out from under the robes of Senators and Judges. Delight—

Excerpted and reprinted from *Aspects of the Novel* (New York: Harcourt, Brace, 1927), 199–203.

top-gallant delight is to him, who acknowledges no law or lord, but the Lord his God, and is only a patriot to heaven. Delight is to him, whom all the waves of the billows of the seas of the boisterous mob can never shake from this sure Keel of the Ages. And eternal delight and deliciousness will be his, who coming to lay him down, can say with his final breath—O Father!—chiefly known to me by thy rod—mortal or immortal, here I die. I have striven to be Thine, more than to be this world's or mine own. Yet this is nothing: I leave eternity to Thee: for what is man that he should live out the lifetime of his God?

I believe it is not a coincidence that the last ship we encounter at the end of the book before the final catastrophe should be called the Delight; a vessel of ill omen who has herself encountered Moby Dick and been shattered by him. But what the connection was in the prophet's mind I cannot say, nor could he tell us.

Immediately after the sermon, Ishmael makes a passionate alliance with the cannibal Queequeg, and it looks for a moment that the book is to be a saga of blood-brotherhood. But human relationships mean little to Melville, and after a grotesque and violent entry, Queequeg is almost forgotten. Almost—not quite. Towards the end he falls ill and a coffin is made for him which he does not occupy, as he recovers. It is this coffin, serving as a life-buoy, that saves Ishmael from the final whirlpool, and this again is no coincidence, but an unformulated connection that sprang up in Melville's mind. *Moby Dick* is full of meanings: its meaning is a different problem. It is wrong to turn the Delight or the coffin into symbols, because even if the symbolism is correct, it silences the book. Nothing can be stated about *Moby Dick* except that it is a contest. The rest is song.

[The Vastness of *Moby-Dick*]

John Erskine

It is usual to say that Herman Melville's *Moby Dick* is a unique story. It suggests nothing before it in American literature nor in European, and it has had no successful imitators. It makes upon the reader a peculiar emotional effect like that of no other book. But it is usual to say also that Melville was not, after all, a great writer. He couldn't repeat this success in other kinds of stories, or at least he never did, and even in *Moby Dick* his methods are often long-winded and crude. Both criticisms are easy for the reader to follow. The story grips us, and we know it is great, but when our attention is directed to minor flaws, we have to admit them.

The flaws, however, are very minor, and it is pedantic to worry over them in a masterpiece of the first order. What the adverse critic forgets to notice is that *Moby Dick* is not a novel, but a poem. Though written in prose it has the power of a great epic—that is, it gathers up our emotions around a central figure, a central incident, and one central mood. Those who read it as a novel might defend their approach by saying that the life of the whaler, and the manners and customs of Bedford and Nantucket are here portrayed faithfully, and that the humors and small details of ordinary life, on the whaler and ashore, are set down in the conversational tone of modern realism. Once convinced that the book is a novel, such readers proceed to find fault with those parts of it which by all standards of novel writing are weak and ineffectual. But if we begin the other way about and recognize first of all the poem in the book, we shall end as most critics now do, in admiration of the genius which could incorporate in a work of such magnificent beauty so much that is homely, whimsical, and matter-of-fact.

To call the book a poem is not a fantastic apology for it. We are beginning to realize that more than one American writer of the early periods left us so-called novels which make the effect of poetry—Cooper's *Deerslayer* is an illustration. But *Moby Dick* leads them all in the vastness of the impression it makes. In moments of enthusiasm we like to say that it is the greatest of sea stories. While we read, the ocean, all the oceans, seem to spread around us. In that immense space a handful of men hunt for one particular whale, one fish out of all the seas, and, terrible thought! we begin

Excerpted and reprinted from *The Delight of Great Books* (Indianapolis: Bobbs-Merrill, 1928), 223–33.

to understand that the great whale is hunting for one man on that one ship. Nothing can keep them apart. Here perhaps is an image of fate simpler and more awful than we can find in ancient story. Not peculiarly American, of course—rather a universal image. The American pictures in the book belong to the shore, to the ports of time and space from which these mariners come. On the sea the characters resolve into human nature, the horizons melt into infinity. One begins to reckon in broad terms by height and depth, and the purpose and the peril of the voyage begin to focus in the ancient poet's sentence, "There is that Leviathan."

*   *   *

What is the one large effect which this prose poem tries to make? Moby Dick, the white whale, is after all the focus of the story rather than the main subject of it. When you have read the book several times and it has begun to haunt your memory, you realize that the central theme of it is the sea—the sea, and all vast aspects of nature. In early American literature nature was more than once treated as a theme in itself, without regard to the spiritual meanings nature suggests. This direct treatment is rarer in modern literature than one might suppose. For many men nature is a language of morality, even a vehicle of divine revelation. Wordsworth found his moral evil and good in the impulses which flowers, fields and mountains gave him. Our own Emerson, from his earliest book to his latest essay, saw in nature glimpses of the Over-soul, aids to man's comfort and power, and a language with which he could talk. The unquestioned truth in these points of view sometimes blinds us to the fact that nature can also be enjoyed or studied for itself alone. It is true that the stars, the sea, the fields and the flowers furnish us a kind of scale against which to measure the human stature. Yet there are moments when we enjoy mountains or fields with no secondary meanings, when the greenness and the freshness of a spring day, or the silver of a moonlight night, enter our souls as an absolute experience. Fenimore Cooper excelled in rendering nature in this bare simplicity. He portrayed in Leatherstocking a man of high morals; but Leatherstocking's love of nature was not Wordsworth's. His character grew out of his early training— indirectly, that is, from books and from tradition. He went to nature only for an atmosphere which he loved, and in which he could feel at ease. The story of his retirement from the settlements, as the line of civilization advanced, and his retreat into the spaces of the prairie, is one of the most poetic renderings the world has of man's love of nature for herself alone.

The same love, though in a far more tragic key, permeates *Moby Dick*. In the very first pages it is suggested somewhat casually by the young narrator. "Call me Ishmael," he begins. Years ago, he tells us, having little money and finding nothing on shore to interest him, he decided to visit the watery parts of the world. Whenever civilization palled upon him, he learned to mend his soul by going to sea. What he got from his voyages was not a moral lesson in the ordinary sense; rather a spiritual new birth, from revisiting infinite space.

Many a poet through the centuries has turned to the sea as to one aspect of nature which seems to resist men's moralizing tendency. In the splendid close of *Childe Harold's Pilgrimage,* Byron emphasizes our inability to leave a trace on the waters. The shores keep the wreck of civilizations, and are scarred by human history; the waters are now as they were at the dawn of creation. Morally so, as well as physically. Our feeble philosophies of cause and effect seem thin indeed in an open boat, or on a fragile raft in mid-ocean. This absolute self-sufficiency of the waters is not easy to render in words. Cooper himself could not do it, however skilful he was in suggesting the infinite beauty of nature ashore. Conrad, our modern story-teller of the sea, is most successful when he shows us his heroes caught in a storm or a hurricane—that is, in some special and local manifestation of the waters which can be described as a problem for particular men at a special moment. But the awful stretch of waters in their normal state, rolling beyond eyesight, almost beyond reach of thought—this, few poets have rendered.

The surface of the ocean as we see it even from the deck of the comfortable liner, places beneath our eyes the mystery of space, that one infinity which besieges even the most materialistic kinds of thought. Space can have had no beginning, as it can have no end. Matter might be annihilated, but how can we do away with space? It can have no boundary in the universe, or we should be compelled to imagine something tangible and physical built up around it. Herbert Spencer and many less famous men have recorded the sort of terror which space inspires in the mind that broods upon it too long.

Something of this awful grandeur Melville has incorporated in his book, and it is his success in conveying this mood to the reader which sets him apart from other writers. The whale is the image of the sea, if you choose, of this mysterious and terrible space, but the sea is the image of nothing but itself, and after the last page is read, the picture which remains with us is of the undisturbed waters below which Ahab, the monster and the strong ship have disappeared for ever. Melville repeats this image of the vastness of the sea, playing variations on it, but letting us forget it in no part of the story.

[Melville and Dostoevski]

Grant Overton

It might be urged that here, too, the matter-of-fact reader can have his way, that he can read *Moby Dick* purely as the story of a whaling voyage with an exciting chase of the White Whale brought to the height of climax, the whole marred or improved, according to his taste, by much lore of the sea and more lore of whaling. This is evidently in the mind of E. M. Foster when he begins a brief discussion with the remark: "*Moby Dick* is an easy book, as long as we read it as a yarn or an account of whaling interspersed with snatches of poetry." But, in fact, has anybody ever been able to read it in that fashion? Probably not. The great length of the book, the extent to which it is interpenetrated by fantasy, the nature of that fantasy, make it seem extremely improbable that the rationally-interested or literal-minded ever persevere to the end. Doubtless such readers read skippingly; perhaps the other class of readers also skip, each accepting what the other puts aside. But the difference must be that to the one sort, Melville's book is an exasperating way of acquiring facts about one of mankind's disused occupations; to the rest of us, it is all manner of things else.

So many, indeed, that there is no exact agreement upon them. Mr. Forster would have it that *Moby Dick* is one of a few specimens to which he attaches the term "prophecy."

*   *   *

Who are the prophets? Mr. Forster names four—Dostoevski, Emily Brontë, D. H. Lawrence, and Melville. Tracing cause and effect from ground denied to him, we may feel a further distinction possible and desirable. Is there not a considerable distinction between Dostoevski and Melville, on the one hand, and Emily Brontë and D. H. Lawrence on the other? The extreme rational mind, called upon to define the difference, might make short work of it by saying that the Russian and the American were more than a little mad, whereas the Englishwoman and Englishman were queer—more than a little queer, no doubt, but still within sanity. We can feel the difference, in a sense less narrow, but our definition can hardly be so glib. Dostoevski and Melville, we may affirm, have nothing whatever to do with realism—do we

Excerpted and reprinted from *The Philosophy of Fiction* (New York: D. Appleton, 1928), 228–31.

not feel it to be so? Their ships, rooms, *personæ*, waters and skies, in spite of a certain attentiveness toward the facts of normal vision, are charged with a strangeness of contour, texture, behavior like the strangeness of Blake's art. "Mr. Blake," said his devoted wife, "is always in Paradise." We cannot say that Dostoevski and Melville are always in Paradise, but we are sure that it is because they have not escaped from Hell, or are yet lingering in Purgatory. Dantes, every one of them; they differ from the Italian chiefly in not being cumbered with theological cosmogony, the materials of ordinary life will do. The materials of ordinary life, but distorted by the pressures of truly extraordinary experience, so that when we gaze upon the least thing in the way of furniture in their stories we have the profound uneasiness of Father Brown in one of Chesterton's tales, the deep disturbance because—it may be only a chair or a table—"the shape is wrong."

The shape is always wrong, in the work of these writers, for the procurance of anything like realism in their fiction. But we scarcely feel that this is true of others whom Forster brackets with them. It is not true—is it?—of the background or the foreground in *Wuthering Heights*, nor is it exactly true of much in D. H. Lawrence; the strangeness of *Women in Love* or *The Plumed Serpent* or *Kangaroo* is grounded on a realism with which we have no trouble; it is this realism, in fact, that excessively annoys some readers of Lawrence, for if they could get rid of it, they could be rid of him, they feel.

But the Dostoevskis and the Melvilles have no more realism than children and poets and angels. They are concerned with the invocation of Deity, although they may feel an epiphany to be impossible. Their mood is one of awful certainty even where it is without expectation; they are apocalyptic, tranced. No longer able to instance the *deus ex machina,* they are unforgetful that *deus in machina movet*; and while most of mankind are become unable to see the god for the machine, they can scarcely perceive the machine for the god agitating it, to them visibly and constantly. Their reports of the machine are somehow unrecognizable, their realism is confronted by Reality. And all their fiction moves toward an apotheosis, or a series of apotheoses, of the Divine Will.

[Like *Wuthering Heights*]

Virginia Woolf

*W*uthering Heights again [like *War and Peace*] is steeped in poetry. But here there is a difference, for one can hardly say that the profound poetry of the scene where Catherine pulls the feathers from the pillow has anything to do with our knowledge of her or adds to our understanding or our feeling about her future. Rather it deepens and controls the wild, stormy atmosphere of the whole book. By a master stroke of vision rarer in prose than in poetry people and scenery and atmosphere are all in keeping. And, what is still rarer and more impressive, through that atmosphere we seem to catch sight of larger men and women, of other symbols and significances. Yet the characters of Heathcliff and Catherine are perfectly natural; they contain all the poetry that Emily Brontë herself feels without effort. We never feel that this is a poetic moment, apart from the rest, or that here Emily Brontë is speaking to us through her characters. Her emotion has not overflowed and risen up independently, in some comment or attitude of her own. She is using her characters to express her conception, so that her people are active agents in the book's life, adding to its impetus and not impeding it. The same thing happens, more explicitly but with less concentration, in *Moby Dick*. In both books we get a vision of presence outside the human beings, of a meaning that they stand for, without ceasing to be themselves. But it is notable that both Emily Brontë and Herman Melville ignore the greater part of those spoils of the modern spirit which Proust grasps so tenaciously and transforms so triumphantly. Both the earlier writers simplify their characters till only the great contours, the clefts and ridges of the face, are visible. Both seem to have been content with the novel as their form and with prose as their instrument provided that they could remove the scene far from towns, simplify the actors and allow nature at her wildest to take part in the scene. Thus we can say that there is poetry in novels both where the poetry is expressed through the characters and again where the poetry is expressed not so much by the particular character in a particular situation, like Natasha in the window, but rather by the whole mood and temper of the book, like the mood and temper of *Wuthering Heights* or *Moby Dick* to which the characters of Catherine or Heathcliff or Captain Ahab give expression.

Excerpted and reprinted from "Phases of Fiction," *Bookman* [New York] 69 (June 1929), 408–9.

247

In *A la Recherche du temps perdu,* however, there is as much poetry as in any of these books; but it is poetry of a different kind. The analysis of emotion is carried further by Proust than by any other novelist; and the poetry comes, not in the situation, which is too fretted and voluminous for such an effect, but in those frequent passages of elaborate metaphor, which spring out of the rock of thought like fountains of sweet water and serve as translations from one language into another. It is as though there were two faces to every situation; one full in the light so that it can be described as accurately and examined as minutely as possible; the other half in shadow so that it can be described only in a moment of faith and vision by the use of metaphor. The longer the novelist pores over his analysis, the more he becomes conscious of something that forever escapes. And it is this double vision that makes the work of Proust to us in our generation so spherical, so comprehensive. Thus, while Emily Brontë and Herman Melville turn the novel away from shore out to sea, Proust on the other hand rivets his eyes on men.

[Pure Allegory]

JOHN GOULD FLETCHER

It is customary among literary critics to devote attention to Melville's remarkable style, and to stress the point that Dostoevsky's major novels are nothing but glorified detective stories. It is true that Melville possessed a style that in its measured eloquence was the equal and sometimes the superior of his models, De Quincey and Sir Thomas Browne, and that—at its best—makes the style of Hawthorne shrivel into insignificance. It is true also that all of Dostoevsky's great works centre about a commonplace murder, and that he uses the most elementary devices of suspense and horror to heighten our interest about this murder. But the significant thing is that neither Melville's long purple passages, surcharged with descriptive power, by which he makes you see every detail of his scenes in an unearthly light, nor Dostoevsky's interminable hysteric conversations, in which each of his characters tries in turn to lay bare the inmost criminal secret of his or her soul, are anything more than skilful devices to set out the heart of the subject, which is in both cases the complete, candid, and terribly disillusioned revelation of the workings of the naked and helplessly-entangled human soul. Both carried pure character-creation to a point beyond that which any other writer has attempted, except perhaps Shakespeare in "Hamlet"; and both, like Shakespeare in "Hamlet," were obsessed by their characters, and obsessed above all by the "mystery of iniquity," the infinite perversion and moral deformity of humankind.

It is possible to show how this is so only by a direct comparison of the masterpiece of both men. "The Brothers Karamazov" is outwardly, at least, the story of the murder of a wealthy landowner by his sons. But a moment's examination of the character of old Karamazov, the landowner in question, will convince us that no such man as old Karamazov could possibly exist in actual flesh. He transcends all human limitations. He is not only a coarse wine-bibber,and an avaricious miser with his money, like Dostoevsky's own father, but an unbridled sensualist, a cynic, a sentimentalist, and a buffoon—none of which Dostoevsky's father ever was. He is, in short, an encyclopædia of all Russian vices, is in fact, a symbol of that Old Russia which Dostoevsky saw had to be put to death. And as such, he triumphs in

Excerpted and reprinted from *The Two Frontiers: A Study in Historical Psychology* (New York: Coward-McCann, 1930), 260–66.

249

life and death over his sons. The oldest, Ivan, who is also the noblest, sees his faith in God and man destroyed by the monstrous conduct of his father, and goes insane; the second, Dmitri, follows a crooked path of sensuality and sentimentality, but is redeemed by some traits of generosity for which he has to suffer; the youngest of all, Alyosha, fancies that he has gained redemption and become "a new man" by entering a monastery, but in the end has to admit that he too is in essence "Karamazov." The actual murder is consummated by Smerdyakov, the unacknowledged offspring of Karamazov himself and a gutter-drab; he hangs himself, and Dmitri has to suffer the penalty. The end of the book leaves Dostoevsky questioning alike human and divine justice; there is no solution, except perhaps in suffering, and the shout of "Hurrah for Karamazov!" with which the story closes, may conceal an even deadlier irony.

Melville's "Moby Dick" is very different as regards setting, but its import is even more clear. Here we have what purports to be the story of a whaling-cruise. But in fact the story from beginning to end is pure allegory, thinly disguised with masses of irrelevant detail about whales and whaling. Moby Dick, the White Whale, whose killing is the special aim of the ship's cruise, is nothing but a symbol: a symbol of the unearthly, unconquerable, superhuman—and after all is said and done, strangely beautiful—power of evil. He exists in every sea of the world, but it is precisely in the "Pacific," in the heart of a noonday calm, that he is found. He has been sighted before, but never without disaster; has been hunted by others, but has always escaped. Captain Ahab, master of the ship that is now seeking him, has been disabled by him, in a previous encounter, having lost one leg. This Captain Ahab is Melville's symbol of the human will in its highest and most courageous aspect; the human will that, not having been able to conquer evil by fair means, in direct battle, now strives to do so by unhallowed ones. By a stroke of superb genius, Melville makes him master even of the souls of simple savages; his three chief harpooners are respectively a South Sea Islander, a Negro, and an American Indian. His control over his three mates, all of whom represent some shade of manly courage, is also practically absolute. Moby Dick is duly hunted, and destroys the ship and Ahab alike in a scene whose magnificence of prose and mounting terror alike have no parallel in anything written by man. The only person who has foreseen the inevitable tragedy is an idiot boy, to whom no one pays attention; the only one who survives it is the outcast, Ishmael, who tells the story.

Here, too, the parallel with Shakespeare is inevitable. As Dostoevsky recalls "Hamlet," and in part "Othello," so Melville recalls the Shakespeare of "Macbeth" and "King Lear." If we can suppose a Lear endowed with superhuman force, who instead of wandering out upon the heath and raving, feeds his insanity with the steady thought of revenge, and at last sets out, backed by others, to accomplish it, we get in this Lear a complete picture of Ahab. He is undaunted, so long as his ship lasts, ready to match weapons with God Himself. Only when his ship goes down before the battering onrush of the superhuman power behind Moby Dick does Ahab momentarily give way; and then but to recover and hurl another unavailing harpoon at his antagonist. Ship and captain alike go down in the struggle, and the last thing seen is a topmast pennon floating above the waters, with a sky-hawk entangled in its folds: "And so the bird of heaven with his whole captive form enfolded in the flag of Ahab, went down with his ship which, like Satan, would not sink to hell till she had dragged a living part of heaven along with her, and helmeted herself in it." "Then all collapsed and the great shroud of the sea rolled on as it rolled five thousand years ago." To the problem of evil Melville has no more an answer, then, than Dostoevsky. He can but suggest that if evil conquers, it is so much the worse for God who lets evil conquer; a solution to which Dostoevsky might have answered in the words of Kirillov in "The Possessed," that God in that case was dead, and man must become God. That Melville adds his favourite tag "all is vanity," to this conclusion would seem to Dostoevsky an impertinence. "We have to live nevertheless," he might have retorted; a fact poor Melville often neglected to take into account.

Before Melville arrived at this conclusion, that the world was more evil than good, he too had striven to portray the ideal human type of his dreams. Jack Chase in "White Jacket" (who is significantly made an Englishman) is the apotheosis of Melville's type; the bluff, hearty, pleasant Anglo-Saxon blend of Pagan and Puritan. Perhaps it was his own wavering between England and America (where the bluff, hearty, pleasant type is but too frequently in practice a hypocrite and a bully to boot) that made Melville select for his life's loyalty, this sort of being, and not continue his search into the deeper waters of the human soul; certainly it was his own reticent prudery in sexual matters—a prudery not shared by the great Russian with whom his name is here linked—that made him hesitate before what must have been the final statement of his problem. What that statement might have been, "Pierre" exists to show; Melville in the end meant to portray evil as seductive but ruinous, and good as purely negative and helpless. The public would have none of this, and Melville decided to keep silent about the dangerous secret of his own philosophy. That he did not continue to write was America's second great disaster in the field of culture; following on the Civil War, it was a double fatality scarcely paralleled elsewhere, and certainly not in Russia. But in his transformation of the realistic adventure story into the "allegory of Good and Evil" Melville perhaps pointed the way to American authors as yet unborn.

LITERARY INFLUENCES
AND AFFINITIES
◆

A Whale Laboratory

CHARLES ROBERTS ANDERSON

Unfortunately, since the logbook of the *Acushnet* for 1841–1845 has not yet been found, little is known of this cruise from official records.* Indeed, a search for the facts behind *Moby-Dick* would perhaps be as misguided as it would be futile. Biographers and critics have in general contented themselves with an examination of the style of the book and an interpretation of its symbolism. As others have pointed out, Melville undoubtedly went to Sir Thomas Browne, Rabelais, and many others as his masters, and he may have drawn even his original inspiration and theme, as has been suggested, from the brief narrative of John Reynolds, "Mocha Dick or the White Whale of the Pacific," published in 1839.[1] It is interesting to discover in this connection that, although the white whale itself has usually been treated as symbolical rather than real, there is at least one account of the actual capture of a white whale, which lends probability to Melville's supposedly fanciful creation:

> As a whaler, the Platina won considerable fame by taking the only pure white whale that was ever captured. One hot day in August, 1902, the old bark, under command of Captain Thomas McKenzie, of New Bedford, was rolling along in the lazy swell of the Atlantic in about 35 north latitude and 53 west longitude, her voyage half over, when whales were sighted. Three boats were lowered, which made for a large sperm whale. The whale sounded and was down a long time. When he came up, he was near the vessel. Captain McKenzie, who was at the masthead on the bark, saw that it was a pure white whale; the first he had ever seen in his thirty years whaling experience. The men in the boats were, fortunately, not aware of the fact, for sailors have a superstitious dread of white whales. . . .
>
> Sperm whales of great age have been taken that were spotted with white, and with the under part of their heads entirely white, but the Platina's whale was pure white from head to tail. Captain McKenzie, from his lofty station, could see the whale under water nearly half a mile away.
>
> One may follow all the works of fiction and histories of whaling and he

Excerpted and reprinted from *Melville in the South Seas* (New York: Columbia University Press, 1939), 36–46. Reprinted by permission.
*The abstract log of the *Acushnet* was subsequently discovered in the National Archives, Department of Agriculture, by Wilson Heflin and Jay Leyda (ed. note).

will not find of [sic] any white whale having been killed by a whaleman, excepting in Herman Melville's novel, "Moby Dick." To the mate of the bark Platina, Andrew W. West, therefore, belongs the honor of having killed the only pure white sperm whale ever caught.[2]

The present study, however, is more concerned with Melville's technique of composition than with vague resemblances of style, or with possible inspirations and confirmations of his subject matter. A brief glimpse into his whale laboratory, therefore, should prove instructive, not so much for the purpose of discovering literary sources as for the opportunity of watching the composer at his work. With the scholarly display of a serious antiquarian and cetologist, Melville lists in the "Extracts" that preface Moby-Dick no less than fourscore authorities—scientific, historical, and literary—upon which he drew, remarking subsequently: "Nor have I been at all sparing of historical whale-research when it has seemed needed."[3] For specimens of this research, it will be sufficient to examine two whaling chronicles, which he cites in the text as well as in the "Extracts."

J. Ross Browne's Etchings of a Whaling Cruise could not have failed to attract Melville's attention and approval, for, in addition to its reliable information, it strikes a congenial note in the preface: a plea to better the condition of seamen in the whale fishery as Dana's book had done for the merchant marine. This theme of reform runs throughout the volume in a series of grievances and complaints which sounds the burden of Typee, Omoo, and White-Jacket, as well as Moby-Dick. For example, Browne, who sailed from Fairhaven, July 19, 1842, on a whaling cruise to the Pacific in the Styx, recounts an occasion when his captain had fleeced some South Sea natives of a boatload of wood; and with the indignation of Typee he declares:

It is treatment like this that renders the natives treacherous and hostile. There has been more done to destroy the friendly feelings of the inhabitants of islands in the Indian and Pacific Oceans towards Americans, by the meanness and rascality of whaling captains, than all the missionaries and embassies from the United States can ever atone for.[4]

Mistreatment of the sailors themselves he condemns with equal vigor in a passage which brings to mind the first part of Omoo:

While visiting the ports [of the Pacific] for the purpose of recruiting, the crews of whale ships are often found in a state of lax discipline; both captains and crew take this opportunity to lay their complaints before the consuls, who are much troubled with them, and frequently at a loss to understand and pass upon the merits of the case. The crews usually complain of bad provisions, short allowance, and bad usage; in some cases, I have heard them assert that they felt their lives in danger from the outrageous conduct of the captain; and in one instance even the officers joined in the complaint. The captain, on the other hand, believed that there was a conspiracy on foot to poison him.

Many Americans are found on the different islands, who have been turned ashore from whale ships, or left because they have broken their liberty a single time, near the end of the voyage.[5]

At Zanzibar the difficulties on board Browne's ship came to a head. Driven to desperation by hard fare and brutal treatment, the seamen decided to desert in a body. The mutiny was poorly planned, however, and the captain succeeded in starving his oppressed crew into submission, although Browne, with the aid of the American consul, procured a substitute and left the ship on June 1, 1843.[6] These extracts, which read like passages culled from the darker pages of *Typee* and *Omoo*, lend color to Melville's extraordinary recital of similar experiences; and, even if they did not serve as actual sources for him in writing, they at least prompted his memory and fired his resentment. In a digression of some ten pages, mixed with these complaints against the whale fishery, Melville might also have found the theme of his *White-Jacket* anticipated:

It is a disgrace to the American flag that the barbarous system of flogging, now permitted in our vessels, has not long since been abolished. A glorious navy is ours; a glorious whaling fleet have we when such a system is suffered to exist. What a spectacle of Republican perfection we present to the world!

. . . We have now a naval aristocracy the most arrogant and despotic, perhaps, in the world. We have a whaling marine in which cruelty and despotism are fostered with special care. . . .

[And he concludes:] There is no class of men in the world who are so unfairly dealt with, so oppressed, so degraded, as the seamen who man the vessels engaged in the American whale fishery.[7]

Etchings of a Whaling Cruise, moreover, furnishes matter more pertinent to the actual text of *Moby-Dick* than this mere similarity of purpose and attitude. In this volume Melville must have found much whale-lore— history, anatomy, and anecdote—that was admirably suited to his needs. For example, the yarn of the murdered sailor, which Browne relates under the caption of "Bob Grimsley's Ghost," may have been the germ of Melville's "Town-Ho's Story," for both are concerned with a deadly feud between a mate and a seaman, resulting in a near-mutiny, and both are prefaced by description of a "gam" on shipboard—a get-together between the crews of two ships that pass each other at sea.[8] Further, the constant bickering and frequent rows between the captain and the first mate on board the *Styx* parallel the running feud that Melville describes between Captain Ahab and Starbuck; indeed, the episodes actually ended similarly on both ships, for Browne's captain put his mate ashore at one of the Seychelles Islands for refusing to submit to his tyranny, whereas the mate of the *Acushnet* had a fight with his captain and went ashore at Payta, Peru, as Melville himself records, though he does not bring the quarrel to this climax in *Moby-Dick*.[9]

Again, more specifically, Browne's description of "cutting in and trying out"—the process of extracting the oil from the whale's blubber—corroborates Melville's and gives proof, if any be needed, that he was writing authentically of the technique of whaling.[10] For such facts, of course, Melville had no reason to resort to printed authorities. But there are several scenes sketched in this connection that show a striking similarity between the two authors. Browne, for example, gives a picture of the crew feasting at night, while the oil is being "tried out":

> About the middle of the watch they get up the bread kid, and, after dipping a few biscuit in salt water, heave them into a strainer, and boil them in oil. It is difficult to form any idea of the luxury of this delicious mode of cooking on a long night-watch. Sometimes, when on friendly terms with the steward, they make fritters of the brains of the whale mixed with flour, and cook them in the oil. These are considered a most sumptuous delicacy. Certain portions of the whale's flesh are also eaten with relish, though, to my thinking, not a very great luxury, being coarse and strong. . . . [But he confesses] I have eaten whale-flesh at sea with as much relish as I ever ate roast-beef ashore.[11]

Melville shows an equal interest in "The Whale As a Dish." When the second mate indulges his "unprejudiced" appetite in a supper of steak cut from the small of the whale, Melville stops to comment:

> That mortal man should feed upon the creature that feeds his lamp, and, like Stubb, eat him by his own light, as you may say; this seems so outlandish a thing that one must needs go a little into the history and philosophy of it. . . .
>
> The fact is, that among his hunters at least, the whale would by all hands be considered a noble dish, were there not so much of him; but when you come to sit down before a meat-pie nearly one hundred feet long, it takes away your appetite. Only the most unprejudiced of men like Stubb, nowadays partake of cooked whales.
>
> . . . But the spermaceti itself, how bland and creamy that is; like the transparent, half jellied, white meat of a cocoa-nut in the third month of its growth, yet far too rich to supply a substitute for butter. Nevertheless, many whalemen have a method of absorbing it into some other substance, and then partaking of it. In the long try-watches of the night it is a common thing for the seamen to dip their ship-biscuit into the huge oil-pots and let them fry there awhile. Many a good supper have I thus made.
>
> [Then follows the final delicacy.] In the case of a small Sperm Whale the brains are accounted a fine dish. The casket of the skull is broken into with an axe, and the two plump, whitish lobes being withdrawn (precisely resembling two large puddings), they are then mixed with flour, and cooked into a most

delectable mess, in flavor somewhat resembling calf's head, which is quite a dish among some epicures; and every one knows that some young bucks among the epicures, by continually dining upon calves' brains, by and by get to have a little brains of their own, so as to be able to tell a calf's head from their own heads; which, indeed, requires uncommon discrimination. [12]

The only noticeable difference between the two accounts is a difference in attitude, Browne being the more straightforward and unblushing epicure. Perhaps the Ganesvoort–Melville palate gagged at the public confession of a relish for whale steak; and perhaps the philosopher of 1851 could not forego a sly thrust at the epicure of 1841, so forcefully recalled to his mind by Browne's description.

A second scene on this same night reveals a more significant debt that Melville owed to *Etchings of a Whaling Cruise*. Browne's account follows:

A "trying-out" scene is the most stirring part of the whaling business, and certainly the most disagreeable. . . . We will now imagine the works in full operation at night. Dense clouds of lurid smoke are curling up to the tops, shrouding the rigging from the view. The oil is hissing in the try-pots. Half a dozen of the crew are sitting on the windlass, their rough, weather-beaten faces shining in the red glare of the fires, all clothed in greasy duck, and forming about as savage a looking group as ever was sketched by the pencil of Salvator Rosa. The cooper and one of the mates are raking up the fires with long bars of wood or iron. The decks, bulwarks, railing, try-works, and windlass are covered with oil and slime of black-skin, glistening with the red glare from the try-works. Slowly and doggedly the vessel is pitching her way through the rough seas, looking as if enveloped in flames. . . . The idlers . . . entertain themselves spinning yarns, singing songs, etc., and calculating the time by the moon.

. . . A trying-out scene has something peculiarly wild and savage in it; a kind of indescribable uncouthness, which renders it difficult to describe with anything like accuracy. There is a murderous appearance about the blood-stained decks, and the huge masses of flesh and blubber lying here and there, and a ferocity in the looks of the men, heightened by the red, fierce glare of the fires, which inspire in the mind of the novice feelings of mingled disgust and awe. But one soon becomes accustomed to such scenes and regards them with the indifference of a veteran in the field of battle. I know of nothing to which this part of the whaling business can be more appropriately compared than to Dante's pictures of the infernal regions. It requires but little stretch of the imagination to suppose the smoke, the hissing boilers, the savage-looking crew, and the waves of flame that burst now and then from the flues of the furnace, part of the paraphernalia of a scene in the lower regions. [13]

Here, again, in his workshop-reading Melville evidently found the inspiration for one of his most brilliant passages. For this unpretentious sailor's memorandum reads strikingly like the rough draft of the unforgettable

chapter in which Melville likens the "Pequod" to a fire ship at sea; but if
Browne's picture gave the cue, it was Melville's magic that wrought the
transformation from the merely pictorial to the dramatic:

> By midnight the works were in full operation. We were clear from the
> carcase; sail had been made; the wind was freshening; the wild ocean darkness
> was intense. But that darkness was licked up by the fierce flames, which at
> intervals forked forth from the sooty flues, and illuminated every lofty rope in
> the rigging, as with the famed Greek fire. The burning ship drove on, as if
> remorselessly commissioned to some vengeful deed. So the pitch and
> sulphur-freighted brigs of the bold Hydriote, Canaris, issuing from their
> midnight harbours, with broad sheets of flame for sails, bore down upon the
> Turkish frigates, and folded them in conflagrations. . . . Like a plethoric
> burning martyr, or a self-consuming misanthrope, once ignited, the whale
> supplies his own fuel and burns by his own body. Would that he consumed his
> own smoke! for his smoke is horrible to inhale, and inhale it you must, and
> not only that, but you must live in it for the time. It has an unspeakable,
> wild, Hindoo odour about it, such as may lurk in the vicinity of funereal
> pyres. It smells like the left wing of the day of judgment; it is an argument
> for the pit. . . .
>
> The hatch, removed from the top of the works, now afforded a wide
> hearth in front of them. Standing on this were the Tartarean shapes of the
> pagan harpooneers, always the whale-ship's stokers. With huge pronged poles
> they pitched hissing masses of blubber into the scalding pots, or stirred up the
> fires beneath, till the snaky flames darted, curling, out of the doors to catch
> them by the feet. The smoke rolled away in sullen heaps. To every pitch of the
> ship there was a pitch of the boiling oil, which seemed all eagerness to leap
> into their faces. Opposite the mouth of the works, on the further side of the
> wide wooden hearth, was the windlass. This served for a sea-sofa. Here
> lounged the watch, when not otherwise employed, looking into the red heat
> of the fire, till their eyes felt scorched in their heads. Their tawny features,
> now all begrimed with smoke and sweat, their matted beards, and the
> contrasting barbaric brilliancy of their teeth, all these were strangely revealed
> in the capricious emblazonings of the works. As they narrated to each other
> their unholy adventures, their tales of terror told in words of mirth; as their
> uncivilized laughter forked upward out of them, like the flames from the
> furnace; as to and fro, in their front, the harpooneers wildly gesticulated with
> their huge pronged forks and dippers; as the wind howled on, and the sea
> leaped, and the ship groaned and dived, and yet steadfastly shot her red hell
> further and further into the blackness of the sea and the night, and scornfully
> champed the white bone in her mouth, and viciously spat round her on all
> sides; then the rushing *Pequod*, freighted with savages, and laden with fire,
> and burning a corpse, and plunging into that blackness of darkness, seemed
> the material counterpart of her monomaniac commander's soul.[14]

Certainly no one, not even Browne himself could carp at an appropriation
handled in such a masterly manner. But it is such dramatic passages as these,

tacitly presented as autobiography, that have misled Melville's biographers. For it was at the conclusion of this scene that Melville declared: "Uppermost [in my mind] was the impression, that whatever swift, rushing thing I stood on was not so much bound to any haven ahead as rushing from all havens astern"—a declaration frequently quoted as the true explanation of "Why Ishmael Went to Sea."[15]

Finally, the portrait that Browne draws of his tyrannical captain may have served in some measure as the prototype of Melville's mad commander, Ahab. In both instances, the authors had their curiosity aroused by the rapturous, awe-stricken terms in which the owners of the two ships had spoken of their captains; and, in both instances, these same captains prolonged the suspense by failing to appear on deck until the ships were well at sea. When finally revealed, the commander of the *Styx* was at least imposing enough to have struck fire from Melville's imagination as he read:

> Picture to yourself a man . . . [of] cold blue eyes, and a shrewd, repulsive expression of countenance; of a lean and muscular figure, rather taller than the ordinary standard, with ill-made, wiry limbs, and you have a pretty correct idea of Captain A——. . . . When he gave orders, it was in a sharp, harsh voice, with a vulgar, nasal twang, and in such a manner as plainly betokened that he considered us all slaves of the lowest cast, unworthy of the least respect, and himself our august master.

To readers of *Moby-Dick,* the figure that Melville has created of moody, stricken Ahab—who "looked like a man cut away from the stake, when the fire has overrunningly wasted all the limbs without consuming them," and who "stood before them with a crucifixion in his face, in all the nameless regal overbearing dignity of some mighty woe"—is distinctly reminiscent of "Captain A——" in more than the provocative initial.[16] And the latter's speech to his crew, in which he lays down the program of his despotism, brings to mind the stirring scene when Ahab musters his crew and in a fiery speech pledges them to the fulfillment of his mad vengeance against Moby-Dick.[17] Perhaps the whaling world had many overbearing masters who might have served as models for Melville, but the captain of the *Styx* is at least a fair specimen of what he had to draw from, though Ahab himself towers above them all by reason of the monomaniacal obsession that motivates his tyranny.

Sometimes in the composition of *Moby-Dick* Melville worked even closer to his originals than has been demonstrated thus far. "I know of only four published outlines of the great Sperm Whale," he says, and of these "by great odds, Beale's is the best." Thomas Beale's *Natural History of the Sperm Whale* is undoubtedly the handbook that Melville found most useful in his "historical whale-research." Here he found an ample sketch of the whaling industry from its inception with numerous quotations from the older chroniclers, a detailed anatomy and an authoritative natural history of the sperm whale, and a full account of the art of whaling as demonstrated on a typical voyage. A single sample—on the history, nature, and uses of ambergris—will indicate how adequate Melville found this source-book, and how directly he gathered his materials from it:

> Although ambergris, even during the sixteenth century, appeared to be much valued as a mercantile commodity by the English, it is curious that we knew nothing of its source, and very little of the use which was made of it in other countries. . . .
>
> In 1791, the attention of government was drawn to this subject, in order to discover if it could be more frequently found. . . . Captain Coffin was examined at the bar of the House of Commons on the subject, and stated that he had lately brought home 362 ounces, troy, of this costly substance, which he had found in the anus of a *female* sperm whale that he had captured off the coast of Guinea, and which he stated was very bony and sickly. . . .
>
> "The use of ambergris," says Brande [Brande's *Manual of Chemistry*, p. 594], "in Europe is now nearly confined to perfumery. . . . Our perfumers add it to scented pastiles, candles, balls, bottles, gloves, and hair powder; and its essence is mixed with pomatum for the face and hands. . . . In Asia and part of Africa, . . . considerable use is also made of it in cooking. . . . A great quantity of it is also constantly brought by the pilgrims who travel to Mecca, probably to offer it there . . . in the same manner as frankincense is used in Catholic countries. . . ."
>
> Ambergris appears to be nothing but the hardened fæces of the spermaceti whale, which is pretty well proved from its being mixed so intimately with the refuse of its food (the squids' beaks). . . .
>
> [Quoting from Sir Thomas Browne:] . . . "in vain it was to rake for ambergris in the paunch of this leviathan, . . . insufferable fetor denying that inquiry; and yet if, as Paracelsus encourageth, ordure makes the best musk, and from the most feted substances may be drawn the most oderiferous essences, all that had not Vespasian's nose might boldly swear here was a substance for such extractions."[18]

Compare Melville:

> Now this ambergris is a very curious substance, and so important as an article of commerce, that in 1791 a certain Nantucket-born Captain Coffin was examined at the bar of the English House of Commons on that subject. For at that time, and indeed until a comparatively late day, the precise origin of ambergris remained, like amber itself, a problem to the learned; . . . ambergris is soft, waxy, and so highly fragrant and spicy, that it is largely used in perfumery, in pastiles, precious candles, hair-powders, and pomatum. The Turks use it in cooking, and also carry it to Mecca, for the same purpose that frankincense is carried to St. Peter's in Rome. . . .
>
> Who would think, then, that such fine ladies and gentlemen should

regale themselves with an essence found in the inglorious bowels of a sick whale! Yet so it is. . . .

I have forgotten to say that there were found in this ambergris certain hard, round, bony plates, which at first Stubb thought might be sailors' trowsers buttons; but it afterwards turned out that they were nothing more than pieces of small squid bones embalmed in that manner.

Now that the incorruption of this most fragrant ambergris should be found in the heart of such decay; is this nothing? Bethink thee of that saying of St. Paul in Corinthians, about corruption and incorruption; how that we are sown in dishonour, but raised in glory. And likewise call to mind that saying of Paracelsus about what it is that maketh the best musk.[19]

The various refinements and recastings by which Melville fused these isolated fragments of raw material into a more disciplined unity are alone sufficient to stamp the finished product as his own; but he was not content with the mere facts and figures of perfumery. He used this borrowed account of ambergris to refute the odious stigma that "whalemen [can] be recognized, as the people of the middle ages affected to detect a Jew in the company, by the nose"; and, growing eloquent, he declares that, for fragrance, a sperm whale can be likened to "a musk-scented lady [who] rustles her dress in a warm parlor" or to "that famous elephant, with jewelled tusks, and redolent with myrrh, which was led out of an Indian town to do honour to Alexander the Great."

This glimpse into Melville's workshop, however, pretends to show no more than the fingers and thumbs of the compositor turning the pages of his copy, the amateur cetologist poring over his authorities. The magic that transforms these inert elements into the living drama of *Moby-Dick*—"the hell-fire in which the whole book is broiled"—is another matter. To the philosopher and the psychologist must be left the task of investigating the sources consulted by the searching eyes of Melville when they were turned inward to the microcosm of his own mind or outward to the macrocosm of moral symbols through which Moby-Dick ploughs his way.

Notes

1. See pp. 13–14.
2. Anon., "New Bedford Whalers."
3. *Moby-Dick*, II, 208. The volumes listed by Melville as having been consulted in the preparation of his masterpiece comprise the best authorities on the subject of whaling that were available in 1850. Further, a modern whaling expert pays convincing tribute to his knowledge and accuracy: "There is one writer of whaling fiction whose book may be taken seriously and unquestioningly. There could be no truer picture of whaling or finer story of the sea than Herman Melville's 'Moby Dick'. Melville knew his subject." (See [Clifford W.] Ashley, [*The Yankee Whaler* (Boston, 1926)] p. 106.)
4. Browne, pp. 262–263. That Melville was acquainted with this volume is evidenced

by the numerous references that he made to it. And the chances are strong that he was the author of the anonymous review of it in the New York *Literary World*, I, 105–106 (March 6, 1847). [Willard Thorp verified this guess when he discovered the manuscript of the review in the Duyckinck Collection of the New York Public Library while preparing *Herman Melville: Representative Selections*, 1938 (ed. note).] The reviewer called attention to the realism, the "unvarnished facts" in this "truthfully and graphically sketched . . . voice from the forecastle," saying that it does for the whale fishery what Dana's book did for the merchant marine. The brutal tyranny of the captain of Browne's *Styx* is specifically pointed out. (See Melville's letter to E. A. Duyckinck on February 3, 1847—MS. in the New York Public Library—promising to review a book just published by Harpers; Browne's volume was the first Harpers' book to be reviewed in the *Literary World* after that date.)

5. Browne, p. 560, quoting from Wilkes's narrative of a voyage on the *Vincennes*.

6. *Ibid.*, pp. 302–327.

7. *Ibid.*, pp. 496, 504, and *passim*.

8. *Ibid.*, pp. 76–96. Compare *Moby-Dick*, I, 310–330.

9. Browne, pp. 105–106, 249–250, 492. Compare *Moby-Dick*, I, 203–205; II, 242–244, 290–293.

10. Browne, pp. 51–61, 127–135. Compare *Moby-Dick*, II, 25–38, 47–52, 177–180.

11. Browne, pp. 62–63.

12. *Moby-Dick*, II, 20–24.

13. Browne, pp. 60–64.

14. *Moby-Dick*, II, 178–182.

15. Weaver, for example, in his latest critical remarks on Melville, again quotes this declaration as the true explanation of "Why Ishmael Went to Sea," describing Melville's South Sea jaunt as "a retreat from life, from reality and outward experience, from the world which has [*sic*] so early disappointed and blighted his soul" (Weaver, *Journal*, p. iv).

16. Browne, pp. 22–23. Compare *Moby-Dick*, I, 152–155. Weaver (*Melville*, p. 137) says: "Though in *Moby-Dick* Melville makes several references to J. Ross Browne's *Etchings of a Whaling Cruise* . . . he owes no debt to J. Ross Browne. Melville and Browne wrote with purposes diametrically opposed."

17. Browne, pp. 35–37. Compare *Moby-Dick*, I, 200–210. It was probably just such high-flown rhetoric as adorns this speech that an English reviewer was analyzing when he remarked, with some fitness, that Melville's Ahab "raves by the hour in a lingo borrowed from Rabelais, Carlyle, Emerson, newspapers transcendental and trans-Atlantic, and the magnificent proems of our Christmas pantomimes" (see "Sir Nathaniel").

18. Beale, pp. 131–135.

19. *Moby-Dick*, II, 161–162.

Lear and Moby-Dick

Charles Olson

"Which is the best of Shakespeare's plays?
I mean in what mood and with
what accompaniment do you like the sea best?"
—Keats, *Letter to Jane Reynolds*
14 Sept 1817

I propose a Melville whose masterpiece, *Moby-Dick,* was actually precipitated by Shakespeare. Shakespeare's plays became a great metaphor by which Melville objectified his own original vision. What was solvent within Melville Shakespeare, in the manner of a catalytic agent, precipitated. Melville had brought his first five books out of suspension but the constant if subtle presence of Shakespeare in *Moby-Dick* and *Pierre* suggests that Melville needed just the fine metal of Shakespeare. The need of some such reagent Melville himself recognizes in the essay called "Hawthorne and His Mosses":

> I somehow cling to the strange fancy, that, in all men, hiddenly reside certain wondrous, occult properties—as in some plants and minerals—which by some happy but very rare accident (as bronze was discovered by the melting of the iron and brass at the burning of Corinth) may chance to be called forth here on earth. . . .

Melville and Shakespeare melted together at just such a Corinth, and *Moby-Dick* was the result.

Weak eyes kept Melville from any full and intimate knowledge of Shakespeare until his twenty-ninth year, the year before *Moby-Dick* was begun. In February, 1849, he wrote to Evert Duyckinck:

> I have been passing my time very pleasantly [pleasurably] here. But chiefly in lounging on a sofa (a la the poet Grey) & reading Shakespeare. It is an edition in glorious great type, every letter whereof is a soldier, & the top of every "t" like a musket barrel. Dolt & ass that I am I have lived more than 29 years, & until a few days ago, never made close acquaintance with the divine William. Ah, he's full of sermons-on-the mount, and gentle, aye, almost as Jesus. I take such men to be inspired. I fancy that this moment

Reprinted from *Twice a Year*, no. 1 (Fall–Winter 1938), 165–89. Copyright 1990 by the Estate of Charles Olson. Reprinted by permission.

Shakespeare in heaven ranks with Gabriel, Raphael, and Michael. And if
another Messiah ever comes he'll [twill] be in Shakespeare's person.—I am
mad to think how minute a cause has prevented me hitherto from reading
Shakespeare. But until now, any [every] copy that was come-atable to me,
happened to be [in] a vile small print unendurable to my eyes which are tender
as young sperms [sparrows]. But chancing to fall in with this glorious edition,
I now exult over it, page after page.*

Melville read his Shakespeare as a genius reads, sure of his own perceptions.
A creative spirit of his magnitude has, at twenty-nine, set his experience in
order, even though he has not achieved the power to communicate that
experience fully. It follows, too, from this coherence of self that he reads in
others his own vision, not theirs. Melville had already used the more active
experience of his life in *Typee, Omoo, Redburn,* and *White-Jacket.* The vast
archipelago of *Mardi,* written in 1847 and 1848, contained most of
Melville's vision of life and though he was to clarify much that is indistinct
there and expand that vision, the outlines of it are apparent. Much of the
"truth" he found in Shakespeare he had found in himself. The necessity of
Melville's own genius led him to this remark in the Hawthorne essay: "There
are minds that have gone as far as Shakespeare into the universe." Like any
creator he had instinctively this self-assurance, a temperature of his own. In
1849 he did not need Shakespeare to form his vision, though Shakespeare
could enrich it; what he needed most Shakespeare could help him to—the
free articulation of that vision.

From the first rush of Melville's reading Shakespeare emerged a
Messiah, as he put it to Duyckinck, "full of sermons-on-the-mount, and
gentle, aye, almost as Jesus." Melville throughout his life ascribed such
divinity to truth tellers, be they Solomon, Shakespeare or Jesus. After this
first enthusiasm, in a second letter to Duyckinck, Melville voices a fuller
judgment of Shakespeare and what he loses in spontaneity he gains in
definition. For he first states here a criticism central to all his later published
passages on Shakespeare. It keeps him this side idolatry. Here it shapes itself:

I would to God Shakespeare had lived later, & promenaded in Broadway.
Not that I might have had the pleasure of leaving my card for him at the
Astor, or made merry with him over a bowl of the fine Duyckinck punch; but
that the muzzle which all men wore on their souls in the Elizabethan day,
might not have intercepted Shakespeare's free [full] articulations, for I hold it
a verity, that even Shakespeare was not a frank man to the uttermost. And,

*For the original use of this set of Shakespeare and of Melville's annotations in it I wish to thank
Mrs. Frances Osbourne; for permission to publish it, Harvard University; and for the Duyckinck
letters, the New York Public Library. For innumerable permissions I thank Mrs. Eleanor Melville
Metcalf. [In quotations from the letters to Duyckinck we have supplied in brackets corrected
transcriptions of words but not of spelling and punctuation (ed. note).]

indeed, who in this intolerant universe is, or can be? But the Declaration of Independence makes a difference.

In the Hawthorne essay, a year later, Melville writes:

> In Shakespeare's tomb lies infinitely more than Shakespeare ever wrote. And if I magnify Shakespeare, it is not so much for what he did do as for what he did not do, or refrained from doing. For in this world of lies, Truth is forced to fly like a scared white doe in the woodlands; and only by cunning glimpses will she reveal herself, as in Shakespeare and other masters of the great Art of Telling the Truth,—even though it be covertly and by snatches.

In his copy of the plays themselves, when Shakespeare muzzles truth-speakers, Melville is quick to underscore the line or incident. In *Antony and Cleopatra,* for example, Melville checks Enobarbus' blunt answer to Antony's correction of his speech.

> That truth should be silent I had almost forgot.

In *Lear,* Melville underscores the Fool's insistence, in answer to Lear's angry threat of the whip:

> Truth's a dog must to kennel; he must be whipp'd out, when
> Lady the brach may stand by th' fire and stink.

The very language of the Hawthorne essay is heard from the Fool's mouth.

But Melville's words on the necessary silence of truth, even in a Shakespeare, imply more than this ultimate limitation of all truth-tellers. These passages contain a particular measure of Shakespeare himself, and plucked out it will help to define Melville's approach to Shakespeare. Melville as an artist chafed at the bonds of representation. His work up to *Moby-Dick* was a progress toward the concrete and after *Moby-Dick* a breaking away. It might be reasoned that his final renunciation of the form of the novel resulted from just such irritation in him at the need for dramatic location of truth. The more Melville pushed toward abstraction, the less was he artist and the more "a searcher for Truth." This recognized, Melville's demand for a more explicit Shakespeare, a more complete master of the great Art of Telling the Truth, is self-revelatory. Melville would have Shakespeare less the playwright, although Shakespeare's deeper dramatic significance was not lost upon him. Melville could have been more "content with the still, rich utterance of a great intellect in repose." Then, more directly, he would have "the spiritual truth as it is in that great genius." Melville read for

> those occasional flashings-forth of the intuitive Truth in him; those short, quick probings at the very axis of reality.

That "intuitive Truth" was the truth as Melville saw it. He finds truth in the mouths of the "dark" characters, Hamlet, Timon, Lear and Iago, for blackness fixed and fascinated Melville. Through such dark men Shakespeare

> craftily says, or sometimes insinuates the things which we feel to be so terrifically true, that it were all but madness for any good man, in his own proper character, to utter or even hint of them!

It is from "the infinite obscure of his background" that those "deep far-away things" in Shakespeare emerge, like the world that first morning emerging from chaos. Melville remarks this "blackness" and centers upon it to define Shakespeare. Madness, villainy and evil are called up out of the vasty depths of the plays as though Melville's pencil were the wand of black magic. Melville fastens on this darker side of Shakespeare: to use Swinburne's comment on *Lear*, it is not the light of revelation but the darkness of revelation which Melville finds most profound in Shakespeare. He was to write in *Moby-Dick:*

> Though in many of its aspects the visible world seems formed in love, the invisible spheres were formed in fright.

II

A thorough and imaginative dissection of *Moby-Dick* will discover the deep impact of *Lear* upon Melville. The use of *Lear* is pervasive and, as far as any generalization can stand, the most implicit of any Shakespeare play. That its use is so implicit serves merely to enforce a law of the imagination, for what has stirred Melville's own imagination most deeply is heaved out, like Cordelia's heart, with most tardiness. In one place Melville does directly and significantly speak of the play—in the Hawthorne essay. There, it is to Lear's speeches particularly that he points to example Shakespeare's insinuations of "the things we feel to be so terrifically true":

> Tormented into desperation, Lear, the frantic king, tears off the mask, and speaks the same [sane]* madness of vital truth.

And his copy of the play is marked more heavily than all the other plays but *Antony and Cleopatra*. Of the characters, the Fool and Edmund receive the

---

*Melville himself informed Sophia Hawthorne that "the same madness of vital truth" (as it appeared in *The Literary World*) should be "the sane madness of vital truth." See Eleanor Melville Metcalf, *Herman Melville: Cycle and Epicycle* (Harvard, 1953), 91–92. [Ed. note]

most attention. I have said Melville found his own words in the Fool's mouth, when the Fool cries, "Truth's a dog must to kennel." He found it in other speeches of that "boy," such a one as this:

> . . . nay, an thou canst not smile as the wind sits,
> Thou'lt catch cold shortly.

For Melville sees the Fool as the Shakespeare he would have liked more of—one from whom the cunning glimpses of Truth come forth, not one who refrained from hinting what he knew. And we shall learn from *Moby-Dick* how imaginatively Melville felt the Fool's humanizing effect upon proud Lear and thus how central he becomes to the whole poetic and dramatic conception of the play.

Melville is obsessed by Edmund who took such fierce quality in the lusty stealth of nature and who, in his evil, leagued with that world whose thick rotundity Lear would strike flat. The sources of this man's evil and his qualities obviously attract the writer who is likewise drawn to Goneril, and to an Iago—and who creates a Jackson in *Redburn* and a Claggart in *Billy Budd*. Melville is fascinated by positive qualities in the depraved: in Edmund, his courage and his power of attracting love. When Edmund outfaces Albany's challenge, denies he is a traitor, and insists he will firmly prove his truth and honor, Melville footnotes the passage: "The infernal nature has a valor often denied to innocence." And when Edmund is dying he forgets Lear and Cordelia, looks upon the bodies of Goneril and Regan, and consoles himself: "Yet Edmund was belov'd." This Melville heavily checks, marveling at love for such a selfish creature by two such selfish women. Here is a twisting ambiguity in the nature of man, a compounding of good in evil—Evil beloved. Throughout the play Melville turns over like ambiguities. He puts a trembling question mark beside Edmund's fraught promise:

> Some good I mean to do
> Despite mine own nature.

When Regan calls Gloucester "Ingrateful fox!" Melville writes: "Here's a touch Shapespearean—*Regan* talks of *ingratitude!*" He is again confounded by the ironic web of good and evil, and the close and blood-chilling double meaning of Shakespeare's language in the scene of Gloucester's blinding strikes him finally dumb, after he gives way to a last exclamation—"Terrific!" For this play, in which Shakespeare has made a world almost generated by the agents of evil if not by primal evil itself, threw Melville back to first causes. The origins of evil were Melville's own preoccupation. In his concentration upon an Edmund, a Goneril, and the whole dark world revealed in *Lear* we learn one large reason why the play lies at the heart of the

relation of Melville and Shakespeare and thus directly behind the creation of
Moby-Dick.

Melville did find answers in the darkness of *Lear*. Not in the weak
goodness of an Albany, who thinks to exclude evil from any good by a remark
as neat and corrective as those of Eliphaz in the *Book of Job*:

> Wisdom and goodness to the vile seem vile;
> Filths savor but themselves.

The ambiguities do not resolve themselves by such "right-mindedness."
Albany is a Starbuck—and not in such men, guarded against life as they are
by the protective tissue of accepted morality, did Melville look for the
answers. He turned rather to men who like Job suffered—to Lear and Edgar
and Gloucester. Judged by his markings upon the scene in which
Edgar discovers, with a hot burst in his heart, his father's blindness, Melville
perceives what suggests itself as a symbol so inherent to the play as to
leave one amazed it has not been more often observed by the critics—that to
lose the eye and capacity for sight, to lose the physical organ, "vile jelly,"
is to gain spiritual percipience. The crucifixion in *Lear* is not of the limbs
on a crossbeam, but of the eyes put out, the eyes of pride which confuse
the feeling and smother the emotions. Lear himself, in the storm speech
to the "Poor naked wretches," senses it, but Gloucester blind speaks
it: "I stumbled when I saw." Gloucester aches to see his son Edgar again
and without knowing that poor Tom is his son, he has his wish—"to see
thee in my touch." He gives Tom his purse and gives him the words of a
lesser Lear who senses now with spiritual sight and knows what wretches
feel:

> Let the superfluous and lust-dieted man,
> That slaves your ordinance, that will not see
> Because he does not feel, feel your pow'r quickly.

Melville checks this speech and within it underscores *"that will not see
Because he does not feel."* In little, this is the purgatorial dispensation of
the whole play. Melville finds in this dispensation, in the stricken goodness
of Gloucester and Edgar, who in suffering feel and thus probe more closely
to the truth, the echo of himself in Shakespeare. His ponderous heart feels
the agony of life. The necessity of feeling, the fertility of the heart for the
head, gives all the life and point to Melville's criticism and creation. He
understood what Keats meant when he called the Heart the Mind's Bible. In
the Hawthorne essay Melville insists upon this importance of the great heart
to the great intellect. What Melville lays down there as a law of criticism and

applies to Hawthorne and Shakespeare is throughout his own writing a philosophy of life:

> For it is not the brain that can test such a man; it is only the heart. You cannot come to know greatness by inspecting it; there is no glimpse to be caught of it, except by intuition; you need not ring it, you but touch it, and you will find it is gold.

Thus the tragedy of *Lear* passed before Melville's eyes and in agony entered his soul. The world Shakespeare has drawn out of the "infinite obscure" and created in the image of terror and beauty is kin to Melville's own perceptions. He will use it as an *immediate obscure* around his own world of *Moby-Dick*. Ishmael remains at the end to tell the tale of Ahab's tragedy. That part of Ishmael that was Melville must have felt strongly the rightness of Kent's epitaph upon his master:

> Vex not his ghost. O, let him pass! He hates him
> That would upon the rack of this tough world
> Stretch him out longer.

III

The real burgeonings of the Shakespeare reading can be found in Melville's own conceptions: what is peculiarly clear is that after reading Shakespeare Melville found the shape in which he could make his own vision most apprehensible—*Moby-Dick*. The past—and it included Shakespeare— was usable: "all that has been said but multiplies the avenues to what remains to be said." It is beautifully right to find what seem to be rough jottings for *Moby-Dick* in the Shakespeare set itself. With dramatic aptness, they are written upon the last fly-leaf of the last volume, the one containing *Lear,—Othello* and *Hamlet*. I transcribe them as accurately as possible:

> Ego non baptizo te in nominee Patris et
> Filii et Spiritus Sancti—sed in nomine
> Diaboli.—madness is undefinable—
> It & right reasons† extremes of one,
> —not the (black art) Goetic but Theurgic magic—
> seeks converse with the Intelligence, Power, the
> Angel.

---

†Concerning Olson's inconsistent transcriptions—the correct "reasons" here and the incorrect "reason" later in the essay, see the "Historical Note" in the Northwestern-Newberry edition of *Moby-Dick*, ed. Harrison Hayford, Hershel Parker, and G. Thomas Tanselle (1988), 650. [Ed. note]

The Latin is but a longer form of what Melville told Hawthorne to be the secret motto of *Moby-Dick*. In the novel Ahab howls it as an inverted benediction upon the harpoon tempered in savage blood:

Ego non baptizo te in nomine patris, sed in nomine diaboli.*

The change in wording from the notes to the novel is of extreme significance. It is no mere gesture to economy of phrase. In that change we witness the process of creation going on before our eyes, for the removal of Christ and the Holy Ghost, "Filii et Spiritus Sancti" is the mechanical act mirroring the imaginative one. Of necessity, from Ahab's world, both Christ and the Holy Ghost are absent. For Ahab moves and has his being in a world to which They and what They import are inimical: remember, Ahab fought a deadly scrimmage with a Spaniard before the altar at Santa, and spat into the silver calabash. The conflict in Ahab's world is sharp and abrupt, more than between Satan and Jehovah, closer to the old dispensation than the new. It is the outward symbol of the inner truth that the name of Christ is uttered but once in the book and then it is torn from Starbuck, the only possible man to use it, at a moment of anguish, the night before the fatal third day of the chase. Ahab himself conjures up his own evil world. He himself uses black magic to achieve his vengeful ends. With the very words "in nomine diaboli" he believes he utters a Spell and performs a Rite of such magic.

The Ahab-world is closer to *Macbeth,* among Shakespeare's plays, than to *Lear*. In it the supernatural is accepted. Fedallah moves in it as freely as the Weird Sisters in *Macbeth,* and before his first entrance, Ahab has reached that identification with evil to which Macbeth out of fear evolves within the play itself. The agents of evil give both Ahab and Macbeth a false security through the same device, the unfulfillable prophecy. Ahab's tense and nervous language is sometimes more like Macbeth's than Lear's. Both Macbeth and Ahab have a common hell of wicked, sleep-bursting dreams, and the torture of isolation from humanity they both endure. The correspondence of these two evil worlds of Macbeth and Ahab is sharp. In both the divine has little place. Melville intended certain exclusions and Christ and the Holy Ghost were two of them. Ahab, alas, could not even baptize in the name of the Father. He could only do it in the name of the Devil.

That is the Ahab-world, and it is wicked. Melville meant exactly what he wrote to Hawthorne when the book was consummated:

"I have written a wicked book, and feel as spotless as the lamb."

For Melville's "wicked book" is the drama of Ahab, his hot hate for the White Whale, and his vengeful pursuit of that whale from the moment the

---

*"I do not baptize thee in the name of the father, but in the name of the devil."

ship plunges like fate into the Atlantic. It is that action, and precisely that action only; it is not the complete novel called *Moby-Dick*. For the *Moby-Dick* universe is something different, and in that difference can be discovered the reason why Melville felt "spotless as the lamb." The rough notes we are exploring will yield the secret up. What follows the black blessing in the name of the devil has a hidden logic likewise revelatory of the book's conception: "madness is undefinable." Two plays from which the thought might have sprung are in the very volume in which it is found: *Lear* and *Hamlet*. Of the three modes of madness in *Lear*—the King's, the Fool's, and Edgar's—which if any is definable? But we need not rest on supposition about what Melville drew from *Lear,* or from *Hamlet,*—for *Moby-Dick* includes both Ahab and Pip. Melville forces his analysis of Ahab's mania to incredible distances, only himself to admit that "Ahab's larger, darker, deeper part remains unhinted." Pip's is a more fathomable idiocy: "his shipmates called him mad." Melville challenges this description, refuses to leave Pip's madness dark and unhinted, and declares: "So man's insanity is heaven's sense."

This emphatic comment is a significant key which resolves apparent difficulties in the last sentence of the notes in the Shakespeare volume:

> It & right reason extremes of one,—not the (black art)
> Goetic but Theurgic magic—seeks converse with the
> Intelligence, Power, the Angel.

Obviously "it" is the "madness" of the previous sentence. "Right reason," less familiar to the 20th century, meant more to the last, for in the Coleridge-Kant terminology "right reason" described the highest range of the intelligence, in contrast to "understanding." Melville himself used the phrase in *Mardi* and what he does with it there will deeply discover what meaning it had for him in these cryptic notes. These are the words in *Mardi*:

> Right reason, and Alma (Christ), are the same; else Alma, not reason, would we reject. The Master's great command is Love; and here do all things wise, and all things good, unite. Love is all in all. The more we love, the more we know; and so reversed.

Now, returning to the notes, if we recognize the phrase "not the Goetic but Theurgic magic" as parenthetical, the sentence yields up some clarity: "madness" and its apparent opposite "right reason" are the two extremes of one way or attempt or urge to reach "the Intelligence, Power, the Angel," or quite simply God. Indeed, the adjectives of the parenthesis bear this reading out. "Goetic" might derive from Goethe and thus *Faust,* but its source is probably the Greek "Goetos," meaning variously trickster, juggler, and, as here, magician,—Plato called literature "Goeteia"! Wherever Melville got it, he means it, as he says, for the "black art." In sharp contrast "Theurgic" is an accurate term for a kind of occult art of the Neoplatonists in which, through self-purification and sacred rites, the aid of the divine was evoked. In thus opposing "Goetic" and "Theurgic" Melville is using a distinction as old as Chaldea between black and white magic, the one of demons, the other of saints and angels, one evil, the other benevolent. For white or "Theurgic magic," like "madness" and "right reason," seeks God, while the "black art Goetic" invokes only the devil.

Thus implemented we can return to *Moby-Dick*. In the Ahab-world there is no place for "converse with the Intelligence, Power, the Angel." Ahab cannot seek it, for understood between him and Fedallah is a compact as binding as Faust's with Mephistopheles. Both Ahab and Faust may be seekers after truth but Melville's assumption is that a league with evil closes the door to truth. For Ahab's art, as long as his hate survives, is black—and "not the black art Goetic" seeks true converse. "Madness," on the contrary, does; and Pip is mad, possessed by an insanity which is "heaven's sense." When the little negro Pip almost drowned, his soul went down to wondrous depths and there he "saw God's foot upon the treadle of the loom, and spoke it." Through that ironic accident of madness Pip, of all the crew, becomes "prelusive of the eternal time" and thus achieves the converse Ahab has denied himself by his blasphemy. The chapter on "The Doubloon" drama- tizes the attempts on the part of the chief active characters to reach truth. In that place Starbuck, in his "mere unaided virtue," is revealed to have no abiding faith: he retreats before "Truth," fearing to lose his "righteous- ness." . . . Stubb's jollity and Flask's clod-like stupidity blunt the spiritual. . . . The Manxman has mere superstition, Queequeg mere curiosity. . . . Fedallah worships the doubloon evilly. . . . Ahab sees the gold coin solipsisticly: "three peaks as proud as Lucifer," and all named "Ahab." Even here Pip alone has true prescience, naming that doubloon the "navel" of the ship—"Truth" its life.

"Right reason" is the other way to God. It is the way of man's sanity, the pure forging of his intelligence in the smithy of life. To understand what use Melville made of "right reason" in *Moby-Dick* two characters, both inactive, have to be brought forth. The one who most closely corresponds to "right reason" is Bulkington. Melville describes him once early in the book, when he enters "The Spouter-Inn," a man "six feet in height, with noble shoulders, and a chest like a coffer-dam," in the deep shadows of whose eyes "floated some reminiscences that did not seem to give him much joy." In the "Lee Shore" chapter Bulkington is explicitly excluded from the action of the book, but not before Melville has, in ambiguities, divulged his symbolic significance. For Bulkington is Man, who by "deep, earnest thinking" puts out to sea, scorning the land, convinced "in landlessness alone resides the highest truth, shoreless, indefinite as God." For the rest of the Pequod's voyage Bulkington remains a "sleeping-partner" to the action. He is the secret member of the crew, below deck always, like the music under the earth in *Antony and Cleopatra*, strange. He is the crew's heart, the sign of their paternity, the human thing, and by that human thing alone can they reach their apotheosis. What Bulkington means will be made abundantly clear when we shall face the crew's function in *Moby-Dick*.

There remains Ishmael. Melville framed Ahab's action, and the parts Pip, Bulkington, and the rest of the crew played in that action, within a narrative told by Ishmael. Too long in criticism of the novel Ishmael has been confused with Herman Melville himself. Ishmael is fictive, imagined, as are Ahab, Pip and Bulkington, not so completely perhaps, for the very reason that he is so like his creator. But he is not his creator: he is a chorus through whom Ahab's tragedy is seen, by whom what is black, and what is white magic is made clear. Like the Catskill eagle Ishmael is able to dive down into the blackest gorges and soar out to the light again. He is passive and detached, the observer, and thus his separate and dramatic existence is not so easily felt. Unless his choric function is recognized, however, some of the vision of the book is lost. When he alone survived the wreck of the Pequod, he remained, after the shroud of the sea rolled on, to tell more than the wicked story. And that story is not, like Ahab's self-created world, in essence evil and privative, a thing of blasphemies and black magic, but in essence love and positive, where the humanities may flower, and man (the crew), by Pip's or by Bulkington's way, reach God. By this use of Ishmael Melville achieved a kind of catharsis which he intended. Melville—and thus the reader—could feel "spotless as the lamb." Ishmael has that cleansing ubiquity of the chorus in all drama. He alone hears Father Mapple's sermon out. He alone saw Bulkington and knew him. He it was who learned the secrets of Ahab's blasphemies from the prophet of the fog, Elijah. He moaned for Pip and understood his God-sight. And he cried forth the glory of the crew's humanity. He tells *their* story and *their* tragedy as well as Ahab's and thus creates the *Moby-Dick* universe in which the Ahab-world is, by the necessity of life, *included*.

For life has its way even with Ahab,—he changes, and with him his world. Melville had drawn upon another myth than Shakespeare's to create his dark Ahab, that of both Marlowe and Goethe: the Faust legend. But he alters the archetypal Faust fable and in the change I think the workings of Lear and the Fool in Melville's consciousness can be discerned. The change comes in the relation of Captain Ahab to Pip. Ahab does not die in the tempestuous agony of Faustus pointing to Christ's blood and crying for His mercy, but he dies with a stolid acceptance of his damnation. Even before the final chase for the White Whale he resigns himself to his fate. His solipsism is most violent and his hate most engendered the night of "The Candles" when he raises the burning harpoon over his crew. It is a night of storm. The setting is *Lear*-like. But Ahab, unlike Lear, does not in that night of storm discover his love for his fellow wretches. On the contrary, that night and in that storm Ahab uncovers his whole hate and commits a greater blasphemy than his defiance of sun and fire and evil lightning. He turns the harpoon, forged and baptized for the inhuman Whale alone, upon his own human companions, the crew, and brandishes that harpoon of hate over them. This act, judged by the ultimate values we shall discover Melville gave to the crew and, through them, to the *Moby-Dick* universe, is Ahab's greatest blasphemy. The morning after the storm Ahab is most subtly dedicated to his malignant purpose when he gives the lightning-ruined binnacle a new needle. Melville marks this pitch of his egotism:

> In his fiery eyes of scorn and triumph, you then saw Ahab in all his fatal pride.

But in a very few hours the change in Ahab sets in and Pip—or the shadow of Pip—is the agent of the change. Like a reminder of Ahab's soul he calls to Ahab that same day after the storm and Ahab, advancing to help, cries to the sailor who has seized Pip, "Hands off that holiness." For the first time Ahab spontaneously offers to help another human being. At that very moment Ahab speaks Lear's phrases:

> Thou touchest my inmost centre, boy; thou art tied to me by cords woven of my heart-strings. Come, let's down.

From this moment, though Ahab continues to curse the gods for their inhumanities, his tone is richer, quieter, less angry and strident. He even questions his former blasphemies, for a bottomed sadness of the humanities grows in him as Pip lives with him in the cabin. There occurs an efflorescence of the humanities that Peleg insisted Ahab possessed on the day Ishmael signed for the fatal voyage. Peleg refuted Ishmael's fears of his captain's wicked name, revealed that Ahab has a wife and a child and concluded:

> . . . hold ye then there can be any utter, hopeless harm in Ahab? No, no, my lad; stricken, blasted, if he be, Ahab has his humanities!

Those humanities Ahab had set aside in his hate for the White Whale, just as he forgot, as he paced the deck in restless and feverish anger at night, how his sharp heel of whale-bone rapping the deck waked his crew and his officers. The aroused Stubb complains, but unlike Pip he cannot call back Ahab's thoughtfulness. After Ahab orders him like a dog to kennel, Stubb's only impulse is to go down on his knees and pray for the hot old man because he feels Ahab has so horribly amputated himself from human feelings.

Pip continues to be, mysteriously, the agent of this bloom once it has started: "I do suck most wondrous philosophies from thee!" Ahab even asks God to bless this Pip and save him. But before he asks that, he threatens to murder Pip, Pip so weakens his revengeful purpose. Though Pip recedes in the last chapters, the suppleness he has brought out of old Ahab continues to grow. Pip is left in the hold as though Ahab would down his soul. But above decks Ahab is no longer the proud Lucifer. He asks God to bless the captain of the Rachel, the last ship they meet before closing with Moby-Dick, the very vessel which picks up Ishmael after the tragedy. Even his voice has a different note: "a voice that prolongingly moulded every word." He gives into Starbuck's hands his "life line," when he prepares a basket lookout for himself to sight Moby-Dick. The hawk takes Ahab's hat when Ahab is perched aloft there, without a word from the Ahab who dashed the quadrant upon the deck. This running sap of his humanities gives out its last shoots in "The Symphony" chapter: it will be enough to observe that in this chapter Ahab asks God to destroy what has been from the first his boast: "God! God! God! . . . stave my brain!" He has turned to Starbuck and talked about that wife and child Peleg had talked to Ishmael of. And if this apple, his last and cindered, drops to the soil, his revenge is now less pursued than resigned to. Ahab's thoughts are beyond the whale, upon easeful death.

In the three days' chase he becomes an intense, tightened, controlled, almost grim man. He sets himself outside humanity still, but he is no longer arrogant, only lonely: "Cold, cold—I shiver!" After the close of the second day, when the Parsee cannot be found, he withers. His last vindictive shout is but to rally his own angers, which are lost like the harpoon tempered by blood and lightning. Again he turns to Fate, the handspike in his windlass: "The whole act's immutably decreed." That night he does not face the whale. He turns his "heliotrope glance" back to the east, waiting the sun of the fatal third day like death. It is Macbeth in his soliloquy of resignation to tomorrow, before Macduff will meet and match him. On the third day the unbodied winds engage his attention for the first time in the whole voyage. Even after the White Whale is sighted Ahab lingers to look for the last time over the sea, to consider his ship and how it must outlast him, to say goodbye to his masthead. He voices to Starbuck his vibrant foreknowledge of death. The prophecies are fulfilled. In his last speech he moans that his ship perishes without him:

> Oh, lonely death on lonely life! Oh, now I feel my topmost greatness lies in my topmost grief.

With his old curse dead on his lips he rushes to the White Whale. The last words spoken to him from the ship had been Pip's: "O master, my master, come back!" Though Pip could not save him he did bring back Ahab's humanities. Their resurrection in Ahab throws over the tragic end a veil of grief, relaxes the tension of hate, and permits a sympathy for the stricken man that his insistent diabolism up to the storm would not have evoked.

Thus the end of this fire-forked tragedy is enriched by a pity even in the very jaws of terror.

This lovely association of Ahab and Pip is not unlike the relations of Lear to both the Fool and Edgar. What Lear learns of their suffering through companionship with them in the storm helps him to shed his pride, for he has felt what wretches feel. Beyond this, Lear, his hedging and self-deluding authority gone, sees wisdom in their profound unreason and he becomes capable of learning from his Fool just as Ahab does from his cabin-boy. In *Lear* Shakespeare has taken the conventional "crazy-witty" and brought him to an integral place in much more than the plot, to a central point of the whole poetic and dramatic conception of the play. Melville grasped the development of the character Shakespeare achieves in *Lear*. From it came some suggestion for Pip and his influence upon Ahab. Someone may object that Pip is mad, not foolish. Even in Shakespeare the gradations subtly work into one another. In *Moby-Dick* Pip is both the jester and the idiot. Before he is frightened out of his wits he and his tambourine are cap and bells to the crew. His soliloquy upon their midnight revelry has the sharp, bitter wisdom of the Elizabethan fool. And his talk after his "drowning" is parallel not only to the Fool and Edgar, but to Lear himself. A remark in *Moby-Dick* throws a sharp light over what has just been said and over what remains to be said. Melville comments on Pip:

> all thy strange mummeries not unmeaningly blended with the black tragedy of the melancholy ship, and mocked it.

Pip mocked that tragedy, for by his madness he had seen God.

IV

Thus these rough manuscript notes of blasphemy, madness and magic which Melville jotted down in his copy of Shakespeare lead into the splintered heart of *Moby-Dick*. Melville conceived his action as dark and tragic. He constructed it aware of dramatic values. Obviously *Moby-Dick* is a novel and not a play. Both its structure and its meaning can finally be understood only if it is regarded as prose narrative. But just as the meaning of the action has roots deep in Shakespeare so has the shape. Melville's "mighty book" was to be a prose tragedy, a novel organized not epically but dramatically. The documentation lies in the pages of the book. The "Epilogue," itself a dramatic device, opens with these words: "The drama's done. Why then here does anyone step forth?" It is but the last of a series of phrases scattered throughout the text. Melville's "mighty theme" was to be "the black tragedy of the melancholy ship." Before Ahab is brought into the action, the creation of such a character is "dramatically regarded"—"a mighty pageant creature, formed for noble tragedies." After Ahab has started the chase for Moby-Dick Melville admits himself a "tragic dramatist" faced with the problem, "so important in his art," of making a Nantucket sea-captain the equal of emperors and kings. To such an artist, man is "a wonder, a grandeur, and a woe." Under such phrases, like a palimpsest, lie the deeper truths of *Moby-Dick's* kinship to drama—structure and movement, and conception.

The book's movement is dramatic and has a rise and fall comparable to an Elizabethan tragedy. The first twenty-two chapters, in which Ishmael, the chorus, narrates the preparations for the voyage, are precedent to the action and prepare for it. Chapter XXIII is an interlude: Bulkington—"right reasons"—is excluded from this evil tragedy. With the next chapter the book's drama begins. This first act of the drama ends in the tensions of the "Quarter-Deck" chapter, the first precipitation of action, which brings together for the first time Ahab, the crew, and the purpose of the voyage—the chase of the White Whale. All the descriptions of the characters, all the forebodings, all the hints are brought to their first manifestation. Another interlude follows in which Ishmael expands upon "Moby-Dick" and "The Whiteness of the Whale." Merely to summarize what follows, the book then moves up to the meeting with the *Jeroboam* and her mad prophet Gabriel (Chapter LXXI), and after that, in a third swell, into the visit of Ahab to the *Samuel Enderby* to see her armless captain (Chapter C). The pitch of the action of the book comes in the storm scene, called "The Candles." From that point on Ahab comes to repose in his fate in a manner remarkably like Shakespeare's heroes in the fifth act. The character who comes to mind here is Macbeth, the line is Edgar's: "Ripeness is all." In this final movement too, Moby-Dick appears. It is a mistake to think of the Whale as the antagonist in the usual dramatic sense, for in this novel the antagonist is actually the subtle demonisms of life and Moby-Dick but the more assailable mass of them. In fact, the physical whale is more comparable to death's function in the Elizabethan tragedy than to the antagonist's: when Moby-Dick is encountered first, he is in no flurry, but quietly gliding through the sea, "a mighty mildness of repose."

But *Moby-Dick* contains things impossible to any stage. It contains a ship the "Pequod," whales, Leviathan, and the vast sea itself. In the making of most of his books Melville naturally used such materials. In *Moby-Dick* Melville integrates this material as he never had before nor was to again. The voyage of the "Pequod" is not like that of the "Highlander" or the "Neversink." The whaling material is stowed away in *Moby-Dick* as Melville did not manage the ethnology of *Typee*. While the book is getting under weigh—that is, in the first forty-eight chapters—Melville allows only four "scientific" chapters on whaling to appear. Likewise, as the book sweeps to its tragic close in the last thirty chapters, Melville rules out all such exposition. The body of the book contains the bulk of the whaling material. But Melville carefully controls these chapters, skillfully breaking them up:

for example, the eight vessels the "Pequod" meets slip in and cut between the matter of whales. The whaling chapters are dynamically a part of the movement and function like the comic plot of an Elizabethan play. They serve to relax the tension of Ahab's pursuit of the Whale. Actually and deliberately they brake the movement of the plot itself.

The devices of drama are most patent. Stage directions appear through-out the book. Other critics have noticed the soliloquies; I do not think anyone has called attention to the specific use of the Elizabethan soliloquy to the skull in Ahab's mutterings to the sperm whale's head in Chapter LXX. Even properties are used in precisely their theatrical way. Ahab smashes his quadrant like Richard his mirror. Of them all, the doubloon is most important, for it becomes the navel of the book in Chapter XCIX. Here the imagery, the thought, the characters, the drama and the events, both precedent and previsioned, are centered. The most sustained sequence of these devices occurs at the end of what I have likened to a "first act," culminating in a chapter which is printed in the form of a play. The sequence runs thus:

Chapter XXXVI. The Quarter-Deck. (Enter Ahab: Then all.)

Chapter XXXVII. Sunset. (The cabin; by the stern windows; Ahab sitting alone, and gazing out.)

Chapter XXXVIII. Dusk. (By the mainmast; Starbuck leaning against it.)

Chapter XXXIX. First Night-Watch. Fore-Top. (Stubb solus, and mending a brace.)

Chapter XL. Midnight, Forecastle, Harpooneers and Sailors. (Foresail rises and discovers the watch standing, lounging, leaning, and lying in various attitudes, all singing in chorus.)

Within the device of the soliloquy the most subtle presence of Elizabethan speech is felt. In fact, it is precisely in the soliloquy, especially as Ahab uses it, that the too frequent and facile comparison of Melville's prose to blank verse has some point. Too often, when the comparison is made general, it arises from a dislike of Melville's prose. In fact, the remark denies Melville his prose which is rhetoric in its widest and best sense. Such rhetoric subsumes both the cadences and the acclivities of Melville's prose. Ahab's "nervous, lofty" language is integrally used by Melville in his novel. In the soliloquies it is staggered and broken speech, fractured like that of Shakespeare's tragic hero whose speech like his heart often cracks in the agony of the fourth and fifth act.

The long ease and sea swell of Ishmael's narrative prose contrasts this short, rent language of Ahab. This opposition in cadence is part of the whole counterpoint of the book. It adumbrates the part the two characters play, for Ishmael is passive, Ahab active. More than that, this double cadence arises from and returns to the whole concept of the book revealed by the jottings in the Shakespeare copy—the choric Ishmael can, like the Catskill eagle, find the light, but Ahab, whose only magic is Goetic, remains in darkness. The contrast in the prose repeats the theme of calm and tempest which runs through the novel. Without exception action rises out of calm, whether it is the first chase, the appearance of the Spirit Spout, the storm, or the final chase precipitously following "The Symphony." The book has a deeply imagined systolic and diastolic pulsation, as though of the universe itself. Upon it depends much of the dramatic movement of the novel.

V

Melville had, in the Hawthorne essay, prepared the way for himself by ridiculing the idea that the literary genius in America would "be a writer of dramas." Critically he advanced what creatively he proved:

> . . . great geniuses are part of the times, they themselves are the times, and possess a corresponding colouring.

What the times gave Melville was whaling and democracy. What Melville gave his times was *Moby-Dick*. From the whaling industry, which America made distinctly her own, Melville drew his central figure, in his own words, "a poor old whale-hunter," a man of "Nantucket grimness and shagginess." Out of such stuff he had to make his tragic hero. He faces his difficulties. He knows he is denied "the outward majestical trappings and housings" Shakespeare had for his Lear and his Macbeth. And he cries:

> Oh, Ahab! what shall be grand in thee, it must needs be plucked at from the skies, and dived for in the deep, and featured in the unbodied air!

From what he knew of poetic tragedy and what he observed of human experience he sensed that Ahab must be given Richard's "hollow crown." Ahab's is the Iron Crown of Lombardy, but he wears it uneasily, for its jagged edge formed from a nail of the Crucifixion, galls him. He makes him "a khan of the plank, and a king of the sea, and a great lord of leviathans." He isolates him in "a Grand-Lama-like exclusiveness." His inward qualities are imagined with no less regard for the necessities of tragedy. Ahab is the captain of the "Pequod" because of "that certain sultanism of his brain." He is proud and morbid, willful and vengeful. His pride tempts him to worship fire and swear to strike the sun. Egotistically he takes upon himself revenge and denies his humanities. Because Melville had the metaphysical mind, he caused Ahab's hate to focus upon the imperceptible. Not man but all the hidden forces that terrorize man must be assailed by his Timon. That hate and that inhumanity involves his crew, and Moby-Dick drags that crew to their death as well as Ahab to his, a collapse of a hero through solipsism which brings down a world.

Ahab's majesty and size is common to the whole *Moby-Dick* universe; the scope and space of the sea; the swell of the prose; the whale, the crew, and the ship itself. The White Whale is Leviathan—no more need be said. He swims the sea with other whales who bear royal names, Timor Tom, Morquan King of Japan. Melville saw the need for a kingdom and subjects for Ahab. Humorously and seriously the whales are made a kingdom. The whaling material is more exactly used for this purpose than as "ballast," in Van Wyck Brooks' phrase, for an epic. At one point Melville challenges the declaration that "whaling has no aesthetically noble associations"; in that place he calls a chief glory of whaling the liberation of South America and the "establishment of the eternal democracy" there. The "Pequod" is made, through age and decoration, what Ahab himself is, "a mighty pageant creature, formed for noble tragedies." The description of her ends:

> A noble craft, but somehow a most melancholy! All noble things are touched with that.

That vessel has a crew which is the census of the world. In the swift and skillful shift from "Islanders" to "Isolatoes" they change from a realistic crew to one highly symbolic. They become an "Anacharsis Clootz deputation," an embassy of the human race to the democratic assembly not of the Constituante, but of God. Melville makes Pip their deputy. When he suffers his madness, he goes before them to "the great quarter-deck on high." Like Pip the crew is capable of the sight of God. But they have that capacity, not through madness like Pip, but through their common humanity. They are all incipient Bulkingtons, able to seek converse with "the Intelligence, Power, the Angel," by the mode of "right reason." Their humanity empowers them. Ahab yearns at the close of the book for that humanity. He wants to possess again what Richard has when his "divine" kinship [kingship?] is gone: "I live with bread like you, feel want, taste grief, need friends." The crew perishes with Ahab, but the long arc of Ahab's hate has returned to what makes them all common, their hearts and their humanities. Melville makes his meaning clear in one radiant passage:

> . . . this august dignity I treat of, is not the dignity of kings and robes, but that abounding dignity which has no robed investiture. Thou shalt see it shining in the arm that wields a pick or drives a spike; that democratic dignity which, on all hands, radiates without end from God; Himself! The great God absolute! The centre and circumference of all democracy! His omnipresence, our divine equality!
>
> If, then, to meanest mariners, and renegades and castaways, I shall

hereafter ascribe high qualities, though dark; weave round them tragic graces; if even the most mournful, perchance the most abased, among them all, shall at times lift himself to the exalted mounts; if I shall touch that workman's arm with some ethereal light; if I shall spread a rainbow over his disastrous set of sun; then against all mortal critics bear me out in it, thou just Spirit of Equality, which hast spread one royal mantle of humanity over all my kind!

In that declaration the crew are made citizens of a tragic world which is Melville's peculiar creation. Though he gives them "tragic graces" and "robed investiture" much as he added the necessary dramatic and tragic cubits of stature to the ship, the whales, and Ahab, he makes that robed investiture "one royal mantle of humanity." A "great democratic God" grants it to them. In spite of the matter and manner of tragedy which Melville drew from Shakespeare—structure and device, theory and characterization—Melville gives tragedy his own coloring through this passage from the lips of the choric Ishmael.

For Melville in *Moby-Dick* has worked out what may be called a concept of democratic prose tragedy. He was writing in a country unlike Shakespeare's, in a country where an Andrew Jackson could be "hurled higher than a throne," because a political theory called "democracy" had led men to think themselves "free" of aristocracy. Melville wanted to think that the Declaration of Independence gave him more searoom in which to tell the truth, but he like Pierre learned that such "freedom," of itself, did not follow America's political independence. For he saw that freedom, either political or social, is, as he put it in *Mardi*, "only good as a means, is no end in itself." Democracy, to Melville, merely gave man his chance to be just—in politics, society *and* intimate human relations. In the Hawthorne essay he asks that America recognize "those writers who breathe that unshackled, democratic spirit of Christianity in all things." He weds democracy with Christianity because he seems to see both ideally freeing man from his own and his fellow's oppression, leaving man "unshackled." In this sense democracy practically implements the Christian ideal. Ishmael can, therefore, call to a "great democratic God"—"thou just Spirit of Equality"—to bear out the use of a whaler's crew, simple workers, skippered by a poor old whale-hunter for the purposes of a prose tragedy.

Such is the "colouring" of the book, "corresponding" to the America of 1850, nothing more. For Melville, in *Moby-Dick*, to the making of which Shakespeare was so important, delivers the American spirit he got from his times and the democratic ideal, unshackled and Christian, over to Man. The "lamb" Melville thought spotless may, to him, be that Lamb of God, Christ, and he may, out of the America of 1850, choose to call humanity "democratic." But we must finally free that vision from such vocabulary to possess its whole truth. At the end of the book, in the heart of the Whale's destruction, the crew and Pip and Bulkington and Ahab all lie down together, "All scatt'red in the bottom of the sea." They *are* all citizens, their state is humanity, and what they find, in tragedy, is that the "humanities" are their kingship and their glory. The citizenship of human suffering, which is of no country, neither kingly caste nor representative government, gives *Moby-Dick* its meaning, as it does *Job* or *Lear*. For human storms not states are the stuff of creation. Shakespeare knew it deeply and from that man Melville learned.

The Revenger's Tragedy

F. O. Matthiessen

His liberation in *Moby-Dick* through the agency of Shakespeare was almost an unconscious reflex. Unlike Emerson he discussed at no point the origins and nature of language. The great philologian Jacob Grimm had, as Renan was to perceive, arrived at mythology through his investigation of speech. [1] Words and fables became finally inseparable for him, and he sought their common source in the most primitive and most profound instincts of the race, in its manner of feeling and imagining. It may be said of Melville that he intuitively grasped this connection. In his effort to endow the whaling industry with a mythology befitting a fundamental activity of man in his struggle to subdue nature, he came into possession of the primitive energies latent in words. He had already begun to realize in the dream-passages of *Mardi* that meaning had more than just a level of sense, that the arrangement of words in patterns of sound and rhythm enabled them to create feelings and tones that could not be included in a logical or scientific statement. But he did not find a valuable clue to how to express the hidden life of men, which had become his compelling absorption, until he encountered the unexampled vitality of Shakespeare's language.

We have already observed that other forces beside Shakespeare conditioned his liberation. Thomas Browne had taught him that musical properties of prose could help increase its symbolical richness. Carlyle's rhetoric may have drugged him into obscurities, but it had also the value of helping him rediscover what the Elizabethan dramatists had known, that rhetoric did not necessarily involve a mere barren formalism, but that it could be so constructed as to carry a full freight of emotion. But his possession by Shakespeare went far beyond all other influences, and, if Melville had been a man of less vigor, would have served to reduce him to the ranks of the dozens of stagey nineteenth-century imitators of the dramatist's stylistic mannerisms. What we actually find is something very different: a man of thirty awakening to his own full strength through the challenge of the most abundant imagination in history. Since Melville meditated more creatively on Shakespeare's meaning than any other Amer-

Excerpted and reprinted from *American Renaissance: Art and Expression in the Age of Emerson and Whitman* (London and New York: Oxford University Press, 1941), 423–35. Copyright 1941 by Oxford University Press, Inc. Reprinted by permission.

ican has done, it is absorbing to try to follow what the plays meant to him, from the superficial evidence of verbal echoes down through the profound transformation of all his previous styles.

Shakespeare's phrasing had so hypnotized him that often he seems to have reproduced it involuntarily, even when there was no point to the allusion, as was the case with the 'tiger's heart.'[2] On other occasions he enjoyed a burlesque effect: in omitting from his account such dubious specimens as the Quog Whale or the Pudding-headed Whale, he says that he 'can hardly help suspecting them for mere sounds, full of leviathanism, but signifying nothing.' He came closer to the feeling of the original passage when he found an equivalent for the gravedigger in the ship's carpenter, at work on a new whale-bone leg for Ahab, who had broken his former one by jumping into his boat. Melville had marked Hamlet's answer to the King's demand for Polonius: 'But, indeed, if you find him not within this month, you shall nose him as you go up the stairs into the lobby.' Now he transferred that to the situation where the carpenter, sneezing over his job, since 'bone is rather dusty, sir,' is told by Ahab: 'Take the hint, then; and when thou art dead, never bury thyself under living people's noses.'

You could trace such kaleidoscopic variations of Shakespeare's patterns throughout this book, since, once you become aware of them, you find fragments of his language on almost every page. Even Ishmael's opening remark about having 'no money in my purse' probably re-echoes *Othello*. 'The Spirit Spout,' that scene when a whale was sighted eerily by moonlight, and which, incidentally, was one of the episodes wherein Mrs. Hawthorne read an allegorical significance that Melville said he did not intend, seems to owe something of its enchanted atmosphere to the last act of *The Merchant of Venice*, if you can judge from the effect that is built up to by the phrase, 'on such a silent night a silvery jet was seen.' The end of *Othello* is more integral to the account of Moby-Dick's former assault upon Ahab; but, as an instance of how Melville's imagination instinctively reshaped its impressions to suit his own needs, it is to be noted that

> Where a malignant and a turban'd Turk
> Beat a Venetian and traduced the state,

is altered to: 'No turbaned Turk, no hired Venetian or Malay, could have smote him with more seeming malice.' On such levels, where the borrowed material has entered into the formation of Melville's own thought, the verbal reminiscences begin to be significant. What he implied by calling the crew 'an Anacharsis Cloots deputation' is made sharper by the addition that they are going 'to lay the world's grievances at the bar from which not very many of them ever come back.' The hidden allusion to Hamlet's 'bourn' from which 'no traveller returns,' serves to increase our awed uncertainty over what lies before them.

The most important effect of Shakespeare's use of language was to give Melville a range of vocabulary for expressing passion far beyond any that he had previously possessed. The voices of many characters help to intensify Ahab's. For instance, as he talks to the blacksmith about forging his harpoon, he finds the old man 'too calmly, sanely woeful . . . I am impatient of all misery . . . that is not mad.' This seems to have drawn upon the mood of Laertes' violent entrance, 'That drop of blood that's calm proclaims me bastard'; or since it has been remarked that 'Ahab has that that's bloody on his mind,' it probably links more closely to Hamlet's 'My thoughts be bloody, or be nothing worth.' The successive clauses, with their insistent repetitions, 'Thou shouldst go mad, blacksmith; say, why dost thou not go mad?' have built upon the cadences of Lear. Finally, as Ahab takes up the blacksmith's statement that he can smooth all dents, and sweeping his hand across his own scarred brow, demands, 'Canst thou smoothe this seam?,' Melville has mingled something of Lady Macbeth's anguish with her husband's demand to the physician, 'Canst thou not minister to a mind diseased?'

In view of Shakespeare's power over him, it is not surprising that in 'The Quarter Deck,' in the first long declaration from Ahab to the crew, Melville broke at times into what is virtually blank verse, and can be printed as such:

> But look ye, Starbuck, what is said in heat,
> That thing unsays itself. There are men
> From whom warm words are small indignity.
> I meant not to incense thee. Let it go.
> Look! see yonder Turkish cheeks of spotted tawn—
> Living, breathing pictures painted by the sun.
> The pagan leopards—the unrecking and
> Unworshipping things, that live; and seek and give
> No reasons for the torrid life they feel!

That division into lines has been made without alteration of a syllable, and though there are some clumsy sequences, there is no denying the essential pattern. Nor is this a solitary case. Ahab's first soliloquy begins:

> I leave a white and turbid wake;
> Pale waters, paler cheeks, where'er I sail.
> The envious billows sidelong swell to whelm
> My track; let them; but first I pass.

Starbuck's meditation opens the next chapter:

> My soul is more than matched; she's overmanned;
> And by a madman! Insufferable sting . . .

The danger of such unconsciously compelled verse is always evident. As it wavers and breaks down again into ejaculatory prose, it seems never to have belonged to the speaker, to have been at best a ventriloquist's trick. The weakness is similar in those speeches of Ahab's that show obvious allusions to a series of Shakespearean characters. The sum of the parts does not make a greater whole; each one distracts attention to itself and interferes with the singleness of Ahab's development.

Emerson had thought about this problem. Writing in his journal in 1838 about the experience of having re-read *Lear* and *Hamlet* on successive days, he did not feel obliged to assume his platform manner, and to call for the emergence of a super philosopher-poet. He was lost in wonder at 'the perfect mastery' of the architectural structure of these wholes. Yet they faced him as always with the question of the derivative literature of his own country, since he knew that, despite all his admiration, he could not construct 'anything comparable' even to one scene. 'Set me to producing a match for it, and I should instantly depart into mouthing rhetoric.'

That Melville so departed on many occasions may hardly be gainsaid. Yet *Moby-Dick* did not become another *Prince of Parthia*. This first tragedy by an American, composed in 1759 by Thomas Godfrey, a young Philadelphian, foreshadowed the romantic conventions that still were prevailing on the stage in Melville's day. It set its scene in a country of whose life its author knew nothing, at the beginning of the Christian era. It passed over contemporary themes, with which, as an officer in the militia shortly to undertake the expedition to Fort Duquesne, Godfrey was to become better acquainted. But even if he had written his tragedy after he had gone as a tobacco factor to North Carolina—where he was to die of a sunstroke at twenty-seven—it is improbable that he would have brought his poetry nearer home. For it resumed the debate between love and honor where Dryden had left off, and made its lines a pastiche of familiar quotations from Shakespeare, and of some less familiar from Beaumont and Fletcher. By the time of Boker the manner had been more subtly assimilated, but the main problem still remained unsolved. Emerson came near to suggesting its resolution in his journal of 1843:

> Do not write modern antiques like Landor's *Pericles* or Goethe's *Iphigenia* . . . or Scott's *Lay of the Last Minstrel*. They are paste jewels. You may well take an ancient subject where the form is incidental merely, like Shakespeare's plays, and the treatment and dialogue is simple, and most modern. But do not make much of the costume. For such things have no verity; no man will live or die by them. The way to write is to throw your body at the mark when your arrows are spent, like Cupid in Anacreon. Shakespeare's speeches in *Lear* are in the very dialect of 1843.

No matter whether Shakespeare's language seems to us anything but 'simple,' Melville's feeling that such words spoke to him directly of life as he knew it called forth from him an almost physical response. The first result might be that he started to write high-flown speeches entirely under the dramatist's spell. But they did not remain mere posturing, since he was able 'to throw his body at the mark.' The weight of his experience backed up what he wanted to do with words. He knew what he was about in the way he prepared the reader for the improbability of Ahab's diction. He stated that there were instances, among the 'fighting Quakers' of Nantucket, of men who, 'named with Scripture names—a singularly common fashion on the island,' had in childhood naturally imbibed 'the stately dramatic thee and thou of the Quaker idiom.' Such men were substantially schooled in the 'daring and boundless adventure' of whaling; they were led, 'by the stillness and seclusion of many long night-watches in the remotest waters,' to think 'untraditionally and independently.' Moreover—and here is a telling factor that operated on Melville as well as on Ahab—they received 'all nature's sweet or savage impressions fresh from her own virgin voluntary and confiding breast,' and had come, 'thereby chiefly, but with some help from accidental advantages, to learn a bold and nervous lofty language.'

In Melville's case the accident of reading Shakespeare had been a catalytic agent, indispensable in releasing his work from limited reporting to the expression of profound natural forces. Lear's Fool had taught him what Starbuck was to remark about poor Pip, that even the exalted words of a lunatic could penetrate to the heavenly mysteries. But Melville came into full possession of his own idiom, not when he was half following Shakespeare, but when he had grasped the truth of the passage in *The Winter's Tale* that 'The art itself is nature,' when, writing out of his own primary energy, he could end his description of his hero in language that suggests Shakespeare's, but is not an imitation of it: 'But Ahab, my captain, still moves before me in all his Nantucket grimness and shagginess; and in this episode touching emperors and kings, I must not conceal that I have only to do with a poor old whale-hunter like him; and, therefore, all outward majestical trappings and housings are denied me. Oh, Ahab! what shall be grand in thee, it must needs be plucked at from the skies, and dived for in the deep, and featured in the unbodied air!' The final phrase seems particularly Shakespearean in its imaginative richness, but its two key words appear only once each in the plays, 'featured' in *Much Ado* ('How wise, how noble, young, how rarely featured'), 'unbodied' in *Troilus and Cressida* ('And that unbodied figure of the thought That gave't surmised shape'), and to neither of these usages is Melville indebted for his fresh combination. The close concatenation of 'dived' and 'plucked' is probably dependent upon their presence of Hotspur's

> By heaven methinks it were an easy leap,
> To pluck bright honour from the pale-fac'd moon,

> Or dive into the bottom of the deep,
> Where fathom-line could never touch the ground,
> And pluck up drowned honour by the locks.

But Melville has adapted these verbs of action so entirely to his own usage that they have become his possession as well as Shakespeare's.

In driving through to his conception of a tragic hero who should be dependent upon neither rank nor costume, Melville showed his grasp of the kind of art 'that nature makes,' and fulfilled Emerson's organic principle. His practice of tragedy, though it gained force from Shakespeare, had real freedom; it did not base itself upon Shakespeare, but upon man and nature as Melville knew them. Therefore, he was able to handle, in his greatest scenes, a kind of diction that depended upon no source, and that could, as Lawrence noted, convey something 'almost superhuman or inhuman, bigger than life.' This quality could be illustrated at length from the language of 'The Grand Armada' or 'The Try-Works' or the final chase, or from Ishmael's declaration of what the white whale signified for him. One briefer example of how Melville had learned under Shakespeare's tutelage to master, at times, a dramatic speech that does not encroach upon verse, but draws upon a magnificent variety and flow of language, is Ahab's defiance of fire:

> Oh! thou clear spirit of clear fire, whom on these seas I as Persian once did worship, till in the sacramental act so burned by thee, that to this hour I bear the scar; I now know thee, thou clear spirit, and I now know that thy right worship is defiance. To neither love nor reverence will thou be kind; and e'en for hate thou canst but kill; and all are killed. No fearless fool now fronts thee. I own thy speechless, placeless power; but to the last gasp of my earthquake life will dispute its unconditional, unintegral mastery in me. In the midst of the personified impersonal, a personality stands here. Though but a point at best; whenceso'er I came; whereso'er I go; yet while I earthly live, the queenly personality lives in me, and feels her royal rights. But war is pain, and hate is woe. Come in thy lowest form of love, and I will kneel and kiss thee; but at thy highest, come as mere supernal power; and though thou launchest navies of full-freighted worlds, there's that in here that still remains indifferent. Oh, thou clear spirit, of thy fire thou madest me, and like a true child of fire, I breathe it back to thee.

The full meaning of that speech can be apprehended only in its context in the tumultuous suddenness of the storm, and in relation to Ahab's diabolic bond with the fire-worshipping Parsee. Even in that context it is by no means clear exactly how much Melville meant to imply in making Ahab regard the fire as his father, and presently go on to say: 'But thou art my fiery father; my sweet mother, I know not. Oh, cruel! what hast thou done with her? There lies my puzzle.' Immersed in primitive forces in *Moby-Dick,* Melville soon learned that—as he made Ishmael remark concerning 'the gliding great demon of the seas of life'—there were 'subterranean' levels deeper than his understanding could explain or fathom. But whatever the latent radiations of intuition in this passage, they emanate from a core of articulated thought. Here, if Emerson's prejudice against the novel had only allowed him to see it, was the proof that the dialect of mid-nineteenth-century America could rise to dramatic heights. That does not mean that any American ever spoke like this, any more than Elizabethans talked like Lear; but it does mean that the progressions of Melville's prose are now based on a sense of speech rhythm, and not on anybody else's verse. The elaborate diction should not mislead us into thinking that the words have been chosen recklessly, or merely because they sounded well. For they are combined in a vital rhetoric, and thereby build up a defense of one of the chief doctrines of the age, the splendor of the single personality. The matching of the forces is tremendous: the 'placeless,' 'supernal power,' a symbol of the inscrutable mystery which Ahab so hates, is set over against his own integrity, which will admit the intrusion of nothing 'unintegral,' and which glories both in its 'queenly' magnificence and in the terrible violence of its 'earthquake life.' The resources of the isolated man, his courage and his staggering indifference to anything outside himself, have seldom been exalted so high.

The verbal resources demonstrate that Melville has now mastered Shakespeare's mature secret of how to make language itself dramatic. He has learned to depend more and more upon verbs of action, which lend their dynamic pressure to both movement and meaning. A highly effective tension is set up by the contrast between 'thou launchest navies of full-freighted worlds' and 'there's that in here that still remains indifferent.' The compulsion to strike the breast exerted by that last clause suggests how thoroughly the drama has come to inhere in the words. Melville has also gained something of the Shakespearean energy of verbal compounds ('full-freighted'); and something, too, of the quickened sense of life that comes from making one part of speech act as another—for example, 'earthquake' as an adjective, or the coining of 'placeless,' an adjective from a noun.

But Melville's new ripeness of power should not be thought of solely in relation to his drama. It is just as apparent in his narrative, as can be suggested very briefly by one of his many Biblical allusions, which for once he makes not for solemnity but to heighten humor. He is just finishing his chapter on 'The Tail': 'Dissect him how I may, then, I but go skin deep; I know him not, and never will. But if I know not even the tail of this whale, how understand his head? much more, how comprehend his face, when face he has none? Thou shalt see my back parts, my tail, he seems to say, but my face shall not be seen. But I cannot completely make out his back parts; and hint what he will about his face, I say again he has no face.'

The effect of that burlesque is to magnify rather than to lessen his theme, not to blaspheme Jehovah, but to add majesty to the whale. Melville's inner sureness was now such that it freed his language from the constrictions that had limited *White Jacket*. He had regained and reinforced the gusto of *Typee* on a level of greater complexity. Whether or not he consciously intended to symbolize sex in the elemental energies of fire or of the white whale, when he wanted to deal with the subject directly he did not resort to guarded hints, but handled very simply the Whitmanesque comradeship between Ishmael and Queequeg. In 'The Cassock' he could also write a chapter about the heroic phallus of the whale.

5. The Matching of the Forces

In tracing the effect of Shakespeare on Melville's language, perhaps not enough attention was given to the equally obvious marks left by the dramatist on the composition of scene after scene. Some of the results are lumbering enough, particularly the interludes of 'comic relief': the character-part of the black cook Fleece; Stubb's account, in a chapter called 'Queen Mab,' of a queer dream in which he had been kicked by Ahab; the scraps of talk between the crew to offset the outer and inner tempests. All these seem so derivative in their conception that the humor runs thin. Melville was much more adept at handling some of Shakespeare's serious devices, since these were more in tune with his own temper. Fedallah's elaboration of the seemingly impossible things that must happen before Ahab can die is reminiscent of Birnam wood and Dunsinane. Ahab feels assured for this voyage when he is told that the Parsee will perish before him, and will appear again after death, and that 'hemp only' can kill Ahab. But it turns out that Fedallah, who is drowned by Moby-Dick's onslaught on the second day of the chase, *is* seen again, pinioned incredibly in the entangled lines on the whale's back. It also happens that in Ahab's final darting of his harpoon into his enemy, the line runs foul, catches him around the neck, and propels him instantly to his grave.

A more effective since less labored derivation adds intensity to the moment when Ahab pledges the crew to his purpose in the harpoon-cups. For he also makes the three mates cross their lances before him, and seizes them at their axis, 'meanwhile glancing intently from Starbuck to Stubb, from Stubb to Flask.' The cellarage scene where Hamlet compelled Horatio and Marcellus to swear on his sword was operating on the construction here. This is also the juncture when Fedallah's spectral laugh is heard from the hold, a counterpart of Hamlet's father's Ghost. An oddly transformed allusion, which shows again how deeply Shakespeare's words had entered into Melville's unconscious, is added by Ahab. He breaks off to say to the boy who has brought the grog, in a recombination of some of Hamlet's remarks to the Ghost: 'Ha! boy, come back? bad pennies come not sooner.' An important contrast between such allusions and those of our age of more conscious craft, those in *The Waste Land* or *Ulysses,* is that Melville did not intend part of his effect in this scene to depend upon the reader's awareness of his source. Indeed, from the way he handles that source here, he seems to have been only partly aware himself of its pervasive presence. His attention was wholly taken up with the effort to pour this energy into a new mould of his own.

But fascinating as the study of some of these configurations can be, they still leave us on the periphery of Melville's interest. The reason why his borrowings did not constitute a series of romantic tableaux was because they were only the by-product of the effort to engage in his own terms with what he had perceived to be the central problems of tragedy. The common denominator he found between Shakespeare and Hawthorne is illuminating. He marked in *The Seven Gables* many of Hawthorne's contrasts between the 'big, heavy, solid unrealities' of Judge Pyncheon's wealth and power, and the core of his real nature. The same 'contraries,' as Melville called them, struck him more than any other element in his reading of Shakespeare: the incongruous and often heartrending discrepancies between appearance and truth. An editor's note that he underlined in *All's Well* suggests Hawthorne's attitude towards the Judge. Designed to elucidate the remark,

> Good alone
> Is good without a name: vileness is so,

it concluded, 'and so vileness would be ever vile, did not rank, power, and fortune, screen it from opprobrium.'

Melville followed Shakespeare's diverse treatments of these 'contraries' through play after play. He noted them particularly in Timon's disillusioned discovery of the difference between the conduct of men towards him when he was rich and when he was poor. To judge from his pencil marks, he was absorbed by the theme of *Measure for Measure,* which is made explicit on many occasions, as in the Duke's observation:

> O, what may man within him hide,
> Though angel on the outward side!

He also marked Othello's torture at the ambiguity of appearance:

> By the world,
> I think my wife be honest and think she is not,
> I think that thou art just and think thou art not.
> I'll have some proof.

He underlined Cordelia's statement to her sisters after her disastrous truthfulness in the opening scene,

> Time shall unfold what plaited cunning hides.

But Melville was aware, in that play particularly, of the desperate odds against which truth had to battle; and when Regan called Gloucester, 'Ingrateful fox!' he added, 'Here's a touch Shakespearean—*Regan* talks of *ingratitude.*'

Such passages were in his mind when he stated in his essay on Hawthorne that 'through the mouths of the dark characters of Hamlet, Timon, Lear, and Iago, he craftily says, or sometimes insinuates the things which we feel to be so terrifically true, that it were all but madness for any good man, in his own proper character, to utter, or even hint of them.' Melville believed that 'the same madness of vital truth' was spoken also by Lear's Fool. Therefore, when dealing with the eerie wisdom in Pip's lunacy, he declared that 'man's insanity is heaven's sense,' words that practically state the theme of Emerson's 'Bacchus' or of Emily Dickinson's lyric which begins,

> Much madness is divinest sense
> To a discerning eye.

This insistence that what is hidden from common sense may be revealed to intuitive vision is the poetic mode of asserting the Kantian contrast between Understanding and Reason. Its most imaginative expression had been made by Blake, in whose work, significantly, Melville was to find a strong attraction in his later years, at a time when it was still not widely known in America. Emerson's madness always kept a gentle decorum; and though Emily Dickinson's comprehension of Shakespeare's treatment of good and evil was undoubtedly as keen as Melville's, her own drama, however intense, remained personal and lyric. Melville's greater horizon of experience, the vigorous thrust of his mind, and the strength of his passion carried him, as similar attributes had carried Blake, into wider and more dangerous waters.

It may be a coincidence that the four characters whom he linked together as the voicers of violent truth are the very four who left the most lasting mark on his own searching of experience. When the terror of the storm scenes is re-enacted on the *Pequod,* Ahab's fierceness owes something of its stature to Lear. Moreover, one of the crucial elements in the evolution of the old captain is his relation with Pip, a relation that, in its interplay of madness and wisdom, is endowed with the pathos of the bond between the King and his Fool. In *Pierre* Melville made his own kind of response to the view held by Coleridge and Emerson that this was the age of Man Thinking, and tried to create an American *Hamlet.* The misanthropic mood of *The Confidence Man,* exposing the mockery of all other 'trust' save that of the cash-nexus, is Melville's own realization of Timonism. And what we shall find to be his most recurrent type of evil character—from Jackson, the sailor whose sinister will so terrified young Redburn, to Claggart, the master-at-arms in *Billy Budd*—is one whose malignity seems to be stirred most by the envious sight of virtue in others, as Iago's was.

Even from such a brief summary it is clear that we have arrived at the point where we are no longer dealing with an ordinary 'influence,' but with a rare case, in which Shakespeare's conception of tragedy had so grown into the fibre of Melville's thought that much of his mature work became a re-creation of its themes in modern terms. But we can best approach the meaning of Ahab's tragedy if we leave the Shakespearean strain in abeyance for a while, and try to apprehend Melville's own awakening sense of the meaning of sin, of suffering, and of the 'boundless sympathy with all forms of being,' to which he had responded so eagerly in Hawthorne as well as in Shakespeare. As he wrote to Duyckinck after his first expression of enthusiasm at hearing Emerson lecture: 'Nay, I do not oscillate in Emerson's rainbow, but prefer rather to hang myself in mine own halter than swing in any other man's swing.' As he grew more dissatisfied with Emerson's inadequacy, he seized upon Shakespeare and Hawthorne as allies. Yet his 'sense of Innate Depravity and Original Sin' did not remain just what he found in Hawthorne. A fundamental reason for some transmutation was that, unlike Hawthorne, he did not confine himself to moral and psychological observation, but launched out into metaphysics. The background of Calvinistic thought over which Hawthorne's imagination played served to keep his brooding interpretation within a coherent frame. He dwelt on the contrast between appearance and reality, but his quiet disillusion accepted their inexplicability; he did not expect the hard facts of life to swerve one foot in the direction of the idealists' hopes. Melville could be neither so cool nor restrained. Though deeply impressed by the firmness of the Puritans' conception of evil, his mind had moved away from any fixed system of theology. Unchecked by formal education, a far more passionate temperament than Hawthorne's drove him to speculate. He felt compelled to search out the truth for himself, even while he recognized, in a growing wildness and turbulence, that it was as unfathomable as the sea.

Notes

1. See Renan's preface to the translation of Grimm, *De l'Origine du Langage* (1859).
2. In view of the enormous impression that *King Lear* made upon him, it is possible that even his chapter title 'Knights and Squires' was suggested by Goneril's 'Here do you keep a hundred knights and squires.'

[Melville's Style]

RICHARD CHASE

In discussing Melville's style, writers like Matthiessen, Sedgwick, and Olson have pointed out several influences: chiefly, Shakespeare, Sir Thomas Browne, and the Bible. It is clear by now that whatever may be said for or against Melville's style, he was a consciously "literary" writer, not, as used to be said, an unlettered or "natural" genius. Henry James, it could once be said, was a "literary" writer, whereas Melville was simply a great talent with no special professional sense of his medium. We can now see that Melville was fully as "literary" as James, if by "literary" we mean conscious of style (which is not to imply that Melville is the equal of James as a stylist).

Melville had other models of style besides the great English authors. One of these was the popular American rhetoric and oratory of his own time. And whereas this accounts for much of what one objects to in Melville's prose—its occasional clumsiness, its purposeless inflation, its vagueness, its jargon—it also accounts for many of his most felicitous passages. A glance at such a story as *The Obedient Wife,* written in 1840 by an anonymous author for the popular New York journal *Spirit of the Times,* will demonstrate how dependent Melville sometimes was on this sort of prose:

> There is an old story of a man who had married a young lady, and who had a friend somewhat skeptical as to the obedient tendency of the wife's disposition, much to the dissatisfaction of the Benedick, who strongly asserted, and warmly asseverated, that his will was law, and that she never by any chance disobeyed any wish or injunction of his.
>
> "Have you ever tried her in that respect?" said his friend.

There are long passages in Melville which sound just like this. It is, of course, very consciously literary. The writer feels that he would be less literary if he wrote "who had a friend somewhat skeptical of his wife's obedience" instead of "somewhat skeptical as to the obedient tendency of his wife's disposition." It is a genuine low-Melvillian trick; and so is the delicious reference to the "Benedick," the toying with "asserted" and

Excerpted and reprinted from *Herman Melville: A Critical Study* (New York: Macmillan, 1949), 86–94, by permission of Macmillan Publishing Company. Copyright 1949 Richard Chase; copyright renewed © 1976 by Frances W. Chase.

"asseverated," and the magniloquent humor of "Have you ever tried her *in that respect?*" The following passage, also from the *Spirit of the Times,* might easily have been written by him who tells the story of *Typee* or *Omoo* or *Mardi.*

> When we got up and rubbed our eyes, to our great disappointment we found that neither day nor wind would suit for *"Snipe Shooting",* so we sat down to our salt shad and our rye coffee, as disconsolate as Israel's maids of yore beside Babylon's waters. Looking out on the glittering expanse of Shinnecock Bay, we gazed with feelings of envy on the clam-men at anchor in their graceful whaleboats, who never knew the *ennui* arising from want of occupation, and were now engaged in destroying the happiness of many a bivalve's family circle with their merciless rakes. . . . After dinner,—a repetition of our morning's enticing fare,—we sat down to enjoy a quiet smoke. "Pooh! Pish! Psha!" muttered L——, a stately old bachelor.
>
> "Damn the day," exclaimed B——, who was an irascible ditto, not reflecting for a moment that Providence would be unwilling to increase the torrid state of the air by adding the hyper-temperature of the infernal regions. As for myself I don't exactly remember what I did, but I believe I ejected a mouthful of smoke and whistled.

Truly Ishmaelian is the philosophical humorist who here ejects his mouthful of smoke. The writer of this passage is a very literary writer, highly conscious of his allusions, careful to use a French word, proud of saying "the hyper-temperature of the infernal regions." He is jocular, reflective, acutely conscious of words. Carefully he constructs a mask of rhetoric and places it between the reader and that which is being described, hiding or merely obscuring the truth behind his featureless style. Probably he is not aware that this style *is* featureless, that what he takes to be a rich humorous-serious involution of phrase is really, much of it, blank and meaningless jargon.

There arose in this country in the 1830's and 1840's a most violent spirit of magniloquence. Oratory was one of the accomplishments of the folk hero. "I can outspeak any man," was one of Crockett's boasts. An orotund native oratory, full of bombast, humorous mythology, and rough American-isms, emerged, as if by necessity, to express the tumultuous feelings of the people. This oratorical language, which could be heard in various forms in tall talk, in congressional addresses, in sermons and written literature, had its effect on Melville, as did the milder humorous jargon we have glanced at above. As H. L. Mencken observes, the native rhetoric had its influence on Whitman and Mark Twain (he does not mention Melville), helping to set them apart from the conventional writers of the time, who looked back to the style of Addison and Johnson. The distinction must have been brought home to Melville in the 1850's, when he began to send short stories to literary magazines; one editor, distressed by Melville's style, suggested that he try to emulate Addison.

The following, from Mark Twain's *Life on the Mississippi,* will demonstrate the style in its more purely egomaniac mode:

> Whoo——oop: I'm the old original, iron-jawed, brass-mounted, copper-bellied corpse-maker from the wilds of Arkansas! Look at me! I'm the man they call Sudden Death and General Desolation! Sired by a hurricane, dam'd by an earthquake, half-brother to the cholera, nearly related to the small-pox on the mother's side! Look at me!

If this was an expression of the Manifest Destiny of the folk personality, its political-historical counterpart could be heard in the House of Representatives, in such speeches as the following:

> MR. SPEAKER: When I take my eyes and throw them over the vast expanse of this expansive country: when I see how the yeast of freedom has caused it to rise in the scale of civilization and extension on every side; when I see it growing, swelling, roaring, like a spring freshet—when I see all *this,* I cannot resist the idea, Sir, that the day will come when this great nation, like a young schoolboy, will burst its straps, and become entirely too big for its boots.
>
> Sir, we want *elbow-room*—the continent—the *whole* continent—and nothing *but* the continent! And we will have it! Then shall Uncle Sam, placing his hat upon the Canadas, rest his right arm on the Oregon and California coast, his left on the eastern sea-board, and whittle away the British power, while reposing his leg, like a freeman, upon Cape Horn! Sir, the day *will*—the day *must* come!

These words of "General Buncombe" have their counterparts in Melville's books, though Melville is never so vulgar a phraseologist as the General. The feeling of power, openness, space, and freedom is the central emotion in many of Melville's best passages, and as any reader of *Moby-Dick* will know, Melville purges the mood of exaltation of all vulgarities, of mere power worship, muscle-flexing, or intoxication with the *mystique* of force and space. About such a piece of oratory as the one quoted above, he would have been of two minds: he would have deplored the jingoism and the mindlessness of the sentiments; but at the same time he would have felt a deep sympathy with the speaker. In *Mardi* he had satirized just such an orator. In that book he represents his travelers as stopping off in Washington to visit the Senate. They hear a speech by a senator from the West. Roaring like a wild beast and smiting his hip with one hand and his head with the other, the speaker proceeds thus (I substitute real names for Melville's mythical ones):

> I have said it! the thunder is flashing, the lightning is crashing! already there's an earthquake in England! Full soon will the King discover that his diabolical machinations against this ineffable land must soon come to naught. Who dare not declare that we are not invincible? I repeat it, we are. Ha! ha!

> The audacious King must bite the dust! . . . Ha! ha! I grow hoarse; but
> would mine were a voice like the wild bull's . . . that I might be heard from
> one end of this great and gorgeous land to its farthest zenith; ay, to the
> uttermost diameter of its circumference.

The felicity of Melville's parody indicates clearly enough that he was aware of the
false and dangerous emotions lying beneath this kind of oratory—despite the
fact that he was himself not entirely proof against the oratorical mood. This kind
of "screaming" caused him many doubts about the American future and
convinced him that America might be throwing away all the opportunities of its
wonderful youth even as it enthusiastically celebrated its own new-found
confidence. He saw two aspects of the American spirit. He feared, on the one
hand, that America would never be more than the "braggadocio" of the world.
He hoped, on the other hand, that America was like "St. John, feeding on
locusts and honey, and with prophetic voice, crying to the nations from the
wilderness." Both of these possibilities he detected in the rough and fulsome
cadences of American speech.

In *Moby-Dick* the language of the screamer is transmuted, when
Melville is at his best, into an exalted apostrophe to power, space, and
freedom. The mood is at once lyric in its poignancy and epic in the large
nobility of its vision. The mood is not brutal or blind or chaotic or
megalomaniac. It is serene and joyful, with the serenity and joy which follow
upon the sense of great power controlled and great violence purged. It is the
mood expressed by Father Mapple at the end of his sermon (which is itself
perhaps the high point of American oratory):

> Delight is to him—a far, far upward and inward delight—who against
> the proud gods and commodores of this earth, ever stands forth his own
> inexorable self. Delight is to him whose strong arms yet support him, when
> the ship of this base, treacherous world has gone down beneath him. Delight
> is to him who gives no quarter in the truth and kills, burns, and destroys all
> sin though he pluck it out from under the robes of Senators and Judges.

The style of *Moby-Dick* is a rhythm of three basic styles: the style of fact,
the style of oratorical celebration of fact, the style of meditation moving toward
mysticism. A passage from the chapter called "Nantucket" will document this:

> What wonder that these Nantucketers, born on a beach, should take to
> the sea for a livelihood! They first caught crabs and quohogs in the sand;
> grown bolder, they waded out with nets for mackerel; more experienced, they
> pushed off in boats and captured cod;

these are facts; but gradually the reader's attention is led away from fact
toward a vision of size and power; the speech becomes metaphorical; the field
of observation opens out:

and at last, launching a navy of great ships on the sea, explored this watery world; put an incessant belt of circumnavigations around it; peeped in at Bering's Straits; and in all seasons and all oceans declared everlasting war with the mightiest animated mass that has survived the flood; most monstrous and most mountainous! That Himmalehan, salt-sea Mastodon, clothed with such portentousness of unconscious power, that his very panics are more to be dreaded than his most fearless and malicious assaults!

Note the quality of the images. The "incessant belt of circumnavigations" for size, and for the cyclical route of the voyager; "peeped in" for vision; "the flood," one of Melville's favorite symbols for the primal sense of power and space; "Himmalehan," image of the mountain; the "Mastodon" with his "portentousness of unconscious power," a phallic, imperial, and masculine image.

As the rhythm of the style turned upward and outward into space, Melville would have had the sensations he expressed in another chapter: "One often hears of writers that rise and swell with their subject, though it may seem but an ordinary one. How then with me, writing of this Leviathan? Unconsciously my chirography expands into placard capitals. Give me a condor's quill! Give me Vesuvius' crater for an inkstand! Friends, hold my arms!" And, then, Melville writing in full possession of his power, there follows the celebration of the Nantucketers:

> And thus have these naked Nantucketers, these sea hermits, issuing from their ant-hill in the sea, overrun and conquered the watery world like so many Alexanders parcelling out among them the Atlantic, Pacific, and Indian oceans, as the three pirate powers did Poland. Let America add Mexico to Texas, and pile Cuba upon Canada; let the English overswarm all India, and hang out their blazing banner from the sun; two thirds of this terraqueous globe are the Nantucketer's. For the sea is his; he owns it, as Emperors own empires; other seamen having but a right of way through it. . . . *There* lies his home; *there* lies his business, which a Noah's flood would not interrupt, though it overwhelmed all the millions in China. He lives on the sea as prairie cocks in the prairie; he hides among the waves, he climbs them as chamois hunters climb the Alps.

The "hermits, issuing from their ant-hill" give us an image of the "return" to the world after a "withdrawal." The "blazing banner," the sun—the sun under which the conquerors and patriarchs, the "naked Nantucketers," divide the oceans among them. The active forces here are all masculine; the feminine quantities are acted *upon*. Not far under the surface is a metaphor expressing the primeval scene of capture and division of the spoils. The whalemen are the rapers of the world. The "prairie" gives us another image of space, reminding us that the Pacific is an extension of the American land frontier. "He hides among the waves" we may read "he withdraws into the trough, the valley"; then, hunting the elusive game, he "climbs the Alps"—that is, he returns.

The style there modulates toward reflection and quiet:

> For years he knows not the land; so that when he comes to it at last, it smells like another world, more strangely than the moon would to an Earthsman.

In these words there is an abrupt sense of loss, of the need to turn back. The celestial symbol is now the moon, a feminine symbol. The faculty of sensation now invoked is smell; the inward, possessive, animal sense now replaces the projective, aspiring, and conquering one.

And then the introversion, with a reminder that a brutal power surges under the peaceful surface of meditation as it does under the delight of the oratorical mood.

> With the landless gull, that at sunset folds her wings and is rocked to sleep between the billows; so at nightfall, the Nantucketer, out of sight of land, furls his sails, and lays him to his rest, while under his very pillow rush herds of walruses and whales.

Again the idea of loss: the "land*less* gull." Notice also that the style is here recapitulating the Fall; two words help to accomplish it: "sun*set*" and "night*fall*." The feeling of a downward motion out of space is invoked, and the sensation of inwardness: the folded wings, the furled sails, the female gull asleep in the trough of the waves. The kinaesthetic sense of horizontality and relaxation is achieved by "lays him to his rest"; and the passage leaves us with the idea of femininity, sleep, and dream; a dream, it may be, of time and the process of nature, the eternal, recapitulant rush of walruses and whales.

Melville's epic style is a rhythm which flows through a life cycle, embodying itself in the appropriate images. At the beginning of the above description of the Nantucketers, we have the style emerging from a context of fact. In the middle of the passage, the style has opened out into the full moon of light and space. The energy, the flight, of the day declines into the myth and fantasy of the afternoon, which in turn modulates into darkness, toward sleep and dream.

"My numerous fish documents"

Howard P. Vincent

The cetological center of *Moby-Dick* begins almost like a formal essay, with bibliography, definition, and classification, except that Melville's tone is mocking and his procedure high-spirited. He was free from precedents; the bibliography of whaling was haphazard in the eighteen-fifties, and even today there is no complete bibliography on the subject.[1] Melville was not a professional scholar, but he wanted to find accurate and authoritative facts. He worked well against odds. His own library in Pittsfield was probably quite small, but he was fortunate to have free access to Evert Duyckinck's large library and to the collections of the New York Library Society, of which he was a member. The student of whaling may be grateful for Melville's diligence in research; the reader of *Moby-Dick* is rewarded by Melville's ingenious and imaginative use of his facts.

If the general structure of "Cetology" seems formal, the details were highly informal. The following list of authors is impressive, but one must admit that it does not meet elementary bibliographical requirements:

> Nevertheless, though of real knowledge there be little, yet of books there are a plenty; and so in some small degree, with cetology, or the science of whales. Many are the men, small and great, old and new, landsmen and seamen, who have at large or in little, written of the whale. Run over a few:—The Authors of the Bible; Aristotle; Pliny; Aldrovandi; Sir Thomas Browne; Gesner; Ray; Linnaeus; Rondeletius; Willoughby; Green; Artedi; Sibbald; Brisson; Marten; Lacépède; Bonneterre; Desmarest; Baron Cuvier; Frederick Cuvier; John Hunter; Owen; Scoresby; Beale; Bennett; J. Ross Browne; the Author of Miriam Coffin; Olmstead; and the Rev. T. Cheever. But to what ultimate generalizing purpose all these have written, the above cited extracts will show.

If one were to read what these men said about whales and whaling, one would be well along in understanding the subject. Few people have done so, and certainly Melville himself was acquainted with most of these men by name only, not with their works. No library then accessible to him along the entire Eastern seaboard contained all the titles on his list, and very few

Excerpted and reprinted from *The Trying-Out of MOBY-DICK* (Boston: Houghton Mifflin, 1949), 126–35. Reprinted by permission. Footnote numbering has been altered.

libraries today contain the majority of these names.[2] Nor does Melville say that he *had* read them; he merely lists them. But the hasty reader gathers the impression that Melville's list was compiled from firsthand investigation. Such was not the situation. Melville took the larger number of his references from Thomas Beale's *Natural History of the Sperm Whale.* Every author up to J. Ross Browne is mentioned or quoted in Beale's work. And rapid research shows that whereas Melville did consult, and use, all the authors from J. Ross Browne to the end of the list, he probably used none of the early ones. At no place in *Moby-Dick* does Melville display the slightest familiarity with the whaling materials gathered by Aristotle, Artedi, Green, Willoughby, Aldrovandi, and Ray, although there is much usable information to be had from them. Certainly, had Melville seen the outlandish whale pictures in Aldrovandi he would have mentioned them sarcastically in his chapters on whaling iconography.

Melville was not at ease in foreign languages.[3] He may have had a slight reading knowledge of Latin and French, recalled from studies at high school, but he obviously did not know those languages or others well enough to work his way through the important whaling documents written in Dutch, French, Latin, and German. His satire of Scoresby's familiarity with the Dutch writers, for instance, suggests that Melville was conscious of his own ignorance. More generally than students have realized, Melville relied on secondary sources; but so blandly does he quote Cuvier, Linnaeus, and others that we credit him with primary research, when investigation shows that he had dexterously removed his allusions from citations in Beale, Bennett, Browne, or Scoresby, Jr. Therefore, when Melville says, "I have swam through libraries," we must take his remark with reservations. Fortunately, the whaling authors which he could find, or did use, were first-rate authorities. Melville's full boast is, in a way, justified: "I have swam through libraries and sailed through oceans; I have had to do with whales with these visible hands; I am in earnest; and I will try." Research among the best available books on whaling, personal experience on the whaling grounds, and a supreme literary skill—what better qualifications could one have for writing a "whaling voyage"? And add a penetrating vision of the tragedy of life and we have *Moby-Dick.*

Five books furnished Melville with the bulk of his whaling data. These books play such an important part in the discussion to follow that a few words about each is in order.

The primary source book for Melville in composing the cetological section of *Moby-Dick* was Thomas Beale's *Natural History of the Sperm Whale.* Melville secured his personal copy on 10 July, 1850, paying Putnam's $3.38.[4] The care with which he read the book is attested by the many checkmarks throughout the book as well as the comments scribbled in the margins. It is a good book, still required reading for cetologists. Even by 1850 it had achieved the status of an authority. In 1843 a reviewer said that

Beale "supplies by far the most copious and satisfactory information on the subject"; and Beddard, writing in our century, called the *Natural History* "the classic in its [the whale's] habits and pursuits." Melville's praise is in fundamental agreement with these two critics. Linking Beale with Bennett, Melville wrote:

> There are only two books in being which at all pretend to put the living sperm whale before you, and at the same time, in the remotest degree succeed in the attempt. Those books are Beale's and Bennett's; both in their time surgeons to the English South-Sea whale-ships, and both exact and reliable men. The original matter touching the sperm whale to be found in their volumes is necessarily small; but so far as it goes, it is of excellent quality, though mostly confined to scientific description.

Melville's specific debts to Beale will be enumerated at length; his general debt—and probably to Bennett, also, though to a much smaller degree—was in his arrangement of whaling materials in chapter groups. Beale's fifteen headings: "External form and peculiarities of the Sperm Whale," "Habits of the Sperm Whale—Feeding," "Swimming," "Breathing," "Other actions of the Sperm Whale," "Herding, and other particulars of the Sperm Whale," "Nature of the Sperm Whale's Food," "Anatomy and Physiology of the Sperm Whale" (divided into twenty-five sections, which leave no part of the whale undescribed), "Of Spermaceti, etc.," "Of Ambergris," "Rise and Progress of the Sperm Whale Fishery," "Description of the Boats, with various Instruments employed in the capture of the Sperm Whale," "Chase and capture of the Sperm Whale," "Of the 'cutting in' and 'trying out,'" "Of the favourite places of resort of the Sperm Whale," were followed, except for necessary variations in narrative structure, by Melville in *Moby-Dick*.[5] Comparing the chapter headings of *Moby-Dick* with this list from Beale, one sees how closely Melville followed, either by accident or design, Beale's grouping. At the same time one notices how freely Melville adapted the groupings to the demands of art, and how his love of metaphor compelled him to change Beale's prosaic wording into graphic figures of speech: e.g. "the battering ram" and "the Heidelburgh Tun" for Beale's "Of the Cranium" and "Of the lower jaw." If, as Melville objected, Beale was limited by his scientific approach, Melville in borrowing from him readily remedied that defect.

When Melville coupled Bennett with Beale as "exact and reliable," he might have added that his personal obligation to Frederick Debell Bennett's *A Whaling Voyage Round the Globe, from the Year 1833 to 1836* (London, 1840) was second only to his debt to Thomas Beale's *Natural History of the Sperm Whale*. Both men, as Melville stated, had written from firsthand knowledge; although they were not professional whalemen, they had at least taken a field trip to the haunts of the sperm whale to see and to dissect the great fish for themselves. Unlike the whalemen, neither Beale nor Bennett was inclined to spin a pretty yarn, nor were they, too, like many scientists, inspired to speak at second hand. Lacépède, Bonneterre, and other cetologists, had done no more whaling than Simple Simon; in contrast, Beale and Bennett went out to the whale to report objectively what they saw, to sift with care that which they heard. In the history of whale research they have an important place; in the history of the American novel they unwittingly played a part.

We have already recognized Melville's debt to Browne's *Etchings of a Whaling Cruise,* in that it was the book which probably led Melville to preparatory research for a whaling book. Why Melville did no more than list Browne without further comment is puzzling. Either he must have felt that Browne's book was essentially a *rifacimento* of other writers' labors, or he may have thought that he had sufficiently recognized *Etchings* in the review which he wrote for Duyckinck's *Literary World.* Or perhaps Melville was embarrassed by the similarities of passages in *Moby-Dick* to passages in *Etchings.* We shall study these similarities shortly.

Melville's fourth source book, the Reverend Henry T. Cheever's *The Whale and His Captors* (1850), contributed much less to *Moby-Dick* than did those of Beale, Bennett, and Browne. It may be that the book appeared too near the composition of *Moby-Dick* for Melville to bother with incorporating many of Cheever's suggestions. But the lively and dramatic account of the whale fishery helped Melville out in at least two places in his own whaling epic.

The sperm whale and the sperm-whale fishery were the subject of four books written in the fifteen years preceding *Moby-Dick.* Melville knew them well; he acknowledged their merits; and yet his was a well-considered remark, and true, when he wrote: "As yet, however, the sperm whale, scientific or poetic, lives not complete in any literature. Far above all other hunted whales, his is an unwritten life." He meant that Beale, Bennett, Browne, and Cheever together had the parts; no one had the whole. For Melville was creating that book at the time.

One other source book was invaluable to Melville, but it did not deal with the sperm whale. Writing a book about the sperm-whale fishery, Melville employed his skill in praising the Cachalot to the derogation of its chief rival, the Right Whale of Arctic waters. (And embarrassingly, this valuable book dealt almost exclusively with the Greenland Whale.) To counteract this potent book, Melville, taking a suggestion from Thomas Beale's words in the *Natural History of the Sperm Whale*—

> The Greenland whale, or *Balaena mysticetus,* has so frequently been described in a popular manner, that the public voice has long enthroned him as monarch of the deep, and perhaps the dread of disturbing such weighty matters as a settled sovereignty and public opinion may have deterred those

best acquainted with the merits of the case from supporting the more legitimate claims of his southern rival to this pre-eminence—

transformed Beale's words into a stirring announcement of his whaling intention in *Moby-Dick*:

> And here be it said, that the Greenland whale is an usurper upon the throne of the seas. He is not even by any means the largest of the whales. Yet, owing to the long priority of his claims, and the profound ignorance which, till some seventy years back, invested the then fabulous or utterly unknown sperm-whale, and which ignorance to this present day still reigns in all but some few scientific retreats and whale-ports; this usurpation has been every way complete. Reference to nearly all the leviathanic allusions in the great poets of past days, will satisfy you that the Greenland whale, without one rival, was to them the monarch of the seas. But the time has at last come for a new proclamation. This is Charing Cross; hear ye! good people all,—the Greenland whale is deposed,—the great sperm whale now reigneth!

This chronicler of the despised Greenland Whale was William Scoresby, Jr., author of the two-volume classic, *An Account of the Arctic Regions with a History and Description of the Northern Whale Fishery* (1820). His learned study, a storehouse of materials, was plundered by Melville. Scoresby has justly been called the father of Arctic science. He is certainly the outstanding English authority on the Greenland whaling fishery, and his two closely packed volumes are the fullest account of whaling ever written by a genuine whaleman gifted with scientific caution and restraint. Immediately after publication, *An Account of the Arctic Regions* became the standard whaling reference. Most of the popular accounts of whaling published in the periodical press from 1820 to 1850 took their information straight from Scoresby,[6] often not acknowledging the source and not even changing the wording. Even today after the researches of one hundred years, the value of his book is almost as great as in 1820. While perhaps no whaling library is complete without Beale and Bennett, the cornerstone of that library must be Scoresby's *An Account of the Arctic Regions*.

Melville's admiration for Scoresby was genuine but grudging. He was, Melville admitted, "a real professional harpooner and whaleman. . . . On the separate subject of the Greenland or right-whale, he is the best existing authority." Why then did Melville seize several opportunities to satirize or parody the saintly old whaleman's pages—parody the entire point of which is partly hidden? Perhaps Melville was amused at the explorer's lack of humor. Another artistic defect, to Melville, was that Scoresby had packed his volumes heavily with dry and often irrelevant fact. He did not bother to marry fact to human history. Lastly, since Scoresby was the celebrant of the Right Whale, rival to the Sperm Whale in the attention of the public, Melville's campaign to glorify the Sperm Whale made it necessary, he felt, for him to laugh at anything concerned with *Balaena mysticetus*. "Scoresby," Melville wrote in reproof, "knew nothing and says nothing of the great sperm whale, compared with which the Greenland whale is almost unworthy mentioning." For this reason does Scoresby posthumously suffer the slings of outrageous satire in *Moby-Dick*.

A Melville dig at Scoresby is before us in "Cetology." In classifying whales, Melville mentioned the narwhale[7]—a fish found only in Arctic waters which Melville knew nothing about at first hand. For whatever information Melville picked up about narwhales, he seems to have relied almost completely on Scoresby's long description and his engraved plate of the narwhale. Not satisfied with using Scoresby's information, Melville insisted on his secret joke, with heavy humor calling Scoresby "Charley Coffin" and giving Scoresby's account a humorous twist of fact. For instance, in describing the narwhale's peculiar long horn, Scoresby had added a suggestion as to its use:

> it is not improbable but it may be used in piercing thin ice for the convenience of respiring, without being under the necessity of retreating into open water. It cannot, I conceive, be used as many authors have stated, in raking their food from the bottom of the sea.

Taking this passage into *Moby-Dick* Melville made characteristic additions:

> What precise purpose this ivory horn or lance answers, it would be hard to say. It does not seem to be used like the blade of the sword-fish and bill-fish; though some sailors tell me that the Narwhale employs it for a rake in turning over the bottom of the sea for food. Charley Coffin said it was used for an ice-piercer; for the Narwhale, rising to the surface of the Polar Sea, and finding it sheeted with ice, thrusts his horn up, and so breaks through.

And then came the extra touch Melville always felt called upon to add:

> But you cannot prove either of these surmises to be correct. My own opinion is, that however this one-sided horn may really be used by the Narwhale—however that may be—it would certainly be very convenient to him for a folder in reading pamphlets.

Scoresby will help out Melville several times, and on each occasion Melville will satirize him under a pseudonym. "Charley Coffin" and "sailors" are but the beginning.

The five whaling books by Thomas Beale, the Reverend Henry Cheever, J. Ross Browne, Frederick Debell Bennett, and William Scoresby, Jr., by no means close the list of Melville's "numerous fish documents."[8] They are, however, with the addition of Olmstead's *Incidents of a Whaling Voyage*, the key books for studying the cetology of *Moby-Dick*. They will be referred to frequently in this study. From them Melville borrowed facts and ideas with lavish freedom, his strange mind ticketing the oddest materials for development in his whaling novel. Melville's borrowings do not in any way make him liable to the charge of plagiarism; whatever he took he transformed; the practice and authority of Shakespeare, his great master, gave sanction to his method of transfer. Out of Beale's and Bennett's sows' ears Herman Melville made silk purses. Imagination amended bare and unpromising fact. In Goethe's words to Eckermann:

> It is, in fact, utter folly to ask whether a person has anything from himself, or whether he has it from others; whether he operates by himself, or operates by means of others. The main point is to have a great will, and skill and perseverance to carry it out.

And an organizing, enlivening imagination.

Notes

1. A modern bibliography is badly needed. Most students must depend on the "List of Sources" appended to the various modern studies of whales and whaling. There is, however, a superb critical bibliography covering the printed materials to 1840 by Joel Asaph Allen, "Preliminary List of Works and Papers Relating to the Mammalian Orders Cete and Sirenia," *Bulletin of the United States Geological and Geographical Survey of the Territories,* VI (1881), [399]–562. In compiling his bibliography Allen made use of D. Mulder Bosgood's *Bibliotheca Ichthyologia et Piscatoria* (Harlem, 1873).

2. The finest collecting of whaling and piscatorial books in America, so far as I know, is the Fearing Collection in the Harvard College Library. The New Bedford Public Library, the Library of Congress, and the New York Public Library have excellent if less extensive holdings.

3. Such a statement would explain why he made such little use, *if any,* of Frederick Cuvier's valuable whale book, *De l'histoire naturelle des cétaces, ou recueil et examen des faits dont se compose l'histoire naturelle de ces animaux* (Paris, 1836).

4. This valuable book was bought in 1945 by Mr. Perc Brown, of Montclair, New Jersey. He has generously allowed me to examine the volume and to copy Melville's markings and notes. Unfortunately, at some time in its history, a vandal erased many of Melville's pencil markings; but since not many words were erased—the vandal objected more to the checkmarks—and since by holding the book to the light one may see where the erasures occurred, it is still possible to follow Melville through the book. It is to be hoped that a future examination of the markings under infra-red rays may bring out some of these erasures.

Melville owned what is called the second edition of Beale. In reality it is a first edition. Printed in 1835, the so-called first edition was but a little pamphlet of sixty pages out of which grew the expanded and altered *Natural History.* This 1835 edition is quite rare; the 1839 is not.

5. Melville of course varied Beale's sequence to suit his own convenience, discussing the subjects listed by Beale in an order as follows, roughly: 1, 15, 13, 7, 2, 14*a,* 8, 4, 3, 6, 10, 9, 14*b,* and 5, 8, 11, and 12 variously.

6. The accounts of the whale fishery published in *The Mariner's Library, or Voyager's Companion* (Boston, 1840), pp. 331–346, and *The Mariner's Chronicle: Containing Narratives of*

the Most Remarkable Disasters at Sea (New Haven, 1834), pp. 410–12, are but two instances of unacknowledged "borrowings" from Scoresby which I have seen.

7. No. 210 of the Hull Museum Publications has a discussion of narwhale tusks which is interesting; even better is Morton P. Porsild, "Scattered Observations on Narwhales," *Journal of Mammalogy,* III (1922), 8–12. Melville also knew, but apparently did not use, the discussion of narwhale anatomy in William Scoresby's *Journal of a Voyage to the Northern Whale-Fishery* (Edinburgh, 1823), pp. 136–42.

8. Although I have examined all the numerous fish documents, especially those prepared for a general public, I have not found satisfactory evidence that Melville borrowed from them. One of the most helpful to him would have been Henry William Dewhurst's *The National History of the Order Cetacea, and the Oceanic Inhabitants of the Arctic Regions* (London, 1834), written by a careful scientist retelling as fully and as entertainingly as possible the facts about whales and whaling. For instance, he mentions on page 54 that the Dutch whalemen at Smeerenberg had hot rolls for breakfast, information which had Melville seen he would scarcely have neglected (cp. "The Decanter"). Dewhurst's book also has information on whale skeletons and fossils which Melville obviously had not read in preparation of his chapters on these subjects. The rarity of this book today (at least in the United States) may indicate a similar rarity in Melville's day.

Characters and Types

Nathalia Wright

In addition to furnishing Melville with the original Ishmael the Old Testament gave him also a model for his most celebrated character: Captain Ahab, who is named for King Ahab, seventh king of Israel after the division of the tribes.[1] In fact, King Ahab's story and that of his predecessor, King Jeroboam, account for an entire group of persons in *Moby-Dick:* Ahab, Fedallah, Starbuck, Elijah, Gabriel, Macey, and the *Jeroboam* and the *Rachel*.

The *Pequod's* Captain Ahab is associated with his Biblical namesake at the outset of the narrative. Acquainting Ishmael with his history, Peleg reminds the young sailor that "'Ahab of old, thou knowest, was a crowned king!'" To this the Presbyterian Ishmael replies: "'And a very vile one. When that wicked king was slain, the dogs, did they not lick his blood?'"[2] Whereupon, begging him never to repeat this remark, Peleg relates the circumstances of Ahab's being so named and the predictions which have followed him:

> "Captain Ahab did not name himself. 'Twas a foolish, ignorant whim of his crazy, widowed mother, who died when he was only a twelvemonth old. And yet the old squaw Tistig, at Gay Head, said that the name would somehow prove prophetic. And, perhaps, other fools like her may tell thee the same. I wish to warn thee. It's a lie."[3]

Despite Peleg's valiant protest, the prophecy about Captain Ahab does not prove to be a lie. Not only the tragic end of his life but the essential duality of his character also is foreshadowed in the Old Testament story. For the picture of King Ahab which emerges in I Kings is a composite of two points of view: that of the sources, according to which he was an able and energetic ruler, and that of the didactic compiler, who saw him also as a dangerous innovator and a patron of foreign gods.

King Ahab's political shrewdness is evident in the series of alliances he made with surrounding kingdoms, his accruing wealth in the ivory palace he built. He married the princess Jezebel of Phoenicia, made peace with Jehoshaphat of Judah, and, according to Assyrian inscriptions, furnished

Excerpted and reprinted from *Melville's Use of the Bible* (Durham, N.C.: Duke University Press, 1949), 61–68. Reprinted by permission. Footnote numbering has been altered.

Ben-hadad of Damascus with troops against Assyria. Being in his turn attacked by Ben-hadad, he concluded his victory by sparing his enemy's life and arranging for each kingdom to have bazaars in the capital of the other. The alliance was thus one of trade and commerce, and as such was violently opposed by the prophetic party of Israel. It lasted, according to the Biblical record, only three years. When hostilities with Damascus were renewed, Ahab was slain in battle, defending his kingdom. It was then that the dogs, as Ishmael ghoulishly remembered, licked his blood.

Like the king of Israel, the captain of the *Pequod* is shrewd in his secular associations. As a captain he is able and courageous; as a whaleman he is successful, for forty years temporizing with the great dangers of the deep for the wealth which it yields. The very evidence of this success is fantastically like that in King Ahab's story: Captain Ahab, too, lives in an ivory house, "the ivory *Pequod*" as it is often called, tricked out in trophies of whale bones and teeth from profitable voyages. Yet in the end trade is no less treacherous to the captain than to the king. Perhaps it could not be otherwise. For as Ishmael's account testifies, its nature is to be now a friend and now an enemy, and the best merchants are, like Bildad and Starbuck, strictly utilitarian. To this category Ahab apparently belonged until his last voyage, which, incidentally, was to have taken three years, just the length of time which King Ahab's bazaars in Damascus lasted. But the *Pequod's* last voyage, unlike its others, is not entirely commercial, and the blame for its disaster must be divided. From the morning on which Captain Ahab nails up the golden doubloon as a prize for Moby-Dick, it becomes a pursuit through invisible waters of an immortal spirit. And a duel is begun between the prudent Starbuck and the haunted Ahab. For Ahab cannot compromise. In the realm in which he hunts the white whale there are no alliances with the enemy. His voyage is disastrous when, in the midst of a profitable whale hunt, he becomes involved in the unequivocal pursuit of supernatural truth.

All this recalls the second nature of King Ahab, an able politician but in the religious sphere a patron of foreign gods. It is on this account that Ishmael remembers him as "vile" and "wicked." In the Biblical narrative Ahab offended Jehovah by introducing the Phoenician Baal as one of the gods of Israel at the time he married Jezebel of Phoenicia, whose father, according to Josephus, was a priest of Astarte. It appears that Ahab never intended thus to displace but only to supplement Jehovah. But Jehovah, who claimed the exclusive right to Israel's worship, tolerated no alliances with neighboring gods, or even with neighboring kings. He never forgave Ahab for sparing Ben-hadad's life. With Jehovah an enemy was always an enemy. And so he contrived with false prophets to bring King Ahab to destruction. Like the captain of the *Pequod*, King Ahab attempted to compromise in an uncompromising realm.

Indeed, Peleg's epithet for Captain Ahab is perhaps a better description of King Ahab than any in the Book of Kings: "'a grand, ungodly, god-like man.'"[4] Like King Ahab, he worships pagan gods. His particular deity is the spirit of fire, and he adores other objects of this cult: the light, the sun, the stars. His harpooner is a fire-worshiping Zoroastrian, Fedallah, the Parsee. In the midst of the typhoon Ahab invokes the fire already burning at the mastends, whereupon it leaps thrice its height—a feat itself which is a match for Elijah's calling down the fire on Mount Carmel to confound King Ahab's Baalite prophets. Finally, as though all this were not "ungodly" enough, Captain Ahab tempers the whale barbs not in water but in the heathen blood of Tashtego, Queequeg, and Daggoo. His voice is lifted defiantly to heaven, in what Melville told Hawthrone was the very motto of the book: "'Ego non baptizo te in nomine patris, sed in nomine diaboli!'"[5]

Of course, Ahab's death is not an instance of divine retribution in the orthodox sense. A romantic paganism is part of his nature, and not the least element of which he is compounded is Milton's Satan himself. The epithets applied to him by Ishmael and Starbuck—"infidel," "impious," "diabolic," "blasphemous"—describe a towering rebel who is akin to all other rebels in history, King Ahab among them.

Yet when in this character Captain Ahab does meet death, it is through hearkening, like King Ahab, to false prophecy. In the case of King Ahab it was the jealous Jehovah who betrayed him. Before trying to recover Ramoth-Gilead, which was in the hands of his old enemy, the King of Damascus, Ahab consulted his four hundred prophets. They promised him victory. But Micaiah, "a prophet of the Lord," who was summoned at the request of Ahab's ally, Jehoshaphat, said he would be slain. To explain this discrepancy in the two prophecies, Micaiah then related a vision he had, in which Ahab's prophets were revealed to be divinely inspired liars. On this occasion he saw Jehovah enthroned and surrounded by angels, and heard him call for someone who would persuade Ahab to engage in the fatal battle. For Ahab's death had apparently already been determined, and to the divine inquiry a spirit appeared who said: "I will go forth, and I will be a lying spirit in the mouth of all his prophets."[6] But in spite of Micaiah's story, Ahab believed the words of the false prophets, and thus deluded went to his death.

A false prophet contributes also to Captain Ahab's death. He is Fedallah, who appears increasingly in this role in the last of *Moby-Dick*. His actual prophecy, however, sounds less like an echo of the Bible than of *Macbeth,* with Birnam Wood moving to Dunsinane. Cryptically Fedallah predicts that before Ahab dies he must see two hearses on the sea—the first not made by mortal hands, the second made of American wood. He promises even then to precede his captain as pilot, and concludes by assuring Ahab that only hemp can kill him. All this is an accurate forecast of the tragic end, but it fatally deceives Ahab, who sees in it an assurance of victory.

On the other hand, there is no end to the honest prophecies that are made to Captain Ahab. The balance of influence is reversed in the two stories. King Ahab had four hundred false prophets and one who was true, but Melville sees to it, with characteristic irony, that Captain Ahab defies all creation in order to believe his single malevolent angel. The pleadings of Starbuck, the ravings of the mad Gabriel, the testimony of ships which have met the whale, the whisperings of his own heart, and a host of omens in nature—all these he ignores, heeding only Fedallah.

Starbuck, in the intimate relation he bears to his captain, also has an antecedent in the original Ahab story. With his frenzied attempts to conciliate the powers which Ahab is determined to alienate he suggests the God-fearing Obadiah, governor of King Ahab's house, who, when Jezebel persecuted the Israelite prophets, concealed a hundred of them in a cave and sustained them there until the danger was past. He was on good terms, too, with the prophet Elijah.

This prophet, the great Tishbite who denounced King Ahab and Queen Jezebel, provided Melville with the name for the pock-marked lunatic whom Ishmael and Queequeg encounter twice before sailing. As the two avidly listen, he enumerates the strange tales which have been told about Captain Ahab and insinuates that not only he but the entire crew of the *Pequod* will never return from the voyage. The significance of his name can hardly have escaped the Biblically astute Ishmael, who calls him a "prophet" and exclaims portentously as they leave the creature, "Elijah!"

Possibly Ishmael remembered that the actual words of the prophet Elijah to King Ahab include a curse, which in the Books of Kings is habitually pronounced upon the wicked kings of Israel: "[I] will make thine house like the house of Jeroboam the son of Nebat."[7] Its meaning is devastatingly clear. Jeroboam, the first king of Israel after the tribal division, though actually a courageous opponent of the tyrant Solomon, is charged in the Old Testament with fostering sacrilegious rituals and sacrifices in the new kingdom. For his offense Jehovah allowed his son to die and vowed to destroy his dynasty. And so the wicked successors of Jeroboam were described as walking "in all the way of Jeroboam the son of Nebat, and in his sin wherewith he made Israel to sin,"[8] and were promised the same punishment. Jeroboam is thus not only a forerunner, but his fate is a forecast of the fates of all the kings who followed him, including King Ahab.

And for this predecessor of King Ahab the *Jeroboam* in *Moby-Dick*, a predecessor of the *Pequod*, is named. Of the four vessels met by the *Pequod* which have already encountered Ahab's quarry, the *Jeroboam* is the first. Her fate is prophetic. It is a message of warning to all who follow, articulated by Gabriel and vindicated by the *Samuel Enderby*, the *Rachel*, the *Delight*, and at last the *Pequod*. The *Jeroboam's* pursuit of Moby-Dick has resulted in the loss of her mate and may in some mysterious way be responsible for the epidemic among her crew, but the whale has escaped. And so the other four vessels, pursuing the same course, meet similar misfortunes, without slaying Moby-Dick.

The "utter-wreck" of the *Pequod,* in its turn, was probably made inevitable by Melville's own flair for spectacle, but the corroboration for it is complete in the stories of King Jeroboam and King Ahab. Compared with the partial losses of the *Jeroboam,* the *Enderby,* the *Rachel,* and the *Delight,* the destruction of the *Pequod* is appalling indeed. But it is a fitting end for the monomania of Ahab, which none of the other captains shared. So in the case of King Ahab the account of his death is elaborated by more details of violence than are to be found in that of any of the Israelite kings before him. The reason is not far to seek. He vexed Jehovah more than all the rest: ". . . and Ahab did more to provoke the Lord God of Israel to anger than all the kings of Israel that were before him."[9]

Without doubt, the seventh king of Israel was a memorable man. Melville did not soon forget him. When in *Clarel* he cast about for a figure to describe the appearance of two of the pilgrims, Mortmain and Rolfe, he found it in the story he had used long before.

> Mortmain aloof and single sat—
> In range with Rolfe, as viewed from mat
> Where Vine reposed, observing there
> That these in contour of the head
> And goodly profile made a pair,
> Though one looked like a statue dead.
> Methinks (mused Vine), 'tis Ahab's court
> And yon the Tishbite; he'll consort
> Not long, but Kedron [*sic*] seek.[10]

Ahab's prophet, too, lingered in his memory, recalled by the surly Mortmain, "the Gileadite In Obadiah's way."[11] A wise man was still solitary, still an inhabitant of the desert.

Notes

1. This, of course, does not preclude the possibility that Melville got the name of Ahab from another source and then developed the Biblical analogy, as he did in *Israel Potter.* In J. Ross Browne's *Etchings of a Whaling Cruise* "Captain A——" of the *Styx* bears a distinct resemblance to Captain Ahab of the *Pequod* (Anderson, *op. cit.,* p. 43).

2. *Moby-Dick,* I, 99.

3. *Ibid.,* I, 100.

4. *Ibid.,* I, 99.

5. *Ibid.,* II, 261.

6. I Kings 22:22.

7. *Ibid.*, 21:22, *et passim.*

8. *Ibid.*, 16:26, *et passim.*

9. *Ibid.*, 16:33.

10. *Clarel,* II, 55–56.

11. *Ibid.*, II, 150. See also I, 313, where Mortmain is associated with the brook Cherith, beside which Elijah lived.

Poetic and Epic Influences of *Paradise Lost*

Henry F. Pommer

"The secrets of the currents in the seas have never yet been divulged, even to the most erudite research."

—Moby-Dick, *I, 226.*

At times during the preceding chapter it has probably seemed strange that prose works should be compared at such length with poems. Actually, of course, we have been dealing chiefly with prose marked by many of the characteristics of poetry, and with poetry which lacks some of the most obvious and superficial aspects of verse, such as rhyme and emphasis on the line as a unit. Nor could this study be by any means the first to call Melville an author of poetic prose, or *Moby-Dick* an epic. In fact, Melville himself was the first to link his masterpiece with poetry.

> The "whaling voyage" . . . will be a strange sort of a book, tho', I fear; blubber is blubber you know; tho' you may get oil out of it, the poetry runs as hard as sap from a frozen maple tree.[1]

And in the finished book itself he wrote, significantly,

> Now it remains to conclude the last chapter of this part of the description by rehearsing—*singing*, if I may—the romantic proceeding of decanting off [leviathan's] oil.[2]

In our own century, John Erskine has made the statement about Ahab's tale that

> when we say that this story is a poem rather than a novel, we mean that its art consists not in reproducing pictures of the outside of life, such as we can call faithful, but rather in preparing our minds for an effect of emotion, so that at the end there will be a powerful catharsis, or release of feeling. . . .
>
> Though written in prose it has the power of a great epic—that is, it gathers up our emotions around a central figure, a central incident, and one central mood.[3]

Excerpted and reprinted from *Milton and Melville* (Pittsburgh: University of Pittsburgh Press, 1950), 50–63. Reprinted by permission of the University of Pittsburgh Press. © 1950 by University of Pittsburgh Press.

Sealts, Mumford, Forsythe, and F. B. Freeman[4] too have used *epic* in connection with *Moby-Dick*, and Padraic Colum enlarges on the same theme by defining the book as an epic

> in the sense of compositions that have a far-reaching theme, a high and singular style, a multiplicity of interest, a tragic and heroic outlook. . . . If Melville had consciously proposed to himself to make an epic of man's invasion of the oceans, his theme and his handling of it could hardly, it seems to me, be different.[5]

Certainly *Moby-Dick* fits Erskine's definition of poetry and Colum's definition of epic, but what about other definitions? To what degree do these authors use the words *poem* or *epic* in a very loose fashion, and to what degree are they prepared for close examination? Students of the dramatic structure of *Paradise Lost* and of *Moby-Dick* have, independently of one another, published conclusions which merit some comparison,[6] but there seem to have been no sustained attempts to analyze the influence of the epic type on Melville's work. The whole of such an analysis lies beyond the proper scope of this book, but it is necessary to enumerate some qualities of poetry and of epic held in common by Milton's poem and Melville's novel. In doing so one might demonstrate the remarkable extent to which the statements just quoted about *Moby-Dick* apply to *Paradise Lost* and, vice versa, how true *Moby-Dick* are statements like this by Addison, made in a criticism of Milton:

> Besides the hidden Meaning of an Epic Allegory, the plain literal Sense ought to appear probable. The story should be such as an ordinary Reader may Acquiesce in, whatever Natural Moral or Political Truth may be discovered in it by Men of greater Penetration.[7]

In lieu of such demonstrations, this chapter will emphasize certain specific similarities in technique which again indicate at least a Miltonic flavor, and perhaps a Miltonic influence. The roles of the heroes, Satan and Ahab, however, must be considered in a later section.

Alliteration is one of Melville's most frequently used borrowings from the poets. Sometimes, as in the first of the following quotations, he uses it to link merely a pair of words; sometimes, as in the second, he unites a number of words, now with inartistic bluntness, again with merriment. On still other occasions, however, alliteration furthers the more serious ambitions of his art, as it did with Milton.

> *H*overingly *h*alting, and dipping on the wing, the white sea-fowls *l*ongingly *l*ingered over the agitated pool that he left.

> What *b*itter *b*lanks in those *b*lack-*b*ordered marbles which cover no ashes.

It was while gliding through these latter waters that one serene and moonlight night, when all the waves rolled by like scrolls of silver; and, by their soft, suffusing seethings, made what seemed a silvery silence, not a solitude: on such a silent night a silvery jet was seen far in advance of the white bubbles at the bow.[8]

Obviously no use of italics could adequately point out the lovely interfusions in this "liquid sea of sound."[9] Of all the poets who might have influenced Melville towards such unusual sound-painting in prose,

undoubtedly the pre-eminent influence is that of Milton, who through his wonderfully perfected, musical, and yet so weighty language, held Melville in his thrall all his life. Like Melville, Milton also had an extremely delicate ear for consonance and sound values.[10]

One device which adds immeasurably to the beauty of the long, suspended sentence last quoted from Melville is its fundamentally iambic rhythm. Melville's lapses or risings into such a beat have been frequently commented on,[11] and parts of *Moby-Dick* have been printed as more than passable blank verse.[12] One passage which I believe has not previously been printed in its natural pentameter lines is about the *Pequod's* blacksmith:

Harkening to these voices, East and West,
By early sunrise, and by fall of eve,
The blacksmith's soul responded, Ay, I come!
And so Perth went a-whaling.[13]

Just as in "The Paradise of Bachelors" Melville used the rhythm of "Il Penseroso," so here in *Moby-Dick* he used that of Milton's epics, achieving something far subtler than just an iambic pentameter rhythm—a Miltonic ring. Weber says that

Melville's tendency is in general towards a fundamentally iambic prose rhythm as it found its ideal form in Miltonic heroic verse and in dramatic blank verse.[14]

It is true, of course, that much of Melville's rhythmic prose has a Shakespearean tone to it,[15] but in weighing Shakespeare's influence against Milton's it is important to remember that Melville did not become intimately acquainted with Shakespeare until after he had written his first iambic prose, and after he had read Milton with some attention. It was on February 24, 1849, that Melville wrote to Duyckinck,

Dolt & ass that I am I have lived more than 29 years, & until a few days ago, never made close acquaintance with the divine William. . . . I am mad to think how minute a cause has prevented me hitherto from reading Shakespeare.[16]

One month before that statement Melville had signed the preface to *Mardi*,[17] and the book appeared for sale in London only twenty days after the letter was written.[18] Consequently it was well before his intimacy with Shakespeare that Melville wrote this blank verse in prose:

> As when from howling Rhœtian heights,
> The traveller spies green Lombardy below,
> And downward rushes toward that pleasant plain;
> So, sloping from long rolling swells,
> At last we launched upon the calm lagoon.[19]

But in this liquid passage we have not only rhythm, alliteration, and an indefinable timbre, which are reminiscent of Milton; we have also an epic simile.

> If we look into the Conduct of *Homer, Virgil* and *Milton*, as the great Fable is the Soul of each Poem, so to give their Works an agreeable Variety, their Episodes are so many short Fables, and their Similes so many short Episodes.[20]

Thus wrote Addison. Melville continued this epic tradition throughout *Moby-Dick*. Sometimes he put his epic similes into iambic pentameter patterns. When this is so, his rhythmic prose is most markedly Miltonic, just as his most Shakespearean tones occur in dramatic speeches. In the separate forms of simile and dialogue, Melville's fabric bears the stamp of the finest master in English of each form:

> As the unsetting Polar star,
> Which through the live-long, Arctic, six months' night
> Sustains its piercing, steady, central gaze;
> So Ahab's purpose now fixedly gleamed down
> Upon the constant midnight of the gloomy crew.[21]

As with Milton's, Melville's epic similes are occasionally elaborated at greater length, and sometimes they are grouped close to one another,[22] as with these examples from the same paragraph:

> As a pilot, when about losing sight of a coast, whose general trending he well knows, and which he desires shortly to return to again, but at some further point; like as this pilot stands by his compass, and takes the precise bearing of the cape at present visible, in order the more certain to hit aright the remote, unseen headland, eventually to be visited: so does the fisherman, at his compass, with the whale. . . . And as the mighty iron leviathan of the

modern railway is so familiarly known in its every pace, that, with watches in their hands, men time his rate as doctors that of a baby's pulse; and lightly say of it, the up train or the down train will reach such or such a spot, at such or such an hour; even so, almost, there are occasions when these Nantucketers time that other leviathan of the deep.[23]

Like these last, some of Milton's similes had been drawn from everyday life,[24] and like others of Milton's some of Melville's were drawn from travel, history, and other learned or unusual sources.[25]

One critic who has briefly analyzed Melville's use of Homeric similes to add bulk and stature to the White Whale and his pursuer, has continued,

He had made one or two flat attempts to handle . . . [similes] in *Mardi*; and his general interest in Homer was to be shown several years later by his frequent markings in Arnold's essay on how to translate him, and by his enthusiasm for Chapman's version. But what Melville had learned in *Moby-Dick* that he had not known in *Mardi* came not from Homer, but from his own assimilation of the organic principle. He had learned how to make beauty . . . functional, for, unlike most borrowers, he did not let his Homeric similes remain mere ornaments.

The flatness of the similes in *Mardi* is certainly open to question. And surely in addition to Melville's "own assimilation of the organic principle," or as an aid to it, one should mention the example of Milton. Milton was not the artist to use Homeric similes for "mere ornaments," and Melville must have learned much of Homer's art through Homer's presence in *Paradise Lost*.

The critic continues,

There could hardly be a more integral way of giving body to Ahab's *hubris* than by the image of the towering elm about to call down heaven's thunderbolt.[26]

The reference is to another iambic passage:

As in the hurricane that sweeps the plain,
Men fly the neighborhood of some lone,
Gigantic elm, whose very height and strength
But render it so much the more unsafe,
Because so much the more a mark for thunderbolts;
So at those last words of Ahab's
Many of the mariners did run
From him in a terror of dismay.[27]

Such a figure is most justly praised for its functionalism, but there is no very great step to this simile from the following one in *Paradise Lost*:

> Millions of Spirits for his fault amerc'd
> Of Heaven, and from eternal splendours flung
> For his revolt; yet faithful . . . stood,
> Their glory wither'd: as when Heaven's fire
> Hath scath'd the forest oaks, or mountain pines,
> With singed top their stately growth, though bare,
> Stands on the blasted heath.[28]

There is one other device for which Melville has been given credit which he should share with Milton and others. A claim that the interior monologue appeared first in modern literature in 1886 has been refuted by pointing out that

> three complete chapters in [*Moby-Dick*] . . . and many other passages, are but lengthy soliloquies which, in modern parlance, we should call interior monologues, since they are not spoken but represent the thought processes of . . . characters.[29]

As has already been indicated, some of Melville's soliloquies appear to find their prototypes in Shakespeare's. Yet there is a slight step from dramatic monologue to fictional thought. Consequently, in this respect Shakespeare is not so immediate a source as is Milton, who had already taken that step, using, in his own extended narrative, soliloquies precisely like Melville's.[30] Satan, Adam, and Eve are in all such cases said to have spoken, though that they spoke merely in silence to themselves can be presumed on the basis of this line preceding Adam's first reaction to Eve's trespass:

> First to himself he inward silence broke.[31]

In such monologues as well as in other speeches of their characters, as also in passages of exposition, both Milton and Melville show a further similarity—frequent bursts of emotion expressed in passages of pathos. Milton himself breaks out,

> O! when meet now
> Such pairs, in love and mutual honour join'd?

or

> How didst thou grieve then, Adam!

or he has Eve apostrophize,

> O flowers
> That never will in other climate grow![32]

Melville was apparently equally surcharged with emotion, which his romanticism vented in such exclamations as

> Oh! ye whose dead lie buried beneath the green grass!
> Oh, Ahab! what shall be grand in thee, it must needs be plucked at
>   from the skies.

Or a character calls,

> Oh! thou clear spirit of clear fire, whom on these seas I as Persian once
>   did worship.[33]

Weber says of this aspect of Melville's style,

> That which we meet in the rest of literature let us say as emphasis, must be considered as more or less formal rhetorical technique. That is in large measure the case with Milton. To be sure it is just his lofty pathos which leads directly over to the subjective outbreak of feeling typical of romanticism. Therefore we sense behind many pathetic passages in Melville's works the great example of Milton.[34]

In addition to the alliteration, rhythm, similes, soliloquies, and pathos which *Paradise Lost* and *Moby-Dick* have in common[35]—superimposed on similarities of vocabulary and sentence structure—there are some miscellaneous likenesses in techniques or structure. Melville's tale, for instance, begins in the middle of Ahab's feud with the White Whale, as Milton's begins in the middle of Satan's story; and both stories are marked by physical conflict and by traditional epic taunts and boastings. Furthermore, in both narratives the initially predominant character loses importance as another major figure, the author's intended hero, gains the stage: Ishmael fades as Ahab brightens, and Satan fades before Mankind. In both works the endings are revealed early by hints and statements of the outcome,[36] but the actual working out of the conclusions is delayed by digressions and interpolations, which strict classicists might wish expunged from each.[37] Melville digresses on whaling and Milton on theology and cosmology, while both halt to talk about themselves and are happy in their mixtures of science with pseudo-science. "The Town-Ho's Story" is a narrative within a narrative, as are Raphael's and Michael's longest speeches, with the same interruptions of the inner narratives to remind us of their dependence on the main story. The flow from the personal to the central to the peripheral and back again is very free. But in all cases, the apparent delays of the central action are necessary to the creation, in characters and readers, of understandings or attitudes vital to proper reactions when the climaxes arise.

Yet none of these matters, true parallels though they are, are essential to an epic.[38] An epic is to be identified not by similes or metaphors or a descent into hell, but by other less superficial characteristics. Those less superficial characteristics we are now in a position to discuss. In considering them we must focus our attention more sharply than ever on *Moby-Dick*, to the exclusion of Melville's other works, and we shall judge *Moby-Dick* not by what critics of Melville think an epic should be, but by what Lascelles Abercrombie, a critic of the epic, thinks an epic is. Nor will it seem necessary to point out in detail that *Paradise Lost* is an epic, and that, as the epic which Melville probably knew better than any other, it may well have influenced him in making *Moby-Dick* the generously epic book that it is.

One of the basic requirements for an epic is a story—but not any story whatsoever. The story of a true epic cannot be that of a *Rape of the Lock*, or, to come closer to home, of a *Mardi* or of a *Pierre*. The story of a true epic must not merely have "an unmistakable air of actuality"; it must be "something which indisputably, and admittedly, *has been* a human experience," whether it tells of "legendary heroism . . . or [of] actual history, as in Lucan and Camoens and Tasso."[39] Does *Moby-Dick* meet these qualifications? Certainly Melville's descriptions of whales and of the whaling industry have "an unmistakable air of actuality" established by his skill as an author but based on his experiences as a whale-hunter and on his wide reading in the literature of whaling. It is equally certain that the chief events of *Moby-Dick* were closely modeled upon happenings "which indisputably and admittedly" have been human experiences. During the first half of the nineteenth century, accounts of scores of whaling, trading, exploring, and missionary voyages were published, and through them ran tales of unusually vicious whales, of captains who long hunted a particular whale, and of ships sunk by whales.[40] Furthermore, the whaling industry was a major part of American economic life, and as such it influenced man's actions and thoughts to an extent best suggested by stating that it held much the same relationship to the 1830's, 40's, and 50's that aviation has held to the 1920's, 30's, and 40's.[41] Perhaps we cannot maintain that Melville's book is an epic to the extent that it uses "some great story which has been absorbed into the prevailing consciousness" of its author's country,[42] but certainly the physical environment in which his characters move was an actual one, familiar through experience or report to many of Melville's countrymen. And, by way of parenthesis, the sense of geographical scope in *Moby-Dick* is fully as great as that in *Paradise Lost*. They are both "large" stories as well as long ones.

But of course an epic is not merely a book telling a story which has an air of actuality and a background of authenticity. That story must be well and greatly told.[43] Whether *Moby-Dick* is a story well told might be determined by its popularity among adolescents as a tale of adventure. Whether it is greatly told might be determined by its popularity with adults. Or we might agree that by good and great telling we mean that the author of an epic must turn a mass of confused splendors into a grand design, forcing the parts "to obey a single presiding unity of artistic purpose." Such unity is not, of course, merely an external affair. The only thing "which can master the perplexed stuff of epic material into unity . . . is, an ability to see in particular human experience some significant symbolism of man's general destiny." The epic poet must, therefore, not merely accept the generally held facts of his era, but he must transfigure them so that they will symbolize not life itself, but some manner of life. That manner of life, based on courage, should reflect the accepted unconscious metaphysic of the author's age.[44]

It seems no more necessary to prove at this point that *Moby-Dick* has a significance beyond that of the loss of a ship than to prove that *Paradise Lost* tells of more than a battle in Heaven and the eating of an apple. Indeed, the very wealth of affirmations as to just what *Moby-Dick* and *Paradise Lost* do symbolize proves that they symbolize something or nothing, and the latter alternative few will accept. It is relevant, however, to note that John Freeman, Melville's English biographer, has found *Moby-Dick* and *Paradise Lost* to have the same larger significance:

> "That intangible malignity which has been from the beginning . . . all the subtle demonisms of life and thought"—it is this and these that haunt Ahab's heart as they haunt Melville. . . .
> > Of man's first disobedience and the fruit
> > Of that forbidden tree whose mortal taste
> > Brought death into the world and all our woe
> > With loss of Eden—
> this is Melville's theme as it was Milton's, but the name of the great enemy is not Lucifer, but Leviathan. The never-to-be-ended combat typified by Milton's Lucifer and Archangels is typified as boldly by Melville's Moby-Dick and Captain Ahab. Vindicating his pride against almightiness, Lucifer is overthrown but unsubdued; but vindicating his perverted spirit against a malignity not less perverse, Ahab is slain by the White Whale.[45]

With equal profit we can come at the same conclusion from another opinion. Abercrombie writes that in *Paradise Lost* "the spirit of man is equally conscious of its own limited reality and of the unlimited reality of that which contains him and drives him with its motion—of his own will striving in the midst of destiny: destiny irresistible, yet his will unmastered."[46] God is Milton's symbol for the unlimited reality which contains man. Is not the White Whale a symbol for the same concept? Milton, true to his age, thought of irresistible destiny in terms of a divine power centered in God. Melville, equally true to his age, thought of irresistible destiny in terms of the mysterious powers of unleashed nature, best symbolized by the most powerful animate creation of nature. God was still the consciously or outwardly worshipped power of 1851, but the unconscious metaphysic of Melville's age—the age of land and sea frontiers, of growing materialism, of the exploitation of nature, and of the pre-Darwinian cuts at revelation—that metaphysic held nature as its deity to worship and to fear.

Such a manner of life—or indeed any manner of life—is best portrayed in literature through people who live, through convincing characters. It is, therefore, a further requirement of an epic that it contain at least one figure "in whom the whole virtue, and perhaps also the whole failure, of living seems superhumanly concentrated." Through that figure will be symbolized much of the meaning of the epic, and he will be its hero.

Three chapters earlier, during a discussion of the inner affinity which existed between Melville and Milton, mention was made of Melville's sharing Milton's repugnance to the traditional trappings of the military hero. From that discussion, however, should not have been inferred the notion that Melville's and Milton's characters are not heroic. Although they may lack the outward marks of Homer's heroes, they have much of their spirit: their courage and their individuality. Especially is this true of the Satan of the first six books of *Paradise Lost*, and of Ahab. They illustrate remarkably well what Abercrombie says of the morals of an heroic age:

> In Homer, for instance, it can be seen pretty clearly that a "good" man is simply a man of imposing, active individuality; . . . he who rules is thereby proven the "best." And from its nature it must be an age very heartily engaged in something; usually in fighting whoever is near enough to be fought with.

And was not a large part of the America of the nineteenth century experiencing an heroic age? Were not the Calhouns, the Thoreaus, the Astors manifesting in their very different ways that theirs was a time for "vehement private individuality freely and greatly asserting itself," even though "the assertion is not always what we should call noble"? It is relevant to note that the heroic age does not, as a rule, last very long, and that it is succeeded by "a comparatively rigid and perhaps comparatively lustreless civilization"?[47] Some of these questions can be answered only with greater perspective than we now have. Certainly the answers to them are not intended to lead to the conclusion that the century of Andrew Jackson and James Fiske was identical in spirit with the century of Achilles and Odysseus. Nevertheless, it may be valuable to think of Ahab as the hero of an epic. To do so may cast new light on the hero, on the epic, and on what the author of the epic may have learned from previous epics. A man can be a hero of primitive courage using either a sword or a prayer to God or an injunction, and fighting for either brute or spiritual or financial dominance.

To notice similarities leads, however, only half the way to wisdom's house. The rest of the way is reached by recognizing the significance of dissimilarities. There is much significance in the differences between Adam and Achilles. There is perhaps equal significance in the differences between both of them and Ahab, and between earlier epics and *Moby-Dick*. For example, that Adam in Paradise is in command of one of God's works, whereas Ahab in the Pacific is in command of a capitalistic business enterprise is not unrelated to certain theological and economic differences between Milton and Melville as individuals, and between the ages in which they lived. Meanings for other differences have already appeared in this study, and more will appear before the end.

There remains the necessity for this chapter to consider the fact that an epic poet, dealing with a story and a significance, should set them out in as lofty poetry as he can achieve.[48] Certainly Milton created *Paradise Lost* with lofty poetry. Did Melville so create *Moby-Dick*?

Much of *Moby-Dick* cannot by any sane standards be called poetry. It may be very competent prose, but it is not poetry. Yet for being prose it should, probably, be praised, not condemned, since its matter is matter best treated in prose. And perhaps it is entirely appropriate that large parts of a modern epic should be written in prose. Perhaps continuous verse is to be required of only those epics written in an age when verse is the dominant form of literary expression. In an age when prose is dominant, perhaps we should expect prose epics. Yet however this may be, some passages of *Moby-Dick* are written in a style so unlike that of most of the book that it seems to deserve a special name. "Verse" is not appropriate, but "prose-poetry" or "poetry" suggest themselves. Certainly the matter of these passages is much like the matter from which Milton and others have created unquestioned poetry. Certainly the manner of these passages has the elevation, even the ritualism, of *Paradise Lost*. And in these passages appear many of the characteristics of vocabulary, of sentence structure, and of alliteration, rhythm, similes, soliloquies, and pathos which we have termed Miltonic.

As has been mentioned from time to time, numerous of these characteristics are ones which Raymond Dexter Havens used as criteria of Milton's influence on English poetry. What, we may ask, is the final tally? Three characteristics of *Paradise Lost* Havens considered valueless in determining Milton's influence on authors who had read pre-Miltonic poetry, but valuable in determining why poetry sounded Miltonic. These three are repetitions of words or phrases, cumulations of the same parts of speech, and the use of adjectives ending in *-ean* or *-ian* and derived from proper nouns. All of these we have found in *Moby-Dick* and others of Melville's works. Of the nine characteristics more peculiar to Milton's epic, seven are these: inversions of natural word order, omissions of words not needed to convey the meaning, parentheses and apposition, the use of one part of speech as another, a vocabulary marked by archaisms and borrowings, generous use of proper nouns, and unusual compound epithets. Every one of these also marks Melville's style to a greater or less degree. The two traits which I have not listed are "dignity, reserve, and stateliness"; and "the organ tone, the sonorous orotund."[49] These two are also found in Melville. Moreover, the two following quotations illustrate not only the dignity and sonorousness to complete Havens' tally, but also support the contention that like other epic writers Melville set out his story and its significance in lofty poetry:

Where unrecorded names and navies rust, and untold hopes and anchors rot; where in her murderous hold this frigate earth is ballasted with bones of millions of the drowned; there, in that awful water-land, there was thy most familiar home.

I turn my body from the sun. What ho, Tashtego! let me hear thy hammer. Oh! ye three unsurrendered spires of mine; thou uncracked keel; and only god-bullied hull; thou firm deck, and haughty helm, Pole-pointed prow,— death-glorious ship! must ye then perish, and without me? Am I cut off from the last fond pride of meanest shipwrecked captains? Oh, lonely death on lonely life! Oh, now I feel my topmost greatness lies in my topmost grief. Ho, ho! from all your furthest bounds, pour ye now in, ye bold billows of my whole foregone life, and top this one piled comber of my death! Toward thee I roll, thou all-destroying but unconquering whale; to the last I grapple with thee.[50]

The present study has, of course, emphasized links between Milton and Melville which fell outside the purpose of Havens' analysis. Iambic rhythm, epic similes, suspensions, compounds of *all* and *un-*, and general epic characteristics are perhaps the most important of these, but the sum of them must be totaled if one is to grasp the full significance of A. S. W. Rosenbach's statement that Melville "could write with . . . the grandeur of Milton."[51] To repeat, this study does not have to do with a case of conscious imitation, nor with an unconscious, unadulterated assimilation. To some indeterminable extent it does deal with the fact that "the books . . . [which] really spoke to Melville became an immediate part of him to a degree hardly matched by any other of our great writers in their maturity."[52] It also deals with that close, attentive reading, whereby "one great Genius often catches the Flame from another, and writes in his Spirit, without copying servilely after him."[53]

Finally, let us, after all, use a method mentioned many pages earlier. In reading the first quotation, let us think how true of Melville's style is this description originally made of Milton's; and, in reading the second, let us think how true of *Paradise Lost* is the already familiar sentence concerning *Moby-Dick*:

[Melville's] style, despite his employment of a verse form identical with the Elizabethan dramatists, stands at an opposite pole from that of Shakespeare and his colleagues. [Melville's] . . . language, unlike theirs, has little relish of the speech of men. Where their anomalies are colloquial and idiomatic, his are the product of a preference for the unusual and recondite, in vocabulary and construction, which leads him to archaism on the one hand, and to the substitution of foreign idiom, particularly Latin, for native on the other. Sometimes not even classical or earlier English example can be alleged. [Melville] . . . is simply carving for himself, remoulding and creating with fine disregard for precedent. In general, [Melville's] . . . style may be described as almost uniquely literary and intellectual. Freighted with learning and bookish phrase, elaborate in construction, often alien in vocabulary, it achieves a uniform effect of dignity and aloofness and becomes a perfect medium for the restrained and elevated yet intensely passionate personality of its author.[54]

[*Paradise Lost*] is a symphony, every resource of language and thought, fantasy, description, philosophy, natural history, drama, broken rhythms, blank verse, imagery, symbol, are utilized to sustain and expand the great theme.

As Addison wrote in an essay on Milton,

The Learned Reader cannot but be pleased with the Poet's Imitation of Homer.[55]

The sequence of imitation and the pleasure of learned readers were both augmented by Melville's echoing of Milton.

Notes

1. H.M. to Richard H. Dana, Jr., May 1, 1850 (Harrison Hayford, "Two New Letters of Herman Melville," *Journal of English Literary History*, XI [March, 1944], 76–83; p. 79).

2. *Moby-Dick*, II, 184.

3. John Erskine, *The Delight of Great Books* (Indianapolis, 1928), pp. 230, 223.

4. Sealts, *Melville's Reading in Ancient Philosophy*, p. 23; Mumford, *Melville*, p. 181; *Pierre*, ed. Forsythe, p. xxxii; *Billy Budd*, ed. Freeman, p. 73.

5. Padraic Colum, *A Half-Day's Ride* (N.Y., 1932), pp. 175–176.

6. *E.g.*, James Holly Hanford, "The Dramatic Element in *Paradise Lost*," *Studies in Philology*, XIV (April, 1917), 178–195; Matthiessen, *American Renaissance*, pp. 414–421.

7. Addison, *Spectator*, No. CCCXV, p. 72.

8. *Moby-Dick*, II, 335; I, 44, 293. Weber calls the last quotation "epischer Prosa" (*Stilistische Untersuchung*, p. 17).

9. *Redburn*, p. 323.

10. Weber, *Stilistische Untersuchung*, pp. 34–35.

11. *E.g.*, George C. Homans, "The Dark Angel: The Tragedy of Herman Melville," *New England Quarterly*, V (October, 1932), 699–730; p. 715: "At times, like its companions, *Moby-Dick* seeks the level of blank verse rhapsody."

12. Matthiessen, *American Renaissance*, p. 426. Padraic Colum has analyzed and printed other passages as "conventionally epical . . . prose," blank verse, polyphonic prose, and free verse (*Half-Day's Ride*, pp. 176–179).

13. *Moby-Dick*, II, 257. Here and below I have capitalized the initial letters of the "lines."

14. Weber, *Stilistische Untersuchung*, p. 22.

Master as . . . {Milton} was of all the resources of verse, he was less an innovator in "numbers" than in other things. Every important characteristic of his versification which is capable of being defined, isolated, and catalogued is to be found in the plays of Shakespeare and the lesser Elizabethans [Havens, Influence of Milton, *p. 86].*

15. Particularly the examples just referred to in Matthiessen.

16. H.M. to E.A.D., February 24, 1849 (*Selections,* ed. Thorp, p. 370).

17. *Mardi,* I, [vii].

18. Minnigerode, *Personal Letters of Melville,* pp.137–138.

19. *Mardi,* II, 272. Iambic rhythm immediately precedes and follows this selection, and occurs elsewhere in *Mardi* (II, 54, 120, 375–377).

20. Addison, *Spectator,* No. CCCIII, p. 58. Italics in original.

21. *Moby-Dick,* II, 318.

22. Four extended similes for a frigate are presented in succession in *White Jacket,* pp. 94–95.

23. *Moby-Dick,* II, 343–344.

24. *Ibid.,* I, 54; II, 97, 263, 345. *P.L.,* I, 594 ff., 768 ff.

25. *Moby-Dick,* I, 344, 346–347; II, 127; *Clarel,* II, 75. *P.L.,* I, 203 ff., 230 ff., 287 ff., 302 ff., 338 ff.; IV, 159 ff.

Melville's pronounced poetic and impressionistic comparisons from nature and animal life unite him with romanticism, while his many geographic, historic, folk-loric, Biblical, and mythological comparisons indicate a continuation of the rhetorical tradition of the Renaissance (Rabelais, Lyly, Shakespeare, Marlowe, Milton; also Carlyle) [Weber, Stilistische Untersuchung, p.139].

26. Matthiessen, *American Renaissance,* p. 461. Italics in original.

27. *Moby-Dick,* II, 284. The last four lines present, of course, some unimportant variations from a strict iambic pentameter pattern.

28. *P.L.,* I, 609–615. See also James Whaler, "The Miltonic Simile," *Publications of the Modern Language Association,* XLVI (December, 1931), 1034–1074.

29. N. Bryllion Fagin, "Herman Melville and the Interior Monologue," *Am. Lit.,* VI (January, 1935), 433–434; p. 433.

30. *P.L.,* IV, 32 ff.; IX, 99 ff., 794 ff., 896 ff.

31. *Ibid.,* IX, 895.

32. *Ibid.,* VIII, 57–58; XI, 754, 273–274.

33. *Moby-Dick,* I, 44, 183; II, 281.

34. Weber, *Stilistische Untersuchung,* pp. 127–128. On p. 176 Weber mentions again "das wuchtige Pathos Miltons."

35. Nor should it be forgotten that other of Melville's works bear incidental likenesses to Milton's epic. In *Mardi* (II, 120), for example, Melville introduces a speech with this sentence fragment of ablative absolutes:
Some remedies applied, and the company grown composed, Babbalanja thus. . . . Milton also introduced speeches with sentence fragments and *thus* (*P.L.,* IV, 610, 634, 834, 885, etc.).

36. *Moby-Dick,* I, 76, 81, 85, 100; *P.L.,* III.

37. Addison, *Spectator,* No. CCXCVII, pp. 46–47. A more charitable view is implied in No. CCCXXXIII, p. 100.

38. Lascelles Abercrombie, *The Epic* (London, [1914]), p. 52. This book is the basis for much of the following discussion.

39. *Ibid.,* pp. 39, 45.

40. Pommer, "Melville and the Wake of the *Essex,*" pp. 290–292.

41. Charles Olson, *Call Me Ishmael* (N.Y., [1947]), pp. 16–25; Sedgwick, *Melville,* pp. 89–91; Weaver, *Melville,* pp. 135–159.

42. Abercrombie, *Epic,* p. 39. Cf. More, "The Theme of *Paradise Lost,*" p. 239: "An epic . . . must be built upon a theme deeply rooted in national belief."

43. *Ibid.,* p. 42.

44. *Ibid.,* pp. 17, 39, 69–70. Cf. More, "The Theme of *Paradise Lost,*" pp. 239–240:

"The development of . . . [an epic] theme must express, more or less symbolically, some universal truth of human nature . . . The poet himself need not be fully conscious of this deeper meaning."

45. John Freeman, *Herman Melville* (N.Y., 1926), pp. 116–117.
46. Abercrombie, *Epic,* p. 80.
47. *Ibid.,* pp. 50, 13, 12, 7.
48. *Ibid.,* p. 39.
49. Havens, *Influence of Milton,* pp. 85, 80–85, 80.
50. *Moby-Dick,* II, 38, 366.
51. Rosenbach, *An Introduction to . . . Moby-Dick,* p. 6.
52. Matthiessen, *American Renaissance,* p. 122.
53. Addison, *Spectator,* No. CCCXXXIX, p. 102.
54. Hanford, *Milton Handbook,* pp. 293–294.
55. Addison, *Spectator,* No. CCCXXVII, p. 90; italics in original.

[Melville's Humor]

JANE MUSHABAC

Part of the sustained achievement of *Moby-Dick* is that Melville has not only found exactly the subject to talk about, but a way of talking about it. One of his distractions in earlier novels was finding a form when available ones such as the travel narrative and the sentimental novel were wrong—unresilient and constricting. Richard Chase has suggested forms and motifs which Melville found in American folklore;[1] these indeed were instrumental in liberating Melville's humor by providing him a way to talk about his very American subject. I suggest, however, that American folklore is only one part, the final part, of what Melville was absorbing and building upon. This was the whole tradition of prose humorists who, from the Renaissance on, played with the excitement of the opening of the frontier, of land and knowledge, of the new man of infinite potentials. Indeed, Melville is not only relieved to find available to him all the forms of the past, but even seems to enjoy the showmanship of incorporating and building upon all the male frontier monologues he knew and admired: the Renaissance tall tale of Rabelais; the melancholy anatomy of Burton; the humorous novel of sensibility/cock-and-bull story of Sterne; the humorous essay of sensibility of Lamb, De Quincey, and Irving; and finally the periodical tall tale or twister of popular American culture.

In his extravaganza, Rabelais gave Melville a way of spelling out the feeling of prodigiousness and bounty that is at the heart of frontier humor. Rabelais created Gargantua and Pantagruel, giants of body, mind, and heart who are described in an affectionate extravagant vernacular and sprung from native folk legend. Like Pantagruel, the whale in Melville's book is a vast creature, described and admired in a spirited colloquial tongue, one who as an infant consumes in a day thousands of gallons of milk, and as an adult, travelling whither he pleases and turning up everywhere, takes the whole world for his province. Moby Dick, in addition, as one particular whale, is sprung very consciously from native legend and, like Pantagruel, is male, important, and importantly dressed in white. Gargantua's enterprising love of learning and independent thinking meanwhile has encouraged Ishmael's bragging, central to *Moby-Dick*, of the grand sweep and scope of his research and knowledge. And so contagious is the love of learning in Rabelais's book

Excerpted and reprinted from *Melville's Humor: A Critical Study* (Hamden, Connecticut: Archon Books, 1981), 89–110. Reprinted by permission. Footnote numbering has been altered.

that even Panurge, obscene practical joker that he is, first wins Pantagruel's heart in the beginning of their long friendship by saying that he is hungry in thirteen languages. Is this perhaps why Ishmael in his overture to his reader translates *whale* into thirteen languages?

For all the friendship and affection, however, neither in Rabelais nor in Melville is the bounty strictly benign. At heart also it is an aggressiveness, not just threatening women, but men and sheep, too, and in this regard Panurge's practical jokes were sources for Melville's inclusion of Stubb's in *Moby-Dick*. Alcofrybas also, let us recall, is always on hand as the subservient fellow so small he could live for six months in Gargantua's throat without that giant even noticing. Indeed this important episode in Rabelais is related to the image of man being swallowed by the whale that figures so large in the mythology behind *Moby-Dick*. Giants, in short, are wonderful but they may swallow you, just as all the marvelous dreams of man's democratic and egalitarian potential may swallow you and leave you a "pale loaf-of-bread" faced steward (*MD* 130), tremblingly serving at the "Cabin Table" the voracious, superb, baronial "giants" (*MD* 133), the harpooners.

The great throat swallows, the great mouth talks. Rabelais's book, like Melville's afterwards, is a teasing ventriloquistic performance. Panurge through three volumes only wishes to know whether he should marry or not, as Pip later in an incident central to *Moby-Dick* only wants to know if he is supposed to jump from the whaleboat or not. All they both get is talk—long, endlessly pompous, contradictory sermons. Moving from physician to poet to philosopher to lawyer to scholar in one book, and from First Congregationalist to Shakespearean soliloquizer to Poor Richard to a tale teller in Peru in the other is a sign that none of the oracles' advice can shield us from uncertainties, particularly because all the ventriloquism is served up with a sexual and religious teasing. Indeed Rabelais helped liberate Melville's humor in this regard. Pantagruel's buoyant sexuality, St. Victor's vast pornographic library, Panurge's making a shambles of feminine niceties and sexual pieties: these are all a great source for Melville in *Moby-Dick*. In *Mardi*, Melville had backed off into a prudish irritability. Here, however, he does not hesitate. In addition to the wide open jokes of a book about "sperm" and a tale of a tail, we get a quiet succession of teasing innuendoes and one-liners about unicorns, prizes to queens, and elephants in the marketplace softly caressing ladies' "zones."

That Melville had Rabelais in mind for a many-sided teasingly heretical independence is clear from a crucial chapter that he borrowed from Rabelais, the whiteness chapter—about Pantagruel wearing, and Moby Dick being, white.[2] The business of these chapters is a theatrical redefinition of the word *white*, Rabelais and Melville each ceremoniously rejecting meanings from the past, insisting upon his own interpretation of things, and officiously cataloguing all the evidence supporting his view. If Melville emphasizes dread to Rabelais's joy, we should keep in mind that Rabelais in that chapter tells us that the "lion, who with his only cry and roaring affrights all beasts, dreads and feareth only a white cock,"[3] and ends by speaking of white as the color of a joy so extreme you could die from it. Similarly Melville in his milk-white steed gives us a creature of royal magnificence which, like that of the Milky Way itself, affrights us, but only by being the greatest of spectacles of this universe. It is certainly true that Rabelais never emphasizes the dread which haunts Melville's novel, that atheism to Rabelais never seems the truly terrifying spectre it does to Melville, that Melville in turn takes Rabelais's catalogue of the previous meanings of white up past Rabelais, through Coleridge (and Poe) to his own. We do have a contrast in tone and fable between the two books. But in some basic concept of the bounty of the universe and of the sociability of friendships like those of Pantagruel and Panurge, Gargantua and Pantagruel, in the excitement of gigantic man as a New World creature of possibilities, and the bounty of nature's gallons of milk, white and endless—Melville found a great source in Rabelais.

Robert Burton gave *Moby-Dick* not just the form of the anatomy,[4] but his subject and a purpose, to cure his own melancholy by writing. "When I first took this task in hand," Democritus, Jr. writes, "this I aimed at: to ease my mind by writing, for I had a heavy heart and an ugly head, a kind of imposthume in my head, which I was very desirous to be unladen of, and could imagine no fitter evacuation than. Besides I might not well refrain, for one must needs scratch where it itches."[5] Ishmael goes to sea for the same reason: "It is a way I have of driving off the spleen, and regulating the circulation. Whenever I find myself growing grim about the mouth: whenever it is a damp, drizzly November in my soul . . . especially whenever my hypos get such an upper hand of me. . . . This is my substitute for pistol and ball. With a philosophical flourish Cato throws himself upon his sword; I quietly take to the ship" (*MD* 12). One for his anatomy, the other for his journey, the purpose is the same, to drive off the spleen, the ugliness in the head, the haziness around the eyes, the heaviness of the heart. Indeed in *Moby-Dick*, as in *The Anatomy of Melancholy*, the imposthume of the head is a central obsession; it is not incidental that Ishmael, while he turns to other things, enjoys leaving the sperm whale's prodigious head hanging on the *Pequod*'s side for, as in Burton, the story begins with a prodigious head (the persona's) caught, suspended, and turned into a helpless monstrosity waiting upon its master. "Too many heads" (*MD* 25), says the landlord of the Spouter Inn, and Melville loves to let us see the steam rising both from whales' heads and philosophers'. "While composing a little treatise on Eternity, I had the curiosity to place a mirror before me . . ." (*MD* 313), Ishmael writes.

Democritus, Jr., we should note, by legacy has good reason for his melancholy. The original Democritus, Burton reminds us, was nothing less than the patriarch of those "Copernical giants";[6] he was the radical scientist who conceived of the universe as all in perpetual atomical motion. The original Ishmael also was no mere anonymous orphan and outcast, but the father of a whole new tribe, a whole new heretical religion, Islam. Melville, in choosing such a name, is following Burton's suit here as the later spate of humorists, by the way, will not. By legacy, then, in both Burton and Melville, it is as if at the start of their books, both men are beyond pat and hackneyed orthodoxies ranging from the Senecan to the Christian. No wonder their heads are steaming and prodigious. No wonder also in both works the speakers at once brag of being a free man born, a schoolmaster, a lording anatomist—and a fool, a slave, a prisoner. "Who aint a slave?" (*MD* 15), Ishmael teases at one point, while Democritus, Jr., "the free man born," tells us that "we are slaves and servants, the best of us all," that he is a giddy fool giving us his "confused lump," his "phantastical fit," and asks "What's our life but a prison?"[7] One needs to know a lot and to be a perseveringly independent thinker in order to have achieved the full title of vulnerability to the chaos of the mind and this universe.

The cure for the imposthume in the head is much the same in both works. Ishmael, like Democritus, Jr., consoles himself with absorption in some monumental all-defying project; it hardly matters that one uses a voyage at sea and the other a voyage of the mind. Ishmael's voyage after all is only grist for his mill, and Democritus, Jr. in his anatomy also, among an eventual myriad of proposed remedies, recommends voyages. Democritus, Jr. takes his readers in fact on a whirlwind tour in "A Digression of Air" to "many strange places, Isthmuses, Europeuses, Chersones, creeks, havens, promontories, straits, lakes, baths, rocks, mountains, places and fields, where Cities have been ruined or swallowed, battles fought, creatures, Sea-monsters, remora, minerals, vegetals."[8] The important thing about the cure is that neither the wonders of travel nor the spectacles of the extravaganza anatomy are mere curatives to the disease, but its cause to begin with. In a popular American song, a doctor prescribes lime and coconut for the patient who is sick from drinking lime and coconut. The madness itself is a product of the original excitability. What Melville borrows from Burton is the underlying preposterousness of the cure. Burton cites Felix Plater, who went on a seven-year voyage to rid himself of the chattering Aristophanic frogs in his belly, but what are Burton's *Anatomy* and Melville's *Moby-Dick* but more frogs chanting splendid impossible "wicked" nonsense, "Breccex, Coax, coax, oop, oop," a fine promiscuity of erudition and jabber, of fancy scientific words and slang. What indeed is the whole anatomy but "never a barrel better herring?"[9]

Comparing Burton's central proof that all men are mad with Melville's that whaling is noble gives us a concrete image of how all this works out through the two books. Just as Burton makes up an absurd list of exceptions to prove the rule, such as Monsieur Nobody and the Stoics who must be mad for not being so, Ishmael as the "advocate" conjures up a great melodramatic courtroom scene in which, to vindicate the nobility of whaling, a hodge-podge of absurd logic, grandiose allusion, and general fast-talking is thrown at the reader while the speaker works himself into a frenzy of assertion. Burton's frenzy is quieter and more archaic in its tone, but he is doing the same thing.

> No dignity in whaling? The dignity of our calling the very heavens attest. Cetus is a constellation in the South! No more! Drive down your hat in presence of the Czar, and take it off to Queequeg! No more! I know a man that, in his lifetime, has taken three hundred and fifty whales. I account that man more honorable than that great captain of antiquity who boasted of taking as many walled towns. [MD 101]

The odd thing is that while the rowdy exaggeration would seem to undermine the argument, the more it parodies itself, the more it nonetheless convinces us. Say no more, indeed! All men are mad! Whaling is noble! Can we possibly disagree? Can we possibly not submit to the acataleptic fervor? The Burtonesque geological sandwiches of *Mardi* have expanded. The whole of *Moby-Dick*, with its perpetual fossil whales, cetologies, and masthead exhaustive researches, endlessly anatomizes the whale, the whaleship, and this watery world.

Laurence Sterne's *Tristram Shandy*[10] is a rewriting and reshaping of Burton's *Anatomy* which gave Melville another handle for *Moby-Dick*. That Tristram writes in the same vein as Democritus, Jr. is clear. "If 'tis wrote against anything,—'tis wrote," Tristram says of his book, "against the spleen."[11] Sterne, however, has made several shifts. Dropping Burton's discreetness, he has revived Rabelais's open sexual and religious teasing in time to encourage Melville to do the same. In addition, Sterne has turned Burton's dignified melancholic philosopher into the domesticated pathetic men of the Shandy household, who are as infatuated with learning as Democritus, Jr. ever was but, in addition, ceremoniously castrated and mechanized, deprived of their noses and names. Indeed, since Melville was responding as much to Sterne as to Burton, it is crucial that we do not speak of Melville's fixation on unmanning without reference to its central place in all the Sterne-based humorous male monologues of the nineteenth century.

Most importantly, however, Sterne has tightened Burton's unwieldy extravaganza *consolatio* to the form at its core, the novel of sensibility/cock-and-bull story, a form surely, by the way, the English ancestor of the American twister. It is most of all the form of Sterne's novel that Melville has worked from; for Sterne's book, unlike Burton's, devotes itself to a series of plotted splenetic events. From the very opening when Walter is interrupted by his wife to every other event of irritation that follows, *Tristram Shandy*'s plot itself is hardly more than a series of disconnections and exasperations.

It is in this conceptual sense that Melville's book is a novel of sensibility. The author is not only willing to dispel his own hypos—morbid blues—but to expiate them, not with a plot built upon a series of frustrations, but with a plot centered on one major exasperation. Indeed the word *exasperation* occurs regularly in the book, like a chime, beginning with the picture of the exasperated whale impaling itself upon the dismantled masts of a ship, like Cato upon his sword. Luther Mansfield has noted a perverse skepticism in Melville's interpreting Cato's great act of courage as mere cure for the spleen.[12] This, however, is the humorist's perspective, establishing from the start a vision of man as a creature beset by hypos and exasperations, and needing continually to get himself from one to the next. So we see other whales, later in the novel, their hunters in the midst of "the serene, exasperating sunlight"; we hear of Ahab's "intellectual and spiritual exasperations," and of Radney at a crucial moment being in a "corporeally exasperated state" (*MD* 159, 160, 212). One may object that all this suggests tragic recognition rather than the exasperation of sensibility. We would not speak, however, of Oedipus or Antigone or Lear as being *exasperated*. The word connotes something unheroic and essentially melodramatic; it describes a creature literally *roughened up*—and by the extremes, not of hubris, but of hypos. We cannot be surprised when Melville turns this sensibility inside out, showing us sulking right whales with their embarrassingly limp lower jaws hanging down, or punning about grim old bull whales who will fight you "like grim fiends exasperated by a penal gout" (*MD* 330).

This is not to say that Sterne and Melville do not have their differences, and use the cock-and-bull story/novel of sensibility in different ways. Melville's humor is grounded in a way that Sterne's is never intended to be; Melville is utterly determined to take the hypo, spleen, and exasperation to their sharpest, so that we most need the humor that is the staple of the book, so that it is in no way gratuitous. Nonetheless, there is a certain similarity that is important, not just incidental. The final thing we must say about Ahab is astonishing to come upon. We have seen him described as one sullen animal after another—all comparisons that are grim jokes on man's idealization of his misery. Even further, however, what we must come to terms with is the hum: "While the mate was getting the hammer, Ahab, without speaking, was slowly rubbing the gold piece against the skirts of his jacket, as if to heighten its lustre, and without using any words was meanwhile lowly humming to himself, producing a sound so strangely muffled and inarticulate that it seemed the mechanical humming of the wheels of his vitality in him" (*MD* 142).

This is balder than the confidence man later humming to himself an "opera snatch" (*TCM* 61) as he goes down the hall to gull the old miser. This is closer to Henri Bergson's mechanical man at the root of all humor.[13] This is related to Walter Shandy's winding up the clock and his marital relations the same one night a month at the opening of Sterne's book. Ishmael too will become the mechanical man of warp and woof, the mere shuttle in "The Mat-Maker," as does the carpenter at the end of the book in a short, brilliant sketch. Finally Moby Dick also in the last moment before Ahab's death: "Suddenly the waters around them slowly swelled in broad circles; then quickly upheaved, as if sideways sliding from a submerged berg of ice, swiftly rising to the surface. A low rumbling sound was heard; a subterraneous hum; and then all held their breaths; as bedraggled with trailing ropes, and harpoons, and lances, a vast form shot lengthwise, but obliquely from the sea" (MD 464). Melville's mechanical exasperated creature—man or beast, cock and bull—is a creature of sensibility and grim humor. Melville takes the joke of the hypo absolutely and deliberately to its limit, but the pattern in which he does so is the novel of sensibility/cock-and-bull story.

It was in Thomas De Quincey's book that Melville found this sensibility gone to seed. Indeed, De Quincey often uses the word *sensibility* to describe the extreme hypos which pushed him to his own extreme remedy, opium addiction. The braggadocio of extremism, the determination to encounter the worst, provided a model, a novel of grim humor, which we cannot be surprised that Melville found "wondrous" in 1849. Specifically, De Quincey's book, *Being an Extract from the Life of a Scholar* (as it was subtitled), gave Melville a monologue of a man proudly miserable in the midst of his myriad of books, a monologue of a modern worried child of Burton and Johnson. De Quincey, much like Ishmael after him in the Spouter Inn, begins with a deliberate and clumsy attempt to produce an amusing situation, his trunk willfully spiriting itself downstairs as he tries to steal away quietly from the house where he is staying. Buffoonery, however, gives way quickly to the mainstream of his confessional and the steadier wryness of passages like the one in which De Quincey peremptorily asks an artist to paint a cottage in order to spell out a theory of happiness ineluctably tied to a demand for a good strong terrible winter. That Melville enjoys this approach is suggested by his taking up the same theme in very similar language:

> But here is an artist. He desires to paint you the dreamiest, shadiest, quietest, most enchanting bit of romantic landscape in all the valley of the Saco. What is the chief element he employs? . . . Go visit the Prairies in June, when for scores of miles you wade knee-deep among Tiger-lilies . . . what is the one charm wanting? . . . there is not a drop of water there! Were Niagara but a cataract of sand, would you travel your thousand miles to see it? [MD 13]

In De Quincey the article, the goods, is winter; in Melville, it is water. In Melville also, however, his theory of happiness resounds to cold outdoors as Ishmael and Queequeg sit up in bed together "very nice and snug, the more so since it was so chilly out of doors. . . . The more so, I say, because truly to enjoy bodily warmth, some small part of you must be cold. . . .

For the height of this sort of deliciousness is to have nothing but the blanket between you and your snugness and the cold of the outer air. Then there you lie like the one warm spark in the heart of an arctic crystal" (*MD* 55). Melville takes up De Quincey's playful perversity here by conscientiously reasoning upon a subject that boils down to a question of taste. Indeed, it seems Melville not only had De Quincey in mind, but deliberately enlarged upon the bit. Melville must have water nearby his cottage in the happy valley, he will tolerate no fire on his most wintry of eves, and, above all, he wants his nose cold.

It is in Melville's chapter 35 that De Quincey's opium is introduced. Ishmael tells us riding in the masthead produced a trance very much like that produced by opium. The trance in turn produces a giddy, wry monologue with historical, philosophical, and emotional commentary upon mastheads; with a mock earnestness cataloguing all possible entrants in that category; teasing pious narrators like Scoresby; and above all celebrating the snugness of this cold, vulnerable, lonely perch which might easily throw a man to his watery death hundreds of feet below. The masthead, indeed, with its opiumlike trance, is Melville's De Quinceyan cottage of happiness par excellence, perfectly fit out to supply the theory of happiness. Here we not only deny ourselves fire, counterpane, and tea (although Ishmael chides the arctic Scoresby for omitting to mention his flask), but windows, walls, and roof.

Indeed, finally here is the difference between De Quincey's and Melville's wry humor of vast vulnerability, of being out in the cold—that De Quincey actually takes a drug to induce his giddy wryness, whereas Ishmael induces his own without help from any of the beverages which humorists have so depended upon to soothe their melancholy souls. In *Moby-Dick*, Melville leaps from the standard humorists' ploy of drinking a beverage to mentally fixating on one. The liquid in *Moby-Dick* is water, but instead of physically drinking it, Ishmael mentally takes it in and becomes obsessed with it, as if he has taken the whole "watery world" and got drunk on it. In contrast to De Quincey, because his trance is only opium-like, and not actually opium-induced, Melville has all the freedom of its intense vision and all the depths of its vulnerability which are the realm of the humorist, but none of the disadvantages. "That De Quincey is a very conscious (at . . . moments one would say conscientious) humorist is obvious," writes Jean-Jacques Mayoux. "What seems to me much less certain is that he knows the way his humor is going, or that he guides it."[14] Melville does guide his book's humor; neither Melville as author nor Ishmael as narrator-humorist is forced into the bondage produced by a chemical actually in the blood. Thus the fine wryness that is so spotty in De Quincey—as in the footnote in which he earnestly discusses whether a druggist may "evanesce," or tosses off a thought about it being a disagreeable thing to die—is intrinsic to Melville's work and steady in it. Similarly, where disturbing childhood events such as a trance over the death of a sister may sprawl out cloyingly over pages of "Suspira Profundis," Ishmael's trance over the loss of his dinner, a very similar type of evocation of a child's utter sense of isolation in an adult world, passes within a page or two, evoking the traumatic material from which humor is built, but never pressing it, providing a source for the humor without ever getting out of control.

Much more in control than De Quincey, although turning the game from deliberately confronting to deliberately evading the extremes of human vulnerability, is Charles Lamb. Elia is an important source for Ishmael. Elia is male, a bachelor, melancholy, domesticated, all oddities and quirks, and pleasures and displeasures, yet overridingly sociable and amiable, with affection especially for other ornery types like his grumbling housekeeper. Elia besides is a customshouse thrall, "poor Elia," who is continuously drawing our attention to the pathetic distance between man's illusion of mental control and the actuality of dependency and slavery, between theory and practice: "My theory is to enjoy life, but the practice is aginst it."[15] Elia, all sensibility, consoles himself with the joys of roast pig and plum pudding. Sympathetically he pokes fun at our Caledonian earnestness. Indulgently he lets himself out for wandering in the "twilight of dubiety" where he will "cry halves" for the bits of truth that he may find, allowing himself only "hints and glimpses," "crude essays at a system," "wanderings" in the maze of possibilities, for "truth presents no full face," a "feature or side face at most."[16]

Ishmael, like Elia, is male, a bachelor, in his own way on board ship domesticated, puttering about among the try-pots and all his likes and dislikes, making friends with other isolatoes—those ornery and intimidating, but ultimately most affectionate, types. Ishmael, too, tells us his foibles and his loves: for whaling, chowder, forbidden seas, cannibals, following funerals, the whale as a dish, confidential chats, dipping his biscuit, holding mock debates, unraveling parodic dissertations and anatomies upon the whale who never shows his face, and turning over his endless thinking as neither infidel nor believer. Ishmael, the whaleship thrall, takes up Lamb's crude "essay" in both its meanings. Duyckinck was one critic to notice the essayistic quality of many of *Moby-Dick*'s chapters,[17] and indeed in this perspective we may recognize them as fine examples of humorous essays— monologue bits in the method of Lamb, Hazlitt, De Quincey, and Irving. In addition, however, Ishmael in all his staggering ambition is in a constant hubbub of crude attempts—essays—at a system. "I am in earnest and I will try" (*MD* 118), he says of his cetological system, that vast array of surly mouths and seductive young bulls. "I try all things; I achieve what I can" (*MD* 291), he says while hopelessly phrenologizing the whale whose head turns out to have no face, just as its spout turns out to be only a mist. Ishmael always busies himself with his desire "to approve myself omni-sciently exhaustive" (*MD* 378), as if one could, through mere well-meaning conscientiousness, actually sort out all the chaos of the universe, and as if he had caught onto exactly the "system" of how that was to be done.

Like Elia, Ishmael is always dishing up some earnestness to respond to the absurdity. "That mortal man should feed upon the creature that feeds his lamp, and, like Stubb, eat him by his own light, as you may say; this seems so outlandish a thing that one must needs go a little into the history and philosophy of it" (*MD* 254). One must? Even if Melville were speaking of actual history, we could not assume that the history of a thing can remove its absurdity. Melville is not even speaking of actual history, however, but making up ludicrous prescriptions of blubber as nutritious for infants, and letting calves' heads, helpless upon the carving board, look up quoting Shakespeare into the face of their executioner. In Melville as with Lamb, ideas are mere absurd pretensions and consolations against the darkness, until heads themselves become things to pity. "Meantime, there was a terrible tumult. Looking over the side, they saw the before lifeless head throbbing and heaving just below the surface of the sea, as if that moment seized with some momentous idea; whereas it was only the poor Indian unconsciously revealing by those struggles the perilous depth to which he had sunk" (*MD* 288). The poor Indian, the poor head, the poor essayist. The joke is that we are creatures possessed by the idea that our heads can save us, and as a result possessed by our heads, which in turn are possessed by momentous uncontrollable ideas.

The problem, however, is that man must worship something. In "The Whale as a Dish," Ishmael takes a different line from Elia in his "Dissertation on Roast Pig." One insists upon giving us a full history and philosophy, the other a dissertation on origins. Both, however, are playing on a finger-licking-good self-indulgence, both establishing the absurdity of a lyricism—and an erudition—devoted to succulence. But what is this infatuation? Let us recall that Ishmael, early in *Moby-Dick,* in an aside on the glory of being paid, says, "I never fancied broiling fowls;—though once broiled, judi-ciously buttered, and judgmatically salted and peppered, there is no one who will speak more respectfully not to say reverentially, of a broiled fowl than I will. It is out of the idolatrous dotings of the old Egyptians upon broiled ibis and roasted river horse, that you see the mummies of those creatures in their huge bake-houses, the pyramids" (*MD* 14). "Idolatrous dotings" is the key. Lamb's whole dissertation on roast pig builds playfully and quietly up to the image of the pig on the platter as meek and beautiful as Christ on the cross. De Quincey told us he worshipped his druggist. We not only are what we eat; we worship what we eat. But only because in the "twilight of dubiety" what else shall man worship?

We must not omit to notice an important difference between Elia and Ishmael, which gave Melville an opening to improve upon his model. Elia says of Negroes that he is drawn to them but he "would not spend his good nights with them." Ishmael, very much as if in reply to Elia upon this exact point, immerses himself in the comic predicament of being forced to spend his good night with the terrible apotheosis of the Negro, a tattooed, shrunken-head-toting cannibal. It is crucial that Ishmael resolves this confrontation in a kind of marriage, so that his night becomes a good night indeed, but it is characteristic too of Ishmael that he takes his humorist self as far into his depths as possible. The humorously joyous denouement of Ishmael's encounter with the black cannibal prefigures, of course, the joy of Ishmael's surviving the encounter with the white whale. That the ship and all its crew descend into the maelstrom (to used Poe's phrase) or over the verge of the Descartian vortex (to use Melville's) is awesome in its horror, but then no humorist worth his salt can avoid calling upon the horrors of the deep, the vacuities beyond man's seeming mental grasp. Elia seems very much at the core of Melville's conception of Ishmael, even if Melville has consciously taken Elia a good deal further.

Washington Irving was another humorist essayist who seems to have been in Melville's mind during the writing of *Moby-Dick*. We may notice details that Melville lifts from Irving, such as Plato's "honey head,"[18] and Manhattan as the isle of "Manhattoes."[19] We may notice that as Irving has written about the Neversink Indians (thus giving Melville the shipname for *White-Jacket*), so Irving had written at length about the Pequod Indians. More to the point, however, Irving's pathetic schoolmaster Ichabod Crane, as well as the Burtonesque bachelor Geoffrey Crayon, provided humorous prototypes for Ishmael; and the tyrannical peg-legged Peter Stuyvesant provided one for Ahab. We must say immediately, of course, that Irving's tyrant turns out to be most kindhearted after all, and Irving's pathetic types are often thin in their appeal, resting too much upon their settings, or rallying a bit too easily after all. Ichabod, for instance, after the headless horseman fright, goes to the city and becomes, within sentences, a successful businessman. Nonetheless, Irving seems to have been in Melville's mind as a novice of an artist. It is as if Melville becomes Irving and survives him, becomes him and transcends him. In "Bartleby," we may see the relationship between the two authors more clearly. For the moment, let us simply note that it must have been important to Melville to find an American working the Democritan extravaganza vein of humor in its romantic essay form.

Considering the Americanness of *Moby-Dick*, it was certainly important that Melville found, in addition to Irving, a thriving American periodical humor which he could tap. Indeed, no one questions the essential Americanness of *Moby-Dick*. That the brave, generous, and dependable Queequeg is called a "George Washington cannibalistically developed" (*MD* 52) sets the mood. All the whalemen, be they from whatever lands or tribes, are George Washington's progeny, translations of the idea of America—just as the showmanship of "The Masthead" chapter, like all Melville's writing, takes us home to America with a final absurd masthead of George Washington on a pedestal. The question is exactly what did Melville take from developing American humor to flesh out the Americanness of his book, and to develop his own humor to its quickest, brightest level.

Richard Chase makes some important suggestions along these lines.[20] He points out that Melville borrows American folk figures—Ishmael, for example, being a composite of the Yankee, the frontiersman, the comic Promethean demigod of a trickster, the jack-of-all-trades like Sam Slick, and finally the elusive soliloquizing yarn-spinner. Stubb is a typically American screamer, using the standard techniques of the American trickster, razzing Negroes and gulling Europeans; and finally out of the comic realm, Ahab is the ultimate screamer, a folkloric embodiment of Manifest Destiny, an American Prometheus. For both his central fable and its spin-offs, Melville also uses, Chase tells us, the American predilection for comic metamorphosis, an instantaneous transformation back and forth that makes the whale into an albino and then into a god; the story's heroes into titans, beasts, and machines; men into animals and back again, as Ahab is made into a grizzly and Ishmael into a May grasshopper. It is only the beginning to recall that Crockett, for one, was half-horse, half-alligator, and half-man, or that he went so far as to call himself an entire zoological institute. Chase shows that in *Moby-Dick*, Melville was working from a grab bag of standard American tall tales built upon exaggeration, sudden or eventual violation of the laws of nature, or the whimsy that shows the utter impracticality of human endeavor.

Within this typically American flight of fantasy, Chase finds a very American emphasis on and undercurrent of fact and practicality, so strong that it sometimes camouflages the fantasy, just as Ahab being above all a successful whaling captain is in good part what wins the loyal adherence of his crew. This underlying bias toward fact is as responsible for the workings of the central fable as it is for the book's whole style. This style has its roots in P. T. Barnum showmanship, American magniloquent oratory, and the theatre of the 1830s and 1840s in which a blank mask, omnipresent from the Yankee pedlar, allows the tale-teller to move freely back and forth from sales pitch to scientific razzmatazz to dramatic action.

Two problems arise with the suggestions Chase made in 1949. To begin with, it was Chase's ultimate point about all this material that Melville exploits Americana to provide a fabric for his historical-tragic allegory, the comic material giving a "low enjoying power"[21] to the higher stuff as Melville transmutes "the language of the screamer" into an apostrophe "to space and freedom."[22] The P. T. Barnum hoax, Chase says, Melville turns inside out. Barnum was exploiting the desire of the audience to be comforted by the destruction of any fierce emotion. Melville, on the contrary, uses his hoax to insist on that emotion. When Melville neither transmutes nor turns inside out the Americana, Chase feels its tastelessness needs apology. For example, regarding Stubb's callous gulling of Fleece, Chase explains that, unpleasant as this sort of play may be, we must accept it as cultural fact.

The main problem with Chase's analysis, however, is that most of what Chase refers to as distinctly American is simply essentially humorous. The American folk tradition, we should realize, is only one part of the background of the comic trickster Prometheus. The European literature which Melville read was full of comic Prometheuses and demigods, like Pantagruel inventing his omnipotent Pantagruelion, Panurge inventing his *libertin* tricks, or de Bergerac inventing his moon machine and calling himself a Prometheus as a result. The literature was full as well of pure rogues and tricksters, from Lazarillo to Volpone to Mosca. For sources of Ishmael as a soliloquizing monologuist, we have already said much here of his literary paternity—Alcofrybas, Democritus, Jr., Tristram Shandy, Elia, and Geoffrey Crayon. The comic metamorphosis, too, is only partially American. We have not only the tall tale of Renaissance humor to cite, but the humorist's whole game of *what I desire I am.* Humor depends upon continuous expansions and contractions, continually thrown back to back. Democritus, Jr. is a free man and a slave, Panurge a giant of desire and cowardice—and later Alice in Wonderland will be a giant, then after a sip of "Drink Me," a mite. The only particularly American characteristic of Melville's metamorphoses may be the predominance of animals in the transformations. Otherwise, the shuffling back and forth is simply the humorist's insistence on writing as he pleases, showing he is boss, submitting to no logic or dogma, continually indulging his fantasies.

Finally to recognize that the showmanship of a literary-scientific extravaganza is not merely American, we need only mention *Gargantua and Pantagruel, The Anatomy of Melancholy,* and *The Historical and Critical Dictionary.* In each of those works of peremptory showmanship, the author is, above all, determined to outdo anything prior in scope and method, as well as to suggest continually the farce of this sort of determination. This is what makes it so important to see beyond the Barnum roots of Melville's humor; while with Chase we may condemn the ultimately shabby artistry of a P. T. Barnum, we may respect and admire the shaggy dog encyclopedias of such great writers as Rabelais, Burton, and Bayle. Their hoaxes need not be turned inside out; their humor needs no "transmuting." The actually literary literary-scientific extravaganza is built upon a fundamental bleakness and the "fierce emotion" it can inspire. It is built upon the uncertainty that Panurge faces, the slippery road on which the patriarchs walk, the bleak lot of a Lazarillo, the whiteness of acatalepsy, the all pervasiveness of mad melancholy, and the trance, finally, of opium. It is always there, that atheistical whiteness. In short, as Chase seems to have begun to suggest in his few pages in 1955 on *Moby-Dick*,[23] humor need not be, and in fact is not, a stepping-off point for this book. It is its center.

Still, once we have recognized that American humor only added one more element to the humor that is central to *Moby-Dick,* let us see what that element is. First of all, America provided the allusive materials for many of Melville's exaggerations and reversals. As a white American, Ishmael need not spell out that he is a free man born, but may jump ahead to the turnaround of "who aint a slave?" So, too, while the squire and Lazarillo or Volpone and Mosca, as master and servant types appropriate to their era, gull each other by turns, it is only fitting that in America, the two parties turning tables on each other—the Cabin Table, for one—should be white and black, or American and European, or Lakeman and Vineyarder. It is fitting also that Melville's metamorphoses jump back and forth not only from erudition to slang, or from rhapsody to the thump, or from piety to phallicism, but from man to animal; America was a land in which the animals were only then in the process of being subdued, conquered, and exterminated. In addition to the incidentals, however, American humor did indeed provide a grab bag of yarns and twisters to help Ishmael, a sort of King Midas, transform details into braggadocio. More importantly, the yarn helped Melville shape the central fable as a fish story of one man hunting down one particularly monstrous fish. Melville uses the yarn to transform and tighten the spacious voyage of Rabelais, the anatomy of Burton, the encyclopedia of Bayle, the rambling novel of Sterne; and he uses it to open up the small essay of sensibility, the melancholic sketch of De Quincey, Lamb, and Irving.

But beyond the paraphernalia for quick allusiveness which humor always demands, and beyond the form both peripheral and central of the yarn or twister, Melville gets something which is distinctively American, a game of immediacy. The American hallmark of *Moby-Dick*'s humor is a certain journalistic predilection that moves us from Rabelais's fantasy of the giant Pantagruel drinking thousands of pails of milk a day to the actuality of a whale sucking that much from its dam; from Rabelais's fantasy of Pantagruel's arch of triumph to the actual six-foot-long pride of the whale. Chase had hinted at this essentially American aspect when he spoke of the particularly American reliance on fact and practicality. Practicality is too broad because all humor depends upon the play between the lofty and the banal, the theory and the practice, the soaring desire and the menial actuality. The fact part is right, however, and crucial. In the Renaissance frontier humor springing from the explorations of that era, the New World is very much in people's minds and very strong in creating the braggadocio and self-parody of that literature, but the authors themselves are not actually *in* the New World. With the earlier non-American humorists, the idea of the frontier is what sets them going, but with those in America, it is as if the joke has been suddenly accelerated and escalated into actuality. In American humor, we are not just given the remote idea or the willful fantasy, but the literal physical frontier, the experience of the land, the Indians, the animals, and the sea.

It is the periodical journalistic aspect which Melville borrowed most from American humor, a certain literal-mindedness, a stubbornness of the person's insistence on having been there. *And I only am escaped to tell you* is part of the song: I alone was there and saw it with my own eyes. That the almanac, periodical book of timely and pragmatic knowledge as well as of humor and entertainment, was the standard American household book is not surprising, nor is it that the humor there is that of factual experience and deposition braggadocio. In the excerpts given above in chapter 2, Robert Thomas was in raptures that *he was there*, and that those "Fifty years!" which America had just lived through were surely the greatest in all history. This spirit rendered humorously gives us the "Deposition of Varmifuge," the literalness of the joker insisting he has seen the sea serpent with his own eyes, and giving us his ostentatiously legal statement; the misspelling used in the piece even forms a sort of verbal literalness, the insistence on sticking as close to reality—via phonetics—as one can possibly get. And finally in the famous Crockett excerpt, we get not just the practicality of how an American typically takes the impossible in hand for his survival, and not just the sense of his being present at the Creation, but of his having initiated it. To see that Melville was responding to this spirit, we may look at central chapters like "The Affidavit," which reveal the book as the bragging deposition that it is. Ishmael calls himself at one point "a veritable witness" (*MD* 373); at another he speaks of procuring for every snow crystal "a sworn affidavit" (*MD* 231). I cannot help thinking that, finally, part of the fun of the title *Moby-Dick* was that the word *dick* in the slang of Melville's day—not yet into the explicitness of our own time—not only signaled fellow (as in Tom, Dick, and Harry), and the dictionary, but declaration or affidavit.[24] *Moby-Dick* is Ishmael's wordy bragging, in fact, "I was there, ladies and gentlemen, this man was there and saw all this with his own eyes."

Although as a doctor, Rabelais teases us with a lot of close-up physicality, he has a certain distance from the low life he describes. Burton, one feels, has isolated himself in his study. Even Sterne and the Romantic essayists have a certain remove. In Melville's humor, however, if only to be able to brag that you were there in the most complete fashion, you are forever "putting your hand into the tar-pot" (*MD* 14); *Moby-Dick* is a total immersion in universal social, economical, political, and physical realities. The central conflict gives us all the innards of fish cleaning and fish stories, while it plays off a history of the peaking of one of America's first extraordinarily successful commercial enterprises. Melville's Ishmael, too, is not only directly at the masthead watching over all the watery world, not only at the helm once with the entire survival of the ship at his hand, not only in the whaleboat privy to the inner circles of the whales copulating and giving suck, but in chapter after chapter on board ship wresting the oil from the captured whale, at the end of the monkey rope, and with his hands, his whole body immersed in the smell and realities of the whale. Indeed the humor of "A Squeeze of the Hand" is that the exultant image of the felicitous brotherhood of mankind is pinned to the most physical and inane of immersions.

Melville is never afraid of getting his hands wet or dirty. His very American humor not only anatomizes the world and presents a melancholic idiosyncratic persona, but gets "these visible hands" (*MD* 118) into the actual physicalities of the whale—and squeezes. Yet, and this is important too, for it makes the whole difference, American as Melville was in his deposition, in his bragging journalistic immersion, at the same time, by his leaning on and listening to earlier and highly literary voices, he avoids the reductionism, provinciality, and claustrophobia of American periodical and almanac humor, whose joke of literalness and insistence on petty regionalist rivalry can quickly begin to pall.

Finally, then, *Moby-Dick*'s giddy sense of triumph evolves out of Melville's building upon a tradition of the giddy sense of triumph. It rests upon his awareness that he is building upon other humorous literature that has gone before, quickening the European fantasy with an American eye for physical and economic realities, sustaining the American quick turn of periodical humor by giving it a longer form and a substantial vision, broadening the American game of provincial literalness with a truly literary and catholic teasing and sense of play. Besides, however, doing all of this, we may ask if Melville adds anything to the long line of developing humor, or whether his whole achievement lies simply in impersonating and stretching. To be sure, the building itself is characteristically Melville's. That he takes everything he looks at into the superlative of the modern, and metamorphoses all that he has read into the present, is itself the game of his humor. In addition, however, it is the intensity of the hug which brings all of Melville's book into focus and distinctively shapes his originality. Against a frame of absolute universality, Melville opens up what he calls the "spheres" of "fright" and "love" (*MD* 169) to two sustaining hugs, Ishmael and Queequeg at one end, Ahab and Moby Dick at the other. To transform the humorous male monologues of the past into his present, and impose upon them the preposterous hug: here is the achievement of Melville's humor in *Moby-Dick*.

Notes

1. Chase, *Herman Melville*, pp. 64–102.
2. Whitney Hastings Wells, "*Moby-Dick* and Rabelais," *Modern Language Notes* 38 (1923): 123. Wells notes the borrowing but makes no comment on it. The chapter in Rabelais is book 1, chapter 10, "Of That Which Is Signified by the Colours White and Blew."
3. Rabelais, *The Lives, Heroic Deeds and Sayings*, pp. 30–31.
4. Northrop Frye's "Theory of Genres," in *Anatomy of Criticism* (1957), pp. 243–341, especially pp. 312–14, helpfully classifies *Moby-Dick* as a romance-anatomy, pointing out that the usual critical approach to the form of such works as *Moby-Dick* "resembles that of the doctors in Brobdingnag, who after great wrangling finally pronounced Gulliver a *lusus naturae*. It is the anatomy in particular that has baffled critics, and there is hardly any fiction writer deeply influenced by it who has not been accused of disorderly conduct." It is odd that

few critics have referred to Frye's useful concept; and yet at the same time we must note that it is important to distinguish, as Frye does not, between Menippean satire and the melancholy anatomy.

5. Burton, *Anatomy of Melancholy*, p. 16.

6. Ibid., pp. 11, 425.

7. Ibid., pp. 11, 529, 24, 103, 530.

8. Ibid., p. 411.

9. Ibid., p. 64.

10. We are not certain what Melville had read of *Tristram Shandy* before writing *Moby-Dick*. We know that in 1849 he first read and enjoyed immensely a few chapters of that novel, and by the time he wrote "Cock-A-Doodle-Doo!" he felt familiar enough with it to speak of it as a remedy for melancholy, in much the way Burton before or Irving after would traditionally speak of their beloved books as cures for hypos. We know also that America was saturated with Shandyisms—that, like Samuel Johnson, Sterne was in the air. Luther Mansfield even suggests that Melville may have gotten many of his stunts from an intermediary, Southey's *Doctor*, a popular romantic rehashing of Sterne which contains prefatory matter labeled "History and Romance Ransacked for Resemblances and Non-Resemblances to the Horse of Dr. Daniel Dove." (Although Sealts does not list Southey, see Richard Moore, "A New Review by Melville," *American Literature* 47 (1975): 265–70, which suggests Melville reviewed Southey's *Commonplace Book* in *The Literary World*.) Mansfield sets us in the wrong direction by suggesting that Melville took up these stunts only to change them into serious mood-setting devices. Mansfield is closer in his linking of Ishmael and Queequeg's bedtime chats with Mr. and Mrs. Shandy's "beds of justice"; Luther Mansfield and Howard Vincent, explanatory notes to Herman Melville, *Moby-Dick* (1952), pp. 570, 579–80, 624 et al.).

11. Sterne, *Tristram Shandy*, p. 265.

12. Mansfield and Vincent, explanatory notes, pp. 593–94, n. line 16: "Melville seems to have perversely misinterpreted the classic Roman as *l'homme fatal* of romantic literature. . . . Perhaps here too, Melville experienced a skeptical failure to understand such virtuous faith and courage as the classical tradition attributed to Cato."

13. Henry Bergson, "Laughter," in *Comedy*, with an introduction by Wylie Sypher (1956), pp. 59–190.

14. Jean-Jacques Mayoux, "De Quincey: Humor and the Drugs," in *Veins of Humor*, ed. Harry Levin (1972), p. 123. This, incidentally, is one of the best essays written on the subject of humor.

15. Lamb to Wordsworth, 20 March 1822, *The Portable Charles Lamb*, p. 156.

16. Lamb, "Imperfect Sympathies," pp. 279–80.

17. Evert (and George?) Duyckinck, "Melville's Moby Dick; or, The Whale," New York *Literary World* 9 (15 November 1851): 381–83 and (22 November 1851): 403–4, reprinted in Parker, *The Recognition of Herman Melville*, p. 41.

18. Mansfield and Vincent, explanatory notes, p. 773. See also p. 681.

19. Harrison Hayford and Hershel Parker, eds., *Moby-Dick* (1967), p. 12, n. 3.

20. Chase, *Herman Melville*, pp. 64–102.

21. Ibid., p. 100: "As patriots we may enjoy with Melville his excursions into American folklore. It was for him, a healthy impulse. Like Ahab, he was gifted with the high perception; without it *Moby-Dick* would lack the over-all structure of its universal-historical allegory. Yet underneath the high perception, supporting and nourishing it, Melville knew there must be a low enjoying power. This he sought and found in the folk spirit of his country."

22. Ibid., p. 91.

23. Chase, *The American Novel*, pp. 93–113. "The essential voice of Melville is to be heard in the half humorous, subtly erotic lyric tone which is peculiar to *Moby-Dick* [p. 111]."

24. See Eric Partridge, *Dictionary of Slang and Unconventional English*, 7th ed. (1970), p. 218; and John S. Farmer and W. E. Henley, *Dictionary of Slang and Its Analogues* (1965). The curious thing is how several slang meanings of the word did seem to surface in print suddenly in 1860: the affidavit or declaration, the dictionary or overly fine language, and the male sexual organ. (It seems fair to assume that the slang existed in speech before it was documented in print.)

Melville and Emerson's Rainbow

MERTON M. SEALTS, JR.

When Melville began *Moby-Dick* early in 1850, he not only knew something of Emerson but was familiar as well with major European authors from Plato to Goethe whose works significantly influenced American Transcendentalism. Emerson once remarked of the Transcendentalists that perhaps they agreed only "in having fallen upon Coleridge and Wordsworth and Goethe, then on Carlyle, with pleasure and sympathy" (*W*, X, 342). By this token Melville too could be charged with Transcendentalist leanings in 1850 and 1851, though in fact he read all of these authors as he read Emerson: with fundamental reservations.

Of the four writers Emerson names, Melville had "fallen upon" Coleridge early in 1848, when he bought a two-volume edition of the *Biographia Literaria*, and he also owned a heavily marked 1839 edition of Wordsworth's poetry.[1] A direct reflection of his recent reading in 1848 and 1849 is his caricature of the "transcendental divine" in *White-Jacket*, a book written at top speed along with the earlier *Redburn* in the summer of 1849 to repair losses in standing and income attending the unpopular *Mardi*. The chaplain's sermons were as "ill calculated to benefit the crew" of his vessel as *Mardi* to please the average reader. Like the author of *Mardi*, the chaplain had tasted of "the mystic fountain of Plato; his head had been turned by the Germans; and . . . White-Jacket himself saw him with Coleridge's Biographia Literaria in his hand" (p. 155). Both the chaplain and Melville must also have been reading Andrews Norton, that distinctly *anti*transcendental divine who in 1839 had attacked Emerson's Divinity School Address as "the latest form of infidelity"; the chaplain's allusion to an obscure tract by Tertullian and Ishmael's later references in *Moby-Dick* to Gnostic thought apparently come from Melville's own knowledge of Norton's *magnum opus, The Evidences of the Genuineness of the Gospels* (1844), as Professor Thomas Vargish has demonstrated.[2] Perhaps Melville had been reading Norton as well as Emerson while visiting the Shaws during the previous winter.

In the fall of 1849, when Melville was on his way to Europe, he could hold his own in talking "German metaphysics" with a shipboard companion, George Adler, whose philosophy he immediately identified as "Col-

Excerpted and reprinted from *Pursuing Melville, 1940–1980: Chapters and Essays* (Madison and London: University of Wisconsin Press, 1982), 267–70. Reprinted by permission. Footnote numbering has been altered.

eridgean."[3] By this time he was interested enough in German writers to buy Goethe's *Auto-Biography* in London and to borrow his *Wilhelm Meister* from Duyckinck after his return to New York;[4] during the summer of 1850, when he was already at work on *Moby-Dick*, he also borrowed three of Carlyle's writings.[5] However much or little of Emerson Melville had read by 1850 and 1851, he obviously knew other Transcendental scripture, and it seems safe to say that his reading of one book in particular—Carlyle's *Sartor Resartus*, with its central idea of "all visible things" as "emblems" of the invisible, and of Nature itself as *"the living visible Garment of God"*[6]—had at least as much to do with the symbolism of *Moby-Dick* as anything in the "Language" chapter of Emerson's *Nature*.

There was a basic reservation in Melville's mind that kept him from giving more than passing allegiance to any form of philosophical idealism, whether he found it in Plato or Proclus or in their modern successors— Carlyle, Goethe, and Emerson. In *Mardi* his Babbalanja had spoken of external nature as something neutral toward mankind rather than benevolent, and in *Moby-Dick* Ishmael makes the dismaying comment that though "in many of its aspects this visible world *seems* formed in love, the invisible spheres *were* formed in fright" (p. 169; emphasis added). Both Ishmael and Ahab, like idealists generally, are of course incurable analogists—so, for that matter, were Hawthorne and the supposedly anti-Transcendental Poe. But Ahab, as Leon Howard has said, is "an imperfect Transcendentalist";[7] "All visible objects," he agrees, "are but as pasteboard masks"—yet "sometimes" he thinks "there's naught beyond" (p. 144).[8] Between such opposite negations, as walls, Melville's own being was also swung.

As Melville worked on *Moby-Dick* at Pittsfield during the fall of 1850 and most of the following year, the Hawthornes were in residence at Lenox, some seven miles away. He had a number of opportunities to discuss Emerson and Transcendentalism with both Hawthorne and his wife; Mrs. Hawthorne had known Emerson before her marriage in 1842 and the Hawthornes' occupancy of the Old Manse in Concord. On at least one occasion Melville and Hawthorne talked of Thoreau (*Log*, I, 407), whom Melville was reading late in 1850, and Emerson may have figured as well when they tackled what Melville called "the Problem of the Universe," discussing "metaphysics" and indulging in "ontological heroics" (*Letters*, pp. 121, 125, 133). Melville's visits to the Hawthornes' cottage sometimes lasted overnight. "He was very careful not to interrupt Mr Hawthorne's mornings," Sophia Hawthorne reported; morning was the time when her husband did his writing. Melville "generally walked off somewhere," she explained, "—& one morning he shut himself into the boudoir & read Mr Emerson's Essays in presence of our beautiful picture."[9]

The ideas of their sometime neighbor in Concord possibly meant more to Sophia Hawthorne than to her husband, who after their marriage, as he wrote in "The Old Manse," came to admire Emerson "as a poet of deep beauty and austere tenderness, but sought nothing from him as a philosopher."[10] Melville valued her judgment and once told her, in response to her praise of *Moby-Dick*, that with her "spiritualizing nature" she saw "more things than other people" (*Letters*, p. 146). She did not specify which of "Mr Emerson's Essays" occupied Melville during that particular morning at the cottage, which can probably be dated early in September of 1850.[11] Although she could have meant *Essays* or *Essays: Second Series*, she could just as well have been thinking of Emerson's writings in general. By this time the Hawthornes owned presentation copies of every book Emerson had then published, from the first edition of *Nature*, given her when she was Sophia Peabody, to the most recent.[12] While telling Melville of her friendship with the Emersons, she may have shown him any or all of these books. What he read that morning, given his probable familiarity by this time with the Essays of 1841 and 1844, was more likely something later—either *Nature, Addresses, and Lectures*, which had appeared in September of 1849 while he was preparing to sail for Europe, or *Representative Men*, published early in 1850 while he was still abroad.[13]

The case for *Representative Men* as the book Melville read at the Hawthornes' turns on a number of close verbal parallels between Emerson's book and passages both in *Moby-Dick* and in Melville's correspondence of 1850 and 1851. His letters to Hawthorne make occasional references traceable to his recent reading, and where Transcendental writers are involved there are characteristic reservations: Carlyle's *Sartor Resartus*, for example, with its "Everlasting No" and "Everlasting Yea," and "some of Goethe's sayings, so worshipped by his votaries." In each case Melville raises an objection. "All men who say *yes*, lie," he retorted, not only to Carlyle but to the affirmative and optimistic tendencies of the age in general; "the grand truth about Nathaniel Hawthorne" is that *he* "says NO! in thunder" (*Letters*, p. 125). Goethe's pantheistic maxim *"Live in the all"* is simply "nonsense" to "a fellow with a raging toothache," Melville writes—only to add in a postscript that there is "some truth" in "this 'all' feeling," and that "what plays the mischief with the truth is that men will insist upon the universal application of a temporary feeling or opinion" (*Letters*, p. 131). Emerson as an intellectual aristocrat was probably in the back of his mind when he wrote with evident distaste about an idea which "some men have boldly advocated and asserted," that of "an aristocracy of the brain" (*Letters*, pp. 126–127). The one man he names as doing so is not Emerson but Schiller, whose thinking is specifically bracketed with Emerson's in *The Confidence-Man* (p. 215), and in this same letter there is an apparent echo of *Representative Men*.[14]

I now believe that Melville also read *Nature, Addresses, and Lectures*, either at the Hawthornes' or at some later time. Unlike Professor Beidler, I have been unable to satisfy myself that he knew *Nature* itself, however, nor have James Duban, Marvin Fisher, and Beryl Rowland convinced me that Emerson's Divinity School Address, which is printed in this same volume, influenced either *Pierre* or "The Two Temples."[15] Christopher Sten compares Bartleby and the lawyer in Melville's "Bartleby, the Scrivener" with the idealist and the materialist in "The Transcendentalist" and "The Conservative," two of Emerson's lectures that are also in the 1849 volume; he sees the story as "Melville's Dead Letter to Emerson."[16] Although I do not find Sten's general parallels conclusive, I have traced a much-quoted passage in *Moby-Dick* to a strikingly similar passage in "The Transcendentalist,"[17] and I am sure that Melville remembered one of Emerson's most telling images, that of "rare and gifted men" as "superior chronometers," when he composed Plotinus Plinlimmon's "Lecture First," on "Chronometricals and Horologicals," in *Pierre*.[18]

Notes

1. On Melville's purchase of *Biographia Literaria*, see *Melville's Reading*, p. 52: No. 154. He also knew something of both Coleridge's poetry and Wordsworth's: see his reference to "The Ancient Mariner" in a note to Chapter 42 of *Moby-Dick*, "The Whiteness of the Whale" (p. 165), and to Wordsworth in Chapter 11 of *White-Jacket* (p. 40); Thomas F. Heffernan, "Melville and Wordsworth," *American Literature*, 49 (November 1977), 338–351.

2. On Melville's possible use of Norton, see Thomas Vargish, "Gnostic *Mythos* in *Moby-Dick*," *PMLA*, 81 (June 1966), 272–277. He also read about the Gnostics in Pierre Bayle's *Historical and Critical Dictionary*, which he bought in Boston in March or April of 1849; see *Melville's Reading*, p. 39: No. 51, and "Melville and the Platonic Tradition," pp. 298, 308 below.

3. *Journal of a Visit to London and the Continent by Herman Melville 1849–1850*, ed. Eleanor Melville Metcalf (Cambridge: Harvard University Press, 1948), p. 5.

4. *Melville's Reading*, p. 62: No. 228. Melville's interest in Goethe was perhaps stimulated by his conversations on shipboard with Adler, who sent him a translation of *Iphigenia in Tauris* early in 1851 (No. 229). If Melville read "Goethe; or, The Writer" in *Representative Men* at some time in 1850, as there is reason to believe he did, it is possible that reading Emerson's discussion of *Wilhelm Meister* (*W*, IV, 227–280) led him to borrow Goethe's novel (No. 230) from Duyckinck in the late summer of that year.

5. *Melville's Reading*, pp. 47–48: Nos. 121–123. Melville first borrowed *Sartor Resartus* and *On Heroes, Hero-Worship, and the Heroic in History*, probably in June or July, and then Carlyle's translation of *German Romance*, probably in August or September.

6. For the quoted phrases, see Thomas Carlyle, *Sartor Resartus*, ed. William Savage Johnson (Boston: Houghton Mifflin Company, 1924), pp. 51 and 39. Julie Ann Braun has studied "Melville's Use of Carlyle's *Sartor Resartus*: 1846–1857" (Diss. University of California at Los Angeles 1967). Morse Peckham, arguing that in *Moby-Dick* "the various styles are derived from various stages of Romanticism, just as the ideas are," discusses relations between the book and Emersonian Transcendentalism, the poetry of Wordsworth, and particularly "The Rime of the Ancient Mariner" and *Sartor Resartus;* see his "Hawthorne and Melville as European Authors," in *Melville and Hawthorne in the Berkshires: A Symposium*, ed. Howard P. Vincent (Kent, Ohio: Kent State University Press, 1968), pp. 58–60.

7. Introduction to *Moby-Dick or, The Whale* (New York: The Modern Library, 1950), p. xiii.

8. On the contrast between Ahab's view of nature and Emerson's, see E. J. Rose, "Melville, Emerson, and the Sphinx," *New England Quarterly*, 36 (June 1963), 249–258.

9. Eleanor Melville Metcalf, *Herman Melville: Cycle and Epicycle* (Cambridge: Harvard University Press, 1953), p. 91; *Log*, II, 925. The "boudoir," according to Rose Hawthorne Lathrop, *Memories of Hawthorne* (Boston and New York: Houghton, Mifflin and Co., 1897), p. 185, was a small sitting room on the first floor of the cottage overlooking lake, meadow, and mountains and furnished with pictures and bookshelves; the "beautiful picture" was an engraving of Raphael's *Transfiguration* that Emerson and Elizabeth Hoar had given Mrs. Hawthorne before her marriage. At Lenox, the engraving first hung "over the ottoman" in the drawing room, as Mrs. Hawthorne told her mother in a letter of 23 June 1850; see Julian Hawthorne, *Nathaniel Hawthorne and His Wife*, 2 vols. (Boston: James R. Osgood and Company, 1884), I, 368. When Melville and Evert Duyckinck visited the Hawthornes on 8 August 1850, it had evidently been moved to the "boudoir"; see Duyckinck's letter to his wife, 9 August 1850, in Luther Stearns Mansfield, "Glimpses of Herman Melville's Life in Pittsfield, 1850–1851: Some Unpublished Letters of Evert A. Duyckinck," *American Literature*, 9 (March 1937), 34.

10. "The Old Manse," in *Mosses from an Old Manse* (Columbus: Ohio State University Press, 1974), p. 31.

11. Leyda, *Log*, II, 924–925, dates the visit as "September 5–6."

12. Emerson sent presentation copies of *Nature* and the 1841 *Essays* to Sophia Peabody (*JMN*, V, 263; VII, 546). To Hawthorne he sent *Essays: Second Series, Poems, Nature, Addresses, and Lectures*, and *Representative Men* (*JMN*, IX, 129, 456; XI, 156, 189).

13. Melville probably read what the *Literary World* said about the two books during his absence. In reviewing *Nature, Addresses, and Lectures* (V, No. 144 [3 November 1849], 374–376) Duyckinck contrasted Emersonian self-reliance with Christian self-renunciation, mentioning in conclusion his "horror" at Emerson's "irreverent blasphemy, his cool, patronizing way of speaking" of Christ. The review of *Representative Men* (VI, No. 158 [9 February 1850], 123–124), which consists largely of extracts from the book, calls it "Mr. Emerson's best work," but objects that Emersonian self-reliance, "this stoicism of the nineteenth century," leads ultimately to "moral indifference." In his later review of *Moby-Dick*, it will be recalled, Duyckinck deplored traces in Ishmael of "the conceited indifferentism of Emerson."

14. Here Melville writes of the "fastidious" feeling which an aristocrat may develop, "similar to that which, in an English Howard, conveys *a torpedofish thrill* at the slightest contact with a social plebeian" (*Letters*, p. 126; emphasis added); there are comparable passages in Melville's *Clarel*, I.xxiii.78–80, and *Billy Budd, Sailor*, p. 98. Emerson declares in his chapter on "Napoleon" that Napoleon's "absorbing egotism was deadly to all other men. It resembled the torpedo, which inflicts a succession of shocks on any one who takes hold of it . . . until he paralyzes and kills his victim" (*W*, IV, 257–258). Emerson probably derived the figure in turn from the *Meno* of Plato, a work that Melville knew also (see "Melville and the Platonic Tradition," pp. 326–327 and 335 below). In Plato's dialogue Meno compares Socrates with "that broad sea-fish, called the torpedo; for that too produces a numbness in the person whoever approaches and touches it." See the Bohn edition of *The Works of Plato*, 6 vols., first published in 1848–1854, III, 18; this is the edition Melville alludes to in *Billy Budd, Sailor*, p. 75.

At least one passage of *Moby-Dick* obviously echoes *Representative Men*. In Chapter 80, "The Nut," Melville refers to the "German conceit, that the vertebræ are absolutely undeveloped skulls" (p. 294); Goethe, according to Emerson, "assumed that one vertebra of the spine might be considered as the unit of the skeleton: the head was only the uttermost vertebræ transformed" (*W*, IV, 275). Further parallels between *Representative Men* and Melville's later writings are discussed below, and other apparent echoes of Emerson essays are also noted in "Melville and the Platonic Tradition," pp. 316–317 and 317–319 below and note 57, p. 393.

15. James Duban, "The Spenserian Maze of Melville's *Pierre*," *ESQ*, 23 (4th Quarter

1977), 217–225—especially pp. 221–222; Marvin Fisher, "Focus on Melville's 'The Two Temples': The Denigration of the American Dream," in *American Dreams, American Nightmares*, ed. David Madden (Carbondale and Edwardsville: Southern Illinois University Press, 1970), pp. 76–86, and *Going Under: Melville's Short Fiction and the American 1850s* (Baton Rouge and London: Louisiana State University Press, 1977), pp. 51–61; Beryl Rowland, "Melville Answers the Theologians: The Ladder of Charity in 'The Two Temples,'" *Mosaic*, 7 (Summer 1974), 1–13, especially pp. 7–10.

16. Christopher Sten, "Bartleby the Transcendentalist: Melville's Dead Letter to Emerson," *Modern Language Quarterly*, 35 (March 1974), 30–44.

17. With "The Transcendentalist," *W*, I, 339–340, on Locke and Kant, compare *Moby-Dick*, Chapter 73, where the Pequod is laboring under the double burden of a sperm whale's head ("Locke's," says Ishmael) and a right whale's ("Kant's") hanging from her sides. See "Melville and the Platonic Tradition," pp. 317–319 below.

18. "The Transcendentalist," *W*, I, 358; *Pierre*, pp. 210–215. "Bacon's brains were mere watch-maker's brains," according to Plinlimmon; "but Christ was a chronometer" (p. 211). In "The Transcendentalist," Emerson cites Timoleon as one of several examples of individuals who refuse "all measure of right and wrong except the determinations of the private spirit" (*W*, I, 336–337). William H. Shurr, "Melville and Emerson," *Extracts: An Occasional Newsletter* (The Melville Society), No. 11 (May 1972), p. 2, compares Melville's late poem "Timoleon," observing that though Plutarch and other sources "enriched the development of Melville's thought in this poem, . . . Emerson's essay clearly provides the suggestion."

Melville and the Platonic Tradition

Merton M. Sealts, Jr.

II. From *Mardi* to *Moby-Dick*

During the opening months of 1849, when Melville was shuttling between New York and Boston while awaiting the birth of his first child and the publication of *Mardi*, he found time to do some significant reading. In Boston he bought a new edition of Shakespeare and an old set of Bayle's *Dictionary;* in New York during March he ordered the thirty-seven volumes of Harper's Classical Library from his publisher and then or later he probably bought William Gowans' new edition of Plato's *Phædon.*[1] His letters to Duyckinck written at Boston refer to his purchase of the Shakespeare and Bayle and also mention the *Phædon;* his familiarity with all of these works is evident in *Redburn* and *White-Jacket*, the two books he drove himself to write during the spring and summer of 1849 once it had become clear that *Mardi* was unsuccessful with both the critics and the public.

The familiar name of Sir Thomas Browne also turns up in Melville's correspondence of this period in association with both Plato and Emerson. After Melville had heard Emerson lecture in February of 1849 and praised him to Duyckinck as "a great man," Duyckinck must have replied with an unfavorable comparison of the essayist with Browne; Melville's response, in a letter of 3 March, reads like a passage from *Mardi*:

> Lay it down that had not Sir Thomas Browne lived, Emerson would not have mystified—I will answer, that had not Old Zack's father begot him, Old Zack [General Zachary Taylor] would never have been the hero of Palo Alto. The truth is that we are all sons, grandsons, or nephews or great-nephews of those who go before us. No one is his own sire. (*Letters*, p. 78)

As we know, Melville had already linked Browne with Plato in composing *Mardi*, and in another letter to Duyckinck he did so again. "I bought a set of Bayle's Dictionary the other day," he wrote on 5 April, "& on my return to New York intend to lay the great old folios side by side & go to sleep on them . . . with the Phaedon in one hand & Tom Brown[e] in the other"

Excerpted and reprinted from *Pursuing Melville, 1940–1980: Chapters and Essays* (Madison and London: University of Wisconsin Press, 1982), 297–317. Reprinted by permission. Footnote numbering has been altered.

(*Letters*, pp. 83–84). There are allusions to Plato in both *Redburn* and *White-Jacket*, and "the Phædon"—spelled as in the title of Gowans' new edition—is specifically named in *White-Jacket* and again in *Moby-Dick*.

Since Melville kept his promise of "no metaphysics" in *Redburn* (*Letters*, p. 86), there is little from Plato in that short book about a sailor's first voyage. In Chapter 49, describing young Carlo and his hand-organ, is an allusion to Book IV of the *Republic* already noted: the idea of that "glorious Greek of old" that the human soul is "essentially a harmony" (p. 249).[2] Chapter 58 is concerned with death at sea, a topic that leads Redburn to remark that "in every being's ideas of death, and his behavior when it suddenly menaces him, lies the best index to his life and his faith."

> Though the Christian era had not then begun, Socrates died the death of the Christian; and though Hume was not a Christian in theory, yet he, too, died the death of the Christian,—humble, composed, without bravado; and though the most skeptical of philosophical skeptics, yet full of that firm, creedless faith, that embraces the spheres. Seneca died dictating to posterity; Petronius lightly discoursing of essences and love-songs; and Addison, calling upon Christendom to behold how calmly a Christian could die; but not even the last of these three, perhaps, died the best death of the Christian. (p. 291)

In this passage, which in subject matter and tone anticipates Ishmael's meditations on death in *Moby-Dick*, is the first mention of the name of Socrates in Melville's published works or surviving letters. The allusion in such a context suggests that he was thinking of "the Phaedon"; in his next book, dealing with life aboard a man-of-war, his White-Jacket characterizes the old sailor Ushant, who "was wont to talk philosophy," as "a sort of sea-Socrates" (p. 353) and describes the ship's chaplain as a "transcendental divine" who "learnedly" alludes to "the Phædon of Plato" (p. 155) and to both Plato and Socrates (p. 157). White-Jacket himself seems to know the *Republic*, like Redburn; he echoes the same passage in Book X on fate and free choice that Melville had drawn upon in Chapter 175 of *Mardi* for Bardianna's "Ponderings."[3]

From these several allusions to Platonic themes and to Socrates, in Melville's correspondence and in both *Redburn* and *White-Jacket*, I conclude that Plato was still fresh in his mind during the spring and summer of 1849, either because he remembered his reading of the year before while he was at work on *Mardi* or because he was then rereading at least one or two of the dialogues. In view of his consistent spelling "Phaedon" and his further allusions to that dialogue in *Moby-Dick*, I am reasonably sure that he was using Gowans' new edition, and from this point on I shall therefore follow the same spelling and cite Gowans' 1849 text.[4] As for the other dialogues, it seems likely that by the time of Melville's removal from New York to Pittsfield in the late summer of 1850 he had begun to acquire his own copies of *The Works of Plato* in the new Bohn edition, translated in six volumes by Henry Cary, Henry Davis, and George Burges, which in *Billy Budd, Sailor*, he was to call "the authentic translation" (p. 75).[5] The first three volumes, published in 1848, 1849, and 1850, would have been available to him by the time he finished *Moby-Dick* in 1851;[6] in a letter to Hawthorne written in response to Hawthorne's praise of that book he made an unmistakable allusion to the *Symposium*, or *Banquet*, which is included in the third volume. There Alcibiades gives his celebrated account of Socrates' outer ugliness and inward beauty (III, 561–564); in a similar vein Melville's letter declares that Hawthorne

> did not care a penny for the book. But, now and then as you read, you understood the pervading thought that impelled the book—and that you praised. . . . You were archangel enough to despise the imperfect body, and embrace the soul. Once you hugged the ugly Socrates because you saw the flame in the mouth, and heard the rushing of the demon,—the familiar,—and recognized the sound; for you have heard it in your own solitudes. (*Letters*, p. 142)

Given such clear evidence that Melville was reading Plato in Pittsfield, I shall therefore cite the text of the Bohn edition from this point on in quoting from Plato's works other than the *Phædon*.[7] In turning to Platonism in *Moby-Dick* I shall first consider Ishmael, who went to sea "with the Phædon . . . in his head" (p. 139); then Ahab, whom Melville repeatedly associated with the thought and imagery of the *Republic;* and finally the implications of Platonic thought for the book as a whole—as Melville conceived it and as it appears to the modern reader.

(1) *Ishmael.* In "The Mast-Head," Chapter 35 of *Moby-Dick*, the narrator Ishmael addresses a half-humorous warning to Nantucket shipowners against

> enlisting in your vigilant fisheries any lad with lean brow and hollow eye; given to unseasonable meditativeness; and who offers to ship with the Phædon instead of Bowditch in his head. Beware of such an one, I say; your whales must be seen before they can be killed; and this sunken-eyed young Platonist will tow you ten wakes round the world, and never make you one pint of sperm the richer. (p. 139)

Is Ishmael then a Platonist? By his own confession, he too "kept but sorry guard" while on duty at the mast-head. "With the problem of the universe revolving in me, how could I—being left completely to myself at such a thought-engendering altitude,—how could I but lightly hold my obligations to observe all whale-ships' standing orders, 'Keep your weather eye open, and sing out every time.'"

Yes, Ishmael himself is one of those "absent-minded young philosophers," the very "Platonists" he warns against, at least at the beginning of his voyage. Therefore he too runs the risk of losing his identity by taking "the mystic ocean at his feet for the visible image of that deep, blue, bottomless soul, pervading mankind and nature," as he puts it in this same chapter,[8] and of having his spirit ebb away "to whence it came" and so forgetting the material world altogether. "But while this sleep, this dream is on ye," he cautions himself and other philosophical idealists,

> move your foot or hand an inch; slip your hold at all; and your identity comes back in horror. Over Descartian vortices you hover. And perhaps, at mid-day, in the fairest weather, with one half-throttled shriek you drop through that transparent air into the summer sea, no more to rise for ever. Heed it well, ye Pantheists! (p. 140)

As we soon learn from the opening chapters, Ishmael may also be taken as a successor to Taji and his questing companions in *Mardi*. There is no Yillah in his thoughts, however. For him, "meditation and water are wedded for ever" (p. 13), and the sea itself is his special image for what he calls "the ungraspable phantom of life" (p. 14). Moreover, he seems preoccupied with death and dying. Going to sea, he tells us, is his "substitute for pistol and ball. With a philosophical flourish Cato throws himself upon his sword; I quietly take to the ship" (p. 12). As a professed reader of the *Phædon* he should of course know that "a man enlightened by philosophy ought to die with courage," as Socrates reminds his friends in that dialogue, which Cato was reading before his suicide. "True philosophers make it the whole business of their lives to learn to die" (*Phædon*, p. 57). Ishmael goes farther, however, in actively courting death by going to sea, and now, being moved to undertake his first whaling voyage by "the overwhelming idea of the great whale himself" (p. 16), he has come to behold still more images in his "inmost soul"—"endless processions of the whale, and, midmost of them all, one grand hooded phantom, like a snow hill in the air" (p. 16), that anticipates what he is yet to learn about the death-dealing White Whale, Moby Dick himself.

Even before Ishmael embarks from Nantucket, while he is visiting Father Mapple's chapel for seamen in New Bedford, he reads in its memorial tablets "the fate of the whalemen who had gone before me. Yes, Ishmael, the same fate may be thine," he reflects, for "there is death in this business of whaling—a speechlessly quick chaotic bundling of a man into Eternity" (p. 41). It is just at this point, as he is thinking of death and Eternity, that Ishmael's Platonism first begins to emerge. "But what then?" he asks, rhetorically, going on to answer his own question in unmistakably Platonic language.

> Methinks we have hugely mistaken this matter of Life and Death. Methinks that what they call my shadow here on earth is my true substance. Methinks

that in looking at things spiritual, we are too much like oysters observing the sun through the water, and thinking that thick water the thinnest of air. Methinks my body is but the lees of my better being. In fact take my body who will, take it I say, it is not me. And therefore three cheers for Nantucket; and come a stove boat and stove body when they will, for stave my soul, Jove himself cannot. (p. 41)

A little-noticed article of 1933 by H. N. Couch, commenting on Ishmael's striking figure of "oysters observing the sun through the water," cites a parallel to this passage in the *Phædon*.[9] There Socrates tells of two earths: the one where mortals dwell and "another pure earth above the pure heaven where the stars are, which is commonly called æther. The earth we inhabit is properly nothing else but the sediment of the other." We mortals

fancy we inhabit the upper part of the pure earth . . . , as if one dwelling in the depths of the sea, should fancy his habitation to be above the waters; and when he *sees the sun and stars through the waters*, should fancy the sea to be the heavens. . . . This is just our condition, we are mewed up within some hole of the earth, and fancy we live at the top of all, we take the air for the true heavens, in which the stars run their rounds. And the cause of our mistake, is our heaviness and weakness, that keep us from surmounting this thick and muddy air. (*Phædon*, pp. 160–161)

The Platonism in Ishmael's words, which like those of Socrates in the *Phædon* concern the limitations of mortal men's spiritual vision, Couch regarded as "too patent to be the chance creation of a similar figure by an independent mind." He suggested an unconscious reproduction of the image on Melville's part, believing that Melville would not have brought *oysters* into the context "if his memory had served him better." Actually his memory had ranged elsewhere in Plato, a fact which escaped the notice of Couch in his citation of only the single parallel with the *Phædon*.

In the *Phaedrus* as well as in the *Phædon* Socrates discusses the impediment to the soul of its mortal frame—"this which we now carry about with us and call the body, fettered to it like an *oyster* to its shell" (Bohn, I, 326; emphasis added).[10] Here is the probable source of Ishmael's phraseology. The notion that "my body is but the lees of my better being" is strongly reminiscent of Socrates' theme in the two dialogues, culminating in the *Phædon* with his reply to Crito's inquiry regarding an appropriate burial: "But how will you be buried?" "Just as you please," answers Socrates, "if you can but catch me, and if I do not give you the slip." For, as he goes on to explain, Crito "confounds me with my corps[e]; and in that view asks how I must be buried. . . . [W]hen he sees my body burnt or interred" he should "not despair, as if I suffered great misery, and say at my funeral, that Socrates is laid out, Socrates is carried out, Socrates is interred. . . . You should . . . say, that my body is to be interred. That you may inter as you please" (*Phædon*, pp. 172–173). In exactly this same vein is Ishmael's remark in *Moby-Dick:* "take my body who will, take it I say, it is not me."[11]

Going back to the passage first quoted from the *Phædon*, we find there that Socrates, after first observing that "our heaviness and weakness . . . keep us from surmounting this thick and muddy air," continues as follows:

> *If any could mount up with wings to the upper surface*, he would no sooner put his head out of this gross air, than he would behold what is transacted in those blessed mansions; *just as the fishes skipping above the surface of the water, see what is done in the air in which we breathe*, and if he were a man fit for long contemplation, *he would find it to be the true heaven* and the true light; in a word, to be the true earth. (*Phædon*, p. 161; emphasis added)

With a characteristic touch, Melville also adapted the suggestion of this remark to the motif of *Moby-Dick*. "With a frigate's anchors for my bridle-bits and fasces of harpoons for spurs," Ishmael exclaims in a later chapter, 57, "would I could mount that whale and *leap the topmost skies, to see* whether *the fabled heavens* with all their countless tents really lie encamped *beyond my mortal sight!*" (p. 233; emphasis added). Here man's mortal vision and the question of life after death are Ishmael's subjects, as they were for Socrates in the *Phædon*, but the skeptic in him—and in Melville himself—cannot speak of an afterlife with the sure conviction of the Greek philosopher; for him the heavens are *fabled* heavens still.

In reviewing the passages from both Melville and Plato we see that in a single paragraph of *Moby-Dick* Melville's Ishmael is sufficiently a Platonist to be able to draw readily on two separate passages of the *Phædon* and one of the *Phaedrus*, combining three related images, and to introduce a further recollection of the longest of the passages nearly two hundred pages later in his narrative. In each passage Socrates is discussing either the impediment to the soul of the mortal body, the prospect of an afterlife, or both; what is taken over into *Moby-Dick* centers on a single vivid picture that was easily adaptable to its new context. Thus Socrates' lifeless body is not Socrates, and Ishmael's body is not Ishmael. Again, a fish's clouded vision and an oyster fettered to its shell combine into "oysters observing the sun through the water," and a fish emerging from the sea to behold the earth becomes a man riding a leaping whale to behold the heavens, as Socrates said a man might do could he "mount with wings to the upper surface."

That two of these instances concern the sea is understandable enough, for one need not read far in Melville to become aware of the quick play of his mind about anything touching either the sea or ships. In another borrowing from the *Phædon* he manages to make a maritime application of that "speculative indifference as to death" that Ishmael characterizes as "Platonian" (p. 284).[12] "All men, except the philosophers, are only brave and valiant through fear," Socrates remarks (*Phædon*, p. 67), and in *Moby-Dick* the conventionally minded Starbuck bears out his observation: as first mate of the Pequod he will have no man in his boat "who is not afraid of a whale" (p. 103). But Ishmael takes Socrates' point: "if you be a philosopher," he affirms, "though seated in the whale-boat, you would not at heart feel one whit more of terror, than though seated before your evening fire with a poker, and not a harpoon, by your side" (p. 241).

Later in the narrative, however, Ishmael appears to lose his allegiance to Socrates and the *Phædon*. Although he speaks at one point of his "doubts of all things earthly, and intuitions of some things heavenly" (p. 314), his faith in the beneficence of the spiritual realm is anything but Platonic once the voyage is under way and Ahab secures a pledge from the crew to join him in hunting the White Whale to his death. In the *Phædon* Socrates had affirmed that the soul is "an invisible being, that goes to a place like itself, marvellous, pure, and invisible, . . . and returns to a God full of goodness and wisdom" (*Phædon*, pp. 96–97). "Though in many of its aspects this visible world seems formed in love," Ishmael declares, he goes on to state without qualification that "the invisible spheres were formed in fright" (p. 169). This flat rejection of idealistic doctrine comes in Chapter 42, "The Whiteness of the Whale," which follows the crew's oath of allegiance to Ahab: now, he says, "Ahab's quenchless feud seemed mine" (p. 155). Whiteness for Ishmael is "at once the most meaning symbol of spiritual things" and yet "the intensifying agent in things the most appalling to mankind"; for him and for his readers it raises unanswerable questions:

> Is it that by its indefiniteness it shadows forth the heartless voids and immensities of the universe, and thus stabs us from behind with the thought of annihilation, when beholding the white depths of the milky way? Or is it, that as in essence whiteness is not so much a color as the visible absence of color, and at the same time the concrete of all colors; is it for these reasons that there is such a dumb blankness, full of meaning, in a wide landscape of snows—a colorless, all-color of atheism from which we shrink? (p. 169)

Once Ishmael commits himself to Ahab's quest he ceases to be the dreamy "young Platonist" of "The Mast-Head." Thoughts of atheism and annihilation, of which "the Albino whale" is the fitting symbol (p. 170), have replaced the *Phædon* in his head, and he makes few additional references to Plato or Platonism in the remaining chapters. One of them is in Chapter 78, where Queequeg rescues Tashtego from perishing within "the secret inner chamber and sanctum sanctorum" of a sperm whale's head. Ishmael can recall "only one sweeter end":

> —the delicious death of an Ohio honey-hunter, who seeking honey in the crotch of a hollow tree, found such exceeding store of it, that leaning too far over, it sucked him in, so that he died embalmed. How many, think ye, have likewise fallen into Plato's honey head, and sweetly perished there? (p. 209)[13]

(2) *Ahab.* If one thinks of Ishmael as playing a role in *Moby-Dick* like Taji's as the narrator of *Mardi*, then Ahab stands in relation to Ishmael as Babbalanja stood with respect to Taji. Like Babbalanja, Ahab is driven by a demon, "the gliding great demon of the seas of life" (p. 162)—"that demon phantom that, some time or other, swims before *all* human hearts" (p. 204; emphasis added). The words are Ishmael's, but the possession, or obsession, is Ahab's.

> All that most maddens and torments; all that stirs up the lees of things; all truth with malice in it; all that cracks the sinews and cakes the brain; all the subtle demonisms of life and thought; all evil, to crazy Ahab, were visibly personified, and made practically assailable in Moby Dick. He piled upon the whale's white hump the sum of all the general rage and hate felt by his whole race from Adam down; and then, as if his chest had been a mortar, he burst his hot heart's shell upon it. (p. 160)

Like Taji, Babbalanja, and Ishmael himself, moreover, Ahab is in part a philosophical idealist, a Platonist, even something of a transcendentalist, and his own words have what Ishmael in another context calls "a transcendental and Platonic application" (p. 372). Witness what he tells Starbuck, his first mate, in Chapter 36:

> "All visible objects, man, are but as pasteboard masks. But in each event—in the living act, the undoubted deed—there, some unknown but still reasoning thing puts forth the mouldings of its features from behind the unreasoning mask. If a man will strike, strike through the mask! How can the prisoner reach outside except by thrusting through the wall? To me, the white whale is that wall, shoved near to me. Sometimes I think there's naught beyond. But 'tis enough. He tasks me; he heaps me; I see in him outrageous strength, with an inscrutable malice sinewing it. That inscrutable thing is chiefly what I hate; and be the white whale agent, or be the white whale principal, I will wreak that hate upon him." (p. 144)

Citing this speech by Ahab to Starbuck and the crew, Michael E. Levin, in the fullest and most challenging comment to date on the Platonic strain in *Moby-Dick*,[14] has recently called attention to "some overall similarities between Ahab and Plato's paradigm philosopher, Socrates." Both, as he notes, are old, "perhaps in conformity with Plato's belief that only a man of advanced age is prepared to grasp the Forms"—those supreme principles that stand at the very head of the Platonic hierarchy of ideas developed in Books VI and VII of the *Republic*. ("Ahab has not studied mathematics or harmony," which Plato's Socrates prescribes there as essential preparation for philosophical dialectic, "but he has in his way studied astronomy," as Levin remarks.)

Both Ahab and Socrates

are men of extraordinary physical endurance: Socrates standing at Potidaea, Ahab standing "for hours and hours . . . gazing dead to windward" in a gale so violent that the crew have lashed themselves to the rail. Both have fathered children when old. In sum, for both Ahab and Socrates physical and spiritual fortitude are of a piece. Finally, Ahab compares himself to a prisoner of this world in his first exchange with Starbuck: "How can the prisoner reach outside except by thrusting through the wall? To me, the white whale is that wall." (p. 65)

Ahab's comparison of himself to a prisoner has at least two Platonic analogues. One is Socrates' image in the *Phædon* of the soul imprisoned in the body—"glued" inside of it, in Ishmael's phrase (p. 137). The other, which is more applicable to Ahab's immediate point, is the allegory of the cave in Book VII of the *Republic,* which illustrates the plight of men who are prisoners of the limited world of sense experience: chained within the cave, they can see only shadows cast upon a wall by physical objects moved between that wall and the flickering light of a fire. But the philosopher, as Socrates explains, is like a prisoner removed from the cave and taught to behold not only real objects but ultimately the sun itself. In Levin's words, he "ascends from the dark realm of illusion into the light of knowledge, there to discover the source of being and goodness" (p. 61). The sequel requires him to reenter the cave in order to govern those incapable of making the ascent—men who may well misunderstand his motives and resist his good offices. In *Moby-Dick*, Levin argues, Ahab's spiritual progress exactly reverses Plato's upward movement from darkness to light: "Ahab descends from the illusion of light into the profundity of darkness, there to discover the evil reality beneath the 'masks' of everyday life. Like the Socratic philosopher, Ahab returns to the realm of illusion, where he is thought mad by those who have never left—but he brings them darkness instead of enlightenment" (p. 61). In short, his story is the myth of the cave *inverted*.

In support of his reading of *Moby-Dick* Levin cites a series of passages that illustrate a consistent pattern of imagery involving light and darkness. "Truth and profundity," he finds, "are always identified with darkness; light, and the sun, with shallowness and illusion" (pp. 67–68). Moreover, he suggests that Ahab's apparent madness, the result of his encounter with dark reality, is "underscored" by Melville through what happens to Pip—"a miniature Ahab," as Levin calls him.

Pip, like Ahab, has been transformed by a glimpse into the dark essence of things: "carried down alive to wondrous depths . . . among the joyous, heartless, ever-juvenile eternities, Pip . . . saw God's foot upon the treadle of the loom, and spoke it; and therefore his shipmates called him mad." Thus, "from that hour the little negro went about the deck an idiot; such, at least, they said he was." Here we have . . . the suggestion that Pip (and Ahab) are not mad at all—it is the blind crew that misperceive the return of the man transformed by knowledge. (pp. 66–67)

Finally Levin, like Ahab and Ishmael before him, must confront Moby Dick himself, whom he comes close to identifying with the Platonic Forms even though he is properly cautious about Melville's own intentions. The White Whale, as he notes, seems preternatural—especially in the "unearthly conceit" of whalemen that he is "not only ubiquitous, but immortal (for immortality is but ubiquity in time)." Here Levin is quoting Ishmael in Chapter 41 (p. 158); one thinks too of Babbalanja's remark in *Mardi* that "true thoughts . . . are ubiquitous; . . . they were in us, before we were born" (p. 397; see p. 283 above). "Ubiquity," according to Levin, is "the very mark" of the Platonic Forms, the attribute that

gives them their distinctive ontological and explanatory role and . . . makes them single abstract rather than scattered concrete objects. Melville could not have intended anything so flatly literal as making the whale out to be a Form; but its ubiquity does suggest that the whale, like the Forms, inhabits some ulterior reality from which it sends out manifold projections, none of which are more than partially adequate. (p. 67)

He adds that Melville may be emphasizing that latter point through Ishmael's insistence that "there is no *earthly* way of finding out precisely what the whale really looks like" (p. 228; emphasis added).

That Levin is correct in recognizing what he calls "Melville's high regard for the *Republic* and especially the *Phaedo*" (p. 62) is amply borne out by what has been reviewed here—from *Mardi, Redburn,* and *White-Jacket* as well as from *Moby-Dick.* He is well aware that there is more to Ahab and to the book as a whole than inverted Platonism; as he admits himself, his reading "risks imposing an allegorical pattern so mechanically that it rubs the texture of narrative suggestion threadbare and compresses character down to a single dimension" (p. 61). This is finely said at the very outset. Moreover, in concluding his presentation he is willing to grant that neither Melville nor any other author consciously *intended* "the meaning we attribute to him," though he has proposed the reading he offers because "I have found it impossible to understand *Moby-Dick* without attending to the dark inverted Platonism that moved Melville himself." Melville's "particular use of light imagery," he maintains, was "cued" by "its appropriateness to the pessimistic dualism jockeying with much else for position in his mind" (p. 71).

To understand that "pessimistic dualism," I would add, we must remember also that for Ahab—and for Melville—there were many things in heaven and earth undreamt of in Plato's philosophy. Not Platonism but Zoroastrianism, Gnosticism, and perhaps even Hinduism "cued" the most powerful imagery of light and dark in the entire book: that in Ahab's defiant address to the "white flame" of the corpusants in Chapter 119, "The Candles."

> "Oh! thou clear spirit of clear fire, whom on these seas I as Persian once did worship . . . ; I now know that thy right worship is defiance. To neither love nor reverence wilt thou be kind. . . . Come in thy lowest form of love, and I will kneel and kiss thee; but at thy highest, come as mere supernal power; and though thou launchest navies of full-freighted worlds, there's that in here that still remains indifferent. . . . Light though thou be, thou leapest out of darkness; but I am darkness leaping out of light, leaping out of thee! . . . But thou art but my fiery father; my sweet mother, I know not. . . . Thou knowest not how came ye, hence callest thyself unbegotten; certainly knowest not thy beginning, hence callest thyself unbegun. I know that of me, which thou knowest not of thyself, oh, thou omnipotent! There is some unsuffusing thing beyond thee, thou clear spirit, to whom all thy eternity is but time, all thy creativeness mechanical. . . . I leap with thee; I burn with thee; would fain be welded with thee; defyingly I worship thee!"
> (pp. 416–417)

Back of this impassioned defiance lay Melville's reading in a wide variety of primary and secondary works ranging far beyond Greek philosophy; one of the most influential, Pierre Bayle's *Historical and Critical Dictionary,* he had bought in 1849 at the same time that he was reading Plato, Browne, and Emerson.[15] This very eclecticism is in keeping with Melville's injunction in *Pierre* against letting any "one great book . . . domineer with its own uniqueness upon the creative mind"; instead, "all existing great works must be federated in the fancy" as "simply an exhilarative and provocative" to the aspiring writer. "Even when thus combined," moreover, they will constitute "but one small mite, compared to the latent infiniteness and inexhaustibility" in the author himself (p. 284).

(3) *"Like a magician's glass."* Both Ahab and Ishmael, though steeped in Platonism as they so obviously were, would subscribe only in part to what Levin identifies as three of its principal tenets (pp. 62–63). First, to borrow Levin's convenient phrasing, Plato's "sharp distinction between a realm of appearance and a realm of reality" means that "genuine knowledge (of reality) requires active transcendence of appearance." But here one remembers Ishmael's insistence throughout the book that no man has ever really known "the living whale," that formidable being which,

> in his full majesty and significance, is only to be seen at sea in unfathomable waters; and afloat the vast bulk of him is out of sight, like a launched line-of-battle ship. . . . And the only mode in which you can derive even a tolerable idea of his living contour, is by going a whaling yourself; but by so doing, you run no small risk of being eternally stove and sunk by him.

> Wherefore, . . . you had best not be too fastidious in your curiosity touching this Leviathan. (pp. 227–228)

Again in a later chapter Ishmael restates his basic position that whatever knowledge of the whale a man can grasp is not transcendental or absolute but relative and existential: "Only in the heart of quickest perils; only when within the eddyings of his angry flukes; only on the profound unbounded sea, can the fully invested whale be truly and livingly found out" (p. 378).

Ahab is more of an absolutist, though even he cannot be sure whether the whale is but a whale or the intermediate "agent" of some higher and necessarily malevolent power (p. 144). "Sometimes" he thinks "there's naught beyond" the realm of appearance that he variously calls the "unreasoning mask" or imprisoning "wall" of visible objects: as he puts it in Chapter 125, "The dead, blind wall butts all inquiring heads at last" (p. 427). (One recalls Media's reminder to Babbalanja in *Mardi*: "you mortals dwell in Mardi, and it is impossible to get elsewhere.") Still, Ahab continues to adhere to what Levin distinguishes as Platonism's second tenet: "reality is mind-like." Here Ahab is the consistent idealist: "Oh! how immaterial are all materials!" he cries in Chapter 127. "What things real are there, but imponderable thoughts?" (pp. 432–433). "All the things that most exasperate and outrage mortal man," he complains, are intangible—"bodiless" (p. 461). But Ishmael, whenever he forgets "our horrible oath" to hunt Moby Dick, draws apart from Ahab as well as from his own earlier Platonism, and in Chapter 94, speaking in the narrative present, he makes this distinctly non-Platonic affirmation:

> For now, . . . by many prolonged, repeated experiences, I have perceived that in all cases man must eventually lower, or at least shift, his conceit of attainable felicity; *not placing it anywhere in the intellect or the fancy;* but in the wife, the heart, the bed, the table, the saddle, the fire-side, the country. (p. 349; emphasis added)

Ishmael's "shift" from the realm of intellect to the realm of tangible entities is a repudiation of the Platonic scale of values and the idealistic assumption that "goodness comes from the source of being"—Levin's third tenet of Platonism. What feelings he has about "the source of being" are apparent in "The Whiteness of the Whale." As for Ahab, it is *evil*, not goodness, that he attributes to ultimate reality; his quarrel with the cosmos itself carries him even beyond Platonism in "The Candles" and eventually to his death in "The Chase." The alternatives, it would seem, are to come to terms with the realm of appearance, as Ishmael recommends, or to transcend it—and transcendence is *not* to be attained in this life. "We can never arrive at the wisdom we court till after death," even Socrates admits in the *Phædon* (p. 63); "Our souls are like those orphans whose unwedded mothers die in bearing them," says Ahab: "the secret of our paternity lies in their grave, and we must there to learn it" (p. 406)[16]

In *Moby-Dick* Melville has dramatized this dilemma that confronts all mortals by creating both Ishmael and Ahab and sending them to sea, there to front Moby Dick. Each is meditative, philosophical, even idealistic, but each in his own way is both more and less than a Platonist. Certain aspects of Ahab's idealism, for instance, seem less like that of the Platonic dialogues than what Melville himself had encountered in the thought of his nineteenth-century contemporaries. "O Nature, and O soul of man!" Ahab exclaims at one point, "how far beyond all utterance are your linked analogies! not the smallest atom stirs or lives in matter, but has its cunning duplicate in mind" (p. 264); this is essentially the conception of symbolic correspondence between matter and spirit to be found in Carlyle and Emerson. Again, both Ahab and Ishmael as nineteenth-century characters are intensely subjective almost to solipsism, as the Greeks were not. In "The Doubloon," Chapter 99, Ishmael reports how seven men of the Pequod, ranging from Ahab to Pip, in turn see themselves projected in the gold coin Ahab has nailed to the mainmast. "Some certain significance lurks in all things," Ishmael himself muses, "else all things are little worth, and the round world itself but an empty cipher" (p. 358). His implication is that "significance" may well lie in the eye of the beholder; Ahab is even more explicit. "The round gold," he soliloquizes aloud,

> "is but the image of the rounder globe, which, like a magician's glass, to each and every man in turn but mirrors back his own mysterious self. Great pains, small gains for those who ask the world to solve them; it cannot solve itself. Methinks now this coined sun wears a ruddy face; but see! aye, he enters the sign of storms, the equinox! and but six months before he wheeled out of a former equinox at Aries! From storm to storm! So be it, then. Born in throes, 'tis fit that man should live in pains and die in pangs! So be it, then! Here's a stout stuff for woe to work on. So be it, then." (pp. 359–360)

What Ishmael and Ahab say in this chapter is written large throughout *Moby-Dick* in terms of its dominant symbol, the sea. To go to sea, as Ishmael tells us from the beginning, is to search for truth; he makes the point most plainly in Chapter 23, "The Lee Shore"—a chapter echoing Emerson[17]— when he sets forth "that mortally intolerable" principle that

> all deep, earnest thinking is but the intrepid effort of the soul to keep the open independence of her sea; while the wildest winds of heaven and earth conspire to cast her on the treacherous, slavish shore[.]
>
> But as in landlessness alone resides the highest truth, shoreless, indefinite as God—so, better is it to perish in that howling infinite, than be ingloriously dashed upon the lee, even if that were safety! (p. 97)[18]

Moving along what I like to think of as the "horizontal" axis of *Moby-Dick*, Ishmael's narrative carries forward the continuous quest that Melville had begun in *Typee*, a quest that in *Mardi* was extended into what Taji calls "the world of mind" (p. 557). By the time of *Moby-Dick*, however, this horizontal movement was displaying a tendency to circle back on itself. The helmsman Bulkington, the "tall, new-landed mariner" memorialized in "The Lee Shore," is a man "who in mid-winter just landed from a four years' dangerous voyage," had "unrestingly push[ed] off again for still another tempestuous term. The land seemed scorching to his feet" (p. 97). He may well be the very steersman whom Ahab is addressing in Chapter 52—"Up helm! Keep her off round the world!"—when Ishmael comments:

> Round the world! There is much in that sound to inspire proud feelings; but whereto does all that circumnavigation conduct? Only through number-less perils to the very point whence we started, where those that we left behind secure, were all the time before us.
>
> Were this world an endless plain, and by sailing eastward we could for ever reach new distances, and discover sights more sweet and strange than any Cyclades or Islands of King Solomon, then there were promise in the voyage. But in pursuit of those far mysteries we dream of, or in tormented chase of that demon phantom that, some time or other, swims before all human hearts; while chasing such over this round globe, they either lead us on in barren mazes or midway leave us whelmed. (p. 204)

Here Ishmael is voicing an idea recurrent in Melville's later thought: that whether for the individual or for the race, progress is a delusion. He returns to the theme in Chapter 98, which includes a reference to metempsychosis far different from anything in *Mardi:*

> hardly have we mortals by long toilings extracted from this world's vast bulk its small but valuable sperm; and then, with weary patience, cleansed ourselves from its defilements, and learned to live here in clean tabernacles of the soul; hardly is this done, when—*There she blows!*—the ghost is spouted up, and away we sail to fight some other world, and go through young life's old routine again.
>
> Oh! the metempsychosis! Oh! Pythagoras, that in bright Greece, two thousand years ago, did die, so good, so wise, so mild; I sailed with thee along the Peruvian coast last voyage—and, foolish as I am, taught thee, a green simple boy, how to splice a rope! (p. 358)[19]

To the degree that the voyage of the Pequod is the figurative representation of a philosophical quest, the death of Ahab and survival of Ishmael—whether by fate, necessity, or chance, which for Ishmael has "the last featuring blow at events" (p. 185)—may seem to have alternative implications, though I would not reduce *Moby-Dick* to the level of a cautionary tale. Instead, I prefer to return the discussion to the issue of idealistic subjectivism by way of what I call the "vertical" axis of *Moby-Dick,* which begins with the "water-gazers" of Chapter 1.

> Why is almost every robust healthy boy with a robust healthy soul in him, at some time or other crazy to go to sea? Why upon your first voyage as a passenger, did you yourself feel such a mystical vibration, when first told that you and your ship were now out of sight of land? Why did the old Persians hold the sea holy? Why did the Greeks give it a separate deity, and make him the own brother of Jove? Surely all this is not without meaning. And still deeper the meaning of that story of Narcissus, who because he could not grasp the tormenting, mild image he saw in the fountain, plunged into it and was drowned. But that same image, we ourselves see in all rivers and oceans. It is the image of the ungraspable phantom of life, and this is the key to it all. (pp. 13–14)

"The story of Narcissus," with all its implications for other "plunges" in *Moby-Dick*—young Platonists teetering above the water at the mast-head, Tashtego actually falling into the whale's head, Pip "carried down alive to wondrous depths," the Pequod ultimately stove and sunk by Moby Dick, with Ishmael himself "escaped alone to tell thee" (p. 470)—has earlier analogues in Melville's writing. Yoomy in *Mardi* "soars" while Babbalanja "dives"; Melville himself told Duyckinck in 1849, with Emerson in mind, "I love all men who *dive*," going on to praise "the whole corps of thought-divers, that have been diving & coming up again with bloodshot eyes since the world began" (*Letters,* p. 79). When he wrote *White-Jacket* later in that same year he ordained a sea-change for his title character through a fall from a yard-arm of the Neversink (Chapter 92). In *Moby-Dick* there are innumerable references to all that lies below the surface of the ocean, which to the idealistic pantheist of Chapter 35 symbolizes "that deep, blue, bottomless soul, pervading mankind and nature";

> and every strange, half-seen, gliding, beautiful thing that eludes him; every dimly-discovered, uprising fin of some undiscernible form, seems to him the embodiment of those elusive thoughts that only people the soul by continually flitting through it. (p. 140)

Is the ocean a Neoplatonic soul of the world, or only the projecting mind of the beholder? Ishmael cannot finally say, though the question has obviously occurred to him and to Melville. Beneath the track of the Pequod "rush herds of walruses and whales" (p. 63); in that "everlasting terra incognita" (p. 235) swims what both Ishmael and Fleece call accursed, the shark (pp. 235, 252);[20] and there too glides Moby Dick.

What thoughts the White Whale "embodies" for Ahab we know, and we know too, through physical analogies reported by Ishmael, how much

Ahab has come to resemble outwardly the projected image of his inner torment, for both are old and wrinkled, humped and scarred. But for Ishmael, by contrast, what he associates with whales in general and Moby Dick in particular is not fixed and set. Instead, his conceptions continually shift as he moves from rumors and superstitions about the whale through actual experience as a whaleman to his first glimpse of Moby Dick himself. During much of the narrative he of course shares Ahab's hatred for the White Whale, though in such later chapters as 94, "A Squeeze of the Hand," he has already moved somewhat apart from Ahab and from Ahab's unchanging obsession. In Chapter 96, "The Try-Works," he partly casts off Ahab's spell, his power of blackness; there is perhaps even a faint recollection of the allegory of the cave as Ishmael cries:

> Look not too long in the face of the fire, O man! Never dream with thy hand on the helm! Turn not thy back to the compass; accept the first hint of the hitching tiller; *believe not the artificial fire*, when its redness makes all things look ghastly. Tomorrow, *in the natural sun*, the skies will be bright; those who glared like devils in the forking flames, the morn will show in far other, at least gentler, relief; *the glorious, golden, glad sun, the only true lamp—all others but liars!*
>
> Nevertheless the sun hides not Virginia's Dismal Swamp, nor Rome's cursed Campagna, nor wide Sahara, nor all the millions of miles of deserts and of griefs beneath the moon. *The sun hides not the ocean, which is the dark side of this earth, and which is two thirds of this earth.* So, therefore, that mortal man who hath more of joy than sorrow in him, that mortal man cannot be true—not true, or undeveloped. With books the same. (pp. 354–355; emphasis added)

Ishmael concludes this deliberate weighing of light against dark with a characteristic injunction that in its imagery of diving and soaring recalls both *Mardi* and Plato's *Phaedrus:*

> Give not thyself up, then, to fire, lest it *invert thee, deaden thee, as for the time it did me.* There is a wisdom that is woe; but there is a woe that is *madness.* And there is a Catskill eagle in some souls that can alike *dive down* into the blackest gorges, and *soar out* of them again and become invisible in the sunny spaces. And even if he for ever flies within the gorge, that gorge is in the mountains; so that even in his lowest swoop the mountain eagle is still higher than other birds upon the plain, even though they soar. (p. 355; emphasis added)

The same effort to weigh and balance and a recurrence of the idea of subjective projection are both apparent when we examine Ishmael's glimpses of whales in the later chapters of his narrative. In Chapter 86, describing the "peaking of the whale's flukes," he is moved to remark that "in gazing at such scenes, it is all in what mood you are in; if in the Dantean, the devils will occur to you; if in that of Isaiah, the archangels" (p. 317). A chapter later, in "The Grand Armada," his mood is less Dantean than Platonic once again. Through water "to a considerable depth exceedingly transparent" he is looking down at "the nursing mothers of the whales":

> as human infants while suckling will calmly and fixedly gaze away from the breast, as if leading two different lives at the same time; and while yet drawing mortal nourishment, be still *spiritually feasting upon some unearthly reminiscence;*—even so did the young of these whales seem looking up toward us, but not at us. (p. 325; emphasis added)

But it is another sight altogether in Chapter 133 when Moby Dick himself at last appears:

> A gentle joyousness—a mighty mildness of repose in swiftness, invested the gliding whale. Not the white bull Jupiter swimming away with ravished Europa clinging to his graceful horns; his lovely, leering eyes sideways intent upon the maid; with smooth bewitching fleetness, rippling straight for the nuptial bower in Crete; not Jove, not that great majesty Supreme! did surpass the glorified White Whale as he so divinely swam.
>
> On each soft side . . . the whale shed off enticings. No wonder there has been some among the hunters who namelessly transported and allured by all that serenity, had ventured to assail it; but had fatally found that quietude but the vesture of tornadoes. Yet calm, enticing calm, oh, whale! thou glidest on, to all who for the first time eye thee, no matter how many in that same way thou may'st have bejuggled and destroyed before.
>
> And thus, through the serene tranquillities of the tropical sea, . . . Moby Dick moved on, still withholding from sight the full terrors of his submerged trunk, entirely hiding the wrenched hideousness of his jaw. But soon the fore part of him slowly rose from the water; for an instant his whole marbleized body formed a high arch, like Virginia's Natural Bridge, and warningly waving his bannered flukes in the air, the grand god revealed himself, sounded, and went out of sight. (pp. 447–448)

What Ishmael is setting before us here is no Platonic Form. In this climactic passage Moby Dick is a tangible and believable whale whose emergence before our eyes has been prepared for in some way, directly or obliquely, by every chapter of Ishmael's long narrative. The majesty of the White Whale as he finally appears to us is first of all the majesty of physical nature itself, with all the ambiguous mingling of beauty and terror that pertains to the natural world. At the same time, our realization that he has risen from the depths of the sea, out of what seems to some the very soul of that world, may suggest still further implications—if one attends to the specific imagery of the passage and relates it to the book's metaphysical and theological dimensions. Here as elsewhere Moby Dick carries attributes not of the Forms but of divinity, itself both beautiful and terrible; yet Ishmael has already provided the basis for alternative readings, either naturalistic or subjective, of what the White Whale is and does. Ahab's obviously subjective vision of his antagonist and all the variations on the Narcissus myth we have noted throughout Ishmael's narrative suggest that the whale and the water in which he swims are like the doubloon and the round globe itself: mirrors of each man's "own mysterious self." Whether qualities and values are "actually inherent" in any natural object, whales included, or whether they are merely "laid on from without"—to borrow phrases from "The Whiteness of the Whale" (p. 170)—is an epistemological issue that Ishmael never finally decides. Taken subjectively, metaphysically, or even on the purely physical level, the White Whale remains ambiguous for him to the final chapter, where Ahab meets his death, the Pequod sinks, and the sea, like a shroud, rolls on "as it rolled five thousand years ago" (p. 469).

Between the writing of *Mardi* and the writing of *Moby-Dick*, during the years when he also turned out *Redburn* and *White-Jacket*, Melville developed from an author who entertained philosophical ideas into a full-fledged philosophical novelist. In *Mardi* the characters talk philosophy; in *Moby-Dick*, for good or for ill, both Ahab and Ishmael put their philosophy to the test of experience in the course of Ahab's doomed quest for Moby Dick. In *Mardi* Taji is narrator, protagonist, and quester all in one and Babbalanja is the inveterate philosopher; in *Moby-Dick* the narrator's role falls to Ishmael but both he and Ahab have their own stories in which each is at once protagonist, quester, and philosopher as well. If the book is "the tragedy of Captain Ahab," John Halverson has remarked, "it is also the novel of Ishmael."[21]

"A philosophical novelist like Melville," says Michael Levin in his analysis of *Moby-Dick* as inverted Platonism,

> supplies something generally lacking in the formal development of a philosophical system: what it is like to experience the world as the system represents it. The system-builder's job is to refine his system, give reasons for accepting it, and perhaps draw from it some practical consequences. A novelist like Melville is trying to articulate the world as seen through the lens of the system. He need not even subscribe to the system to appreciate its interest as an aesthetic object—perhaps not Ahab but the sceptical Ishmael speaks for Melville. (pp. 61–62)

"What it is like to experience the world" as a philosophical idealist is a state of mind and feeling that Melville first communicated with genuine success in *Moby-Dick* with Ishmael and Ahab, though he had dramatized elements of idealistic thought in a line of characters extending from Taji and Babbalanja through the vignette of the unnamed "transcendental" chaplain of *White-Jacket*. Levin recognizes a difference between Ahab, with his philosophy of ultimate blackness, and "the sceptical Ishmael," but he does not analyze the

movement of Ishmael's narrative and therefore takes no account of Ishmael's [7]
inclination toward Platonism in the opening chapters, his loss of idealistic
faith once his allegiance is transferred from Socrates to Ahab, or his ultimate
awareness of what Emerson meant when he wrote in "Experience" that "Life
is a train of moods like a string of beads":

> as we pass through them they prove to be many-colored lenses which paint the
> world their own hue, and each shows only what lies in its focus. . . . We
> animate what we can, and we see only what we animate. Nature and books
> belong to the eyes that see them. It depends on the mood of the man whether
> he shall see the sunset or the fine poem. There are always sunsets, and there
> is always genius; but only a few hours so serene that we can relish nature or
> criticism.[22]

"Oh! time was," Ahab soliloquizes, "when as the sunrise nobly spurred me,
so the sunset soothed. No more. This lovely light, it lights not me; all
loveliness is anguish to me, since I can ne'er enjoy" (p. 147). "It is all in what
mood you are in" when you behold the whale, Ishmael tells us, as though his
subjectivism were Emerson's; it is not a doctrine he had learned from the
Phædon.

Does Ahab speak for Melville in such passages, or does Ishmael? The
reader need not choose; the advantage of "this method of philosophising in
dialogues," as Melville had read in Montaigne, is the opportunity to deliver
"from several mouths . . . the diversity and variety" of an author's "own
fancies." Ahab's philosophy, like his purpose in pursuing Moby Dick, is
fixed—"laid with iron rails," as he says, "whereon my soul is grooved to run"
(p. 147); Ishmael's is far more flexible. "So far gone" is Ahab "in the dark side
of earth," as he himself realizes, "that its other side, the theoretic bright one,
seems but uncertain twilight to me" (p. 433). Ishmael will grant that "the
dark side of this earth" (which he identifies with the ocean) is "two thirds of
this earth," but there is another side as well, where the natural sun outshines
the artificial fire of the Pequod's try-works. "Give not thyself up, then, to
fire," he tells us, "lest it invert thee, deaden thee; as for the time it did me";
though there is "a wisdom that is woe," there is also "a woe that is madness."

From Ahab's mouth, as from Babbalanja's in *Mardi* when Azzageddi is
in the ascendant, come Melville's own darker, deeper fancies; "for any good
man, in his own proper character, to utter, or even hint of them," in the
words of "Hawthorne and His Mosses" (1850), "were all but madness."[23] At
one remove from Ahab (and from Moby Dick) stands Ishmael, for Melville
and for us. He too knows what madness is, having more than "a mouthful
of brains," in Melville's phrase. He is both poet and philosopher—Yoomy as
well as Babbalanja—and can soar as well as dive; it is he who survives the
wreck to report the Pequod's voyage.

Notes

1. On the Shakespeare, the Bayle, and Harper's Classical Library, see *Melville's Reading*, p. 93: No. 460; p. 39: No. 51, and p. 349 above; pp. 51–52: No. 147. As for the *Phædon*, Gowans was a New York bookseller where in 1847 Melville had bought a volume that was once his father's (*Melville's Reading*, p. 45: No. 103; p. 37 above); in the *Literary World* for 17 March 1849 appeared an advertisement for Gowans' *Phædon: or, a Dialogue on the Immortality of the Soul. By Plato. Translated from the Original Greek by Madam Dacier. With Notes and Emendations. To Which is Prefixed the Life of the Author, by Fenelon* (New York: William Gowans, 1849). Melville was in New York between 2 and 15 March 1849, according to a letter written by Hope Savage Shaw quoted in Joyce Deveau Kennedy and Frederick J. Kennedy, "Elizabeth Shaw Melville and Samuel Hay Savage," *Melville Society Extracts*, No. 39 (September 1979), p. 4; he first mentioned "the Phaedon" in a letter of 5 April (*Letters*, pp. 83–84).

Another "*Phædon*" translated from the German of Moses Mendelssohn (London, 1789) would have been available to Melville at the New York Society Library, according to its 1850 *Catalogue*, p. 294, but Gowans' more recent publication seems the likelier text. Duyckinck, it might be noted, owned a copy of an earlier English version of the Dacier rendering (New York, 1833), but there is no record of Melville's borrowing it.

2. See pp. 291–292 above and p. 388, note 21.

3. See p. 293 above and p. 389, note 25, which quotes the passage from *White-Jacket*, Chapter 75.

4. Parenthetically within the text as "*Phædon*."

5. London: Henry G. Bohn, 1848–1854. In *Billy Budd, Sailor*, Melville quotes a definition of "natural depravity" from what he calls a "list of definitions" that is to be found in the Bohn edition (VI, 143) but is lacking in later nineteenth-century translations by Whewell and Jowett. See p. 333 below and note 77, p. 395.

6. On 27 January 1849 the New York bookseller John Wiley advertised the first volume in the *Literary World;* this volume includes the *Apology, Crito, Phaedo, Gorgias, Protagoras, Phaedrus, Theaetetus, Euthyphron,* and *Lysis.* The second volume (1849) includes the *Republic, Timaeus,* and *Critias;* the third (1850), the *Meno, Euthydemus, Sophist, Statesman, Cratylus, Parmenides,* and *Banquet.*

7. Parenthetically within the text as "Bohn."

8. Elsewhere he writes of the sea as "the great mundane soul" (p. 201).

9. H. N. Couch, "*Moby Dick* and the *Phaedo*," *Classical Journal*, 28 (February 1933), 367–368.

10. A note in the Hendricks House edition of *Moby-Dick*, p. 614, correctly identifies Melville's source for the image of "oysters," citing the Jowett translation of the *Phaedrus.* Overlooking Couch's article, the note also proposes Plato's allegory of the cave in Book VII of the *Republic* as Melville's further source in the passage.

11. In "The Mast-Head," Ishmael refers to the soul as "glued inside of its fleshly tabernacle," the body (p. 137); his image may have come from Cary's translation of a passage in the *Phaedon* where Socrates speaks of the soul as "bound and glued to the body" (Bohn, I, 86). (The Gowans *Phædon*, p. 102, uses the phrase "tied and chained" at this same point.)

12. To Ishmael, the sperm whale appears elsewhere as a "Platonian leviathan" (p. 228); Melville probably knew from *Anthon's Classical Dictionary* that the name Plato (Πλατών, from πλατύς, "broad") was given the Greek philosopher "from either the breadth of his shoulders or of his forehead." In the present passage Ishmael sees the sperm whale as "a Platonian, who might have taken up Spinoza in his latter years"; the right whale, with his "enormous practical resolution in facing death," he sees as "a Stoic" (p. 284). Ishmael's tone here may be light, but

the distinction between Platonists and Stoics was a real one for Melville himself. In *Mardi*, it will be recalled, Babbalanja quotes the Stoic Seneca, the "antique pagan" of Chapter 124, as well as Bardianna (p. 280 above), and either he or Media differentiates Athenians from Spartans as "meditative philosophers" rather than "enduring stoics" (p. 526; see p. 288 above).

13. It has not been observed that Melville's phrase "Plato's honey head" recalls an old tradition—one that he may have come across in William Browne's *Britannia's Pastorals*, which he borrowed from Evert Duyckinck in 1850 (*Melville's Reading*, p. 44: No. 91). In Book I, Song 2, lines 439–440, Browne writes:

> And as when Plato did i' th' cradle thrive,
> Bees to his lips brought honey from their hive. . . .

The head as a "hive" is an image Melville later applied both to Benjamin Franklin in Chapter 7 of *Israel Potter* and to Babo in "Benito Cereno" (1855). Franklin, called a "household Plato" (as noted above), has a "hive of a head," and Babo's severed head is a "hive of subtlety"; see *Complete Stories*, p. 353.

14. Michael E. Levin, "Ahab as Socratic Philosopher: The Myth of the Cave Inverted," *ATQ: The American Transcendental Quarterly*, No. 41 (Winter 1979), pp. 61–73; further reference to this article will be made parenthetically within the text. Levin is a member of the Department of Philosophy, The City College of The City University of New York.

15. *Melville's Reading*, p. 39: No. 51, and p. 349 above; see "Melville and Emerson's Rainbow," p. 263 above. Melville's knowledge of Gnosticism seems to have come both from Bayle and from Andrews Norton; see Millicent Bell, "Pierre Bayle and *Moby-Dick*," *PMLA*, 66 (September 1951), 626–648; and for specific comment on the passage just quoted, Thomas Vargish, "Gnostic *Mythos* in *Moby-Dick*," *PMLA*, 81 (June 1966), 272–277. On Melville and Zoroaster, see Dorothee Metlitsky Finkelstein, *Melville's Orienda* (New Haven and London: Yale University Press, 1961), pp. 152–164; on Ahab's notion of worship by defiance, see H. B. Kulkarni, *Moby-Dick: A Hindu Avatar. A Study of Hindu Myth and Thought in "Moby-Dick"* (Logan, Utah: Utah State University Press, 1970), pp. 36–38. As Levin himself remarks (p. 66), Melville's out-of-the-way learning at the time of *Moby-Dick* led him to note in a new copy of the Bible that certain books of the Apocrypha combined Platonism and Judaism; see also *Melville's Reading*, pp. 40–41: No. 62; and *Log*, I, 370.

16. Although quotation marks are absent from the received text at this point, the passage quoted follows a paragraph on Ahab and precedes companion meditations attributed to Starbuck and Stubb. I take the words to be Ahab's.

17. See "Melville and Emerson's Rainbow," p. 264 above.

18. The antithesis of sea and land is recurrent in *Moby-Dick*. In Chapter 58, for example, Ishmael draws "a strange analogy": "as this appalling ocean surrounds the verdant land, so in the soul of man there lies one insular Tahiti, full of peace and joy, but encompassed by all the horrors of the half known life. . . . Push not off from that isle, thou canst never return!" (p. 236).

19. Here as in *Mardi* Melville was probably drawing on Sir Thomas Browne, who wrote in *Religio Medici:* "I cannot believe the wisdom of Pythagoras did ever positively, and in a literal sense, affirm his metempsychosis" (*Works*, II, 55). In *Moby-Dick*, compare Chapter 114: "There is no steady unretracing progress in this life; we do not advance. . . . [O]nce gone through, we trace the round again" (p. 406, in a paragraph I attribute to Ahab; see note 45 above). In "I and My Chimney" (1856) the narrator likens his home to "a philosophical system": "Going through the house, you seem to be forever going somewhere, and getting nowhere. . . . [I]f you arrive at all, it is just where you started"; see *Complete Stories*, p. 389.

20. "Queequeg no care what god made him shark; wedder Fejee god or Nantucket god; but de god wat made shark must be one dam Ingin" (p. 257).

21. John Halverson, "The Shadow in *Moby-Dick*," *American Quarterly*, 15 (Fall 1963), 444. Halverson's entire essay (pp. 436–446) investigates the abundant shadow imagery of the book in terms of psychological archetypes; he remarks incidentally that "Jung did not discover the shadow side of man. Among countless earlier instances, let Plato's black horse of the *Phaedrus* parable suffice as an example" (p. 436). Melville's imagery is closest to Plato's when Ishmael is dealing with Fedallah in Chapter 130. The crew of the Pequod seem uncertain "whether indeed he were a mortal substance, or else a tremulous shadow cast upon the deck by some unseen being's body" (p. 438). Ahab and Fedallah gaze upon one another "as if in the Parsee Ahab saw his forethrown shadow, in Ahab the Parsee his abandoned substance." Sometimes he appears as Ahab's slave, Ishmael declares; "again both seemed *yoked together*, and an unseen tyrant driving them" (p. 439; emphasis added).

22. Emerson, *Works*, III, 50.

23. Melville had in mind Shakespeare as speaking his own thoughts through the "mouths" of his "dark characters" in the tragedies; see "Hawthorne and His Mosses" in *The Norton Anthology of American Literature*, ed. Ronald Gottesman et al., 2 vols. (New York and London: W. W. Norton & Company, 1979), I, 2061.

[The Influence of Carlyle]

Leon Howard

During the latter part of 1850 Melville was also reading Carlyle. He borrowed *Sartor Resartus* and *Heroes and Hero-Worship* from Duyckinck's library shortly before he went on his vacation and Carlyle's translation of German Romances shortly before he moved to Pittsfield. He may have been interested in the last two because their titles suggested a possible usefulness in developing the Romantic elements in his book, but, though they may have had some effect upon his style, it was *Sartor Resartus* which was to have an important influence upon the evolution of *Moby-Dick*.

Like James Russell Lowell and other contemporaries, Melville appears to have been attracted by the rhetoric of Carlyle's sardonic humor before becoming interested in the substance of his book. He had been attracted by Sir Thomas Browne and Robert Burton and by Duchat's translation of Rabelais while writing *Mardi* and was reading Richter in translations by both Noel and Carlyle. But, though he respected Emerson as a "thought-diver," he was suspicious of Transcendental philosophy; and he had no conception of the *Bildungsroman* which Carlyle, in his own peculiar way, was introducing into English literature. Yet his own tendency toward sardonic humor and rhetorical extravagance enabled him to appreciate an author who could identify his own thoughts and emotions with a hero named Teufels-dröckh, express them in language of Shakespearean extravagance, and become the wandering outcast of his own dark mind with a sense of heroic self-confidence rather than Byronic guilt.

*   *   *

Ahab's emblematic universe was certainly more directly out of *Sartor Resartus* than out of the lecture on Mahomet. His best expression of it is in his words to Starbuck in "The Quarter-Deck" (36): "All visible objects, man, are but as pasteboard masks. But in each event—in the living act, the undoubted deed—there, some unknown but still reasoning thing puts forth the mouldings of his features from behind the unreasoning mask." This is very close to Teufelsdröckh's conviction that "all visible things are emblems; what thou seest is not there on its own account; strictly taken, it is not there

Excerpted and reprinted from *The Unfolding of MOBY-DICK*, ed. James Barbour and Thomas Quirk (Glassboro: The Melville Society, 1987), 39–43.

at all: Matter exists only spiritually, and to represent some Idea, and *body* it forth." Furthermore, Ahab's attitude toward it came directly from *Sartor*. He did not see the material universe as God's shadow, as Mahomet did, or as the manifestation of some more abstract divine Spirit as Teufelsdröckh came to see it. He saw it through the eyes of Carlyle's hero in the first stage of an experience equivalent to a Christian "conversion"—when he became aware of evil and felt that it was the strongest force in the universe, yet was determined to resist and overcome it. Carlyle's hero followed the conventional Christian's progress through the slough of despond to the Beulah land of the "Everlasting Yea." Ahab died a heroic death at the height of his defiance.

Carlyle also influenced Melville's more recognizably personal meditations on philosophical matters. If he took Carlyle's advice to close his Byron and open his Goethe, the Goethe who most affected his novel came directly from *Sartor Resartus* in the form of the Earth-spirit in *Faust* as it had appeared in Carlyle's chapter on "The World Out of Clothes." This was the image of the Creator, weaving "on the roaring Loom of Time" the visible universe as the living garment of God. Melville adopted it almost literally for his "weaver-god" in "A Bower in the Arsacides" (102). But Melville also used it in two other chapters in an imaginative way which surely came after the literal fancy. In "The Castaway" (93) it became the more abstract and greater god, indifferent to weal or woe, who was above and behind the demiurge of *Faust* (of chap. 102); and when Pip saw "God's foot on the treadle of the loom, and spoke it," "his shipmates called him mad." In "The Mat-Maker" (47) the god disappeared altogether, leaving "the Loom of Time" as a frame for fate, free-will, and chance as the individual used his shuttle to weave the woof of free-will into the warp of necessity while the indifferent batten tightened the weave, more or less, with its random blows. It is this sort of speculation about the three-fold possibility of causation which provides the philosophical background for Ahab's final outburst of determination, just before the chase begins: "Is Ahab, Ahab? Is it I, God, or who that lifts this arm?"

In other chapters of the narrative conclusion (106 ff.), when Carlyle had a stronger influence upon Melville's imagination than upon his style, we find a similar blossoming of literal suggestiveness into fullblown symbolism. This is particularly evident in three chapters in this section (118, 119, 124) which seem to have blossomed out of *Sartor Resartus*. Two of these, "The Quadrant" and "The Needle," seem to be literal amplifications of a metaphor which represented Carlyle's hero, after "Getting Under Way" on his spiritual quest, were represented in a nautical situation: "Quitting the common Fleet of herring-busses and whalers, where indeed his leeward, laggard condition was painful enough, he desperately steers off, on a course of his own, by a sextant and compass of his own." It is applicable both to the author's procedure and Ahab's behavior. Melville sends the *Pequod* off the original course he knew from his own experience into strange seas he had never visited. Ahab renounces the guidance of the sun by dashing his quadrant to the deck just as Shakespeare's Richard II dashes his looking-glass to the ground for showing him a face that once was "like the sun." In chapter 124, when the polarity of the compass needle is reversed by lightning, Ahab makes his own compass; and in chapter 125, when the log is lost, he produces his own means for dead-reckoning by ordering the blacksmith to forge a new one.

The climax of Carlyle's suggestive influence upon Melville's imagination occurred in chapter 119, "The Candles," in which his own recent personal experience, his feeling for Shakespearean drama, the literal implications of a metaphor from *Sartor*, and a Carlylean hero genuinely akin to Ahab all combined to enable him to heighten his drama and weave into it not only his romantic hero but also the Byronic orientalism he had found difficult to manage in his earlier narrative. The chapter deals with the typhoon at the height of its awesome fury, the appearance of the corpusants or St. Elmo's fire which Melville had seen for the first time on his voyage home from England, and the reappearance of the Parsee who had slipped out of the book with the beginning of the Beale section. The metaphor is contained in Carlyle's reference to Teufelsdröckh's "Spiritual New-birth" as his "Baphometic Fire-baptism" and said that "the fire-baptised soul, long so scathed and thunder-driven . . . finds its own Freedom" in that feeling which was "its Baphometic Baptism." The adjective (derived from a medieval corruption of "Mahomet") was a peculiar one, but Melville would have found its metaphorical implications fully revealed in another book he had borrowed from Duyckinck at the time he borrowed *Sartor Resartus*—Carlyle's *On Heroes and Hero-Worship*. There Carlyle represented Mahomet, "The Hero as Prophet," as a "fiery mass of Life," a "strong wild man," with "a strong untutored intellect" who scorned "formulas and hearsays" and "was alone with his own soule and the reality of things." He could see the Truth behind material appearances, and his wild followers "must have seen what kind of man he *was*, let him be *called* what you like."

Carlyle placed in contrast to the calculating morality of Bentham and Paley in his own day "that grand spiritual fact" which he said "had burnt itself," as in flame-character, into the wild Arab soul: "That man's actions were of *infinite* moment to him, and never die or end at all; that man, with his little life reaches upwards as high as Heaven, downwards low as Hell." "As in flame and lightning . . . awful, unspeakable, ever present in him": and "bodied forth" in the symbols, "Heaven and Hell." Such a characterization might apply to Ahab at the height of the typhoon, holding the lightning in his hand while defying and also worshipping it and such a character Melville, beset by necessity of utilitarian calculations, might have dreamed of being himself. But it was the fire imagery which brought together the German professor, the Arabian prophet, and the American sea-captain—and enabled the Parsee, the romantically conceived fire-worshipper, to slip back into the story so naturally that he hardly seems to have been out of it. "Kneeling in Ahab's front, but with his head bowed away from him," the Parsee, no more than a snaggle-toothed phantom up to now, becomes Ahab's footstool for the fire ceremony and his familiar intimate thereafter.

[Sources of *Moby-Dick*]

Hershel Parker

It seems most likely that Melville started to write *Moby-Dick*, on the pattern of his five earlier books, as a sailor-voyager's firsthand account of his experiences and observations, ashore and aship, amid ways of life strange at first to him and still strange to his stay-at-home readers. Beginning with Charles R. Anderson in the 1930's, [1] scholars have established that, as in the earlier books, some of the materials in *Moby-Dick* were autobiographical, some borrowed and reshaped from other works, and some invented. For *Typee, Omoo, Redburn* and *White-Jacket* many documents of several kinds permit a check upon what parts of the books are fictional and what are autobiographical, but the evidence about what is autobiographical in *Moby-Dick* is very slight. The shipmate, Henry F. Hubbard, to whom Melville gave one of his textually flawed but nevertheless precious sets of *The Whale*, in his one marginal comment identified Pip as Backus, a crew member on the *Acushnet* (though not one who sailed from Fairhaven), and recalled Backus's leap overboard from a whaleboat headed by the second mate, John Hall. Aside from Hubbard's tantalizing notation there is little evidence to prove that any of the characters on shore or on the *Pequod* were based on real people. (The only convincing exception is Father Mapple, for whom Father Edward Taylor of Boston supplied more than a hint.) To be sure, Melville used many of his own experiences in characterizing his narrator, implying that Ishmael came as he did from an old-established family in the land and had been a country schoolmaster, and giving Ishmael (or himself in his narrative voice) allusions to the same range of European travel he had made in 1849—London, Paris, the Rhine. Melville truthfully (if discreetly) referred to an "acquaintance" of his as "Commodore J———" (the real Commodore Jones) and truthfully named the real John D'Wolf of Dorchester, Massachusetts, as his uncle. The similarities (and differences) could be extended. While it appears that in the June 27, 1850, letter to Richard Bentley (see p. 621) Melville misrepresented his years of service as a harpooneer, if not also the degree to which he would recount his own

Excerpted and reprinted from *Moby-Dick; or, The Whale*, ed. Harrison Hayford, Hershel Parker, and G. Thomas Tanselle (Evanston and Chicago: Northwestern University Press and The Newberry Library, 1988), 635–47. Copyright ©1988 by Northwestern University Press and the Newberry Library. Reprinted by permission. Footnote numbering has been altered.

experiences in the book, he had at least served on whaleships that, in fact, hunted whales, lost whales, caught whales, cut whales up and tried them out, cleaned up the bloody and greasy decks (which had been heaped with parts of whale heads and other recently living debris), stowed away the signs of trying out, lost men to desertion and death, and met and gammed with other ships.

Even before he went whaling Melville had in all likelihood read and heard many facts and stories about the whale fishery, mainly from newspaper and magazine items devoted to what was, after all, a major part of the national economy as well as a regular source of newsworthy events. Just before he sailed to Liverpool the popular New York magazine, the *Knickerbocker* (May, 1839), printed J. N. Reynolds's "Mocha Dick: or the White Whale of the Pacific: A Leaf from a Manuscript Journal," an account that readers found both enthralling and memorable. (The magazine was available nationally; Melville's uncle in Albany, Peter Gansevoort, seems to have kept up a subscription to it.) Reynolds presented the somber story of an obsessive hunt in a classic "frame story" situation, where a witness to the wild events told it to the writer afterwards, when the danger was over—an oceanic equivalent of the technique T. B. Thorpe used a few years later in his comic-mythic hunt story, "The Big Bear of Arkansas," and Melville himself was to use in "The Town-Ho's Story" (chap. 54 of *Moby-Dick*). Mocha Dick was real, "an old bull whale, of prodigious size and strength," "*white as wool,*" and he shared other attributes with Moby Dick:

> From the period of Dick's first appearance, his celebrity continued to increase, until his name seemed naturally to mingle with the salutations which whalemen were in the habit of exchanging, in their encounters upon the broad Pacific; the customary interrogatories almost always closing with, 'Any news from Mocha Dick?'

The mate who narrates the story within the frame closes with the death of Mocha Dick, the longest whale he had ever seen, and profitable to the killers, yielding an extraordinary "one hundred barrels of clear oil." Significantly, the battle-scarred Mocha Dick was a near-legendary beast as well as profitable: "not less than twenty harpoons did we draw from his back; the rusted mementos of many a desperate encounter." Even more significant for Melville's uses, he was reported as sighted in the years following his death, and after the publication of Reynolds's story. A reviewer of *Moby-Dick* recalled that every "old 'Jack-tar' " knew the story in one form or another, and in 1839–43 the young jack-tar Herman Melville had good chances to know it, or part of it, from print or from sailors' yarns, and perhaps even then had chances to retell it. As a whaleman Melville had participated in one of the most remarkable literary phenomena of his time, the frontier-training of writers, in which ordinary Americans confronted natural horrors and wonders, far from home, and came back, when they were lucky, to tell tall tales about their experiences, or truthful tales so extraordinary that stay-at-home people would take them as false. Melville said he had based the narrative in *Moby-Dick* on certain wild legends of the whale fishery, but he could as well have based it on tales that his own careful inquiries had established as true stories, however wild. Some such stories, to be sure, were passing into legendary status, among them, recent scholars are finding, a good number of stories of hunting great white whales in the Pacific.[2]

Simply by being months at a time on a whaleship Melville heard (along with sailor songs, jokes, proverbs, and miscellaneous tall tales) a range of whaling stories from the other members of the crew, some stories surely more than once, and—starved for news—avidly heard fresh stories or fresh versions of old stories from crews of other whaling ships encountered in the open waters or ports of the Pacific. Such an assertion would be true of any whaleman, but it happens that Melville in "What I know of Owen Chace &c" put on record how he learned that a whale had sunk Chase's ship, the *Essex*:

> When I was on board the ship Acushnet of Fairhaven, on the passage to the Pacific cruising-grounds, among other matters of forecastle conversation at times was the story of the Essex. It was then that I first became acquainted with her history and her truly astounding fate.

The *Acushnet*'s second mate, Mr. Hall, had served with Chase on another ship, and was a source of information, and in the Pacific the *Acushnet* gammed with a ship on which Melville met a teenage son of Chase who let him read a copy of his father's *Narrative of the Most Extraordinary and Distressing Shipwreck of the Whale-Ship Essex, of Nantucket; Which Was Attacked and Finally Destroyed by a Large Spermaceti-Whale, in the Pacific Ocean; with an Account of the Unparalleled Sufferings of the Captain and Crew during a Space of Ninety-Three Days at Sea, in Open Boats; in the Years 1819 & 1820* (New York: Gilley, 1821). A decade afterwards he recalled the special qualities of the experience: "The reading of this wondrous story upon the landless sea, & close to the very latitude of the shipwreck had a surprising effect upon me."

A constant of Melville's mind was that a book he read remained associated with the time and the place he read it. It would have been one thing to read "Mocha Dick" ashore in New York state, another to hear the story on the ocean. Similarly, stories he heard ashore in Tahiti and Honolulu may have produced surprisingly different effects from those he experienced as he read whaling books in Manhattan in the spring of 1850. Cases in point are the real sailor adventures, analogues to "The Town-Ho's Story" (chap. 54), which Wilson L. Heflin discovered could readily have come to Melville's attention, either at sea or in Honolulu. Melville must have heard excited versions of the sensational story of a one-man rebellion on the New Bedford whaler *Nassau*, in 1843, during which Luther Fox fatally wounded the mate by all but severing his leg with a mincing knife, for he was in Honolulu when the *Nassau* entered the harbor, and full news accounts were printed there. Quoting *Omoo* on the custom of hanging around jails in the islands for companionship and news, Heflin reasonably suggests that Melville may have gone to the jail at the fort and talked to Fox, who was from Rensselaerville, near Albany, and no cold-blooded murderer to be shunned but a self-appalled naif who had committed a hotheaded manslaughter because no one had ever taught him that he would not lose his pride of manhood if he backed down after he had boldly taken his stand. Melville may well have known other real-life stories Heflin discovered (one involves a fact that sounds like tall talk in "The Town-Ho's Story": a swordfish could stab a ship and cause a leak), and chances are that he heard whaling stories on the frigate *United States* as well.

Melville's reading of his whaling sources for *Moby-Dick* may have gone at least as far back as May 27, 1839, when the Albany *Argus* printed "Method of Taking the Whale" from the British surgeon Thomas Beale's *The Natural History of the Sperm Whale to Which Is Added a Sketch of a South-Sea Whaling Voyage in Which the Author Was Personally Engaged* (London: Van Voorst, 1839), including the powerful passage about the death flurry of the immense creature, mad with his agonies. If Melville missed that sample of Beale, he had another chance to read it when the West Troy *Advocate* devoted two columns to "Method of Taking the Whale" on October 23, 1839 (a few months after it reprinted one of his own "Fragments"). As far back as 1840 he read *Two Years Before the Mast*, a minor source. More than two columns (taken from the New Hampshire *Courier*) were devoted to Dana's book in the West Troy *Advocate* on December 16, 1840—about the time he was making his decision to sign on a whaler. His first reading of Owen Chase's *Narrative* (under the evocative circumstances already described) took place in July or August of 1841.

Melville's subsequent reading in his frigate's library and in libraries ashore had exposed him to more whaling information, and well before he started writing his own whaling voyage he owned some of the source-books or at least was already familiar with them. Around the first of February, 1847, he got a copy of J. Ross Browne's *Etchings of a Whaling Cruise, with Notes of a Sojourn on the Island of Zanzibar. To Which Is Appended a Brief History of the Whale Fishery; Its Past and Present Condition* (New York: Harper & Brothers, 1846) in order to review it in the *Literary World* (March 6, 1847). During the early stages of his work on *Mardi* he had a copy of Frederick Debell Bennett's *Narrative of a Whaling Voyage round the Globe, from the Year 1833 to 1836. Comprising Sketches of Polynesia, California, the Indian Archipelago, etc. with an Account of Southern Whales, the Sperm Whale Fishery, and the Natural History of the Climates Visited* (London: Bentley, 1840). By April 28, 1849, he knew at least one of William Scoresby, Jr.'s works on the North Atlantic fishery, the *Journal of a Voyage to the Northern Whale Fishery; Including*

Researches and Discoveries on the Eastern Coast of West Greenland . . . in . . . 1822 (Edinburgh: Constable, 1823), the source for the "level lodestone" passage in "The Needle" (chap. 124), since he made offhand mention of it in his *Literary World* review of Cooper's *The Sea Lions*. In that review he also referred to Charles Wilkes's *United States Exploring Expedition. During the Years 1838 . . . 1842. Under the Command of Charles Wilkes, U.S.N.* (Philadelphia: Sherman, 1844–46), another source for *Moby-Dick*, which he had bought in April, 1847, for work on *Mardi*.[3] Early in 1850 Melville also had at hand in his working library some information about the natural history of whales, including the *Penny Cyclopædia of the Society for the Diffusion of Useful Knowledge* (London: Charles Knight, 1843), with its long article "Whales" which cited and paraphrased whole passages from the standard work by Thomas Beale (in "Sources," see Kendra Gaines). We know only a sample of the works Melville had access to, and new sources are still turning up.

A striking fact is that Melville did not seek out whaling sources during his sojourn in London, not proof but certainly a good indication that while he was there and at the time he left he had no idea of writing a whaling book any time soon. Very likely the return voyage itself so stirred his memories that he decided then, or soon after he reached New York, that his next book would be based on the most adventurous episodes left from his sea-going years, his whaling experiences. Although he could start writing from his memories and his imagination, he needed every source he could lay hands on, for even when writing about events he had lived through he habitually relied on printed works as prompt books to remind him of things worth writing about and to suggest ways they might be served up to readers. At the outset Browne was useful for "the story pattern, the scenes employed, the structure in the presentation of whaling information," important borrowings even though Melville often supplemented these parts from other books.[4] With his own memories and with Browne open before him, Melville could have gotten under weigh. Because he had lived by whaling routines far longer than he experienced the naval routines he had described in *White Jacket*, he could infuse those experiences and observations into his work and even tardily transform a particular section of the manuscript which was based upon some printed source.

To the books already in his library he added others, such as the Rev. Henry T. Cheever's *The Whale and His Captors; or, The Whaleman's Adventures, and the Whale's Biography, as Gathered on the Homeward Cruise of the "Commodore Preble"* (New York: Harper & Brothers, 1849), which became a major source. Some of Cheever's chapter titles advertised useful passages for Melville's borrowing: "Authentic Tragedies and Perils of the Whaling Service" and "Yarns from the Experience of Old Whalemen." James Barbour names the following chapters as being derived at least in part from Cheever: 45 ("The Affidavit"); 48 ("The First Lowering"); 59 ("Squid"); 61 ("Stubb kills a

Whale"); 73 ("Stubb and Flask kill a Right Whale"); 78 ("Cistern and Buckets"); 81 ("The Pequod meets the Virgin"); 87 ("The Grand Armada"); and 91 ("The Pequod meets the Rose-bud"). In "The Affidavit" Melville took from Cheever evidence for two basic points: that a whaling captain seeking a particular whale would have a chance of finding it and that a whale could sink a ship. In other words, the purpose of the chapter, which seems to date initially from an early stage of the composition, before the stage of writing about the natural history of the whale, was to establish the plausibility of someone's (presumably an officer's) quest for a particular whale and to establish as well the plausibility of a catastrophe like that which befell the *Essex*—the sinking of a ship by a whale, in all likelihood by the particular whale being sought. Howard P. Vincent (1949) thought that perhaps Cheever's book was published too late for Melville to make much use of it, but Barbour pointed out that it was copyrighted in 1849; it was in fact published late in 1849 and reviewed along with *Redburn* while Melville was abroad.

Bennett's *A Whaling Voyage round the Globe* is another source Melville used extensively in both the whaling chapters and the chapters on the natural history of whales. Melville used Bennett in "The Affidavit" to supplement Cheever, drawing from him names of legendary whales. In that chapter, first writing before he received his own copy of Chase's *Narrative* but after seeing many "stupedly abbreviated" accounts of it, Melville used Cheever for the account of the sinking of the *Essex*, but supplemented him with Bennett. Barbour believes that in "The Grand Armada" Melville also combined information from Cheever and Bennett, taking the "harrowing ride" from Cheever and the observations of the "boudoir and nursery scenes" from Bennett. Some other sources include: Francis Allyn Olmsted, *Incidents of a Whaling Voyage. To Which Are Added Observations on the Scenery, Manners and Customs, and Missionary Stations, of the Sandwich and Society Islands* (New York, 1841); J. C. Hart, *Miriam Coffin, or the Whale-Fishermen: A Tale* (New York, 1834)[5]; Obed Macy, *The History of Nantucket; Being a Compendious Account of the First Settlement of the Island by the English; Together with the Rise and Progress of the Whale Fishery; and Other Historical Facts Relative to Said Island and Its Inhabitants* (Boston: Hilliard, Gray, 1835); W. A. G., *Ribs and Trucks, from Davy's Locker; Being Magazine Matter Broke Loose, and Fragments of Sundry Things In-edited* (Boston: Charles D. Strong, 1842); Captain James Colnett, *A Voyage to the South Atlantic and round Cape Horn into the Pacific Ocean, for the Purpose of Extending the Spermaceti Whale Fisheries, and Other Objects of Commerce, by Ascertaining the Ports, Bays, Harbours, and Anchoring Births, in Certain Islands and Coasts in Those Seas at Which the Ships of the British Merchants Might Be Refitted* (London, 1798); Pierre Bayle, *An Historical and Critical Dictionary* (London, 1710); John Kitto, *A Cyclopædia of Biblical Literature* (Edinburgh, 1845). Some chronology of the use Melville made of some of these sources can be established; for instance, the fact that he says in "The Affidavit" that he had not yet learned particulars of the destruction of the *Union* by a whale must mean that he had not yet acquired (or read through) Macy's book, where (as Anderson pointed out) they do occur.

The consensus of scholars is that Melville wrote for some two or three months without having ready access to the basic books about whales—as opposed to whaling—although he had access to passages from Thomas Beale's standard work, as quoted or subsumed in other sources, among them Browne's *Etchings*, Cheever's *The Whale and His Captors*, and one of his hard-worked reference tools, the *Penny Cyclopædia*. From the New York Society Library on April 29, 1850, he borrowed the two volumes of Scoresby's *An Account of the Arctic Regions, with a History and Description of the Northern Whale Fishery* (Edinburgh: Constable, 1820), two days before he wrote Dana that he was "half way" in the whaling voyage (and kept them out for over a year, until June 14, 1851). Much of Scoresby's book was of little use to Melville because it dealt with the Northern (Atlantic) fishery for the right whale and from a British point of view, but he took from it incidental information on topics such as the head and spiracle of the right whale, the narwhale's use of its tusk, and the way ships in the Holland fishery are fitted out. Furthermore, Scoresby's stuffy and pious tone proved so irritating or amusing that Melville treated him as a stooge whenever he plundered him (as he had mocked the good missionary William Ellis while plundering his *Polynesian Researches* in *Omoo*), repeatedly contriving comic names for the imaginary authorities to whom he attributed particular bits of poor Scoresby's information. As Leon Howard says, Melville probably ordered Beale about the time he borrowed Scoresby, judging from the fact that on July 10, 1850, he received the copy that Putnam had imported for him from London. The week before he left for Pittsfield, therefore, Melville had books to quarry both for whaling and for whales, although, as Sections II and III have shown, he did not immediately settle into using those books.

Beale's scholarly volume was only a decade old, but long quotations from it had already made their way into encyclopedias and into books on whaling, as well as into newspapers and magazines; Melville was far from the first to recognize Beale as the standard source on the natural history of the whale, and to some extent on whaling. As Melville expected when he ordered the book, he found Beale useful for information which he could quote and assimilate into his manuscript.[6] After he received his copy, if not before, he realized that Beale would also give him such an abundance of materials that he could give the impression of having read far more reference books than had in fact come his way. Howard P. Vincent instances "Cetology" (chap. 32), where Melville quotes "four cetological experts all alluding to the mystery of whale groupings" (Scoresby, Cuvier, Hunter, and Lesson):

> although they sound as though Melville had surgically removed them directly
> from their original contexts, they had actually been quoted together on an

unnumbered page in the front part of Beale's *Natural History of the Sperm Whale*; instead of ransacking a large whaling library, Melville had merely lifted his authorities from Beale's convenient cache of quotations.

Four experts from one page is over and above what a plunderer should expect, but otherwise this example of Melville at work is as characteristic as it is vivid. Yet Melville's claim in this chapter to having "swam through libraries" in his quest for whaling authorities is followed by a list of authorities taken from the *Penny Cyclopædia*, not from Beale. Little about Melville's use of sources in *Moby-Dick* can be described simply.

Melville's working methods have complicated all attempts to chart his progress on his manuscript by the evidence of his use of sources. The problem is that in a given chapter he might use a single source, and in widely differing ways, as simple as using it only as a "prompt book" to jog his memory, to remind him of a topic, scene, or process from which to take off on his own without identifiable borrowing, or perhaps as complicated as cannibalizing a little or a lot of its pattern, matter, or wording.[7] In another chapter he might use only one source at first then come back and use further sources, then use the first source again. In a third chapter he might use two or more sources from the start, and he might well use Beale (for instance) at second or third hand, or in a now unknown copy, so that it becomes incautious, and possibly fallacious, for a scholar to date all of Melville's uses of Beale after July 10, 1850. Furthermore, in the course of Melville's writing what started as a patch of one or two sentences or a paragraph may have ended up either pretty much at their original length, or expanded but kept in the same location, or expanded and spread through a chapter, or spread into one or more other chapters, placed earlier or later.[8] Failure to take this process into consideration has led some scholars to sort the information about Melville's use of whaling sources into too rigid a schematization.

Most reviewers did not recognize the whaling sources, but they did see the main literary sources. It was plain to the British reviewers of *Mardi* and *The Whale* (and to the best American reviewers of *Mardi* and *Moby-Dick*) that Melville was a remarkably literary sea-writer. (See Section VII). The books these well-educated reviewers were reminded of were precisely the "old Books" that Melville had borrowed from Duyckinck and had commented on with such surprising intelligence. By the count of Mary K. Bercaw in *Melville's Sources*, critics (from reviewers through present academic critics) have named more than a hundred and sixty works as Melville's sources for *Moby-Dick*, more than a source for every chapter, if that had been the way Melville worked. A value of Bercaw's historical recapitulation is that it allows one to restate obvious propositions, some of which tend to be shuffled aside. By general agreement, the literary works most important to Melville in *Moby-Dick* include the Bible and classics of English literature (along with some European classics, in translation), but they also include some of "the books that prove most agreeable, grateful, and companionable" because they are picked up "by chance here and there": "those which seem put into our hands by Providence; those which pretend to little, but abound in much" (*White-Jacket*, chap. 41). Yet Melville had a way of taking hold of even the classics providentially, as when he discovered a large-print edition of Shakespeare just when he was both intellectually ready to grapple with the plays and had days and days when he did not have to do much else besides look in at his wife and newborn son, and read.

For Melville nothing fell into the category of required reading, and any attempt to systematize the sometimes routine and other times idiosyncratic twists he made of his literary sources risks ending up in fatuous reductiveness. With that gesture toward mitigating the critical sin of oversimplification, we report in this paragraph some of what the best authorities have concluded about literary influences on *Moby-Dick*. It was pervasively influenced by the Bible (in particular the Book of Job, providing an analogue for Ahab's quarrel with God, and the Book of Jonah, providing an analogue for Ishmael's less defiant method of coming to terms with the universe); by Shakespeare's plays (where King Lear and other tragic heroes provided models for Ahab); by Milton's *Paradise Lost* (from which Melville took some of Ahab's qualities as satanic opponent); by Marlowe's *Doctor Faustus* and Goethe's *Faust* (for analogues of demonic temptation and heroic obsession); by Robert Burton, whose *Anatomy of Melancholy* served as this pondering-man's textbook on morbid psychology; by Sir Thomas Browne, that cracked-archangel (for seductive prose rhythm serving a dumbfoundingly self-possessed idiosyncrasy); by Thomas Hope's *Anastasius; or, Memoirs of a Greek* (for hints at Ishmael's twists of mind and actions, not least for a ceremonial marriage between men); by Mary Shelley's *Frankenstein* (for a prolonged revenge pursuit); by Dante (for an anatomy of human sinfulness); by Pierre Bayle's dictionary and Montaigne's essays (for their worldly-wise skepticism which braced him against superficial pieties); by Coleridge's lecture on *Hamlet* (for the crucial definition of the Shakespearean hero that he worked into "The Ship" [chap. 16]); by Carlyle, especially *Sartor Resartus* but also *Heroes and Hero-Worship* (for a sardonic verbal playfulness and a depiction of the physical universe as emblematical, but also hints for Ahab from the depiction of Cromwell); by Sterne's *Tristram Shandy* (for liberating game-someness toward the lofty task of bookmaking); by De Quincey's *Confessions* (for the Malay whose Asiatic associations were infused into Fedallah and his boat's crew, and for the apparently inimitable prose style which to Melville was as natural as his own breath). Any such list has at least the virtue of reminding readers of the obvious—that in Melville's own resolve (*Pierre*, bk. 21.i) "to give the world a book, which the world should hail with surprise and delight," his reading—from Shakespeare to Scoresby, from Milton to Macy, from Bayle to Beale—flowed into a "contributary stream:"

A varied scope of reading, little suspected by his friends, and randomly acquired by a random but lynx-eyed mind, in the course of the multifarious, incidental, bibliographic encounterings of almost any civilized young inquirer after Truth; this poured one considerable contributary stream into that bottomless spring of original thought which the occasion and time had caused to burst out in himself.

We have dealt in this section with only a few of the books that formed the "considerable contributary stream" pouring into Melville's "bottomless spring of original thought" which burst out in him as he worked on *Moby-Dick*.

Notes

1. From the late 1920's into the 1930's, forerunning any inquiry about how *Moby-Dick* was written, pioneering Melville scholars conducted overlapping biographical researches, fragmentary, mostly solitary, and too often secretive (as individualistic academic usage seems to require). Active then were Henry A. Murray, John H. Birss, Robert S. Forsythe, and Charles Olson, who all projected larger works on Melville which proved abortive, along with Charles R. Anderson, Luther S. Mansfield, and Willard Thorp, who completed important studies. They all published findings that proved relevant to the composition of *Moby-Dick*, but did not focus their discoveries on genetic questions. Their work that has proved most relevant to genetic study of *Moby-Dick* was the documentation of Melville's extensive reading, and their discovery of his surprising uses of his reading. While this section is in part indebted to their initial discoveries, and their work underlies the theories reported in the first part of Section V, it draws most heavily on several later contributions: Wilbur S. Scott, Jr.'s Princeton Ph.D. dissertation on "Melville's Originality" (1943), directed by Willard Thorp; Howard P. Vincent's *The Trying-Out of MOBY-DICK* (1949); Sumner W. D. Scott's Chicago Ph.D. dissertation, "The Whale in *Moby-Dick*" (1950); the Luther S. Mansfield and Howard P. Vincent edition of *Moby-Dick* (1952); and James Barbour's UCLA Ph.D. dissertation, "The Writing of *Moby-Dick*" (1970).

2. In his journal on February 19, 1834, Ralph Waldo Emerson recorded that a seaman, a fellow-passenger in a stagecoach, had told "the story of an old sperm whale which he called a white whale which was known for many years by the whalemen as Old Tom & who rushed upon the boats which attacked him & crushed the boats to small chips in his jaws, the men generally escaping by jumping overboard & being picked up. A vessel was fitted out at New Bedford, he said, to take him. And he was finally taken somewhere off Payta head by the Winslow or the Essex." In "Sources" see Janez Stanonik, F. De Wolfe Miller, and Joel Myerson.

3. We use full or nearly full titles at a first or an early naming of Melville's whaling sources because each subtitle is (by definition) a more succinct guide to the nature and scope of the book than we could provide in another way.

4. See Barbour (1970), p. 90; also Vincent (1949) and Howard (1951 and 1987). These chapters have been cited as deriving at least in part from J. Ross Browne's *Etchings*: 1 ("Loomings"); 3 ("The Spouter-Inn"); 16 ("The Ship"); 22 ("Merry Christmas"); 24 ("The Advocate"); 29 ("Enter Ahab; to him, Stubb"); 31 ("Queen Mab"); 35 ("The Mast-Head"); 36 ("The Quarter-Deck"); 40 ("Midnight, Forecastle"); 48 ("The First Lowering"); 53 ("The Gam"); 54 ("The Town-Ho's Story"); 65 ("The Whale as a Dish"); 69 ("The Funeral"); 73

("Stubb and Flask kill a Right Whale"); 81 ("The Pequod meets the Virgin"); and 96 ("The Try-Works").

5. *Miriam Coffin* was the subject of "A Predecessor of *Moby-Dick*" (1934), the first article Leon Howard wrote on Melville.

6. Vincent, Howard, Barbour, and others have cited these as the chapters most influenced by Beale: 24 ("The Advocate")—for a long account, quoted by Beale, on the "importance of the southern whale fishery"; 32 ("Cetology"), discussed below; 41 ("Moby Dick"); 42 ("The Whiteness of the Whale"); 44 ("The Chart"); 45 ("The Affidavit"); 47 ("The Mat-Maker"); 51 ("The Spirit-Spout"); 52 ("The Albatross"); 55 ("Of the Monstrous Pictures of Whales"); 56 ("Of the Less Erroneous Pictures of Whales"); 57 ("Of Whales in Paint; in Teeth; . . ."); 59 ("Squid"); 60 ("The Line"); 61 ("Stubb kills a Whale"); 65 ("The Whale as a Dish"); 68 ("The Blanket"); 71 ("The Jeroboam's Story"); 74 ("The Sperm Whale's Head"); 76 ("The Battering-Ram"); 77 ("The Great Heidelburgh Tun"); 78 ("Cistern and Buckets"); 79 ("The Prairie"); 80 ("The Nut"); 82 ("The Honor and Glory of Whaling"); 83 ("Jonah Historically Regarded"); 85 ("The Fountain"); 86 ("The Tail"); 88 ("Schools and Schoolmasters"); 89 ("Fast-Fish and Loose-Fish"); 90 ("Heads or Tails"); 91 ("The Pequod meets the Rose-bud"); 92 ("Ambergris"); 95 ("The Cassock"); 99 ("The Doubloon"); 101 ("The Decanter"); 102 ("A Bower in the Arsacides"); 103 ("Measurement of the Whale's Skeleton"); 104 ("The Fossil Whale"); and 105 ("Does the Whale's Magnitude Diminish?"). Melville (see Vincent) used Beale for learned information in the chapters on the pictures of whales (55–57) and the fossils and skeletons (102–105). Howard (1987) concluded that only three chapters show the influence of both Browne and Beale: Chapters 48 ("The First Lowering"), 65 ("The Whale as a Dish"), 81 ("The Pequod meets the Virgin").

7. In the introduction to the Hendricks House *Omoo* Harrison Hayford was the first to work out Melville's use of sources in this genetic way.

8. An extant manuscript example of the whole course of one of Melville's expansion processes, where the material remained in a single place, may be found in the growth of Chapter 14 of *The Confidence-Man* from a single sentence into the forty-sentence chapter. See the Northwestern-Newberry edition, pp. 413–68.

THE WHALE, AHAB,
AND ISHMAEL

◆

Moby-Dick

LEWIS MUMFORD

M oby-Dick is a story of the sea, and the sea is life, "whose waters of deep woe are brackish with the salt of human tears." Moby-Dick is the story of the eternal Narcissus in man, gazing into all rivers and oceans to grasp the unfathomable phantom of life—perishing in the illusive waters. Moby-Dick is a portrait of the whale and a presentation of the demonic energies in the universe that harass and frustrate and extinguish the spirit of man. We must gather our own strength together if we are to penetrate Moby-Dick: no other fable, except perhaps Dante's, demands that we open so many doors and turn so many secret keys; for, finally, Moby-Dick is a labyrinth, and that labyrinth is the universe.

*   *   *

. . . Moby-Dick stands by itself as complete as the Divine Comedy or the Odyssey stands by itself. Benedetto Croce has correctly taught us that every work of art is indeed in this same position: that it is uniquely what it is, and cannot be understood except in terms of its own purpose. If, for purely practical reasons, we ignore this in dealing with the ruck of novels and stories, because their inner purpose is so insignificant, we must respect it strictly when we confront a work that does not conspicuously conform to the established canons; for, needless to say, an imaginative work of the first rank will disclose itself through its differences and its departures, by what it originates, rather than by what it is derived from or akin to. Had Melville seriously sought in Moby-Dick to rival the work of Trollope or Reade or Dickens, had he simply desired to amuse and edify the great bourgeois public that consumed its three-decker novels as it consumed its ten-course public dinners, and wanted no delay in the service, no hitch in the round of food, drink, toasts, speeches, and above all, no unaccustomed victuals on such occasions, then Moby-Dick would have been a mistake and failure. But one cannot count as a failure what was never an attempt. Moby-Dick does not belong to this comfortable bourgeois world, any more than horse-hair shirts or long fasts; it neither aids digestion nor increases the sense of warm drowsy good nature that leads finally to bed: and that is all there is to it.

Excerpted and reprinted from *Herman Melville* (New York: Harcourt, Brace, 1929), 158–95.

The same criticism that disposes of the notion that Moby-Dick is a bad novel, by admitting freely that it is not a novel at all, equally disposes of its lack of verisimilitude. Although Melville was at first challenged on his facts, such as the ramming of the Pequod by Moby-Dick, events were just as kind to his reputation here as they were in the case of Typee: for while Moby-Dick was on the press, news came of the sinking of the whaler Ann Alexander by the ferocious attack of a whale. No one of authority has attempted to quarrel with Melville's descriptions of the life and habits of whalemen and the whale: the testimony of every observer is that Melville left very little for any one else to say about the subject. This does not, however, dispose of the charge; for those who are wisely captious of Melville here will confine themselves to saying that no such crew ever existed, no such words ever passed human mouth, and no such thoughts could enter the mind of a Nantucketer, as entered Ahab's.

Again, one is tempted to grant the objection; for it makes no difference in the value of Moby-Dick as a work of art. In the realistic convention, Moby-Dick would be a bad book: it happens that the story is projected on more than one plane, and a good part of it belongs to another, and equally valid, convention. Melville himself was aware of the difference, and early in the book he calls upon the Spirit of Equality, which has spread its royal mantle of humanity over all his kind, to defend him against all mortal critics "if, then, to the meanest mariners, and renegades, and castaways, I shall hereafter ascribe high qualities, though dark; weave round them tragic graces; if even the most mournful, perchance the most abased among them all shall at times lift himself to the exalted mounts; if I shall touch that workman's arm with some ethereal light; if I shall spread the rainbow over his disastrous set of sun." Now, the convention in which Melville cast this part of Moby-Dick was foreign to the nineteenth century; obscure people, like Beddoes, alone essayed it: to create these idealized figures called for such reserves of power that only minor poets, for the most part, unconscious of their weaknesses, attempted the task.

The objections to Melville's use of this convention would be fair enough if, like the minor poets, he failed; but, through his success, one sees that the limitations of naturalism are no closer to reality than the limitations of poetic tragedy; and, on the contrary, Melville's valiant use of this convention enabled him to present a much fuller picture of reality than the purely external suggestions of current realism would have permitted him to show. What we call realism is a method of approaching reality: an external picture of a Cowperwood or a Gantry may have as little human truth in it as a purely fanciful description of an elf: and the artist who can draw upon more than one convention is, at all events, free from the curious illusion, so common in the nineteenth century, alike in philosophy, with its pragmatism in science, with its dogmatic materialism, and in imaginative writing, with its realism, that this convention is not limited, and so far arbitrary, but the very stuff and vitals of existence. The question to settle is not: Did an Ahab ever sail from Nantucket? The question is: Do Ahab and Stubb and Starbuck and Tashtego live within the sphere where we find them? The answer is that they are tremendously alive; for they are aspects of the spirit of man. At each utterance, one feels more keenly their imaginative embodiment; so that by the time Ahab breaks into his loftiest Titanisms, one accepts his language, as one accepts his pride: they belong to the fibre and essence of the man. Ahab is a reality in relation to Moby-Dick; and when Melville projects him, he ceases to be incredible, because he is alive.

We need not concern ourselves particularly with those who look upon Moby-Dick solely as a sort of World's Almanac or Gazetteer of the Whaling Industry, unhappily marred by the highly seasoned enticements of the narrative. This criticism is, indeed, but the other side of the sort of objection I have disposed of; and it tells more about the limitations of the reader than it does about the quality of Moby-Dick. For the fact is that this book is a challenge and affront to all the habits of mind that typically prevailed in the nineteenth century, and still remain, almost unabated, among us: it comes out of a different world, and presupposes, for its acceptance, a more integrated life and consciousness than we have known or experienced, for the most part, these last three centuries. Moby-Dick is not Victorian; it is not Elizabethan; it is, rather, prophetic of another quality of life which Melville had experienced and had a fuller vision of in his own time—a quality that may again come into the world, when we seek to pass beyond the harassed specialisms which still hold and preoccupy so many of us. To fathom this quality of Melville's experience and imagination, we must look a little deeper into his myth and his manner of projecting it. What is its meaning? And first, in what manner is that meaning conveyed to us?

8

Moby-Dick is a poetic epic. Typographically, Moby-Dick conforms to prose, and there are long passages, whole chapters, which are wholly in the mood of prose: but in spirit and in actual rhythm, Moby-Dick again and again rises to polyphonic verse which resembles passages of Webster's in that it can either be considered as broken blank verse, or as cadenced prose. Mr. Percy Boynton has performed the interesting experiment of transposing a paragraph in Pierre into excellent free verse, so strong and subtle are Melville's rhythms; and one might garner a whole book of verse from Moby-Dick. Melville, in Moby-Dick, unconsciously respects Poe's canon that all true poetry must be short in length, since the mood cannot be retained, unbroken or undiminished, over lengthy passages, and if the form itself is preserved, the content nevertheless is prose. But while Poe himself used this dictum as an excuse for writing only short lyrics, Melville sustained the poetic mood through a long narrative by dropping frankly into prose in the intervening while. As a result, he was under no necessity of clipping the emotions or of bleaching the imaginative colours of Moby-Dick: like a flying-boat, he rises from the water to the air and returns to the water again without losing control over either medium. His prose is prose: hard, sinewy, compact; and his poetry is poetry, vivid, surging, volcanic, creating its own form in the very pattern of the emotional state itself, soaring, towering, losing all respect for the smaller conventions of veracity, when the inner triumph itself must be announced. It is in the very rhythm of his language that Ahab's mood, and all the devious symbols of Moby-Dick are sustained and made credible: by no other method could the deeper half of the tale have been written. In these poetic passages, the phrases are intensified, stylicized, stripped of their habitual associations. If occasionally, as with Shakespeare, the thought itself is borne down by the weight of the gold that decorates it, this is only a similar proof of Melville's immense power of expression.

Both Poe and Hawthorne share some of Melville's power, and both of them, with varying success, wrought ideality and actuality into the same figure: but one has only to compare the best of their work with Moby-Dick to see wherein Melville's great distinction lies. The Scarlet Letter, The House of the Seven Gables, William Wilson, like most other works of fiction, are melodic: a single instrument is sufficient to carry the whole theme; whereas Moby-Dick is a symphony; every resource of language and thought, fantasy, description, philosophy, natural history, drama, broken rhythms, blank verse, imagery, symbol, are utilized to sustain and expand the great theme. The conception of Moby-Dick organically demands the expressive interrelation, for a single total effect, of a hundred different pieces: even in accessory matters, like the association of the Parsee, the fire-worshipper, with the death of Ahab, the fire-defier, or in the makeup of the crew, the officers white men, the harpooneers the savage races, red, black, brown, and the crew a mixed lot from the separate islands of the earth, not a stroke is introduced that has not a meaning for the myth as a whole. Although the savage harpooneers get nearest the whale, the savage universe, it is Ahab and the Parsee, the European and the Asiatic, who carry the pursuit to its ultimate end—while a single American survives to tell the tale!

Melville's instrumentation is unsurpassed in the writing of the last century: one must go to a Beethoven or a Wagner for an exhibition of similar powers: one will not find it among the works of literature. Here are Webster's wild violin, Marlowe's cymbals, Browne's sonorous bass viol, Swift's brass, Smollett's castanets, Shelley's flute, brought together in a single orchestra, complementing each other in a grand symphony. Melville achieved a similar synthesis in thought; and that work has proved all the more credible because he achieved it in language, too. Small wonder that those who were used to elegant pianoforte solos or barrel-organ instrumentation, were deafened and surprised and repulsed.

What is the meaning of Moby-Dick? There is not one meaning; there are many; but in its simplest terms, Moby-Dick is, necessarily, a story of the sea and its ways, as the Odyssey is a story of strange adventure, and War and Peace a story of battles and domestic life. The characters are heightened and slightly distorted: Melville's quizzical comic sense is steadily at work on them, and only Ahab escapes: but they all have their recognizable counterparts in the actual world. Without any prolonged investigation one could still find a Starbuck on Nantucket or a Flask on Martha's Vineyard—indeed, as Mr. Thomas Benton's portraits properly indicate, queerer fish than they.

On this level, Moby-Dick brings together and focusses in a single picture the long line of sketches and preliminary portraits Melville had assembled in Typee, Omoo, Redburn, and White-Jacket. As a story of the sea, Moby-Dick will always have a call for those who wish to recapture the magic and terror and stress and calm delight of the sea and its ships; and not less so because it seizes on a particular kind of ship, the whaler, and a special occupation, whaling, at the moment when they were about to pass out of existence, or rather, were being transformed from a brutal but glorious battle into a methodical, slightly banal industry. Melville had the singular fortune to pronounce a valedictory on many ways of life and scenes that were becoming extinct. He lived among the South Sea Islanders when they were still pretty much as Captain Cook found them, just before their perversion and decimation by our exotic Western civilization. He recorded life on a man-of-war half a generation before the sail gave place to steam, wood to armour-plate, and grappling-irons to long-range guns. He described life on a sailing-packet before steam had increased the speed, the safety, and the pleasant monotony of transatlantic travel: and finally, he recorded the last heroic days of whaling. Moby-Dick would have value as first-hand testimony, even if it were negligible as literature. If this were all, the book would still be important.

But Moby-Dick, admirable as it is as a narrative of maritime adventure, is far more than that: it is, fundamentally, a parable on the mystery of evil and the accidental malice of the universe. The white whale stands for the brute energies of existence, blind, fatal, overpowering, while Ahab is the spirit of man, small and feeble, but purposive, that pits its puniness against this might, and its purpose against the blank senselessness of power. The evil arises with the good: the white whale grows up among the milder whales which are caught and cut up and used: one hunts for the one—for a happy marriage, livelihood, offspring, social companionship and cheer—and suddenly heaving its white bulk out of the calm sea, one comes upon the other: illness, accident, treachery, jealousy, vengefulness, dull frustration. The South Sea savage did not know of the white whale: at least, like death, it played but a casual part in his consciousness. It is different with the European: his life is a torment of white whales: the Jobs, the Aeschyluses, the Dantes, the Shakespeares, pursue him and grapple with him, as Ahab pursues his antagonist.

All our lesser literature, all our tales of Avalon or Heaven or ultimate redemption, or, in a later day, the Future, is an evasion of the white whale: it is a quest of that boyish beginning which we call a happy ending. But the old Norse myth told that Asgard itself would be consumed at last, and the very gods would be destroyed: the white whale is the symbol of that persistent force of destruction, that meaningless force, which now figures as the outpouring of a volcano or the atmospheric disruption of a tornado or again as the mere aimless dissipation of unused energy into an unavailable void—that spectacle which so disheartened the learned Henry Adams. The whole tale of the West, in mind and action, in the philosophy and art of the Greeks, in the organization and technique of the Romans, in the precise skills and unceasing spiritual quests of the modern man, is a tale of this effort to combat the whale—to ward off his blows, to counteract his aimless thrusts, to create a purpose that will offset the empty malice of Moby-Dick. Without such a purpose, without the belief in such a purpose, life is neither bearable nor significant: unless one is polarized by these central human energies and aims, one tends to become absorbed in Moby-Dick himself, and, becoming a part of his being, can only maim, slay, butcher, like the shark or the white whale or Alexander or Napoleon. If there is no God, exclaims Dostoyevsky's hero, then we may commit murder: and in the sense that God represents the totality of human purpose and meaning the conclusion is inevitable.

It is useless to derive man's purposes from those of the external universe; he is a figure in the web of life. Except for such kindness and loyalty as the creatures man has domesticated show, there is, as far as one can now see, no concern except in man himself over the careless motions and accidents that take place in nature. Love and chance, said Charles Peirce, rule the universe: but the love is man's love, and although in the very concept of chance, as both Peirce and Captain Ahab declare, there is some rough notion of fair play, of fifty-fifty, of an even break, that is small immediate consolation for the creature that may lose not the game, but his life, by an unlucky throw of the dice. Ahab has more humanity than the gods he defies: indeed, he has more power, because he is conscious of the power he wields, and applies it deliberately, whereas Moby-Dick's power only seems deliberate because it cuts across the directed aims of Ahab himself. And in one sense, Ahab achieves victory: he vanquishes in himself that which would retreat from Moby-Dick and acquiesce in his insensate energies and his brutal sway. His end is tragic: evil engulfs him. But in battling against evil, with power instead of love, Ahab himself, in A.E.'s phrase, becomes the image of the thing he hates: he has lost his humanity in the very act of vindicating it. By physical defiance, by physical combat, Ahab cannot rout and capture Moby-Dick: the odds are against him; and if his defiance is noble, his methods are ill chosen. Growth, cultivation, order, art—these are the proper means by which man displaces accident and subdues the vacant external powers in the universe: the way of growth is not to become more powerful but to become more human. Here is a hard lesson to learn: it is easier to wage war than to conquer in oneself the tendency to be partial, vindictive, and unjust: it is easier to demolish one's enemy than to pit oneself against him in an intellectual combat which will disclose one's weaknesses and provincialities. And that evil Ahab seeks to strike is the sum of one's enemies. He does not bow down to it and accept it: therein lies his heroism and virtue: but he fights it with its own weapons and therein lies his madness. All the things that Ahab despises when he is about to attack the whale, the love and loyalty of Pip, the memory of his wife and child, the sextant of science, the inner sense of calm, which makes all external struggle futile, are the very things that would redeem him and make him victorious.

Man's ultimate defence against the Universe, against evil and accident and malice, is not by any fictitious resolution of these things into an Absolute which justifies them and ultilizes them for its own ends: this is specious comfort, and Voltaire's answer to Leibniz in Candide seems to me a final one. Man's defence lies within himself, not within the narrow, isolated ego, which may be overwhelmed, but in that self which we share with our fellows and which assures us that, whatever happens to our own carcasses and hides, good men will remain, to carry on the work, to foster and protect the things we have recognized as excellent. To make that self more solid, one must advance positive science, produce formative ideas, and embody ideal forms in which all men may, to a greater or less degree, participate: in short, one must create a realm which is independent of the hostile forces in the universe—and cannot be lightly shaken by their onslaught. Melville's method, that of writing Moby-Dick, was correct: as correct as Ahab's method, taken literally, that of fighting Moby-Dick, was fallacious. In Moby-Dick, Melville conquered the white whale in his own consciousness: instead of blankness there was significance, instead of aimless energy there was purpose, and instead of random living there was Life. The universe *is* inscrutable, unfathomable, malicious, *so*—like the white whale and his element. Art in the broad sense of all humanizing effort is man's answer to this condition: for it is the means by which he circumvents or postpones his doom, and bravely meets his tragic destiny. Not tame and gentle bliss, but disaster, heroically encountered, is man's true happy ending.

9

Here, it seems to me, is the plainest interpretation of Melville's fable, and the one he was partly conscious of in the writing of it. But a great book is more a part of its milieu than either the writer or his public knows; and there is more in Moby-Dick than the figure of man's heroic defiance of brute energy, and evil, and the high gods.

In another sense, the whale stands for the practical life. Mankind needs food and light and shelter, and, with a little daring and a little patience, it gains these things from its environment: the whale that we cut up, dissect, analyze, melt down, pour into casks, and distribute in cities and households is the whale of industry and science. The era of whaling which opened only in the late seventeenth century is timed with the era of modern industry; and in the very year Melville wrote Moby-Dick, 1851, industry and science were announcing their triumphs in that great cock-crow of the Crystal Palace Exhibition in London. Side by side with this purpose, which secures man's material existence, is another set of purposes which, though they sometimes take advantage of the means offered by the practical life, as Ahab takes advantage of his sordid crew and ordinary whaling to carry out his private revenge, run counter to the usual flow of our daily efforts. The white whale cannot be met and captured by the usual means; more than that: to fulfil man's own deeper purposes, the captains of the spirit must oppose the prudence of Starbuck and the common sense of Stubb. Material sustenance, home, comfort, though their pursuit occupy the greater part of the daily round of humanity, are sometimes best forgotten and set at naught: indeed, when nobler human purposes are uppermost, they must be set at naught. He who steadily seeks to preserve life and fortify it must be ready to give up his life at a moment's notice when a fellow creature is in danger: he who would provide others with daily bread must be prepared to go hungry if the wheat that would nourish him is needed for the planting. All the more does this hold in the affairs of the spirit. When the human spirit expands itself to the uttermost, to confront the white whale and hew meaning and form from the blank stone of experience, one must reverse all the practical maxims: earth's folly, as Melville says, is Heaven's wisdom, and earth's wisdom is Heaven's greatest disaster.

The crew of the vessel seek the ordinary whale: they are after comfort and contentment and a greater share of the "lay"; but the Ahabs seek danger and hardship and a lay that has no value in terms of material sustenance and magnificence. And the paradox, the hard paradox, is this: both purposes are essential: Ahab could not set out at all without the aid of Peleg and Bildad and Charity and his harpooners and sailors, and they, for their part, would never know anything except sluggish routine were they not at times stirred up to great efforts by purposes they do not easily understand or consciously accept. Yet: there is an Ahab in every man, and the meanest member of the crew can be awakened to the values that Ahab prizes: given a storm and a stove boat, and the worst rascal on shipboard may be as magnificent as Odysseus. All men live most intensely when they are moulded by such a purpose—or even, wanting that, by an enterprise that counterfeits it. Art, religion, culture in general, all those intangible triumphs of the spirit that are embodied in forms and symbols, all that spells purpose as opposed to senseless energy, and significance as opposed to routine—these efforts develop human life to its fullest, even when they work contrary to the ordinary standards of the world.

There, it seems to me, is another meaning in Ahab's struggle with Moby-Dick. He represents, not as in the first parable, an heroic power that misconceives its mission and misapplies itself: here he rather stands for human purpose in its highest expression. His pursuit is "futile" because it wrecks the boat and brings home no oil and causes material loss and extinguishes many human lives; but in another sense, it is not futile at all, but is the only significant part of the voyage, since oil is burned and ships eventually break up and men die and even the towers of proud cities crumble away as the buildings sink beneath the sand or the jungle, while all that remains, all that perpetuates the life and the struggle, are their forms and symbols, their art, their literature, their science, as they have been incorporated in the social heritage of man. That which is useful for the moment eventually becomes useless; the mummy's food and drink shrivel away or evaporate: but that which is "useless," the graven image or the tomb itself, continues to nourish the spirit of man. Life, Life purposive, Life formative, Life expressive, is more than living, as living itself is more than the finding of a livelihood. There is no triumph so petty and evanescent as that involved in capturing the ordinary whale: the nineteenth century made this triumph the end and object of all endeavour; and it put the spirit in chains of comfort and material satisfaction, which were heavier than fetters and harder to bear than the stake. By the same token, there is no struggle so permanent and so humanly satisfactory as Ahab's struggle with the white whale. In that defeat, in that succession of defeats, is the only pledge of man's ultimate victory, and the only final preventive of emptiness, boredom, and suicide. Battles are lost, as Whitman cried, in the same spirit that they are won. Some day the physical powers of man may be commensurate with his utmost spirit, and he will meet Leviathan on even terms.

10

The epic and mythic quality of Moby-Dick has been misunderstood because those who examined the book have thought of the epic in terms of Homer, and the myth itself in relation to some obvious hero of antiquity, or some modern folk-hero, a Washington, a Boone, raised to enormous dimensions. "The great mistake seems to be," as Melville said in his essay on Hawthorne, "that even with those Americans who look forward to the coming of a great literary genius among us, they somehow fancy he will come in the costume of Queen Elizabeth's day; be a writer of dramas founded upon old English history or the tales of Boccaccio. Whereas, great geniuses are parts of the times, they themselves are the times and possess a corresponding colouring."

Now, Moby-Dick was written in the best spirit of the nineteenth century, and though it escaped most of the limitations of that period, it escaped with its finest qualities intact. Heroes and gods in the old sense, as Walt Whitman plainly saw, had had their day: they fitted into a simpler scheme of life and thought, and a more credulous sort of attitude; so far from representing the ultimate triumph of the human imagination, from which the scientific mode of thought was not merely a departure but a falling off, the old myths were but the product of a juvenile fantasy. One might still use these figures, as Milton used an Arcadian image to express the corruptions of the Established Church; but they stood for a mode of consciousness and feeling remote from our modern experience. Science did not, as has been foolishly believed, destroy the myth-making power of man, or reduce all his inner strivings to bleak impotence: this has been the accidental, temporary effect of one-sided science, serving, consciously or not, a limited number of practical activities. What the scientific spirit has actually done has been to exercise the imagination in finer ways than the autistic wish—the wish of the infant possessed of the illusion of power and domination—was able to express. Faraday's ability to conceive the lines of force in a magnetic field was quite as great a triumph as the ability to conceive fairies dancing in a ring: and, as Mr. A. N. Whitehead has shown, the poets who sympathized with this new sort of imagination, poets like Shelley, Wordsworth, Whitman, Melville, did not feel themselves robbed of their specific powers, but rather found them enlarged and refreshed.

One of of the finest love-poems of the nineteenth century, Whitman's Out of the Cradle Endlessly Rocking, is expressed in such an image as Darwin or Audubon might have used, were the scientist as capable of expressing his inner feelings as of noting "external" events: the poet haunting the sea-shore and observing the mating of the birds, day after day following their life, could scarcely have existed before the nineteenth century. In the seventeenth century, such a poet would have remained in the garden and written about a literary ghost, Philomel, and not about an actual pair of birds: in Pope's time, the poet would have remained in the library and written about the birds on a lady's fan. Almost all the important works of the nineteenth century were cast in this mode and expressed this new imaginative range: they respect the fact: they are replete with observation: they project an ideal realm in and through, not over, the landscape of actuality. Notre Dame might have been written by an historian, War and Peace by a sociologist, The Idiot might have been created by a psychiatrist, and Salammbô might have been the work of an archaeologist. I do not say that these books were scientific by intention, or that they might be replaced by a work of science without grave loss; far from it. I merely point out that they are conceived in the same spirit; that they belong to a similar plane of consciousness. Much as Melville was enriched by the Elizabethan writers, there is that in Moby-Dick which separates him completely from the poets of that day—and if one wants a word to describe the element that makes the difference, one must call it briefly science.

Now, this respect for fact, as opposed to irresponsible fantasy, did not of course exist for the first time in the nineteenth century: Defoe had this habit of mind in quite as great a measure as Melville: what is important is that in the nineteenth century it was for the first time completely wedded to the imagination. It no longer means a restriction, a dried-up quality, an incompleteness; it no longer deifies the empirical and the practical at the expense of the ideal and the aesthetic: on the contrary, these qualities are now completely fused together, as an expression of life's integrated totality. The symbolism again becomes equal to the reality. Hercules no longer serves in this way: although originally he was doubtless as full of immediate relationships as whaling; and a more complex and diffuse symbol—like Kutuzov's army in War and Peace—is necessary. Had Milton sought to tell this parable of Melville's, he would probably have recast the story of Jonah and the whale, making Jonah the hero; but in doing so he could not help losing all the great imaginative parallels Melville is able to work out, through using material hitherto untouched by previous myth or history. For Ahab's hate and the pursuit of the whale is only one part of the total symbol: the physiological character of the whale, its feeding, its mating, its whole life, from whatever sources Melville drew the data, is equally a part of it. Indeed, the symbol of Moby-Dick is complete and rounded, expressive of our present relations to the universe, only through the passages that orthodox criticism, exercised on lesser works and more meagre traditions, regards as extraneous or unimportant!

Moby-Dick, then, is one of the first great mythologies to be created in the modern world, created, that is, out of the stuff of that world, its science, its exploration, its terrestrial daring, its concentration upon power and dominion over nature, and not out of ancient symbols, Prometheus, Endymion, Orestes, or mediaeval folk-legends, like Dr. Faustus. Moby-Dick lives imaginatively in the newly broken soil of our own life: its symbols, unlike Blake's original but mysterious figures, are direct and explicit: if the story is bedded in facts, the facts themselves are not lost in the further interpretation. Moby-Dick thus brings together the two dissevered halves of the modern world and the modern self—its positive, practical, scientific, externalized self, bent on conquest and knowledge, and its imaginative, ideal half, bent on the transposition of conflict into art, and power into humanity. This resolution is achieved in Moby-Dick itself: it is as if a Shakespeare and a Bacon, or, to use a more local metaphor, as if an Eakins and a Ryder, had collaborated on a single work of art, with a heightening of their several powers. The best handbook on whaling is also—I say this scrupulously—the best tragic epic of modern times and one of the fine poetic works of all time.

That is an achievement; and it is also a promise. Whitman went as far in his best poems, particularly in the Song of Myself; and, with quite another method, Tolstoy went as far in War and Peace, Dostoyevsky in the Brothers Karamazov; Hardy, less perfectly, approximated it perhaps in The Dynasts; but no one went further. It is one of the great peaks of the modern vision of life. "May God keep us," wrote Blake, "from single vision and Newton's sleep." We now perhaps see a little more clearly what Blake's enigmatic words mean. In Moby-Dick Melville achieved the deep integrity of that double vision which sees with both eyes—the scientific eye of actuality, and the illumined eye of imagination and dream.

11

I have dwelt for a little on some of the meanings of Moby-Dick; but this does not exhaust the matter. Each man will read into Moby-Dick the drama of his own experience and that of his contemporaries: Mr. D. H. Lawrence sees in the conflict a battle between the blood-consciousness of the white race and its own abstract intellect, which attempts to hunt and slay it: Mr. Percy Boynton sees in the whale all property and vested privilege, laming the spirit of man: Mr. Van Wyck Brooks has found in the white whale an image like that of Grendel in Beowulf, expressing the Northern consciousness of the hard fight against the elements; while for the disciple of Jung, the white whale is the symbol of the Unconscious, which torments man, and yet is the source of all his proudest efforts.

Each age, one may predict, will find its own symbols in Moby-Dick. Over that ocean the clouds will pass and change, and the ocean itself will mirror back those changes from its own depths. All these conscious interpretations, however, though they serve the book by approaching its deeper purpose, do not, cannot, quite penetrate the core of its reality. Moby-Dick has a meaning which cannot be derived or dissociated from the work itself. Like every great work of art, it summons up thoughts and feelings profounder than those to which it gives overt expression. It introduces one, sometimes by simple, bald means, to the depths of one's own experience. The book is not an answer, but a clue that must be carried further and worked out. The Sermon on the Mount has this quality. It does not answer all the difficult problems of morality, but it suggests a new point of view in facing them: it leads one who is sufficiently moved to follow through all the recesses of conduct which can be influenced by mildness, understanding, and love, but not otherwise. So with Moby-Dick: the book itself is greater than the fable it embodies, it foreshadows more than it actually reflects: as a work of art, Moby-Dick is part of a new integration of thought, a widening of the fringe of consciousness, a deepening of insight, through which the modern vision of life will finally be embodied.

The shadow cast by Moby-Dick throws into obscurity not merely the sand-hills, but likewise some of the mountains, of the last three centuries. Noting the extent of that shadow, one begins to suspect how high the mountain itself is, and how great its bulk, how durable its rock.

In Nomine Diaboli*

Henry A. Murray

Next to the seizures and shapings of creative thought—the thing it-self—no comparable experience is more thrilling than being witched, illumined, and transfigured by the magic of another's art. This is a trance from which one returns refreshed and quickened, and bubbling with unenvious praise of the exciting cause, much as Melville bubbled after his first reading of Hawthorne's *Mosses*. In describing *his* experience Melville chose a phrase so apt—"the shock of recognition"—that in the thirties Edmund Wilson took it as the irresistibly perfect title for his anthology of literary appreciations. Acknowledging a shock of recognition and paying homage to the delivering genius is singularly exhilarating, even today—or especially today—when every waxing enthusiasm must confront an outgoing tide of culture.

In our time, the capacities for wonder and reverence, for generous judgments and trustful affirmations, have largely given way, though not without cause surely, to their antipathies, the humors of a waning ethos: disillusionment, cynicism, disgust, and gnawing envy. These states have bred in us the inclination to dissect the subtlest orders of man's wit with ever-sharper instruments of depreciation, to pour all values, the best confounded by the worst, into one mocking-pot, to sneer "realistically," and, as we say today, "assassinate" character. These same humors have disposed writers to spend immortal talent in snickering exhibitions of vulgarity and spiritual emptiness, or in making delicate picture-puzzles out of the butt-ends of life.

In the face of these current trends and tempers, I, coming out of years of brimming gratefulness for the gift of *Moby-Dick*, would like to praise Herman Melville worthily, not to bury him in a winding-sheet of scientific terminology. But the odds are not favorable to my ambition. A commitment of thirty years to analytic modes of thought and concepts lethal to emotion has built such habits in me that were I to be waked in the night by a cry of "Help!" I fear I would respond in the lingo of psychology. I am suffering from one of the commonest ailments of our age—trained disability.

*An essay read at the exercises to commemorate the centennial of the publication of *Moby-Dick* (William College, September 3, 1951).

Reprinted from *New England Quarterly* 24 (December 1951), 435–52. Reprinted by permission of Mrs. Henry A. Murray.

The habit of a psychologist is to break down the structure of each personality he studies into elements, and so in a few strokes to bring to earth whatever merit that structure, as a structure, may possess. Furthermore, for reasons I need not mention here, the technical terms for the majority of these elements have derogatory connotations. Consequently, it is difficult to open one's professional mouth without disparaging a fellow-being. Were an analyst to be confronted by that much-heralded but still missing specimen of the human race—the normal man—he would be struck dumb, for once, through lack of appropriate ideas.

If I am able to surmount to some extent any impediments of this origin, you may attribute my good fortune to a providential circumstance. In the procession of my experiences *Moby-Dick* anteceded Psychology, that is, I was swept by Melville's gale and shaken by his appalling sea dragon before I had acquired the all-leveling academic oil that is poured on brewed-up waters, and before I possessed the weapons and tools of science—the conceptual lance, harpoons, cutting irons, and what-nots—which might have reduced the "grand hooded phantom" to mere blubber. Lacking these defenses I was whelmed. Instead of my changing this book, this book changed me.

To me, *Moby-Dick* was Beethoven's *Eroica* in words: first of all, a masterly orchestration of harmonic and melodic language, of resonating images and thoughts in varied metres. Equally compelling were the spacious sea-setting of the story, the cast of characters and their prodigious common target, the sorrow, the fury, and the terror, together with all those frequent touches, those subtle interminglings of unexampled humor, quizzical and, in the American way, extravagant, and finally the fated closure, the crown and tragic consummation of the immense yet firmly-welded whole. But still more extraordinary and portentous were the penetration and scope, the sheer audacity of the author's imagination. Here was a man who did not fly away with his surprising fantasies to some unbelievable dreamland, pale or florid, shunning the stubborn objects and gritty facts, the prosaic routines and practicalities of everyday existence. Here was a man who, on the contrary, chose these very things as vessels for his procreative powers—the whale as a naturalist, a Hunter or a Cuvier, would perceive him, the business of killing whales, the whale-ship running as an oil factory, stowing-down, in fact, every mechanism and technique, each tool and gadget, that was integral to the money-minded industry of whaling. Here was a man who could describe the appearance, the concrete matter-of-factness, and the utility of each one of these natural objects, implements, and tools with the fidelity of a scientist, and, while doing this, explore it as a conceivable repository of some aspect of the human drama; then, by an imaginative tour de force, deliver a vital essence, some humorous or profound idea, coalescing with its embodiment. But still more. Differing from the symbolists of our time, here was a man who offered us essences and meanings which did not level or depreciate the objects of his contemplation. On the contrary, this loving man exalted all creatures—the mariners, renegades, and castaways on board the *Pequod*—by ascribing to them "high qualities, though dark" and weaving round them "tragic graces." Here, in short, was a man with the myth-making powers of a Blake, a hive of significant associations, who was capable of reuniting what science had put asunder—pure perception and relevant emotion—and doing it in an exultant way that was acceptable to skepticism.

Not at first, but later, I perceived the crucial difference between Melville's dramatic animations of nature and those of primitive religion-makers: both were spontaneous and uncalculated projections, but Melville's were in harmony, for the most part, with scientific knowledge, because they had been recognized as projections, checked, and modified. Here, then, was a man who might redeem us from the virtue of an incredible subjective belief, on the one side, and from the virtue of a deadly objective rationality, on the other.

For these and other reasons the reading of *Moby-Dick*—coming before Psychology—left a stupendous reverberating imprint, too lively to be diminished by the long series of relentless analytical operations to which I subsequently subjected it. Today, after twenty-five years of such experiments, *The Whale* is still *the* whale, more magnificent, if anything, than before.

Before coming to grips with the "mystery" of *Moby-Dick* I should mention another providential circumstance to which all psychologists are, or should be, forever grateful, and literary critics too, since without it no complete understanding of books like *Moby-Dick* would be possible today. Ahead of us were two greatly gifted pioneers, Freud and Jung, who, with others, explored the manifold vagaries of unconscious mental processes and left for our inheritance their finely-written works. The discoveries of these adventurers advantaged me in a special way: they gave, I thought, support to one of Santayana's early convictions, that in the human being imagination is more fundamental than perception. Anyhow, adopting this position, some of us psychologists have been devoting ourselves to the study of dreams, fantasies, creative productions, and projections—all of which are primarily and essentially emotional and dramatic, such stuff as myths are made of. Thus, by chance or otherwise, this branch of the tree of psychology is growing in the direction of Herman Melville.

To be explicit: psychologists have been recognizing in the dream figures and fantasy figures of today's children and adolescents more and more family likenesses of the heroes and heroines of primitive myths, legends, and fables—figures, in other words, who are engaged in comparable heroic strivings and conflicts, and experiencing comparable heroic triumphs or fatalities. Our ancestors, yielding to an inherent propensity of the mind, projected the more relevant of these figures into objects of their environment, into sun, moon, and stars, into the unknown deeps of the sea and of the earth, and into the boundless void of heaven; and they worshipped the most potent of these projected images, whether animal or human, as super-beings, gods, or goddesses. On any clear night one can see scores of the more luminous of such divinities parading up and down the firmament. For example, in Fall and Winter, one looks with admiration on that resplendent hero Perseus and above him the chained beauty, Andromeda, whom he saved from a devouring monster, ferocious as Moby-Dick. Now, what psychologists have been learning by degrees is that Perseus is in the unconscious mind of every man and Andromeda in every woman, not, let me hasten to say, as an inherited fixed image, but as a potential set of dispositions which may be constellated in the personality by the occurrence of a certain kind of situation. Herman Melville arrived at this conclusion in his own way a hundred years ago, sooner and, I believe, with more genuine comprehension than any other writer.

An explanation of all this in scientific terms would require all the space permitted me and more. Suffice it to say here that the psychologists who are studying the elementary myth-makings of the mind are dealing with the germy sources of poetry and drama, the fecundities out of which great literature is fashioned. Furthermore, in attempting to formulate and classify these multifarious productions of the imagination, the psychologist uses modes of analysis and synthesis very similar to those that Aristotle used in setting forth the dynamics of Greek tragedy. In these and other trends I find much encouragement for the view that a rapprochement of psychology and literary criticism is in progress, and that it will prove fruitful to both callings. As an ideal meeting ground I would propose Melville's world of "wondrous depths."

To this Columbus of the mind, the great archetypal figures of myth, drama, and epic were not pieces of intellectual Dresden china, heirlooms of a classical education, ornamental bric-a-brac to be put here and there for the pleasure of genteel readers. Many of the more significant of these constellations were inwardly experienced by Melville, one after the other, as each was given vent to blossom and assert itself. Thus, we are offered a spectacle of spiritual development through passionate identifications. Only by proceeding in this way could Melville have learnt on his pulses what it was to be Narcissus, Orestes, Oedipus, Ishmael, Apollo, Lucifer. "Like a frigate," he said, "I am full with a thousand souls."

This brings me to the problem of interpreting *Moby-Dick*. Some writers have said that there is nothing to interpret: it is a plain sea story marred here and there by irrelevant ruminations. But I shall not cite the abundant proof for the now generally accepted proposition that in *Moby-Dick* Melville "meant" something—something, I should add, which he considered "terrifically true" but which, in the world's judgment, was so harmful "that it were all but madness for any good man, in his own proper character, to utter or even hint of." What seems decisive here is the passage in Melville's celebrated letter to Hawthorne: "A sense of unspeakable security is in me this moment, on account of your having understood the book." From this we can conclude that there *are* meanings to be understood in *Moby-Dick*, and also—may we say for our own encouragement?—that Melville's ghost will feel secure forever if modern critics can find them, and, since Hawthorne remained silent, set them forth in print. Here it might be well to remind ourselves of a crucial statement which follows the just quoted passage from Melville's letter: "I have written a wicked book." The implication is clear: all interpretations which fail to show that *Moby-Dick* is, in some sense, wicked have missed the author's avowed intention.

A few critics have scouted all attempts to fish Melville's own meaning out of *The Whale*, on the ground that an interpretation of a work of art so vast and so complex is bound to be composed in large measure of projections from the mind of the interpreter. It must be granted that preposterous projections often do occur in the course of such an effort. But these are not inevitable. Self-knowledge and discipline may reduce projections to a minimum. Anyhow, in the case of *Moby-Dick*, the facts do not sustain the proposition that a critic can see nothing in this book but his own reflected image. The interpretations which have been published over the last thirty years exhibit an unmistakable trend towards consensus in respect to the drama as a whole as well as many of its subordinate parts. Moreover, so far as I can judge, the critics who, with hints from their predecessors, applied their intuitions most recently to the exegesis of *The Whale*, can be said to have arrived, if taken together, at Melville's essential meaning. Since one or another of these authors has deftly said what I clumsily thought, my prejudices are strongly in favor of their conclusions, and I am whole-hearted in applauding them, Mr. Arvin's[1] most especially, despite their having left me with nothing fresh to say. Since this is how things stand, my version of the main theme of *Moby-Dick* can be presented in a briefer form, and limited to two hypotheses.

The first of them is this: Captain Ahab is an embodiment of that fallen angel or demi-god who in Christendom was variously named Lucifer, Devil, Adversary, Satan. The Church Fathers would have called Captain Ahab "Antichrist" because he was not Satan himself, but a human creature possessed of all Satan's pride and energy, "summing up within himself," as Irenaeus said, "the apostasy of the devil."

That it was Melville's intention to beget Ahab in Satan's image can hardly be doubted. He told Hawthorne that his book had been boiled in hell-fire and secretly baptized not in the name of God but in the name of the Devil. He named his tragic hero after the Old Testament ruler who "did more to provoke the Lord God of Israel to anger than all the Kings of Israel that were before him." King Ahab's accuser, the prophet Elijah, is also resurrected to play his original rôle, though very briefly, in Melville's testament. We are told that Captain Ahab is an "ungodly, god-like" man who is spiritually outside Christendom. He is a well of blasphemy and defiance, of scorn and mockery for the gods—"cricket-players and pugilists" in his eyes. Rumor has it that he once spat in the holy goblet on the altar of the Catholic Church at Santa. "I never saw him kneel," says Stubb. He is associated in the text with scores of references to the Devil. He is an "anaconda of an old man." His self-assertive sadism is the linked antithesis of the masochistic submission preached by Father Mapple.

Captain Ahab-Lucifer is also related to a sun-god, like Christ, but in reverse. Instead of being light leaping out of darkness, he is "darkness leaping out of light." The *Pequod* sails on Christmas Day. *This* new year's sun will be the god of Wrath rather than the god of Love. Ahab does not emerge from his subterranean abode until his ship is "rolling through the bright Quito spring" (Easter-tide, symbolically, when the all-fertilizing sun-god is resurrected). The frenzied ceremony in which Ahab's followers are sworn to the pursuit of the White Whale—"Commend the murderous chalices!"—is suggestive of the Black Mass; the lurid operations at the try-works is a scene out of Hell.

There is some evidence that Melville was re-reading *Paradise Lost* in the summer of 1850, shortly after, let us guess, he got the idea of transforming the captain of his whale-ship into the first of all cardinal sinners who fell by pride. Anyhow, Melville's Satan is the spitting image of Milton's hero, but portrayed with deeper and subtler psychological insight, and placed where he belongs, in the heart of an enraged man.

Melville may have been persuaded by Goethe's Mephistopheles, or even by some of Hawthorne's bloodless abstracts of humanity, to add Fedallah to his cast of characters. Evidently he wanted to make certain that no reader would fail to recognize that Ahab had been possessed by, or had sold his soul to, the Devil. Personally, I think Fedallah's rôle is superfluous and I regret that Melville made room for him and his unbelievable boat-crew on the ship *Pequod*. Still, he is not wholly without interest. He represents the cool, heartless, cunning, calculating, intellectual Devil of the Medieval myth-makers, in contrast, to the stricken, passionate, indignant, and often eloquent rebel angel of *Paradise Lost*, whose rôle is played by Ahab.

The Arabic name "Fedallah" suggests "dev(il) Allah," that is, the Mohammedans' god as he appeared in the mind's eye of a Crusader. But we are told that Fedallah is a Parsee—a Persian fire-worshipper, or Zoroastrian, who lives in India. Thus, Ahab, named after the Semitic apostate who was converted to the orgiastic cult of Baal, or Bel, originally a Babylonian fertility god, has formed a compact with a Zoroastrian whose name reminds us of still another Oriental religion. In addition, Captain Ahab's whale-boat is manned by a crew of unregenerate infidels, as defined by orthodox Christianity, and each of his three harpooners, Queequeg, Tashtego, and Daggoo, is a member of a race which believed in other gods than the one god of the Hebraic-Christian Bible.

Speaking roughly, it might be said that Captain Ahab, incarnation of the Adversary and master of the ship *Pequod* (named after the aggressive

Indian tribe that was exterminated by the Puritans of New England), has summoned the various religions of the East to combat the one dominant religion of the West. Or, in other terms, that he and his followers, Starbuck excepted, represented the horde of primitive drives, values, beliefs, and practises which the Hebraic-Christian religionists rejected and excluded, and by threats, punishments, and inquisitions, forced into the unconscious mind of Western man.

Stated in psychological concepts, Ahab is captain of the culturally repressed dispositions of human nature, that part of personality which psychoanalysts have termed the "Id." If this is true, his opponent, the White Whale, can be none other than the internal institution which is responsible for these repressions, namely the Freudian Superego. This then is my second hypothesis: Moby-Dick is a veritable spouting, breaching, sounding whale, a whale who, because of his whiteness, his mighty bulk and beauty, and because of one instinctive act that happened to dismember his assailant, has received the projection of Captain Ahab's Presbyterian conscience, and so may be said to embody the Old Testament Calvinistic conception of an affrighting Deity and his strict commandments, the derivative puritan ethic of nineteenth-century America, and the society that defended this ethic. Also, and most specifically, he symbolizes the zealous parents whose righteous sermonizings and corrections drove the prohibitions in so hard that a serious young man could hardly reach outside the barrier, except possibly far away among some tolerant, gracious Polynesian peoples. The emphasis should be placed on that unconscious (and hence inscrutable) wall of inhibition which imprisoned the puritan's thrusting passions. "How can the prisoner reach outside," cries Ahab, "except by thrusting through the wall? To me, the White Whale is that wall, shoved near to me . . . I see in him outrageous strength, with an inscrutable malice sinewing it." As a symbol of a sounding, breaching, white-dark, unconquerable New England conscience what could be better than a sounding, breaching, white-dark, unconquerable sperm whale?

Who is the psychoanalyst who could resist the immediate inference that the *imago* of the mother as well as the *imago* of the father is contained in the Whale? In the present case there happens to be a host of biographical facts and written passages which support this proposition. Luckily, I need not review them, because Mr. Arvin and others have come to the same conclusion. I shall confine myself to one reference. It exhibits Melville's keen and sympathetic insight into the cultural determinants of his mother's prohibiting dispositions. In *Pierre,* it is the "high-up, and towering and all-forbidding . . . edifice of his mother's immense pride . . . her pride of birth . . . her pride of purity," that is the "wall shoved near," the wall that stands between the hero and the realization of his heart's resolve. But instead of expending the fury of frustration upon his mother, he directs it at Fate, or, more specifically, at his mother's God and the society that shaped her. For he saw "that not his mother had made his mother; but the Infinite Haughtiness had first fashioned her; and then the haughty world had further molded her; nor had a haughty Ritual omitted to finish her."

Given this penetrating apprehension we are in a position to say that Melville's target in *Moby-Dick* was the upper middle-class culture of his time. It was *this* culture which was defended with righteous indignation by what he was apt to call "the world" or "the public," and Melville had very little respect for "the world" or "the public." The "public," or men operating as a social system, was something quite distinct from "the people." In *White Jacket* he wrote: "The public and the people! . . . let us hate the one, and cleave to the other." "The public is a monster," says Lemsford. Still earlier Melville had said: "I fight against the armed and crested lies of Mardi (the world)." "Mardi is a monster whose eyes are fixed in its head, like a whale." Many other writers have used similar imagery. Sir Thomas Browne referred to the multitude as "that numerous piece of monstrosity"; Keats spoke of "the dragon world." But closest of all was Hobbes: "By art is created that great Leviathan, called a commonwealth or state." It was in the laws of this Leviathan, Hobbes made clear, that the sources of right and wrong reside. To summarize: the giant mass of Melville's whale is the same as Melville's man-of-war world, the *Neversink*, in *White Jacket*, which in turn is an epitome of Melville's Mardi. The Whale's white forehead and hump should be reserved for the world's heavenly King.

That God is incarnate in the Whale has been perceived by Mr. Stone,[2] and, as far as I know, by every other Catholic critic of Melville's work, as well as by several Protestant critics. In fact, Mr. Chase[3] has marshalled so fair a portion of the large bulk of evidence on this point that any more from me would be superflous. Of course, what Ahab projects into the Whale is not the image of a loving Father, but the God of the Old Dispensation, the God who brought Jeremiah into darkness, hedged him about, and made his path crooked; the God, adopted by the fire-and-brimstone Puritans, who said: "With fury poured out I will rule over you." "The sword without and the terror within, shall destroy both the young man and the virgin." "I will also send the teeth of beasts upon them." "I will heap mischiefs upon them." "To me belongeth vengeance and recompense."

Since the society's vision of deity, and the society's morality, and the parents and ministers who implant these conceptions, are represented in a fully socialized personality by an establishment that is called the Superego—Conscience as Freud defined it—, and since Ahab has been proclaimed "Captain of the Id," the simplest psychological formula for Melville's dramatic epic is this: an insurgent Id in mortal conflict with an oppressive cultural Superego. Starbuck, the First Mate, stands for the rational realistic Ego which is overpowered by the fanatical compulsiveness of the Id and dispossessed of its normally regulating functions.

If this is approximately correct, it appears that while writing his greatest work Melville abandoned his detached position in the Ego from time to time, hailed "the realm of shades," as his hero Taji had, and, through the mediumship of Ahab, "burst his hot heart's shell" upon the sacrosanct Almighty and the sacrosanct sentiments of Christendom. Since in the world's judgment, 1851, nothing could be more reproachable than this, it would be unjust, if not treacherous, of us to reason *Moby-Dick* into some comforting morality play for which no boldness was required. This would be depriving Melville of the ground he gained for self-respect by having dared to abide by his own subjective truth and write a "wicked book," the kind of book that Pierre's publishers, Steel, Flint, and Asbestos, would have called "a blasphemous rhapsody filched from the vile Atheists, Lucian and Voltaire."

Some may wonder how it was that Melville, a fundamentally good, affectionate, noble, idealistic, and reverential man, should have felt impelled to write a wicked book. Why did he aggress so furiously against Western orthodoxy, as furiously as Byron and Shelley, or any Satanic writer who preceded him, as furiously as Nietzsche or the most radical of his successors in our day?

In *Civilization and its Discontents* Freud, out of the ripeness of his full experience, wrote that when one finds deep-seated aggression—and by this he meant aggression of the sort that Melville voiced—one can safely attribute it to the frustration of Eros. In my opinion this generalization does not hold for all men of all cultures of all times, but the probability of its being valid is extremely high in the case of an earnest, moralistic, nineteenth-century American, a Presbyterian to boot, whose anger is born of suffering, especially if this man spent an impressionable year of his life in Polynesia and returned to marry the very proper little daughter of the Chief Justice of Massachusetts, and if, in addition, he is a profoundly creative man in whose androgynic personality masculine and feminine components are integrally blended.

If it were concerned with *Moby-Dick*, the book, rather than with its author, I would call *this* my third hypothesis: Ahab-Melville's aggression was directed against the object that once harmed Eros with apparent malice and was still thwarting it with presentiments of further retaliations. The correctness of this inference is indicated by the nature of the injury—a symbolic emasculation—that excited Ahab's ire. Initially, this threatening object was, in all likelihood, the father, later, possibly, the mother. But, as Melville plainly saw, both his parents had been fashioned by the Hebraic-Christian, American Calvinist tradition, the tradition which conceived of a deity in whose eyes Eros was depravity. It was the first Biblical myth-makers who dismissed from heaven and from earth the Great Goddess of the Oriental and primitive religions, and so rejected the feminine principle as a spiritual force. Ahab, protagonist of these rejected religions, in addressing heaven's fire and lightning, what he calls "the personified impersonal," cries: "But thou art my fiery father; my sweet mother I know not. Oh, cruel! What hast thou done with her?" He calls this god a foundling, a "hermit immemorial," who does not know his own origin. Again, it was the Hebraic authors, sustained later by the Church Fathers, who propagated the legend that a woman was the cause of Adam's exile from Paradise, and that the original sin was concupiscence. Melville says that Ahab, spokesman of all exiled princes, "piled upon the whale's white hump the sum of all the general rage and hate felt by his whole race from Adam down." Remember also that it was the lure of Jezebel that drew King Ahab of Israel outside the orthodoxy of his religion and persuaded him to worship the Phoenician Astarte, goddess of love and fruitful increase. "Jezebel" was the worst tongue-lash a puritan could give a woman. She was Sex, and sex was Sin, spelled with a capital. It was the Church periodicals of Melville's day that denounced *Typee*, called the author a sensualist,and influenced the publishers to delete suggestive passages from the second edition. It was this long heritage of aversion and animosity, so accentuated in this country, which banned sex relations as a topic of discourse and condemned divorce as an unpardonable offense. All this has been changed, for better and for worse, by the moral revolutionaries of our own time who, feeling as Melville felt but finding the currents of sentiment less strongly opposite, spoke out, and with their wit, indignation, and logic, reinforced by the findings of psychoanalysis, disgraced the stern-faced idols of their forebears. One result is this: today an incompatible marriage is not a prison-house, as it was for Melville, "with wall shoved near."

In *Pierre* Melville confessed his own faith when he said that Eros is god of all, and Love "the loftiest religion of this earth." To the romantic Pierre the image of Isabel was "a silent and tyrannical call, challenging him in his deepest moral being, and summoning Truth, Love, Pity, Conscience to the stand." Here he seems to have had in mind the redeeming and inspiring Eros of Courtly Love, a heresy which the Medieval Church had done its utmost to stamp out. *This*, he felt convinced, was *his* "path of God," although in the way of it he saw with horror the implacable conscience and worldly valuations of his revered mother.

If this line of reasoning is as close as I think it is to the known facts, then Melville, in the person of Ahab, assailed Calvinism in the Whale because it blocked the advance of a conscience beneficent to evolutionary love. And so, weighed in the scales of its creator, *Moby-Dick* is not a wicked book but a *good* book, and after finishing it Melville had full reason to feel, as he confessed, "spotless as the lamb."

But then, seen from another point, *Moby-Dick* might be judged a wicked book, not because its hero condemns an entrenched tradition, but because he is completely committed to destruction. Although Captain Ahab manifests the basic stubborn virtues of the arch-protestant and the rugged individualist carried to their limits, *this* god-defier is no Prometheus, since all thought of benefiting humanity is foreign to him. His purpose is not to make the Pacific safe for whaling, nor, when blasting at the moral order, does he have in mind a more heartening vision for the future. The religion of Eros which might once have been the secret determinant of Ahab's undertaking is never mentioned. At one critical point in *Pierre* the hero-author, favored by a flash of light, exclaims, "I will gospelize the world anew"; but he never does. Out of light comes darkness: the temper of Pierre's book is no different from the temper of *Moby-Dick*. The truth is that Ahab is motivated solely by his private need to avenge a private insult. His governing philosophy is that of nihilism, the doctrine that the existing system must be shattered. Nihilism springs up when the imagination fails to provide the redeeming solution of an unbearable dilemma, when "the creative response," as Toynbee would say, is not forthcoming, and a man reacts out of a hot heart—"to the dogs with the head"—and swings to an instinct—"the same that prompts even a worm to turn under the heel." This is what White Jacket did when arraigned at the mast, and what Pierre did when fortune deserted him, and what Billy Budd did when confronted by his accuser. "Nature has not implanted any power in man," said Melville, "that was not meant to be exercised at times, though too often our powers have been abused. The privilege, inborn and inalienable, that every man has, of dying himself and inflicting death upon another, was not given to us without a purpose. These are the last resources of an insulted and unendurable existence."

If we grant that Ahab is a wicked man, what does this prove? It proves that *Moby-Dick* is a *good* book, a parable in epic form, because Melville makes a great spectacle of Ahab's wickedness and shows through the course of the narrative how such wickedness will drive a man on iron rails to an appointed nemesis. Melville adhered to the classic formula for tragedies. He could feel "spotless as the lamb," because he had seen to it that the huge threat to the social system, immanent in Arab's two cardinal defects—egotistic self-inflation and unleashed wrath—was, at the end, fatefully exterminated, "and the great shroud of the sea rolled on as it rolled five thousand years ago." The reader has had his catharsis, equilibrium has been restored, sanity is vindicated.

This is true, but is it the whole truth? In point of fact, while writing *Moby-Dick* did Melville maintain aesthetic distance, keeping his own feelings in abeyance? Do we not hear Ahab saying things that the later Pierre will say and that Melville said less vehemently in his own person? Does not the author show marked partiality for the "mighty pageant creature" of his invention, put in *his* mouth the finest, boldest language? Also, have not many interpreters been so influenced by the abused Ahab that they saw nothing in his opponent but the source of all malicious agencies, the very Devil? As Mr. Mumford has said so eloquently, Ahab is at heart a noble being whose tragic wrong is that of battling against evil with "power instead of love," and so becoming "the image of the thing he hates." With this impression imbedded in our minds, how can we come out with any moral except this: evil wins. We admit that Ahab's wickedness has been cancelled. But what survives? It is the much more formidable, compacted wickedness of the group that survives, the world that is "saturated and soaking with lies," and their man-of-war God, who is hardly more admirable than a primitive totem beast, some oral-aggressive, child-devouring Cronos of the sea. Is this an idea that a man of good-will can rest with?

Rest with? Certainly not. Melville's clear intention was to bring not rest, but *unrest* to intrepid minds. All gentle people were warned away from his book "on risk of a lumbago or sciatica." "A polar wind blows through it," he announced. He had not written to soothe, but to kindle, to make men leap from their seats, as Whitman would say, and fight for their lives. Was it the poet's function to buttress the battlements of complacency, to give comfort to the enemy? There is little doubt about the nature of the enemy in Melville's day. It was the dominant ideology, that peculiar compound of puritanism and materialism, of rationalism and commercialism, of shallow, blatant optimism and technology, which proved so crushing to creative evolutions in religion, art, and life. In such circumstances every "true poet," as Blake said, "is of the Devil's party," whether he knows it or not. Surveying the last hundred and fifty years, how many exceptions to this statement can we find? Melville, anyhow, knew that *he* belonged to the party, and while writing *Moby-Dick* so gloried in his membership that he baptized his work *In Nomine Diaboli*. It was precisely under these auspices that he created his solitary masterpiece, a construction of the same high order as the Constitution of the United States and the scientific treatises of Willard Gibbs, though huge and wild and unruly as the Grand Canyon. And it is for this marvel chiefly that he resides in our hearts now among the greatest in "that small but high-hushed world" of bestowing geniuses.

Here ends this report of my soundings in *Moby-Dick*. The drama is finished. What became of its surviving author?

Moby-Dick may be taken as a comment on the strategic crisis of Melville's allegorical life. In portraying the consequences of Ahab's last suicidal lunge, the hero's umbilical fixation to the Whale and his death by strangling, the author signalized not only his permanent attachment to the *imago* of the mother, but the submission he had foreseen to the binding power of the parental conscience, the Superego of middle-class America. Measured against the standards of *his* day, then, Melville must be accounted a *good* man.

But does this entitle him to a place on the side of the angels? He abdicated to the conscience he condemned and his ship *Pequod*, in sinking, carried down with it the conscience he aspired to, represented by the sky-hawk, the bird of heaven. With his ideal drowned, life from then on was load and time stood still. All he had denied to love he gave throughout a martyrdom of forty years, to death.

But "hark ye yet again—the little lower layer." Melville's capitulation in the face of overwhelming odds was limited to the sphere of action. His embattled soul refused surrender and lived on, breathing back defiance, disputing "to the last gasp" of his "earthquake life" the sovereignty of that inscrutable authority in him. As he wrote in *Pierre,* unless the enthusiast "can find the talismanic secret, to reconcile this world with his own soul, then there is no peace for him, no slightest truce for him in this life." Years later we find him holding the same ground. "Terrible is earth" was his conclusion, but despite all, "no retreat through me." By this dogged stand he bequeathed to succeeding generations the unsolved problem of the talismanic secret.

Only at the very last, instinct spent, earthquake over, did he fall back to a position close to Christian resignation. In his Being, was not this man "a wonder, a grandeur, and a woe?"

Notes

1. Newton Arvin, *Herman Melville* (New York, 1950).
2. Geoffrey Stone, *Melville* (New York, 1949).
3. Richard Volney Chase, *Herman Melville: A Critical Study* (New York, 1949).

Moby-Dick: Work of Art*

WALTER E. BEZANSON

Among those who still read books there are few who do not know at least the outward adventure of Ishmael, the young whaleman: how he signed with his South Seas friend, Queequeg, to go aboard the fated *Pequod;* what happened when Captain Ahab enchanted his crew into hunting down the White Whale "on both sides of land, and over all sides of earth, till he spouts black blood and rolls fin out"; and how the "god-bullied hull" of the *Pequod* at last went down before the battering brow of Moby Dick, who smashed in the ship, sending them all to drown—"O Christ! to think of the green navies and the green-skulled crews!"—all, that is, but Ishmael, who lived to tell the tale. Some readers, looking beyond the simpler narrative, take *Moby-Dick* as *vade mecum,* in our peculiarly bedeviled times searching out what its ethical imperatives may be. Still other readers help to multiply its influence through scholarship and art; for in addition to shaking down a white snowstorm of books, essays, and commentaries, *Moby-Dick* has inspired fine poems by Hart Crane and W. H. Auden, illustrations by Rockwell Kent and Boardman Robinson, paintings by Gil Wilson, a concerto by Ghedini, several radio dramas, two old-time films of flickering merit (who could forget the anguished, silent groaning of John Barrymore?); and from time to time good artists and directors are tempted to produce a *Moby-Dick* opera, a *Moby-Dick* ballet, and a good (if the temptations could be resisted) *Moby-Dick* movie. Then, too, readers of *Moby-Dick* are almost inevitably drawn to reading something about Melville himself: his memorable Pacific adventures, his immersion in the rich world of books and ideas, his complex spiritual and psychological history, and the nearly unique decline and recovery of his subsequent reputation.

All these matters have their attractions, and will continue to have them. Yet underlying them all is at once a simpler and a more complex attraction—the fact that the book is a work of art, and that it is a work of art of a most unusual sort. Curiously enough, it is precisely here that our reading and scholarship have been least adequate. Interest in *Moby-Dick* as

Read at Oberlin College on November 13, 1951, at exercises to commemorate the one hundredth year of publication of Moby-Dick.

Reprinted by permission from *Moby-Dick Centennial Essays*, ed. Tyrus Hillway and Luther S. Mansfield (Dallas: Southern Methodist University Press, 1953), 30–58.

direct narrative, as moral analogue, as modern source, and as spiritual autobiography has far outrun commentary on it as a work of art. A proper criticism of so complex a book will be a long time in the making and will need immense attention from many kinds of critics. In the meantime I am struck by the need just now for contributions toward a relatively impersonal criticism directed at the book itself. The surrounding areas—such as *Moby-Dick* and Melville, *Moby-Dick* and the times in which it was made—are significant just because the book is a work of art. To ask what the book means is to ask what it is about, and to ask what it is about is in turn to ask how art works in the case at hand.

My remarks are therefore in this direction. Beginning with a look at the materials out of which *Moby-Dick* is created, we shall explore the means of activation and some of the forms that contain and define them. The three roadmarks we shall follow are *matter*, *dynamic*, and *structure*.

I

By *matter* I mean here the subject (or subject matter) in the gross sense. *Moby-Dick* has as its gross subject not Indian fighting or railroad building but whaling.

Any book about mid-nineteenth-century American whaling must in some fashion or other deal with certain phenomena, artifacts, and processes. There they are, and they must be used or the book is not about whaling. A rough inventory of data would include at least the following areas:

NATURAL WORLD: The *seas and oceans*, covering three-fifths of the globe: on the surface—tides, currents, winds, and weather; under the surface—countless forms of life of extreme diversity. Marine animals of the order *Cetacea*, ranging from small dolphins and porpoises to whales, the largest form of life in earth history (up to 125 tons). The Sperm Whale (*Physeter Macrocephalus*): one of the larger varieties (up to 75–85 feet), wrapped in a fat blanket (blubber) like other whales but unique in carrying a pool of pure spermaceti oil (up to 500 gallons) in his great square head; protects himself with rows of ivory teeth and the slap of his tail (20 feet across), or dives to the sea bottom; known to attack great objects which threaten him.

HISTORICAL WORLD: *Man*, a prolific, social, land animal constantly in search of animal, mineral, and vegetable resources for survival and use. *Seventeenth century*: discovering the use of whale products, especially the oil for lighting, man begins to bring to bear on the pursuit of whales the technologies developed in transportation and war. *Nineteenth century*: the United States, a newly created and powerfully expanding democracy in the early stages of capitalism, builds a whaling fleet of over seven hundred vessels and commits itself to a sea frontier that girdles the globe. New Bedford, Nantucket, and Sag Harbor become the world centers for the pursuit of sperm whales.

ARTIFACTS: *The whale-ship:* a wooden vessel, length about 105 feet, beam about 28 feet; three vertical masts (foremast, mainmast, mizzenmast), each with four horizontal yards (crosspieces); rigged to the yards more than thirty separate sails, each named for identification. *Nautical equipment:* windlass, capstan, chocks, pins, block and tackle, pumps; lines for handling sails, anchors, cargo. *Navigation equipment:* chronometer, quadrant, compass, charts, log and line, wheel or tiller; for finding location and keeping on course. *Spaces:* below decks two levels of compartments, including forecastle bunkroom for the crew and cabins aft for the captain and mates; storage quarters for food, water, whaling gear, casks, shooks (staves and barrel heads); sail and chain lockers, blubber room, holds for the cargo. *Pursuit equipment:* whaleboats of cedar planking, length 25 feet; plank seats for five oarsmen, platforms bow and stern for harpooner and boatsteerer; five pair of oars, steering oar, harpoons, lances, waif poles (for signal flags), line tubs, assorted gear. *Processing equipment:* try-works (deck furnaces), kettles, forks, spades, mincing knives, etc.

TECHNIQUES: innumerable skills demanded by all artifacts, especially ship and boat handling, maintenance, attack, butchering.

SOCIAL ORGANIZATION: *In the background:* Yankee owners who furnish capital and artifacts for voyages, to whom the products of voyages are returnable for sale at a profit. *In the foreground:* a ship's company of about thirty-five men brought aboard under individual contracts giving each a percentage of the profits (lay) according to his skill with men or artifacts. *The hiearchy*, in descending order of authority: absentee owners; captain, three mates, three harpooners, boat crews, blacksmith, cooper, cook, cabin boy. *Politics:* manhandling.

OBJECT OF VOYAGE: in three or four years' time to sight, chase, kill, and process into oil as many whales as possible, returning to port safely with a profitable cargo.

These are the given elements of whaling as a major industry in nineteenth-century America. They may be thought of as simply existing in nature and experience; we have been thinking of them independent of communication, though they are necessarily written down here. In art, however, communication is the heart of the matter; and the subject of whaling, it chances, offers good historical instances of some planes on which the communication problem may be conceived.

Looking back into nineteenth-century Anglo-American history, we find at least four different levels of communication on whaling. The first was that of the typical whaling logbook. A whaleman's log was a record kept for the owners by the mates or captain; it consisted of daily entries giving the ship's position, weather, landfalls, ships sighted or hailed, whales taken and their size (expressed in barrels of oil), crew desertions, injuries, deaths, etc. What any of this felt like or meant, except in terms of navigation and trade, was purposely excluded. The whaler's log was meant to be an abstraction of group experience in terms of pragmatic ends.

A second level was that of the standard histories. The aim here was the compilation of reliable data on the natural history of the whale (as part of the zoölogical record) or on the happenings in the fishery (as a contribution to economic history). Classic examples of the histories that had wide circulation in the second quarter of the nineteenth century include Thomas Beale's *Natural History of the Sperm Whale* (1835, 1839), Frederick Bennett's *A Whaling Voyage Round the Globe, from the Year 1833 to 1836* (1840), and William Scoresby's *An Account of the Arctic Regions with a History and Description of the Northern Whale Fishery* (1820). Empirical knowledge set the aims and limits for such books as these, too; their meaning and function were conditioned by the rise of the life sciences and of inductive historiography.

A third level of communication was the simple transcription of generalized personal experience. Americans who had never been whaling were interested to know something of the representative experiences of the seventeen thousand men engaged in the American fisheries in the 1840's. So came the reports of scenes and adventures, of duties and dangers, in books like J. Ross Browne's *Etchings of a Whaling Cruise* (1846) and the Reverend Henry Cheever's *The Whale and His Captors; or the Whaleman's Adventures and the Whale's Biography* . . . (1849). Such books were records of outward experience to whose general validity any ex-whaleman could testify. They were the journalism of the whaling industry, written by the Lowell Thomases and John Gunthers of the day (or perhaps one should say *Jonah* Gunthers, as no doubt he would have called his book *Inside the Whale*).

A generous distance beyond these logbooks, histories, and personal narratives lies the problem of fiction. When Melville was composing *Moby-Dick* in 1850 and 1851 he did not hesitate to make quite shameless use of all the books just named, as well as others, in the preparation of his own. Reading for facts and events, for recall and extension, he took on an enormous cargo of whaling matter. But facts are not fiction. In *Moby-Dick* the inert matter of whaling has been subjected to the purposes of art through a dynamic and a structure.

II

By the term "dynamic" I mean the action of forces on bodies at rest. The whaling matter in *Moby-Dick* is in no sense at rest, excepting as here or there occurs a failure in effect. For the most part the stuff and data of whaling are complexly subject to the action of a force which can be defined and illustrated. So too is the whole narrative base of the book, which is something far more than a record of what anyone aboard the *Pequod* would agree had happened. There is a dynamic operating on both matter and narrative which distinguishes *Moby-Dick* from logs, journals, and histories.

One of two forces, or their combination, is commonly assumed to provide the dynamic of *Moby-Dick*. The first, of course, is Captain Ahab, the dark protagonist, the maimed king of the quarter-deck whose monomania flows out through the ship until it drowns his men—mind and (finally) body. That he is the dominant "character" and the source of "action" seems obvious. The reader's image of him is a lasting one. Is Ahab the dynamic?

The alternative force, it is commonly assumed, is Moby Dick himself, that particular white "spouting fish with a horizontal tail" about whom legend and murmured lore have woven enchantments, so that he looms a massive phantom in the restless dreams of the *Pequod's* captain and crew. His name gives the novel its title. He is prime antagonist of the tale. Is Moby Dick the dynamic?

Both these interpretations have their uses, especially when taken together in a subject-predicate relation. But there is a third point of view from which neither Ahab nor the White Whale is the central dynamic, and I find it both compelling and rewarding, once recognized. This story, this fiction, is not so much about Ahab or the White Whale as it is about Ishmael, and I propose that it is he who is the real center of meaning and the defining force of the novel.

The point becomes clearer when one realizes that in *Moby-Dick* there are two Ishmaels, not one. The first Ishmael is the enfolding sensibility of the novel, the hand that writes the tale, the imagination through which all matters of the book pass. He is the narrator. But who then is the other Ishmael? The second Ishmael is not the narrator, not the informing presence, but is the young man of whom, among others, narrator Ishmael tells us in his story. He is simply one of the characters in the novel, though to be sure a major one whose significance is possibly next to Ahab's. This is forecastle Ishmael or the younger Ishmael of "some years ago." There is no question here of dual personality or *alter ego*, such as really exists, for instance, in Poe's "William Wilson" or Conrad's "The Secret Sharer." Narrator Ishmael is merely young Ishmael grown older. He is the man who has already experienced all that we watch forecastle Ishmael going through as the story is told.

The distinction can be rendered visual by imagining, for a moment, a film version of the novel. As the screen lights up and the music drops to an obbligato we look on the face of narrator Ishmael (a most marvelous face, I should judge), and the magic intonation begins:

> Call me Ishmael. Some years ago—never mind how long precisely—having little or no money in my purse, and nothing particular to interest me on shore, I thought I would sail about a little and see the watery part of the world. It is a way I have of driving off the spleen, and regulating the circulation. Whenever I find myself . . .

And as the cadenced voice goes on, the face of the Ishmael who has a tale to tell fades out, the music takes up a brisk piping air, and whom should we see tripping along the cobbled streets of New Bedford, carpetbag in hand, but forecastle Ishmael. It is a cold winter's night, and this lonely young man is in search of lodgings. For very soon now he plans to go a-whaling.

Meanwhile we hear the voice, always the magic voice, not of the boy we watch with our eyes, but of one who long since went aboard the *Pequod*, was buried in the sea and resurrected from it. This voice recounts the coming adventures of young Ishmael as a story already fully experienced. Experienced, but not fully understood; for as he explicitly says: "It was the whiteness of the whale that above all things appalled me. But how can I hope to explain myself here; and yet, in some dim, random way, explain myself I must, else all these chapters might be naught." So we are reminded by shifts of tense from time to time that while forecastle Ishmael is busy hunting whales narrator Ishmael is sifting memory and imagination in search of the many meanings of the dark adventure he has experienced. So deeply are we under the spell of the narrator's voice that when at last the final incantation begins—"'And I only am escaped alone to tell thee'. . . . The drama's done. . . . "—then at last, as forecastle Ishmael floats out of the *Pequod's* vortex, saved, we look again on the face of Ishmael narrator. And we realize that for many hours he has been sitting there and has never once moved, except at the lips; sitting in profound reverie, yet talking, trying to explain "in some dim, random way" what happened, for "explain myself I must."

The distinction between the function of the two Ishmaels is clear. Yet it would be a mistake to separate them too far in temperament. Certainly young Ishmael is no common sailor thoughtlessly enacting whatever the fates throw his way. He is a pondering young man of strong imagination and complex temperament; he will, as it were, become the narrator in due time. But right now he is aboard the *Pequod* doing his whaleman's work and trying to survive the spell of Ahab's power. The narrator, having survived, is at his desk trying to explain himself to himself and to whomever will listen. The primary use of the distinction is to bring the narrator forward as the essential sensibility in terms of which all characters and events of the fiction are conceived and evaluated. The story is his. What, then, are some of his primary commitments of mind and imagination as he shapes his story through one hundred and thirty-five chapters?

As a lover of laughter and hilarity, Ishmael delights in the incongruities. Of whales, for instance: whales spout steam because they think so much; they have no nose, but don't really need one—there are no violets in the sea; they are very healthy, and this is because they get so much exercise and are always out of doors, though rarely in the fresh air; and they like to breakfast on "sailor tarts, that is whaleboats full of mariners." Ishmael has too a deep belly laugh for the crudities and obscenities that mark the life of animal man, making much more than is proper of some talk about gentlemen harpooning ladies, relishing a Rabelaisian remark about "head winds" versus "winds from astern," and penning a memorable canonization of a rarely discussed part of the anatomy in "The Cassock." But as a purveyor of the "genial, desperado philosophy," his most characteristic humor is that of the hyena laugh: he begins his tale with a mock confession of suicidal impulses; he sends young Ishmael running to his bunk after his first encounter with a whale to make out his will; he reports that some sailors are so neat that they wouldn't think of drowning "without first washing their faces"; and he delights in Queequeg's solemn decision, when he seems mortally ill, whereby the good savage suddenly "recalled a little duty ashore, which he was leaving undone; and therefore . . . changed his mind about dying." Beneath Ishmael's mask of hypochondria is the healthy grimace of a man who stands braced to accept "the universal thump" and to call out: "Who ain't a slave?" To Ishmael "a good laugh is a mighty good thing, and rather too scarce a good thing; the more's the pity."

As narrator Ishmael betrays a passion for all faraway places and things, "Patagonian sights and sounds," imagined cities, fabled heroes, the sepulchers of kings. His rich imagination is stirred by all that is secret, mysterious, and undecipherable in the great riddles of mankind. He both cherishes and mocks the great systems of the philosophers, the operations of "chance, free will, and necessity," the great religions and heresies of the past. His fascination with ancient lore and wisdom runs from Adam to Zoroaster; to help tell his tale he marshals the great mythic figures of past centuries and all black-letter commentaries thereon.

His temperament is complex. If one of its facets, that of the "Sub-Sub-Librarian," has an antiquarian glint, another glows with the love of action. Each cry from the masthead alerts him from dreamy speculations to the zest of the hunt. Every lowering away starts his blood pounding. He is a superb narrator of the frenzied strivings of the boat crew as they press in for the kill, chanting their terror and competence as they enter "the charmed, churned circle" of eternity. When the death-deed is done, when the whirl slowly widens, he takes up the song of dismemberment. For the weapons of the chase, the red tools of slaughter, the facts of procedure, he has an insatiable curiosity. Cutting in, trying out, stowing down—the whole butcher-slab routine of processing the dead whale he endows with ritual certainty, transforming dirty jobs into acts of ceremonial dignity. Ishmael's voice translates the laughter and wild deeds of the bloody crew into the ordered rites of primitive tribal priests.

Narrator Ishmael has an instinct for the morally and psychologically intricate. He presses close in after the intertwinings of good and evil, tracks down the baffling crisscross of events and ideas, ponders their ambiguities and inversions. He is keen for a paradox and quick to see polarities—so keen in fact that the whole experience seems a double vision of what is at once noble and vile, of all that is lovely and appalling. This two-fold sensitivity marks his probings into the life-images of those he has known—whether in his grand-scale exposition of the "ungodly, god-like man, Captain Ahab" or in the compassionate recollection of little Pip, for a time lost overboard in the "heartless immensity" of the sea, and gone divinely mad from it. Whether noting that Queequeg's tomahawk-pipe "both brained his foes and soothed his soul" or contemplating "the interlinked terrors and wonders of God," he turns the coin both ways. He makes it a crisis of the first order that young Ishmael, both a brooder and a good companion, was drawn with the rest of the crew by the dark magnetic pull of the captain's monomania, wavering between allegiance to that uncommon king—Ahab—and to "the kingly commons"—the crew. Only the traumatic revulsion on the night of "The Try-Works" saved young Ishmael—"a strange (and ever since inexplicable) thing" which the narrator now explains symbolically: "Give not thyself up, then, to fire, lest it invert thee, deaden thee; as for the time it did me."

Above all one notes the narrator's inexhaustible sense of wonder. Wonder at the wide Pacific world, with its eternal undulations; wonder at the creatures of the deep; wonder at man—dreamer, doer, doubter. To him in retrospect the whale has become a mighty analogue of the world, of man, of God. He is in awe before the whale: its massive bulk, tiny eyes, great mouth, white teeth; its narrow throat and cavernous belly; the spout; the hump; the massed buttress of its domed head; the incomparable power and magic of its fanning, delicate tail. It is wonder that lies at the center of Ishmael's scale of articulation, and the gamut runs out either way toward fear and worship.

Enough of evocation. Every reader of *Moby-Dick* can and will want to enlarge and subtilize the multiple attributes of Ishmael. The prime experience for the reader is the narrator's unfolding sensibility. With it we have an energy center acting outward on the inert matter of nature and experience, releasing its possibilities for art. Whereas forecastle Ishmael drops in and out of the narrative with such abandon that at times a reader wonders if he has fallen overboard, the Ishmael voice is there every moment from the genesis of the fiction in "Call me Ishmael" to the final revelation of the "Epilogue" when "The drama's done." It is the narrator who creates the microcosm and sets the terms of discourse.

But this Ishmael is only Melville under another name, is he not? My suggestion is that we resist any one-to-one equation of Melville and Ishmael. Even the "Melville-Ishmael" phrase, which one encounters in critical discussions, though presumably granting a distinction between autobiography and fiction, would seem to be only a more insistent confusion of the point at stake unless the phrase is defined to mean either Melville or Ishmael, not both. For in the process of composition, even when the artist knowingly begins with his own experience, there are crucial interventions between the act that was experience and the re-enactment that is art—intrusions of time, of intention, and especially of form, to name only a few. Which parts of Ishmael's experience and sensibility coincide with Melville's own physical and psychological history and in just what ways is a question which is initially only tangential to discussion of *Moby-Dick* as a completed work of art.

III

But what of structure? That there is a dynamic excitation in *Moby-Dick* sympathetic readers have not denied. Is the effect of Ishmael's energy, then, simply to fling the matter in all directions, bombarding the reader with the accelerated particles of his own high-speed imagination? Is Ishmael's search for "some dim, random way" to explain himself not merely a characterization of the complexity of his task but also a confession of his inadequacy to find form? The questions are crucial, for although readers will presumably go on reading *Moby-Dick* whichever way they are answered, the critical reader will not be encouraged to keep coming back unless he can "see" and "feel" the tension of controlling forces.

To an extraordinary extent Ishmael's revelation of sensibility is controlled by rhetoric. Throughout the tale linguistic versatility and subtle rhythmic patterns exploit sound and sense with high calculation. Almost at random one chooses a sentence: "And ever, as the white moon shows her affrighted face from the steep gullies in the blackness overhead, aghast Jonah sees the rearing bowsprit pointing high upward, but soon beat downward again towards the tormented deep." It is a successful if traditional piece of incantation with its rising and falling movements manipulated to bring a striking force on the qualitative word "aghast." Its mood is typically Gothic-romantic (pictorial equivalents would be certain passages from Poe or the sea-paintings of Ryder), but structurally its allegiance is to the spacious prose of the seventeenth century. Although the passage is from Father Mapple's sermon, it is in no way unrepresentative; there are scores of sentences throughout *Moby-Dick* of equal or greater rhetorical interest.

Of the narrative's several levels of rhetoric the simplest is a relatively straightforward *expository* style characteristic of many passages scattered through the cetological accounts. But it is significant that such passages are rarely sustained, and serve chiefly as transitions between more complex levels of expression. Thus a series of expository sentences in the central paragraph of the chapter on "Cutting In" comes to this point: "This done, a broad, semicircular line is cut round the hole, the hook is inserted, and the main body of the crew striking up a wild chorus, now commence heaving in one dense crowd at the windlass." Whether it cannot or will not, Ishmael's sensibility does not endure for long so bare a diction: "When instantly, the entire ship careens over on her side; every bolt in her starts like the nail-heads of an old house in frosty weather; she trembles, quivers, and nods her frighted mastheads to the sky." The tension is maintained through a following sentence, strict exposition returns in the next, and the paragraph concludes with an emotionally and grammatically complex sentence which begins with exposition, rises to a powerful image of whale flesh hoisted aloft where "the prodigious blood-dripping mass sways to and fro as if let down from the sky," and concludes with a jest about getting one's ears boxed unless he dodges the swing of the bloody mess. Even in the rhetorically duller chapters of exposition it is a rare paragraph over which heat lightning does not flicker.

A second level of rhetoric, the *poetic*, is well exemplified in Ahab's soliloquy after the great scene on the quarter-deck. As Matthiessen has shown, such a passage can easily be set as blank verse:

> I leave a white and turbid wake;
> Pale waters, paler cheeks, where'er I sail.
> The envious billows sidelong swell to whelm
> My track; let them; but first I pass.

Because the rhythms here play over an abstract metrical pattern, as in poetry, they are evenly controlled—too evenly perhaps for prose, and the tone seems "literary."

Quite different in effect is a third level of rhetoric, the *idiomatic*. Like the poetic it occurs rather rarely in a pure form, but we have an instance in Stubb's rousing exordium to his crew:

> "Pull, pull, my fine hearts-alive; pull, my children; pull, my little ones . . . Why don't you break your backbones, my boys? . . . Easy, easy; don't be in a hurry—don't be in a hurry. Why don't you snap your oars, you rascals? Bite something, you dogs! . . ."

Here the beat of oars takes the place of the metronomic meter and allows more freedom. The passage is a kind of rowing song and hence is exceptional; yet it is related in tone and rhythm to numerous pieces of dialogue and sailor talk, especially to the consistently excellent idiom of both Stubb and young Ishmael.

One might venture a fourth level of rhetoric, the *composite*, simply to assure the inclusion of the narrator's prose at its very best. The composite is a magnificent blending of the expository, the poetic, the idiomatic, and whatever other elements tend to escape these crude categories:

> The Nantucketer, he alone resides and riots on the sea; he alone, in Bible language, goes down to it in ships; to and fro ploughing it as his own special plantation. *There* is his home; *there* lies his business, which a Noah's flood would not interrupt, though it overwhelmed all the millions in China. He lives on the sea, as prairie cocks in the prairie; he hides among the waves, he climbs them as chamois hunters climb the Alps. For years he knows not the land; so that when he comes to it at last, it smells like another world, more strangely than the moon would to an Earthsman. With the landless gull, that

at sunset folds her wings and is rocked to sleep between billows; so at nightfall, the Nantucketer, out of sight of land, furls his sails, and lays him to his rest, while under his very pillow rush herds of walruses and whales.

The passage is a great one, blending high and low with a relaxed assurance; after shaking free from the literary constrictions of the opening lines, it comes grandly home. And how does it relate to event and character? Ishmael's memory of the arrival at Nantucket, a mere incident in the movement of the plot, is to Ishmael now an imaginative experience of high order; and this we must know if we are to know about Ishmael. The whole chapter, "Nantucket," is a prose poem in the barbaric jocular vein, and it is as valuable a part of the documentation of Ishmael's experience as are the great "scenes." It is less extraneous to the meaning of the book than are many of the more average passages about Captain Ahab. The same could be said for other great passages of rhetoric, such as the marvelous hymn to spiritual democracy midway in "Knights and Squires." The first level of structure in *Moby-Dick* is the interplay of pressure and control through extraordinarily high rhetorical effects.

Beneath the rhetoric, penetrating through it, and in a sense rising above it, is a play of symbolic forms which keeps the rhetoric from dropping into exercise or running off in pyrotechnics. The persistent tendency in *Moby-Dick* is for facts, events, and images to become symbols. Ahab makes the most outright pronouncement of the doctrine of correspondences on which such a tendency depends, and to which almost all characters in the book are committed: "O Nature, and O soul of man! how far beyond all utterance are your linked analogies! not the smallest atom stirs or lives on matter, but has its cunning duplicate in mind." No less sensitive to symbolic values than Ahab is the young Ishmael in the forecastle. It is he who unfolds moral analogues from the mat-making, from the monkey-rope, from squeezing the case. He resembles Ahab in his talent for taking situations "strongly and metaphysically."

So on down the roster of the crew, where symbols and superstitions blend. Can there be any doubt that it is above all the enfolding imagination of the narrator which sets and defines the symbolic mode that pervades the entire book? From the richly emblematic theme of "meditation and water" in the opening chapter, to the final bursting of the "black bubble" of the sea which releases young Ishmael, the narrator sets the symbolic as the primary mode of self-examination and communication. He is predisposed to see events, however incidental, as "the sign and symbol" of something larger. To Ishmael "some certain significance lurks in all things, else all things are little worth, and the round world itself but an empty cipher. . . ."

Most commonly the symbols begin with a generative object: a waif-pole, a coin, a compass needle, a right-whale's head. The symbolic events begin with a chance incident: the dropping of his speaking trumpet by the Captain of the *Goney* (the nameless future), finding ambergris in a blasted whale (unexpected sweetness at the core of corruption), the chasing of the *Pequod* by Malay pirates (the pursuer pursued). Both give the tale solidity, for the objects and events are objects and events before they become meanings. But all the symbols do not rise out of tangible referents. We have to take into account also the narrator's love for "a furious trope" which often far exceeds the simple metaphorical function of comparison; the thing to which analogy is made—a pyramid, an elephant, a Leyden jar, a bird, a mythic figure—may itself enter the circle of symbolic values through recurrent reference. Thus the imagery brings scope to the limited range of symbols available on board the *Pequod*. Whereas the object-symbols in a sense carry the "plot," elucidating the experience of young Ishmael, Ahab, the mates and crew (as well as serving the narrator), the image-symbols chiefly reveal the psyche of the narrator through images of procreation and animality, mechanization and monomania, enchantment and entombment.

Though simpler objects, events, or images may connote primarily some one thing, as a shark means rapacious evil, most symbols which Ishmael develops in his narration express a complex of meanings which cannot easily be reduced to paraphrase and are not finally statable in other than their own terms. So it is with the *Pequod* herself and the ships she passes, with the root metaphors of earth, air, fire, and water which proliferate so subtly; and so it is with the most dynamic word-image-symbol of the tale: "white" (or "whiteness"). Their meanings are not single but multiple; not precisely equatable but ambiguous; not more often reinforcing than contradictory. The symbolism in *Moby-Dick* is not static but is in motion; it is in process of creation for both narrator and reader. Value works back and forth: being extracted from objects, it descends into the consciousness; spiraling up from the consciousness, it envelops objects.

Symbolism is so marked a characteristic of the narrator's microcosm that it is possible to phrase Ahab's tragedy not only in moral, social, and psychological terms, but in "structural" terms as well. Clearly Ahab accepts the symbolic as a source of cognition and of ethics. It was a symbolic vision that brought him on his quest, as no one senses with stronger discomfort than Starbuck, who stands alone in his sturdy, limited world of facts and settled faith. Yet the tragedy of Ahab is not his great gift for symbolic perception, but his abandonment of it. Ahab increasingly reduces all pluralities to the singular. His unilateral reading of events and things becomes a narrow translation in the imperative mood. Unlike young Ishmael, who is his equal in sensitivity but his inferior in will and authority, Ahab walls off his receptiveness to the complexities of experience, replacing "could be" or "might be" with "must." His destruction follows when he substitutes an allegorical fixation for the world of symbolic potentialities.

Ishmael's predilection for keying his narrative in the symbolic mode suggests another aspect of structure. *Moby-Dick* lies close to the world of dreams. We find the narrator recalling at length a remembered dream of his childhood. Stubb attempts a long dream-analysis to Flask after he has been kicked by Ahab. It is not strange, then, that young Ishmael's moment of greatest crisis, the night of the try-works when he is at the helm, should be of a traumatic order. More subtly, numerous incidents of the narrative are bathed in a dream aura: the trancelike idyll of young Ishmael at the masthead, the hallucinatory vision of the spirit spout, the incredible appearance on board of the devil himself accompanied by "five dusky phantoms," and many others. The narrator's whole effort to communicate the timeless, spaceless concept of "The Whiteness of the Whale" is an act of dream analysis. "Whether it was a reality or a dream, I never could entirely settle," says the narrator of his childhood dream; and so it was with much of what occurred aboard the *Pequod*. Ishmael's tale is to be listened to in terms of a tradition that runs from Revelation to *Finnegan's Wake*. Dream sense is an important mood in *Moby-Dick*; and dream form, to the extent there is such a verbal form, is an incipient structural device of the book. At regular intervals the narrator, in his intense effort to explain himself, resorts to a brief passage in which there is a flashing concentration of symbols that hold for a moment and then disappear. It is a night device for rendering daytime experience, and in *Moby-Dick* it happens again and again.

Any rigorous definition of structure must lead us on to consider the nature and relation of the constituent parts. Since the tale is divided into "parts" by the narrator himself (135 chapters, plus prefatory materials and "Epilogue"), one cannot escape considering the extent to which individual chapters themselves are structural units. We shall have to pass over such chapters, probably the largest group, as are devoted to the movement of narrative or to character analysis; the form here falls in a general way within the customary patterns of novelistic structure. Two chapter forms, however, are sufficiently non-novelistic to invite comment, the first of these being the dramatic. The term "dramatic" is here used in a technical, not qualitative sense, and refers to such devices of the playwright's script as italicized stage directions, set speeches with the speaker named in capitals, straight soliloquies, and dialogue without commentary. More than a tenth of the chapters are in this sense dramatic, some ten having strictly dramatic form without narrative intrusion, and another half-dozen or so using some script devices along with the narrative. The most successful of the strict-form group is certainly "Midnight, Forecastle," a ballet-like scene which superbly objectifies the crew in drunken exaltation over the quest. But the two greatest are in the second group. "The Quarter-Deck," Ishmael's curtain-raising treatment of the quest theme, is a triumph of unified structure, conceived with extreme firmness and precision of detail. The powerful dramatic structure of the chapter—prologue, antiphonal choral address, formal individual debate, and group ceremonial—is a superb invention on free-traditional lines, unhampered by stage techniques yet profiting from them. The other great dramatic scene, a counterpart to "The Quarter-Deck" both thematically and structurally, is the massive Ahab-and-his-crew scene late in the book, "The Candles." The chapter is not so firmly conceived as its forerunner; and this, rather than its subject matter, is what brings it dangerously close to seeming overwrought and a bit out of hand. The key to the structure here lies in the narrator's word "tableau," a dramatic device of considerable currency in nineteenth-century America. As the primary symbols of fire and whiteness melt hotly into each other for the first time, we see a series of memorable tableaux lit by storm lightning and corposant flames between "intervals of profound darkness." The piece is a series of blinding kaleidoscopic flashes which reveal the alarmed mates, the primitives in their full demonic strength, Ahab in a fury of ritual power. The "enchanted" crew, which near this same quarter-deck had made its jubilant pledge, now hangs from the rigging "like a knot of numbed wasps"; and when Ahab brandishes his burning harpoon among them (an unstated completion of the image), "the mariners did run from him in a terror of dismay." The two chapters, "The Quarter-Deck" and "The Candles," are twin centers of gravity in ordering the structure of the Ahab theme. The two fields of force are possibility and necessity, and Ahab's shift is from initial ecstasy to final frenetic compulsiveness.

A second unusual element of chapter structure in *Moby-Dick* grows out of the sermon form. Most famously there is Father Mapple's sermon (chapter ix), a piece of sustained eloquence in the idiomatic-composite style. From his *text* in Jonah the old sailor-preacher moves at once to two *doctrines* (the Christian pattern of sin and repentance, and the hardness of obeying God); enters a highly imaginative narrative *explication* of the Biblical story; comes next to *applications* and *uses* (that the congregation shall take Jonah as "a model for repentance" and the preacher shall "preach the Truth to the face of Falsehood"); and concludes with an *exhortation* (the very subtly constructed incantation on the double-themed coda of Woe and Delight). Somewhat buried away in another chapter, "Stubb's Supper," is the shorter sermon in which Fleece, the Negro cook, one night preaches to the sharks in a seriocomic vein. As he peers over the *Pequod's* side with his lantern at the murderous feasting down below, Fleece addresses his "congregation" first as "Fellow-critters," then as "Belubed fellow-critters," and finally as "Cussed fellow-critters," the final imprecation sharpening Fleece's ominous doctrine that "all angel is not'ing more dan de shark well goberned." The structural pattern, especially in its repetitive address, is clearly derived from the folk tradition of the Negro sermon.

These are not the only two "sermons" in *Moby-Dick*. Although the free essay tradition from Montaigne to Hazlitt provides a more comfortable prototype for the more loosely ordered speculative chapters, most of these have a prophetic or protestant vein that pulls them over toward the sermon tradition. Again and again throughout the narrative a chapter comes to its climax in a final paragraph of moral exhortation (Mapple) or imprecation

(Fleece). Nor should we forget that young Ishmael's crisp moral analogues (above) start with symbols and end as parables. It is especially interesting to note that some of the cetological chapters can be analyzed in terms of sermon structure. In "The Line," for instance, the narrator takes hemp for his text, makes a full-scale explication of its history and uses, gives admonitions on its subtleties and dangers, and concludes with a full-scale application of the doctrine that "All men live enveloped in whale-lines." In "The Blanket" the text is whale blubber; and preacher Ishmael comes inevitably to the doctrine of internal temperatures, raising it to a high exhortation (Mapple) and then cutting it down with three lines of wry counterstatement (Fleece). Nor is it hard to identify text, inferences, uses, doctrine, and admonition in the brief "sermon" the narrator preaches over the peeled white body of a whale in "The Funeral." The technique lies midway between the Protestant sermon of the nineteenth century and the tradition of the digressive-antiquarian essay.

Coming to the problem of the mutual relation of the chapters in *Moby-Dick*, we can observe several tendencies, of which *chapter sequences* is one. The simplest sequence is likely to be one of narrative progression, as in "The Chapel," "The Pulpit," and "The Sermon," or in the powerful concluding sequence on "The Chase": "First Day," "Second Day," "Third Day." Or we get chapter sequences of theme, as in the three chapters on whale paintings. Or again sequences of structural similarity: the five chapters beginning with "The Quarter-Deck" all use dramatic techniques, as do the four beginning with "The Candles." More typical than strict sequences, however, are the *chapter clusters* in which two or three (or five or six) chapters are linked by themes or root images, other chapters intervening. For example, chapters xlii, li, lii, and lix make a loose cluster that begins with "The Whiteness of the Whale" and carries through the white apparitions in "The Spirit-Spout," "The Albatross," and "Squid." Similarly, later in the narrative, fire imagery becomes dominant, breaking out in young Ishmael's fire-dream ("The Try-Works") and running intermittently until the holocaust of Ahab's defiance ("The Candles"). In addition to sequences and clusters there are also widely separated *balancing chapters*, either of opposites ("Loomings" and the "Epilogue") or of similars ("The Quarter-Deck" and "The Candles"); here the problem is infinitely complex, for the balancing units shift according to the standard of comparison: theme, event, root image, structure, and so forth. Two points can be made in tentative summary of this complex aspect of structure: there are definable relations between any given chapter and some other chapter or chapters; and these relations tend to be multiple and shifting. Like the symbols, the chapters are "in process."

Looking beyond chapter units and their interrelations we find the most obvious larger structural effect in the narrative line of the book, such as it is, which records the preparations for going on board, leaving port, encountering adventures, and meeting some final consequence. Along this simple linear form of The Voyage occur two sets of events: the whale killings and the ship meetings. The question is whether either of these event groups performs more for the structure than the simple functions of marking the passage of time and adding "interest." Of the whale pursuits and killings some ten or more are sufficiently rendered to become events. They begin when the narrative is already two-fifths told and end with the final lowerings for Moby Dick during which the killers are themselves killed. The first lowering and the three-day chase are thus events which enclose all the whaling action of the novel as well as what Howard Vincent has aptly called "the cetological center," and the main point I wish to make about the pursuits is that in each case a killing provokes either a chapter sequence or a chapter cluster of cetological lore growing out of the circumstances of the particular killing. The killings in themselves, except for the first and last, are not so much narrative events as structural occasions for ordering the whaling essays and sermons. Their minimized role is proof enough, if any were needed, that Ishmael's tale is not primarily a series of whaling adventures.

Much more significant structurally than the killings is the important series of ship meetings also occurring along the time line of the voyage. The nine gams of the *Pequod* are important in several ways, of which three might concern us here. First of all, even a glance at the numbers of the chapters in which the gams occur shows a clear pattern: the first two are close together; the central group are well spaced (separated by an average of twelve chapters, with not very wide divergences); the last two are close together. The spatial pattern looks like this:

$$1 \; 2 \qquad 3 \qquad 4 \qquad 5 \qquad 6 \qquad 7 \qquad 8 \; 9$$

This somewhat mechanical pattern is a stiffening element in the structure of the book, a kind of counterforce, structurally, to the organic relationship of parts we have been observing. The gams are bones to the book's flesh. Secondly, their sequence is meaningful in terms of the Ahab theme. The line of Ahab's response from ship to ship is a psychograph of his monomania showing the rising curve of his passion and diagraming his moral hostility. The points on the graph mark off the furiously increasing distance between Ahab and the world of men. And thirdly, their individual meanings are a part of the Ishmael theme. Each ship is a scroll which the narrator unrolls and reads, like a prophet called to a king's court. They provide what Auden calls "types of the relation of human individuals and societies in the tragic mystery of existence," though his superbly incisive reading of each type is perhaps too narrowly theological and does scant justice to either the tone of the episodes (are not the *Jungfrau* and *Rosebud* accounts hilariously comic and ironic?) or their rich amplitude of meanings. The ships the *Pequod* passes may be taken as a group of metaphysical parables, a series of biblical analogues, a masque of the situations confronting man, a pageant of the humors within men, a parade of the nations, and so forth, *as well as* concrete and symbolic ways of thinking about the White Whale. Any single systematic treatment of all of the ships does violence to some of them. The gams are symbolic, not allegorical.

It is time in fact to admit that our explorations of structure suggest elaborate interrelations of the parts but do not lead to an overreaching formal pattern. For the reader predisposed to feel that "form" means "classical form," with a controlling geometric structure, *Moby-Dick* is and will remain an aesthetically unsatisfying experience. One needs only to compare it with *The Scarlet Letter*, published a year and a half earlier, to see how nonclassical it is. If this is the sort of standard by which one tries to judge *Moby-Dick*, he will end by dismissing it as one of the more notable miscarriages in the history of literary lying-in. But surely there is no one right form the novel must take—not the one used by Hawthorne, not even the form, one might wryly add, perfected by James. For Hawthorne the structural frame of reference was neoclassical; for Melville it was romantic.

To go from *The Scarlet Letter* to *Moby-Dick* is to move from the Newtonian world-as-machine to the Darwinian world-as-organism. In the older cosmology the key concepts had been law, balance, harmony, reason; in the newer, they became origin, process, development, growth. Concurrently biological images arose to take the place of the older mechanical analogies: growing plants and life forms now symbolized cosmic ultimates better than a watch or the slow-turning rods and gears of an eighteenth-century orrery. It is enough for our purposes to note that the man who gave scientific validity to the organic world view concluded the key chapter of his great book, *The Origin of Species*, with an extended image of "the great Tree of Life . . . with its ever branching and beautiful ramifications." It was a crucial simile that exploited not the tree but the tree's growth.

Of course the poets had been there first. Coleridge had long since made his famous definition of organic form in literature. The roots of his theory had traveled under the sea to the continent of Emerson, Thoreau, and Whitman (as Matthiessen brilliantly showed in *American Renaissance*), where they burst into native forms in the minds of a few men haunted simultaneously by the implications of the American wilderness, by the quest for spiritual reality, and by the search for new literary forms. *Moby-Dick* is like Emerson's *Essays* and *Poems*, like *Walden*, like *Leaves of Grass*, in its structural principles. In the literature of the nineteenth century it is the single most ambitious projection of the concept of organic form.

Recharting our explorations we can see now where we have been. The matter of *Moby-Dick* is the organic land-sea world where life forms move mysteriously among the elements. The dynamic of the book is the organic mind-world of Ishmael whose sensibility rhythmically agitates the flux of experience. The controlling structure of the book is an organic complex of rhetoric, symbols, and interfused units. There is no over-reaching formal pattern of literary art on which *Moby-Dick* is a variation. To compare it with the structure of the Elizabethan play, or the classical epic, or the modern novel is to set up useful analogies rather than congruous models. It is a free form that fuses as best it can innumerable devices from many literary traditions, including contemporary modes of native expression. In the last analysis, if one must have a prototype, here is an intensively heightened rendition of the logs, journals, and histories of the Anglo-American whaling tradition.

Organic form is not a particular form but a structural principle. In *Moby-Dick* this principle would seem to be a peculiar quality of making and unmaking itself as it goes. The method of the book is unceasingly genetic, conveying the effect of a restless series of morphic-amorphic movements. Ishmael's narrative is always in process and in all but the most literal sense remains unfinished. For the good reader the experience of *Moby-Dick* is a participation in the act of creation. Find a key word or metaphor, start to pick it as you would a wild flower, and you will find yourself ripping up the whole forest floor. Rhetoric grows into symbolism and symbolism into structure; then all falls away and begins over again.

Ishmael's way of explaining himself in the long run is not either "dim" or "random." He was committed to the organic method with all its possibilities and risks. As he says at the beginning of one chapter: "There are some enterprises in which a careful disorderliness is the true method." And at the beginning of another chapter we have an explicit image whose full force as a comment on method needs to be recognized: "Out of the trunk, the branches grow; out of them, the twigs. So, in productive subjects, grow the chapters."

IV

From our considerations of *Moby-Dick* a few simple, debatable propositions emerge. More accurately they are, I suppose, the assumptions which underlie what has been said. The first is that *nature*, ultimately, is chaos. Whatever order it has in the mind of God, its meaning is apparent to man only through some more or less systematic ordering of what seems to be there. The second is that *experience* is already one remove from nature; filtered through a sensibility, nature begins to show patterns qualified by the temperament and the culture of the observer. And the third is that *art*, which is twice removed from nature, is a major means for transforming experience into patterns that are meaningful and communicable. As in part it is the function of religion to shape experience for belief and conduct, and of science to organize nature for use and prediction, so it is the business of art to form man's experience of nature for communication. In art the way a thing is said is what is being said. To the maker the form is completion; to the receiver it is possibility. Art is an enabling act for mankind without which life may easily become meager, isolated; with it the mind can be cleared and the spirit refreshed; through it memory and desire are rewoven.

The great thing about fiction, which is simply the telling of a story in written words, is that it is fiction. That it is "made up" is not its weakness but, as with all art, its greatest strength. In the successful work of fiction certain kinds of possibilities, attitudes, people, acts, situations, necessities, for the first and last time exist. They exist only through form. So it is with *Moby-Dick*—Ishmael's vast symbolic prose-poem in a free organic form. From *olim erat* to *finis* is all the space and time there is.

Ahab's Greatness: Prometheus as Narcissus

Thomas Woodson

In the popular mind *Moby-Dick* has always been Ahab's book. A spectacular, melodramatic old sea captain, a literary cousin of Long John Silver and Captain Hook, embarks on an excitingly fateful voyage of revenge. Of course he is thwarted, but after all he is not likeable enough to succeed. The reader's vicarious daring is satisfied and his awe of the white whale lingers on.

Literary critics, more concerned with the intellectual issues raised by Melville's art than with the adventurous plot, have turned their attention from Ahab to Ishmael, the author's narrator and spokesman. Ahab, who at first seemed an arch-romantic self-projection, we now tend to see as a case-study of Romantic "madness," an American counterpart of the Victorian monstrous egotist typified by Emily Bronte's Heathcliff. He is also seen as an incarnation of the Romantic "dark" hero, rebellious towards the bourgeois world, alienated from the comforts of traditional faith, pitting himself against all obstacles to reach and rifle the secrets of the Infinite and Absolute. He is most frequently compared to Milton's Satan, Byron's Manfred and Goethe's Faust. Such a figure calls forth ethical judgments, most often unfavorable ones. The archaic Elizabethan rhetoric Melville has put in Ahab's mouth brings to mind such morally excessive hero-villains as Macbeth and Richard III, Tamerlane and Faustus. Various writers have accused Ahab of embodying the dark Puritan hatred of nature, the nineteenth-century capitalist greed for forceful acquisition, and even the insane persuasiveness of a twentieth-century dictator.

All these characterizations are certainly just in some measure; Ishmael's more prudential and speculative approach to the voyage allows us to accept the horrible truths of the story with a greater hopefulness and self-respect than if Ahab completely dominated our perception of it. But we still have to come to terms with Ahab. To dismiss him as a madman, a Satan or a Byronic egotist is too simple. For instance, much has been made of his Biblical name; "Ahab of old," says Peleg to Ishmael, "was a crowned King!" and Ishmael answers: "And a very vile one. When that wicked King was slain, the dogs, did they not lick his blood?"(77)[1] But in many ways our Ahab is no more comparable with the Old Testament schemer and murderer than is Ishmael

Reprinted from *ELH* 33, no. 3 (September 1966), 351–69. Reprinted by permission of the Johns Hopkins University Press.

with his primal namesake, whose hand was to be against every man, and who signaled his bitterness by mocking God. Ishmael insists that Ahab is a great man, a tragic hero; it seems appropriate here to reexamine his character with sympathy towards this judgment, leaving the ethical atmosphere in the background, and concentrating on what actually is said about him in Ishmael's narrative and in his own words.

The most fruitful starting-point for study of Ahab's personality is not, perhaps, Captain Peleg's description of him to Ishmael, but Ishmael's later meditation on the hierarchy of rank on a whaler (Chapter 33, "The Specksynder"). Ishmael observes that Ahab "sometimes masked himself" behind the "forms and usages" of rank, the "external arts" of practical power, but that these are not the true index of his greatness. Ishmael speaks here in his role as "tragic dramatist" rather than as plebeian observer of his dictatorial captain. As a dramatist he struggles to put into words what haunts him still about Ahab: "But Ahab, my Captain, still moves before me in all his Nantucket grimness and shagginess; . . . I must not conceal that I have only to do with a poor old whale-hunter like him; and, therefore, all outward majestical trappings and housings are denied me. Oh, Ahab! what shall be grand in thee, it must needs be plucked at from the skies, and dived for in the deep, and featured in the unbodied air!" (p. 130.) It would be possible to take the last phrases of this statement ironically, were it not for Ishmael's obvious preference for democratic "shagginess" over "majestical trapppings." Ahab's true greatness will not be contained or exposed in forms, trappings, housings. It is harder to find, but (Ishmael's urgent tone insists) it must be found.

The angle of approach to Ahab I am proposing depends upon the ramifications of these phrases: "plucked at from the skies, and dived for in the deep, and featured in the unbodied air!" What is really vital is Ahab's relationship to the great forces of nature; Ishmael can only know Ahab through the "bold and nervous lofty language" which, he has already told us, Ahab himself learned by "receiving all nature's sweet or savage impressions fresh from her own virgin voluntary and confiding breast," thereby becoming "a mighty pageant creature, formed for noble tragedies" (Chapter 16, "The Ship," p. 71). Ahab was "formed" by the language of nature, but this is a different kind of "form" than that given by human culture. Paradoxically, nature's language seems not available to man, since Ishmael finds no "voluntary and confiding breast" from which to learn it, but only the empty immensities of sea and sky. He must "pluck" and "dive" for knowledge which he mistakenly presumes Ahab to possess already.

Above all, Ishmael must "feature" Ahab's greatness "in the unbodied air." He must create verbally a face for Ahab in the unsubstantial, phantasmal world of the air. Much later Ahab announces defiantly that he *does* in fact exist in the mode Ishmael here prescribes for him. "In the midst of the personified impersonal, a personality stands here" (Chapter 119, "The

Candles," p. 417). Man must affirm his own uniqueness in order to exist as man. This affirmation is of itself heroic and tragic, both for character and dramatist.

Thus Ishmael links himself to Ahab in an underlying way. Ahab's self-assertion, however excessive and immoral in social terms, is necessary to the imaginative logic of the novel. Ishmael's plucking and diving to feature him are verbal counterparts of Ahab's destructive quest for Moby-Dick. In this sense Melville, standing behind Ishmael directly and Ahab obliquely, has "written a wicked book."[2] And Ishmael's desperate search for words is really parallel to Ahab's "bold and nervous lofty language" which, as we soon learn, has *not* brought him definite knowledge of nature's secrets: the virgin teases and deludes; she "absolutely paints like the harlot, whose allurements cover nothing but the charnel-house within" (Chapter 42, "The Whiteness of the Whale," p. 170). Ahab, addressing the captured whale's head, senses the inadequacy of all human language to the problem he insists on solving: "O Nature, and O soul of man! how far beyond all utterance are your linked analogies! (Chapter 70, "The Sphinx," p. 264). Similarly, Ishmael, after an extended essay on the featureless face of the whale, gives up in despair: ". . . how may unlettered Ishmael hope to read the awful Chaldee of the Sperm Whale's brow? I but put that brow before you. Read it if you can." (Chapter 79, "The Prairie," p. 293).[3]

Ahab's most extended statement of his problem, it is universally recognized, comes in the "Quarterdeck" chapter. Insisting to Starbuck that he is intent on more than "vengeance on a dumb brute," Ahab reveals his belief that ". . . in each event . . . in the living act, the undoubted deed . . . there, some unknown but still reasoning thing puts forth the mouldings of its features from behind the unreasoning mask" (p. 144). He goes on to characterize Moby-Dick as "the unreasoning mask," the white wall which Nature has "shoved near" to him. Nature's intelligent creativity, then, is not the body of the whale but the essential "features" of itself which it seems to reveal in a mysterious way "from behind." If we can trust Melville's use of "features" here to correspond to "featured" in the passage about Ahab's greatness, both whale and whale-hunter possess a hidden and ultimately dynamic existence; Ahab in chasing Moby-Dick feels himself to be "thrusting through the wall," the "pasteboard mask" of mere external form. Ishmael in writing about Ahab, feels he must "pluck" and "dive" in sky and sea to understand the real Ahab behind the mask of "forms and usages."

Ahab talks of the "mouldings" of Nature's essential features. This curious word seems to mean the forming power, that which creates patterns and forms in matter. The word is typical of the stylistic idiosyncrasy of *Moby-Dick* Thornton Wilder has pointed to, Melville's coinage of plural gerunds.[4] I would guess that Melville's choice of "mouldings" in this context stems from his reading of *King Lear,* and particularly from Lear's magnificent apostrophe to the elements during the storm on the heath in Act III, scene 2:

> You sulph'rous and thought-executing fires,
> Vaunt-couriers of oak-cleaving thunderbolts,
> Singe my white head! And thou, all-shaking thunder,
> Strike flat the thick rotundity o' the world!
> Crack Nature's moulds, all germens spill at once
> That makes ingrateful man!

While Lear's speech is tonally closer to Ahab's address to the fire in the "Candles" chapter much later, Ahab here implies a similar "thought-executing" violence: "the living act, the undoubted deed" he soon explains as "the unrecking and unworshipping things that live; and seek, and give no reasons for the torrid life they feel!"

According to this evidence Ahab, no less than Ishmael, is a Romantic naturalist believer in an interflow of spiritual and mental energy between the human mind as perceiver and the phenomena of nature as the objects of perception. While nature may appear as an impenetrable mystery (epitomized by the "unbodied air"), unsubstantial and "impersonal," it is also the mask-like creation of "some unknown but still reasoning thing," which "moulds" and gives body and form to it. The "impersonal" is "personified," Ahab puts it in the "Candles" chapter. Hence Ahab's quest for Moby-Dick, in whom he has found that "all the subtle demonisms of life and thought . . . were visibly personified, and made practicably assailable" (Chapter 41, "Moby-Dick," p. 160). Ahab's "mad" purpose is to destroy that which he seeks. In this he responds to the power of nature as he understands it. To live, to create a substantial body of oneself, is to destroy the *other*: man finds behind nature a competing mind and creative force; in order to become himself, man must destroy this competing other. To repeat and complete a quotation from Ahab I gave earlier: "O Nature, and O soul of man! how far beyond all utterance are your linked analogies! not the smallest atom stirs or lives on matter, but has its cunning duplicate in mind" (p. 264). Although Ahab seems here only to endorse an orthodox Romantic faith in the interinanimation of mind and nature (for example, Emerson's "Me" and "Not-Me"), by avoiding the syntactic parallel of "matter" to "mind," by claiming that each atom "lives *on* matter," he announces his belief that to live (to "stir") is to destroy, to feed on that which is outside the self. Ishmael comes to understand this outlook in a much more general way when he speaks of the "universal cannibalism of the sea; all whose creatures prey upon each other, carrying on eternal war since the world began" (Chapter 58, "Brit," p. 235–36). But for Ahab the mind is a cannibal as well as the body. And perhaps the greatest of Melville's achievements in writing *Moby-Dick* is to make us see in Ahab the naked dramatic identity of creative and destructive impulses within the human soul.

The notion that nature can be treacherously destructive is certainly not Ahab's secret—all the characters, even Starbuck, earnestly subscribe to it—but only Ahab sees it as a challenge to the essence of his being. It would be possible to show how each of the other voyagers refuses to see what Ahab sees, but it seems best to let one extreme case illustrate Melville's thinking about the opposite alternative to the personality of Ahab: the carpenter, whose breadth of experience leads Ishmael to wonder if he possesses "some uncommon vivacity of intelligence. But not precisely so. For nothing was this man more remarkable, than for a certain impersonal stolidity as it were; impersonal, I say; for it so shaded off into the surrounding infinite of things, that it seemed one with the general stolidity discernible in the whole visible world; which while pauselessly active in uncounted modes, still eternally holds its peace, and ignores you, though you dig foundations for cathedrals. Yet was this half-horrible stolidity in him, involving, too, as it appeared, an all-ramifying heartlessness . . ." (Chapter 107, "The Carpenter," p. 388). The carpenter's stolidity is a kind of muteness, an inability to express himself (evidenced in the next chapter by his soliloquy, which says nothing). The carpenter is "the personified impersonal" in human form. Ahab addresses him half-mockingly as "manmaker" and "Prometheus," requesting him to construct a heartless mechanical man with "about a quarter acre of fine brains": a creation which, because of its inhumanity, could withstand the malicious power of nature.[5] Similarly, as the chase nears its end Ahab sees the entire crew, and particularly his direct subordinates Starbuck and Stubb as "mechanical" men, mere metallic instruments of his own will encountering the opposing will embodied in Moby-Dick.[6]

One phrase in Melville's description of the carpenter is particularly interesting: "the surrounding infinite of things." Whereas Ahab's greatness was to be "featured in the unbodied air," the carpenter's "impersonality" shades off into a world of bodies without sensible life. While Ahab is to become more human, more tragic, as he emerges from the infinite dead world of matter, the carpenter fades out of view back into this world, into the meaninglessness Ishmael contemplated in "The Whiteness of the Whale" as the "colorless, all-color of atheism before which we shrink" (Chapter 42, p. 169).

In making this distinction between Ahab and the carpenter I have assumed an opposition in meaning between "personality" and "things."[7] It would follow from the whole pressure of Western intellectual history—from Descartes and Locke to Hume and Kant to Coleridge and Emerson—that Melville would accept the assumption of a cleavage between mind and matter. The "Descartian vortices" Ishmael discovers in the sea from "The Masthead," as well as Ahab's comments on "linked analogies," support this conclusion. But a close reading of *Moby-Dick* brings out interesting information about Melville's use of the word "thing," and particularly about that word when it is put in Ahab's mouth. For example, to go back to the "Quarterdeck" passage, he there describes his cosmic opponent as "some unknown but still reasoning thing," repeating the word a few sentences later: "that inscrutable thing is chiefly what I hate; and be the white whale agent, or be the white whale principal, I will wreak that hate upon him" (p. 144). In terms of my distinction, a "reasoning thing" is a contradiction. But again, a bit later in the same speech he speaks of the pagan sailors as "unrecking and unworshipping things, that live; and seek, and give no reasons for the life they feel" (p. 144). Once more, in the same chapter, Ahab overcomes the objecting minds of Starbuck, Stubb and Flask: "It seemed as though, by some nameless, interior volition, he would fain have shocked into them the same fiery emotion accumulated within the Leyden jar of his own magnetic life. The three mates quailed before his strong, sustained, and mystic aspect. . . . 'In vain!' cried Ahab; 'but, maybe, 'tis well. For did ye three but once take the full-forced shock, then mine own electric thing, *that* had perhaps expired from out me . . .'" (pp. 145–46). The last of these instances seems to obliterate any clear separation between Ahab ("I," "a personality") and his enemy world ("the unbodied air," "the surrounding infinite of things"). The word "thing" connotes a vagueness which defies my effort to catch and define it, unless Ahab himself contains the malicious, inscrutable force he opposes. The power within him is described as vaguely as the power of nature ("some nameless, interior volition"), and the imagery pictures his mind as a mechanical force, a magnet, an "electric thing" which shocks in a thoroughly physical manner.

Is Ahab a "thing?" Is he simply a source of physical energy, a spark of voltage opposing a similar electrical charge housed in Moby-Dick? If so, my previous defense of Ahab's humanity is invalid. The various metaphors and similes Melville uses in describing Ahab give abundant support to our seeing a consistently "mechanical" Moby-Dick. Early in the book he is compared to a cannonball, a pyramid, a hurricane, a railway train, a mortar, and a tornado. Later we see him as a javelin, a mechanical vice, a seam of iron, an anvil, a splintered helmet, a scythe, a piece of steel.[8] At a crucial point in the final chase of Moby-Dick he sees himself as "a braver thing—a nobler thing" than the wind (p. 461).

Nevertheless, Ahab's greatness consists in his selfhood, his humanity. He fascinates us as a character partially because his literary integrity, his identity as a personality, is so consistently in danger of destroying itself. Aware that he destroys the spiritual independence of Starbuck and Stubb, he further recognizes the inhumanly destructive "thing" within himself. He contains within himself the fierce, wild energy of nature. It is no sterile convention of epic style which leads Melville to compare Ahab to a giant tree, to a mountain, a river, a volcanic crater and, finally to the sea itself.[9] All these are substantial bodies which can "feature" the book's hero "in the unbodied air," though none of them can exhaust his meaning or reach to his essence.

Ishmael confessed to looking forward with dismay to his task of characterizing and explaining Ahab. After the crucial "Quarterdeck" scene he devotes several chapters to an analysis of Ahab's purpose and of what can be said about his opponent, the White Whale. This analysis concludes with "The Chart," a chapter which relates Ahab's private goals to those of the crew, and which ends by characterizing him as "a Prometheus." Since so many interpretations (including this one) of *Moby-Dick* rely so heavily on that mythological identification, it should be worthwhile to quote and examine the entire paragraph carefully:

> Often, when forced from his hammock by exhausting and intolerably vivid dreams of the night, which, resuming his own intense thoughts through the day, carried them on amid a clashing of phrensies, and whirled them round and round in his blazing brain, till the very throbbing of his life-spot became insufferable anguish; and when, as was sometimes the case, these spiritual throes in him heaved his being up from its base, and a chasm seemed opening in him, from which forked flames and lightnings shot up, and accursed fiends beckoned him to leap down among them; when this hell in himself yawned beneath him, a wild cry would be heard through the ship; and with glaring eyes Ahab would burst from his state room, as though escaping from a bed that was on fire. Yet these, perhaps, instead of being the unsuppressable symptoms of some latent weakness, or fright at his own resolve, were but the plainest tokens of its intensity. For, at such times, crazy Ahab, the scheming, unappeasedly steadfast hunter of the white whale; this Ahab that had gone to his hammock, was not the agent that so caused him to burst from it in horror again. The latter was the eternal, living principle or soul in him; and in sleep, being for the time dissociated from the characterizing mind, which at other times employed it for its outer vehicle or agent, it spontaneously sought escape from the scorching contiguity of the frantic thing, of which, for the time, it was no longer an integral. But as the mind does not exist unless leagued with the soul, therefore it must have been that, in Ahab's case, yielding up all his thoughts and fancies to his one supreme purpose; that purpose, by its own sheer inveteracy of will, forced itself against gods and devils into a kind of self-assumed, independent being of its own. Nay, could grimly live and burn, while the common vitality to which it was conjoined, fled horror-stricken from the unbidden and unfathered birth. Therefore, the tormented spirit that glared out of bodily eyes, when what seemed Ahab rushed from his room, was for the time but a vacated thing, a formless somnambulistic being, a ray of living light, to be sure, but without an object to color, and therefore a blankness in itself. God help thee, old man, thy thoughts have created a creature in thee; and he whose intense thinking thus makes him a Prometheus; a vulture feeds upon that heart for ever; that vulture the very creature he creates. (pp. 174–75)

This is a difficult passage to follow, primarily because of the clumsiness of the grammatical references and the abstractness of Melville's distinction between "characterizing mind" and "eternal living principle or soul."[10] Behind the passage seems to be a distinction between thinking and feeling, some such psychological insight as Hawthorne's famous (and sometimes confusing) separation of "head" and "heart." But this rhetorical overflow of qualifications blunts the clarity of the distinction; the repeated "which's," "this's," "these's" and "the latter" make the passage difficult reading; it is hard to tell which idea is subject of a given clause, and which is object. To make matters worse, the soul is first an "agent," then a "principle"; Ahab's "tormented spirit" (presumably the soul) glares from his "bodily eyes," but his body (or is it his soul?) is at the same moment "a vacated thing."

Even so, the general sense of the characterization is clear. Ahab's "one supreme purpose" (destroying Moby-Dick) attains "a kind of self-assured, independent being" which takes control of his "characterizing mind." This mind is a fire, imaged as the chasm of hell "from which forked flames and lightning shot up"; this mind can "grimly live and burn"—its life is its self-consuming burning, while the soul, "the eternal living principle," "the common vitality," escapes as the body of Ahab escapes from the confinement of the cabin and the bed "that was on fire."

The passage does not make clear whether the mind or the soul is the *real* Ahab. Is the soul "a vacated thing," and the mind a "frantic thing?" Has his mind driven his soul out of his being in a Faustian bargain for power and intellectual strength? Then the mind is "vacated" by the soul, and is a "blankness in itself" because it cannot "color" the moral life of conscience. As his thoughts become dreams, they are no longer controlled by his "characterizing mind," and flood over his reasoning, "charting" abilities; he becomes "a formless somnambulistic being," a subject parallel in meaning to the object Ishmael originally despaired of "featuring."

If my speculations here seem as tortured as Melville's prose, it is to contend that Ahab as Prometheus is not simply a devil who has lost what Captain Peleg called "his humanities." Ahab is a divided man, self-alienated and confused by the very uncertainty of his relation to his world. Just as Ahab here (or an aspect of him) is "a ray of living light, to be sure, but without an object to color," so the verbal process which gradually forms the book *Moby-Dick* is a ray of living light searching frantically to make language *form* something out of itself.

Ahab is Prometheus, not stealing fire from the gods, but suffering the agony of an internal vulture. In fact, Melville's version of the myth is peculiarly Romantic and modern in that all the action is internalized—the fire and the vulture both exist within the hero's mind. The vulture is Ahab's purpose, which destroys him; but the object of the quest, the humanizing fire, is synonymous with the vulture. It is the essence of Ahab's experience that man is frustrated by an inadequacy within himself; either he fails utterly to join himself to an external significance, to a "reasoning thing" which "features" itself, and his "ray of living light" becomes "a blankness in itself"; or life allows an easy, sliding, deceptive identification and fusing of mind and thing, as self becomes "thing," and the light becomes the fire and the vulture both, collapsing all life-giving distinctiveness in a suicidal cannibalism.

It is on these terms, it seems to me, that Ahab becomes one of the most interesting of Romantic intellectual heroes. Nineteenth-century man, so earnestly obsessed with extending his mental and physical control over all the vast deserts and oceans of the planet, confronts more starkly than his predecessors the *otherness* of nature, and part of him recoils in terror. At the same time he exuberantly revives his faith in irrational knowledge, in the mysterious correspondence of mind and matter; he absorbs nature into himself, coloring it with his own spirit: the result is solipsism. Ahab is peculiar in that he carries on both of these processes with full awareness of the dangers of both. He is a Prometheus whose fire consumes him; carrying out Ishmael's prophecy from the first chapter, he is also a Narcissus, "who because he could not grasp the tormenting, mild image he saw in the fountain, plunged into it and was drowned" (p. 14).

An important imaginative tendency in *Moby-Dick* is, then, the tormenting identification and fusion of Ahab with Moby-Dick. Out of his "tormented sleep" Ahab once imagines himself as successfully completing his purpose: "Oh Moby Dick, I clutch thy heart at last!" (Chapter 123, "The Musket," p. 423). To "clutch" the whale's heart is like (too much like) "grasping" the self-image in the fountain, just as Melville must have felt it to be agonizingly like "plucking" Ahab's greatness from the skies. Life, Ishmael tells us, is an "ungraspable phantom"; Ahab knows this; he admires the carpenter's vice, pinching his hand in it, because "I like a good grip; I like to feel something in this slippery world that can hold, man" (Chapter 108, "Ahab and the Carpenter," p. 390). But later he laments in soliloquy: "Oh! how immaterial are all materials! What things real are there, but imponderable thoughts?" (Chapter 127, "The Deck," p. 432–33). Hence his obsession with "things," though they be "inscrutable" or "unknown but still reasoning," as in the "Quarterdeck" chapter. If "thoughts" and "things" can connect and unite, without denying the separateness of each other, then Ahab is himself substantially real. But Ahab is haunted by the unknowability of "things," and turns desperately to solipsism. He asks the carpenter: "How dost thou know, that some entire, living, thinking thing may not be invisibly and uninterpenetratingly standing precisely where thou now standest; aye, and standing there in thy spite?" (Chapter 108, "Ahab and the Carpenter," p. 391). Here the "vacated thing," "the blankness" of a self-consuming Prometheus, and the haunting phantom of a tormented Narcissus become one.

Ahab's desperate defiance, I have implied, is really an intimate part of

Melville's own urge to write *Moby-Dick*. It is understandable that a writer grappling with such a problem should resort to a turbulent, sometimes logically incoherent style. Alfred Kazin, in a brilliant "introduction" to the book's meaning, has noted in the style a "peculiarly loping quality, as if it were constantly looking for connectives, since on the subject of the whale no single word or statement is enough."[11] Thorton Wilder's observation about Melville's coinage of verbal nouns and adjectival adverbs (". . . the whale shed off *enticings*," ". . . the last *whelmings intermixingly* poured themselves over the sunken head of the Indian at the mainmast," pp. 447, 469, italics mine), points to a similar purpose: the style converts naming words (nouns, adjectives) into actions (verbs, adverbs), trying to bring every object to life, desperately projecting animation into "things" and fighting the "blankness" it senses within itself.

It is in the characterization of Ahab that we notice the mocking trickiness of language as it strives to thwart the style's affirmative urge. Peleg's description of him as a "grand, ungodly, god-like man" (p. 76) begins this pattern by both affirming and denying Ahab's grasping of the divine. He is "god-like" (and Promethean) in that he *creates* his own image of the world, but is "ungodly" in that he rebels against his existence as a *creature* of forces beyond his control. The same sort of word-play mocks him in the final sentence of the passage on his "intolerably vivid dreams of the night": . . . thy thoughts have *created* a *creature* in thee; . . . that vulture the very *creature* he *creates*." Stylistically Ahab's tragedy consists in his failure to keep saying "I" meaningfully; striving to remain the grammatical subject of his world, who acts upon objects or "things" and creates or destroys them, he constantly lapses into the passivity of an object, acted upon, created or destroyed. Early in the book he defines his identity by playing with the word which tells what Moby-Dick has done to him: "I now prophesy that I will dismember my dismemberer" (Chapter 37, "Sunset," p. 147). A moment earlier in the same soliloquy, he attempts to convert the creaturely connotations of "madness" into independent creative action: "They think me mad—Starbuck does; but I'm demoniac, I am madness maddened. That wild madness that's only calm to understand itself." In these moments of bravado he thinks he understands himself by enlisting language against the "personified impersonal" opposing him. But actually he is continually in doubt of his identity. His own name mocks and haunts him, as he gradually comes to give it a talismanic significance. Observing the symbols on the doubloon, he confidently announces to himself: "All are Ahab," but later he is jolted by Starbuck's warning: "Let Ahab beware of Ahab." In his most profound moment of self-doubt in "The Symphony," he asks: "Is Ahab, Ahab? Is it I, God, or who, that lifts this arm?" Finally after the second day of the chase, he reasserts his name, but now in the context of a world empty of personality, able only to *be* by repeating his name: "Starbuck, of late I've felt strangely moved to thee; ever since that hour we both saw—thou know'st what, in one another's eyes. But in this matter of the whale, be the front of thy face to me as the palm of this hand—a lipless, unfeatured blank. Ahab is forever Ahab, man. This whole act's immutably decreed" (pp. 359, 394, 445, 459). This spectrum of statements reveals the word "Ahab" to mean "everything" (absorbing all significance into itself) or "nothing" (drained of any intrinsic meaning by the pull of extrinsic forces). Ahab is never sure whether he is everything or nothing. Narcissistically he says of the doubloon, "this round gold is but the image of the rounder globe, which, like a magician's glass, to each and every man in turn but mirrors back his own mysterious self. Great pains, small gains for those who ask the world to solve them; it cannot solve itself." (Chapter 99, p. 359.) The world cannot "solve" or understand itself, but Ahab is willing to try. The mystery of things and the mystery of self become the same problem to him.

The mocking ambiguity of language is present even in the naming of Ahab's ship, the *Pequod*. The fierce and warlike New England Indian tribe for which the ship is named was called by its neighboring tribes the "Pequots," or "destroyers." As Ishmael notes, the Pequots are now "as extinct as the ancient Medes": the "destroyers" were destroyed, and the same fate awaits Ahab and his crew. The ship itself, "a thing of trophies, a cannibal of a craft," decked out to resemble the whale it pursues, is simultaneously a symbol of Moby-Dick and of Ahab, of the ambiguity of "destroyer" and "destroyed." There is a similar grim joke in Ishmael's characterization of the Nantucket whale-hunters as "fighting Quakers . . . Quakers with a vengeance" (Chapter 16, "The Ship," pp. 67, 71). As a "Quaker," Ahab is supposed to tremble before the power of God, but as a whaler he causes the whales to tremble. But finally, of course, his destroying power is itself destroyed; asserting his divinity as the active subject of his world, he is driven back to becoming its suffering object.

Ahab finally comes to understand what is happening to him. In a conversation about "The Log and Line" with the Manxman, he says: "'Twill hold, old gentleman. Long heat and wet, have they spoiled thee? Thou seem'st to hold. Or, truer perhaps, life holds thee, not thou it." As usual, Ahab thinks as a symbolist, linking the old sailor by analogy to the rope. But this very imaginative process turns the sailor into a "thing," a creature of "life" and a grammatical object. Learning that the sailor was born "in the little rocky Isle of Man," Ahab continues his symbolic speculations, unable to resist the pun which makes them universal and personal: "Here's a man from Man; a man born in once independent Man, and now unmanned of Man; which is sucked in—by what? Up with the reel! The dead, blind wall butts all inquiring heads at last . . ." (Chapter 125, p. 427). It is interesting that the "dead, blind wall" (identified in "The Quarterdeck" with Moby-Dick) is now actively "butting," no longer merely an obstacle to be thrust through to reach the "unknown but still reasoning thing." Later, at the conclusion of the chase, "the solid white buttress" of Moby-Dick's forehead (another "lipless, unfeatured blank") smites the ship's bow, and destroys it (Chapter 36, p. 144; Chapter 135, p. 468).

It is apparent that in the later chapters of the book Ahab becomes both more and more fiercely assertive and more and more fatalistic. Critics have attacked him for inconsistency, but it seems more accurate to see him as more clearly understanding the division in himself between the humanity which wants to say "I" and the hard truth that the mirroring world makes him into a "thing." His address to the fire in "The Candles" reveals his narcissistic Prometheanism. He tells the crew: "the white flame but lights the way to the white whale," identifying fire with whale. But he needs a closer identification, out of which he can free himself from his oppressive creatureliness: "I would fain feel this pulse, and let mine beat against it; blood against fire." As he "fronts" the "personified impersonal," he hopes to "stand" more distinctly as a human personality, defined by his "blood" against the fire. He touches the flames: "I own thy speechless, placeless power; said I not so? Nor was it wrung from me; nor do I now drop these links. Thou canst blind; but I can then grope. Thou canst consume; but I can then be ashes . . ." Ahab recognizes the insignificance of man's self-making—he can only "grope," can only "be ashes"; these are minimal assertions. He goes on to turn language against itself: "Light though thou be, thou leapest out of darkness; but I am darkness leaping out of light, leaping out of thee." According to all traditional symbolism darkness is formless and empty; Ahab in his despair seeks to invert this meaning, but he cannot. His dilemma is complete: to be someone, he must be nothing.

But he is heartened by his human power of speech, the power by which he has asserted the "speechless, placeless power" of the fire. He presses this advantage: "I know that of me, which thou knowest not of thyself, oh, thou omnipotent. There is some unsuffusing thing beyond thee, thou clear spirit, to whom all thy eternity is but time, all thy creativeness mechanical. Through thee, thy flaming self, my scorched eyes do dimly see it." In characterizing the opposing power of nature as "unsuffusing," Ahab achieves a small victory. To suffuse is to spread, to cover, to fill the formless with substance. This the human imagination can do, but the essential force of nature cannot. Ahab accordingly concludes his speech by verbally *becoming* the fire, the repellant otherness he defies: "Leap! leap up, and lick the sky! I leap with thee; I burn with thee; would fain be welded with thee; defyingly I worship thee!" (Chapter 119, pp. 416–17). In this peculiar way he does "feature" himself in the "unbodied air."

Alfred Kazin has defined the unique literary effect of *Moby-Dick* as Melville's ability to "make you feel that he knows, as a writer, what it is like to be the eyes of the rock, the magnitude of the whale, the scalding sea, the dreams that lie buried in the Pacific. It is all, of course, seen through human eyes—yet there is in Melville a cold, final, ferocious hopelessness, a kind of ecstatic masochism, that delights in punishing man, in heaping coals on his head, in drowning him."[12] Ahab's eyes and voice are the most eloquent vehicles of this "ecstatic masochism." Melville establishes this effect through Ahab's imagery. A particularly striking pattern is one probably derived from the rural New England setting in which Melville wrote the book. Describing Moby-Dick's spout to the harpooneers, Ahab compares it to "a whole shock of wheat" (p. 143). Later Ishmael says of Ahab's mutilation: "Moby Dick had reaped away Ahab's leg, as a mower a blade of grass in the field" (p. 160). Through these comparisons the man and the whale change places; they are alternately the mower (the destroyer of life) and the thing mowed. This ambiguity returns at the end of Ahab's poignant speech to Starbuck in "The Symphony": "But it is a mild, mild wind, and a mild looking sky; and the air smells now, as if it blew from a far-away meadow; they have been making hay somewhere under the slopes of the Andes, Starbuck, and the mowers are sleeping among the new-mown hay. Sleeping. Aye, toil we how we may, we all sleep at last on the field. Sleep? Aye, and rust amid greenness, as last year's scythes flung down, and left in the half-cut swaths . . ." (p. 445). Gradually, as Ahab feels his nostalgic mood dissipate into the brutal present reality of the chase, he changes from the sentient human mower into the rusting scythe, becoming only a used-up "thing" in a world of cold wintry desolation.

His despair at becoming a scythe, the instrument of the implacable anti-human life-force, is matched and extended by the imagery of the "Chase" chapters. There, finally, Ahab identifies with the air and the sea, with the restless, aimless, eternal motions of wind and waves. Whereas earlier he thought analogically, following the traditional religious identification of wind with the human breath of inspiration ("Would now St. Paul would come along that way, and to my breezelessness bring his breeze," Chapter 70, p. 264), now he faces the wind with primitive directness as an equal force in a world of forces: "Were I the wind, I'd blow no more on such a wicked, miserable world. I'd crawl somewhere to a cave, and slink there. And yet, 'tis a noble and heroic thing, the wind! who ever conquered it? . . ." (Chapter 135, p. 460). This Lear-like "madness" reveals the elemental nakedness of man's place in nature. On the last day Ahab tells Starbuck: "Some men die at ebb tide; some at low water; some at the full of the flood;—and I feel now like a billow that's all one crested comb" (p. 462). A conventional metaphor suddenly becomes a statement of identity. Ahab's human energy, he now realizes hopelessly but defiantly, has no more force upon the impenetrable rock-like nature of things than that of a momentary wall of water. He repeats the image in his final speech: "Oh, lonely death on lonely life. Oh, now I feel my topmost greatness lies in my topmost grief. Ho, ho! from all your furthest bounds, pour ye now in, ye bold billows of my foregone life, and top this one piled comber of my death!" (p. 468). This "one piled comber" breaks upon the whale, as the whale's "predestinating

head" breaks upon the ship; ". . . then all collapsed, and the great shroud
of the sea rolled on as it rolled five thousand years ago." Like the ship, like
the wave, Ahab's personality collapses, slipping back into the undifferentiated oneness of the empty sea. His vulture-like mind consumes itself; the
"tormenting, mild" image of himself he saw in the water fades as the ripples
left by a dropping pebble fade into ever-widening circles. But the mighty
voice remains; Ishmael still plucks at the sky and dives into the deep to make
it heard.

Ahab's character is a unique feature of American Romanticism; not one
or all of Poe's and Hawthorne's dark Gothic isolatoes can match him.
Melville has taken the imagination far down an endless corridor with Ahab
(though he evidently intended to lead Pierre Glendinning even farther). The
Ahab who stands facing the fiery corpusants is really a "representative man"
(to appropriate Emerson's phrase), as representative of the American Romantic imagination as Henry Thoreau standing on the shores of Walden,
announcing: "I went to the woods because I wished to live deliberately, to
front only the essential facts of life . . . I wanted to live deep and suck out
all the marrow of life, to live so sturdily and Spartan-like as to put to rout
all that was not life, to cut a broad swath and shave close, to drive life into
a corner, and reduce it to its lowest terms. . . ." Thoreau's stubborn
recognition of the reality of "things" combines with his insatiable appetite
for experience: "If you stand right fronting and face to face to a fact, you will
see the sun glimmer on both its surfaces, as if it were a cimeter, and feel its
sweet edge dividing you through the heart and marrow. . . . Be it life or
death, we crave only reality."[13] Ahab's career stems from the same faith, the
same craving, but as he knows it the dividing edge is not sweet. To stare
with Ahab into the heart of the fire is to see life reduced to its lowest terms
with an impact Thoreau could barely imagine.

Walt Whitman sometimes felt the force of an Ahab-like narcissism, as
in "As I Ebb'd with the Ocean of Life":

> I too Paumanok,
> I too have bubbled up, floated the measureless float,
>   and been washed on your shores,
> I too am but a trail of drift and debris,
> I too leave little wrecks upon you, you fish-shaped
>   island.

Whitman's imagination of disaster is like Thoreau's, particular and fully
naturalistic. Thoreau knows what it feels like to be an animal, or a fish, or
a bird; Whitman knows the pull of the infinite ocean, its power to turn a
healthy body into "sea-drift," atomized "little wrecks." But only Ahab
knows the ultimate emptiness on the other side of the mirror; at the end he
sees himself reduced to a billow, to a brief disturbance on the blank surface

of "things." Like the wake of the unconquered whale, he is "a thing writ on water" (Chapter 134, p. 453). It is through Melville's awareness of such a potential evanescence in human speech itself that we should see his featuring of Ahab.

Notes

1. Page references are to the Norton Critical Edition of *Moby-Dick*.
2. There are, of course, many passages in *Moby-Dick* which will not support the intensity of tone I evoke here. Ishmael plays other roles, and other characters occasionally divert us from Ahab's moral centrality. But Melville's famous remarks to Hawthorne about his "secret motto" and "wicked book" indicate Ahab's importance to him. My emphasis here on the common problems of Ahab, Ishmael and Melville is anticipated (as are other aspects of my argument) by Charles Feidelson, *Symbolism and American Literature* (Chicago, 1953), pp. 27–35. I am further indebted for comments and suggestions to my colleagues William Charvat, Julian Markels and Joan Webber.
3. Ishmael also comments on the formlessness of the whale's appearance and the consequent impossibility of understanding it in Chapter 55, "Of the Monstrous Pictures of Whales," p. 228; and Chapter 86, "The Tail," pp. 317–18.
4. Thornton Wilder, "Towards an American Language," *Atlantic Monthly*, 190 (July, 1952), 36.
5. For a different view of this passage, see Richard Chase, *Herman Melville* (New York, 1949), pp. 47–48. According to Chase, Ahab willingly transforms himself into a mechanical monster. But Ahab's heavy, mockingly ironic tone indicates to me that he rejects the mechanical man as a grim joke.
6. See pp. 438, 452, 459.
7. It is true that the English language did not demand in Melville's day, any more than it does now, such an opposition. While the OED gives a definition of "thing" as "a being without life or consciousness, an inanimate object, as distinguished from a person or living creature," it also gives much more general definitions, e.g.: "That which exists individually (in the most general sense, in fact or in idea); that which may be in any way an object of perception . . . ; a being, an entity (including persons, when personality is not considered)."

A concordance to *Moby-Dick* would probably reveal that in a majority of instances Melville uses "thing" in a general, innocuous way. But even in casual usage "thing" seems naturally to oppose whatever is essentially human, as in Emerson's dictum: "The one thing in the world, of value, is the active soul." The tone here is not far from that of another Emersonian phrase: "the ghastly reality of things." An interesting case where the casual meaning becomes suddenly serious is this moment in Emerson's "Ode: Inscribed to W. H. Channing":

> Boston Bay and Bunker Hill
> Would serve things still;
> Things are of the snake.

All the major American Romantic writers seem to have been aware of this potential explosiveness in style.
8. Pp. 112, 115, 144, 147, 160, 193, 358, 400, 403, 435, 442, 445, 463.
9. E.g., pp. 110, 111, 418, 438; 161, 400; 443; 462.
10. For an analysis of this paragraph which focuses on Ishmael's epistemological problems, see Paul Brodtkorb, Jr., *Ishmael's White World: A Phenomenological Reading of Moby Dick* (New Haven, 1965), pp. 62–81.

11. Alfred Kazin, "Introduction" to the Riverside Edition of *Moby-Dick* (Boston, 1956); reprinted in *Contemporaries* (Boston, 1962) and in *Melville: A Collection of Critical Essays,* ed. Richard Chase (Englewood Cliffs, N.J., 1962), p. 47.

12. Kazin, *Melville: A Collection of Critical Essays,* p. 46.

13. Henry David Thoreau, "Where I Lived and What I Lived For," in *Walden; Writings* (Boston, 1906), Vol. II. 100–101, 109.

"Loomings": Yarns and Figures in the Fabric

Harrison Hayford

A linked image cluster that recurs throughout Melville's works also figures centrally in the initial chapter of *Moby-Dick*. My aim in this essay is to demonstrate how some recurrent items ("images") and topics ("motifs") in "Loomings" carry a few basic strands of thought ("themes") in the book; how these elements relate to each other; and also how they relate to syntax, rhetoric, and such larger elements as the book's characters, plot, and thought. My analysis takes up elements as they occur locally in Chapter I and relates them to similar elements in other parts of the work. The immediate effect of my discussion is to illustrate the dense imaginative coherence of *Moby-Dick*. Its images, motifs, and themes are yarns closely woven into figures in its fabric, as the chapter title "Loomings" can be taken to imply. [1]

Somewhat arbitrarily, I focus my discussion on the element of character. Specifically, I focus on Ishmael and on the ways in which the elements I analyze show similarities and differences between him and Ahab. My critical strategy is to take the narrative, from its opening sentence "Call me Ishmael," as altogether the work of Ishmael, its ostensible narrator, and to interpret all its elements as coming from Ishmael and hence characterizing Ishmael, not Melville. In this way the dense imaginative coherence is transferred from the book and its author to the mind of Ishmael as its ground and cause. In this perspective, the action of the work takes place in the observing and participating mind of Ishmael. His mind "contains" the tragedy of Ahab as Ishmael confronted it some years ago in experience and now confronts it once again in the telling. Of course this approach is not new, for perhaps the chief discovery criticism has made in the interpretation of *Moby-Dick* in the past generation is to recognize the presence and centrality of Ishmael. Most earlier critics had overlooked him altogether because they were so taken by Ahab and the White Whale. [2] A close corollary perception has been recognition of the thematic importance of the juxtaposition between Ishmael and Ahab. Both points are now usually taken for granted in interpretations of the book, however at odds readings may otherwise be. Neither point, though, entails taking the whole work as

Reprinted from *Artful Thunder: Versions of the Romantic Tradition in Honor of Howard P. Vincent*, ed. Robert J. DeMott and Sanford E. Marovitz (Kent: Kent State University Press, 1975), pp. 119–37. Reprinted by permission.

Ishmael's—a strategy I am adopting here provisionally and only for convenience.

One further bit of strategy needs a word. All along I refer to Ahab in the present tense. This is the way we usually discuss a fictional character, since we imagine him dramatically alive as we read, though the narrative is told in past tense and we may know the story ends with his death. In *Moby-Dick* Ishmael only occasionally makes any point of Ahab's being already dead and gone, and for my purposes no harm is done by my not doing so. On the other hand, since it is of more consequence that Ishmael is narrating in the present tense, I use tenses for him that distinguish between Ishmael at the time of the *Pequod*'s voyage and Ishmael at the later time he is telling about it. What is involved in Ishmael-then vs. Ishmael-now is the quite unsettled interpretive problem of Ishmael's development in character and outlook.[3] It is not part of my purpose to deal with this problem here. Let me simply declare that in my reading he did not change and has not changed, from then to now, in his essential nature. Ishmael is forever Ishmael. Call him Ishmael.

I

In *Moby-Dick* Ishmael plays the role—a frequent one in Melville's writings—of sympathetic but perplexed observer. What he chiefly confronts and observes is the tragedy of Ahab in his revengeful attack upon the great White Whale. In this perspective the book's early chapters are preparation for Ahab. Before Ahab's appearance, Ishmael builds up in them the physical and conceptual worlds which make probable Ahab's character, his language, his thought, and his actions. In "Loomings" Ishmael starts on his narrative way as participant and observer. As he tells the story, his manner with words, his habitual ways of perceiving and dealing with situations, his preoccupations of thought, all reveal his character. Through these means the first chapter begins to establish the grounds both of Ishmael's sympathy with Ahab and of the differences between them that mark his dissociation from Ahab.

An initial similarity between Ishmael and Ahab is the way both of them turn every object, situation, and person they confront into a problem, one which cannot be solved, a mystery whose lurking meaning cannot be followed to its ultimate elucidation. This habit of mind shapes the rhetorical form of the first chapter; and many later chapters also take the shape of their development from it. Chapters of exposition, especially, often treat their subjects as problematical and end up by declaring them inexplicable. But narrative chapters, too, are frequently constructed on a pattern of confrontation-exploration-nonsolution of a problem.

Simply in vocabulary items, apart from context, this propensity of

Ishmael's is illustrated. In this very first chapter, for example, wonder and mystery are constantly being evoked, at the same time that inability to solve or to understand is being declared. One running series of words connotes wonder and mystery: *magic, enchanting, romantic, tranced, charm, mystical, marvelous, secretly, portentous and mysterious, marvels, wonder-world, hooded phantom.* Intertwined with these words runs another series denoting or evoking inability to solve or identify: *ungraspable, invisible, secretly, unaccountable, unimaginable, undeliverable.* The two series continue intertwined throughout the book, and as vocabulary items alone they imply not only a habit of Ishmael's perception but a major thematic proposition of the book: life—the cosmos and everything in it taken as a microcosm—confronts man as a compelling but insoluble mystery.

In the first chapter, Ishmael sets out to tell the story of this particular whaling voyage. But no further along than his third sentence, the narrative mode shades into exposition, as Ishmael begins explaining his reasons not only for having gone on this voyage but for his voyaging in general. And then, by the end of the first paragraph, the reasons themselves have come to require explanation; the problem has arisen of communicating some sense of his feelings toward the ocean, feelings which, though nearly universal, are not easy for him to convey in statements. Already the narrative has generated what I take to be a basic motif of the book: that of confronting an insoluble problem.

Why he went to sea has become, in the telling, a problem to Ishmael. Initially it is a problem in communicating just what it is that he felt and feels, but soon it becomes something of a problem to himself. For to Ishmael, as to Ahab, motives have lower and yet lower layers. While Ishmael is developing this problem of his motivation it splits into three successive questions: 1. Why does he go to sea? (paragraphs 1–6) 2. Why does he go as a common sailor? (paragraphs 7–11) 3. And why did he go that voyage on a whaler rather than on a merchant ship? (paragraphs 11–14)

As Ishmael deals with each of these three questions through the rest of the chapter, he shows further traits of mind and patterns of reaction which he shares with Ahab. But in his treatment of each question, and especially of the second, he also reveals traits which set him off from Ahab, and which, indeed, define a crucial distinction between them.

II

To answer his first question—why he goes to sea (initially why he went on this particular voyage)—Ishmael begins with two immediately assignable conditions, both of them negative and somewhat aimless rather than positive reasons: he had little money in his purse and nothing in particular to interest him on shore. Then he adds his general motive for going to sea not only on that voyage but at various times: he says it is a way he has of driving off the spleen—driving off spells of melancholy—and a substitute for his impulses toward violence against others or himself whenever he feels depressed. But actually his motives on that and other such occasions, he realizes, reach deeper than these personal ones, specific or general; there is something universal in them. For nearly all men, he says, share his feelings towards the ocean.

Next, to suggest that which he cannot analyze in what he declares is an almost universal feeling towards the ocean, he leaps at once (paragraph 3) from declarative statements to a series of parallel analogies couched in imperatives and interrogatives. He exhorts us to confront, and, if we can, to explain the meaning of a series of analogical situations, stated in various images. The basic motif these situations exemplify is confrontation: in each situation men are drawn toward water, gaze fixedly upon it, and meditate its mystery. They come in crowds, "pacing straight for the water, and seemingly bound for a dive." And "They must get just as nigh the water as they possibly can without falling in." This motif of confronting a mystery implies a consequent motif: that of self-destruction. For one may come too close to the fascinating object, the water—may take a dive or fall in. This implication becomes explicit in the climactic analogy of the series: "Surely all this is not without meaning. And still deeper the meaning of that story of Narcissus, who because he could not grasp the tormenting, mild image he saw in the fountain, plunged into it and was drowned." The water-gazing analogies coincide with the plot shape of *Moby-Dick:* Ahab with the crew of the *Pequod* thrusts off from land into the ocean, and in his effort to grasp a tormenting image, the White Whale, plunges in and is drowned. "But," says Ishmael, here in the first chapter commenting on the plunge of Narcissus, "that same image, we ourselves see in all rivers and oceans. It is the image of the ungraspable phantom of life; and this is the key to it all." This Narcissus analogy indeed is the "key" to a thematic argument of the book: something in man, now as throughout his history, forces him to confront the mystery of life, to pursue that phantom; but it is "ungraspable"; and the man who goes too far in the effort, who crowds too close upon the mystery, destroys himself. Such is Ahab's pursuit of Moby Dick, and such is his fate.

Ishmael, likewise, feels the attraction of the phantom. In the final words of this chapter he declares that "one grand hooded phantom, like a snow hill in the air" swayed him to his purpose of embarking on the whaling voyage. Similarly, the Spirit Spout is later a "phantom" luring the *Pequod* and her crew on and on (Ch. 51). After Ahab had revealed his purpose on this voyage, Ishmael realized, at least dimly, what the end must be. His shouts, he says, went up with the rest. "A wild, mystical, sympathetical feeling was in me; Ahab's quenchless feud seemed mine." But Ishmael "while yet all arush to encounter the whale, could see naught in that brute but the deadliest ill" (Ch. 41). And again Ishmael comments, "But in pursuit of those far mysteries we dream of, or in tormented chase of that demon phantom that, some time or other, swims before all human hearts; while chasing such over this round globe, they either lead us on in barren mazes or midway leave us whelmed" (Ch. 52).

Later Ahab shows repeatedly that he too realizes what Ishmael indicates from the beginning; that the issue of such an aggressive quest can only be self-destruction. For a single example, when Captain Boomer, who has lost an arm to Moby Dick, warns Ahab that "He's best let alone; don't you think so, Captain?" Ahab replies, "He is. But he will still be hunted, for all that. What is best let alone, that accursed thing is not always what least allures. He's all a magnet!" (Ch. 100).

Yet this first chapter makes a decisive point about Ishmael. Despite the magnetic attraction he feels towards the mystery which lures one on to destruction, he is still not by nature disposed, like Ahab, to press up so close to it as to plunge in and drown. This difference, a decisive one, between Ishmael's nature and Ahab's is manifested in several ways in the first chapter. For one thing, it is evident in Ishmael's second reason for going to sea at all, since the voyage was—as his voyages still are—his conscious substitute for aggressive action, for expressing his frustrations destructively on others or himself, either by "deliberately stepping into the street, and methodically knocking people's hats off" or by following funerals (to the graveyard) or stabbing or shooting himself. To him, going to sea is not in itself aggressive; it is rather his "substitute for pistol and ball." Even at the outset, Ishmael half-consciously recognizes death may be the ultimate goal of his journey. Omens, icons, and monuments of death attend his progress on this voyage, as they do Ahab's, and cannot swerve him from his purpose to take ship.

III

The second question Ishmael raises is why he goes to sea as a common sailor. Although, unlike his first and third questions, this question presents no problem to Ishmael, his treatment of it leads again to definition of the same distinction between himself and Ahab. In this second section of the chapter (paragraphs 7–11) the difference comes out more fully, but so does an essential similarity. Ishmael feels as strongly as does Ahab a sense of personal dignity, heightened by pride, and he too is galled by the weight of indignities which superiors impose upon his body, mind, and spirit. But from the beginning, where he tells of his custom of going to sea as a "simple sailor" rather than as an officer, he announces his habitual acceptance of subordinate positions, indeed (as if he had a choice) his settled preference for them. At the same time, he displays his feeling that this subjection is one he shares with men in general, that his lot merges with the common lot of men, all of whom, he says, are slaves or victims in one way or another and should therefore help each other endure their common lot. Ahab's parallel perception of humanity's general suffering gives him no comfort and only exacerbates his sense of outrage.

The section is couched in motifs that are recurrent in *Moby-Dick*, of which the leading and dominant one is that of the inferior-superior relationship, involving the acceptance or rejection of imposed authority. Associated motifs include money; food; bodily impairment or injury; injustice or insult; antiquity; masonry and massive objects; personal dignity; and family. All are constituents of the image cluster I referred to earlier as recurring throughout Melville's works.

When Ishmael goes to sea, he explains, he never goes as a passenger, because to do so requires a purse. Nor does he go as an officer, for he abominates all honorable, respectable posts and responsibilities and will not identify himself with them. First, the motif of money which comes in the second sentence of the chapter ("having little or no money in my purse") appears again: "you must needs have a purse, and a purse is but a rag unless you have something in it"; then the money motif is dropped until it recurs at the end of the section in the image of "paying" (paragraph 10).

Next (still in paragraph 7) the motif of food develops, in the image of Ishmael's rejecting the possibility of shipping as cook. Though a cook is "a sort of officer on ship-board," with "considerable glory," Ishmael explains that "I never fancied broiling fowls;—though once broiled, judiciously buttered, and judgmatically salted and peppered, there is no one who will speak more respectfully, not to say reverentially, of a broiled fowl than I will." Here motifs of food, authority, and bodily impairment are linked as they often are in the book. In his joshing way, Ishmael seems merely to be saying he has never cared to cook fowls, though once they are properly cooked and seasoned he has a very good appetite for them. The motifs he employs, however, carry in undercurrent the more generalized theme that he does not take pleasure as superiors (here reductively made comic as "cooks") do, from subjecting the bodies of inferiors ("fowls") to radical physical impairment ("broiling")—though once the bodies so treated have by such official and legal process ("judiciously," "judgmatically") been dignified and transformed, he is respectful, almost reverential toward them, in a way inverting superior and inferior. In short, he does not care to be a superior to inflict the physical hurt, but once it has been, as it were, legally and duly done he accepts and respects the result. He is as willing as anyone to "swallow" and "stomach" it. In a jocose second sentence, Ishmael quickly recapitulates the same motifs: food (victimized bodies eaten), authority, reverence—but twines them now with two further motifs, of antiquity and of massive masonry, in a single compressed image: "It is out of the idolatrous dotings of the old Egyptians upon broiled ibis and roasted river horse, that you see the mummies of those creatures in their huge bake-houses the pyramids." The general effect of this analogy, as of those in the earlier paragraphs, is to universalize the personal attitude Ishmael has just stated by associating it with a parallel instance in antiquity, one which (in "mummies" and "pyramids") has preserved and monumentalized the situation through the ages.

The arc of feeling traversed in the two sentences about cooking and eating fowl becomes thematically characteristic in *Moby-Dick*. Ishmael repeatedly moves from opposing ("I abominate . . .") a physically threatening person, object, or situation that is somehow "superior," to reconciling himself with it ("no one will speak more respectfully . . ."). And the particular motifs that carry the theme restate it repeatedly in the book. The motifs of food and eating are often linked to the motif of a superior in situations which are treated in a humorous tone, and sometimes the superior is embodied as a comic figure in authority, or has an attendant comic figure. Such a situation occurs in the next chapters when Ishmael confronts the cannibal Queequeg (who might eat him!) and ends up smoking and eating with him and even "married" to him. Another occurs when Ishmael and Queequeg eat their chowders under the dominating eye of shrewish Mrs. Hussey, who is scolding a man as the eating scene begins and who takes away Queequeg's harpoon as it ends (Ch. 15). Another is the scene in which the mates silently eat at table with the domineering Ahab, to be followed by the savage harpooneers attended by comic Dough-Boy (Ch. 34). And still another, the most fully developed, is that in which Stubb masticates his whale steak (cooked too much for his taste) while humorously baiting Old Fleece the comic black cook into delivering a sermon to a congregation of sharks who are also devouring a whale's body (Ch. 64. Cf. also Ch. 65 on "The Whale as a Dish").

Now very likely the reading I have just given seems somewhat far-fetched, particularly in its generalizing the specific imagery of broiling, salting, and peppering a fowl into a motif designated as "bodily impairment." And it would really be only a facile translation if that motif did not become a central theme in *Moby-Dick*. In Ishmael's outer and inner worlds, of whaling and of consciousness, a major theme is that living bodies, animal and human, are subjected to physical outrage, to all the possible range of injury, maiming, mangling, destruction—to the "horrible vulturism of earth." Victimizers act upon victimized bodies, superiors upon inferiors. The central instance is Ahab's dismemberment when his leg is reaped away by the White Whale's jaw; and the sustained context is the whaling world, in which bodies of men and animals are given to mutual injury and destruction in the normal course of existence, in the whole routine of chase, slaughter, and dismemberment—the hunter's and butcher's bloody work that is the whaleman's life and may be his death when the persecuted whale retaliates on his body.[4] In this destructive bodily collision of whaleman and whale the relationship of superior-inferior shifts, from one passage to another, in ways that depend as much on Ishmael's perspective and mood as on any facts of the immediate instance. He recognizes this world's general condition of mutual bodily victimization and identifies at different times either with superior or inferior, with biter or bitten. And often, as in the sentences just examined, his initial sympathy with the inferior, whose body is victimized, shifts, and he accepts the superior's victim as now transmuted into "food." The generalized motif of such a shift in feeling can be termed reconciliation.

Despite such strategies of reconciliation with the superior, however, Ishmael is habitually and characteristically on the side of the inferior. He feels victimized and his feeling of being put upon is carried by constant bodily images in the flow of his narration. He is unusually conscious of his own body, and in the course of the first chapter he names many of his bodily parts, functions, sensations, positions, and actions. Often he expresses his feelings in images of bodily discomfort or malfunction: "driving off the spleen, and regulating the circulation," "growing grim about the mouth," "a damp, drizzly November in my soul," "hazy about the eyes," "over conscious of my lungs"—these occur with some frequency.

Ishmael's signing on as a simple sailor, he admits, entails subjection to authority and an affront to his self-respect and family pride as well as the relinquishment of his own superior authority as a schoolmaster. "True, they rather order me about some. . . . And at first, this sort of thing is unpleasant enough. It touches one's sense of honor, particularly if you come of an old established family in the land. . . . And more than all, if just previous to putting your hand into the tar-pot, you have been lording it as a country schoolmaster, making the tallest boys stand in awe of you." Evidently Ishmael's sensitivity is rubbed raw on precisely the same point as Ahab's. Both resent the indignity of being ordered about, of being thumped and punched by superiors, particularly because each feels the pride of distinguished lineage and is accustomed to order tall fellows about and make them stand in awe. Ahab's sensitivity is exposed to the metaphysical thumping and punching of the gods, and the distinguished lineage he feels is not literal but the metaphysical dignity of the race of man, human dignity. Unlike Ahab, however, Ishmael has nonaggressive strategies for alleviating such indignities. Here, his first strategy is recourse to the folk wisdom of "grin and bear it," fortified by the book wisdom of Stoic philosophy; the transition from schoolmaster to sailor is a keen one requiring "a strong decoction of Seneca and the Stoics to enable you to grin and bear it." Furthermore, patience helps; for even this feeling of indignity "wears off in time."

Another jocular gambit of alleviation takes up the next paragraph (paragraph 9). Suppose some "old hunks of a sea-captain" does order Ishmael to sweep the decks (an indignity to an able seaman since this broom business is the prescriptive province of the boys, as we learn in Chapter 54)—what does this indignity amount to, weighed in the scales of the New Testament?

Or does Ishmael's prompt obedience make the archangel Gabriel think less of him? And finally,

> Who ain't a slave? Tell me that. Well, then, however the old sea-captains may order me about—however they may thump and punch me about, I have the satisfaction of knowing that it is all right; that everybody else is one way or other served in much the same way—either in a physical or metaphysical point of view, that is; and so the universal thump is passed round, and all hands should rub each other's shoulder-blades and be content.[5]

In both the physical and metaphysical points of view, this recognition of universal slavery, this "thump," enrages Ahab past endurance and impels his physical attack upon the whale and his metaphysical attack upon whatever powers may stand behind the whale. But from the first, although Ishmael is as sensitive as Ahab to the indignity of physical subordination, he declares strategies, if not principles, of nonaggression: Stoic endurance, New Testament and democratic equality in suffering and slavery, fellow-feeling and mutual help—such are his remedies. Only too late does Ahab catch a glimpse through Pip, of something resembling Ishmael's insight into the emollient effect of shared suffering, of mankind full of sweet things of love and gratitude.

Another of Ishmael's remedies, evident from the first paragraph and one which in the end may be the most important of all, is the saving practicality of his humor. From the beginning the tone of his voice has been varied and flexible. Its serious flow yields to rifts of humor which usually break the tension just when the topic has become most serious and its tone most magniloquent. In the first paragraph a swelling exaggeration of language and structure creates a suspicion that ultimately he will not take altogether solemnly his own feelings and motives which are real enough but overdramatized: "Whenever . . . ; whenever . . . ; whenever . . . ; and especially whenever . . . ; then. . . ." The suspicion is at once confirmed by the next sentence where the irreverent wording of the qualifying alliterative phrase "With a philosophical flourish" reduces Cato's classical suicide to mock heroism in contrast to Ishmael's own underplayed sensible substitute, "I quietly take to the ship." In this middle section of the chapter, directly after the peroration of the first section (the series of analogies ending with the high-keyed climactic image of Narcissus which is "the key to it all"), his tone relaxes into jocularity all through the four and a half paragraphs (7–11) just discussed. As Ishmael discourses, his fluid consciousness is marked by varying tones and never settles into the monotone of a single attitude. His range does not reach the heights or the depths of Ahab's noble monomania, though it at times approaches them; he is brought back to a habitable mid-region by his humorous sense of his own practical situation, which allows him to take "a strong decoction of Seneca and the Stoics" to help him "grin and bear it." This practical humorousness is a saving quality Ishmael shares with Stubb, the second mate, a quality that distinguishes them both from Ahab in the high seriousness of his tragic nobility.

By these strategies of attitude and tone, then, the tension of the chapter's middle section is relaxed and resolved. But in diminuendo Ishmael goes on to advance two further reasons for shipping as a sailor rather than as a passenger or officer. Both of these involve the motif of inferior-superior. In each of them he now argues in consciously sophistical rhetoric that the inferior is really the superior. His tone is jocular, but, as often, its jocularity barely veils his underlying hostility to anybody in a position of social and economic superiority. Passengers, as financially superior to sailors, are dealt with in the linked motifs of money-injustice. For passengers, so his resumed argument runs, must pay when they go to sea, whereas sailors are paid—and paying is the most uncomfortable infliction the two orchard-thieves, Adam and Eve, entailed upon their descendants. "But *being paid*,—what will compare with it?" Even here, however, Ishmael turns the thought against those above him: momentarily it is he, a poor sailor, not they, enjoying the felicity of being paid. But—so his thought runs on—to receive much pay leads to wealth, and wealth leads to destruction, for money is "the root of all earthly ills," and "on no account can a monied man enter heaven." And he moralizes, "How cheerfully we consign ourselves to perdition!"

In this last line of thought two motifs are twined: that of money (coupled with injustice) and that of self-destruction, in the image of consigning ourselves to perdition. The first paired motif, that of money-injustice, comes in for fuller development in the following chapter in Ishmael's lack of money for a night's lodging and in the passage about Lazarus and Dives. The second, that of self-destruction in the image of damnation or going-to-hell, first appears as such here but will often recur. For the whole voyage of the *Pequod* is, in fact, Ahab's wilful self-consignment to perdition. Of this fact we are reminded throughout the book, both directly and indirectly, even to the final scene where the ship "sinks to hell."

Ishmael's last reason for shipping as a common sailor rather than in any position of honor is a humorously specious one that again develops the inferior-superior motif, reversing the positions. His reason is that the Commodore on the quarter-deck aft gets the air he breathes only at second hand from the forecastle sailors. The schoolmaster's learnedly indecorous joke, turning on the Pythagorean maxim to avoid eating beans, covertly vents contempt on the officers. "In much the same way do the commonalty lead their leaders in many other things, at the same time that the leaders little suspect it." At the end of the section, thus, analogizing from the sailors' station forward on the ship (of state) as she sails, Ishmael transforms the sailor-followers into "leaders" and the officer-leaders aft into "followers"—so the last shall be first and the first, last.

IV

At this point in the chapter (in the middle of paragraph 11), Ishmael by the foregoing strategies has handled two of the three questions into which he divides the problem of his going to sea. Now he takes up his final question: why did he go that voyage on a whale-ship? Why, having repeatedly smelt the sea as a merchant sailor did he then go on a whaling voyage? (Note that this is the only one of the three questions that refers solely to the *Pequod*'s voyage, not to the motivations for Ishmael's voyages in general.) With this question, too, Ishmael deals in the recurrent motifs. He posits his motivation as a mystery. The dominant motif is that of the supernatural, while linked to it is that of injustice (or wrong) in the form of mystery-deception, or mystery-concealment. As Ahab characteristically does, Ishmael generalizes this particular question back into the problem of the universe—what he later calls "the universal problem of all things" (Ch. 64).

Why he took it into his head to go this time on a whaling voyage is a puzzle to Ishmael, one which is answerable only as part of the cosmic mystery, and which he deals with in a series of linked images. In the first witty image, Ishmael declares semi-seriously that he is secretly dogged and unaccountably influenced by an "invisible police-officer of the Fates," who can better answer than anyone else. His going whaling was doubtless his fate, or his predestined lot—in a second image "part of the grand programme of Providence that was drawn up a long time ago." For himself, he cannot tell (continuing the second image and showing some of his customary irreverence for high authorities over him) why it was that "those stage managers, the Fates," put him down for "this shabby part of a whaling voyage" when they assigned to others "magnificent parts in high tragedies" and to still others parts in comedies and farces. Here there lurks some irony on Ishmael's part, for on this whaling voyage high tragedy is indeed to be enacted (as well as comedy and farce), though the tragic role in it is to be Ahab's, not Ishmael's. But Ahab is a transfigured, transvaluated, common old whaleman exalted to the heights in a "democratic" tragedy. And Ahab, too, is convinced, as he cries to Starbuck, that his role was determined by the Fates: "This whole act's immutably decreed.—'Twas rehearsed by thee and me a billion years before this ocean rolled. . . . I am the Fates' lieutenant; I act under orders" (Ch. 134). Whatever motives of their own the Fates may have had in assigning Ishmael his part (Ishmael refrains from exploring that byway!), they cunningly presented to him, under various disguises, certain illusory motives as his own, into which he thinks he can now see a little way. Some of these motives, as he now recalls them in images of characteristic connotation, were: the curiosity "roused" in him by the "portentous and mysterious" monster, "the overwhelming idea of the great whale himself";

the "undeliverable, nameless perils" and "attending marvels" of the whale; the "torment" of his own "everlasting itch for things remote." These images associate the coming voyage with the motif of confrontation—the numinous fascination of the mysterious, here, as often, embodied in the massive and associated with the perilous (the danger of destruction from approaching it too close). Ishmael, like Ahab, like all men in their degree, feels this attraction. He feels, too, its frequently associated quality of forbiddenness. Paradoxically, to move toward the region where all these qualities coalesce is to respond actively to an attraction which is at the same time forbidden; he says (in active verbs), "I love to sail forbidden seas and land on barbarous coasts." But unlike Ahab, Ishmael by his characteristic strategy again dissolves into sociality the aggressive, implied motive of invasion. To his sociality of feeling the barbarous horrors themselves will turn out to be just fellow "inmates" of this prison world: "Not ignoring what is good, I am quick to perceive a horror, and could still be social with it—would they let me—since it is but well to be on friendly terms with all the inmates of the place one lodges in."

So far as Ishmael can see into his motives when he confronts them as a problem, the foregoing were his reasons. "By reason of these things, then, the whaling voyage was welcome." But there is a still lower layer—for he realizes that these felt motives only "cajoled" him into "the delusion that it was a choice resulting from my own unbiased freewill and discriminating judgment." The climactic and final image of the chapter reasserts Ishmael's conviction that his motives were somehow imposed upon him as a passive receiver: "The great floodgates of the wonder-world swung open, and in the wild conceits that swayed me to my purpose, two and two there floated into my inmost soul, endless processions of the whale, and, midmost of them all, one grand hooded phantom, like a snow hill in the air." By the syntax of this sentence Ishmael becomes the passive recipient of conceits that "float" into his "inmost soul" from some exterior source; he is "swayed" by them rather than being their active originator. This image of something "floating" into the mind is one more metaphor (perhaps for an experiential sensation, perhaps for a metaphysical concept) to explain the same process Ishmael alluded to above in the theatrical image as a cleverly deceitful casting operation of the stage-managing Fates: "the springs and motives which being cunningly presented to me under various disguises, induced me to set about performing the part I did."

Here, indeed, the imagery brings up one of the major themes of *Moby-Dick*. In most general terms the theme may be defined as the problem of free will, of responsibility for one's actions. Already in this chapter the theme has been broached in three different metaphors, or concepts. First it was introduced as discussed above, under the image of "magnetic virtue," the attraction of water. Then it appeared under the loosely equivalent image or concept of "the Fates" and "Providence," with supplementary allusion to an "invisible police-officer of the Fates," who is evidently a sort of special daemon or supervisory angel put into modern dress and so comically demeaned as a petty official who "dogs" one. Finally, it is restated here in terms of the sensation of a psychological process, of something "floating" into the consciousness from outside—a metaphor evidently derived from a conceptual system of "atmospheric influences" frequently invoked elsewhere in *Moby-Dick* (and at great length in *Pierre,* where the etiology of motivation is examined with great intensity). Of all three images—magnetic influences, Fates or Providence, and "atmospheric influences"—the common denominator is their postulation of exterior forces determining the action of the mind. The mind is essentially their passive instrument, and its subjective sense of "a choice resulting" from "unbiased freewill and discriminating judgment" is only a "delusion" cunningly contrived and made pleasant by invisible superior powers.

The syntax of many sentences in the chapter supports the tenor of these metaphors in the motif of active-passive, and it here bears out Ishmael's explicit declaration that he has no free will. Many passive verb constructions and dissociations of self occur. In the opening paragraph, for example, a kind of struggle goes on in Ishmael between what he feels happening independently in him ("I find myself growing grim about the mouth"; "it is a damp, drizzly November in my soul"; "I find myself involuntarily pausing"; "hypos get such an upper hand of me") and his assertive will opposing it ("a way I have of driving off the spleen"; "it requires a strong moral principle to prevent me"). In this sentence, the syntactical structure declares the control of Ishmael's active will in the struggle, for that assertion is placed in the main clause; but the declaration is only that he must get away to sea "as soon as I can," and "quietly take to the ship." The forces are still working upon him, even in his supposition that he "chose" this evasion of the aggression and suicide towards which they are driving him; for in passively ("quietly") taking to ship, as in welcoming the whaling voyage, he is actually shipping on Ahab's aggressive mission, which leaves him in "abandonment" at the end (in the last words of his epilogue), "another orphan."

V

This discussion of "Loomings" has, I hope, illustrated what I called at its beginning the dense imaginative coherence of *Moby-Dick*, the close weaving of yarns in the figures of its fabric. I suppose readers have been at least as uneasily aware all along as I have of the limitations of some of my strategical assumptions, and especially do I sense the artificiality of my main working assumption that everything in the book is coming to us from its narrator Ishmael. When one should ascribe such elements as imagery, syntax, rhetoric, and their implications for thought and character in *Moby-Dick* to the fictional narrator Ishmael and when to his creator Melville is, I suspect, perhaps more a matter of critical strategy and relevance than of inherent propriety. If readers have noticed points in the discussion where taking such linguistic elements to characterize Ishmael seems unusually arbitrary, such points may indicate where it might have been better to assign them to Melville instead. Ultimately, this must somehow be done if sense is to be made of such recurrent images, motifs, and themes as I have been most concerned with displaying, especially since those which figure centrally in "Loomings" and the rest of *Moby-Dick*, where Ishmael is narrator, also permeate the whole of Melville's work from *Typee* to *Billy Budd*, where of course he is not. The total imaginative coherence of these works must have as its ground the mind of Melville, as author of them all.

Notes

1. On August 1, 1969, Herman Melville's 150th birthday was celebrated at Kent State University. Of course Howard P. Vincent was the organizer as he has indefatigably been, alone and with others, of so many such occasions, from the great Williamstown one in 1951, for the 100th birthday of *Moby-Dick*, to the Paris one of May, 1974. It was at his instigation that I delivered a paper at Williamstown in 1951 titled "Melville's Prisoners," in which I set out a peculiar image cluster I had found in Melville's works. It was also at his instigation that I delivered a paper at Kent in 1969 titled "Birthdays of Herman Melville," of which a razeed version of the paper now offered was substantially the central section. (A tape recording preserves the whole ebullient session at which it was presented.) I hope Howard will think it an appropriate offering, because it was worked up for him in the first place, because it may remind him of that happy Kent occasion, and because (in spite of his efforts over the years of our long association) it is the only offshoot of my larger study, the long-in-process *Melville's Prisoners*, yet to reach print.

2. I believe William Ellery Sedgwick, in *Herman Melville: The Tragedy of Mind* (Cambridge, Mass.: Harvard University Press, 1944), was the first critic to discuss Ishmael equally with Ahab. It was Howard Vincent who contributed as much as anyone else to this delineation of Ishmael's role, in *The Trying-Out of Moby-Dick* (1949). Others who have pursued this line of interpretation include Walter Bezanson, "*Moby-Dick*: Work of Art," Tyrus Hillway and Luther Mansfield, eds., *Moby-Dick Centennial Essays* (Dallas: Southern Methodist University Press, 1953), pp. 30–58; Merlin Bowen, *The Long Encounter* (Chicago: University of Chicago Press, 1960); Paul Brodtkorb, *Ishmael's White World* (New Haven: Yale University Press, 1965); and Edgar Dryden, *Melville's Thematics of Form* (Baltimore: Johns Hopkins Press, 1968). Most recently, the approach attributing all to Ishmael is systematically followed in Robert Zoellner's full length treatment of *Moby-Dick, The Salt-Sea Mastodon* (Berkeley: University of California Press, 1973), whose basic assumption is that "every word of *Moby-Dick*, including even the footnotes, comes from Ishmael rather than Melville" (p. xi).

3. For example, refer to Carl Strauch, "Ishmael: Time and Personality in *Moby-Dick*," *Studies in the Novel*, I (Winter, 1969), 468–483.

4. Robert Lowell, in "The Quaker Graveyard in Nantucket," restated this theme accurately and magnificently.

5. In *The Salt-Sea Mastodon* Robert Zoellner calls this "universal thump" concept a "central preoccupation of *Moby-Dick*" (p. 54).

The Meaning of the Whale

Edward F. Edinger

With the crew all committed to the destruction of Moby-Dick, we must now turn to the question: What is the meaning of this mighty whale, the central character of the book? The problem is that the whale has too many meanings. Melville has gone to great trouble to provide an almost boundless network of associations to amplify the image of the whale. The whale and its multitude of meanings becomes a Cretan labyrinth wherein one is almost sure to lose himself. The amplification process begins before the narrative itself in the extracts concerning whales that Melville has collected from the literature and mythologies of the world. This collection of general and mythological associations to the whale, together with much other evidence in the book proper, indicates that Melville had discovered on his own the amplification method and used it to gain entrance to the collective unconscious.

Amplification as developed by Jung is a fundamental procedure in the process of uncovering and analyzing the unconscious. According to this procedure, dreams and other psychic images are used to initiate a series of associations which enlarge the meaning of the initial image and provide it with a context. The method of amplification has two aspects, personal amplification and general amplification. The first step, personal amplification, is done by asking the patient to express his spontaneous feelings, thoughts, and memories pertaining to his personal life that come to mind concerning the given image. The totality of these personal associations to all the elements in a dream provide the personal context of the dream and often lead to a significant meaning. The second step is general amplification. This is done by the psychotherapist on the basis of his own knowledge. General amplification provides the collective, archetypal associations to the dream elements. It is here that the therapist's knowledge of the collective or objective psyche is put to use. When a dream contains an archetypal image or theme, the therapist demonstrates this by presenting parallel imagery from mythology, legend, and folklore. General amplification establishes the collective context of the dream and enables it to be seen as referring not only to a personal psychic problem but also to a general, collective problem

Excerpted and reprinted from *Melville's MOBY-DICK: A Jungian Commentary* (New York: New Directions, 1978), 73–80. Copyright © 1978 by Edward F. Edinger. Reprinted by permission of the New Directions Publishing Corp.

common to all human experience. General amplification introduces one to the collective or archetypal psyche and at the same time helps the process of disidentifying the ego from the archetypal psyche.

Poetry and imaginative literature have always used amplification and analogy to suggest depths of meaning that would otherwise be missed. However, *Moby-Dick* is a particularly fine and far-reaching example of the amplification process. The entire book can be seen as an elaborate amplification of the psychological meaning of the whale and whale hunting. Since this is the case, it will be obviously impossible to circumscribe the meaning of the whale in a brief descriptive account. Melville himself has forewarned us concerning the impossibility of painting the portrait of the whale. After reviewing the various attempts to capture the reality of the whale in pictures, all of which fail in some respects, he concludes:

> For all these reasons, then, any way you may look at it, you must needs conclude that the great Leviathan is that one creature in the world which must remain unpainted to the last. True, one portrait may hit the mark much nearer than another, but none can hit it with any very considerable degree of exactness. So there is no earthly way of finding out precisely what the whale really looks like. And the only mode in which you can derive even a tolerable idea of his living contour, is by going whaling yourself; but by doing so, you run no small risk of being eternally stove and sunk by him. Wherefore, it seems to me you had best not be too fastidious in your curiosity touching this Leviathan. (Chapter 55)

Melville gives us the same warning when he talks about the dangers of the sea, the whales' habitat. He catalogs the terrors of the sea and continues:

> Consider the subtleness of the sea; how its most dreaded creatures glide under water, unapparent for the most part, and treacherously hidden beneath the loveliest tints of azure. Consider also the devilish brilliance and beauty of many of its most remorseless tribes, as the dainty embellished shape of many species of sharks. Consider, once more, the universal cannibalism of the sea; all whose creatures prey upon each other, carrying on eternal war since the world began.
>
> Consider all this; and then turn to this green, gentle, and most docile earth; consider them both, the sea and the land; and do you not find a strange analogy to something in yourself? For as this appalling ocean surrounds the verdant land, so in the soul of man there lies one insular Tahiti, full of peace and joy, but encompassed by all the horrors of the half known life. God keep thee! Push not off from that isle, thou canst never return! (Chapter 58)

Here we have the compensatory opposite to Bulkington's attitude, "in landlessness alone resides the highest truth" (Chapter 23). The sea and the whale convey the same terrors and evoke the same warnings because they are different images to symbolize the same psychological fact. We do indeed find a "strange analogy" to something inside ourselves. The sea and the whale represent the primordial unconscious psyche which contains the aboriginal energies of life—numinous, awesome, and terrible. The sea is the collective unconscious and the whales that inhabit it are its major contents, the archetypes. The green island surrounded by the sea is the ego, the structural order of consciousness. Although an encounter with whales is dangerous, threatening drowning or dissolution of the conscious personality (psychosis), for the whaleman, the hero, whales are a vitally necessary source of energy to light the lamps of civilization. They must be hunted out, killed, and dismembered so that their raw natural energies can be transformed and applied to the uses of civilization—the purposes of the conscious discrimi-nating personality. The whaling industry is thus a paradigm of the heroic effort of human consciousness to confront and transform the raw and aboriginal energies of the psyche.

The life of the whale hunters has many similarities to primitive hunting societies, and something of the same psychology applies to both. A primitive hunting group tends to have one animal on which it relies for sustenance, and its attitude toward this animal is a reverent one. This was true, for instance, of the Blackfoot Indians and the buffalo. The buffalo hunt is surrounded with sacred rite and ceremonial. Campbell writes: "Where the animal rites are properly celebrated by the people, there is a magical, wonderful accord between the beasts and those who have to hunt them. The buffalo dance properly performed insures that the creatures slaughtered shall be giving only their bodies, not their essence. . . . The hunt itself, therefore, is a rite of sacrifice, sacred and not a rawly secular affair."[1]

It was considered safe to kill particular buffaloes only if the reverent relation to the "great buffalo" is maintained. The "great buffalo" is the prototypical or essential animal; the eternal form or Platonic Idea of the species. "He is a figure of one more dimension than the others of his herd; timeless and indestructible. . . . He is a manifestation of that point, principle, or aspect of the realm of essence from which the creatures of his species spring."[2]

These considerations fit quite closely the hunting of whales in Moby-Dick. The whale hunters must kill whales for their own livelihood. But among all the whales in the ocean there is one special white whale, the "great" whale who will not permit himself to be captured. As with the "great Buffalo" of the Blackfoot who is timeless and indestructible, Moby-Dick was thought to be ubiquitous and immortal. He was the collective whale soul, the essential, eternal whale of which all other whales are only ephemeral manifestations. The sacred, special character of Moby-Dick is indicated by his whiteness. White or albino animals are typically considered sacred. Melville notes this fact, giving as examples the sacred white elephant of the Orient and the sacred white dog of the Iroquois.

To hunt the sacred white whale in the same way as all other whales are hunted is a sacrilege, a blasphemy, as Starbuck said. It represents a denial of the primitive hunter's religious attitude toward his victim. An assault on Moby-Dick is an assault on the very concept of the sacred. Now we begin to glimpse one of the fundamental meanings of Ahab's vengeful quest. It symbolizes the psychic dynamism which is responsible for the radical secularization of the modern industrial world. The very notion of the sacred, the numinous, the suprapersonal as a concept or category of experience is being extirpated from modern consciousness. Whales are the primitive, undifferentiated energies of nature; and, as one Melvillian commentator has put it, the whaleship is a machine for the exploitation of nature.[3] But if that exploitation process is turned against the sacred and suprapersonal aspect of man's own inner nature, she will turn against man and destroy him. The primitive attitude is right. When a primitive kills an animal for food or threshes his grain to make bread, he realizes he is sacrificing an aspect of deity. He therefore does it solemnly and religiously. His myths tell him that the animal or vegetation god is willing to offer himself freely as a sacrifice to the needs of men. But if this god-killing is done irreverently, with hybris, the god can turn against man and destroy him by withholding future food.

This may not be good logic for efficient hunting or agriculture, but it is sound psychology. The primitive attitude of natural piety may be considered superstitious and misplaced when applied to the external world; however, it is instinctive wisdom when applied to the inner psychic world. We can contain within us raw, undifferentiated natural life energies. If we are to have a conscious psychic life, it must feed on and transform these elemental energies. The archetypal energy-forms of the collective unconscious must be dismembered and broken down into assimilable units, like Osiris and like a captured whale, if the primordial energies are to be made available for conscious purposes. However, these are suprapersonal energies most aptly described as deities. Hence they must be approached with a religious attitude. Failure to do so is an act of hybris which does not recognize the existence of any power other than the will of the ego. In such a case the ego does not succeed in assimilating the energies of the archetypal form; rather, the archetype assimilates the ego. This is a disaster for the conscious personality. It undergoes a regression and lives out unconsciously the fate of the particular mythological image with which it is identified. And so it was with Ahab.

There can be no doubt that the white whale symbolizes the deity. A definite effort is made to assimilate the god-images of many of the world's mythologies to Moby-Dick. Let us pass some of the evidence in quick review.

Moby-Dick is called a "Job's whale" (Chapter 41), referring to Leviathan in the book of Job, one of the manifestations of Yahweh. The whale is remarked to be one of the incarnations of Vishnu in the Matse Avatar (Chapter 55). The mad sailor, Gabriel, pronounced the white whale to be the

Shaker God incarnated, and he prophesied "speedy doom to the sacrilegious assailants of his divinity" (Chapter 71). When Moby-Dick is first sighted, he is associated with Jupiter. "A gentle joyousness—a mighty mildness of repose in swiftness, invested the gliding whale. Not the white bull Jupiter swimming away with ravished Europa clinging to his graceful horns; his lovely, leering eyes sideways intent upon the maid; with smooth bewitching fleetness, rippling straight for the nuptial bower in Crete; not Jove, not that great majesty Supreme! did surpass the glorified White Whale as he so divinely swam" (Chapter 133). Later, Moby-Dick is called a "grand god": "warningly waving his bannered flukes in the air, the grand god revealed himself, sounded and went out of sight" (Chapter 133).

Much earlier, Ahab had described Moby-Dick as representing the transcendental reality behind the appearance of things. And such transcendental reality is another name for God. "All visible objects, man, are but as pasteboard masks. But in each event—in the living act, the undoubted deed—there, some unknown but still reasoning thing puts forth the mouldings of its features from behind the unreasoning mask. If man will strike, strike through the mask! How can the prisoner reach outside except by thrusting through the wall? To me, the white whale is that wall, shoved near to me." (Chapter 36)

Jung has demonstrated that the various representations of the god-image are expressions of the central archetype of the psyche, what he terms the Self. We must thus conclude that Moby-Dick is a symbol of the Self. One of the features of the phenomenology of the Self is that it is a paradoxical union of opposites. This theme appears in the discussion of the whale's vision. It is stated that the eyes of a whale are located in the sides of his head, and hence they look in opposite directions.

> A curious and most puzzling question might be started concerning this visual matter as touching the Leviathan. But I must be content with a hint. So long as a man's eyes are open in the light, the act of seeing is involuntary; that is, he cannot then help mechanically seeing whatever objects are before him. Nevertheless, any one's experience will teach him, that though he can take in an indiscriminating sweep of things at one glance, it is impossible for him, attentively, and completely, to examine any two things—however large or however small—at one and the same instant of time; never mind if they lie side by side and touch each other. But if you now come to separate these two objects, and surround each by a circle of profound darkness; then in order to see one of them, in such a manner as to bring your mind to bear on it, the other will be utterly excluded from your contemporary consciousness. How is it, then, with the whale? True, both his eyes, in themselves must simultaneously act; but is his brain so much more comprehensive, combining, and subtle than man's, that he can at the same moment of time attentively examine two distinct prospects, one on one side of him, and the other in an exactly opposite direction? (Chapter 74)

The whale can relate to opposites simultaneously and thus transcend or reconcile them. This is one of the features of the Self which distinguishes it most clearly from that lesser center of personality, the conscious ego. Consciousness by its very nature exists by the separation of opposites by acquiring unilateral vision. The Self, the suprapersonal center of the personality has bilateral vision—it incorporates both sides of a pair of opposites in the total view and hence conveys wholeness.

The paradoxical nature of Moby-Dick is considered more extensively in regard to its color symbolism. A long chapter is devoted to discussing the significance of the whiteness of the whale. Although Melville records many of the positive and sacred associations to the color white, they are mentioned only to be discarded. For Melville, whiteness is equated with evil. The conventional meaning of the symbolic antithesis between black and white is reversed. We are told in effect that white is black—an enantiodromia is announced.

A woman once dreamt of Melville's white whale connected with a black whale "very much in the fashion of the Chinese T'ai-chi-t'u." The white whale had a black eye and the black whale a white eye.[4] ☯

For this dreamer, and likewise for Melville, the white whale Moby-Dick poses the archetypal problem of opposites. The Chinese T'ai-chi-t'u symbolizes the reciprocal relationship between two opposing principles. The white fish is Yang, the masculine principle of light, heaven, spirit, action. The black fish is Yin, the feminine principle of darkness, earth, matter, receptivity. According to the Chinese notion, these two primal modes of being are in an alternating relation to one another, each containing the seed of its own opposite.

Moby-Dick is both black and white. It is white so far as its color is concerned. But it is symbolically black in its essential nature. Hence, it is a union of opposites. It is both Yang and Yin. It symbolizes paradoxically both the masculine principle of the father archetype and the feminine principle of the mother archetype. Its whiteness relates it to Yang, the spiritual logos principle and the father archetype, but its womblike, devouring aspects relate it to the mother archetype. I shall discuss these each in turn.

Notes

1. Joseph Campbell, *The Masks of God: Primitive Mythology* (New York: Viking Press, 1959), p. 293.
2. Ibid., p. 292.
3. "So if you want to know why Melville nailed us in *Moby-Dick*, consider whaling. Consider whaling as FRONTIER and INDUSTRY. A product wanted, men got it: big business. The Pacific as sweatshop. Men, led, against the biggest, damnedest creature nature uncorks. The whaleship as factory, the whaleboat the precision instrument." Charles Olson, *op. cit.*, p. 23.
4. Harriet A. Todd, *The Quest in the Works of Herman Melville* (privately printed, 1961), preface.

GENESIS

◆

Unnecessary Duplicates:
A Key to the Writing of *Moby-Dick*

HARRISON HAYFORD

The lock contains no key. Hearing him foolishly fumbling there, the Captain laughs lowly to himself. Chap. 9.

I

Melville introduces the *Pequod*'s carpenter by remarking that if you seat yourself 'sultanically' among the moons of Saturn 'high abstracted man alone' seems 'a wonder, a grandeur, and a woe' but that from the same viewpoint 'mankind in mass' for the most part seem 'a mob of unnecessary duplicates' (ch. 107). Something of the same sort can be said about two such ways of looking at *Moby-Dick*. From an integrative critical viewpoint the book gives a unified impression of wonder, grandeur, and tragic woe. But on close scrutiny many of its compositional elements seem, in ordinary fictional terms, to be 'a mob of unnecessary duplicates'. You could call both views 'sultanically' elevated, since each is way outside any view mundane readers are likely to take of the book. In this essay I am going, arbitrarily enough, to disregard the integrative view and take the second way of looking at it. First I'll point out the curious pattern of duplicates I see in it, and then I'll go on to use this pattern as evidence for a major hypothesis I'll offer about Melville's shifting intentions for some of the central characters in *Moby-Dick* as it developed through several phases during the year and a half he was writing it. I believe these duplicates give us a new key, to add to the several we already have, to fumble with (let's hope not altogether foolishly) as we keep trying to open some of the interlocked complications of the book's genesis, to which there is no master key we know of.

Duplicates begin at once. It takes not one but two chapters to do the narrative job of getting Ishmael started out to see the watery part of the world on his first whaling voyage. Chapter I loses narrative headway after its third sentence, so that chapter 2 must duplicate its job and start him again,

Reprinted from *New Perspectives on Melville*, ed. Faith Pullin (Edinburgh: Edinburgh University Press, 1978), 128–61. Reprinted by permission of the publisher.

as he stuffs a shirt or two in his bag and sets out for a whaling port, New Bedford. But at once there's another duplicate; he tells us he won't sail from that first port but from a second, Nantucket. Moreover, since at New Bedford he misses the Nantucket boat and it's Saturday night he must spend not one but two nights and the intervening Sunday there, getting no closer to a whaleship. The job of the rest of chapter 2 is to deal with his problem of finding an inn. Presumably the inn, like the whole chapter, serves the book's larger fictional purpose of illustrating the whaleman's world as a tyro encounters it; but presenting two whaling ports entails presenting two inns—duplicates breed duplicates. Why need we be shown the whaleman's shore life via *two* inns, one at New Bedford run by an officious humorous landlord, and a second at Nantucket run by an officious humourless landlady? Seeking a suitable inn, Ishmael passes up a couple of 'too expensive and jolly' ones and blunders into and out of a Negro church before he manages to select the Spouter-Inn.

The first of the two problems in the Spouter-Inn (ch. 3) is for Ishmael to find a sleeping-place there. And he finds duplicates, not one place but two, and goes to bed twice, first on a cold narrow bench alone, then in a warm prodigious bed with a harpooneer bedfellow. Why both?

The chapter's second problem is the larger narrative job of introducing an experienced whaleman to become tyro Ishmael's comrade and probably also his mentor in 'this business of whaling'. But the chapter proceeds to introduce not one but two such characters, first Bulkington, then Queequeg—duplicates. Bulkington enters the inn with the *Grampus* crew, just landed from a three years' whaling voyage; he is a 'huge favorite' with the crew and evidently an experienced whaleman. Ishmael describes Bulkington, he says, because he'll be a shipmate—only to explain in an immediate parenthesis and metaphor that he won't: 'This man interested me at once; and since the sea-gods had ordained that he should soon become my shipmate (though but a sleeping-partner one, so far as this narrative is concerned), I will here venture upon a little description of him.' After a portentous description of Bulkington in romantic-heroic terms he is said to slip away unobserved, and we are told 'I saw no more of him till he became my comrade on the sea'. The word 'comrade' applied to Bulkington here is a noteworthy one; it postulates a special personal relationship transcending that of a mere 'shipmate', and later in the book Ishmael applies the word in the singular to only one man, not to Bulkington but to Queequeg (chs 13, 18, 72). At once Bulkington slips away, is missing from the following shore chapters, is seen once more as the ship puts out to sea, and then is altogether absent from the book. Thus he sets a pattern of 'hiding out' that is to be duplicated by several characters who are themselves duplicates. But, oddly, the bulk of chapter 3 is then given over to the spun-out practical-joke introduction of a duplicate comrade.

This duplicate is a second experienced whaleman, a harpooneer, who is missing (a second 'hide out') until near the chapter's end; there, after 'second thoughts' on the part of both landlord and Ishmael, he's accepted as the tyro's literal 'sleeping-partner' that Saturday night. And in the course of Sunday evening, after Ishmael sallies out twice, first for a morning sightseeing stroll then to visit the Whaleman's Chapel and hear Father Mapple's sermon, Queequeg further becomes Ishmael's 'bosom-friend' and is a second time his sleeping-partner. He resolves to accompany Ishmael on his whaling voyage and share his every hap. Ishmael tells us, 'To all this I joyously assented; for besides the affection I now felt for Queequeg, he was an experienced harpooneer, and as such, could not fail to be of great usefulness to one, who, like me, was wholly ignorant of the mysteries of whaling . . .' (chs 4–12).

Monday morning, in chapter 13, Ishmael sets off with Queequeg—'my comrade' as he twice calls him—for Nantucket, to the second whaling port, second inn, second dominating keeper, and even two chowders. The next problem, in chapter 16, is for them to choose a ship and sign aboard. Ishmael had 'not a little relied upon Queequeg's sagacity to point out the whaler best fitted' for their voyage, and certainly Queequeg's novelistic job, as experienced-whaleman mentor, should be to 'be of great usefulness'. Nevertheless, he declares he can't do so, reassigns the job to his little god Yojo, and 'hides out' a second time. Consequently, since he doesn't accompany Ishmael to the docks, not one but two signing-aboard scenes must be presented, first one for Ishmael then another for Queequeg; that is, duplicate chapters (16, 18) must be devoted to business that might have been economically accomplished in a single one.

So tyro Ishmael goes alone and himself decides on the *Pequod*—or duplicates Yojo's pre-decision. In chapter 16, 'The Ship', in which he does so, duplications continue. First, there are duplications with respect to the ship herself. For some of the *Pequod*'s attractive peculiarities are specified here in particulars that are later to be negated by discrepant duplicate specifications. Here, for example, she's said to have 'unpanelled, open bulwarks' all round; but later, off the Cape of Good Hope, the crew seek shelter from the heavy seas 'along the bulwarks in the waist', which must, therefore, be panelled ones (ch. 51). Here, again (as in chapters 96, 123) she's said to sport instead of a turnstile wheel 'a tiller . . . curiously carved from the long narrow lower jaw of her hereditary foe'; but twice later she's given a wheel with spokes (chs 61, 118).

Besides these minor duplications in the ship's details, there are at once major duplicates among characters associated with her, notably in her having not one but three 'captains'. For as Ishmael first goes aboard the *Pequod*, who's in charge? Not, as might be expected, just one agent, owner, or captain to sign him on, but two—both retired Quaker captains who are also the two chief owners, Peleg and Bildad. And—though it's old Captain Peleg who has served for years on the Indian-named ship, who sits in a 'wigwam' of whalebone on her deck, and who has, we're told, done the curious whalebone carving work that dresses her in 'barbaric' apparel—it turns out to be not Peleg but still a third duplicate old Quaker captain, Ahab, who is to be her actual captain in command on the upcoming voyage and who (not Peleg) possesses the most striking piece of whalebone carving, a 'barbaric white leg' which 'had at sea been fashioned from the polished bone of the sperm whale's jaw' (ch. 28). But this third duplicate captain is not to be seen until days after the ship sails; he's said to be sick (like Bulkington and Queequeg he 'hides out'), and so his appearance will require a later separate chapter (ch. 28). The two old Quaker captains who do appear in chapter 16, Peleg and Bildad, so overlap in fictional uses that they may seem to be duplicates as indistinguishable as Rosenkranz and Guildenstern, though they are given individualizing peculiarities. Peleg is a profane 'blusterer' while Bildad is a quiet, pious canter who solemnly declares his fear that impenitent Peleg's leaky conscience will sink him 'foundering down to the fiery pit'. Peleg angrily rejects Bildad's prophecy, rephrasing it in plain English: 'Fiery pit! fiery pit! ye insult me, man; past all natural bearing, ye insult me. It's an all-fired outrage to tell any human creature that he's bound to hell'. But, as it turns out, it is not the first captain, Peleg, with his mild everyday profanities, but the third captain, Ahab, with his outraged sense of the insults and indignities heaped upon the human creature, and with his major blasphemies, who is the one indeed 'bound to hell' and who drives the *Pequod* and all her crew (save one) to 'sink to hell' (ch. 135).

And very soon further duplications of characters follow, centering upon the role of prophet of Ahab's fate. Bildad's prophecy here in chapter 16 makes him the first of seven duplicate prophets, all of whom take up in their various direct or indirect ways the burden of Christian Bildad's initial prediction of a profane captain's hell-bound career (though not Peleg's, it turns out, but Ahab's). After Bildad, these prophets are, in order, three who are introduced ashore—'the old squaw, Tistig, at Gay-head' (ch. 16); an old sailor, Elijah (chs 19, 21); the Parsee Fedallah (who's hiding out in chapter 21); and two more who are introduced at sea, upon Ahab's first appearance, in chapter 28: 'Tashtego's senior, an old Gay-Head Indian among the crew', and 'a grey Manxman . . . , an old sepulchral man'. To these six prophets closely associated with Ahab on shore or ship can be added a seventh encountered on another ship, the crazy Shaker Gabriel, who also warns Ahab to 'beware of the blasphemer's end!' and prophesies, 'thou art soon going that way' (ch. 71).

Among these prophets along Ahab's hell-bound route the most curiously conspicuous duplicates are three Gay-Head Indians (the book uses the place name in several forms as quoted here). The first, the old squaw Tistig, is followed in prophetic role by the old Gay-Head Indian crewman, 'Tashtego's senior', and both of these Gay-Headers know circumstances of Ahab's birth and speak portentously about his career. The old crewman appears only once, and two of the three items of Ahab's history he gives out are later contradicted by discrepant duplicate information: 'Aye, he was dismasted off Japan', he volunteers, 'but like his dismasted craft, he shipped another mast without coming home for it. He has a quiver of 'em'—whereas later it's established that it was on the equator (and not off Japan) that Moby Dick took off Ahab's leg (ch. 130), and also shown that Ahab has no quiver of extras but must order a new one to be made by the carpenter when his original one is wrenched (chs 106, 108). This old Indian crewman, 'Tashtego's senior', never reappears, but his prophetic role is duplicated by Tashtego, 'an unmixed Indian from Gay Head' (ch. 27) who is prominent as one of the *Pequod*'s three pagan harpooneers. 'To look at the tawny brawn of his lithe snaky limbs, you would almost have credited the superstitions of some of the earlier Puritans, and half believed this wild Indian to be a son of the Prince of the Powers of the Air' (ch. 27). It is Tashtego, this third Gay-Head Indian, who at the masthead sights and sings out for the *Pequod*'s first whale and in doing so is described as like a prophet or seer:

> High aloft in the cross-trees was that mad Gay-Header, Tashtego. . . . As he stood hovering over you half suspended in air, so wildly and eagerly peering towards the horizon, you would have thought him some prophet or seer beholding the shadows of Fate, and by those wild cries announcing their coming. (ch. 47)

Months later, when Moby Dick is sighted for the first time, it is Tashtego again at the masthead who 'saw him at almost the same instant that Captain Ahab did' and cried out—just missing award of the doubloon (ch. 133). And on the final day, in the moments of Ahab's fated end when the unanimous prophecy of all these duplicate prophets is fulfilled, it is for some reason the red Indian Tashtego who at Ahab's command is nailing Ahab's red flag of no-surrender to the mast of the fated *Pequod* during the moments when she must 'sink to hell' (ch. 135).

As for the other two prophets introduced ashore before the ship sails, Elijah, though 'crazy', is a true prophet, an 'old sailor chap' who has sailed under Ahab and calls him 'Old Thunder'; he reveals to Ishmael and Queequeg some hints of Ahab's character and history, and warns them of the soul-peril of shipping on the *Pequod*—'that ship'—with him. Elijah also hints the existence of Ahab's false prophet-companion, Fedallah, the Parsee of vague East Indian or else devilish origin, whom Ahab smuggles aboard along with his oriental four-man duplicate boat-crew, to 'hide out' below until the first lowering (ch. 48). Why all these seven duplicate prophets?

At long last chapter 22 gets the *Pequod* hauled out from the Nantucket wharf. The twenty-one shore chapters have already taken up about a fifth of the book—surely a disproportionate share—before the whaling voyage begins, before Ishmael sees anything of the watery part of the world, before the book's tragic protagonist appears, and before its plot and Ahab's mighty antagonist are revealed. There have been two narrative starts, two whaling ports, two inns (and two chowders), two innkeepers, two beds and goings-to-bed, two comrades (one dismissed already), two signings-aboard, two Quaker captain-owners and a third Quaker captain-in-command, four (of an eventual seven) prophets, four hide-outs, and an extra boat-crew. No wonder it has taken so much space, with so much duplication already! Did Melville think the book itself had to be stocked with duplicates just as the *Pequod* had to be provided with 'spare boats, spare spars, and spare lines and harpoons, and spare everythings, almost, but a spare Captain and duplicate ship'? (ch. 20).

Nor does this space-demanding pattern of duplicates cease when the ship has left the wharf. As the *Pequod* is worked out of Nantucket harbour into the open sea, not just one pilot but two are aboard. What need two? Again it is those two old Quaker owner-captains (the ship's commanding Quaker captain, Ahab, still hides out in his cabin); both of them are 'going it with a high hand on the quarter-deck, just as if they were to be joint-commanders at sea, as well as to all appearances in port'. Captain Peleg's first order is one that Captain Ahab significantly duplicates fourteen chapters later, to open the 'Quarter-Deck' scene (ch. 36). Peleg's is an order that by usage a captain would give his mate soon after such a ship got under way—'Call all hands, then. Muster 'em aft here. . . .' This order customarily initiated one or two routines neither of which follows Peleg's order here. On an actual voyage the crew thus mustered aft might be harangued by the captain, who would lay down the purpose of the voyage, the crew's duties, and his own policies; and the mates would choose up men for their watches. (For accounts see Melville's own *Redburn,* or R.H. Dana's *Two Years Before the Mast,* J.N. Reynolds' 'Mocha Dick', and J. Ross Browne's *Etchings of a Whaling Cruise*—works Melville knew and used in writing *Moby-Dick.*) In *Moby-Dick,* however, the all-hands sequence does not get played out normally but is curiously split in two after the duplicate orders in chapters 22 and 36. Profane Captain Peleg (standing in here for Captain Ahab) begins it with his first order to the mate, 'Well, call all hands, then. Muster 'em aft here—blast 'em!' But Peleg, it turns out, doesn't want them all aft for either of the usual routines just mentioned; no, what he wants done there by the 'sons of bachelors' is only to have his whalebone tent struck—scarcely a duty requiring all hands. Apparently something went askew in Peleg's—or Melville's—orders. (Peleg's next order, however, is a proper one, actually requiring all hands, though for duty forward not aft: 'Man the capstan! Blood and thunder!—jump!' This is the order to raise the anchor, an order, indeed, that normally came *before* the order to muster, lest the crew might sober up and desert before the ship got under way.) On the *Pequod*, Captain Ahab's duplicate muster order comes after the ship has been at sea for many days, with the mates and crew doing their regular duties, though, as was just pointed out, no account of choosing up watches (indeed nothing in detail about deck or forecastle life at all) has been given before Captain Ahab, at last out of hiding, appears above hatches (ch. 28). When Ahab 'impulsively' orders the mate to send everybody aft, Starbuck is said to be 'astonished at an order seldom or never given on ship-board except in some extraordinary case' (chs 46, 36). True enough, at *that* stage of a voyage. But what then ensues on the quarterdeck is, in form, one part of the long-overdue normal follow-up of Peleg's order days ago—the captain's harangue to the crew about the voyage's purpose and his own policies—though in *content*, as Starbuck sees and the narrator tells us, Ahab's 'prime but private purpose', is a mad usurpation of any proper purpose and policy. In sum, Melville has his duplicate captains give duplicate muster orders; Peleg's is too early (in harbour) and is not followed by either customary routine; while Ahab's is fourteen chapters too late (at sea) and is followed by a customary but subverted routine. It's as if Ahab took up right where Peleg left off.

And this duplication of orders is not the only or most significant duplication that occurs in the Christmas-day departure chapter. While profane Peleg rips and swears astern at the crew 'in the most frightful manner', Ishmael pauses in his efforts at the capstan forward to think of the perils he and Queequeg are running 'in starting on the voyage with such a devil for a pilot'—though even a tyro whaleman should realize that a *pilot*, soon to go ashore, could offer them no peril on the voyage itself. Then Ishmael feels a 'sudden sharp poke in my rear' and is horrified to see Captain Peleg 'withdrawing his leg' from 'my immediate vicinity'. And he remarks, 'That was my first kick'. Yes, but it's not the first we've heard of Peleg's leg, or the last we'll hear of a kick from a captain. There's in fact some confused duplication of legs and kicks on the *Pequod*. Already in the first signing-aboard scene (ch. 16) Peleg has for some reason called Ishmael's special attention to his leg though apparently it's just a normal leg, Ahab's being the only remarkable one, of whalebone: 'Dost see that leg?—I'll take that leg away from thy stern, if ever thou talkest of the marchant service to me again.' So sure enough, though for another offence, here at up-anchor time Peleg does kick Ishmael with 'that leg'. It's Ishmael's 'first kick', as he says; and, though this expression implies more kicks, it's also his last kick and indeed anybody's last actual kick of the voyage, apart from those Peleg gives in 'using his leg very freely' as the anchor is being raised. Yet, more kicks and kicking soon do follow, but only in a reported dream, including a dream-kick from a captain with a more noteworthy leg than Peleg's. The recipient this time is not Ishmael (a common sailor) but Stubb (an officer—who sounds like a duplicate of the Ishmael of chapter 1) in his 'Queen Mab' dream of his own kicking a pyramid, of being invited to kick a merman's marlinspike-bristling rump, and of having been kicked by Ahab's ivory leg, and in his wide-awake rationalizing of his wisdom in not kicking back (ch. 31). Duplicate legs-and-kicking galore!

In the course of chapter 22 the *Pequod* at last gains an offing in the wintry Atlantic, and the duplicate pilot-captains (the swearing-kicking fearsome Quaker 'devil' Peleg with 'that leg' and the pious Quaker prophet Bildad) both say their reluctant farewells to the ship and both drop into the pilot boat to go ashore, leaving the third and still hidden-out duplicate Quaker captain, the soon-to-be-revealed Satanic Ahab, in command for the voyage.

The *Pequod* is at sea. But the book's duplicative treatment of three central and closely related novelistic jobs still confronts us with questions we might suppose Melville should have settled by this point. These are questions as to its narrator and narrative point-of-view, its protagonist or hero, and the over-all shape of its narrative line—its action or plot. For each of these questions, however, we have already been offered, or are about to be given, several duplicate answers. Nor do duplications of other kinds cease in the sea chapters. I'll leave readers the pleasure of compiling their own lists. Some duplicates are not obvious but no one will overlook the series of deaths and averted near-deaths (I think of it as the 'man-overboard' pattern); or the closely related series of rescues and redeemings by Queequeg already begun ashore; or the series of ship-meetings, sometimes miscalled gams; or the *Pequod*'s final three-day trio of encounters with tragic-hero Ahab's great antagonist; or the duplicate names of that antagonist, the 'White Whale' some call 'Moby Dick'; or the book's own successive duplicate titles, *The Whale* and *Moby-Dick*. But the ones I have just listed in the shore-narrative— taken with the sea-narrative matters they implicate—already give me more duplicates than I can deal with in this essay. As a key, they give me enough, as I try to account for them, to give rise to my major hypothesis about a part of the genetic history of some of the book's characters.

II

Among the duplicate characters, Bulkington and Queequeg are the best pair to begin with, because it's so obvious which of them came first, and because our seeing the compositional ways Melville handled this pair leads us on, by a somewhat devious path, to see the ways he handled the other major duplicate characters, and thus to my major hypothesis: My line of reasoning about the composition stages is simple enough, but since it has to work backwards from what's in the printed book to earlier inferred stages, it will be easier to follow if I list the stages here by numbers and use them all along in my discussion. I provisionally distinguish three stages through which Melville's shore-narrative must have gone—I mean just with respect to this pair of alternate comrades, not to its whole writing history. Stage 1 included neither Bulkington nor Queequeg; Stage 2 added Bulkington; Stage 3 dismissed Bulkington and added Queequeg, ending up as the version printed. All three probably included substages.

In the finished book, Bulkington, unlike any of the other duplicate characters, sticks out as vestigial because in the two early passages that he enters (chs 3, 23) he is assigned the dual roles of comrade and truth-seeker, but is not developed later in either role; indeed, in both passages Melville explicitly dismisses him from appearing in any role at all in the ensuing narrative. The explanation of this anomalous assignment-dismissal procedure must be that two compositional stages are involved in the passages as they stand, that at the earlier (Stage 2) Melville intended him to play these roles but then at the later (Stage 3) changed his intention and revised the passages to dismiss him from both roles, yet for some reason did not discard him, or the passages, altogether.

Not only is Bulkington vestigial, he is one of our duplicates—in chapter 3 he and Queequeg pair in the one-man role of narrator's comrade. Again, the explanation must be that two composition stages are involved. Bulkington must have been either Melville's earlier or his later intended choice for the comrade role; and it is easy to see that he was earlier (Stage 2) than Queequeg, since it was he whom Melville (Stage 3) dismissed and Queequeg whom he kept and developed in this and other chapters.

So far I've distinguished Stages 2 and 3 and in a moment I'll distinguish the still earlier Stage I, at which Melville had not yet got around to assigning the narrator any companion at all. First, however, I want to look more closely at Stage 2, to see what Melville did and didn't have in his shore-narrative about these two characters at that time. We have just seen that in it Bulkington, not Queequeg, was to be the narrator's comrade; so Bulkington was there, but we must infer that Queequeg wasn't. Bulkington was there, presumably, in only the same two passages he occupies in chapters 3 and 23 of the book—meaning those passages as they stood before Melville made the later (Stage 3) revisions by which he dismissed him, from one of them by the curious 'sleeping-partner' parenthesis, and from the other by the two-and-a-half new or recast paragraphs in which he managed both to bury and to praise him.

Well then, at Stage 2, as in the book, Bulkington entered the shore-narrative in the four-paragraph episode in which the narrator reports his coming into the Spouter-Inn with the *Grampus* crew, describes him (because he later became a shipmate), and says he slipped out pursued by the crew and wasn't seen again by the narrator 'till he became my comrade on the sea'. That last clause tells us Bulkington left the shore-narrative then and there and played no further part in it; and I see no good reason to suppose he ever did so. But what about Bulkington at sea? Had Melville already written—or did he later write—any passages for him there? I mean, aside from his standing at the helm (in Stage 2, as now) when the *Pequod* thrust off. Of course he now doesn't appear in the sea-narrative, and so far I can identify only one passage I think Melville wrote for him in it. But I can see further passages Melville *may* have written for him; and I have my major hypothesis to offer in due course about Melville's intentions, when I take up what I believe he did at Stage 3 with the two roles he had assigned at Stage 2 to Bulkington as comrade and as truth-seeker.

Let me regress from Stage 2 for a moment to distinguish Stage 1, the earliest narrative stage I infer from the duplicates I am considering here. In Stage 1, I infer that Melville had in hand a first-person shore-narrative in which Bulkington played no part at all. In it, Melville had evidently not yet assigned his narrator a comrade for the voyage (and possibly not yet the name Ishmael). Since Queequeg, as we've seen, wasn't yet present in Stage 2, he can't have been in this earlier stage either. Bulkington's absence at Stage 1 is inferred from the two compositional procedures by which, in the four-paragraph *Grampus*-crew episode, Melville simultaneously introduced him into and got him right off the Spouter-Inn scene. Clearly, Melville (at Stage 2) inserted that episode into an already-written sequence (first procedure). It is detachable, unintegrated with anything that precedes or follows, a patch designed to introduce Bulkington as the narrator's prospective comrade (though the dramatic whaling-life vignette that encapsules him yields a surplus illustrative value). At the same time, the transparent purpose served by Melville's ending it with Bulkington's disappearance and the narrator's statement (second procedure) that 'I saw no more of him till he became my comrade on the sea' (i.e. with what I've called Bulkington's 'hiding out') was to spare Melville the necessity of incorporating Bulkington more thoroughly into his existing shore-narrative (of Stage 1). Furthermore, that second compositional procedure seems to me to explain the pattern of 'hide outs' by duplicate characters to which I have called attention: of Bulkington, Queequeg, Ahab, and Fedallah with his boat-crew. Each of them, I am saying, was occasioned by Melville's procedure of inserting the character at an early point (or points) into an already-written narrative, and by his then sparing himself the revisional work of writing the character into further passages of that existing narrative by instead supplying some rationalization for the character's not appearing in it but in effect 'hiding out'. Sometimes, however, Melville chose (notably in the case of Queequeg) to write and insert entirely *new passages* about the character. I believe some of the book's most awkward anomalies were induced and some of its best passages inspired in just these ways.

Now I return to the matter of Queequeg's absence from Stage 2 and of what its lean narrative was like then without him; after that I'll go on to the meatier matter of just how much more was involved when Melville was introducing and developing him at Stage 3.

As readers of *Moby-Dick* we may not care much that the vestigial Bulkington was no more important in the Stage 2 shore scenes than he is now; but as readers we do care a great deal about Queequeg, so long known to us in his central, even indispensable, role that we assume Melville must have conceived him as the narrator's comrade from the time he first set pen to paper to write the book. So it's startling to realize, following my line of reasoning, that at Stage 2 Queequeg can't have played any part at all in the shore-narrative. The reason he can't have done so is that his *only* shore role even now is the integral one of narrator's comrade—the role which at that stage Melville had assigned to Bulkington. Well, what can that Stage 2 narrative have been like without him? Can it have stood in anything like its printed form without the extended passages in which Queequeg is so important? Surprisingly, it can, though much abridged. For the most part we can excise him simply by bracketing whatever involves him. (That is to say, conversely, during Stage 3 Melville inserted whatever now involves him, with very little *rewriting*, though a fair amount of new writing, including several new chapters.) And to me at least, the excision of Queequeg from the shore-chapters seems to demonstrate that the curious pattern of duplicates did result, as I'm suggesting, from separate composition stages. For with that excision many of the duplicates in these chapters disappear: the two comrades, two sleeping places (and 'second thoughts'), two signing-aboard scenes—each of these pairs shrinks to a single member. Not only do these duplications disappear, but, of course, so do the wonderful Queequeg matters that swell the number of shore-narrative passages so disproportionately before the narrator finally gets to sea.

Let's follow the book's shore chapters in detail to see what was and wasn't there at Stage 2, judging simply by what's left after excision of the Queequeg (Stage 3) materials. In the Stage 2 Spouter-Inn passage (now in chapter 3) Melville solved each of its two narrative problems—of a sleeping-place and a comrade—only once, not twice (by duplicates) as at Stage 3. When the narrator asked Peter Coffin for a room the landlord simply told him there was 'not a bed unoccupied'. The narrator responded, 'I'll try the bench here'. And after a supper in an adjoining room cold as Iceland, and the landlord's futile attempt to plane the bench smooth, he spent a drafty night on it, in the winter cold that afflicts him throughout the shore and early sea chapters. So much for the sleeping problem. At Stage 2 Melville handled the second problem more simply. He supplied a comrade by inserting the four-paragraph irruption of the *Grampus* crew with the momentary glimpse it gave the narrator of Bulkington, his comrade-to-be, who slipped away leaving him companionless for the rest of the shore-narrative, to reappear at the *Pequod*'s helm in a scene presumably written at Stage 2.

What our excision of Queequeg reveals as not yet present at Stage 2 is of course—besides Queequeg himself—what's now the warm comic heart of the Spouter-Inn chapter, the whole business set off by the landlord's 'second thoughts' practical joke of offering tyro Ishmael half of a harpooneer's blanket. That is, Ishmael's own series of 'second thoughts'—first reluctantly agreeing, then changing his mind and trying the bench, then changing his mind again and consenting to share the harpooneer's bed, then his strange meeting and sensible acceptance of the cannibal, followed by his warm night's sleep. All this, it would seem, was Melville's brilliant comic elaboration by which he wrote the 'hidden-out' Queequeg into the bare Stage 2 narrative he had written earlier for his cold and alienated narrator.

Next morning, at Stage 2, the companionless narrator woke up, breakfasted alone, and strolled alone to see the New Bedford street sights; perhaps he sallied out again to the Chapel alone, as the sky 'changed from clear, sunny cold, to driving sleet and mist', to hear Father Mapple's sermon alone, like the other solitary worshippers. (But more likely the duplicate sally, the Chapel and sermon episode, was inserted at Stage 3.) The only important Stage 3 Queequeg matter that this sequence (now in chapters 4–9) lacked was the whole of chapter 4, where Ishmael wakes up caught in the 'comical predicament' of his sleeping-partner's 'bridegroom clasp', and Queequeg dresses first in his own outlandish way. Elsewhere Melville brought Queequeg into the sequence with only slight revisions and minor insertions: in the first three paragraphs and the last one of chapter 5; in the discrepant reference to him in the first sentence of chapter 6; and in the three adjacent sentences in chapter 7 that briefly and rather implausibly bring the pagan (who's 'given up' on Christians) into the Chapel.

In the remaining shore-narrative at Stage 2, the narrator sailed to Nantucket alone, stayed and ate alone at Mrs Hussey's, signed aboard the *Pequod* alone (as he now does). He encountered Elijah alone. And he sailed alone. A possibility I cannot pursue here is suggested by some of the duplicates I have pointed out: the two whaling ports, two inns, two innkeepers. Perhaps at a very early stage the narrator went to and sailed from only one port, New Bedford. Bulkington's appearing there then popping up on a Nantucket ship might suggest this. But it's an intricate problem. Can the ship—or its earlier duplicate—with all or any of its duplicate captains have at first been from New Bedford? Similarly, can the duplicate prophet Elijah (whose Biblical name, at least, seems dependent on Ahab) have been generated somewhere in the process that induced Ahab's series of prophets? As I have remarked, there were probably substages within the three stages I have needed to distinguish here, perhaps other major stages as well.

As from earlier chapters, Queequeg can be readily excised from the present chapters 10–21. Since he is undetachably central to chapters 10, 11, 12, where his bosom-friendship with Ishmael develops, these chapters belong to Stage 3. The same is true of much of chapter 13, 'Wheelbarrow', with Queequeg's anecdote in comparative anthropology and his rescue of the bumpkin, though its paragraphs 5, 6, and part of 7 may have been part of the Stage I narrative. Chapter 14, 'Nantucket', has no reference to Queequeg (nor does it have the narrative mode or dramatized first-person narrator after its first sentence, and in this, like its twin chapter 6 on New Bedford, it anticipates the imminent fictional truancy of the companions). Queequeg is easily removed from chapter 15, 'Chowder', by bracketing a few phrases and sentences, changing the first-person plural pronouns to singular, and cutting out the byplay with Mrs Hussey about his harpoon. The sequence of chapters 16–18 shows Melville engaging in a compositional procedure we've already observed. I think he already had written at Stage I the scene of the narrator's signing aboard the *Pequod*. Rather than revise it to include Queequeg, what he did, I think, was to write a new passage (the first two and a half paragraphs of chapter 16) in which he provided reasons why Queequeg could not 'be of great usefulness' and choose their ship as he should do in his role of experienced-whaleman mentor: Queequeg assigns Yojo that job and also 'hides out' (a second time) for his 24-hour Ramadan. This procedure kept him out of chapter 16, where Melville might have managed to have him too sign aboard; and it motivated the two fine new comic chapters 17–18, about Queequeg's Ramadan and signing-aboard. From chapters 19–22, Queequeg is again easily removed by cutting out or changing the few words here and there by which Melville (at Stage 3) established his presence. The thematic common denominator of Melville's additions occasioned by his introduction of Queequeg is the contrast of savage and civilized, pagan and Christian; their cumulative effect is an eclectic enrichment of the religious dimensions of the book's world.

So much for the lean narrative of Stage 2 and the startling but negative matter of Queequeg's absence from it. Now I'll move further into the positive matter of just how much more was involved for his central characters while Melville was introducing Queequeg into Bulkington's vacated place as Ishmael's comrade at Stage 3. Above, I called this a 'meatier' matter; and so it was, because it was part of a larger process in which Melville was doing far more than fleshing out the then lean shore-narrative by importing an exotic new comrade and the newly-written passages about him which were not present at Stage 2, when even Bulkington was barely there.

III

The larger process in which Melville was engaged at this point was a multiple reassignment of roles among four of his central characters. I even dare surmise this was the decisive turning-point in their genetic development, and in the definition of the narrator himself. What I've called the major hypothesis of this essay is my formulation of the several interconnected reassignments involved. I'll state the hypothesis now, in two different perspectives, in advance of my presentation of the specific compositional evidence by which I'll later support it. Because up to here I've approached the hypothesis piecemeal, through Melville's treatment of Bulkington and Queequeg, I'll state it first in that perspective.

At Stage 3 of his shore-narrative Melville decided to dismiss Bulking-ton from his dual role of comrade and of truth-seeker, and from any active role in the narrative. He reassigned Bulkington's comrade role to Queequeg, as we've just seen. And he also, I now add, made two further closely-related reassignments which involved two more characters. He reassigned Bulking-ton's truth-seeker role to a newly-invented character (who was even more startlingly absent—in the book 'hiding out'—up to this point)—Ahab. He simultaneously reassigned to Ahab the sea-role of captain of the *Pequod*, taking that commanding role away from the captain who had first held it—Peleg—and reducing Peleg thus to his present shore role as her 'captain' without command, retired chief-mate, and duplicate part-owner and pilot. The narrator, too, was redefined in the reassignment of his comrades.

Now I'll restate the hypothesis from a second perspective (with recognizable reference to the pattern of duplicates I have summarized but still without detailed compositional evidence). The hypothesis is this. Four central characters of *Moby-Dick* were involved, at this crucial stage of the book's development, in a multiple reassignment of roles, which also redefined a fifth, the narrator. (By a 'role' I mean intentions Melville had projected for a character, some of which were actually written but some were still only in his mind, though signalled in what he had written.) In the process of reassignment, each of the four became in certain ways a dupli-cate; but while two of them gained and consequently became major characters, two of them lost and became to a degree vestigial—'unnecessary duplicates'.

The two gainers were Queequeg and Ahab—and, coincidentally, Ishmael himself. Queequeg, up to this point, had not been brought into the shore-narrative; but in its continuation in the already-written sea-narrative he by then was one of the three harpooneers, and was (then as now) usually named and presented there not singly but linked with the other two, though in several passages he already played a separate role and was sometimes individually characterized. Queequeg received from Bulkington at Stage 3 of the shore-narrative the role of Ishmael's comrade; but Melville made him a quite different comrade from what Bulkington would have been, by not assigning him as well the alienated, aggressive component implicit in Bulkington's romantic, truth-seeking role. Instead, Queequeg embodied a reconciling principle. While he brought over with him from the sea-narrative the aggressive filed teeth of a cannibal and the harpoon of a whaleman, he brought also a noble savage's 'calm self-collectedness of simplicity', a tranquil piety, and a capacity for bosom-friendship. His tomahawk-pipe shows the union in him of war and peace. Whereas Bulkington, that unresting voyager (in 'the deep shadows' of whose eyes 'floated some reminiscences that did not seem to give him much joy'), as a comrade would have engaged and heightened Ishmael's own alienated and aggressive tendencies (even while ennobling them), Queequeg caused him to feel 'a melting in me'. 'No more my splintered heart and maddened hand were turned against the wolfish world. This soothing savage had redeemed it' (ch. 10). Queequeg's pagan warmth softened and assuaged the aggressive disaffection from cold Christendom that had driven Ishmael, as a 'substitute for pistol and ball', to take to the ship in midwinter—and did so even before he had found and signed aboard the vindictive *Pequod*! Thus Melville's substitution of Queequeg for Bulkington as the narrator's comrade signalized, or perhaps even precipitated, a reorientation in Ishmael's psychology. And this reorientation was explicitly defined and delimited by Melville's elaboration of the new shore-narrative episodes, told by Ishmael in his own individualized first-person, that dramatize the terms of their likewise individualized bosom-friendship. So Ishmael, too, as an emergently defined fictional character, was a gainer from the reassignment of comrades. At least he gained in the shore segment of the narrative, where Melville elaborated his relationship with Queequeg; however, in the already-written episodes of its sea segment that bring Queequeg and the narrator together Melville did not fully carry through the elaboration of their relationship.

The second (not to count Ishmael), and of course even greater, gainer by the reassigments was Ahab. Up to this decisive point Ahab had simply not existed at all as a character in either the shore or the sea segment of Melville's earlier narrative, but only in large fractions of the potential roles Melville had so far assigned to two other characters, Bulkington and Peleg. (You could say that these fractions of Bulkington and Peleg went into the initial making of Ahab.) From Bulkington, Ahab received the projected role of heroic truth-seeker, with its Gothic and Romantic penumbra of 'noble' traits and its inherent alienated, aggressive component. Possibly he was also given by revision some passages Melville had already written for Bulkington. Just possibly, too, Ahab's quest of the White Whale was to have been Bulkington's—I am not yet sure. From Peleg, on the other hand, Ahab received (purged of original comic overtones) the role of ungodly Quaker commanding captain of the whalebone-apparelled, Indian-named, vindictive *Pequod*; along with the whalebone leg (and whalebone stool?); probably the attendant old Gay-Head devil-associated Indian prophet who gets so duplicated as the narrative goes on; and (if it had indeed been Peleg's not Bulkington's) the hell-bound, devil-involved, vindictive quest of the particular whale who had taken off his fleshly leg, very likely the White Whale some call Moby Dick. So Ahab was, as Peleg aptly said, 'something like me—only there's a good deal more of him'.

The two losers by Melville's reassignments were Bulkington and Peleg. Bulkington's loss was in fact fatal: while in a spiritual sense you could say he 'became' the god-like Ahab in his apotheosis, in the quite literal sense he became only the vestigial description and eulogy which make clear Melville's original intention for his character before reassigning both his roles. One role, as Ishmael's comrade, went to Queequeg (but, as I've said, without its aggressive component). If, as seems likely, Bulkington was also projected to be a harpooneer, perhaps that role too was quite early transferred to Queequeg in the sea-narrative, where some significant passages suggest he was not originally conceived as one. The second loser was Peleg; he is quasi-vestigial, if not unnecessary, because Melville gave his original role as *Pequod*'s sea-commander to Ahab along with his whale-bone appurtenances. Peleg lost to Ahab his whalebone leg (probably his fleshly one was lost, like the *Pequod*'s masts, 'off Japan', just as the no doubt well-informed old Gay-Head Indian said). And so he lost by transfer to Ahab the self-pitying epithet 'a poor pegging lubber'. Also, probably, along with 'that leg' and epithet Peleg lost one letter from his original name (I dare say it): Pegleg—too homely and comic a sailor soubriquet to reassign to the lofty and tragic new captain, to whom Melville gave a Biblical name that 'the old squaw Tistig, at Gay-head', said 'would somehow prove prophetic' (ch. 16). But even so Peleg as a duplicate retains vestiges of all these; he is still 'Captain' Peleg, in half-command of the *Pequod* in dock and in getting her to sea and ordering all hands about. It is still he who did the whalebone carving-work for the ship; who was aboard her (though as mate under Ahab, not captain himself) in that dismasting typhoon off Japan; who has 'that leg' (now of restored flesh—possibly his only gain!) with which he threatens and delivers kicks; and who, despite now having both good legs, does his mildly comic 'roaring' (and perhaps 'hobbling'), 'clattering' about the decks, and profane swearing (including the epithet 'thunder'); and who still has his prophet, Bildad, to tell him he's hell-bound, and also his Indian-named ship *Pequod* and his 'wigwam' as links to Indians, and is himself still a 'devil'.

There, in duplicate summary, is my major hypothesis. Now I pick up my line of reasoning upon the compositional evidence that suggested and supports it, with Bulkington's quietus. Melville carried out his Stage 3 decision to remove Bulkington from both of his roles simply by inserting into the already-written sentence that makes him the narrator's 'shipmate' (at Stage 2) the contradictory parenthesis '(though but a sleeping-partner one, so far as this narrative is concerned)'. Did the metaphor suggest the literal 'sleeping-partner' sequence that introduced his replacement? He also at this time revised the first sea episode, where Bulkington appears at the *Pequod*'s helm, and with a eulogy but no epitaph made that 'six-inch chapter' his 'stoneless grave'. (And thereby too he made Bulkington the first of the duplicate 'man-overboard' casualties who mark the wake of Melville's compositional voyage.) Just why Melville kept these two vestiges of Bulkington rather than discard him altogether one can only guess, and I have now no guess to offer, beyond the humdrum one that Melville, like lesser writers, found it hard to throw away good words he had written.

Bulkington is disposed of in chapter 23, and Ishmael opens chapter 24 saying, 'Queequeg and I are now fairly embarked in this business of whaling'. But no sooner is this said than—in the very same sentence—two abrupt and linked shifts occur: in narrative voice and in presentation of the

Ishmael-Queequeg relationship. Not only does the voice of tyro Ishmael give way to the (duplicate) voice of a veteran and sometimes omniscient whaleman who is only putatively the same tyro Ishmael grown older (several duplicate voices can be distinguished within that unsingle voice, among them Herman Melville's own). Suddenly, also, the narrative mode gives way to the argumentative and expository, and the presentation no longer focuses closely on the experiences of tyro Ishmael and his harpooneer-mentor and comrade Queequeg. From now on the tyro voice is heard only intermittently, in sporadic episodes; and few episodes show the pair engaged in either comradeship or pupil-teacher relationships. Even in those episodes where both Ishmael and Queequeg are included by name or inference they are usually not brought together in any personal interchange—they just don't seem to be aware of each other. Surely, this abrupt double shift, of narrative voice and of presentational focus, between the shore and sea segments of the book is fictionally the most curious oddity among many in *Moby-Dick*. What is the explanation?

On the face of it, one might guess that Melville lost either his interest in the comradeship or his technical control of the materials. Another explanation is more circumstantially genetic. The few scholars who have theorized about the book's genesis have thought, as I do, that it is possible to distinguish various parts of the book as written earlier or later in the course of its composition, that its pages were not necessarily written, by any means, in the order in which they now stand. Whatever their more specific theories may be, however, these scholars have all thought that the shore-narrative, with the Ishmael-Queequeg comradeship, belongs to the earliest distinguishable writing stage. Nobody has seen a means of distinguishing stages within its development as regards Ishmael and Queequeg, as I have just done, though they have seen that anticipatory references to Ahab were inserted. Nor has anybody tried to explain the abrupt double shift between the two parts of the book by hypothesizing that some of the veteran-narrator passages and Ishmael-Queequeg passages in the sea segment were written before not after the relevant tyro-narrator passages in the shore segment, as I am now doing.

But the fact is that the truancy both of the tyro-narrator and of the close comrades (hard on the heels of Bulkington's disappearance) can most plausibly be explained this way. As for Queequeg, the infrequency and spareness of his involvement with Ishmael in the sea chapters means not that Melville lost interest in developing their comradeship, but that, by and large, those passages as they touch on the pair had already been written, before not after, those relevant passages in the shore chapters which include Queequeg and develop their comradeship in detail. Melville certainly made some appropriate revisions and numerous brief insertions in the earlier-written sea-narrative but did not carry through into it the detailed elaboration by which, as I have argued, he had incorporated Queequeg into the shore-narrative. What Melville lost, I venture, was not interest but 'Time, Strength, Cash, and Patience'—maybe heart, too—for continuing the job: near the end of it, in June 1851, he wrote Hawthrone, 'What's the use of elaborating what, in its very essence, is so short-lived as a modern book?'

When Melville imported cannibal Queequeg at Stage 3 into the shore segment of his narrative, he did not invent him at that point as a new character. For Queequeg, as I shall now argue, already had a place in the sea segment of the narrative, from an earlier stage, though not as the narrator's comrade. Examination of compositional details in three scenes involving Ishmael and Queequeg strongly supports this conclusion. The first is representative, the other two central to my argument.

The scene I've taken as 'representative', the mat-making passage in chapter 47, is the first in which Ishmael and Queequeg are brought together since just before the ship sailed, twenty-six chapters back, in chapter 21, where Ishmael expostulated with Queequeg for sitting on a sleeping rigger's 'face'. In the intervening chapters, Queequeg is 'there' in these ways: he is mentioned only once, misnamed by Peleg, in the departure scene, chapter 22; he and Ishmael are named together in the first sentence of chapter 24, and Queequeg is named once in a later paragraph but isn't there; Queequeg's selection as Starbuck's harpooneer is reported in two brief sentences of chapter 27; he's discrepantly grouped with the other barbaric harpooneers, but not named, in chapter 28; he's named, and shown eating in the officers' cabin with the two other savage harpooneers in chapter 34, but Ishmael isn't there, unless by implication he, 'like any mere sailor', can see him through the cabin skylight; he's named casually once in chapter 35 when Ishmael says that he might 'have a chat with Queequeg, or any one else off duty'; he's one of the three harpooneers in Ahab's quarter-deck ritual in chapter 36, where Ishmael is only inferentially present; he's missing from the forecastle midnight roysterings (ch. 40), though the stage directions call for 'Harpooneers'; and he next is named in Ishmael's company in the mat-making passage. This chapter sequence just summarized illustrates Melville's technique of introducing Queequeg's name, without really building him into scenes, and they seem more likely to have been written before than after the shore Ishmael-Queequeg scenes—otherwise there's no reason Melville shouldn't more often have engaged Ishmael and Queequeg in them somehow. And so it goes through the rest of the book. I must ask readers to check for themselves exactly how, in compositional terms, Melville established Queequeg's existence, presence, actions, and only occasionally his involvement with Ishmael.

In the mat-making passage, Ishmael is acting as 'the attendant or page' of Queequeg in weaving a sword-mat for 'our boat'. Perhaps this fits the forecast tyro-mentor relationship well enough, though nothing is said of Queequeg's teaching, or Ishmael's learning, anything—they are just doing it, which suggests that Melville hadn't yet thought of their special mentor-pupil relation when he wrote it. Moreover, no personal interaction of any sort is worded; on the contrary, 'each silent sailor' acts on his own, Queequeg 'idly looking off upon the water', Ishmael weaving his own analogical thoughts. Queequeg is not personalized by so much as one word; in fact only his name, given four times, and his usual epithet the 'savage' (shared with the two other pagan harpooneers) attach him to the passage. Another shipmate—say Bulkington—would do as well, which is to say the passage can have been reassigned to Queequeg by changing these few words from an earlier named or unnamed incumbent. I keep pointing out how inorganically present Queequeg is all along, first to call attention to Melville's relative lack of concern about him, in his special comrade-mentor relation to Ishmael; second, to show the possibility that at a quite early stage Melville wrote many such passages without any particular or individualized characters in mind, and only later assigned names and did more or less 'elaborating'. In the process he may have reassigned roles. I entertain seriously the possibility that earlier Bulkington indeed occupied some of Queequeg's present name slots, so to speak, and was a harpooneer, and I am considering the possibility that some of Ahab's may have been reassigned from Bulkington. I am calling this mat-making passage 'representative' because what is true of its handling of Queequeg simply by name, with no individual detail, turns out, upon examination, to be characteristic of many passages that stick in our minds as presenting the two in a comradely relationship, which in fact nothing in the passage really establishes. Again, I must ask readers to check for themselves.

Two further Queequeg passages, however, are crucial to my argument from compositional detail. On inspection significant details of their wording show pretty conclusively that Melville wrote them before not after he wrote the shore-narrative chapters in which he developed their bosom-friendship.

The monkey-rope episode (ch. 72) is one of those frequent passages where Melville dramatizes his initially present-tense exposition of a whaling routine by attaching it to a particular occasion and to named characters of the *Pequod*'s voyage. Here, as often, the expository mode and purpose come foremost, and the named characters play their part in the scene primarily by virtue of their shipboard station and only secondarily in ways calling on their individual traits (so that Melville might easily have assigned the name of another character of the same station). Here, Queequeg, 'whose duty it was, as harpooneer', was overboard upon the whale's back; Ishmael, 'being the savage's bowsman, that is, the person who pulled the bow-oar in his boat', had the duty of safeguarding his movements by means of the monkey-rope which was attached to both of them. The scene specifies no particular qualities of Queequeg. He is the 'savage' and repeatedly 'poor' Queequeg, like 'poor' Tashtego in the scene of his falling into the whale's head (ch. 78). His special relationship to Ishmael is specified by epithets at two points: the first reference is 'my particular friend Queequeg whose duty it was, as harpooneer . . .'; the second is 'my dear comrade and twin-brother, thought I'. A third reference is Ishmael's comment on Queequeg's Highland costume, a shirt and socks, '. . . in which to my eyes, at least, he appeared to uncommon advantage . . .' In the light of what follows, I argue that Melville later inserted 'my particular friend' and 'my dear comrade', perhaps as well the third reference quoted, and added the comic dramatic scene with Stubb at the end. The third reference does not necessarily presuppose the bosom-friendship, however, and may have been original in the passage. Nothing else in that scene of the chapter is written in a way that presumes or requires the pair to be comrades already. Indeed, the central monkey-rope metaphor, and the way Melville has Ishmael apply it, makes that prior-established bosom-friendship highly unlikely. Furthermore it suggests the likelihood that it was his writing of this scene and this metaphor that opened to Melville the possibility of making the pair bosom-friends in the shore sequence when he removed Bulkington from the comrade role. As Ishmael states his perilous monkey-rope attachment to Queequeg, he develops it into a metaphor: 'So that for better or for worse, we two, for the time, were wedded'. To me it is not conceivable that Melville could write 'for the time, we were wedded'—especially the phrase *'for the time'*—if he had already written the shore chapters in which he dramatized the bosom-friendship of Queequeg and Ishmael, starting off with Queequeg's declaration, 'Henceforth we were married'. 'Henceforth', not 'for the time'. Could Melville have forgotten he'd written—if in fact he had—the paragraph in which Ishmael and Queequeg are compared to 'man and wife', ending with the sentence, 'Thus, then, in our hearts' honeymoon, lay I and Queequeg—a cosy, loving pair'? (ch. 10). And the comic anticipatory marital imagery of chapter 4? And Ishmael's declaration, 'From that hour I clove to Queequeg like a barnacle'? (ch. 13). Nor is that all that's askew in this monkey-rope passage. It goes on from the 'wedded' metaphor to, 'So, then, an elongated Siamese ligature united us. Queequeg was my own inseparable twin brother', and twice repeats the twin figure. If this figure in itself is not incongruous enough with the 'wedded' image, surely its re-insistence that the mere monkey-rope was what tied the pair together, at this late point—weeks, and chapters, after their New Bedford union—thickens the unlikelihood that Melville had already provided that union. No, I must conclude, Melville had not yet written those earlier passages or yet conceived the bosom-friendship they establish.

My third Queequeg scene, on Queequeg in his coffin (ch. 110), is the most telling in its compositional betrayals. Most glaringly, though his bosom-friend is dying, Ishmael is not placed bodily on the scene at all, or even represented as having witnessed it. The focus is not once that of a first-person participating narrator. The pair's special relationship is signalled at only two points, one of eight words early in the chapter, one of a single word near its end. The first is in the single-sentence second paragraph that effects a transition between the expository first and third paragraphs about the process of breaking out leaky casks and Queequeg's catching a fever while performing his routine duties on them in the hold as a harpooneer. (The chapter thus has the same compositional structure, and I think genetic pattern, as 'The Monkey-Rope'.) The sentence reads: 'Now, at this time it was that my poor pagan companion, and fast bosom-friend, Queequeg, was seized with a fever, which brought him nigh to his endless end'. The double epithet and the pronoun 'my' that tie Queequeg to Ishmael here were patently inserted. The epithets' content is contradicted by the whole chapter's detached (though sentimental) omniscient presentation of the death scene. At the second point that ties the (elsewhere) 'cosy, loving pair' the tie is effected in the next-to-last paragraph, when the crisis has passed, by the single word 'my' in 'So, in good time my Queequeg gained strength'—again a patently inserted word. The sentence could do better without it, because 'my' makes an even more abrupt and gratuitous break in point-of-view than the first 'my' above. The absence of Ishmael from the side of his 'fast bosom-friend' is made still more glaring by further compositional details. We are told, 'Not a man of the crew but gave him up'. (Not even 'We all. . . .') Including Ishmael? Did *he* have feelings about it? Why not say so? Then Queequeg has some dying wishes. He wants someone to get him a coffin made. Does he call his 'fast bosom-friend'? No: 'He called one to him . . . , and taking his hand', made his first request—made it of some indefinite 'one'! And the request was transmitted not even by this indefinite 'one' but simply 'was made known aft' in agentless passive voice. When Queequeg is satisfied with his coffin, he tells an indefinite 'one', again, his second dying request—not Ishmael, who should be the only 'one' to rummage his bag on such an errand; no, he 'told one to go to his bag and bring out his little god, Yojo'. Throughout the chapter Queequeg is repeatedly called 'poor' Queequeg, 'savage', 'pagan', 'waning savage', etc., with no word of a more intimate feeling than pity and awe. Even a barnacle would feel more affection and cleave closer! The point of view shifts about (but is never first-person) from that of a disembodied third-person observer into several sentences of close focus on Queequeg's eyes and facial expression observed by a disembodied 'you' (four times), who 'sat by his side', and who fuses into an omniscient sententious authorial 'us' ('let us say'), and declares selfconsciously that 'only an author from the dead' could adequately tell Queequeg's expression. Well, Melville's handling of point-of-view is often wayward enough; but he could scarcely have handled it this way in Queequeg's dying scene had he already written the foregoing shore scenes that bound them as bosom-friends.

A further glaring inconsistency throughout chapter 110 directs me to a new area of genetic questions and possibilities, one which I've hinted in my hypothesis but which I can't do more than outline. It concerns Queequeg as harpooneer and the whole unexplored topic of the role of harpooneers in the book. As noted, Queequeg is a harpooneer in the chapter's third paragraph.

In its middle he gets assistance (in a series of passive constructions, not from Ishmael) in stocking his coffin-canoe with his needs for his eternal voyage, including the iron part of his harpoon; and also at its end, 'poising a harpoon', he said he was fit for a fight. So he's a harpooneer at three spots. But the glaring discrepancy is that Melville has gone out of his way in 'The Specksynder' (ch. 33) to establish the social status of the harpooneer, entailing where he is quartered: 'The grand political maxim of the sea demands, that he should nominally live apart from the men before the mast, and be in some way distinguished as their professional superior; though always, by them, familiarly regarded as their social equal'. A grand distinction, he goes on, 'drawn between officer and man at sea, is this—the first lives aft, the last forward', and in most American whalers 'the harpooneers are lodged in the after part of the ship' and so 'take their meals in the captain's cabin, and sleep in a place indirectly communicating with it'. Why then, does Melville—who has properly shown him and the two other pagan harpooneers eating in the captain's cabin, in chapter 34—show the dying Queequeg, throughout chapter 110, quartered *forward, in the crew's forecastle*? The carpenter is twice said to go 'forward' to the forecastle about his coffin, and Starbuck looked 'down the scuttle' at Queequeg in his coffin. Oddly, it is one of the book's very few forecastle scenes, and dying in it is a harpooneer who belongs aft. (He's also—contrary to whaleship usage—in a hammock; but so are several others, including Ahab and Stubb.) Did Queequeg, at the time Melville wrote his dying scene (at least that layer of it) *belong* in the forecastle, because he was then a common sailor, not yet a harpooneer? This is only the first of many questions the book's compositional details arouse about its harpooneers. Why are there a number of misassignments of harpooneers to the wrong mates' boats? Did Melville nod, or are they vestigial? Why do so many chapters focus on the harpooneer and harpoon? Why did Melville describe his work in progress to his English publisher in late June 1850, as 'illustrated by the author's own personal experience, of two years & more, as a harpooneer'? (As to his own career it was a gross exaggeration; but perhaps this book was to be set up as if that were true.) Such questions suggest a genetic phase of *Moby-Dick* when Melville was projecting a book that would focus both its narrative line and its whaling activities on the harpooneers. And even, it could be, on a harpooneer hero—on Bulkington, whom he intended to be Ishmael's comrade at sea, before he substituted the harpooneer Queequeg. In the opening three paragraphs of 'The Specksynder' (ch. 33), Melville carefully established the harpooneer class of officers as intermediary between crewmen and officers; the harpooneer is in a sense both and thus provides a social bridge between them. Fictionally, in these three paragraphs Melville was preparing the way for some narrative situation that was to follow. But nothing
does follow from it. The chapter in its fourth paragraph drops the harpooneers altogether and with a shaky transition via the topic of

officer-crew relations is soon discussing Ahab's relations with his crew, in highly exalted terms. Some ill-spliced genetic seam divides the chapter into two ill-matched parts. The Specksynder-harpooneer is displaced by the captain: perhaps Bulkington by Ahab? Its first part is the one passage (to which I referred some pages above) that I can now identify as one I think Melville wrote for Bulkington. My suspicion is that these opening paragraphs were setting up Bulkington, Ishamel's comrade-to-be, for a role which involved his harpooneer status between officers and men. If so, several inferences follow. If Bulkington as harpooneer was to be the book's heroic figure, Ishmael as his comrade would have been personally close to the action and the main actor, whereas now he has no plausible close access to Ahab—one reason for the book's curious hiatus in point-of-view, and for the veteran-narrator's (putatively Ishamel's) reporting various matters he could know nothing about. As I've said, I think that Bulkington, in Melville's mind, outgrew his station, 'becoming', in his heroic role, Ahab. For if Bulkington was a heroic harpooneer, at what was his harpoon, in more than a routine whaleman's way, to be pointed? At the White Whale some call Moby Dick? Was that whale among the 'reminiscences that did not seem to give him much joy'? (ch. 3).

But here two trains of my present speculations collide. For my hypothesis, as summarized, points also to Captain Peleg as the duplicate who may have yielded to Ahab in that hell-bound devil-guided quest.

In conclusion, two of Captain Peleg's shore chapters require brief examination to show the compositional signs they betray—apart from what's on the face of matters I've already catalogued—for my notion that as a duplicate Peleg is the vestige of the *Pequod*'s original commanding captain, a large fraction of whom Melville reassigned to Ahab. I need not discuss the first, 'The Ship', (ch. 16) in detail. I think my summary of its duplicates reveals the pattern that suggests Captain Ahab was grafted into the chapter. (Other scholars, using other keys, are in consensus.) I suggest only that readers try the experiment of bracketing out all that refers to Ahab and then looking at the literal words left, to see their changed significance when taken to apply to Peleg: for example, Bildad's first answer to Ishmael's inquiry whether he's captain of the *Pequod*; and the way 'that leg' of Peleg's may have been whalebone; and how his remarks and 'hearty grief' originally could refer to his *own* (not Ahab's) loss of a leg to 'the monstrousest parmacetty that ever chipped a boat'; and so on.

With the hypothesis that Peleg was originally captain, and Ahab nonexistent, readers should continue the bracketing experiment with 'Merry Christmas' (ch. 22). To me its compositional oddities seem enough proof in themselves that at some earlier composition stage Peleg actually sailed on this voyage as the ship's captain. Ishmael would more justifiably fear 'such a devil' as *captain* than as 'pilot' (for Melville a one-word substitution there). Ahab's later supplanting Peleg would have called for only simple revisions in this earlier already-written episode. Ahab's 'hiding out' (as earlier and later)—now an effective device of suspense rationalized by his moody sickness—would be genetically explained by his then non-existence. The four brief direct references to him are local and dissect out neatly. The one indirect reference to Ahab (as an old shipmate of Bildad) would originally in fact have applied even better to Peleg ('in which an old shipmate sailed as captain; a man almost as old as he'), for nowhere else is it said that Bildad and Ahab were old shipmates—whereas Bildad and Peleg are so described in chapters 16 and 22. Peleg's part in the chapter is just what it would be, except for his farewells and leaving the ship at the end. The few revisional words tying Peleg to the stay-at-home role would be simple to insert ('with Peleg'; 'the two pilots'; etc.). Bracketing out the two words 'both dropt' from the passage where both Peleg and Bildad now go over into the pilot boat, leaves the context a perfect statement, as is the whole scene, of Bildad's being the only one who's to go ashore, while Peleg is to go with the ship. Most conclusively, the paragraph about the two captains' reactions at leaving-time is so written that it would make more sense (cutting out references to Peleg's going) if Bildad alone, not Peleg as well, were leaving. The first sentence joins them, but at once moves back, awkwardly, to Bildad alone and develops only his (not Peleg's) feelings: 'It was curious . . . how Peleg and Bildad were affected at this juncture, especially Captain Bildad'. Bildad acts for all the world as if he's giving Peleg a *goodbye* handshake and taking a last (for three years) long look at him by holding up the lantern: '. . . poor old Bildad lingered long; . . . convulsively grasped stout Peleg by the hand, and holding up a lantern, for a moment stood gazing heroically in his face. . . .' Why does he do that, if they are not separating? 'As for Peleg himself' [why 'himself'?], his less emotional behavior fits that of the person going the voyage though 'there was a tear twinkling in his eye when the lantern came too near'. Apart from the easily adjustable farewells to the mates the rest of Peleg's words and actions fit perfectly the situation of his urging Bildad to stop talking and leave them: ' "Come, come, Captain Bildad; stop palavering,—away!" and with that, Peleg hurried him over the side and [both dropt] into the boat'.

Remaining questions are large, my answers uncertain. As to Queequeg's place in the harpooneer mixups, I can only suspect that in his earliest appearances in Melville's sea-narrative he was not yet a harpooneer. Similar discrepancies suggest that Tashtego too may not have originally been a harpooneer. (For example, in the first paragraph of 'The Town-Ho's Story'—chapter 54—he's sleeping forward with the crew.) At some stage, perhaps, Melville conceived the schematic trio of pagan harpooneers and promoted Queequeg and Tashtego, already existing crewmen, into these roles. If so, perhaps it was from Bulkington that Queequeg took over his (you'd think inseparable) harpoon, along with the comrade role? Wasn't Tashtego, the wild Indian harpooneer, generated (by adding the possessive and the word 'senior' to the name 'Tashtego' in his epithet 'Tashtego's senior'?) from the 'old Gay-Head Indian' prophet, who thus became vestigial in his one appearance while the thus-created Tashtego took over his name and Indian-devil role as Ahab's (Peleg's?) original accompanying prophet and his original series of masthead prophetic assignments, a role to be duplicated by all those other prophets, notably Fedallah? More conjectures than I can now resolve.

Finally, if Peleg was to sail as the *Pequod*'s captain, what of Ahab? Simple: he didn't yet exist; he was invented later. Then conversely, with the invention of Ahab what was Melville to do with the original captain? Drown him? (Perhaps; I mean, he could have worked him into the remarkable 'man overboard' series of duplicate deaths and near deaths that, like the so-called 'gams', punctuate the voyage.) Melville's actual solution was to demote and retire him. This solution had the advantage of not requiring Melville to throw away but only to adapt the lively chapters built around him and Bildad. Did the newly created 'grand, ungodly, god-like man', Captain Ahab—who had still further developments to undergo—take up his vengeful quest of the White Whale from this quasi-comic old Quaker 'devil' Captain Peleg, along with his ship—or from the truth-seeking Bulkington? I cannot now tell. And that is only the most pressing of my unanswered questions and loose ends.

IV

Maybe scholarly prudence should have kept me from offering with such apparent confidence this sketch of what I think was a crucial phase in the writing of *Moby-Dick*. Still, I am confident that the unnecessary duplicates do give us a new key to Melville's work on the book. I'm not committed to my hypothesis in detail, and likely enough before it is printed will have reformulated it in some ways. Its essentials, I think, don't conflict with those of the more comprehensive theories already offered by Leon Howard, George Stewart, Howard P. Vincent, James Barbour, and others, who have used different keys, and I believe it can be synthesized with theirs to improve our understanding. All of us must go on with our fumbling—with any combination of keys we can find—at what I've called the interlocked complications of the book's genesis.

Melville wrote a great book. In writing it he worked hard at the job, and during the year and a half his work went on he said so in various ways, both in his letters and in the book itself. Often he identified his writer's job with those of many common workmen, from cooks to ditchers. He introduced his carpenter with remarks I quoted at the beginning. As the carpenter, having made Ahab a duplicate ivory leg, is commanded in chapter 126 to rework the unnecessary coffin he made for Queequeg into its duplicate, the life-buoy that saves Ishmael, and grumbles over his job, isn't Melville describing and grumbling over his own reworking of *Moby-Dick?*

> Are all my pains to go for nothing with that coffin? And now I'm ordered to make a life-buoy of it. It's like turning an old coat; going to bring the flesh on the other side now. I don't like this cobbling sort of business—I don't like it at all; it's undignified; it's not my place. Let tinkers' brats do tinkerings; we are their betters. I like to take in hand none but clean, virgin, fair-and-square mathematical jobs, something that regularly begins at the beginning, and is at the middle when midway, and comes to an end at the conclusion; not a cobbler's job, that's at an end in the middle, and at the beginning at the end.

Note of Acknowledgment

Leon Howard, to whom this essay is offered in professional homage and affectionate friendship, initiated nearly forty years ago our scholarly study of the genesis of *Moby-Dick,* and he has done more than anyone else over the years to advance our understanding of it. George Stewart, Howard P. Vincent, and James Barbour, among others, have made distinguished contributions. In this undocumented essay, none of their works needed to be cited specifically, but I wrote it with their approaches, theories, and discoveries in mind and could not have developed the hypothesis I sketch here without them. I gratefully acknowledge my conscious and unconscious debts to them. Since my approach in the essay happens to be through close examination of compositional peculiarities in the book, with little recourse to outside evidence, the approach used up to now chiefly by George Stewart, I am most immediately indebted to his work. My assumptions about Melville's compositional procedures draw confidence from my own close textual study of *Moby-Dick,* with Hershel Parker and G. Thomas Tanselle, and especially, with Merton M. Sealts, Jr, of his semi-final draft manuscript of *Billy Budd, Sailor,* where similar procedures are demonstrable.

NEW ESSAYS

◆

Moby-Dick and the Impress
of Melville's Learning

JOHN WENKE

On 5 February 1849 Melville turned out to hear a speaker in Boston's Freeman Place Chapel. On the platform Ralph Waldo Emerson lectured on "Mind and Manners in the Nineteenth Century."[1] In the wake of completing *Mardi*, Melville made his first sustained encounter with Emerson at a time when he was immersing himself in Shakespeare's plays. As his letters to Evert Duyckinck attest, Melville included both Emerson and Shakespeare in "the whole corps of thought-divers, that have been diving & coming up again with blood-shot eyes since the world began."[2] While praising Shakespeare to the heavens, Melville qualifies his assessment of Emerson, taking care to distinguish between his "merit" and his "gaping flaw." Part of Melville's energy is directed toward asserting his independence from Emerson's reputed "transcendentalisms, myths & oracular gibberish." While professing that "I do not oscillate in Emerson's rainbow, but prefer rather to hang myself in mine own halter," Melville nevertheless goes on to defend the "brilliant" Emerson against Duyckinck's apparent imputation that Emerson's work is derivative: "Be his stuff begged, borrowed, or stolen, or of his own domestic manufacture he is an uncommon man. . . . Lay it down that had not Sir Thomas Browne lived, Emerson would not have mystified—I will answer, that had not Old Zack's father begot him, Old Zack would never have been the hero of Palo Alto. The truth is that we are all sons, grandsons, or nephews or great-nephews of those who go before us. No one is his own sire" (*Letters*, 78–79). Couched in a simulated dialogue—"Lay it down . . . I will answer"—Melville's allusion to Browne suggests that Melville's attraction to Emerson had less to do with the content of Emerson's thought than with the process of intellection and his own relation to earlier traditions. Though Melville probably went on to read some or all of Emerson's *Essays: First Series*, his primary response is to defend Emerson's practice in light of his own developing aesthetic.[3] Melville's notion that we are "all sons. . . . No one is his own sire" paradoxically liberates him from being anyone's disciple and reinforces his habit to absorb, critique, and

This essay was written specifically for this volume and is published here for the first time by permission of the author.

re-form the work of earlier thinkers. In *Mardi* this process has its roots in Melville's adaptation of the Platonic conception of knowledge as recollection.[4] Babbalanja explains, "The catalogue of true thoughts is but small; they are ubiquitous; no man's property; and unspoken, or bruited, are the same. When we hear them, why seem they so natural, receiving our spontaneous approval? why do we think we have heard them before? Because they but reiterate ourselves; they were in us, before we were born. The truest poets are but mouth-pieces; and some men are duplicates of each other."[5] Babbalanja combines ideational metempsychosis and spontaneous discovery. In *Mardi* Melville is fascinated by the prospect of an abiding consistency in the deep structures of human consciousness; these notions can only be discovered through intuition and reflected through an art that expresses the process of thinking. In February 1849 Emerson appealed to Melville as one more thought-diver recasting the wisdom of the ages in the language of the day, a process that Melville had occasion to study the previous year as he read not only Plato and Browne but also Rabelais, Montaigne, Burton, and Coleridge.[6] In his art Melville was seeking to translate the intellectual materials inspired by his reading into appropriate narrative vehicles. In *Mardi* the interminable philosophical dialogues are scattershot attempts to contain competing perspectives within a narrative framework. At the very least the example of Emerson as lecturer and author would have reinforced Melville's penchant for the dialectical possibilities of literary art, while the plays of Shakespeare would have fed his appetite for dramatizing great ideas through tragic action. Melville's view of art as a process of intellectual reformulation and invention culminates in what I call the assimilative process narrative of Ishmael, while Melville's attraction to the possibilities of tragic characterization culminates in the absolutism of Ahab.

Melville's encounters with Plato and Browne in 1848 and Emerson and Shakespeare in early 1849 provided him with stimulating contexts for dramatizing ideas. In his purchase of Pierre Bayle's *An Historical and Critical Dictionary* Melville recognized an opportunity to extend his researches: indeed he imagined himself peacefully presiding over a three-way textual interchange. In a 5 April 1849 letter to Evert Duyckinck, Melville mentions that he "bought a set of Bayle's Dictionary the other day, & on my return to New York intend to lay the great old folios side by side & go to sleep on them thro' the summer, with the Phaedon in one hand & Tom Brown in the other" (*Letters*, 83–84). This act of self-dramatization exposes Melville's tendency to see his reading as a procreant fusion of disparate materials. The principle of fusion, as it were, is nothing other than the reader's focusing eye and inquiring mind. Indeed Bayle's *Dictionary* may be the world's ultimate book for serendipitous browsing. Flanked by Plato and Browne, Melville may have confronted Bayle's tirade against Spinoza's pantheism, his refutation of the Gnostic heresies, his exploration of Chrysippus' stoicism, and his discussion of Zoroaster's interest in magic. To open any volume to any page is to find the sort of intellectual feast that Melville appreciated. The very layout of the page overwhelms one with the dialectical interstices of argument. In large print Bayle covers the contours of historical narrative—the general matters of biography and thought. In small print the footnotes contain gnarled, often vituperative, commentary replete with etymologies, extracts, and reading lists. In forging one text from many Bayle locates the principle of cohesion in his own adjudication. Melville's very desire to pursue Bayle in the company of Plato and Browne reflects a habit of mind in which any direct statement is prelude to a tangled interplay of competing positions—a quality made most manifest in Ishmael's own meditativeness in such chapters as "The Chapel," "Moby Dick," and "The Whiteness of the Whale." Melville's experience of Bayle reinforced the notion that all argument has roots in historical and literary contexts. Such a condition pertains directly to two of Melville's informing beliefs: first, there are very few thoughts per se; the few true thoughts have been abroad throughout the ages; second, once ascertained through study and/or inspiration, these ideas are the materials that true genius shapes through the process of intellectual activity.

Prior to the composition of *Moby-Dick*, Melville had the good luck to encounter the perfect companion on his voyage to England in the fall of 1849. Like Melville, George J. Adler was coming off a strenuous period of intellectual exertion.[7] Melville was fascinated by Adler's imposing scholarly mind: "He is author of a formidable lexicon, (German & English); in compiling which he almost ruined his health. He was almost crazy, he tells me, for a time. He is full of the German metaphysics, & discourses of Kant, Swedenborg &c. He has been my principal companion thus far."[8] Marovitz examines Adler's epigraphs from Coleridge's *Biographia Literaria*, Plato's *Cratylus*, and Jean Paul Richter's *Levana oder Erziehlehre*, all of which depict "the power of language through literary tradition and through the distinctions that linguistic classification makes possible" (Marovitz, 377). While there is no documentary evidence to suggest that Melville ever read Adler's "Preface," it is highly unlikely that Adler would have avoided his most cherished subjects in conversation. Marovitz plausibly speculates that Melville adapted at least some of Adler's methods and intentions in composing *Moby-Dick*, especially Adler's sense—gleaned from Richter—that "every good grammarian must of necessity, be a partial philosopher" (qtd. in Marovitz, 380). According to Marovitz, Adler stimulated Melville's interest in the "double value of terminology" (381). In *Moby-Dick* Melville's multiple uses of the loom and the sphinx alone suggest the procreant possibilities of seeing objects in a range of associative meanings. Essentially, Adler stimulated Melville's metaphysical predisposition, especially the pursuit of what Melville called "the problem of the universe."[9] In one journal entry Melville relates their conversations to an appropriate Miltonic context. Melville evokes the sedate demons of *Paradise Lost* who

> reason'd high
> Of Providence, Foreknowledge, Will and Fate,
> Fixt Fate, Free Will, Foreknowledge absolute,
> And found no end, in wand'ring mazes lost.[10]

Melville's own words—"Walked the deck with the German, Mr Adler till a late hour, talking of 'Fixed Fate, Free-will, foreknowledge absolute'" (*Journals*, 4)—do not associate him with the dour and tedious futility of Milton's damned; instead Melville seems deft and wry in alluding to the endlessness of human speculation. The allusion indicates Melville's instinct for linking his own endeavors with appropriate textual corollaries. Similarly, not far from land, Melville comments on the rampant seasickness among his fellow passengers, echoing Job and prefiguring his epigraph to *Moby-Dick's* "Epilogue": "A gale of wind, & every one sick. . . . & I alone am left to tell the tale of their misery" (*Journals*, 6).

Melville's relationship with Adler on a voyage at sea constituted a propitious conflation of many elements in his life and work. The trip to England allowed Melville to reexperience his past as sailor, though now he had no work to do. He could rove at will in the rigging. While on his first voyage Melville had labored as a green sailor, he embarked on the present voyage as author and intellectual. Melville took note of the transfiguration: ". . . *then* a sailor, *now* H. M. author of 'Peedee' 'Hullabaloo' & 'Pog-Dog'" (*Journals*, 12; Melville's italics). Removed from wife, children, home, and work, Melville found himself in the experiential position of bachelorhood. He could enjoy the comradeship, the boozing, the intellectual repartee. It must have seemed that Melville was living out the peripatetic life of his questers in *Mardi*. The association of travel and talk informed *Mardi's* structure and it invigorated his mind on the voyage. Indeed the plots of Melville's most single-mindedly philosophical narratives—*The Confidence-Man* and *Clarel*—offer extended variations on the intellectual possibilities of fusing the activity of roving with the permutations of thought.

Once in England, with the band of boon companions broken and plans for extended travel ruptured, Melville spent much of his time sightseeing, meeting potential publishers, and buying books. On his book-buying rambles Melville evinced a recurrent inclination for four kinds of narratives: romance; autobiography; biography; and a fictional hybrid that combines personal narrative and biography. The acquisition of William Godwin's *Caleb Williams* and William Beckford's *Vathek* reflected Melville's interest in the romantic potboiler and the exotic travelogue, respectively, and they point ahead to the composition of *Pierre* rather than *Moby-Dick*. In the genre of autobiography Melville acquired Thomas De Quincey's *The Confessions of an English Opium-Eater*, Goethe's *Autobiography*, and Rousseau's *Confessions*. Melville's interest in biography led him to purchase Boswell's *Life of Johnson*. This interest continued through 1850 when he borrowed Carlyle's

On Heroes, Hero-Worship, and the Heroic in History and probably read all or part of Emerson's *Representative Men*. The hybrid genre of fictionalized autobiography that contains the fictional biography of another person was congenial to Melville's instincts and was reflected in his own writing. At the very least the autobiographically based *Typee, Omoo, Redburn*, and *White-Jacket* all fuse elements of fact and fiction in the cause of synthesizing such disparate generic contexts as travelogue, romance, novel, bildungsroman, satire, anatomy, essay, among others. Similarly, in the biographically based *Israel Potter* and "Benito Cereno" Melville uses personal narrative as the raw materials for inspiring his invention. In this regard Mary Shelley's *Frankenstein* was a notable purchase. In *Frankenstein* Walton's first-person narrative contains the inset narratives of both Frankenstein and the monster. The narrative contours of Shelley's novel find a provocative aesthetic complement in Carlyle's use of multiple narrators in *Sartor Resartus*, which Melville borrowed in June or July 1850.[11]

Of these acquisitions, De Quincey's *Confessions*, Shelley's *Frankenstein*, and Carlyle's *Sartor Resartus* offer the greatest range of suggestive possibilities for understanding the impress of Melville's learning in relation to his auspicious reformulation of *Moby-Dick*. It is my contention that these works, whether read in London, as in the case of De Quincey's *Confessions*, or later, as is probable for *Frankenstein* and *Sartor Resartus*, had the cumulative effect of supplying general and particular suggestions and materials for Melville's transformation of the Peleg/Bulkington "whaling voyage" into the Ishmael/Queequeg/Ahab voyage for Moby Dick.[12] It must be noted, however, that this particular cluster cannot be somehow viewed as a force separate from the inscrutable alchemical process of Melville's genius—a process that was also shaped by Melville's five previous books, his fascination with Shakespeare, his August 1850 discovery of Hawthorne as artist and man, his self-reflexive review of Hawthorne's *Mosses from an Old Manse*, his abiding interest in Emerson's work, among other forces. In viewing the relationship of particular texts to the gestation of *Moby-Dick*, one seeks to identify a symphony of possibilities that has a plausible relation to Melville's finished text. The danger of fixing a single resource as preeminent, as Nina Baym does with Emerson, is that one cuts the Gordian knot of entangled interrelation.[13] As most scholars would agree, source materials not only emerge in distinct topical contexts, but they also change shape and are made the author's own through a process of conscious and unconscious adaptation. Like Ishmael in "The Whiteness of the Whale," one must proceed inductively by way of accumulation: the sum of multiple possibilities does not add up to an answer—or a key—but to an articulation of those elements that might best formulate the best questions. Speculative surmises on De Quincey and Shelley, then, will pave the way for an examination of the possible interweaving of elements in *Moby-Dick*, Emerson's "History," and Carlyle's *Sartor Resartus*.

In a 22 December 1849 London journal entry Melville notes that he "at last got hold of 'The Opium Eater'" (*Journals*, 46). He started this "most wondrous book" immediately and finished it next day (*Journals*, 47). Given to "the sleep of endless reverie, and of dreamy abstraction from life and its realities," De Quincey provides a narrative analogue to Ishmael.[14] Both narrators combine meditative voice and orphaned status—traits that also characterize Rousseau in his *Confessions*. A "homeless vagrant upon the earth before I had accomplished my seventeenth year," De Quincey is alienated from a lost world of familial coherence and grandeur (De Quincey, 54). Thrust forth into psychological exile he must construct an order based upon the "innumerable acts of choice [that] change countenance and are variously appraised at varying stages of life [and] shift with the shifting hours" (De Quincey, 74). The meditative wanderer not only contemplates the flux of experience, but he also perceives that the act of choice circumscribes one's fate. Not only alive to the confluence of freedom and fate, the narrator often speaks in the self-possessed and proprietary tones that evoke Ishmael's comic voice. De Quincey on opium resembles Ishmael on the whale: "And therefore, worthy doctors, as there seems to be room for further discoveries, stand aside, and allow me to come forward and lecture on this matter" (De Quincey, 156). Like Ishmael, De Quincey infuses his observations with humorous and genial assertions of authority: "This is the doctrine of the true church on the subject of opium. . . . I speak from the ground of a large and profound personal experience, whereas most of the unscientific authors who have at all treated of opium . . . make it evident . . . that their experimental knowledge of its action is none at all" (De Quincey, 158). Bereft of traditional faith in a benevolent cosmos, De Quincey ponders a silent universe that haunts the inquiring mind. Like Emerson, Carlyle, and Melville, De Quincey associates the mysteries of creation with the image of the Sphinx: "If in this world there is one misery having no relief, it is the pressure on the heart from the *Incommunicable*. And, if another Sphinx should arise to propose another enigma to man—saying, What burden is that which only is insupportable by human fortitude? I should answer at once—*It is the burden of the Incommunicable*" (De Quincey, 92; his italics). This "insupportable . . . *burden*" provides a possible analogue for Ahab's detestation for whatever force may lurk behind the "pasteboard masks" of material forms. As Ahab exclaims, "That inscrutable thing is chiefly what I hate" (164). In De Quincey's "Incommunicable" may also be a germ of Melville's speculation in *Pierre* on God as the "Voice from Silence."[15]

Melville acquired Mary Shelley's *Frankenstein* on 20 December 1849, though we have no evidence to indicate when he might have read it. Nevertheless, affinities between *Frankenstein* and *Moby-Dick* make it likely that Melville read the novel with care. In pertaining to the characters and voices of Ahab and Ishmael, these affinities support the notion that Shelley's book contributed to Melville's transformation of the "whaling voyage."

Of the most topical nature, Ahab's speech to the Carpenter on how to make a mighty man constitutes a probable adaptation of Frankenstein's plan for making his monster. Ahab addresses the Carpenter as "manmaker" and the Blacksmith as "Prometheus," perhaps alluding to Shelley's presentation of the modern Prometheus, especially the myth of Prometheus *Plasticator*. Ahab remarks, "I do deem it now a most meaning thing, that that old Greek, Prometheus, who made men, they say, should have been a blacksmith, and animated them with fire" (470). As scientist and artist/maker, Frankenstein is obsessed with "bestowing animation upon lifeless matter."[16] He desires "to make the being of a gigantic structure; that is to say, about eight feet in height, and proportionably large" (Shelley, 54). Ahab conflates the myth of Prometheus *Plasticator* with its associative counterpart: the myth of the defiant Titan who stole fire from the gods and gave it to man. Rooted in place though not chained to a rock, Ahab's man would presumably be ready to do battle with the gods. Ahab says, "Hold; while Prometheus is about it, I'll order a complete man after a desirable pattern. Imprimis, fifty feet high in his socks; then, chest modelled after the Thames Tunnel; then, legs with roots to 'em . . . no heart at all, brass forehead, and about a quarter of an acre of fine brains" (470).

Like *Moby-Dick*, Shelley's *Frankenstein* presents a strange sea voyage into the great unknown as a primary narrative structure. Walton's obsession with ultimate knowledge drives him toward the desolate polar world where he meets the questing Frankenstein, who is bent on exacting vengeance by killing the monster he created. As a narrator, Walton intermittently reflects the genial and megalomaniacal qualities of voice that respectively characterize Ishmael and Ahab. At one point Walton seems to prefigure Ishmael's exuberant embrace of the "barbarous," his "everlasting itch for things remote" (7). Walton reports, "I am practically industrious—pains-taking;—a workman to execute with perseverance and labour:—but besides this, there is a love for the marvellous, a belief in the marvellous, intertwined in all my projects, which hurries me out of the common pathways of men, even to the wild sea and unvisited regions I am about to explore" (Shelley, 21–22). Shortly thereafter Walton speaks with the obsessed megalomaniacal voice that may have reminded Melville of Taji and perhaps pointed ahead to Ahab: "But success *shall* crown my endeavours. Wherefore not? Thus far I have gone, tracing a secure way over the pathless seas: the very stars themselves being witnesses and testimonies of my triumph. Why not still proceed over the untamed yet obedient element? What can stop the determined heart and resolved will of man?" (Shelley, 23; her italics).

Not only do Shelley and Melville draw on Promethean materials and present genial and absolutistic narrative voices, but they also present, in at least a limited sense, cautionary tales, which depict the attraction and dangers of attempts to recast the fundamental terms of human existence. Both writers are attracted to the "exceptional natures" capable of spawning such grandiose aspirations.[17] What intrigued Shelley in Walton and Frankenstein, and Melville in Ishmael and Ahab (and Hawthorne and Shakespeare), was the degree to which these figures could strike through commonplace renderings to what Melville called the "vital truth" below the surface.[18] Indeed Walton's assessment of Frankenstein's exceptional nature is very like Melville's judgment on Shakespeare in "Hawthorne and His Mosses," which was composed in early August 1850. Walton remarks, "Sometimes I have endeavoured to discover what quality it is which he possesses, that elevates him so immeasurably above any other person I ever knew. I believe it to be an intuitive discernment; a quick but never-failing power of judgment; a penetration into the causes of things" (Shelley, 29). Melville's description of Shakespeare's quality of mind characterizes the "whole corps of thought-divers" (Letters, 79) that Melville so admired: "But it is those deep far-away things in him; those occasional flashings-forth of the intuitive Truth in him; those short, quick probings at the very axis of reality;—these are the things that make Shakespeare, Shakespeare" ("Mosses," 244). And these are the things—the "quick probings at the very axis of reality"—that could well have united Melville's encounters with Plato, Browne, Montaigne, Rabelais, and Burton during the composition of *Mardi* with his alchemical interaction with Emerson, Shakespeare, Bayle, Browne, Adler, De Quincey, Shelley, and Carlyle (among others) during the gestation and actual composition of *Moby-Dick*.

In mid-July 1850 Melville took his family on a vacation to his Cousin Robert Melvill's farm in Pittsfield. This propitious move took Melville away from the summer heat of New York City, returned him to a place where he spent pleasant summer months as a teenager, and put him in proximity to Hawthorne, whom he met on 5 August. About this time Melville was saying that his whaling book was almost finished. Melville's visit to the Berkshires and his encounters with Hawthorne as man and writer, however, unsettled his creative life. His review of Hawthorne's *Mosses* is as close as he ever came to composing a self-advertising manifesto. In celebrating the possibilities of American literature, Melville summons himself forth as the American Shakespeare. Inflamed with the prospect of tragic vision, Melville considers the "great power of blackness" ("Mosses," 243). At the center of his decision to recast his "whaling voyage" must have been his desire to explore this "great power." Out of this desire the figure of Ahab must somehow have loomed "interweavingly" (215) with the white whale—an inventive symbiosis that reshaped both the voice telling the tale as well as the symbolic context that contained the tale.

Given the teasing possibilities that surround the question of how Melville came to fuse the vestigial and the re-formed narratives of *Moby-Dick*, it is inviting to view "The Mat-Maker" chapter as an exemplary paradigm for speculating on the ways in which the vestigial narrative provided direction and clues for his reconstruction. This chapter seems to reside at the compositional nexus between old and new. Hayford speculates that "The Mat-Maker" was composed prior to the onshore relationship between Ishmael and Queequeg. [19] If this is so, the chapter may have supplied the notion of bringing a tyro-Ishmael together with cannibal Queequeg. It may also have suggested the possibility of extending the symbolic interconnection between phenomenal and noumenal realms as represented in Ishmael's "Loom of Time" into the nautical and weaving contexts suggested by "Loomings." In "The Mat-Maker" Ishmael presents a sublime synthesis of material and spiritual processes—a harmony made evident by the interpretive activity of the perceiving mind. Without question Melville derived the image of "the Loom of Time" from Carlyle's *Sartor Resartus*.[20] But his application of this figure constitutes an adaptation from Plato's Myth of Er in Book X of the *Republic*. In telling the tale of the soul's pre-birth journey, Socrates fashions an elaborate cosmological image that conflates the structure of a ship with the operation of a loom: "this light is the belt of heaven, and holds together the circle of the universe, like the under-girders of a trireme. From these ends is extended the spindle of Necessity, on which all the revolutions turn. The shaft and hook of this spindle are made of steel. . . . Now the whorl is in form like the whorl used on earth."[21] Ship and loom act in unison with the Fates. Unlike Plato, for whom the Fates are absolute, Ishmael argues for the interconnection of apparently disparate elements: "chance, free will, and necessity—no wise incompatible—all interweavingly working together" (215). Melville brings together Carlyle's Loom and Platonic myth with a narrator who makes meaning in the act of thinking. Melville's narrator is alert to the mind's ability to forge symbolic correspondences, even though the next instant may unravel his synthesis. Indeed Tashtego sights a whale and Ishmael drops the "ball of free will" (215).

If "The Mat-Maker" chapter provides a nexus between old and new, it may then make sense to examine ways in which key elements of this chapter—the process narrator, the world as loom, the whale as lure—may have been re-formed in relation to Melville's encounters with works by Emerson and Carlyle, both of whom he seems to have read in the summer of 1850. In the *Mosses* review Melville mentions Emerson with apparent familiarity. In early September 1850 Melville spent a morning at Hawthorne's home reading an unspecified volume of Emerson's work.[22] Whether now or earlier Melville almost certainly read Emerson's "History," the initial piece in *Essays: First Series*. At the very least, "History" provides provocative terms that help describe Melville's achievement in developing voice and symbol in *Moby-Dick*. Like Carlyle (and Plato, Montaigne, Browne, Burton, and Coleridge) Emerson identifies an abiding pool of ideas that transcend historical boundaries. As these thoughts impinge upon a present thinker's consciousness, past and present fuse into a sublime experience of perceptual synthesis: "When a thought of Plato becomes a thought to me,—when a

truth that fired the soul of Pindar fires mine, time is no more."[23] Emerson's
"History" focuses more on the poetic recreation in the present "of a very few
laws" than it does on the studious contemplation of things past (Emerson, 9).
The vital force animating Plato and Pindar generates from the same eternal
Soul pervading Nature. What interests Emerson is the way in which ideas
become part of a thinker's perceptual present and then become translated into
narrative. Emerson's "metempsychosis of nature" allows for the "innumerable
variations" of these abiding ideational structures (Emerson, 8, 9). Consequently Emerson's "History" highlights the centrality of story or fable as a
means of presenting metaphysical concepts. As Emerson argues, "The
philosophical perception of identity through endless mutations of form,
makes him know the Proteus" (Emerson, 18). To evoke the figure of
Prometheus, then, is for Emerson to give expression to "universal verities.
What a range of meanings and what perpetual pertinence has the story of
Prometheus. . . . Prometheus is the Jesus of the old mythology" (Emerson, 17).

Emerson's conflation of the mythic contexts of ancient story and
narrative self-fashioning through the "metempsychosis of nature" provides an
aesthetic parallel to Melville's tendencies in *Moby-Dick*. Most notably the
imperative act of self-naming—"Call me Ishmael" (3)—links present time
and Biblical story to the announcement, if not the inception, of the narrator's
identity, at the same time that it highlights his status as wanderer, outcast,
isolato. Throughout the narrative's unfolding social framework, Ishmael
adapts mythic identities to his purposes. When recounting his story by using
forms that derive from disparate mythologies, most notably Hebraic and
Hellenic, Ishmael appropriates a technique analogous to Emerson's "metempsychosis of nature." Ahab, for example, chases the inscrutable, vicious
"Job's whale" (186), sharply contrasting with Father Mapple's presentation of
the subservient whale of Jonah. In "Stowing Down and Clearing Up"
Ishmael adapts an element of Hellenic mythology. A sailor's initiation into
the world of work can be understood in relation to the transmigration of
souls. The sailors engage in "the severest uninterrupted labors" only to "go
through the whole weary thing again" (429). In a startling observation
Ishmael fuses this "man-killing" process of labor with the eternal recurrence
of old souls in new bodies. As Emerson says, "Time is no more" (Emerson,
15). Under the eye of Ishmael, present time is linked to mythic time: "Oh!
the metempsychosis! Oh! Pythagoras, that in bright Greece, two thousand
years ago, did die, so good, so wise, so mild; I sailed with thee along the
Peruvian coast last voyage—and, foolish as I am, taught thee, a green simple
boy, how to splice a rope!" (429). Though an incidental perception, this
connection is paradigmatic of the myth-making properties of Ishmael's
voice—a voice that insistently reshapes fables and forms into new combina-
tions.

While Emerson's "metempsychosis of nature" in "History" provides at least an exemplary parallel for identifying Ishmael's penchant for infusing his story with mythic signification, Carlyle's wide-ranging dialectical voice in *Sartor Resartus* provides a suggestive foundation for approaching Melville's use of narrative voice in *Moby-Dick*. At one point Carlyle even mentions the Biblical Ishmael in relation to the acquisition of self-reliance: "Thus in the destitution of the wild desert does our young Ishmael acquire for himself the highest of all possessions, that of Self-help."[24] Of special interest to Melville would have been Carlyle's insistence on philosophical play, an attribute Melville would have associated with Rabelais and Burton. An appropriate successor to Plato, Montaigne, Browne, and Bayle, Carlyle would certainly have contributed to Melville's sense of the procreant possibilities of the compositional act. In *Mardi* Melville depicted processes of consciousness as principles of narrative self-fashioning. However uncontrolled a work, *Mardi* first provided a forum within which Melville could link narrative situation and metaphysical speculation. What Melville needed was a way to focus voice and vision. With his emphasis in *Sartor Resartus* on open-ended discussion and dialectical interchange, Carlyle would at least have complemented Melville's growing sense of the aesthetic potential of a narrator who uses the present tense to recount incidents in the very act of trying to understand them. *Moby-Dick* is a fiction in which Ishmael's process narration overcomes distinctions between then and now, there and here in order to bring the reader to experience the processes animating the narrator's perceptual experience. Like Carlyle, Ishmael conflates retrospection and interpretation. The narrative voice, then, is authoritative insofar as it identifies a field of inquiry—Teufelsdröckh's philosophy of clothes or Ishmael's wonder-world of whaling—*and* provisional insofar as the narrator becomes enmeshed in a slippery interpretive activity. The assimilative process narrator highlights the dialectical play of possibility. In *Sartor Resartus* two voices—sometimes three—coexist in a comic display of conjecture. Just as Ishmael claims that in "some enterprises . . . a careful disorderliness is the true method" (361), so too does Carlyle's editor attest to Teufelsdröckh's sporadic illogical assays: "But of true logical method and sequence there is too little. Apart from its multifarious sections and subdivisions, the Work naturally falls into two Parts; a Historical-Descriptive, and a Philosophical-Speculative: but falls, unhappily, by no firm line of demarcation; in that labyrinthic combination, each Part overlaps, and indents, and indeed runs quite through the other" (Carlyle, 26–27). It is inviting to think of *Moby-Dick* as possessing both "Historical-Descriptive" and "Philosophical-Speculative" centers that are "no wise incompatible" (215) and woven by a teasing voice that appears intermittently as participating actor (both tyro and veteran), detached observer, and omniscient commentator.

A key to the connection between Melville and Carlyle is not only to be found in narrative voice but also in the way in which the narrative voice attempts to make meaning in a world rife with symbolic suggestiveness. In one representative passage Carlyle writes, "Rightly viewed no meanest object is insignificant; all objects are as windows, through which the philosophic eye looks into Infinitude itself. . . . All visible things are emblems . . ." (Carlyle, 55; his italics). This passage is echoed in Ahab's "pasteboard masks" speech (164); in his later question, "What things real are there, but imponderable thoughts?" (528); and in Ishmael's claim that "some certain significance lurks in all things, else all things are little worth, and the round world itself but an empty cipher" (430). Teufelsdröckh's philosophy of clothes constitutes a comic celebration of how the outer world of material things is but the woven garment of the spiritual world. In arguing for the correspondence of Nature and Soul, Teufelsdröckh depicts a universal fusion of seen and unseen. Viewed "philosophico-poetically," the world of material forms reflects the ubiquitous hand of the divine weaver (Carlyle, 57). In presenting the relationship of seen and unseen, Teufelsdröckh adopts Goethe's image of the Loom of Time. The artist's holy office is to weave the "garment" whereby God is recognized:

'Tis thus at the roaring Loom of Time I ply,
And weave for God the Garment thou seest Him by. (Carlyle, 42)

Melville would have recognized that Carlyle's book offers a quirky reformulation of Platonic Idealism. The editor even mentions Teufelsdröckh's "high Platonic Mysticism" (Carlyle, 50). Carlyle's extended exegesis on the philosophy of clothes might have suggested ways for Melville to vary his application of distinct correspondences between objects and ideas. In *Moby-Dick*, for example, Melville adapts the image of the loom to multiple contexts. The very word "Loomings" plays on the double-meaning of weaving and nautical vista. The loom is also associated with Melville's use of the imagery of lines. For example, the whale line and the monkey rope, respectively, depict the tenuousness of life and the interdependence among mortals. The image of the loom suggests the literal lines of intersection between phenomenal and noumenal realms. As noted above, the weaving scene in "The Mat-Maker" explicitly connects the social contexts of cooperative labor with the metaphysical contexts of the Loom of Time, an association that is recast in Pip's cosmic vision in "The Castaway." He sees "God's foot upon the treadle of the loom" (414). The loom as image complements Ishmael's activity as process narrator. In this regard the loom is an appropriate image for a world characterized by the interaction of fixity and flux. The loom, in effect, *translates* possibility into fixity, process into product. For Carlyle the philosophy of clothes and the Loom of Time provide ways of discussing a dynamic world of constant and coherent interplay among disparate forces: "I say there is no . . . separation; nothing hitherto was ever stranded, cast aside; but all, were it only a withered leaf, works together with all: is borne forward on the bottomless, shoreless flood of Action, and lives through perpetual metamorphoses" (Carlyle, 54–55). Melville apparently adapts Carlyle's notion of "perpetual metamorphoses" to very different purposes in "A Bower In the Arsacides," where Ishmael describes a beached skeleton of a sperm whale, carved "in strange hieroglyphics" and festooned with verdure from "the great world's loom" (449, 450). In this paradigmatic scene of reading Ishmael confronts the unification of unreadable sign and natural process:

> . . . the industrious earth beneath was as a weaver's loom, with a gorgeous carpet on it, whereof the ground-vine tendrils formed the warp and woof, and the living flowers the figures. All the trees, with all their laden branches; all the shrubs, and ferns, and grasses; the message-carrying air; all these unceasingly were active. Through the lacings of the leaves, the great sun seemed a flying shuttle weaving the unwearied verdure. Oh, busy weaver! . . . the shuttle flies—the figures float from forth the loom; the freshet-rushing carpet for ever slides away. The weaver-god, he weaves; and by that weaving is he deafened, that he hears no mortal voice; and by that humming, we, too, who look on the loom are deafened. (449–450)

In *Sartor Resartus* the "perpetual metamorphoses" become ultimately signs of man's ontological relation to an immanent God; Melville's adaptation, on the contrary, reflects man's experiential separation and cosmic alienation from God. Indeed it is the very driving force of natural process itself that deafens God and man.

The "strange hieroglyphics" of the whale's skeleton indicate Melville's attraction to using Egyptian symbolism to evoke the inscrutable mysteries of the cosmos. Melville would have been alert to the recurrence of such imagery in his reading of De Quincey, Carlyle, and Emerson. Such encounters would have reinforced his penchant for placing the human perceiver before the inscrutable sign. As early as *Typee*, Tommo confronts the natives' indecipherable totems. In *Mardi* the high priest Aleema is covered with hieroglyphic tattoos. In reading De Quincey, Carlyle, and Emerson, Melville probably noted their similar evocations of the Sphinx. A version of De Quincey's Sphinx as sign of "the Incommunicable," Emerson's "old fable of the Sphinx" depicts the dangers which face the strident seeker after truth. In Emerson's figuration the Sphinx puts riddles to every passerby: "If the man could not answer she swallowed him alive. If he could solve the riddle, the Sphinx was slain" (Emerson, 18). This description evokes the Jonah story, the devouring maw of Peleg's "monstrousest parmacetty" (72) as well as Ahab's quest to slay the creature that personifies the cosmic riddle. At the least Emerson's presentation of this myth indicates its easy adaptation to Melville's purposes. In "The Sphinx" chapter Ahab directly addresses the severed whale's head. Unlike Emerson's Sphinx, Ahab's "venerable head" is silent (311). Though having witnessed the mysteries of the deep, the whale hangs dead and dumb. Under the hand of Carlyle in *Sartor Resartus*, the Sphinx excites a similar mystery. To Herr Teufelsdröckh "The Universe . . . was as a mighty Sphinx-riddle, which I knew so little of, yet must rede [*sic*], or be devoured. In red streaks of unspeakable grandeur, yet also in the blackness of darkness, was Life, to my too-unfurnished Thought, unfolding itself" (Carlyle, 98).[25] Carlyle extends the image to discuss the mystery of human ontology: "The secret of Man's Being is still like the Sphinx's secret: a riddle that he cannot rede [*sic*]; and for ignorance of which he suffers death, the worst death, a spiritual" (Carlyle, 41). Ishmael's "one grand hooded phantom, like a snow hill in the air" (7) has associations with "the ungraspable phantom of life"—the ontological and epistemological mysteries evoked in "that story of Narcissus" (5). The whale as Sphinx finds a recurrent imagistic corollary in the whale as unreadable symbol of mystery, especially in the hieroglyphic markings associated with whales in general and Moby Dick in particular. With its "unaccountable masses of shades and shadows" the painting on the wall of The Spouter Inn elicits Ishmael's puzzled meditation on a creature very like a whale, a "long, limber, portentous, black mass of something hovering in the centre . . ."(12). In "The Prairie" the brow of the whale possesses the sphinx-like inscrutability—the very unreadability—of God Himself: "Human or animal, the mystical brow is as that great golden seal affixed by the German emperors to their decrees. It signifies—'God: done this day by my hand'" (346). In embodying the living nexus between phenomenal and noumenal realms, then, the sperm whale emanates "god-like dignity . . . For you see no one point precisely; not one distinct feature is revealed . . . nothing but that one broad firmament of a forehead, pleated with riddles; dumbly lowering with the doom of boats, and ships, and men." The whale's brow presents a language utterly foreign: the silent sounds of the dead Egyptian land. With its haunting surface, the whale paradoxically declares its genius through "his pyramidical silence. . . . Champollion deciphered the wrinkled granite hieroglyphics. But there is no Champollion to decipher the Egypt of every man's and every being's face. . . . how may unlettered Ishmael hope to read the awful Chaldee of the Sperm Whale's brow? I but put that brow before you. Read it if you can" (346–347). Ishmael presents, in effect, the limitations of his powers as process narrator. In describing himself as "unlettered" he surrenders interpretation to the reader.

The blank brow of the whale may be viewed as a synoptic image of the mysterious matrix—the symphony of contrapuntal qualities—that constitutes Melville's *Moby-Dick*. Far from being the narrative of a "whaling voyage," as Melville seems originally to have intended, *Moby-Dick* offers a grand compendium of forces and intentions. In the process of writing Melville became possessed with the idea of writing a great book with a mighty theme. In translating his "multifarious bibliographic" and life experiences into the process of storytelling, Melville seemed to be trying, whether consciously or unconsciously, to fulfill his own dictates, set forth in *Mardi*, for the making of literary monuments. In "Time and Temples" the narrator proclaims that "to make an eternity, we must build with eternities." Melville's materials for invention were frequently literary artifacts—both ancient and contemporary—and like his Promethean artificer in *Mardi*, Melville in *Moby-Dick* combined invention and creative appropriation to make a book "alike durable and new."[26]

Notes

1. Merton M. Sealts, Jr., "Melville and Emerson's Rainbow," in *Pursuing Melville, 1940–1980* (Madison: University of Wisconsin Press, 1982), 258.
2. Herman Melville, *The Letters of Herman Melville*, ed. Merrell R. Davis and William H. Gilman (New Haven: Yale University Press, 1960), 79; hereafter cited as *Letters*.
3. See Sealts, "Emerson's Rainbow" for his discussion of what Melville might have read (263–67).
4. See Sealts, "Melville and the Platonic Tradition," in *Pursuing Melville, 1940–1980*, 283–84.
5. *Mardi*, ed. Harrison Hayford, Hershel Parker, and G. Thomas Tanselle (Evanston and Chicago: Northwestern University Press and The Newberry Library, 1970), 397.
6. See Sealts, "The Platonic Tradition," 281–97, and John Wenke, "'Ontological Heroics: Melville's Philosophical Art," in *A Companion to Melville Studies*, ed. John Bryant (New York: Greenwood Press, 1986), 567–601.
7. See Sanford E. Marovitz, "More Chartless Voyaging: Melville and Adler at Sea," in *Studies in the American Renaissance*, ed. Joel Myerson (Charlottesville: University of Virginia Press, 1986), 373–84. Marovitz comments on "their remarkably compatible psychological states. . . . Perhaps the most crucial correspondence between them—apart from their mutual willingness to participate in extended discussion on the level of metaphysics—is the fact that both men were in need of rest and change after an extremely trying period of sustained intellectual productivity" (375).
8. *Journals*, ed. Howard C. Horsford with Lynn Horth (Evanston and Chicago: Northwestern University Press and The Newberry Library, 1989), 4; hereafter cited as *Journals*.
9. For Melville's other uses of this phrase, see *Letters*, 121, 124, 125, 256. In *Moby-Dick*, ed. Harrison Hayford, Hershel Parker, and G. Thomas Tanselle, (Evanston and Chicago: Northwestern University Press and The Newberry Library, 1988), see 158 and 293. All citations from this text will be noted parenthetically within the body of the essay.
10. John Milton, *Paradise Lost*, ed. Merritt Y. Hughes (New York: Odyssey Press, 1957), Bk. II, lines 558–61.
11. See Merton M. Sealts, Jr., *Melville's Reading* (Columbia: University of South Carolina Press, 1988), for an alphabetized listing of full citations for the aforementioned primary materials.
12. See Harrison Hayford, "Unnecessary Duplicates: A Key to the Writing of *Moby-Dick*," pp. 479–504, above.
13. Nina Baym, "Melville's Quarrel with Fiction," *PMLA* 94 (1979), 909–23.
14. Thomas De Quincey, *The Confessions of an English Opium-Eater* (New York: Illustrated Editions, 1932), 24; hereafter cited as De Quincey.
15. *Pierre*, ed. Harrison Hayford, Hershel Parker, and G. Thomas Tanselle (Evanston and Chicago: Northwestern University Press and The Newberry Library, 1971), 204.

16. Mary W. Shelley, *Frankenstein*, ed. M. K. Joseph (London: Oxford University Press, 1969), 52; hereafter cited as Shelley. I do not mean to suggest that Melville discovered the image of Prometheus in *Frankenstein*. In fact, he evokes Prometheus as artist and maker in *Mardi* (229).

17. I borrow this phrase from Melville's *Clarel*, ed. Walter E. Bezanson (New York: Hendricks House, 1960), I, xxxi, 45.

18. "Hawthorne and his Mosses," in *The Piazza Tales and Other Prose Pieces, 1839–1860*, ed. Harrison Hayford, Alma A. MacDougall, G. Thomas Tanselle, and others. (Evanston and Chicago: Northwestern University Press and The Newberry Library, 1987), 244; hereafter cited as "Mosses."

19. See "Unnecessary Duplicates," pp. 496, above.

20. See Leon Howard, *The Unfolding of MOBY-DICK*, eds. James Barbour and Thomas Quirk (Glassboro, N. J.: The Melville Society, 1987), 39–43, for a brief discussion of Melville and Carlyle.

21. *The Republic*, trans. B. Jowett (New York: Tudor, n.d.) II, 410.

22. See Sealts, "Emerson's Rainbow," 269.

23. *Essays: First Series*, ed. Joseph Slater et al. (Cambridge: Harvard University Press, 1979), 15; hereafter cited as Emerson.

24. *Sartor Resartus* (Boston: Dana Estes, n.d.), 88; hereafter cited as Carlyle.

25. It seems likely that Melville borrowed "the blackness of darkness" from Carlyle and included it in his review of Hawthorne.

26. *Mardi*, 229.

"Its wood could only be American!": *Moby-Dick* and Antebellum Popular Culture

DAVID S. REYNOLDS

Despite growing interest in the historical dimensions of *Moby-Dick*, it has been difficult for scholars to dispel the longstanding myth that Melville was alienated from his contemporary popular culture. Ever since Raymond Weaver portrayed him as the isolated, rebellious "Devil's Advocate," Melville has been generally viewed as an uncharacteristic nay-sayer in an age of progressivist optimism, a mythic stylist exiled from a Philistine culture of utilitarianism and literal-mindedness.

This notion of Melville's distance from his literary and social culture contravenes his own convictions about the symbiotic relationship between art and society. "[G]reat geniuses are parts of the times," he proclaimed in his essay on Hawthorne; "they themselves are the times, and possess a correspondent coloring."[1] He appears to have been particularly responsive to the ephemeral literature of his time and culture. In his semiautobiographical portrait of Pierre Glendinning, he explained that even apparently trivial literature contributed to his author-hero's creativity: "A varied scope of reading, little suspected by his friends, and randomly acquired by a random but lynx-eyed mind . . . poured one considerable contributary stream into that bottomless spring of original thought which the occasion and time had caused to burst out in himself."[2] Melville himself was a lynx-eyed reader quick to discover literary possibilities in randomly acquired minor literature. His reading seems to have been done in the spirit of a character in *White-Jacket* who says that "public libraries have an imposing air, and doubtless contain invaluable volumes, yet, somehow, the books that prove most agreeable, grateful, and companionable, are those we pick up by chance here and there; . . . those which pretend to little, but abound in much."[3]

In fact, it was precisely Melville's *openness* to images from various contemporary cultural arenas—not, as is commonly thought, his *alienation* from his culture—that accounts for the special complexity of *Moby-Dick*. Melville's narrative art was one of wide-ranging assimilation and literary transformation. It reflected his statement in "Hawthorne and His Mosses"

This essay was written specifically for this volume and is published here for the first time by permission of the author.

that the American writer was "bound to carry republican progressiveness into Literature, as well as into Life."[4] A principal misconception about *Moby-Dick* is that its ambiguities stood in opposition to a popular culture that was uniformly tame and moralistic. Actually, antebellum popular culture was full of contradictions and paradoxes that became textually inscribed in Melville's most capacious novel.

The main types of popular writing Melville drew from in *Moby-Dick* were Romantic Adventure fiction, dark reform literature, radical-democrat fiction, and subversive humor.[5] Melville had learned key images and stereotypes from each of these modes by immersing himself in American popular culture as a writer for the mass market earlier in his career. Melville knew that his first two novels were, as he wrote his publisher about *Omoo*, "calculated for popular reading."[6] After soaring to allegorical and philosophical heights in *Mardi*, he again wrote unabashedly for the popular audience in *Redburn* and *White-Jacket*, which he called "two *jobs*, which I have done for money."[7] As dismissive as Melville was about some of this early fiction, he learned much from his forays into popular culture. Taken together, Melville's early works show him to have been a daring experimenter with popular images. The breadth of his experimentation placed him in an ideal position to produce a novel of full cultural representativeness. When Melville is studied in terms of his popular cultural backgrounds, we see the validity of a contemporary reviewer's remark that in *Moby-Dick* he seemed "resolved to combine all his popular characteristics."[8]

In the most basic sense, *Moby-Dick* falls in the category of Romantic Adventure, by far the most popular type of fiction published in America during the two decades immediately prior to the publication of the novel.[9] When Melville described *Moby-Dick* to his British publisher as "a romance of adventure, founded upon certain wild legends in the Southern Sperm Whale Fisheries" (*Letters*, 109), he was placing the novel in the Romantic Adventure category. Despite the twentieth-century reputation of *Moby-Dick* as a premodern metaphysical fiction unusual for its day, it should be noted that contemporary reviews of the novel, which were predominantly favorable, emphasized its divertingly adventurous aspects.

It is understandable that many contemporary reviewers felt comfortable with *Moby-Dick*, because Melville was drawing off a well-established convention of adventurous sea novels. A good amount of fiction about destructive whales or other monstrous creatures had appeared during the 1830s and 1840s. J. N. Reynolds's "Mocha Dick: or The White Whale of the Pacific," a story in the May 1839 issue of the New York *Knickerbocker*, is full of analogies to *Moby-Dick*: both works center on a dramatic chase for a white sperm whale legendary for its indestructibility; both reproduce the salty dialect of whalemen engaged in dangerous pursuit of the white whale; and both utilize this fearless pursuit as a means of illustrating the inherent democratic dignity of the unfavored trade of whaling.[10] Another work that strikingly prefigures *Moby-Dick* is "Whaling in the Pacific. Encounter with a White Whale," a tale published 8 October 1842 in the popular Boston weekly *Uncle Sam*. This story features a dauntless Captain Coffin and his mates (one of them named Starbuck) who one day lower for a white whale that is harpooned but then crushes two whale boats with his jaws and kills several seamen in bloody revenge.

Moby-Dick was also presaged by three popular sea novels quoted in the prefatory "Extracts" to Melville's novel: Joseph C. Hart's *Miriam Coffin* (1834), William Comstock's *The Life of Samuel Comstock, the Terrible Whaleman* (1840), and Harry Halyard's pulp novel *Wharton the Whale-Killer!* (1848). Hart's *Miriam Coffin*, like *Moby-Dick*, is climaxed by a dramatic sequence in which a mate named Starbuck resists his captain's orders to join the chase for a ferocious sperm whale, for he feels the chase is doomed to end in death for all. As it turns out, the whale kills Starbuck and then smashes into the whale ship, causing it to sink and the sailors to flee to lifeboats until they are rescued. *The Life of Samuel Comstock* is a Dark Adventure pamphlet novel—that is, a popular novel that intersperses adventure and philosophical gloom—about a fiercely independent Nantucket lad who, rather like Melville's Ishmael, first is subjected to hypocritical Quakers and later serves under a whale-ship captain described as "passionate, violent, and sometimes tyrannical," always threatening "to nail the men to the deck, if they do not hasten to their duty."[11] *Wharton the Whale-Killer!*, by the popular novelist Harry Halyard, includes a vivid sequence in which a ship's captain offers a reward to the first sailor who can raise a whale; his wager is met when a greenhorn sights a whale from a masthead, initiating a long whale chase, made lively by a swearing mate who grins in the face of destruction, a sequence that culminates in the whale being killed and drawn alongside the ship for cutting in. Also in the novel is an interpolated story of a whale that rams a ship. Since Melville quotes from *Wharton the Whale-Killer!* in his "Extracts," it seems likely that he knew of another Halyard novel, *The Doom of the Dolphin* (also 1848), which featured a grim engraving of huge whale flukes cracking apart splintered boats with terrified sailors flying through the air and other whales hovering near a ship in the background. The scene on which the engraving was based involves several boats that fail in their attempt to kill a sperm whale described as "a regular old white-headed eighty barrel fellow."[12] Another pre-Melvillian Dark Adventure pamphlet novel was *Life in a Whale Ship* (1841), an episodic novel narrated by an old philosophical salt named Romanta. Like *Moby-Dick*, *Life in a Whale Ship* contains detailed anecdotes about gams and ill-fated whale chases, often interspersed with dark philosophical reflections. Melville's images of fate and the Spirit Spout are strikingly anticipated in Romanta's account of a whaling crew who felt that "their doom and every incident attending it was writ out at length previous to that eventful day—that it was revealed to them the moment they struck their whale—that its phantom voice urged them on, and that they had not the desire or the power to disobey," suggesting that "our final fate is revealed to us through its spirit-agent."[13]

Melville's emphasis upon the unparalleled immensity and destructiveness of his white whale can be viewed as part of a growing fascination with monsters of all varieties. There had arisen a wild one-upmanship among popular adventure writers competing against each other to see who could produce the most savage, freakish beast. In *The Raven and the Whale* Perry Miller suggests as a source for Melville's white whale the terrific antediluvian beast described in *Behemoth* (1839), a novel by Melville's New York literary associate Cornelius Mathews. Mathew's monster, however, was only one of several tremendous creatures in popular literature of Melville's day. For example, strange encounters between humans and sea monsters were standard fare in grotesque humor periodicals such as the Crockett almanacs. The 1838 Crockett almanac included a sketch, "Colonel Crockett and the Sea Sarpint," in which Davy Crockett battles a kraken said to be long enough to twist the hair of an angel who straddles the land and the sea. The 1849 Crockett almanac contained a story, "Crockett and the Great Prairie Serpent," about a huge snake, said to be larger than any kraken, whom Crockett wrestles and lashes to death. In the Crockett almanac for 1850, Crockett's nautical friend Ben Harding tells a violent story about a time he and a sailor friend harpooned a whale, climbed aboard a whale's back, and went for a dizzying ride until at last the whale vindictively rammed against their ship, which was saved only when the whale was killed by a lance. The largest monster in antebellum literature was the kraken depicted in Eugene Batchelder's *Romance of the Sea-Serpent, or The Ichthyosaurus* (1849), a bizarre narrative poem about a sea serpent that terrorizes the coast of Massachusetts, destroys a huge ship in mid-ocean, repasts on human remains gruesomely with sharks and whales, attends a Harvard commencement (where he has been asked to speak), shocks partygoers by appearing at a Newport ball, and at last is hunted and killed by a fleet of Newport sailors.

To mention such possible antecedents of *Moby-Dick*, however, is to underscore the originality of Melville's novel. All the above works share a common trait of most Romantic Adventure novels of the day: they trivialize a topic that Melville treats with seriousness and artistic care. In *Miriam Coffin, Samuel Comstock, Life in a Whale Ship*, and Harry Halyard's novels, whaling adventure is included rather arbitrarily as part of meandering narratives that also describe other lively topics such as piracy, doomsaying, battles with South Sea natives, and murder. Even the two works that might seem closest to Melville, "Mocha Dick" and "Encounter with a White Whale," have a flat, neutral quality. As for humorous writings like the Crockett almanacs and Batchelder's *Romance of the Sea-Serpent*, they show just how devoid of probability or significance huge creatures could be when treated by authors interested solely in purveying freaks for antebellum sensation-lovers.

Melville's whale is at once more realistic and more mythic than the monsters of popular literature. On the one hand, Melville includes an unprecedented amount of factual information about the whale in order to counteract what Ishmael calls the "curious imaginary portraits of him which even down to the present day confidently challenge the faith of the landsman" (260). The "plain facts" about whaling are designed to prevent us from dismissing Moby Dick, in Ishmael's words, as merely "a monstrous fable" or "a hideous and intolerable allegory" (205). Even though factual sections of *Moby-Dick* like the "Cetology" chapter are partly tongue-in-cheek, there is clearly a serious intent behind Ishmael's statement that "the various species of whales need some sort of popular comprehensive classification" (136). While this cetological factuality is Melville's rhetorical answer to the haphazard, often inane treatment of monsters in popular culture, his contrasting emphasis on the final indecipherability of sea creatures succeeds in summoning up a sense of mystery he felt was also needed since, as Ishmael laments, "man has lost that sense of the full awfulness of the sea which aboriginally belongs to it" (273). Any rare or mysterious sea phenomenon— squid, sharks, brit—assumes momentous import in the novel, and, as for whales, "the great Leviathan is that one creature in the world which must remain unpainted to the last" (264). The whale's facticity and his ultimate unreadability—both insisted upon with equal vigor in the novel—are crucial to Melville's mission of bringing both solidity and suggestiveness to a topic, the pursuit of monstrous creatures, that had been widely trivilialized in popular culture.

The factual side of whaling, as we know, was known to Melville as a result of his experience aboard whale ships and his reading of contemporary whaling books such as Thomas Beale's *The Natural History of the Sperm Whale* and William Scoresby, Jr.'s *Northern Whale-Fishery*.[14] But Melville's means of achieving what Robert Richardson calls "mythic investiture"—the infusion of natural objects, especially the whale, with mystic otherness[15]—have remained largely unexplained. To find cultural roots for the mythic, richly ambiguous quality of *Moby-Dick* we must look not to Romantic Adventure fiction, which we saw to be generally nonsymbolic and merely adventurous, but to other areas of antebellum popular culture, particularly dark-reform literature and radical-democrat fiction. A principal distinction between *Moby-Dick* and other adventure fiction was Melville's assimilation of a full range of zestful, paradoxical images from such dark popular literature.

The capacity for a richly imagistic work such as *Moby-Dick* had been inherent in American popular culture since the early 1830s, when vehement reformers began coining larger-than-life, mythic metaphors for the social vices they fiercely denounced. Virtually every reform movement of the day—temperance, antislavery, antiprostitution, naval reform, utopian socialism—became notably sensationalized in the hands of popular reformers competing for the attention of an American public increasingly taken with

Dark Adventure novels and crime-filled penny newspapers. The "dark" or "immoral" reformers, as I call them, righteously proclaimed that they were wallowing in foul moral sewers only to scour them clean; but their seamy writings prove that they were more powerfully drawn to wallowing than to cleaning. They scandalized conservatives with their emphasis upon the perverse results rather than the moral remedies of social vice. Some immoral reformers, such as the notorious antiprostitution reformer John McDowall and the dramatic temperance orator John B. Gough, were publicly exposed as opportunistic frauds; others, such as the uncompromising abolitionist William Lloyd Garrison and the labor advocate Mike Walsh, were regularly denounced as "ultraists" who exaggerated the horrific aspects of social ills.

The dark reformers introduced a fierce new rhetoric that featured veil-lifting imagery, mythic metaphors, and post-Calvinist gloom. In popular reform newspapers and pamphlets, vice was regularly described as a "monster" stalking over mountains and rivers, or a "whirlpool" sucking helpless victims to destruction, or an "ocean" threatening to engulf the world, or an all-controlling "fate." Often such analogies had a distinctly pre-Melvillian ring, as when a writer for Garrison's *Liberator*, alarmed by the rise of various social vices in America, wrote: "The whale which swallowed up the recreant prophet [Jonah] may be likened to the many monsters which swallow up the aberrant sinner of our own days," except that "the whales of this latter day are much more voracious than that of old; inasmuch as the whale which swallowed up the prophet Jonah cast him forth again after the third day. But, in our days, when a hapless mortal once gets within the jaws of the monster, he is lost forever; he is not so fortunate as to be vomited forth on dry land."[16] In the dark-reform imagination, modern "whales"—moral vices like drinking and prostitution as well as social injustices such as slavery, poverty, and upper-class hypocrisy—were far deadlier than the biblical one because they seemed ubiquitous and inescapable.

By the time he wrote *Moby-Dick* Melville had gained full exposure to popular reforms, for he had experimented broadly with reform themes and images in his first five novels. In *Typee* and *Omoo* he had assumed a standard reform stance in his exposure of hypocrisy among white Christians on South Sea islands; other reforms he utilized were antiprostitution, temperance, peace reform, and utopian socialism, all of which had been widely debated in the popular press. In *Mardi* such reforms as temperance, socialism, and antislavery provide a backdrop to Melville's pondering of moral paradoxes and social conflict. The popular-oriented *Redburn* is filled with dark-temperance and city-mysteries images of the crassest variety, such as the picture of frivolous rich people and huge dens of sin in the modern city or a sailor's horrid suicide after heavy drinking or the sensational account of another sailor burned alive in flames produced by spontaneous combustion produced by cheap liquor he has drunk. In *White-Jacket* Melville used naval reform as a vehicle for diving into the mire of nineteenth-century social vices and for probing deep ironies in human nature and society.

Having experimented with so many different reform voices in his early novels, Melville had reached a level of stylization whereby reform content was abandoned but reform images and subversive spirit were retained. He wished to fully utilize reform images in the pursuit of truth but, simultaneously, to detach himself from specific reform programs—probably because he realized that in an age of immoral reformers, the reform mode was widely held suspect. As he wrote in a June 1851 letter to Hawthorne: "It can hardly be doubted that all Reformers are bottomed upon the truth, more or less; and to the world at large are not reformers almost universally laughing-stocks?" (*Letters*, 127) Poised between the intensely reformist *White-Jacket* and the ambiguous later novels, *Moby-Dick* shows the reform impulse at last fully divested of didacticism.

Since *Moby-Dick* can be viewed as the culmination of Melville's early permutations of the dark-reform mode, it is understandable that the novel has far more direct references to popular reform movements than even the most reform-minded of his previous novels. Temperance, antislavery, socialism, anti-Catholicism, antiwar—these and other popular reforms provide a wealth of images to Melville in *Moby-Dick*. Ironically, however, the novel does not seem reformist at all. This is because reform imagery has eventually become for Melville a colorful shell, largely devoid of political or didactic content, that can be arranged at will in the overall mosaic of a subversive novel.

This stylization of reform runs throughout the novel. It is visible, for example, in Melville's creative adaptation of dark-temperance imagery. Such imagery abounds in the early scene in which Ishmael witnesses the *Grampus* crew, just home from a three years' voyage, rushing straight into the Spouter-Inn's bar (the entrance to which is a huge whale jaw) and getting drunk on drinks poured by the bartender Jonah, while the temperate Bulkington watches aloof and then disappears. Just as popular reformers had regularly described alcohol as an all-devouring "whale" or all-consuming "poison," so Melville described the *Grampus* crew entering through "jaws of swift destruction" to be served "deliriums and death" by a prophetically named bartender (14). Just as reformers had emphasized the illusoriness of alcohol's pleasures, so Melville writes: "Abominable are the tumblers into which he pours his poison. Though true cylinders without—within, the green goggling glasses deceitfully tapered downward to a cheating bottom" (14). The Spouter-Inn barroom scene shows Melville typically adopting a popular mode as a preparatory literary exercise: just as the bartender pours poisonous drinks to rambunctious sailors who are inside symbolic whale's jaws, so in a sense the dark-temperance mode "pours" *Moby-Dick* by providing Melville with various subversive images.

Melville is now so sensitively attuned to all possible permutations of the dark-temperance mode that he can shift with ease between antitemperance and protemperance stances, giving full moral credence to no single viewpoint and always seeking the rhetorical potentialities of whatever stance he assumes. He sounds antitemperance when he has the comical mate Stubb, a boisterous advocate of grog, snicker at Dough-Boy for giving someone ginger-water; Stubb declares, "There is some sneaking Temperance Society movement about this business" (322). Melville also strikes antitemperance notes when he gives an updated sketch of the biblical rich man Dives, who, "a president of a temperance society . . . only drinks the tepid tears of orphans" (11), and when he ironically depicts Jack Bunger, the captain of the *Samuel Enderby*, as a self-avowed "strict total abstinence man" who nevertheless gets drunk on the sly (440). On the other hand, Melville sounds protemperance in his portrait of the wretched Perth, the blacksmith who had been driven to sea after alcohol had shattered his family and who is now the lonely forger of harpoons for Ahab. Retracing how the insidious "Bottle Conjuror" had torn apart Perth's happy home, Melville calls death "the only desirable sequel for a career like this," and death "is but the first salutation to the possibilities of the immense Remote, the Wild, the Watery, the Unshored"—and so Perth commits a kind of suicide by going to sea on the *Pequod*, where he is left a stolid relic, a man "past scorching," well suited to forge the harpoon that Ahab will baptize in the devil's name and hurl at the white whale (485, 486).

It would be easy enough to run through the entire novel and suggest specific reform influences for other scenes as well. The city-mysteries mode (as popularized in antebellum novels that portrayed crime and desolation in American cities) enhances the gloom of Ishmael's opening entrance into New Bedford, as he stumbles over an ashbox and asks, "[A]re these ashes from that destroyed city, Gomorrah?" (9). Ishmael's ironic query "Who aint a slave?" (6) would seem to owe much to the fiery New York radical Mike Walsh, who in the late 1840s famously universalized the notion of slavery by stressing that *both* Northern wage slaves and Southern chattel slaves were equally oppressed. Sensational anti-Catholic imagery sometimes adds color or irreverence, as when Ishmael asks why a Midwestern Protestant is terrified by the mention of "a White Friar or a White Nun," or when the account of the mincer who wears the whale's cassock (i.e., penis skin), leads to the bawdy pun: "what a candidate for an archbishoprick, what a lad for a Pope, this mincer!" (192, 420). A particularly concentrated grouping of popular reform images occurs in Ishmael's discussion of "fast fish" (things that are considered personal property merely because they happen to be in one's possession): in listing examples of fast fish, Melville brings together typical ironic imagery from antislavery agitation ("Republican slaves"), property-law reform (the widow in the hands of a "rapacious landlord"), socialist and city-mysteries writings (a poor family cheated by a banker; laborers exploited by a rich churchman) (397).

Such individual sources, however, are less important than the overall dark-reform *écriture* that governs the novel. Scholars have long sought historical prototypes for several scenes and characters, but the results have often proven contradictory. Ahab, for instance, has been variously associated with the radical abolitionist Garrison, with Garrison's arch-opponent Calhoun, and with the moderate politician Daniel Webster! Such historical source-study can be constricting, for in fact *Moby-Dick* moves beyond slavery or antislavery, protemperance or antitemperance, to a literary realm in which subversive reform energy and rhetoric, rather than reform message, become the literary artist's central concern. The many explicit reform devices in *Moby-Dick* are pushed toward literariness by Melville's devotion to the subversive images that formed a rhetorical sub-basis of *all* dark-reform writings. Ultimately, Melville in *Moby-Dick* is a gigantic dark reformer, towering above all reform programs but driven by his age's powerful reform impulse. If other reformers (and Melville himself in his earlier fiction) had "lifted the veil" off social corruption or lamented the "pasteboard" artificiality of certain people, Melville has Ahab describe all visible objects as "pasteboard masks" and declare that man's highest goal is to "strike through the mask" (164). In this sense, the object of Ahab's quest is the ultimate dark-reform mythic image, which now has been granted an independent life and an alluringly malevolent will of its own. The white whale brings together all the "whales" swimming in all the turbulent "oceans" of the image-fashioning ultraists. If popular reformers had seen society as a "whited sepulchre" hiding submerged evil, so the white whale is invested with the most apparently benign but most ultimately subversive qualities, suggesting to Ishmael that "all deified Nature absolutely paints like the harlot, whose allurements cover nothing but the charnel-house within" (195). If popular reformers regularly used post-Calvinist images, Melville secularly enacts the Calvinist God itself, as the whole novel culminates in the destruction of Ahab and his crew by the "predestinating head" of Moby Dick, which is alive with "[r]etribution, swift vengeance, eternal malice" (571).

If reform literature supplied Melville with potent, often disturbing images, the allied mode of radical-democrat fiction contributed various paradoxical character types. The group of popular writers I am calling *radical democrats*—most notably George Lippard, A. J. H. Duganne, George G. Foster, and George Thompson—in the 1840s carried both social protest and literary irrationalism to new extremes. Alarmed by widening class divisions and all forms of social oppression, the radical democrats used every degree of literary invective to expose what they regarded as the prevailing depravity of America's ruling class. They translated into nightmarish fiction the prevailing metaphors of dark reform. America in their eyes was no more than a whited sepulchre with rottenness within, a place of appalling "city mysteries." Their exaggerated impulse to "tear away veils" or "strike through masks" produced militant declarations like this one in a Duganne novel:

"[T]errible, terrible will be the reaction, when the veil is torn aside, when the sepulchres, no longer whited, burst forth in their own horror and loathsomeness."[17] Best-selling novels such as Lippard's *The Quaker City* (1844–45), Duganne's *The Knights of the Seal* (1845), Thompson's *New York Life* (1849), and Ned Buntline's *The G'hals of New York* (1850) depicted a topsy-turvy world in which justified outcasts and likable criminals actually seemed more worthy than conventionally virtuous characters, whose probity was held suspect because it reflected an inherently unjust social system. The great conflict in radical-democrat fiction was between the smirking justified criminal and what may be called the oxymoronic oppressor: the outwardly respectable but inwardly corrupt social leader who variously appeared as the churchgoing capitalist, the religious slaveholder, the unctuous reverend rake, and so on. The hero of this fiction was a mixed figure known as the "b'hoy" (street slang for "boy"), the crude yet acute, wicked yet thoroughly likable city youth who had arisen in the street gangs of the Eastern cities and then was mythologized in pamphlet novels and melodramas. These radical-democrat stereotypes reflected deep working-class aggressions and fantasies in the turbulent decade following the crushing economic panic of 1837.

In time, however, radical-democrat literature became notably vulgarized when it was taken up by opportunistic authors who exaggerated gross sensationalism but left behind serious political goals. In the late 1840s, a sudden explosion of cheap pamphlet novels, stimulated mainly by mass publishers' adoption of the new cylinder press, brought about a cheapening of the radical-democrat mode. In the countless pamphlet novels by now forgotten authors like Benjamin Barker, Charles E. Averill, Maturin Murray Ballou, Osgood Bradbury, and George Thompson, the fiery rhetoric and revolutionary themes of radical-democrat fiction became mechanically mass-produced, giving rise to a grisly formula fiction about likable criminals warring against secretly corrupt social rulers, with the b'hoy now presented as merely a punchy, cocksure swaggerer with few vestiges of his former earnestness. Mingled with these grotesque caricatures of radical-democrat types were scenes of almost unparalleled atrocity and perversity, involving lively topics such as blood-drinking, whippings, devilish baptisms, cannibalism, and delirium tremens. How popular was this sensational pamphlet fiction? In 1850 Melville's friend Evert A. Duyckinck ran an article on crime-filled pamphlet novels in the *Literary World* containing the assertion that "the reader who sets out to master all the yellow cover literature of the day, works very hard for a living."[18] Similarly, the Boston critic Edwin P. Whipple lamented that the rage of the hour was "the Romance of Rascality." "According to the philosophy obtaining among the romancers of rascality," Whipple wrote, "the fact that an object creates physical disgust, is the reason why we should take it to our arms; the fact that a man excites moral reprobation, is his claim upon our sympathy."[19]

By the time he wrote *Moby-Dick* Melville's imagination was bristling with the polarities of American radical democracy. He himself had become a kind of likable criminal, one who could write in his June 1851 letter to Hawthorne: "[W]hen you see or hear of my ruthless democracy on all sides, you may possibly feel a touch of a shrink, or something of that sort. It is but nature to be shy of a mortal who boldly declares that a thief in jail is as honorable a personage as Gen. George Washington" (*Letters*, 126–27). He had become a fully American metaphysical outlaw who could place a thief on the same level as George Washington. He could proclaim himself simultaneously the greatest democrat and the greatest misanthrope. He had arrived at the very core of the popular paradox that fused criminality and goodness, iconoclasm and patriotism.

Melville's transformation of popular strategies in *Moby-Dick* is revealed in his willed *fusion* of the justified criminal and the oxymoronic oppressor. True, sometimes he is quite close to the popular radical democrats, as in his satirical portrait of the oxymoronic Captain Bildad, the querulous Quaker and penny-pinching Christian. Because he had immersed himself so completely in the inverted value system of radical democracy, he could now deal convincingly only with paradoxical characters. Throughout *Moby-Dick*, conventionally virtuous figures (the "pious, good man" Starbuck [79], the noble Bulkington, Aunt Charity, Dough-Boy) are doomed to impotency, while richly paradoxical figures (the "swearing good man" Ahab [79], the likable outcast Ishmael, the humane cannibal Queequeg, the whole rollicking *Pequod* crew) control the narrative. But Melville departs from the popular radical democrats by bringing together stereotypes that in popular fiction remain uncompromisingly opposed. Captain Ahab is his central fusing agent. As we have seen, Ahab is the gargantuan immoral reformer tearing away "pasteboard masks." At the same time, he is the sympathetic criminal who is on a seemingly justified vindictive quest and who reflects the inversions of radical-democrat fiction. These inversions in popular fiction had been aptly summed up by an essayist for the *Knickerbocker*: "The heroes of many of the novelists of the present day have almost converted us to the belief that there is no moral incompatibility between a criminal and a judge, and that a series of violations of the law is no obstacle to a man attaining fame, fortune, and honor."[20] Ahab, recognizing the deep moral implications of the sympathetic criminal, uses a similar metaphor when he cries to Starbuck: "Where do murderers go, man! Who's to doom, when the judge himself is dragged to the bar?" (545). Ahab is also the tyrannical oppressor who can only be described oxymoronically as "a swearing good man" and "a grand, ungodly, god-like man" (79). Although he embodies all the wildness and contradictions of these varied popular characters, he does not have their extreme heartlessness. The popular characters' haphazard aims are answered by his unprecedented singleness of purpose; their horrid willingness to murder human beings contrasts with his intent to hunt down a whale; their unmitigated inhumanity differs from his capacity to display occasional "humanities," as when he tearfully recalls his wife and child or when he befriends the hapless cabin-boy Pip.

If Ahab represents a humanized version of the oxymoronic oppressor and the justified criminal, Ishmael is the transformed version of another radical-democrat stereotype: the b'hoy. A figure of both reality and legend, the b'hoy had been an appropriate hero of radical-democrat fiction, since he was a mixture of bad qualities (rebelliousness, egotism, indolence) and good ones (native intelligence, confidence, an inclination to adopt the manners of the upper-class). By 1850, widespread vulgarization of the b'hoy figure in the popular press made this figure seem a great ideal that had gone sour. George G. Foster, a New York journalist in Melville's circle, identified the b'hoy as a representative indigenous character who offered "a rich and certain harvest" for American authors, but he rightly noted that "only the coarser and more vulgar traits," the "faults, vices, and barbarisms" were now being drawn by popular writers who aimed at "enlisting the brutal sympathies and passions of their audiences."[21] In popular melodramas like Benjamin A. Baker's *A Glance at New York in 1848* and in countless pamphlet novels, the b'hoy was little more than a gangster whose amoral violence was a source of crude fun for the antebellum public.

In his portrait of Ishmael, Melville borrows from the b'hoy stereotype. In the opening pages of the novel Ishmael is established as the indigent, loafing, acute, brash, genial New Yorker who plays pranks, hates respectable jobs, and aches for adventure. Melville's contemporary readers surely saw signs of the b'hoy in an unconventional narrator who boasts that he travels not with commodores and who abominates "all honorable respectable toils, trials, and tribulations of every kind whatsoever" (5). Like the typical sensation-loving b'hoy, Ishmael feels "an everlasting itch for things remote" and is attracted by "the wild and distant seas" with their "undeliverable, nameless perils" (7). The images that surround him in the early chapters—images of suicide, funerals, coffins, cannibalism, the gallows, tombstones—place him in the blackly humorous domain familiar to the popular b'hoy. His entire voyage becomes a kind of popular culture text when he imagines "WHALING VOYAGE BY ONE ISHMAEL" squeezed as on a theater poster between sensational headlines about a hotly contested election and a bloody battle in Afghanistan (7).

But in the process of adopting the b'hoy Melville reconstructs him. Ishmael was not the first b'hoy narrator in American fiction, but he was the first pressed in the direction of the humane and the broadly tolerant. He is the b'hoy reconceived by a writer who recognized the universal, fully human potentialities of his own culture's popular images. Ishmael is not merely the "Mose" or "Sikesey"of melodramas and pamphlet novels, the two-fisted b'hoy who mocks aristocrats and gets involved in comical pranks. He is also the flexible, loving youth who stirs our deepest democratic sympathies when he embraces Queequeg, a man he had previously feared as a bloodthirsty cannibal.

Through the developing Ishmael-Queequeg relationship, Melville enriches not only the b'hoy but another stereotype who had figured largely in radical-democrat fiction: the savage non-white. Radical democrats had regularly depicted even the most fierce oppressed peoples and minority groups as more noble than secretly corrupt social leaders. In his characterization of Queequeg, Melville may have been indebted to George Lippard, the most popular radical-democrat novelist of the day. Lippard's best-selling volumes *Blanche of Brandywine* (1846) and *Washington and His Generals* (1847) both had included memorable episodes involving a massive black soldier of the American Revolution, Black Sampson, who slashed through British lines with his tremendous scythe waving and his dog "Debbil" by his side. Radical-democrat egalitarianism had special import in the portrayal of Black Sampson, who is not only poor but also a Negro savage haunted by memories of his former noble stature as the son of the king of an African tribe. Although Lippard sympathetically portrays Sampson as one of the proudest and best soldiers of Washington's army, in typical fashion he permits the Black Sampson episode to degenerate into grotesque black humor. Sampson seizes his giant scythe and rushes into battle, decapitating and dismembering British soldiers with obvious love of gore. He screams to his dog: "We am gwain' mowin' today," and indeed he mows down every soldier in sight.[22] In *Blanche of Brandywine* Lippard writes that such violence exemplifies "the instinct of Carnage . . . which makes a man thirst for blood, which makes him mad for joy, when he steeps his arms to the elbows in his foeman's gore, which makes him shout and halloo, and laugh, as he goes murdering on over piles of dead!"

In portraying Queequeg, Melville takes up where Lippard left off, beginning with violent images but then moving to a dissolution of violence and an affirmation of affectionate brotherhood. Lippard had concluded the Sampson episode with a fiendish picture of his warrior-savage mowing down humans with his tremendous scythe. Melville begins with the deadly scythe and then progresses through various darkly humorous scenes toward a consoling portrait of Queequeg's humaneness. When in Chapter 3 Ishmael enters the Spouter-Inn, he sees hanging on the wall several "heathenish" weapons, the most terrifying of which is "sickle-shaped, with a vast handle sweeping round like the segment made in the new-mown grass by a long-armed mower," making Ishmael wonder "what monstrous cannibal and savage could ever have gone a death-harvesting with such a hacking, horrifying implement" (13). Having initiated the Spouter-Inn sequence with this Lippardian image, Melville remains, through this and the following chapter, in the realm of radical-democrat sensationalism: Queequeg is reported to have trouble selling his heads because "the market's overstocked"; when Queequeg leaps into bed with Ishmael he screams, "Who-e debel you?," and Ishmael in turn yells for the landlord Peter Coffin (18, 23). To this point, the tone of Melville's episode is not distant from the end of Lippard's. The huge deadly sickle, the images of mowing and death-harvesting, the references to decapitation and dismemberment, the word "debel"—all of these images place Melville's episode in the familiar arena of radical-democrat fiction.

Melville, however, prevents the sequence from descending into the merely perverse. Rather than allow his savage character to become a grisly emblem of gleeful carnage, as does Lippard, Melville makes him an emblem of universal love. He is able to do so primarily because he is more open than Lippard to the *reconstructive* possibilities of the radical-democrat vision. Whereas Sampson goes to bloody extremes as a member of George Washington's army, Queequeg at first seems a sanguinary demon but soon is described as "George Washington cannibalistically developed," a pagan savage without "civilized hypocrisies and bland deceits" who becomes admirable because of his tenderness and generosity (50, 51). Melville is able to lift Queequeg out of the mire of sensationalism because he has him embraced by an enriched version of that flexible radical-democrat hero, the b'hoy. The "marriage" of Ishmael and Queequeg is Melville's rhetorical intermerging of two popular characters—the b'hoy and the oppressed non-white—on the ground of common humanity. Melville burrows through the cheapened radical democracy of popular culture to a genuine radical democracy signaled by deep affection between two good-hearted human beings of different races.

Another popular cultural phenomenon relevant to *Moby-Dick* was subversive humor, which appeared variously as Old Southwest humor, radical-democrat humor, and what I term urban humor. Old Southwest humor introduced irreverent outbursts and colloquial boasts by rascalish folk heroes such as Davy Crockett, Nimrod Wildfire, Roaring Ralph Stackpole, and other popular "screamers" or "ring-tailed roarers." Radical-democrat humor, popularized particularly by George Lippard and George Thompson, gave a black edge to American humor, as devilish, downtrodden heroes sneered at a society that always struck them, in their favorite word, as irredeemably "queer." Urban humor, a stylized brand of humor that arose in such periodicals as the *Yankee Doodle* and the *New York Picayune*, travestied all modes of antebellum popular writings—sermons, domestic fiction, Dark Adventure novels, immoral reform, sensational newspapers and pamphlets—with the effect of divesting these modes of any fixed meaning and casting them into the relativist, carnivalized realm of parody and absurdity. Permeating urban humor was the spirit of the age's great master-showman, Phineas T. Barnum, for whom all aspects of American culture, moral or immoral, were equally objects of public display and manipulation. In the various types of native humor, the centrifugal discourse that characterized all American subversive literature reached a bizarre extreme. Mark Twain would later remark that the only truly indigenous American literary form was the tall tale: the exaggerated, virtually structureless string of improbable events related by a vernacular narrator. This kind of willed directionlessness was in fact a common denominator of several indigenous types of subversive humor, all of which featured a rapid succession of inconsequential and absurdly juxtaposed images.

Some of the humorous images in *Moby-Dick* are lifted directly from the pages of popular humor. For example, urban humor directly influenced the characterizations of the black cook Fleece and the crazed cabin-boy Pip. Both are variations upon the Negro preacher featured in William H. Levison's burlesque sermon series published in *The New York Picayune* from 1847 onward and later published in two popular volumes, *Julius Caesar Hannibal* and *Black Diamonds*. Fleece's comic sermon to the sharks in Chapter 64 is an adaptation of the burlesque sermons by Levison's Julius Caesar Hannibal, the pedantic, ill-spoken black preacher who regaled antebellum readers with his darkly humorous discourses (called "black diamonds") on varied topics.[23] Just as Levison's Hannibal inevitably began his sermons with blessings such as "Blubed Sinners" or "Helpluss Brutheren," so Fleece addresses his congregation as "Belubed fellow-critturs" (295). Melville's contemporary readers would have found familiar amusement in the fact that Fleece uses sharks as his text, because Levison's Hannibal had preached funny sermons about many strange animals: the crocodile, the lobster, the monkey, the hog, and the whale. Nor would they have been surprised by Fleece's ultimately cynical message—the horrifying voraciousness of the sharks, symbolizing the cannibalism of humankind and nature—for Hannibal often emphasized human savagery and universal mistrust.

Whereas Levison had popularized what he called "black diamonds"— the darkly humorous sayings of Julius Caesar Hannibal—Melville took the further step of actually creating a black diamond in Pip, a character who emerges from the ocean depths with a dark wisdom that can be best expressed in mad laughter. The connection between Melville's and Levison's characters would have been immediately apparent to antebellum readers, for when Pip is introduced he is compared at length to a diamond. Emphasizing that "this little black was brilliant, for even blackness has its brilliancy," Melville describes the increased brilliancy created by Pip's dreary nautical environment by noting: "[W]hen the cunning jeweler would show you the diamond in its most impressive lustre, he lays it against a gloomy ground, and then lights it up, not by the sun, but by some unnatural gases. Then come out those fiery effulgences, infernally superb; then the evil-blazing diamond, once the divinest symbol of the crystal skies, looks like some crown-jewel stolen from the King of Hell" (412). In time, Pip becomes a kind of living embodiment of the "black diamonds" Hannibal delivers, for the darkest of Hannibal's reflections, pertaining to the relativism of all human viewpoints, is metonymically expressed by the insane cabin-boy in his relativist outburst after conflicting interpretations of the doubloon: "I look, you look, he looks; we look, ye look, they look" (434). Melville has converted the "black diamonds" of one of his age's leading urban humorists, Levison, into a memorable fictional character whose insane wisdom shines luridly over the conclusion of his novel.

Melville's adaptations of Levison are part of a larger strategy in *Moby-Dick* of absorbing all the wilder elements of popular humor. The bizarre, volcanic oaths of Old Southwest humor are transcribed in Peleg's vow that he will "swallow a live goat with all his hair and horns on" and Stubb's boast that he will pull off the devil's tail and sell it as an ox whip (77, 327). The leering sarcasm and nightmarish imagery of popular humorists is captured in the portrayal of Stubb, who embodies the explosive forces of dark humor that fly quickly into the cynical and the chaotic as result of disillusion with perceived reality. Described as "one of those odd sort of humorists, whose jollity is sometimes so curiously ambiguous" (219), the comically churlish, grinning Stubb is particularly derivative of radical-democrat humor in its extreme form. The irony of the radical democrats often went beyond social criticism to dark generalizations about a world that suddenly seemed profoundly awry. The word "queer" had special prominence in the radical-democrat lexicon, for it summoned up the skewed reality that the dark humorists perceived. George Lippard again stands out as the main popular-izer of this word, for his writings are filled with sarcastic comments about the "queer" arrangement of things. "Queer world this!" exclaims a character typically in Lippard's *The Quaker City*. "Don't know much about other worlds, but it strikes me that if a prize were offered somewhere by somebody, for the queerest world a-going, this world of ours might be rigged up nice, and sent in like a bit of show beef, as the premium queer world.[24] So significant was this word to Lippard that in 1849 his reform newspaper, *The Quaker City*, featured a regular weekly column, "It is a Queer World," which reported grotesque social injustices.

For Melville, too, the word "queer" became particularly descriptive of the world as seen from a humorous perspective. When he was in the final stages of *Moby-Dick* he wrote Hawthorne a letter in which he imagined them together in heaven, sipping champagne and singing "humorous, comic songs—'Oh, when I lived in that queer little hole called the world'" (*Letters*, 128). In *Moby-Dick*, this radical-democrat sarcasm surfaces in Ishmael's account of "certain queer times" when the universe seems "a vast practical joke" (226). It is particularly embodied in Stubb, whose favorite word is "queer." When Ahab strikes him and sends him below, Stubb mutters, "It's very queer. . . . It's queer; very queer; and he's queer too; aye, take him fore and aft, he's about the queerest old man Stubb ever sailed with. . . . Damn me, but all things are queer, come to think of 'em" (128). His response to the doubloon is a dismissive "Humph! in my poor, insignificant opinion, I regard this as queer" (432). The ship's carpenter sums up Stubb well when he comments that "Stubb always says [Ahab is] queer; says nothing but that one sufficient little word queer; he's queer, says Stubb; he's queer—queer, queer; and keeps dinning it into Mr. Starbuck all the time—queer, sir—queer, queer, very queer" (472). In addition to parroting the radical democrats' favorite word, Stubb is closely linked to the bizarre, nightmarish imagery of the popular subversive imagination. Two of the strangest moments in *Moby-Dick* pertain to Stubb's overactive, disordered imagination. In Chapter 31 he reports his "queer dream" in which he tries to kick Ahab, who, shockingly, turns into a pyramid, which Stubb pummels with his leg until he is approached by a humpbacked merman, who turns threateningly to show Stubb a back studded with marlinespikes and then, after advising Stubb not to kick the pyramid anymore, seems "in some queer fashion, to swim off into the air" (132). The second strange moment comes when Stubb tries to comment on the doubloon: his remarks are a tangle of shifting, circular astrological readings.

The centrifugal cultural forces embodied in Stubb are also visible in the *Pequod's* crew, particularly in the picture in Chapter 40 of the crew's boisterous revel in the forecastle. The black humor of the radical democrats was often punctuated by scenes of orgies meant to reflect the wildness and savagery lurking below the civilized surfaces of life. In Lippard's *The Quaker City* there is the freakish scene in which drunken characters whip themselves into a frenzy manifested by incoherent exclamations, erotic oaths, and complete noncommunication. It is this kind of disorganized blasphemy that Melville recreates in the forecastle revel. Like much American subversive humor, it firmly dismisses sentimentality (the first Nantucket sailor exclaims, "Oh, boys, don't be sentimental; it's bad for the digestion!" [173]) and proceeds into an inconsequential succession of oaths and jests that include a Lippardian mixture of sexual and dark images, such as warm bosoms, lithe limbs, and dancing on graves. Like so many scenes in popular subversive texts, this one culminates in sadistic threats between bloodthirsty characters who engage in a terrible brawl.

Surveying the popular images and devices in *Moby-Dick*—from Romantic Adventure, reform literature, radical-democrat fiction, and subversive humor—it is safe to call the novel the most broadly absorptive fiction of the antebellum period. Indeed, besides the above connections between *Moby-Dick* and antebellum popular culture, there are other linkages that might be suggested. Melville's use of the tryworks as a symbol of hell, for instance, had been presaged in a *New England Magazine* article, "A Chapter on Whaling," which pointed out that the tryworks by night is "too like Dante's purgatory, to be neglected" by American authors.[25] Ahab's deterministic outcries—for example, "Fool! I am the Fates' lieutenant; I act under orders" (561) or "By heaven, man, we are turned round and round in this world, like yonder windlass, and Fate is the handspike" (545)—seem to echo similar outbursts by popular sea-captains like J. H. Ingraham's Lafitte, who declares: "Fate! Fate! I am the football of circumstances! How often have I been led by my destiny to do deeds at which my soul revolted!"[26] Ahab's devilish baptism of his crew followed a convention in Dark Adventure fiction of the day and in fact was mild when compared with the following typical moments in popular yellow fiction: in Augusta Franklin's *The Sea-Gull; or, The Pirates League!* (1846) initiates into a crime band are forced to gash open their arms with knives, let their blood flow freely into bowls, swear to follow the Evil One, and then kill a young woman; in Robert F. Greeley's *Old Cro' Nest; or, The Outlaws of the Hudson* (1846) a man joining a criminal band has to stab his own arm, write a red cross with blood, and be branded by a scalding iron; in *The Female Land Pirate* (1847) a woman being initiated into a murderers' league is forced to stab a man and write in his blood the oath that she will *"cling to every thing wicked, abjure every thing holy, deny God and the Bible."*[27] Given this popular-cultural background, Melville was actually meliorating horrid popular imagery when he had Ahab puncture the arms of his three harpooners and use their "baptismal blood" to consecrate their quest in the name of the Devil (489).

Melville's melioration of the devilish-ritual motif reflects his general strategy of transforming the merely perverse into the resonantly wicked and suggestively ambiguous. The most horrifying aspect of dark popular literature, especially crime-filled Dark Adventure fiction, is the flat indifference with which the most brutal deeds are performed. In this sense, *Moby-Dick* may be viewed as a rhetorical answer to a body of popular sensational novels that suddenly flooded the market in the late 1840s. One would have to look long in literary annals to find so purely disgusting a succession of popular novels as *The Female Land Pirate* (1847), *Amelia Sherwood; or, Bloody Scenes at the California Gold Mines* (1848), George Lippard's *The Empire City* (1849), Henri Foster's *Ellen Grafton: or the Den of Crime* (1850), and the many novels of the arch-sensationalist George Thompson, including *The House Breaker* (1848), *Venus in Boston* (1849), *The Countess* (1849), and *City Crimes* (1849). The blood that flows through the pages of these novels is always *human* blood, in scenes of murder, torture, cannibalism, and blood-drinking that have unthinkably perverse implications. Typical of the sensibility behind this fiction is the heroine of *The Female Land Pirate*, who kills and maims so many people that, in her words, "I soon learned to look upon a murder as indifferently as a butcher would look upon the death of an animal; so great is the force of habit."[28]

Bloodletting in *Moby-Dick*, in contrast, is carefully calibrated so that it is made meaningful rather than arbitrary or gratuitous. Given Ahab's overwhelming determination to kill Moby Dick, the bloody baptism of his harpoon seems justified. Elsewhere in the novel, Melville gives us potentially gory scenes—for example, Ishmael's night in bed with a hatchet-wielding cannibal, the scuffle after the forecastle revel, Starbuck's pointing the rifle at Ahab—but determinedly avoids bloody violence and in fact makes these scenes preparatory to alternate scenes of deep human togetherness (the "marriage" between Ishmael and Queequeg, the unified commitment of the crew to Ahab's quest, the momentary tearful affection between Ahab and Starbuck). Blood does flow through *Moby-Dick*, but it is the blood of purposefully hunted whales, not of arbitrarily maimed or murdered human beings. Melville provides an outlet for the sanguinary fantasies of his readers by describing gore spouting freely from wounded whales and by having all but one of his sailors killed in the end, but he does not step across the boundary into sadism and inhumanity, as do the popular sensationalists. In fact, the whale hunt is in several senses a deeply *humanizing* experience, since it draws crew members of all races together in a tight teamwork of pursuit, killing, cutting in, and trying out—all the duties of the whaling trade that demand expert individual skill but also constant interdependence. Thus, at key moments in his whaling activities Ishmael deeply senses his radical dependence on others (in "The Monkey-Rope") and his love of his fellow man (in "A Squeeze of the Hand").

Melville's overriding technique in *Moby-Dick* is to allow all the centrifugal, disorienting forces within the American popular mind to be fully released momentarily through structural "escape valves," usually a chapter or a small cluster of chapters, and then, having released some of the subversive steam, disperse its remaining energy through counterbalancing factual chapters or through the powerfully centripetal plot line, main characters, and symbols. Melville could incorporate all his culture's images, from the religious to the sensational, and yet rescue them from their native directionlessness by introducing a centripetal action (the quest for the white whale) with a centripetal object (the whale itself) through a centripetal agent (Ahab, and then the whole crew)—all driven by hope for a centripetal reward, the doubloon fixed to the mast.

Even in fashioning these centripetal images, Melville borrowed from popular culture. For instance, his use of the Biblical names Ishmael and Ahab lend depth and grandeur to common figures such as the b'hoy and the tyrannical captain; and this very fusion of sacrosanct Biblical archetypes with modern-day figures was made possible by a widespread secularization of popular religious culture in nineteenth-century America, a phenomenon also visible in Father Mapple's anecdotal sermon and in Ishmael's homely fantasy of "rows of angels in paradise, each with his hands in a jar of spermaceti" (416). This secularized reapplication of the religious imagery contributed as well to the supernatural overtones of Fedallah, often associated with the devil, and of the white whale itself, a magnificent combination of God and Satan. Another popular phenomenon that greatly aided Melville was pseudosciences such as mesmerism (mind control through what was seen as electrical, magnetic energy) and phrenology and physiognomy (the interpretation of character through the reading of physical characteristics). In the fluid atmosphere of antebellum popular culture, these pseudosciences were handled with unprecedented flexibility and creativity. The popular mesmerists' belief in mind control through electrical fluid was inventively reapplied by Melville to enhance the centripetal quality of his main plot and characters. Ahab is not merely a charismatic sea captain. In antebellum terms, he was one of very few individuals gifted with enough "odic force," or magnetic energy, to govern the wills of others. It was the popular acceptance of control through magnetic force that made possible such statements as "[Ahab] would fain have shocked into them the same fiery emotion accumulated within the Leyden jar of his own magnetic life" (165), or "Ahab kept his magnet at Starbuck's brain" (212), or "a certain magnetism shot into [the harpooners'] congenial hearts from inflexible Ahab's" (518). The popular notion that a mesmerist lost some electrical fluid during a session is reflected in Ahab's declaration, when the three mates look away from him, "'tis well. For did ye three but once take the full-forced shock, then mine own electric thing, *that* had perhaps expired from out of me" (166). Moby Dick, too, is invested with electrical attractiveness when Ahab explains his obsession with the white whale by crying: "He's all a magnet!" (441). As for physiognomy and phrenology, these popular pseudosciences allow Melville to do some fanciful character-reading through descriptions of the whale's face and head. "To scan the lines of his face, or feel the bumps on the head of this Leviathan," Melville writes; "this is a thing which no Physiognomist or Phrenologist has as yet undertaken" (345)—and so he devotes two detailed chapters to a pseudoscientific reading of the facial bumps and vertebra of the whale, aptly concluding that the sperm whale has an unusually large "organ of firmness or indomitableness" (350). Yet another cultural phenomenon that aided Melville's centripetal aims was the railroad, the new mode of transportation, and the factory, the increasingly important locus of economic production. Put to metaphorical use, they perfectly enforce Melville's centripetalism, for Ahab can declare, "The path to my fixed purpose is laid with iron rails, whereon my soul is grooved to run. . . . Naught's an obstacle, naught's an angle to the iron way!" (168). And Ahab's relationship with his crew is vivified by a factory metaphor when he says, "my one cogged circle fits into all their various wheels" (168).

Melville's broad-scale assimilation of popular images greatly complicates the longstanding issue of "meaning" in *Moby-Dick*. The issue becomes even more complex when we keep in mind not only Melville's reapplications of popular cultural phenomena but also his omnivorous gatherings from elite sources. Ahab is, as we have seen, a combination of many popular types; but he is also drawn, as various critics have suggested, from the wicked Ahab of I Kings, Prometheus, Faust, Lear, Milton's Satan, Captain Charles Wilkes, and other figures of fact and legend. Ishmael, likewise, is not merely a refashioned b'hoy but also derives from the old Testament outcast beloved of God, just as Pip resembles Lear's fool, and so on. The white whale is an especially ambiguous repository of popular and archetypal images.

But in all these cases, precise meaning matters less than the dazzling ability of Melville's characters and symbols to radiate meanings. Melville's comprehensive pillaging of classic religious and literary sources reveals his overarching interest in adding resonance and suggestiveness to popular cultural chronotopes that were formless, neutral, or contradictory in their native state. The *Pequod*'s quest for the whale is ultimately self-destructive and the book's truth remains tantalizingly elusive; but this does not place *Moby-Dick* at odds with American culture, as is commonly believed. What distinguishes this novel from its many popular prototypes is that it absorbs numerous American images and treats them not frivolously or haphazardly, as did the popular texts, but instead takes them seriously, salvages them from the anarchically directionless and gives them new intensity and mythic reference. Melville's quest is dangerous, but it is also exhilarating and finally joyful. Upon completing the novel Melville could express his paradoxical feeling of danger and peace by writing to Hawthorne: "I have written a wicked book, and feel spotless as the lamb. Ineffable socialities are in me" (*Letters*, 142). Having written a novel that fully absorbed the subversive forces of his culture, Melville could nonetheless feel warmly calm because he had produced a lasting testament to the creative spirit.

Notes

1. "Hawthorne and His Mosses," *The Piazza Tales and Other Prose Pieces, 1839–1860*, eds. Harrison Hayford, Alma A. MacDougall, G. Thomas Tanselle and others (Evanston and Chicago: Northwestern University Press and The Newberry Library, 1987), 246. "Mosses" first appeared in two installments in the New York *Literary World*, nos. 185–86 (17–24 August 1850). Citations for *Moby-Dick* are from *Moby-Dick; or, the Whale*, ed. Harrison Hayford, Hershel Parker, and G. Thomas Tanselle (Evanston and Chicago: Northwestern University Press and The Newberry Library, 1988), and will be cited parenthetically.

2. *Pierre; or, The Ambiguities*, ed. Harrison Hayford, Hershel Parker, and G. Thomas Tanselle (Evanston and Chicago: Northwestern University Press and The Newberry Library, 1971), 283.

3. *White-Jacket; or, The World in a Man-of-War*, ed. Harrison Hayford, Hershel Parker, and G. Thomas Tanselle (Evanston and Chicago: Northwestern University Press and The Newberry Library, 1970), 169.

4. *The Piazza Tales*, 245.

5. I discuss these and other types of popular antebellum literature at length in *Beneath the American Renaissance: The Subversive Imagination in the Age of Emerson and Melville* (New York: Alfred A. Knopf, 1988). The present article incorporates and expands upon arguments made in *Beneath the American Renaissance*.

6. Melville to John Murray, 29 January 1847, *The Letters of Herman Melville*, ed. Merrell R. Davis and William H. Gilman (New Haven: Yale University Press, 1960), 53; hereafter cited as *Letters*.

7. Herman Melville to Lemuel Shaw, 6 October 1849, *Letters*, 91.

8. New York *Home Journal*, 29 November 1851, reprinted in *MOBY-DICK as Doubloon: Essays and Extracts (1851–1870)*, ed. Hershel Parker and Harrison Hayford (New York: Norton, 1970), 56.

9. In a comprehensive survey of the volumes listed in Lyle Henry Wright's *American Fiction, 1774-1850: A Contribution toward a Bibliography* (San Marino: Huntington Library, 1957), I have found that the number of Romantic Adventure and Subversive novels published in America rose from about 20 percent before 1800 to about 55 percent for the 1841–1850 decade.

10. Reynolds's "Mocha Dick" is conveniently available in *Moby-Dick*, eds. Harrison Hayford and Hershel Parker (New York: Norton, 1967), 571–90.

11. William Comstock, *The Life of Samuel Comstock, the Terrible Whaleman, Containing an Account of the Mutiny, and Massacre of the Officers of the Ship Globe, of Nantucket* (Boston: James Fisher, 1840), 69.

12. *The Doom of the Dolphin; or, The Sorceress of the Sea* (Boston: F. Gleason, 1848), 83.

13. *Life in a Whale Ship* (1841), reprinted as *Romance of the Deep; or the Cruise of the Aeronaut . . . During a Three Years' Voyage in an American Whale Ship* (Boston: Redding and Co., 1846), 25.

14. The most comprehensive discussion of Melville's use of whaling books remains Howard Vincent, *The Trying-Out of Moby-Dick* (Boston: Houghton Mifflin, 1949).

15. Robert D. Richardson, *Myth and Literature in the American Renaissance* (Bloomington: Indiana University Press, 1978), 212–13.

16. *The Liberator*, 22 January 1831.

17. A. J. H. Duganne, *The Knights of the Seal; or, The Mysteries of Three Cities* (Philadelphia: Colon and Adriance, 1845), 112.

18. *The Literary World*, 9 February 1850.

19. E. Whipple, "The Romance of Rascality" (1848), in *One Hundred Years Ago: American Writings of 1848*, ed. James Playstead Wood (New York: Funk and Wagnalls, 1948), 479.

20. *Knickerbocker Magazine*, 8 (October 1836), 619.

21. G. Foster, *New York by Gas-Light* (New York: DeWitt and Davenport, 1850), 109; *New York in Slices* (New York: William H. Graham, 1849), 44.

22. The Black Sampson episode from *Washington and His Generals* is reprinted in *George Lippard, Prophet of Protest: Writings of an American Radical*, ed. David S. Reynolds (New York: Peter Lang, 1986), 123–28. The following quotation from *Blanche of Brandywine* is in Reynolds, *George Lippard, Prophet of Protest*, 286.

23. Typical burlesque sermons are collected in W. H. Levison, *Black Diamonds; or, Humor, Satire, and Sentiment. Treated Scientifically by Professor Julius Caesar Hannibal. A Series of Burlesque Lectures, Darkly Colored. Originally Published in "The New York Picayune"* (New York: A. Ranney, 1855).

24. G. Lippard, *The Quaker City; or, The Monks of Monk Hall* (1845; rpt. New York: Odyssey, 1970), 34.

25. *New England Magazine*, June 1835, 449.

26. Joseph Holt Ingraham, *Lafitte, The Pirate of the Gulf* (New York: Harper & Bros., 1836), 62.

27. *The Female Land Pirate; or, Awful, Mysterious and Horrible Disclosure of Amanda Bannoris* (Cincinnati: E. E. Barclay, 1847), 18.

28. *The Female Land Pirate*, 20.

Moby-Dick and Domesticity

HERSHEL PARKER

Everyone notices that through most of its many pages *Moby-Dick* is a book of men without women. Oddly enough, no one has paid much attention to the fact that the book was written while Melville was living in a household of women. Indeed, until the New York Public Library acquired part of the papers of Melville's sister Augusta in 1983, we have not had the strongest evidence of just how encircled by females Melville was during 1850 and 1851. In reviewing Melville's life, aspirations, and circumstances 1849–1851, this essay explores the possibility that Melville embodied some of his domestic comforts, compromises, and tensions in *Moby-Dick*.

Melville was sheltered and even indulged until his father failed at business in New York City in 1830, then died early in 1832, having taken a humbler place with his brother-in-law and creditor Peter Gansevoort in Albany.[1] Then Melville, twelve years old, was taken out of school and put in a bank as a clerk, and at fourteen put as a clerk in his older brother Gansevoort's hat and fur store.[2] His salary was considered the family's, not his own. At best he barely supported himself by his first grownup jobs at eighteen and twenty, schoolteaching, and despite Gansevoort's bankruptcy in 1837 and his subsequent sickness, Herman had no expectation of ever having to be the man of the family. His shore jobs (relieved by a summer's voyage to Liverpool on a merchant ship in 1839) created in him a fierce hatred of confinement and routine, and at twenty-one he sailed for the ends of the earth where for three or four years he could not possibly help his mother and Gansevoort provide for the other children, and from which at best he would return with only a few dollars in his pocket.[3] His behavior was that of a young man who felt and was made to feel responsible only for himself, not for his family.

Months after Melville's return late in 1844 he started *Typee*, writing in the law office in New York where his brothers Gansevoort and Allan worked, then at Lansingburgh.[4] After Gansevoort as the new Secretary of the American Legation arranged for its publication in London and also secured its American publication early in 1846 (*Log*, 202–203), Herman bestirred himself to be sure he had the American copyright and set himself to

This essay was written specifically for this volume and is published here for the first time by permission of the author.

defend the book against various attacks.[5] During the book's phenomenal publicity Gansevoort suddenly died. The income from *Typee* was too small to be of much help to the family, even if Melville placed some of it in the family coffers. In 1847 Melville turned his initial payment for *Omoo* over to his mother for her and the girls; she was appreciative but hardheaded about the contribution: it was welcome, albeit small.[6]

In 1847, when Herman Melville and his brother Allan married within a few weeks of each other, Herman's father-in-law, Judge Shaw, and Allan's mother-in-law, Mrs. Thurston, set them up in a house on Fourth Avenue with (besides their brides) their mother and four sisters. For the next two years Melville had no responsibilities except to finish *Mardi*, which he had begun before his marriage.[7] He worked on it, with intermittent assiduity, but he embarked upon a regime of reading and entered rather freely into literary life, becoming something of a fixture at all-male gatherings in the editor Evert Duyckinck's house (*Log*, 263). In February 1849, just as *Mardi* was at last off his hands, his son Malcolm was born in Boston (two days before Allan's daughter Maria was born in New York). In the spring of 1849 the failure of *Mardi* caused Melville to abandon his plans to make his next book of comparable importance to his growth as a writer. Having lavished two years of his working life upon *Mardi,* he was ready to defend the "certain something unmanageable" that had driven him on, seeing that unmanageable quality as a mark of greatness.[8] But he acted as a responsible (and perhaps repentant) family man and (only for money, he said) wrote *Redburn* and *White-Jacket* during four months in the summer of 1849, enduring the heat and staying on in New York even during a cholera epidemic (*Log*, 309). A newly discovered contemporary assertion by A. Oakey Hall (later mayor of New York City) refines what we have known: Melville wrote the second of these books in "a score of sittings"—a phenomenal, and self-sacrificial, intensity of labor, even if the truth in twenty "sittings" is that for eight weeks Melville would spend, say, two days laying out his sources, then on the third day write heroically, far past his usual mid-afternoon stopping point.[9]

Biographers have not commented much on what led up to Melville's decision to go to England in the fall (leaving his wife and eight-month-old son), other than asserting that the new copyright ruling in England made him think he could do better selling *White-Jacket* in person there rather than by mail and acknowledging that he deserved a vacation after the extraordinary two-book production of one summer.[10] The New York *Tribune* said that it was Melville's "intention to spend a twelvemonth abroad," and the evidence in his journals, letters, and family correspondence validates this report (*Log*, 318).[11] He was being challenged on his own field of vivid personal travel books by footloose young travel writers like Bayard Taylor while he was at home running out of experiences, except for the unglamorous business of whaling. Having persuaded himself and his family that extensive travel was a necessity, he was planning a grand research tour—a chance to see wonders he could come home and write about. Practicality aside, wanderlust, or simply restlessness, we sometimes forget, was a powerful component of his personality.

Once he got to sea on the *Southampton* on 11 October 1849, Melville had ideal companions. A friend of his friend Evert Duyckinck's was aboard, George Adler, a young scholar of German philosophy and literature, a sort of adjunct professor of modern languages at New York University. Melville wrote in his journal that Adler was "full of the German metaphysics" and discoursed "of Kant, Swedenborg &c."[12] Aboard as ship's doctor was Frank Taylor, a former travel companion of his cousin Bayard Taylor, whom Melville had already met. With Adler he had long talks on "Fixed Fate, Free-will, fore-knowledge absolute"—Milton's list of topics debated by the fallen angels—but the early talks with Taylor were also momentous, particularly one on 15 October:

> This afternoon Dr Taylor & I sketched a plan for going down the Danube from Vienna to Constantinople; thence to Athens in the steamer; to Beyroot & Jerusalem—Alexandria & the Pyramids. From what I learn, I have no doubt this can be done at a comparativ[e]ly trifling expence. Taylor has had a good deal of experience in cheap European travel, & from his knowledge of German is well fitted for a travelling companion thro Austria & Turkey. I am full (just now) of this glorious *Eastern* jaunt. Think of it!—Jerusalem & the Pyramids— Constantinople, the Egean, & old Athens!

Melville's parenthetical "just now" acknowledges the evanescence of his moods, but it cannot disguise his rapturous enthusiasm (*Journals*, 7).

On 18 October Adler was included in some of the travel plans Melville recorded:

> Spent the entire morning in the main-top with Adler & Dr Taylor, discussing our plans for the grand circuit of Europe & the East. Taylor, however, has communicated to me a circumstance, that may prevent him from accompanying us—something of a pecuniary nature. He reckons our expenses at $400. (*Journals*, 8)

Taylor was now the doubtful party, and Melville himself seemed to be the most committed to the tour, which still involved a sweeping loop, through Europe and the Middle East and back (to England?) by some unspecified route, presumably through Spain. The discussions continued, not without vacillations, as Melville recorded on 26 October:

> For a few days passed, Adler & I have had some "sober second thoughts" about our grand Oriental & Spanish tour with Taylor. But tonight, the sight of "Bradshaw's Railway & Steamer Guide" showing the marvellous ease with

which the most distant voyages may now be accomplished has revived—at least in *my* mind,—all my original enthusiasm. Talked the whole thing over again with Taylor. Shall not be able to decide till we get to London. (*Journals*, 9)

Once in London, Melville had to stifle his hopes.

Richard Bentley had lost money on *Mardi*, but on 12 November he kept his agreement to give Melville a hundred pounds at sixty days for *Redburn*, and despite "much anxiety & vexation at the state of the Copyright question" the publisher made a generous offer for *White-Jacket*, two hundred pounds for the first thousand copies, but no advance. Needing an advance if he were to depart on his grand circuit, and a bigger payment than Bentley offered, Melville for several days made a fruitless canvass of publishers ("Historical Note," 603; see also *Journals*, 16–26). On 14 November he called on John Murray, his first publisher, who still kept *Typee* and *Omoo* in print, and Murray sent a messenger to Melville's room for the sheets of *White-Jacket*. That day Melville dined with Taylor, a fellow passenger named McCurdy, and Adler. Melville had described McCurdy as "a sickly youth of twenty bound for the grand tour," at the expense of his father, "a rich merchant of New York." The rich merchant had hoped his son would share a cabin with Melville—about as devoutly as Melville had dreaded the prospect. Now ironically young McCurdy was to have the privilege of going forth with Taylor without Melville and without Adler: "Tomorrow he [Taylor] starts with McC for the East—Jerusalem, &c.—" Murray's decision on *White-Jacket* was negative, and in the next days Melville called successively upon the publishers Colbourn, Longmans, Chapman, Bohn, none of whom equalled Bentley's offer. Nothing in Melville's journal explicitly records a shift in plans under which Rome seemed a realistic destination even after the tour of Eastern Europe and the Near East was renounced, but his entry for 17 November suggests that some such alternative was still alive in his hopes. Colbourn had rejected his demands for *White-Jacket* (two hundred pounds for the first thousand copies—on delivery of the proofs?): "Bad news enough—I shall not see Rome—I'm floored—appetite unimpaired however—so down to the Edinburgh Castle & paid my compliments to a chop. Smoked a long pipe . . ." (*Journals*, 3, 18–20).

In the "Historical Note" to *Moby-Dick* I suggested that rarely had Melville "put himself on record as wanting anything so much as he wanted this prolonged trip to eastern Europe, the Holy Land, and the entire Mediterranean region. He was careful to note that he was homesick for his wife and son, but he was wild to have his *Wanderjahr*" ("Historical Note," 603). I was this emphatic because biographers have discounted the importance of Melville's renouncing his trip, as if his own resolutely jaunty declaration that his appetite was unimpaired meant that he had shrugged off his plans with a chop, a pipe of tobacco, and ale. Mumford (1929), who usually looked for intellectual and emotional intensities, took a rational view of Melville's abandonment of his hopes for a grand tour, constructing a ventriloquistic pastiche from the journal:

> Taylor has a notion of going through the Near East: down the Danube from Vienna to Constantinople—Athens, Beyrut, Jerusalem, Cairo, Alexandria. That would be something neither Polynesia nor the Hudson Valley could give: marvellous, if it were not for the strain on one's purse. . . . One is going to England to get a little ready cash from Bentley or Murray or Moxon on *White-Jacket*: one can't dissipate that in travel. One is tied: there is no getting away from that. One wants to travel far, perhaps; but not with the same old lust and confidence: all paths lead home again.[13]

Leon Howard was even more rational. Quoting the itinerary Taylor and Melville sketched on 15 October, Howard commented:

> But he [Melville] learned before the end of the voyage that Taylor was in worse financial shape than he was, and, as a result, his philosophical conversation [with Adler] was more immediately fruitful than his talk of the Near East.[14]

We have usually taken it for granted that Melville could not seriously have wanted to make a grand tour and we have simplified his psychology by depriving him of any serious disappointment at having to forgo it.

Melville's renunciation of the grand Eastern jaunt and the consolation trip to Rome was soon complicated by a new renunciation that grieved him in a different way. On 13 December, returned from his frugal foray into France, Belgium, and Germany, Melville was handed his mail. A letter from the Duke of Rutland, "sealed with a coronet," invited him "to visit Belvoir Castle at any time after a certain day in January." Melville noted: "Can not go—I am homeward-bound, & Malcolm is growing all the time." On the fifteenth he read over the note, which he had "not fairly perused before," and found it "very cordial," but the date for the proposed visit impossibly distant (*Journals*, 39, 41). On Sunday the 16th he was in turmoil:

> It is now 3. P.M. I have had a fire made & am smoking a cigar. Would that One I know were here. Would that the Little One too were here———I am in a very painful state of uncertainty. I am all eagerness to get home—I ought to be home—my absence occasions uneasiness in a quarter where I must beseech heaven to grant repose. Yet here I have before me an open prospect to get some curious ideas of a style of life, which in all probability I shall never have again. I should much like to know what the highest English aristocracy really & practically is. And the Duke of Rutland's cordial invitation to visit him at his Castle furnishes me with just the thing I want. If I do not go, I am confident that hereafter I shall upbraid myself for neglecting such an opportunity of procuring *"material."* And Allan & others will account me a

ninny.—I would not debate the matter a moment, were it not that at least three whole weeks must elapse ere I start for Belvoir Castle——three weeks! If I could but get over *them!* And if the two images would only *down* for that space of time.————I must light a second cigar & revolve it over again. (*Journals*, 41–42)

At half past six he wrote again: "My mind is made; rather, is irrevocably resolved upon my first determination. A visit into L[ei]cester would be very agreeable—at least very valuable, in one respect, to me—but the Three Weeks are intolerable" (*Journals*, 42). Traveling months in the Mediterranean regions was justifiable as literary research, but lingering three more weeks in England, after he had concluded his financial affairs there, was intolerable to so restless a man. On shipboard, homeward bound, when that "certain day in January" arrived, Melville may well have marked it with a twinge for his renunciation of a chance-of-a-lifetime. Seeing Europe and the Levant (or seeing merely the Eternal City and not the Holy City) would have been richly rewarding, but he would have been only a tourist there, seeing the sites sacred to history, religion, and literature from the outside, the way he saw Paris. Staying in a castle as the valued guest of a Duke (whose language he spoke) would have afforded him unique opportunities of observing the home life of British aristocracy, and it might also have eventuated in correspondence with the Duke or his other guests, and even later visits or association with Britons in New York. Melville was young and unformed enough that such an experience could have altered his life decisively: he would never know. This new renunciation was not eased by the fact that he was strongly drawn toward Lizzie and Malcolm. (Plainly he accepted separation from the rest of the family with more equanimity.)

During his last days in London Melville had some compensation in meeting brilliant literary and artistic men on a common footing, men with a level of achievement and capacities far surpassing most of the men he had met through Duyckinck in New York City. On 19 December 1849, he was memorably entertained: he "dined in Elm Court, Temple, and had a glorious time till noon of night. A set of fine fellows indeed. It recalled poor Lamb's 'Old Benchers'" . . . The Paradise of Batchelors" (*Journals*, 44). The next night he was invited to the Erechtheum Club in St. James's where he encountered "exceedingly agreeable company." When he left London, Melville had a clear—if tantalizing—sense of what literary and artistic life in the great metropolis could be like.

Melville went home because he loved his wife and son and felt a strong sense of duty toward them, but also, surely, because in his lonely lodgings he missed all the comfortable and comforting domesticity he had grown used to since his return from the South Seas. In London he had watched for suitable books for use in case he served up the story of the Revolutionary beggar Israel Potter, but a desire to write that story or any other story was not impelling him homeward. On the unusually long voyage home, however, he seems to have decided to write a book about whaling, and he may well have worked himself into a mood of some urgency by the time he reached home. His reentry into the household was easy. The family was relieved that he had returned home so promptly from what might have been an indefinitely prolonged trip, and reviews of *Redburn* that they had saved for him were almost all favorable. But there was reason for some edginess, for by the time Melville returned the family knew that Sophia was pregnant with her second child, and the prospect of having a third child in the house may well have been enough to tip the balance from thinking that the house was commodious (in 1848) and adequate (in 1849) to thinking that it would be cramped (by the fall of 1850). It was apparent during the early months of 1850 that the household would be disrupted before very long, but Melville probably kept at bay any sense that he had to make an immediate decision about new living arrangements. Perhaps one obvious possibility, to be thought about only when pressed, was that he would purchase (with Lizzie's money but of course in his name) a house in the city for him and Lizzie and Malcolm—or perhaps a house large enough that his mother and sisters (or some of them) might live there also. He retreated to his study, quickly absorbed in his new book, and for three or four months his work habits were indulged the way they had been for three years. As far as we know, he was absolutely free to read and write.

Herman Melville was the only man in the house all day until brother Allan returned home from his law office on Wall Street, and for a variety of reasons he seems to have kept pretty much within the family circle at night. Part of the reason was that the literary cliques of the city were in an uproar, as I have described in the "Historical Note" in *Moby-Dick*. His friend Nathaniel Parker Willis, by publishing in his *Home Journal* part of a letter from Melville about having to retrench his plans, had unintentionally given ammunition that the crooked Thomas Powell used in mocking Melville's thwarted aspirations to make the grand tour. Powell's attack appeared in James Gordon Bennett's New York *Herald*, the chief competitor of Greeley's *Tribune* and a paper that almost everyone looked at, even though it was fashionable to profess disgust at Bennett's sensationalism. Other papers carried stories, partly true, of Melville's attempts to peddle *White-Jacket* "from Whitechapel to Picadilly," and correspondents wrote in to rewrite the record. Worse, his literary friends Duyckinck and Willis were being even more petty than usual, sniping at each other in their papers while their literary opposition sniped indiscriminately at the Duyckinck-Mathews crowd and at Willis. The sight of his name in the February papers, where his private disappointment was paraded in public, must have been embarrassing to Melville, and the sight of his friends' names can hardly have been pleasant ("Historical Note," 606–610).

At least the subsequent commentary on *White-Jacket* was for the most part very favorable. In March some London reviews crossed the ocean and extracts (from London papers and then from advance sheets of the Harper edition) began appearing in American papers, prior to the April reviews. Like *Redburn, White-Jacket,* while not reviewed with universal favor, was generally hailed as a welcome return to the successful pattern Melville had set in *Typee* and *Omoo.*[15] No one in the family could have read a generous sampling of the reviews of *Redburn* and *White-Jacket* without feeling that Melville had redeemed himself. Once the spate of attention in the newspapers and magazines died down, Melville probably suppressed any regrets at his renunciations: the challenge of the manuscript can hardly have been far from all-absorbing, although in this phase it may have kept him close to the emotional intensity of *White-Jacket,* or not much greater than that.

Melville seems to have taken a break from his writing in May or June, for a letter his sister Augusta wrote to Duyckinck in July seems to hint that he went on an excursion to West Point and came back with zestful stories, and the evidence of his borrowing and his purchases of source books is that he was regrouping in early summer, probably having finished what he thought of as some discrete stage of the manuscript (*Log,* 373–77, 379). After his obsessive labor during the summer of 1849, the prospect of working year-round in New York City was more than he could willingly endure. As a pampered child he had always had a vacation with doting grandparents or aunts and uncles, but in his early teens he was given only a week's vacation, and in 1834 Gansevoort said "he was wanted in the store" and would not let him go to his uncle Thomas's farm near Pittsfield even for a week.[16] Maria thought of the farm as an Edenic refuge in the early 1830s, and Herman thought of it the same way. When he stopped off there in the early spring of 1848 his cousin Priscilla recalled that the farm had been his "first love."[17] The glimpse of Pittsfield in 1848 (even during the snows of early April) had revived in him his intense love of the Berkshires, and in June 1850 his mother was there visiting her widowed sister-in-law Mary Melvill (whom she had not seen for years) and undoubtedly writing home (as she and other visitors always did) about the delicious air. Now it was time for Melville to bring the concept of a vacation back into his life, for there was no reason any regrouping on his manuscript could not take place in the Berkshires. He suddenly decided to go to the Melvill place himself. His inconsiderate lack of forethought discommoded his mother, for she had left the farm for a visit to Lansingburgh rather than outstay her welcome, only to hear to her irritation that she could have stayed on, since Herman and Lizzie had decided to come up—and in fact then she did return promptly.[18]

Soon after Melville's arrival at Pittsfield on 10 or 11 July, he left with his cousin Robert Melvill for a two-day wagon ride around the Berkshires. Robert and Herman had been youthful schoolmasters at the same time, but by 1850 Herman was more than a little scornful of Robert, the hapless cousin "Doolittle" in his letter of 13 December.[19] Needing better companionship, Melville invited his editorial friends Evert Duyckinck and Cornelius Mathews to join him at the Melvill place in August 1850, apparently having seen little of them for many months, and looking forward to talking with them of literary issues. Since Mathews had just founded *The Prompter*, a magazine devoted to the drama, Melville may have wanted particularly to talk about something agitating him, such as the supposed unapproachableness of Shakespeare or the oblique way he thought Shakespeare told his darker truths. A fortuitous congregating of literary-minded local men and luminaries from New York and Boston was too remarkable not to take advantage of, and on 5 August Melville contributed to the momentum of the holiday mood during a picnic on Monument Mountain where he and his New York guests were joined by Oliver Wendell Holmes, Nathaniel Hawthorne, and others. After the climb there was dinner at Dudley Field's house in Stockbridge—not Elm Court, Temple, or the Erechtheum Club, St. James's, but grand enough to hold several choice American literary men. Melville was caught off guard by the effect Nathaniel Hawthorne had on him. Having denied himself literary companionship for many months as he worked on the whaling book, he now encountered the only American he could consider his literary equal, and the rapturous essay he wrote on "Hawthorne and His Mosses" for the *Literary World* (17 and 24 August) a few days after their meeting was an assertion of his own aspiration to rival Shakespeare as well as an acknowledgment of the power of Hawthorne's person and of his stories (*Log*, 389; see "Historical Note," 610–17).

In his practical way Leon Howard was sure that Melville went to Pittsfield in order to buy a house in the country, yet all the evidence suggests that he went there for a vacation. Having been self-indulgent during the composition of the ambitious *Mardi*, he had between June 1849 and early July 1850 been responsibly self-denying as a young husband and father should be. By July he had a substantial new manuscript to point to as evidence that he was still being responsible and not self-indulgent—"mostly done," Duyckinck reported in early August (*Log*, 385). In mid-August he probably justified staying on at the Melvill house by finding a little time to work, writing in a hallnook in an upper floor, with a great view of Mount Greylock but without walls or a door.[20] On 29 August Melville's sister Augusta Melville reported to her friend Mary Blatchford that some of their "absentees" had returned to New York but not all: "Herman & Lizzie still prolong their rusticating, & are so happy among the mountains of Berkshire, that it seems impossible to tear themselves away."[21] Melville was prolonging his vacation, not estate-hunting.

The attraction had not been one-sided: Hawthorne had been immediately drawn to Melville, also, to the point of taking the remarkable step of inviting him to stay at the rented cottage at Stockbridge Bowl before he returned to New York. Plainly, Hawthorne had heard nothing of Melville's moving to the Berkshires, for there would have been no need for him to violate his own reclusive habits if Melville were to live nearby. They met twice more in August, and Melville arrived in Lenox for his visit on the morning of 3 September. On the 4th he and Hawthorne spent the day at Uncle Thomas's place before returning to Lenox, where Melville stayed until the morning of the 7th, becoming an intimate of Sophia Hawthorne's as well as her husband's (*Log*, 389–94). During Melville's visit the great topic was the fact that Melville himself was the author of the review of Hawthorne's *Mosses* in the *Literary World* attributed only to a "Virginian." Absolutely nothing in the Hawthornes' records of this visit suggests that they knew Melville was going to move to the Berkshires, yet by the time he returned alone to the Melvill farm Melville may have made momentous plans— certainly he had done so before a few days had passed. Overwhelmed by the renewed power of his much loved Berkshires and comparably overwhelmed by Hawthorne, Melville had decided that his best chance of making the whaling book as great as he dared to think it might be (Shakespeareanly great) was to finish it in a splendid (and for him memory-fraught) natural setting with a darkly alluring (and perhaps even Shakespearean) fellow writer nearby. None of this was logical (however infatuated you are, you do not buy a house to be near another man who is merely renting), but Melville had no solid record of being reasonable about money matters and had misjudged badly his success the last time he made an attempt at literary greatness. He did have a record of vaunting the certain something unmanageable that distinguished the drives of artists like himself. As far as he was concerned, he had been the model of a sacrificial husband and it was time that he had something he wanted.

What he wanted, most likely, was Uncle Thomas's place, but it had been promised in sale (although not sold), so he would (without conducting any rigorous survey of purchasable properties?) take the next best, an adjacent farm with a comparable view, although with a lesser house that would have to be torn down when he built the proper residence for a great American writer, one at a still higher elevation where his writer's tower would command a view of mountain ranges in New York and Vermont. This time he was going to get his way. He was impetuous—determined to buy the Brewster property without waiting to get his father-in-law Lemuel Shaw's money out of the New York house first. Shaw, newly arrived to hold his annual court session in Lenox, went along with his plans, no doubt proud of Herman's recovered reputation and happy to have his daughter only several hours away by a direct railroad line where she could visit him more frequently and he could be sure of seeing her every time he came to Lenox. Shaw advanced the necessary money, and on 14 September Melville bought the Brewster place (*Log*, 395).

The first the Hawthornes heard of this was when Melville rode up in the splendor of the waxing moon (perhaps 19 September, shortly before the full harvest moon of the 21st). Sophia Hawthorne testified to their surprise:

he drove up one superb moonlight night & said he had bought an estate six miles from us, where he is really going to build a real towered house—an actual tower. He is married to a daughter of Judge Shaw Judge Lemuel Shaw, & has a child of year & half—Malcolm. He is of Scotch descent—of noble lineage—of the Lords of Melville & Leven, & Malcolm is a family name. So we shall have him for a neighbour. (*Log*, 925)

More than half of the Melville household packed up posthaste, Kate electing to stay with Allan and Sophia while Maria Melville and her other daughters, Helen, Augusta, and Fanny, chose to go with Herman and Lizzie.[22] Astonished by these developments, George Duyckinck (Evert's brother) on 23 September wrote to a friend:

> Herman Melville has taken us by surprise by buying a farm of 160 acres in Berkshire County. It is mostly woodland which he intends to preserve and have a road through, making it more of an ornamental place than a farm. Part of it is on a hill commanding a view of twenty miles, where he intends eventually to build. He removes at once with his mother and sisters to our great sorrow as the house was one of the pleasantest to visit as I ever came across and we are much attached to them all. (*Log*, 395–96).

Plainly, everything about the purchase of what Melville soon named Arrowhead was impulsive.

Moving disrupted Melville's compositional process more than he could possibly have imagined. Like a reasonable man he made up his mind to put the manuscript aside without complaint during the time it would take for him to get moved to Pittsfield and settled in. He probably pretty much resolved to sacrifice the remainder of September and all of October. The problem came when household chores did not end abruptly at the projected time, and during November Melville became torn between the need to finish settling in and the compulsion to return to his work. Many parts of the household had to be left in disorder, but even so he became increasingly exasperated at not being able to establish a work routine. Some interruptions were caused by his stubborn masculine protectiveness, for he forbade the women to drive the wagon. Every time one of them wanted to go to town or to the old Melvill house (sold but still occupied by the aunt and cousins) she had to wait until Herman was free to drive her. He became unable to control his temper when he was drawn away from the work he had just returned to; perhaps he did not speak rudely, but he let his irritation show. In November when his sister Helen needed to catch a train at a time of day (probably late morning) that in New York had been sacred to his literary labors, he behaved badly—showing his impatience to the point that Augusta felt obliged to send a soothing message to the older sister.[23] Hawthorne was a powerful presence in his mind, tantalizingly near yet, week by week, as Melville settled into life at Arrowhead, unapproachable. Day in and day out, Melville was surrounded by a circle of females.

At Arrowhead, Melville's role in the family changed. In New York he had been young husband and author with a private bedroom for himself and his wife and apparently a separate private study; he was free to go out in the afternoon and at night as he wished, with only minimal obligations as occasional escort of his mother, sisters, sister-in-law, and wife. In New York, Maria Melville had had her hands full with four daughters, two sons and their wives, then two babies, and the shifting complement of servants; besides all that she had her old New York friends and the new circle into which her sons had brought her. As long as Herman was not being criticized in the press she could pretty much ignore him. Once she came to Pitts-field with Herman she was in a familiar environment she thought she could control, and she suddenly became a more conspicuous force in his life than she had been since 1839 or 1840. Maria knew many of the townspeople of Pittsfield from the weeks she had stayed with her brother-in-law and his family in the 1830s, and she found it easy to establish herself socially, beginning, inevitably, with the church. For her and perhaps for Augusta, if not for Helen and Fanny, the world contracted temporarily to the bounds of that village long marked by religious conservatism.[24] Being in so parochial a situation, where the same group of people each week let her know that her famous son's presence was expected at worship, Maria focused her attention on Herman perhaps more than ever before. A son, he deserved more attention than the daughters; a famous man, he deserved to be guided into the safety of Christian piety. Life at Arrowhead gave her the chance to work seriously on Herman's character and immortal soul, and without Allan around to deflect any of his mother's attention, Herman got more than he needed.

Lizzie seems to have deferred to Maria's vast personal experience with hiring and bossing servants (as she later deferred to her knowledge of gardening), and seems to have been content to let Maria take charge of many areas of domestic life. Certainly Lizzie did not pit herself against her mother-in-law, but she may have wanted to escape some of the family tensions when she decamped with Malcolm to spend Thanksgiving with her family in Boston, and stayed on all through December. Melville was forced to evacuate his newly set up study (the room with the best view of Mount Greylock) in order for the women to convert it into a makeshift dining room big enough to accommodate the Melvills for Thanksgiving as well as their own reduced household.[25] In early December his mother got him to church once, and Augusta had hopes that if they did not make too much of their triumph he might return.[26] He was in a trap of his own making. At night there was no available equivalent of strolling down to the Battery to look at the stars, so conflicts tended to fester. He may have been glad to have Lizzie and Malcolm out of the way for a while, but he welcomed their return at the first of the year, and early in January his intensifying need to work undisturbed brought him to the point of letting Augusta and their mother take the horse and wagon on a trial outing, after which he was convinced that they could be trusted to drive safely.[27] He continued to write in something like ideal conditions until late winter.

One chapter of *Moby-Dick* that seems part of the section on whaling processes Melville wrote this winter is "A Squeeze of the Hand." Writing in the Berkshire cold, Melville imagined his narrator in the warm Indian Ocean (or Pacific?). Bound to his desk, pen in his hand, he imagined soothing physical labor (after bitter physical exertion), labor in which his hero could relax his mind in free association (while he himself was concentrating his efforts on his awesome literary task). Surrounded by women, with no man around besides himself, he imagined himself in the warm, soothing task of squeezing the lumps out of the sperm, a task in which his co-laborers were all men and all were united in perfect sociability: "Such an abounding, affectionate, friendly, loving feeling did this avocation beget; that at last I was continually squeezing their hands, and looking up into their eyes sentimentally; as much as to say,—Oh, my dear fellow beings, why should we longer cherish any social acerbities, or know the slightest ill-humor or envy!" What follows is the injunction to "squeeze hands all round," and (more than that) to squeeze ourselves into each other and to "squeeze ourselves universally into the very milk and sperm of kindness" (416). Then comes this reflective paragraph:

> Would that I could keep squeezing that sperm for ever! For now, since by many prolonged, repeated experiences, I have perceived that in all cases man must eventually lower, or at least shift, his conceit of attainable felicity; not placing it anywhere in the intellect or the fancy; but in the wife, the heart, the bed, the table, the saddle, the fire-side, the country; now that I have perceived all this, I am ready to squeeze case eternally. In thoughts of the visions of the night, I saw long rows of angels in paradise, each with his hands in a jar of spermaceti. (416)

The paragraph begins with a wishful exclamation, then proceeds to an explanation of why Ishmael wishes he could keep squeezing that sperm for ever. The cause is his perception (not one readily arrived at, but come to after "many prolonged, repeated experiences") of a change one must make in his notion of attainable happiness. The presupposition is that "man" in early life takes the lofty view that happiness is to be attained through the exercise of the intellect or of the imagination. The long-delayed insight is that "man must eventually lower" that notion; but to use the word "lower" seems invidiously to denigrate the alternative to the intellect and the fancy more than he wants to do, so he substitutes the phrase "or at least shift," without, however, removing the more telling word "lower." Melville says (or has Ishmael say) that in all instances man must make that lowering or at least shifting of expectation, but (this is implicit) only if what he wants is "attainable felicity," attainable happiness. Melville leaves open the possibility that a man may well want something more than happiness, and in that instance he might indeed pursue *something* (not happiness, but perhaps some sort of fame or even glory) through the intellect or the imagination. However, Melville makes his position clear about any man who wants to achieve happiness: the way to do it is through "the wife, the heart, the bed, the table, the saddle, the fire-side, the country." And he has Ishmael insist that having achieved this perception he is "ready to squeeze case eternally."

Ishmael's conclusion (a perhaps provisional decision to do something eternally) is at odds with the parts of the book surrounding (and especially following) "A Squeeze of the Hand," parts where another character, Captain Ahab, makes conspicuously manifest a determination to pursue matters of the intellect and the imagination at whatever cost to the values associated with domesticity. This very chapter, moreover, seems not wholly consistent, for it celebrates (instead of conventional family life ashore) a conspicuous display of sentimental male communion with other men, fellow workmen, where the "horrible oath" is forgotten, lesser grievances and mad feelings are banished, and a universal (male) affection is hailed. All this occurs without a hint that the absence of women undercuts any of the validity of the series of emotions described—or that Melville might have recognized the passage as a fantasy of escaping from the lonely, cramped, frigid conditions in which he was writing—from winter in an isolated Berkshire farmhouse full of women, where even Malcolm was probably still in petticoats.

Chances are that in the late winter or early spring of 1851 Melville (however much he still rued the curtailment of his travels the year before) was exhilarated by what he was writing and content with his working conditions (however ill they comported with what he had projected in early September). When the house in New York was slow in selling, Allan dropped in unannounced in early January and offered to buy Herman out,[28] and then, if not before, Melville buried his wild dream of tearing Arrowhead down and building a real towered house and tried to reconcile the needs of his manuscript with his commitment to act responsibly as the man of the family. Some duties could not be turned off onto Augusta, and he broke off work (one morning?) to drive his mother to the depot in late February or early March. He left her there with her trunk a full hour before the train arrived and drove off as if "his life" depended upon it. His mother wrote to Augusta on March 10: "Herman I hope returned home safe after dumping me & my trunks out so unceremoniously at the Depot—Altho we were there more than an hour before the time, he hurried off as if his life had depended upon his speed, a more ungallant man it would be difficult to find."[29] A part of Melville's aesthetic (and commercial) life probably did in fact depend upon his speed, for he was almost surely frantic to get back to his manuscript before losing the mood that had to be sustained if the interrupted passage were to be finished in anything like the shape it had been growing toward when he had to break off work. Sometime in March, Melville probably learned that Lizzie was pregnant again, and as the weeks went on he was torn by the conflict between his responsibilities as husband, father, and farmer and his aesthetic compulsions and professional aspirations. Maria Melville was not the haughty aristocrat that Melville made Pierre's mother, Mary Glendinning, but she was a supremely bossy woman whose reforming zeal was focused all too sharply on her oldest living son. Going behind Herman's back in March, during her visit to New York, Maria assured Evert Duyckinck that despite her son's earlier refusal she was sure she could persuade him to meet Duyckinck's reasonable request that he have a daguerreotype taken from which his portrait could be engraved for *Holden's Magazine*.[30]

Late winter, 13–14 March, brought Hawthorne to Arrowhead with his daughter Una for much good talk with Melville, and during the first week or so of spring Melville hired men to start building a piazza, probably while the ground was still frozen (*Log*, 407–408).[31] Then spring brought not the simple gardening chores such as Melville had been accustomed to in a rented plot of land in Lansingburgh but serious farm work that had to be done if horse and cow were to be kept in hay and pumpkins over winter and if he were to lay vegetables away for the family. In his impatience to have the money to make the house and outbuildings adequate to his needs, he asked the Harpers for an advance, and when they refused he took the dangerous step of accepting a loan from an old Lansingburgh friend—an act that must have caused great domestic tension, given what we know of Lizzie's outright horror of debt—if he told her about it (*Log*, 410).[32] About the end of April, the week Melville got the loan from his friend, Augusta was released from her duties as copyist so she could visit the Van Rensselaers at the Manor House in Albany, from which luxurious vantage point she fantasized about the "beautiful order" which would have been imposed on Arrowhead by the time she returned: in settling down to work on his manuscript Melville had left Arrowhead all winter in a state far from "beautiful order."[33]

From early spring on through the summer of 1851, Melville's working conditions degenerated. Having committed himself to repaying a large debt in semiannual installments, he seems to have used some of the borrowed money on the risky venture of having his book set in type and stereotyped, beginning the project well before he had written the last hunk of the book. In his attempt to control the printing as well as to keep up with the care of his crops, he had to go to New York and back more than once, and while he was in town he had to work in a makeshift third-floor study (sure to have been miserably airless and hot in June and July) in Allan's new house, which was far uptown (on 31st Street). There during Melville's working hours the other inhabitants were his sister-in-law, his two-year-old niece, his one-year-old niece, and one or two of his sisters (and possibly his mother?) ("Historical

Note," 629–30). Melville had Allan's company again at intervals in evenings, but the location was remote from his old friends as well as very inconvenient to the printers, who were located far downtown with all the other major printing establishments.

In the summer of 1851 Melville was torn between mundane responsibilities for overseeing the actual printing (which he had never before had to deal with) as well as the necessity of going over the proofs to make whatever small insertions and other adjustments he could reasonably make in order to harmonize a book written over many months in such different circumstances under such differing impulses. He was oppressed also by the obligation (however exalted) to write the "tail" of *Moby-Dick*, and every time he came back to Lizzie her pregnancy was farther advanced.

The pressure under deteriorating conditions to meet all the obligations he had undertaken may have pushed Melville to articulate his situation in his manuscript. One chapter of *Moby-Dick* that seems to reflect these harassing circumstances of composition is "The Lee Shore." In all likelihood Melville conceived the character of Bulkington early in 1850, during his first push on the whaling book. Everyone who has paid attention to the anomalies in the text of *Moby-Dick* has concluded that Melville must first have planned for Bulkington to take a much larger role in the book than he in fact allotted him, "The Lee Shore," the chapter in which Melville dismisses Bulkington, was probably written quite late,[34] perhaps even in the summer of 1851, as he was trying to find the time he needed to write the concluding chapters. Chances are great that "A Squeeze of the Hand" was written months before "The Lee Shore," although of course the reader encounters "The Lee Shore" more than three hundred pages (in the Northwestern–Newberry text) before "A Squeeze of the Hand." In dismissing Bulkington from the book by apotheosizing him in a six-inch chapter, Melville was in all probability importing a late state of mind into passages written more than a year before.

In the stress of finishing the labor on the book while torn in several directions, Melville in "The Lee Shore" came down harder on the side of the intellect and the imagination than in a "A Squeeze of the Hand." Here he contrasted the domestic values of the port ("safety, comfort, hearthstone, supper, warm blankets, friends, all that's kind to our mortalities") with landlessness where "alone resides the highest truth, shoreless, indefinite as God." The lure of the values associated with the port is undeniable, but to choose those values is death to any seeker of the highest truth. Through this chapter (and this chapter alone) he made Bulkington stand for a seeker of truth, not a seeker of earthly felicity, and here Melville's narrative voice frenetically celebrates a "mortally intolerable truth," a truth intolerable to mere human beings: "that all deep, earnest thinking is but the intrepid effort of the soul to keep the open independence of her sea; while the wildest winds of heaven and earth conspire to cast her on the treacherous, slavish, shore."

He knew all too well that the mildest winds of home and hearth conspired for the same purpose.

Melville in moving to the Berkshires to finish *Moby-Dick* was gambling that he could achieve the highest development of his intellect and imagination without sacrificing the happiness that could come only through loving domesticity. Despite its being notoriously without major female characters, *Moby-Dick* can be said to be partly "about" an artist and domesticity, and in particular about the rival—and incompatible—claims of creativity and marriage. Rather than achieving or settling for one or the other permanently—open independence or slavish shore life; imagination and intellect or domesticity; earnest pursuit of truth at all costs or else the pursuit of attainable, domestic happiness; creativity or happy marriage—rather than one or the other Melville got neither, in a pure form, even during the Arrowhead phase of his work on *Moby-Dick*, his masterpiece which poignantly embodies his brief intense conviction that he could be a great writer and a responsible family man—that he could have it all.

Notes

1. Jay Leyda, *The Melville Log: A Documentary Life of Herman Melville, 1819–1891*, 2 vols. (New York: Harcourt Brace, 1951), I. 44–46. Reprinted, with a supplement (New York: Gordian Press, 1969). Hereafter cited as *Log*.

2. Hershel Parker, "A Melville Chronology," in *Reading "Billy Budd"* (Evanston: Northwestern University Press, 1990), 179–80.

3. Parker, 180–81.

4. Inscription on wrapper for the draft manuscript of *Typee*, reproduced in the *Melville Society Extracts*, 57 (February 1984), 4.

5. Maria Gansevoort Melville to Augusta Melville, 28 February 1846, NYPL–GL Additions.

6. Maria Gansevoort Melville to Augusta Melville, 17 February 1847, NYPL-GL Additions.

7. "Historical Note," 592–96 and 618–19 in *Moby-Dick*, ed. Harrison Hayford, Hershel Parker, and G. Thomas Tanselle (Evanston and Chicago: Northwestern University Press and The Newberry Library, 1988). Hereafter cited as "Historical Note"; all references to *Moby-Dick* are to this edition and are given parenthetically within the text.

8. Melville to Richard Bentley, 5 June 1849, in *The Letters of Herman Melville*, ed. Merrell R. Davis and William H. Gilman (New Haven: Yale University Press, 1960), 86; hereafter cited as *Letters*.

9. Croton [pseudonym of A. Oakey Hall], "Correspondence, March 29, 1850," in the New Orleans *Commercial Bulletin* (9 April 1850).

10. Leon Howard, *Herman Melville* (Berkeley: University of California Press, 1951), 138.

11. See also Priscilla Melvill to Augusta Melville, 28 January 1850 and 28 February 1850, NYPL–GL Additions.

12. Herman Melville, *Journals*, ed. Howard Horsford with Lynn Horth (Evanston and Chicago: Northwestern University Press and The Newberry Library, 1989). 4; hereafter cited as *Journals*.

13. Lewis Mumford, *Herman Melville* (New York: Literary Guild of America, 1929), 120.

14. Howard, 141.

15. Willard Thorp, "Historical Note," in *White-Jacket*, ed. Harrison Hayford, Hershel Parker, and G. Thomas Tanselle (Evanston and Chicago: Northwestern University Press and The Newberry Library, 1970), 429–435.

16. Julia Melvill to Augusta Melville, 12? September 1834, NYPL-GL Additions.

17. Priscilla Melvill to Augusta Melville, 3 April 1848, NYPL-GL Additions.

18. Maria Gansevoort Melville to Augusta Melville, 27 June 1850, NYPL-GL Additions.

19. Melville to Evert Duyckinck, 13 December 1850, *Letters*, 116.

20. Melville to Evert Duyckinck, 16 August 1850, *Letters*, 111.

21. Augusta Melville to Mary Blatchford, 29 August 1850, NYPL-GL Additions.

22. Kate's staying in New York City is clear in the letter from Augusta Melville to Mary Blatchford, 25 November 1850, NYPL-GL Additions.

23. Augusta Melville to Helen Melville, 22 November 1850, NYPL-GL Additions.

24. [David Dudley Field], *A History of the County of Berkshire, Massachusetts* (Pittsfield: S. W. Bush, 1829), 158 and 174–75.

25. Augusta Melville to Helen Melville, 22 November 1850 and 6 December 1850, NYPL-GL Additions.

26. Augusta Melville to Helen Melville, 6 December 1850, NYPL-GL Additions.

27. Augusta Melville to Helen Melville, 14 January 1851, NYPL-GL Additions.

28. Augusta Melville to Helen Melville, 14 January 1851, NYPL-GL Additions.

29. Maria Gansevoort Melville to Augusta Melville, 10 March 1851, NYPL-GL Additions, excerpted in *Moby-Dick*, "Historical Note," 628.

30. Maria Gansevoort Melville to Augusta Melville, 12 March 1851, NYPL-GL Additions.

31. For the construction of the piazza see Maria Gansevoort Melville to Augusta Melville, 10 March 1851, NYPL-GL Additions.

32. See also Patricia Barber, "Two New Melville Letters," *American Literature*, 69 (November 1977), 418–21.

33. Augusta Melville to Allan Melville, 16 May 1851, Berkshire County Historical Society.

34. See in this volume Harrison Hayford, "Unnecessary Duplicates," 493–94.

Index

♦

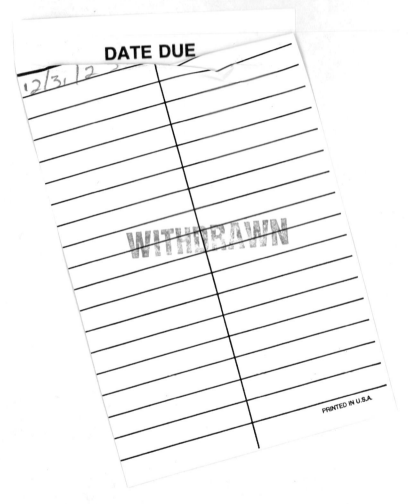

DATE DUE

12/3, 12

WITHDRAWN

PRINTED IN U.S.A.